Dixie Dias

To Karen & Jordan
love
uncle mark

JUDAIC STUDIES SERIES

Leon J. Weinberger, General Editor

Dixie Diaspora

An Anthology of Southern Jewish History

EDITED BY MARK K. BAUMAN

THE UNIVERSITY OF ALABAMA PRESS

Tuscaloosa

Publication of this book is supported in part by a grant from the Southern Jewish Historical Society.

Typeface: New Baskerville

∞

The paper on which this book is printed meets the minimum requirements of American National Standard for Information Sciences-Permanence of Paper for Printed Library Materials, ANSI Z39.48–1984.

Library of Congress Cataloging-in-Publication Data

Dixie diaspora : an anthology of southern Jewish history / edited by Mark K. Bauman.
    p. cm. — (Judaic studies series)
Includes bibliographical references.
ISBN-13: 978-0-8173-1504-7 (cloth : alk. paper)
ISBN-13: 978-0-8173-5291-2 (pbk. : alk. paper)
ISBN-10: 0-8173-1504-7
ISBN-10: 0-8173-5291-0
    1. Jews—Southern States—History.   2. Jews—Southern States—Social conditions.   3. Jews—Southern States—Economic conditions.   4. Jews—Southern States—Politics and government.   5. Jews—Southern States—Identity.   6. Judaism—Southern States—History.   7. Southern States—Ethnic relations.   I. Bauman, Mark K.   II. Series.
    F220.J5D59 2006
    975'.004974—dc22

                                                                                    2005034153

Publications Permissions
Elliott Ashkenazi, "Jewish Commercial Interests Between North and South: The Case of the Lehmans and the Seligmans," *American Jewish Archives* 39 (Spring/Summer 1991): 25–39; published by permission of the American Jewish Archives. Mark K. Bauman, "Role Theory and History: The Illustration of Ethnic Brokerage in the Atlanta Jewish Community in an Era of Transition and Conflict," *American Jewish History* 73 (September 1983): 71–95; courtesy of the American Jewish Historical Society. Canter Brown Jr., "Philip and Morris Dzialynski: Jewish Contributions to the Rebuilding of the South," *American Jewish Archives* 44 (Fall/Winter 1992): 517–39; published by permission of the American Jewish Archives. Mark I. Greenberg, "A 'Haven for Benignity': Conflict and Cooperation Between Eighteenth Century Savannah Jews," *Georgia Historical Quarterly* 86 (Winter 2002): 544–68; published by permission of the Georgia Historical Society. Scott M. Langston, "Interaction and Identity: Jews and Christians in Nineteenth Century New Orleans," *Southern Jewish History* 3 (2000): 83–124; published by permission of the Southern Jewish Historical Society. Eliza R. L. McGraw, "'How to Win the Jews for Christ': Southern Jewishness and the Southern Baptist Convention," *Mississippi Quarterly* LIII, no. 2 (Spring 2000): 209–23; published by permission of *Mississippi Quarterly*. Howard N. Rabinowitz, "Nativism, Bigotry and Anti-Semitism in the South," *American Jewish History* LXXII (March 1988): 437–51; courtesy of the American Jewish Historical Society. Leonard Rogoff, "Is the Jew White? The Racial Place of the Southern Jew," *American Jewish History* 85 (September 1997): 195–230; courtesy of the American Jewish Historical Society. Joshua D. Rothman, "'Notorious in the Neighborhood': An Interracial Family in Early National and Antebellum Virginia," *Journal of Southern History* 67 (February 2001): 73–114; published by permission of the *Journal of Southern History*. Ira M. Sheskin, "The Dixie Diaspora: The 'Loss' of the Small Southern Jewish Community," *Southeastern Geographer* 40 (May 2000): 52–74; published by permission of *Southern Geographer*. Clive Webb, "Closing Ranks: Montgomery Jews and Civil Rights, 1954–1960, *Journal of American Studies* 32 (1998): 463–81; published by permission of *Journal of American Studies*. Deborah R. Weiner, "Jewish Women of the Central Appalachian Coal Fields, 1880–1960: From Breadwinners to Community Builders," *American Jewish Archives Journal* 52 (2000): 10–33; published by permission of the American Jewish Archives. Hollace Ava Weiner, "The Mixers: The Role of Rabbis Deep in the Heart of Texas," *American Jewish History* 85 (September 1997): 289–332; courtesy of the American Jewish Historical Society. Lee Shai Weissbach, "East European Immigrants and the Image of Jews in the Small-Town South," *American Jewish History* 85 (September 1997): 231–62; courtesy of the American Jewish Historical Society. Stephen J. Whitfield, "The Braided Identity of Southern Jewry," *American Jewish History* 77 (March 1988): 363–87; courtesy of the American Jewish Historical Society. Gary P. Zola, "Southern Rabbis and the Founding of the First National Association of Rabbis," *American Jewish History* 85 (December 1997): 353–72; courtesy of the American Jewish Historical Society.

Contents

Introduction: An Anthology of Southern Jewish History   1

PART I. JEWS AND JUDAISM

Introduction to Part I   7

1. A "Haven of Benignity": Conflict and Cooperation Between
   Eighteenth-Century Savannah Jews
   Mark I. Greenberg   12

2. Southern Rabbis and the Founding of the First National
   Association of Rabbis
   Gary P. Zola   33

3. The Mixers: The Role of Rabbis Deep in the Heart of Texas
   Hollace Ava Weiner   55

PART II. SMALL-TOWN LIFE

Introduction to Part II   105

4. East European Immigrants and the Image of Jews
   in the Small-Town South
   Lee Shai Weissbach   108

5. Jewish Women in the Central Appalachian Coal Fields, 1880–1960:
   From Breadwinners to Community Builders
   Deborah R. Weiner   143

6. The Dixie Diaspora: The "Loss" of the Small Southern Jewish Community
   Ira M. Sheskin   165

PART III. BUSINESS AND GOVERNANCE

Introduction to Part III   191

7. Jewish Commercial Interests Between North and South:
   The Case of the Lehmans and the Seligmans
   Elliott Ashkenazi   195

8. Philip and Morris Dzialynski: Jewish Contributions to the Rebuilding
   of the South
   Canter Brown Jr.   209

9. Role Theory and History: The Illustration of Ethnic Brokerage
   in the Atlanta Jewish Community in an Era of Transition and Conflict
   Mark K. Bauman   236

PART IV. INTERACTION

Introduction to Part IV   265

10. Nativism, Bigotry and Anti-Semitism in the South
    Howard N. Rabinowitz   270

11. "Notorious in the Neighborhood": An Interracial Family in Early
    National and Antebellum Virginia
    Joshua D. Rothman   285

12. Closing Ranks: Montgomery Jews and Civil Rights, 1954–1960
    Clive Webb   331

PART V. IDENTITY

Introduction to Part V   353

13. Interaction and Identity: Jews and Christians in Nineteenth Century
    New Orleans
    Scott M. Langston   357

14. Is the Jew White? The Racial Place of the Southern Jew
    Leonard Rogoff   390

15. The Braided Identity of Southern Jewry
    Stephen J. Whitfield   427

16. "How to Win the Jews for Christ": Southern Jewishness and the
    Southern Baptist Convention
    Eliza R. L. McGraw   452

Bibliographical Essay   467

Contributors   475

Dixie Diaspora

Introduction

An Anthology of Southern Jewish History

The year 2004 marked the 350th anniversary of the first permanent Jewish settlement in what became the United States. Yet the Jews who arrived in New Amsterdam in 1654 had been preceded by Joachim Gaunse, mining expert for the Roanoke Colony, who arrived in 1585. Some Crypto-Jews (who practiced Judaism secretly to avoid the Spanish and Portuguese Inquisitions) landed in the southwest even earlier. Savannah and Charleston, along with New York, Newport, Rhode Island, and Philadelphia, housed the first and only congregations in British America. Arguably, in terms of religious change and development, Charleston (the largest Jewish enclave in America from 1800 to 1830) served as the cauldron of American Judaism during its heyday. New Orleans, Richmond, and Baltimore emerged as important centers of Judaism in the mid-nineteenth century. Numerous "firsts" and important events in American Jewish history took place in the South, and Jews from the region played significant roles in national and international Jewish affairs. Nonetheless southern Jews have been depicted by Eli Evans, perhaps the region's most famous chronicler of Jewry, as "The Provincials," a term reflective of their image in much of the historical literature.

Historians have written about southern Jewry since the beginning of historical enquiry into American Jewry. During the 1970s and 1980s anthologies and special issues of the American Jewish Historical Society's journal appeared dedicated to the subfield. But regardless of dramatic quantitative and qualitative output over the last two decades, southern Jewish history remains an exotic aside to many, and its study is more peripheral than integrated. This anthology is designed to expose different audiences to the subfield and particularly to the scholarship of the last twenty-five years, and to encourage the integration of southern Jewish history into American, southern, religious, ethnic, and Jewish history.

Choosing the articles proved difficult, and neither all subjects nor all places could be covered. Selection was based on methodological innovation, how well articles opened discussion of key themes, and how well they complemented each other. Rather than chronology, the articles are organized topically to provide a clearer understanding of contemporary debates and questions.

Although all cannot be treated here, questions historians of southern Jewry ask are those also discussed broadly. These include: What is appropriate periodization? Why did Jews leave their country of origin, particularly when they did? What factors affected emigration? What drew immigrants to America? What cultural baggage did they bring with them and what impact did it have? How did the forces of adaptation and continuity intertwine and unfold? What are the patterns of institutional development and change? How did the majority and minorities react to the Jewish presence? How were Jews influenced by and how did they interact with the host society as well as other Jews in America and overseas?

Because the South can be viewed as a distinctive region, a few final questions arise. If, as Jonathan Sarna has noted (in his introduction to *The American Jewish Experience,* Sarna, ed. [New York, 1997], xiii), "American Jewish history weds together two great historical traditions: one Jewish . . . and the other American," what did Southern tradition add to the marriage? More specifically, to borrow Stephen J. Whitfield's apt image (from his contribution to this anthology) and to mix metaphors, how and to what extent does Southern Jewish history braid three identities: Jewish, American, and Southern? What impact did multiple and fluid identities exert on the behavior of Jews and others?

Information surrounding the answers to these questions bears on the integration of Southern Jewish history into southern history. Where Jews acculturated differently than elsewhere, or their treatment varied from other locations because of southern-specific circumstances, one can document the region's influence on a minority. Conversely, much of Jewish history in the South is neither region-specific nor illustrative of a "Jewishkeit" mode of adjustment defined by generalized Jewish values, traditions, and historical experiences. Here southern historians can describe paths not followed by the Protestant majority, a group often analyzed in an almost deterministic model.

For example, farming dominated the South; yet few Jews became farmers and many of those who did were noted for their business methods and innovation. As merchants, factors, peddlers, shopkeepers, and department store magnates, Jews achieved success by filling economic niches within the agrarian society. They did this while negotiating within a society dominated by racist and prejudicial mores and policies by sometimes accepting societal values and at others bending the boundaries. By studying the varied experiences of Jews and other minorities, a more complete understanding of the South should emerge.

This anthology is divided into five parts: I. Jews and Judaism; II. Small-Town Life; III. Business and Governance; IV. Interaction; V. Identity. Just as in life, overlap occurs. Articles on identity, for example, deal with theology and interaction, and could easily be placed in those parts.

As with all historical writing and human understanding, authors and readers (as well as editors) are influenced by their backgrounds and experiences. Nonetheless we gather and analyze evidence logically to try to comprehend where we have been and thus help us understand who, what, and why we are the way we are today, and where we may be heading in the future. The more I study southern Jewish history the more I realize how much remains to be learned. It has reached the stage where the best way I can describe the story is "yes, but." Yes, Jews may have been more accepted in the South than elsewhere, but frequently they felt and were treated as marginal. Yes, virulent racism against African Americans deflected prejudice against Jews in relative and real terms, but eras of heightened anti-black racism were marked by rising antisemitism and violence against Jews as well. Yes, most Jews in the South supported slavery and the Confederacy, but involvement was filtered through a "Jewish" prism. Yes, the region's Jews did not tend to march and demonstrate as Jews did in the urban/industrial North, but they did campaign for women's rights, black rights, and other unpopular causes more than previously recognized. "Yes, but" history recognizes exceptions, nuance, and ambiguity, terms to consider before drawing absolute conclusions.

Leonard Dinnerstein inspired and assisted me greatly with the development of this anthology. Thanks also go to the very cordial and able staff at The University of Alabama Press.

This book is dedicated to my wife of almost four decades, Sandra (Woolf) Bauman.

I
JEWS AND JUDAISM

INTRODUCTION

Many Jews in colonial America traced their origins to the Portugal and Spain of the Inquisition where they had been forced to practice Judaism secretly. They influenced congregations like Savannah's Mikve Israel and Charleston's Beth Elohim through the adoption of the Sephardic mode of worship and congregational governance. These practices continued even when Jews from the Germanic states and England became the majority. During the transition, however, as Mark I. Greenberg shows, divisions were typical. Ashkenazim were more observant and followed different rites, and were less affluent and educated than their Sephardic brethren. Gradually the Old World demarcations blurred with adjustment to America and upward mobility, and translated into a melding of an American Jewish culture. Nonetheless identity as Jews drew the two together and marked them as alike by the Protestant majority. The patterns recurred with each wave of immigration as those once frowned upon became the aristocracy to later arrivals. Greenberg's article also introduces the influence of European background, the role of the family, the impact of missionaries, and the continued replenishment of Jews and Judaism as immigrants reinvigorated communities. In these and other ways, Jewish community history should be viewed not in isolation but as a story of internal and external forces.

Colonial Jewry was part of a transatlantic Jewry linked by business, family, and religion. But whereas European Jews began modern emancipation in 1790 with the French Revolution, in America, regardless of discriminatory laws, Jews practiced their religion within a relatively tolerant environment. While European Jews were accustomed to governance by Jewish community structures, American Jews freely developed as individuals and through lay-controlled congregations lacking the supervision of ordained rabbis. To Jewish men isolated along the frontier with tenuous religious ties, declining observance and intermarriage became the norm.

By the 1820s in viable Jewish communities, trouble developed over lax observance. Second- and third-generation Americans promoted change in keeping with their desire to rise in society. Their efforts paralleled similar developments in Western Europe. The first reform began in Charleston. Although the Reform Society of Israelites (1824–1838) was short-lived, parent congregation K. K. Beth Elohim (K. K. stands for Kahal Kadosh, or "Holy Congregation") gradually moved toward Reform

Judaism. Borrowing Protestant practices, changes stressed services that could impress Christian visitors and appeal to Americanized Jews. As men spent more time with business and less in synagogue, women played greater roles with Sunday schools, fund raising, and philanthropy, and many reforms reflected their participation.

Not everyone welcomed change. Traditionalists formed Shearith Israel, the first congregation in America to break from a reforming synagogue. Into the 1890s congregations wrestled with the issue of reform versus orthodoxy with religious leaders coming and going as one faction or the other held sway. The South offered its share of both moderate reformers like James K. Gutheim of New Orleans and radical reformers like abolitionist David Einhorn of Baltimore's Har Sinai Verein, in 1842 the first permanent congregation to begin as a Reform synagogue in the United States.

The South boasted many other firsts. During a short, cantankerous career, Abraham Rice, who had been the first ordained rabbi to emigrate to America from Europe, came to loggerheads with those in Baltimore drifting from tradition. Henry W. Schneeberger, one of the first American-born, ordained rabbis, enjoyed more success partly by garnering acceptance in the wider community. His Baltimore congregation, Chizuk-Amuno, had split from the Baltimore Hebrew Congregation in 1871, when the latter joined the Reform ranks. Yet labels and religious identities during the mid- to late-nineteenth century were in flux. Schneeberger advocated Positive Historical Judaism, a precursor to Conservative Judaism. Begun in 1853, Baltimore's Oheb Shalom has been called the first to organize in this quasi-Conservative mold. Simon Tuska, the first graduate of an American university to serve an American congregation, accepted a pulpit in Memphis. The first US Senator of Jewish origin, the first practicing Jew in the US Senate, the first Jewish lieutenant governor, and the first Jew in a state legislature all served in the South. Rather than a filiopietistic exercise, this listing of "firsts" raises the question of what conditions in the South made it conducive to so much innovation.

The first major attempt at institutional unity for American Jewry arose as a response to antisemitism overseas when Papal authorities abducted a Jewish child, Edgara Mortara, after he was secretly baptized by a maid. This case led to the formation of the Board of Delegates of American Israelites, an organization which southern Jews helped establish and which advocated causes like the end to discriminatory provisions in the

North Carolina constitution. Gary P. Zola's article depicts the Conference of Rabbis of Southern Congregations as the prototype for the Union of American Hebrew Congregations (now called the Union for Reform Judaism, or URJ), and further cements the significance of Judaism in the region in relation to the nation. Isaac Mayer Wise, institution builder of Reform Judaism, found welcome allies in the South and West for his moderate reform, and his Hebrew Union College graduates solidified the movement in southern congregations.

Following the Pittsburgh Platform of 1885, most Reform rabbis and their congregations rejected political Zionism when it appeared during the late 1890s. Some continued to do so through the American Council for Judaism, which was established in 1942, even as the Reform movement abandoned the position with its Columbus Platform of 1937 and the position became unpopular because of the Holocaust. Emphasis shifted to social reform and rabbis became leaders as circumstances allowed and dictated.

During much of the nineteenth century many rabbis struggled with their congregations and roles while Isaac Leeser, Wise, and Einhorn attempted to foster unity through personal journalism, institution building, and publications. By the 1890s and early twentieth century the position of the Reform rabbi solidified, and serving in the same pulpit for decades became normal. The rabbis gained prestige by becoming the ambassador to the gentiles and ethnic brokers bridging gaps between various constituencies. Hollace Ava Weiner's article uses these and other categories to describe the behavior of the "Mixers" (rabbis hired more for their ability to mix with the larger community than for their knowledge of Judaism or ritual observance) along the Texas frontier. Here the region was composed not just of blacks and whites but also of Germans and Hispanics. Individuals who found it hard to fit in elsewhere were accepted in isolated congregations and emerged as voices of social justice and culture. What were the different roles of rabbis? How and why did they change over time and in relation to circumstances? What do these factors imply about behavior of congregants and boards, and the relationship between the congregations and the surrounding communities?

Especially from 1881, Eastern European Jews flocked to America to seek economic opportunity and flee Czarist oppression. Many traveled south and west, often via the chain migration pattern described by Hollace Weiner. They brought Orthodox practices and settled in large enough numbers in cities to maintain viable communities. By the early

1900s cities boasted affluent, acculturated-member congregations adjusting to America, and smaller congregations catering to traditionalists typically lower on the socio-economic scale.

In towns, these people often entered communities with small, declining numbers of descendents of the preceding migration. They founded congregations, worked with Jews in surrounding areas to maintain tradition, and/or created compromises with the Reform "German" Jews so that together they could maintain viable institutions.

Jews from the declining Ottoman Empire made inroads in Atlanta and Montgomery during the early twentieth century. Speaking Ladino, a mixture of Spanish and Hebrew, instead of the Yiddish of European Jews, and following their own liturgy, foodways and music, these Sephardim tended to remain relatively isolated from the other Jewish subgroups. They did, however, cooperate with federated Jewish social service agencies and supported Zionism in conjunction with the East European immigrants.

With World War I and the passage of immigrant restriction laws during the 1920s, the stream of immigrants that had repeatedly reinvigorated orthodoxy dried up. Recent immigrants and especially their children rose economically (a rise only delayed by the Depression) and acculturated. During the 1920s and 1930s many of them called for Americanized rabbis able to give English-language sermons. Many other congregations turned Conservative during the late 1930s and after World War II, although some remained Orthodox in cities which could support multiple synagogues. In smaller towns, Orthodox shuls tended to die or enter the Reform or Conservative camps.

Into the 1950s in larger Jewish enclaves, new Orthodox congregations formed in response to the Conservative direction of older congregations or in response to needs of arriving Holocaust survivors and migrants from northern cities. Since the 1950s, many Reform congregations gradually returned to tradition, and Orthodoxy grew tremendously. Around 1968 a wave of congregation formation began (and has not abated) in flourishing Jewish communities. These congregations sometimes split from older congregations that remained in older areas or had grown large, but more often they were formed by migrants from other sections of the country or Russian or Iranian newcomers. A patterns of congregational life and death, unity and factionalism, continue. The student of history may find it interesting to graph the patterns over time to analyze the factors involved with each change and thus gain greater understanding of the present and future.

The three essays in this section and the overall story of Judaism in the south and nation reflect different aspects of cultural transmission and adaptation. Greenberg's essay focuses on continuity and change among Sephardim and Ashkenazim as they Americanize and blend practices and identities. The rabbinical organizations described by Zola and Weiner's circuit riders and the Texas Kallah of Rabbis can be defined as survival mechanisms created in response to fluid conditions. Where Jews stretched across the frontier, such adaptation was essential for continuity. This two-sided sword is critical to the understanding of immigrant behavior.

1
A "Haven of Benignity"

Conflict and Cooperation Between Eighteenth-Century Savannah Jews

Mark I. Greenberg

Savannah's eighteenth-century Jewish settlers have received scholarly attention since the early nineteenth century, but older studies differed in emphasis and quality and were often filiopietistic in nature and thin on analysis.[1] Over the last three decades, several important books and many excellent essays have significantly expanded an understanding of the topic. Incorporating the methodological advances of the new social history, scholars have probed relations between Savannah Jews and Christians, explored Jews' roles in Georgia's development, and corrected inaccuracies in earlier works.[2]

Despite improvements in the field, no single source has integrated the highly diverse and dispersed current scholarship into a single, accessible introduction to the first hundred years of Savannah Jewish history. No author has effectively employed insights from European Jewish history to demonstrate how Portuguese and German cultures, carried across the Atlantic with Savannah's first Jewish immigrants, shaped life in the New World. Nor has any previous historian persuasively explained the periods of conflict and cooperation that characterized relations between Georgia's eighteenth-century Ashkenazic (Germanic) and Sephardic (Iberian) settlers.[3]

On July 11, 1733, forty-one Jews aboard the schooner *William and Sarah* landed in the fledgling Georgia colony.[4] Their harrowing five-month journey had included damage to their boat in the Thames River and a near shipwreck off the North Carolina coast. The weary travelers joined 275 Christian inhabitants already settled on the bluffs above the Savannah River. Only five months earlier James Oglethorpe had landed with a charter from King George II and the financial support of British investors to found a refuge for England's poor. The king hoped that by cultivating the desolate lands of America, the new settlers "might not only gain a comfortable subsistence, but also strengthen the colonies and increase the trade, navigation, and wealth of his realms."[5]

The vessel's journey stemmed from conditions in London's Jewish community. Faced with an influx of poor Jews from Portugal and smaller numbers from Germany, three leaders of London's wealthy Spanish-Portuguese congregation, Bevis Marks, had received commissions from the Georgia Trustees in early 1732 to raise funds among their coreligionists for the colonization effort. The Trustees assumed that collections from London Jewry would support prospective Protestant settlers. London's Jewish elites had other ideas. They viewed the Georgia venture as an opportunity to manage their financial commitment to the poor and alleviate the perceived threat that these newcomers posed to their social status among London Christians.[6]

The prospect of Jews in Georgia upset the Common Council of the Trustees, which never expected that Jews might choose to make the colony their home. Motivated by centuries-old antipathy toward Jews and Judaism, in December 1732 the council voted to bar their entry.[7] The next month it agreed "that no Jews should be sent, and the deputations given them to collect should be revoked. . . . Besides, the report of our sending Jews has prevented several from subscribing to us."[8] Oglethorpe was unaware of these decisions when the group landed at Savannah in July. Taken off guard by their arrival, he sought a legal opinion in Charleston on the subject of Jewish settlement in the colony. The Charleston lawyers held that since the Georgia charter guaranteed liberty of conscience and worship to all newcomers except "papists," Jews had to be admitted. The Georgia leader followed this advice.[9]

The arrival of Jews in Savannah and Oglethorpe's decision to admit them shocked the Common Council in London. The council secretary instructed Oglethorpe in an October letter to prevent the group from taking up permanent residence. "Use your best endeavours [*sic*] that the said Jews may be allowed no kind of settlement with any of the grantees, the Trustees being apprehensive they will be of prejudice to the Trade and Welfare of the Colony."[10] This correspondence crossed a letter from Oglethorpe, written in August, praising the Jews' good conduct, commending especially the skill of passenger Dr. Samuel Nunes Ribeiro, who had provided valuable medical attention to sick colonists during a yellow fever outbreak. Oglethorpe informed the Trustees on August 12 of a "doctor of physick [*sic*] who immediately undertook our people and refused to take any pay for it. He proceeded by cold baths, cooling drinks and other cooling applications."[11] Although the epidemic had killed twenty, or 10 percent of the residents, Nunes "entirely put a stop to it, so that not one died afterwards."[12] The Common Council met, debated, and fumed throughout much of the winter that Jews had arrived without its permission. In January 1734 it reiterated demands that London's Jewish commissioners return their licenses and remove the Jewish settlers from the colony. It was too late. The previous month Oglethorpe had assigned plots of land to fourteen men, and the Jewish arrivals began their new lives.[13]

Despite sharing a common religion and appearing culturally similar to the Trustees, Oglethorpe, and most other Christians, Savannah's early Jews hailed from different European countries, spoke different languages, had different historical experiences, and held dissimilar religious customs and practices. Thirty-four of those onboard the *William and Sarah* were from Portugal and thus of Sephardic background.[14] Nunes served as the group's leader, and his personal story sheds light on Portuguese Jewish history and culture prior to Georgia's colonization.

Dr. Diogo Nunes Ribeiro, as he was known in Portuguese records, belonged to a respected family in the north-central province of Beira. His father served as a procurator of the Customs House and several family members practiced medicine. Among the doctor's prominent patients were Dominicans at the Lisbon monastery and, according to his daughter's memoirs, the Portuguese Grand Inquisitor. Unbeknownst to the Christians around him, Nunes lived a secret life. He was a crypto-Jew, like his ancestors for generations before him.[15]

Nunes's story is part of the complex but fascinating history of Jews on the Iberian Peninsula. In 1492 the Spanish crown completed a four-century-long reconquest of Spain from the Moors, which included forced conversions of its Jews, by compelling the remaining Jewish community to adopt Catholicism or leave the country.[16] Thousands of Jews converted publicly but practiced Judaism behind closed doors. Approximately half of the 100,000 people who chose exile instead of conversion fled to Portugal, but within five years Spain's intolerance had spread across its western border.[17]

In 1497 King Manoel I, seeking to marry the daughter of Ferdinand and Isabella, prohibited Jewish emigration and began forced conversions in Portugal. Promising not to investigate the personal lives of these "New Christians" too closely, Manoel inadvertently fostered development of a large crypto-Jewish community. Crypto-Jews dropped most overt Jewish symbols in order to maintain secrecy. Circumcision, prayer books and shawls *(tallisim)*, Torah scrolls, *mezuzahs*, several public festivals, and the ritual slaughter of animals could not be maintained under close scrutiny. For centuries, Portugal's secret Jews remained cut off from European Jewish life and thus developed religious practices based upon increasingly diluted traditions and curious Jewish-Catholic hybrids passed orally from one generation to the next.[18]

Loose oversight of Portugal's New Christians lasted barely forty years. In 1536 the Inquisition spread to Portugal. For the next three centuries, it sought to root out people who had lapsed back to Judaism or, worse, those who actively encouraged others to return to their ancient faith (judaisers). In 1702 a New Christian arrested and tortured by the Inquisition denounced Nunes as a fellow judaiser. According to the man's secret testimony, Nunes "had persuaded him to declare his faith in the Law of Moses, in which they would save their souls." An August 1703 warrant for Nunes's arrest and the seizure of his property opened a floodgate of new accusations from other New Christians in the Inquisition's custody. One person claimed that Nunes had disclosed his faith to her and had "spoken of the Great Fast (Kipur) and its dispensatory value." Another stated that he had told him about the "Passover of the Hebrews which ought to be kept for 2 or 3 days beforehand." Someone else declared that the doctor came to her house on a medical call "whereat certain practices took place and they declared their faith in the Law of Moses, by keeping sabbaths, not eating pork or shell-fish."[19]

In October 1703, Inquisition officials formally charged Nunes with judaising. According to Inquisitional records, he had separated himself from the Catholic faith, rejected the Trinity and Christ as the true Messiah, and observed various Jewish practices. Nunes denied the charges and attempted to mount a defense against his many secret accusers. Working blindly to reconstruct a list of those who might have enmity toward him, he correctly identified informants with whom he previously had quarreled and attempted to explain the petty motivations for their charges.[20]

Nunes finally succumbed to mounting pressure in July 1704, confessed to twenty acts of judaising, and repented. He admitted that approximately fifteen years earlier another judaiser had convinced him to believe in the Law of Moses and, though he could not practice Jewish ceremonies faithfully, to separate himself from the Catholic faith. He also reported that his own father had urged him to return to the fami-

ly's ancient faith. A month later, Nunes suffered torture on the rack because he had failed to implicate his wife as an accomplice and others with
whom he had clandestinely worshiped. In a September 1704 final judgment, the Inquisitional court upheld its charges against him but offered
leniency in punishment. In the presence of Portugal's Inquisitor-Gen-
eral, Nunes publicly renounced his heresies. He swore to keep the events
of his arrest, incarceration, and trial secret, and he received the holy
sacrament. On November 6, 1704, fifteen months after his original arrest, he was conditionally released from prison but confined indefinitely to Lisbon. The Inquisition had treated Nunes mercifully.[21]

In the days following his ordeal, officials forced the doctor to give testimony against his wife, her parents, and various other relatives. The
scope of new denunciations troubled the Lisbon Inquisition. At the September 1705 *auto da fe* in which his family was punished, one victim was
burned at the stake and sixty-five given lesser sentences.[22] During the
eighteenth century's first two decades, the Inquisition punished more
than two thousand people in Portugal for practicing Judaism. Most received penances and imprisonment, but thirty-seven were burned.[23]

Faced with ever increasing oppression, at least 1,500 impoverished
Portuguese Jews contracted with British and Dutch sea captains for secret passage to England between 1700 and 1735. London's Bevis Marks
Synagogue paid the way for most refugees and supported them after
their arrival. Nunes helped as well. His nephew and countless others fled
thanks to his generosity. Finally, sometime in late spring 1726, Nunes
and seventeen family members boarded a British brigantine anchored
in the Tagus River and joined a growing flood escaping persecution in
Portugal for religious freedom in England. For a short time he practiced
medicine among Bevis Marks' poor. Five years later, he and his extended family comprised one-third of the passengers aboard the *William and
Sarah*. Other once-secret Portuguese Jews accounted for all but eight of
the remaining forty-one settlers to Georgia in July 1733.[24]

Far less is known of the specific European origins or experiences of
the non-Sephardic Jews who arrived with Nunes.[25] Abraham Minis and
family, Benjamin Sheftall and his wife Perla, and bachelor Jacob Yowel
were Ashkenazim—members of the branch of European Jews who had
settled in northwest Europe, initially on the banks of the Rhine.[26] Minis
was probably born in England, though his family likely had migrated
westward from a German state, and Benjamin Sheftall came from Frankfurt an der Oder in Prussia to London about 1730.[27]

No records detail the Sheftalls, Minises, or Yowels in Central Europe, but broad strokes can paint the environment in which they and their families lived before migrating to England sometime prior to 1732. Within the German states, Jews were spread unevenly, living in clusters of several dozen to several hundred people. Ninety percent of these Jews concentrated in small towns or villages where noblemen granted the community rights of residence and physical protection in return for high taxes.[28]

For their economic survival Jews depended almost entirely on trade, yet the ability to earn a living in this sphere was subject to severe limitations. Most crafts were closed to Jews, with the exception of those associated with the Jewish community's basic needs: kosher slaughtering, baking, and making articles for worship. Because officials also prohibited Jews from owning land, earning a living in agriculture was seriously curtailed. Jews clustered in irregular or distressed trades such as secondhand clothing, pawn brokering, peddling, and money lending. Since laws ordinarily prevented Jews from keeping shops, they had to seek out customers or trade illegally from their homes.[29] In rural areas they served as dealers in agricultural products and manufactured goods by exporting produce and livestock to market, importing finished wares required by farmers, and providing needed credit. In poorer regions, city merchants were not likely to grant small-scale and risky loans to unknown debtors or to accept produce in place of cash; therefore, many smallholders depended on Jewish middlemen for the movement of crops and credit between rural and urban areas.[30]

Jewish businessmen's intermediary role in the age of mercantilism made them an indispensable element throughout the German states. Unlike Catholic religious leaders, rabbinic scholars did not denigrate commerce and the profit motive, and thus historically Jews had engaged in commercial pursuits. The weakness of an indigenous capitalist and entrepreneurial class in seventeenth- and eighteenth-century Germanic states prompted princes and government officials to encourage limited Jewish settlement in their territories and to elevate a few Jewish businessmen to positions of economic power within their courts. Here, Jews drew upon an expansive network of coreligionists across Central Europe to provide horses, cattle, and other goods during times of war and to serve as sources for diamonds and precious metals to fund the lavish lifestyles and political machinations of their absolutist monarchs. Horse-trading was an exclusive and prestigious position for a Jew, as every prince wanted a good stable of horses for both civilian and military use.[31]

Virulent anti-semitism and Jews' commercial and credit dealings con-

tributed to constant friction in their relationship with the Christian population, especially the peasantry. Smallholders' seasonal needs often required that they seek loans, yet the uncertainties of a good harvest called
into question their ability to repay. The association of Jewish creditors
with economic ruin lay just below the surface in peasant consciousness
and easily erupted into violence during times of crisis.[32] Economic, social, and political dislocations caused by military conflict also threatened
Jews. During the Thirty Years War (1618–1648) soldiers looted homes
and synagogues and killed thousands of Jews across Central Europe.
Bloodthirsty Cossacks swept through Eastern Europe in 1648 wreaking
havoc in Jewish areas. Jews flooded westward, only to kindle resentment
and anger in their new German homes.[33]

In a world of religious antipathies, economic inequalities, and personal uncertainties, seventeenth-century German Jews found solace in
their synagogues and other communal institutions. Unlike Portugal,
where Jews practiced secretly, Jewish activities in Central Europe occurred openly. The synagogue served as the center of communal life, offering a focal point for worship, study, and celebration. Weddings and
other joyous occasions took place in the courtyard, and dress and residential clustering in the *Judengassen* (Jews' Alleys) made Jews highly visible to their Christian neighbors. The nobility supported Jewish life by
sanctioning *Landjudenschaften,* corporate self-governing bodies set up to
administer Jewish affairs autonomously in each region. Led by a lay
board, the communal organization regulated Jews' religious, social, and
economic lives. Torah study and strict adherence to ancient Jewish customs, including dietary restrictions and Sabbath and holiday observance, were the norm. Frankfurt an der Oder, Benjamin Sheftall's home,
contained a prestigious center of rabbinic learning and a publisher of
Jewish texts.[34]

Two distinct Jewish cultures collided in early eighteenth-century London. Minis, Sheftall, and Yowel felt at home at the German-speaking, orthodox Great Synagogue, located in the heart of the Jewish quarter for
Ashkenazim, Duke's Place.[35] Nunes and four other Sephardic families
that later sailed to Savannah affiliated with the city's Bevis Marks congregation, founded by fellow crypto-Jews in the early seventeenth century. Here fathers and sons underwent ritual circumcision, and husbands and wives remarried according to Jewish law.[36] These actions
reveal their desire to put secrecy behind them and to sanctify their re-
union with Judaism, but they could not erase centuries of isolation. Many

crypto-Jews found it hard to adapt to the Orthodox Judaism practiced in London. Life in the colonies offered a chance to start again.

In the first years following settlement in Georgia, cultural differences between the Ashkenazim and Sephardim threatened to tear Savannah Jewry asunder. Some of the dissimilarities were linguistic. Minis, Sheftall, and Yowel felt most comfortable in German or a German-Hebrew hybrid.[37] The Portuguese knew neither. The arrival of seventy-eight Lutheran refugees from Salzburg in March 1734 reveals that the Ashkenazim had more in common with their fellow Germans than fellow Jews. The Salzburgers received a welcome from Benjamin Sheftall, and either Minis or Yowell.[38] The Reverend John Martin Boltzius, leader of the Salzburgers, noted in his journal the warm reception given to his flock by the two Jews and his future plans for them: "These Jews show a great love for us, and have promised to see us at our settlement, we hope we will preach the Gospel of Jesus Christ to them with good success. They are both born in Germany and speak good German."[39]

John Wesley shared Boltzius's goal for Savannah Jews' conversion, and he recognized Jews' linguistic differences. As an emissary of the Society for the Propagation of the Gospel, Wesley hoped to convert to Anglican Christianity people belonging to other faiths. To this end, he familiarized himself with Richard Kidder's *The Demonstration of the Messias. In Which the Truth of the Christian Religion is defended, especially against the Jews* and "began learning Spanish in order to converse with my Jewish parishioners; some of whom seem nearer the mind that was in Christ than many of those who called him Lord."[40] It is unclear whether Wesley meant that Jews already attended Anglican services or simply that he sought to bring them into the fold. Either way, speaking English to the Sephardim would not suffice. Nunes served as his Spanish teacher, friend, and confidante throughout his short time in Savannah, though no evidence exists that Wesley had any success with his missionary efforts among the group.[41]

Other Christian leaders encountered early Savannah Jews and commented on their internal divisions. In July 1735, Reverend S. Quincy reported from Savannah to his Church of England mission headquarters in London on the Sephardim's and Ashkenazim's differing levels of religiosity. The Portuguese, he believed, had professed Christianity in Portugal or the Caribbean for some time and had dispensed with many Jewish practices. In fact, two young men sometimes came to his church, and thus some people thought them Christians. Quincy could not find out their true religious beliefs, "only that their education in these Countries where they were oblig'd to appear as Christians makes them less rigid and stiff in their way." He believed that the German Jews were much stricter in their religious practices and observance of Jewish law and unlikely to convert. "Their kindness shew'd to Mr. Boltzius and the Saltzburgers [sic], was owing to the Good temper and humanity of the people, and not to any inclination to Change their religion," he opined.[42]

The Reverend Boltzius noted that some Jews referred to themselves as Spanish and Portuguese while others called themselves German Jews. The latter spoke "High German" and differed from the former in their religious services and in "other matters as well." In particular, the Spanish did not adhere closely to Jewish dietary laws and religious ceremonies.[43] In another letter Boltzius wrote that the German Jews wanted to be on good terms with their fellow countrymen and had done them small favors time and again. But as far as religion was concerned, they were unwilling to abandon Judaism, the Salzburgers' efforts to proselytize notwithstanding.[44]

Differences in language and religiosity may have hindered close relations, but they did not prevent Portuguese and German factions from uniting to preserve Judaism in Savannah. Ironically, the various proselytizing efforts underfoot may have pushed the two groups together.[45] In July 1735, following nearly two years of informal worship services held in people's homes, Savannah's Ashkenazic and Sephardic settlers formally gathered to establish Congregation Mickve Israel (Hope of Israel). Continuing in temporary quarters for several more years, Reverend Boltzius reported that services moved to "an old miserable hut" on Market Square (now Ellis Square), where "men and women [sat] separated" and "a boy speaking several languages and especially good in Hebrew is their reader and is paid for his services."[46] The young congregation received a second Torah, a Hanukkah menorah, and books from London's Sephardic community. Benjamin Sheftall purchased land for a Jewish cemetery to bury his infant son according to religious custom, and Savannah's third Jewish institution, a *mikvah* (ritual bath) opened for the congregation's use on April 2, 1738.[47]

Establishing a congregation, cemetery, and ritual bath proved relatively easy compared with efforts to erect a synagogue. Boltzius recorded the years of strife in his correspondence. The Jews "want to build a Synagogue, but the Spanish and German Jews cannot come to terms. I do not know the special reason for this," he wrote in February 1738. The next year he elaborated. "They have no Synagogue, which is their own fault; the one element hindering the other in this regard. The German Jews believed themselves entitled to build a Synagogue and are willing to allow the Spanish Jews to use it with them in common; the latter, however, reject any such arrangement and demand preference for themselves."[48]

Precise reasons for the strife cannot be known for certain, but cultural differences likely dominated.[49] More permanent and thus more significant than informal gatherings in people's homes, the design and operation of a synagogue generated heated debate and intractable divisions. Ashkenazim and Sephardim follow the same basic tenets of Judaism (both view the Babylonian Talmud as their ultimate authority), but significant variations exist in matters of detail and outlook. During worship services, the Torah scrolls are raised at different times in the service, the sanctuary's seating and ark placement have different arrangements, the prayers and their melodies vary in detail, even the Hebrew is not pronounced the same.[50] Given these and other significant cultural distinctions, heated arguments and deadlock on the look and function of a synagogue erupted between factions.

Ironically, a synagogue in Savannah mattered little to the divided factions just a few years later. Despite the addition of thirty-nine Sephardic immigrants from London and the birth of some twenty Jewish children in Georgia between 1733 and 1740, Savannah's Jewish population disintegrated in 1741.[51] Threat of a Spanish invasion during the War of Jenkins' Ear (1739–1742) haunted the Portuguese Jews and precipitated the community's collapse. Reminded of their ancestors' experiences, the Sephardim worried that should Spain conquer the colony, religious persecution would spread to Georgia. Nunes, now seventy-two years old, along with his son and daughter left for Charleston in August 1740. Others soon followed or went to New York. Only the German Sheftall and Minis families remained.[52] Not until 1774 would Savannah Jewry again meet for religious services.

In the decades preceding the American Revolution, Benjamin Sheftall and Abraham Minis prospered. Although both men began in Georgia as farmers, within a short time they had become merchants. In Minis's case, frequent flooding of his land made a life in agriculture unprofitable. In 1736 he began buying beef, pork, and butter from New York to sell to Thomas Causton, the colony's keeper of public stores. During the fighting between Spain and England in 1742, he traveled to New York City to purchase supplies, which he transported to Oglethorpe's forces at Fort Frederica on St. Simons Island.[53] As early as 1752, Sheftall referred to himself as a "storekeeper," and after 1760 legal documents consistently termed him a merchant. Benjamin's son Mordecai achieved considerable success as a merchant and large landowner. By the early 1760s he engaged in timbering, saw milling, shipping, and selling manufactured goods from the Sheftall family's store. Mordecai's half-brother Levi developed a successful tannery near the city in the 1770s.[54]

In 1750 Benjamin Sheftall joined four other men to found the St. George's (or Union) Society to further the education of orphan children. The name "Union" was adopted after the first few years to emphasize that its founders subscribed to varying religions yet were united around the brotherhood of man.[55] The organization's rules commanded members to contribute two pence weekly for the support of an orphan house, to hold regular meetings, and to celebrate the group's anniversary on April 23.[56]

With the outbreak of the Revolution, the city's small Jewish population was well situated economically and socially to hold positions of leadership. Mordecai Sheftall allied himself with Savannah Whigs and served as chairman of the Savannah Parochial Committee (similar to a county Committee of Safety) from 1775 to 1778. Levi Sheftall and Philip Minis (Abraham's son) assisted in the same body. In 1777 Mordecai received a commission as deputy commissary general of the Continental troops in Georgia and South Carolina, as well as commissary general of the Georgia troops, positions that made him a member of the Georgia General Staff. The following year, Maj. Gen. Robert Howe promoted Sheftall, removing the deputy status. Providing troops with food and supplies proved especially difficult because of a lack of public funds throughout the war. In some instances Mordecai purchased goods with his own money and extended credit to the state and federal governments. Philip Minis lent almost $11,000 to the Revolutionary forces, funds that paid salaries and provisions for troops from North Carolina and Virginia.[57]

A sermon by Presbyterian minister John J. Zubly before the Georgia Provincial Congress in July 1775 suggests reasons why Jews actively participated in the colony's struggle for independence and why Georgia conferred important leadership positions on some of them. Zubly admonished the spirit of submission that other religious leaders had preached: "As to the Jewish religion it cannot be charged with favoring despotism. The whole system of that religion is so replete with laws against injustice and oppression; and by one of its rites it proclaimed liberty throughout the land to all the inhabitants thereof."[58]

The unfailing commitment of many Jewish settlers to the Revolution caused them considerable hardship during the war. Most Jews, including Philip Minis, his wife and three children, and Levi Sheftall and family, fled to safety shortly before British troops captured Savannah in December 1778. In doing so, they left homes and businesses to an uncertain fate. Mordecai Sheftall and his fifteen-year-old son Sheftall Sheftall remained behind to fight the British, and Mordecai continued his responsibilities as commissary. They were soon captured and imprisoned on board the British prison ship *Nancy* anchored in the river, in the British-held town of Sunbury, Georgia, and later on the island of St. Johns in Antigua. Upon their release two years later, they moved to the American-held city of Philadelphia where they established ties with local Jews. In autumn 1779 Levi Sheftall and Philip Minis agreed to serve as guides for Commander Charles-Hector (Count d') Estaing and the French fleet during his ill-fated attempt to recapture Savannah. With the fall of Charleston in May 1780 Levi was again on the move—this time to Petersburg, Virginia. Distraught over separation from his family, he accepted a British offer of amnesty, returned to Charleston, and swore loyalty to the king. Savannah's Jews endured the rest of the war scattered in Georgia, Charleston, and Philadelphia.[59]

The departure of British troops from Savannah in July 1782 enabled residents who had fled to return. Mordecai Sheftall and family came back after two years in Philadelphia. While in Pennsylvania, he had purchased the schooner *Hetty* with several associates, outfitted the vessel as a privateer, and captured one British ship as a prize.[60] Back in Georgia, he resumed his Savannah mercantile business and began a campaign to clear Levi of charges that he was a Tory. In August 1785 Levi regained his citizenship and recommenced business activities. Rather than return to tanning and butchering, he used slave labor to develop farmland and timberland. Both Mordecai and Levi were elected to governmental positions following independence: Levi to alderman and fire master; Mordecai to city magistrate, warden, and state legislator.[61]

By 1785 the Minis and Sheftall families were no longer alone. Sephardim settled Savannah again and reconstituted a community moribund for over four decades. Dr. Nunes's sons Moses and Daniel were among the returnees, but most were newcomers. In 1786 the community reestablished Congregation Mickve Israel under shared leadership, and a synagogue opened in a rented house in Broughton Street Lane. Philip Minis and Levi Sheftall served as the congregation's president and trustee, respectively. David Nunes Cardozo held the treasurer's position, and Emanuel De la Motta officiated during prayers. After learning of the incorporation of both an Episcopal and Congregational church by the Georgia General Assembly in late 1789, Mordecai Sheftall recommended in August 1790 that the Jews take advantage of Georgia's religious tolerance and apply for a charter for Mickve Israel. The congregation's adjunta (governing board) authorized Sheftall to appeal to Gov. Edward Telfair, who in November 1790 granted the request.[62]

The rules and regulations governing Mickve Israel, written immediately following incorporation, suggest that the Ashkenazim and Sephardim had learned the art of accommodation. First and foremost, Mickve Israel followed examples set in colonial New York, Newport, and Charleston by adopting the Sephardic mode of worship. On the matter of religious observance inside and outside the synagogue, traditional Judaism prevailed. Men and women sat in separate sections of the sanctuary during services. Those who did not keep the Sabbath were subject to denial of synagogue honors. Engaging in business on the Sabbath or holidays was forbidden. The congregation prohibited its members from marrying outside the faith, and the offspring of mixed marriages were denied a Jewish burial. Finally, the board expected seat holders to eat kosher meat exclusively. The constitution gave the adjunta power to punish transgressors. In March 1792 the synagogue president and board members summoned Isaac Pollock, a Savannah merchant, to appear before them and explain why he had opened his store on the Sabbath.[63] Three years later, in 1795, the adjunta voted to deny two men the right to interment in the Jewish cemetery until they made "such concessions as the parnass [president] and adjunta shall think proper."[64]

What factors facilitated cooperation between Savannah's German and Portuguese Jews in 1790 where dissension had been predominant in the 1730s? Definitive answers are elusive, but it is likely that the composition of the Sephardim in the latter period played a role. Although the Sheftall and Minis families still comprised the bulk of the city's German Jews, the Portuguese-Jewish population was almost entirely different in the post-Revolutionary period. Most of the original Sephardic settlers, described by the Reverends Boltzius and Quincy as nonreligious and confrontational, do not appear on the roster of Mickve Israel's charter members. The dozen or so Sephardic households that purchased pews after incorporation were mostly South Carolina natives and apparently held more conciliatory views and traditional Jewish beliefs than the founding generation.

The influences of time, space, and shared experiences in America also seem to have dampened differences. Portuguese and German Jews lived far from their native lands. Neither Germany's *Landjudenschaften* nor Portugal's Inquisitional courts guided Jewish practice in America. Instead, a half-century of face-to-face interaction, a revolution against the British, and the reality of religious freedom fostered a new American national identity.[65] Mickve Israel's membership reveals the continuity of interaction. Of the twenty Jewish household heads located in the 1830 federal census, fourteen were congregants or the children of members in 1793.[66]

Intermarriage between the two groups also played a role in lessening differences and building understanding. With relatively few Ashkenazic Jews in America in the eighteenth century, the Minis and Sheftall families married Sephardim.[67] Levi Sheftall married Sarah De la Motta, daughter of Emanuel, in 1768; Mordecai Sheftall and Frances Hart married in Charleston; and Philip Minis wed Judith Polock of Newport, Rhode Island, in 1774.[68] As distinctions between the groups broke down and cultures fused, compromise and cooperation increased. It was possible by 1800 to regard the city's Jews as a small, relatively cohesive ethnic community.

At the turn of the nineteenth century Temple Mickve Israel had a dozen families, though numbers increased to eighty persons thirty years later. This growth paralleled Savannah's own development. The city's population increased 50 percent, from 5,166 in 1800 to 7,776 in 1830.[69] The community's expanding size, cooperation among its members, and an increase in financial resources permitted synagogue leaders to begin planning construction of a place of worship. In March 1820 a building committee, comprising Abraham DeLyon, David Leion, Moses and Sheftall Sheftall, and Jacob De la Motta received a grant of land from the city—a lot at the corner of Whitaker Street and Perry Lane—and within four months workers completed construction of Savannah's first synagogue.[70] On June 23, acting cantor Jacob De la Motta led a processional into the new building.

De la Motta's address to the congregation that day demonstrated the existence of a Jewish community with an increasingly shared history and identity in America: "Assembled as we are, to re-establish by commemoration, the Congregation of this remnant, or small portion of the house of Israel; your expectation of a brief sketch of our History, and particularly as connected with a primeval residence in this City, and for many years past . . . shall be realized; and may I trust, it will not be uninteresting, as it will include the well known fact, that many Jews struggled, and sacrificed their dearest interest, for the independence of this country."[71]

The Jews' long history, De la Motta insisted, had much in common with the experience of all Americans: "The dawn of the Revolution, opened to their view, new scenes; and they revolved in their minds, the condition of their forefathers, who toiled and suffered under the yoke of servitude, during the reign of Pharoh. . . . Resolving to separate from the standard of Tyranny, they united with freemen for the general good; [and] contended for the independence of the states."[72] The successful overthrow of British rule and passage of a Constitution codified religious tolerance and protected Savannah Jews' right to practice their religion: "It is *here,* that we are reasonably to expect the enjoyment of those rewards for our constancy and sufferings, as promised by the word of God, when he declared he would not forsake us." To merit the continuation of God's favor and ensure a completion of its promise, De la Motta called for a "rigid adherence to his commandments, and an undeviating pursuit of that path, which by his protection, leads to that external and exalted kingdom, the haven of benignity."[73]

Rhetoric aside, De la Motta's sermon conveyed an important message. Jews had found freedom from religious persecution in America, but with that liberty came considerable change. Nearly one hundred years in Savannah had transformed its Jewish population. From two factions with different national and linguistic backgrounds and religious practices, a relatively cohesive community had taken shape. If in the 1730s Savannah's German Jews appeared to have more in common with the Salzburgers than their Portuguese coreligionists, by the 1820s economic growth, kinship ties, and the Revolution increasingly had brought Jews together for worship and fellowship. Many of these Jews and their descendants would remain in Savannah throughout the antebellum period, to be joined by increasing numbers of arrivals from South Carolina, Germany, and then Eastern Europe.[74] Savannah Jewry would again face considerable internal tension. Eighteenth-century conflict between the Portuguese and Germans would seem insignificant compared with the social and religious battles raging between Eastern European and German Jewry in 1900 Savannah.

Notes

1. Early writings by state and local historians include Capt. Hugh M'Call, *The History of Georgia* (1811–1816; rpt. Atlanta, 1969), 34; William Bacon Stevens, *A History of Georgia,* 2 vols. (1847; rpt. Savannah, 1972), 1:101–04; Charles C. Jones,

Jr., *The History of Georgia*, 2 vols. (Boston, 1883), 1:151–55; William Harden, *A History of Savannah and South Georgia*, 2 vols. (1913; rpt. Atlanta, 1969), 1:44–52; and F. D. Lee and J. L. Agnew, *Historical Record of the City of Savannah* (Savannah, 1869), 2–9. American Jewish historians have also written on the topic. See Leon Hühner, "The Jews of Georgia in Colonial Times," *Publications of the American Jewish Historical Society* 10 (1902): 65–95 (hereinafter cited as *PAJHS*); Hühner, The Jews of Georgia from the Outbreak of the American Revolution to the Close of the 18th Century," *PAJHS* 17 (1909): 89–108; Edmund H. Abrahams, "Some Notes on the Early History of the Sheftalls of Georgia," *PAJHS* 17 (1909): 167–86; Abram Vossen Goodman, *American Overture: Jewish Rights in Colonial Times* (Philadelphia, 1947), 168–200; W. Guenther Plaut, "Two Notes on the History of the Jews in America," *Hebrew Union College Annual* 14 (1939): 575–82.

2. See, for example, David T. Morgan, "Judaism in Eighteenth-Century Georgia," *Georgia Historical Quarterly* 58 (Spring 1974): 41–54 (hereinafter cited as *GHQ*); John McKay Sheftall, "The Sheftalls of Savannah: Colonial Leaders and Founding Fathers of Georgia Judaism," in Samuel Proctor and Louis Schmier with Malcolm Stern, eds., *Jews of the South: Selected Essays from the Southern Jewish Historical Society* (Macon, Ga., 1984), 65–78; B. H. Levy, "The Early History of Georgia's Jews," in Harvey H. Jackson and Phinizy Spalding, eds., *Forty Years of Diversity: Essays on Colonial Georgia* (Athens, 1984), 163–78; Kaye Kole, *The Minis Family of Georgia, 1733–1992* (Savannah, 1992); John C. English, "John Wesley and His 'Jewish Parishioners': Jewish-Christian Relationships in Savannah, Georgia, 1736–1737," *Methodist History* 36 (July 1998): 220–27; and B. H. Levy, *Mordecai Sheftall: Jewish Revolutionary Patriot* (Savannah, 1999).

3. George Fenwick Jones, "Sephardim and Ashkenazim Jewish Settlers in Colonial Georgia," *GHQ* 85 (Winter 2001): 519–37, sought to explain the cultural differences between Savannah Jews of Ashkenazic and Sephardic heritage but left many questions unanswered. Note that "Sephardim" and "Ashkenazim" in Jewish culture are used as proper nouns, plural. The words Sephardic and Ashkenazic are used as adjectives and thus would have been more suitable in the essay's title.

4. According to Malcolm H. Stern's definitive essay, "New Light on the Jewish Settlement of Savannah," *American Jewish Historical Quarterly* 52 (March 1963): 176, forty-two Jews left London aboard one ship; however, Isaac Nunes Henriques's child died at sea. For citations to earlier, erroneous sources, see Jones, "Sephardim and Ashkenazim Jewish Settlers in Colonial Georgia," 519–22.

5. Lee and Agnew, *Historical Record of the City of Savannah*, 2–3.

6. Jacob Rader Marcus, *The Colonial American Jew, 1492–1776*, 3 vols. (Detroit, Mich., 1970), 1:351–52; Levy, "Early History of Georgia's Jews," 164.

7. On the enormous literature exploring the depth and breadth of European anti-semitism, see Susan Sarah Cohen, ed., *Antisemitism: An Annotated Bibliography* (New York, 1987); Bernard Glassman, *Anti-Semitic Stereotypes without Jews: Images of Jews in England, 1290–1700* (Detroit, 1975); Gavin I. Langmuir, *History, Religion, and Antisemitism* (Berkeley, 1990); Lionel B. Steiman, *Paths to Genocide: Antisemitism in Western History* (New York, 1998).

8. John Earl Perceval, *Manuscripts of the Earl of Egmont*, 3 vols. (London, 1920–1923), 1:309, 313.

9. Robert G. McPherson, ed. *The Journal of the Earl of Egmont* (Athens, 1962), 12; Marcus, *Colonial American Jew*, 1:356.

10. Amos Aschbach Ettinger, *James Edward Oglethorpe, Imperial Idealist* (Oxford, 1936), 137.

11. Oglethorpe to Trustees, August 12, 1733, in Mills Lane, ed., *General Oglethorpe's Georgia: Colonial Letters, 1733–1743,* 2 vols. (Savannah, 1975), 1:19–23.

12. Lee and Agnew, *Historical Record of the City of Savannah*, 8–9; R. D. Barnett, "Dr. Samuel Nunes Ribeiro and The Settlement of Georgia," in *Migration and Settlement: Papers on Anglo-American Jewish History* (London, 1971): 63–97; *Manuscripts of the Earl of Egmont, 1:440.*

13. Ettinger, *James Edward Oglethorpe,* 137; Allen D. Candler et al., eds., *The Colonial Records of the State of Georgia,* 32 vols. to date (Atlanta, 1904–), 1:75; E. Merton Coulter and Albert B. Saye, eds., *A List of the Early Settlers of Georgia* (Athens, Ga., 1949). It appears that the fourteen Jews who received land from Oglethorpe had purchased it. On this point, see Levy: "Early History of Georgia's Jews," 168.

14. The word "Sephardic" originates from "Sepharad," the usual Hebrew designation for the Iberian Peninsula. Sephardic Jews descend from those who lived in Spain or Portugal before the expulsions of 1492 and 1496.

15. Richard D. Barnett, "Zipra Nunes's Story," in Bertram Wallace Korn, ed., *A Bicentennial Festschrift for Jacob Rader Marcus* (New York, 1976), 49.

16. An enormous literature exists on the Jews of Spain. See Robert Singerman, comp., *Spanish and Portuguese Jewry: A Classified Bibliography* (Westport, Conn., 1993). The best recent overview is Jane S. Gerber, *The Jews of Spain: A History of the Sephardic Experience* (New York, 1992).

17. David M. Gitlitz, *Secrecy and Deceit: The Religion of the Crypto-Jews* (Philadelphia, 1996), 74.

18. The most comprehensive treatment of crypto-Jewish religious practices appears in Gitlitz, *Secrecy and Deceit.* Other good sources include Norman Roth, *Conversos, Inquisition, and the Expulsion of the Jews from Spain* (Madison, Wis., 1995); B. Netanyahu, *The Marranos of Spain from the Late 14th to the Early 16th Cen-*

tury, 3rd ed. (Ithaca, N.Y., 1999); and Michael Alpert, *Crypto-Judaism and the Spanish Inquisition* (New York, 2001).

19. Barnett, "Dr. Samuel Nunes Ribeiro," 66–68.

20. Ibid., 69–71.

21. Ibid., 71–72.

22. An *auto da fe* (Act of Faith) was a public ceremony intended to show the Church's majesty and the convicted heretic's debasement. On an announced day, people gathered in a city's principal plaza to watch accused prisoners in penitential garments hear their offenses and receive their penance. See Gitlitz, *Secrecy and Deceit,* 21.

23. Barnett, "Zipra Nunes's Story," 47–50.

24. Barnett, "Dr. Samuel Nunes Ribeiro," 77–79, 84; Richard Barnett, "Dr. Jacob de Castro Sarmento and Sephardim in Medical Practice in 18th-Century London," in *Jewish Historical Society of England. Transactions,* 36 vols. (London, 1982), 27:90, 110–11; Stern, "New Light on the Jewish Settlement of Savannah," 176–77.

25. Malcolm H. Stern, "The Sheftall Diaries: Vital Records of Savannah Jewry (1733–1808)," *American Jewish Historical Quarterly* 54 (March 1965): 246–47, offers no details on the family's life prior to arrival.

26. *Encyclopaedia Judaica,* 16 vols. (Jerusalem, 1971), 3:719.

27. Sheftall, "The Sheftalls of Savannah," 66; Kole, *Minis Family of Georgia,* 3; Levy, *Mordecai Sheftall,* 1, 3.

28. Mordecai Breuer and Michael Graetz, *German-Jewish History in Modern Times,* ed. Michael A. Meyer, 4 vols. (New York, 1996), 1:82, 191.

29. David S. Landes, "The Jewish Merchant: Typology and Stereotypology in Germany," *Leo Baeck Institute Yearbook* 19 (1974): 11–13; Breuier and Graetz, *German-Jewish History in Modern Times,* 1:27–43.

30. Monika Richarz, "Emancipation and Continuity: German Jews in the Rural Economy," in Werner E. Mosse, Arnold Pauker, and Reinhard Rürup, eds., *Revolution and Evolution: 1848 in German-Jewish History* (Tübingen, Germany, 1981), 95–96; Werner J. Cahnman, "Village and Small-Town Jews in Germany: A Typological Study," *Leo Baeck Institute Yearbook* 19 (1974): 111.

31. Werner E. Mosse, *Jews in the German Economy: The German-Jewish Economic Elite, 1820–1935* (Oxford, 1987), 24–29; Richarz, "Emancipation and Continuity," 99; Hasia R. Diner, *A Time for Gathering: The Second Generation, 1820–1880* (Baltimore, 1992), 11. For a discussion of court Jews' roles in the German economy, see Breuer and Graetz, *German-Jewish History in Modern Times,* 1:104–26.

32. William Zvi Tannenbaum, "From Community to Citizenship: The Jews of Rural Franconia, 1801–1862" (Ph.D. diss., Stanford University, 1989), 224.

33. Breuer and Graetz, *German-Jewish History in Modern Times,* 1:97–98.

34. Ibid., 1:166–224.

35. Vivian D. Lipman, *Three Centuries of Anglo-Jewish History* (Cambridge, 1961), 54; Todd M. Endelman, *The Jews of Georgian England, 1714–1830: Tradition and Change in A Liberal Society* (Philadelphia, 1979), 47; Cecil Roth, *The Great Synagogue, London, 1690–1940* (London, 1950), 144. Meticulous records kept by London's Sephardic congregation contain no references to Sheftall, Minis, or Yowell, suggesting that if they belonged to a synagogue, it was Ashkenazic.

36. R. D. Barnett, ed., "The Circumcision Register of Isaac and Abraham de Paiba (1715–1775)" in *Bevis Marks Records,* 6 vols. (Oxford, 1940–1997), 4:61–62, 71; Barnett, "Dr. Samuel Nunes Ribeiro," 79, 81–82; Stern, "New Light on the Jewish Settlement of Savannah," 175–76; Richard D. Barnett and Abraham Levy, *The Bevis Marks Synagogue* (Oxford, 1970), 10. A sixth Sephardic couple on the *William and Sarah* remarried in a Jewish ceremony in Amsterdam.

37. Benjamin Sheftall (1691–1765) and his son Levi (1739–1809) kept a diary in Juedisch-Deutsch (Yiddish) from 1733 to 1808. The original did not survive, but two English translations may be found in the Keith Reid Collection at the University of Georgia library. For an annotated version of the two diaries, see Stern, "Sheftall Diaries: Vital Records of Savannah Jewry," 243–77.

38. Stern, "New Light on the Jewish Settlement of Savannah," 184.

39. Boltzius journal entries of March 14, 20, 1734, quoted in Hühner, "Jews of Georgia in Colonial Times," 75–76.

40. John Wesley, *The Journal of John Wesley,* ed. Percy Livingstone Parker (Chicago, 1952), 43.

41. English, "John Wesley and His 'Jewish Parishioners,'" 222–23.

42. Quoted in Stern, "New Light on the Jewish Settlement of Savannah," 184.

43. Letter from Boltzius dated July 3, 1939, in Hühner, "Jews of Georgia in Colonial Times," 76–77.

44. Stern, "New Light on the Jewish Settlement of Savannah," 186.

45. Ibid., 185; Morgan, "Judaism in Eighteenth-Century Georgia," 43.

46. Quote in Levy, "Early History of Georgia's Jews," 169.

47. Saul Jacob Rubin, *Third to None: The Saga of Savannah Jewry, 1733–1983* (Savannah, 1983), 5; Sheftall, "Sheftalls of Savannah," 68.

48. Quoted in Levy, "Early History of Georgia's Jews," 170; Stern, "New Light on the Jewish Settlement of Savannah," 185.

49. Several scholars have cited the social and economic elitism in London's Sephardic community c. 1700 and later Sephardic exclusivity in America to explain early Savannah tensions. As Savannah's Portuguese and German Jews arrived in similar economic conditions and without much exposure to Europe's Sephardic community or its prejudices, this reasoning seems unconvincing. See

Jones, "Sephardim and Ashkenazim Jewish Settlers in Colonial Georgia," 531, 536; and Morgan, "Judaism in Eighteenth-Century Georgia," 44.

50. *Encyclopaedia Judaica,* 14:1168–70.

51. Stern, "New Light on the Jewish Settlement of Savannah," 181–82. At least ten ships brought Jews from London to Savannah between 1733 and 1738, including arrivals on November 12 and December 30, 1733. Philip Minis, born July 11, 1734, is considered the first white male child conceived and born in Georgia. See Kole, *Minis Family of Georgia,* 24.

52. Ibid., 193; Barnett, "Dr. Samuel Nunes Ribeiro and the Settlement of Georgia," 87–88. Jacob Yowell had died in September 1736.

53. Kole, *Minis Family of Georgia,* 3–4; Stern, "New Light on the Jewish Settlement of Savannah," 188–89.

54. Sheftall, "Sheftalls of Georgia," 69, 71–72. Mordecai Sheftall's life is told in considerable detail in Levy, *Mordecai Sheftall.*

55. Hühner, "Jews of Georgia from the Outbreak of the American Revolution to the Close of the 18th Century," 90.

56. Lee and Agnew, *Historical Record of the City of Savannah,* 19, 25, 183–85.

57. "Sheftall, "Sheftalls of Georgia," 73; Kole, *Minis Family of Georgia,* 25; Levy, *Mordecai Sheftall,* 65.

58. Hühner, "Jews of Georgia from the Outbreak of the American Revolution to the Close of the 18th Century," 89.

59. Ibid., 94, 99–103; Sheftall, "Sheftalls of Georgia," 74–75; Kole, *Minis Family of Georgia,* 28.

60. For more on these activities, see Levy, *Mordecai Sheftall,* 85–88.

61. Ibid., 96–97; Sheftall, "Sheftalls of Georgia," 76–77.

62. Rubin, *Third to None,* 39; Morgan, "Judaism in Eighteenth-Century Georgia," 48; Minutes of Congregation Mickve Israel, August 29, 1790, Savannah Jewish Archives, Georgia Historical Society, Savannah.

63. Morgan, "Judaism in Eighteenth-Century Georgia," 50.

64. Rubin, *Third to None,* 47, 50, 52, 55; Jacob Rader Marcus, *American Jewry: Documents, Eighteenth Century* (Cincinnati, 1959), 179; Minutes of Congregation Mickve Israel, October 4, 1791, September 17, 1793, September 20, 1795.

65. Samuel Rezneck, *Unrecognized Patriots: The Jews in the American Revolution* (Westport, Conn., 1975), 48, 60, 203–04, 221.

66. Rubin, *Third to None,* 52; Ira Rosenwaike, *On the Edge of Greatness: A Portrait of American Jewry in the Early National Period* (Cincinnati, 1985), 156.

67. Ira Rosenwaike estimates that as late as 1830 approximately 10 percent of Jewish households in America were German. See Rosenwaike, *On the Edge of Greatness,* 39.

68. Malcolm H. Stern, comp., *First American Jewish Families: 600 Genealogies, 1654–1988,* 3rd ed. (Baltimore, 1991), 267; Kole, *Minis Family of Georgia,* 24.

69. Jacob Rader Marcus, *To Count a People: American Jewish Population Data, 1585–1984* (Lanham, Md., 1990), 52–53; Rosenwaike, *On the Edge of Greatness,* 31; Department of the Interior, Census Office, *Report on the Social Statistics of Cities,* 2 vols. (Washington, 1887), 2:173.

70. Rubin, *Third to None,* 63–64; Minutes of Congregation Mickve Israel, April 25, 1820.

71. Morris Schappes, *A Documentary History of the Jews in the United States, 1654–1875* (New York, 1950), 151.

72. Ibid., 153–54.

73. Ibid., 155.

74. On nineteenth-century Savannah Jewry, see Mark I. Greenberg, "Creating Ethnic, Class, and Southern Identity in Nineteenth-Century America: The Jews Of Savannah, Georgia, 1830–1880" (Ph.D. diss., University of Florida, 1997); Greenberg, "Becoming Southern: The Jews of Savannah, Georgia, 1830–1870," *American Jewish History* 86 (March 1998): 55–75; and Greenberg, "Savannah's Jewish Women and the Shaping of Ethnic and Gender Identity, 1830–1900," *GHQ* 82 (Winter 1998): 751–74.

2
Southern Rabbis and The Founding of The First National Association of Rabbis

Gary P. Zola

The reconstruction of the history of the Central Conference of American Rabbis (CCAR) usually begins with the details of a "Preliminary Meeting" held in Detroit, Michigan, on July 9–10, 1889. At this meeting the rabbis in attendance resolved to form an association to unify the "Rabbis of America" for the purpose of "mutual co-operation, encouragement and support."[1]

As one might suspect, the antecedents of the CCAR may be traced to events that transpired long before the organization's official beginning in 1889. Much has been written about the various rabbinical gatherings in the United States that were, in some sense, precursors to the CCAR: the Cleveland Conference (1855),[2] the Philadelphia Conference (1869), the Rabbinical Literary Association (established in 1880)[3] and, of course, the Pittsburgh Conference (1885). To one extent or another each of these gatherings was intended to serve as an enduring venue by which rabbinical leaders (and, in some instances, the laity too) could work collectively toward addressing many of the vexing questions and challenges they were experiencing. Those who attended these conferences debated the need for liturgical reform and the goals and objectives of contemporary Jewish education as well as a wide range of ritual and philosophical questions. Why did these earlier efforts fail to sustain themselves? Isaac Mayer Wise pointed to a coalescence of factors that had long hindered his early attempts to establish a permanent rabbinical organization: ideological discord, geographical isolation, and a series of intense rabbinical rivalries.[4]

Yet conditions began to change during the last half of the nineteenth century. The Jewish population of the United States grew steadily as did the number of rabbis and Jewish religious leaders. With this rise in Jewish population, American Jewry's religious life became more diverse, more complicated. The need for a semblance of order and communal interaction became more evident. These factors conjoined to make the establishment of an authoritative ecclesiastical body a desideratum for Jews in America.[5]

In his magnum opus, *United States Jewry*, Jacob Rader Marcus emphasizes the fact that by the mid-1880s American rabbis interested in "uniformity" began to organize themselves into regional conferences. Interestingly, two such regional associations began in 1885—one in the South and one in the Northeast. In summarizing the impact of these two regional conferences, Marcus notes: "With a Northern and a Southern fellowship in existence it was inevitable that a Western or Central association would ultimately arise. This new conference was called into being in 1889 by [Isaac Mayer] Wise who had sought to organize and unite the rabbis ever since the late 1840's."[6] While it is difficult to prove the inevitability of a durable national rabbinical conference like the Central Conference, there can be little doubt that the story of these two regional associations provides us with a great deal of helpful information relating to the embryonic stages of the process that ultimately spawned the CCAR—the first permanent rabbinical conference in world Jewry.[7]

The Establishment of an Eastern Conference

Soon after his arrival in this country in 1846, Isaac Mayer Wise (1819–1900) began to advocate a national association of American rabbis.[8] Since the early 1850s gatherings and small leagues of Jewish clergy serving in the same city had organized themselves informally. One of the most important Jewish leaders of the antebellum period, Isaac Leeser (1806–1868), succeeded in unifying the Jewish clergy from five of his city's traditional congregations into the Board of Jewish Ministers of Philadelphia as early as 1861.[9] Leeser's journal, *The Occident,* subsequently noted that the purpose of this board was to "put an end to unauthorized parties interfering in matters which properly belong to acknowledged agents of the people, in which light the minister alone can be regarded." It seems that the vitality of the Philadelphia Board of Jewish Ministers ebbed and flowed until, in 1885, it was unofficially incorporated into an even larger association of Jewish clergy—perhaps the first permanent regional association—centered in New York City.[10]

Toward the close of 1884, a call was issued from six Jewish ministers—already meeting periodically in New York—inviting Jewish clergy from that city *and* "their colleagues as resided within comparatively easy distance of New York" to join in the formation of a "Jewish Ministers Association."[11] The six conveners were Gustav Gottheil (1827–1903), of Congregation Emanu-El; Adolph Huebsch (1830–1884), of Ahavath Chesed; Henry S. Jacobs (1827–1893), of B'nai Jeshurun; Kaufmann Kohler (1843–1926), of Beth El; Frederic de Sola Mendes (1850–1927), of Shaaray Tefila; and his younger brother Henry Pereira Mendes (1852–1937), of Shearith Israel.[12]

On January 19, 1885, 22 men attended the first meeting of this group in New York. Twelve came from communities outside the greater New York metropolitan area, including cities such as Albany, Baltimore, Boston, Newark, New Haven, Philadelphia, Rochester and Syracuse. Significantly, the group resolved to call itself "The Jewish Ministers' Association of America" but despite this expectant name the association never amounted to anything more than a regional organization and was often referred to as the "Eastern Conference of Jewish Ministers" in a variety of unpublished documents.[13]

This newly established Jewish Ministers' Association of America did manage to enlist the cooperation, at least temporarily, of men who inclined toward both the Reformist and the conservative approach to Jewish religious life. This was no mean achievement at the time. Tensions arose between Jewish leaders who believed in religious reform with moderation and those who advocated a more progressive, modernist approach—the so-called radicals. The persistent advance of reform in American synagogues provoked bitter dissension among rabbis and laity as to what was and was not permissible. Sectarian newspapers fanned the flames of these religious controversies and often magnified the level of hostility. By 1884 points of cooperation between the two ideological camps had become exceedingly ephemeral.[14]

The establishment of the Union of American Hebrew Congregations (UAHC) in 1873 and the Hebrew Union College (HUC) in 1875 provided a short-lived hope for holding reform and traditional synagogues —and their rabbis—under one umbrella organization. The conservative wing became increasingly fearful that the UAHC and its college were actually Wise's furtive tools for imposing unwanted radical reforms—most especially a Reform uniformity—on the American synagogue. The radicals, for their part, resented these protests, which they considered baseless charges rooted in local prejudices. Reformers viewed the constant assaults from the conservatives as nothing more than a self-serving pretext for frustrating their hopes for American Jewish unity. Although this controversy found its expression in many parts of the nation, this strife became particularly strident in the Northeast during the 1870s and 1880s, when traditional Jewish sentiments intensified in that region.[15]

Thus it was significant indeed that two of American Judaism's most notable reformers participated in the Eastern Conference: Kaufmann Kohler (1843–1926), the eminent theologian and rabbi of Temple Beth-El in New York City, and David Philipson (1862–1949)—one of HUC's first four ordinees—then serving Har Sinai Congregation in Baltimore. On the other side of the ideological aisle were men such as the scholarly Marcus Jastrow (1829–1903) and the distinguished rabbi Sabato Morais (1823–1897), leaders of the so-called historical school of thought out of which would eventually emerge the Jewish Theological Seminary of America and the Conservative Movement in Judaism. Jastrow and Morais came to New York from Philadelphia, where they served congregations. Both men had been presidents of Philadelphia's Board of Ministers. While in Philadelphia, Jastrow and Morais undoubtedly felt the influence of the remarkable *hazan* Isaac Leeser. As early as 1841 Leeser began pushing for a national union of congregations that would sponsor, among other things, an authoritative ecclesiastical board to license teachers and supervise Philadelphia's Jewish schools.[16]

Even in an opening statement about the association's primary objectives, the conveners of the Eastern Conference attempted to allay concern about the group's raison d'être. Many of the conservatively-inclined leaders—men like Jastrow and Morais—had originally lent their support to the formation of the Union of American Hebrew Congregations and the Hebrew Union College. By 1883, however, they had become leery about Wise and the institutions he headed.[17]

In envisioning this new association the conference organizers sought to reassure all prospective members that their group would neither encroach upon the independence of its clergy members nor threaten the sovereignty of the congregations they served. Organizers declared that the primary purpose of the association was to "promote brotherly feeling and harmony among its members, to be helpful by mutual counsel without fettering individual opinion, and to strive by friendly union and co-operation to advance and strengthen the best interests of Judaism without interference with congregational autonomy."[18]

The Eastern Conference elected the highly regarded Gustav Gottheil as its first president. Gottheil maintained close professional ties with both the reformists and the conservatives, earning the trust of both ends of the ideological spectrum. Gottheil served as the superintendent of the Emanu-El Theological Association, established in 1877, a not-very-successful attempt by the Eastern reformers to establish a rabbinical school of their own in New York. Nevertheless, the fact that Wise selected Gottheil to serve as one of the main speakers at the first ordination ceremony of the Hebrew Union College in 1883 underscored the high regard in which Gottheil was held by the community at large.[19] The opening meeting of the Eastern Conference in January 1885 seemed to have gone quite well. Both reformists and traditionalists presented a variety of scholarly papers. Jastrow delivered a talk on the "Alliance Is-raélite Universelle"; Morais spoke on the subject of "The Jewish Pulpit"; Philipson lectured on "The Hebrew Union College"; Gottheil read a paper entitled "The Drift of Modern Christian Thought"; Frederick de Sola Mendes' subject was "Higher Charity"; and his brother Henry spoke on "The Sphere of Congregational Work." Finally, Kohler delivered what was called "an exhaustive essay" on Sabbath school reform. The East-erners proceeded to appoint a committee to draft a constitution and by-laws to be considered at their next meeting, scheduled to take place in Philadelphia on April 13, 1885.[20]

The Establishment of A Southern Conference

On Tuesday, April 14, 1885, 15 Jewish ministers from various locations in the South gathered in New Orleans. Coming from cities in Alabama, Arkansas, Georgia, Louisiana, Mississippi, Tennessee, and Texas, the del-egates resolved to organize themselves into a Southern association of Jewish clergy to be known as "The Conference of Rabbis of Southern Congregations."[21] Geographically speaking, the maintenance of a per-manent colloquium of Southern rabbis must have been a challenging enterprise. Yet the craving for professional fellowship and the need for mutual support in a largely frontier region made the extra effort worth-while.

The fact that the *second* meeting of the Eastern Conference (April 13, 1885) took place on practically the same day as the founding meeting of the Southern Conference suggests strongly that the activities of the East-ern Conference had prompted or, at the very least, motivated the Jewish clergy of the South to assemble themselves. Although it is impossible to know with certainty how these two regional associations came into being at the same time, there are some likely suppositions.

It is certainly possible that Philipson discussed the conference's activities with three of his former HUC classmates serving Southern congregations in 1885: Henry Berkowitz (1857–1924), class of 1883, leader of a congregation in Mobile, Alabama; Joseph Silverman (1860–1930), class of 1884, rabbi of the then small Dallas congregation Emanu-El; and Joseph Stolz (1861–1941), also ordained in 1884, who was serving in Little Rock, Arkansas. Of course, Kohler—who (as we shall see) tried to ally the Eastern and Southern Conferences—may very well have sparked his Southern colleagues into action. Though the link to the South remains elusive, there was one Southerner whom most of the Northern rabbis knew quite well—the distinguished convener of the Southern Conference, its first president and unquestionably its most venerated member: James Koppel Gutheim (1817–1886).[22]

Gutheim, known as the "High Priest of Southern Judaism," came to the United States in 1843 and worked in New York City as a bookkeeper in his brother's counting room. Soon he began contributing articles to the Anglo-Jewish press. By 1844 Leeser noted Gutheim's potential and praised him in the pages of *The Occident* for having "in so short a time acquired a great facility to express himself so generally correctly in the English language." Leeser's hope that Gutheim would soon be able to devote himself to "advancing the cause of Jewish faith" in America was fulfilled in 1846 when the latter accepted an offer to serve as headmaster of a Talmud Torah school in Cincinnati.[23]

Soon after his arrival in Cincinnati Gutheim became minister of Congregation B'nai Jeshurun, an appointment which launched his career as an American rabbi. Gutheim's proficiency in English made him an appealing personality. At the time, he was one of only a handful of rabbis who could preach in the vernacular. The oldest Jewish congregation in New Orleans, Shangaray Chessed (Gates of Mercy), coaxed him away from Cincinnati in 1849 and the following January (1850) elected him "minister" of that pulpit. Only a few years later (November 1853) Nefutzot Yehudah (Dispersed of Judah)—a New Orleans congregation receiving financial support from wealthy Jewish philanthropist Judah Touro—enticed Gutheim to move across town for a handsome annual salary of $2,000.[24]

In 1868 Congregation Emanu-El brought Gutheim to New York to serve alongside their distinguished senior rabbi, Rev. Dr. Samuel Adler, as its English preacher. During the four years he spent in New York, a sojourn which signaled his official association with Reform Judaism, Gutheim produced a number of publications, including numerous articles in the Anglo-Jewish press, a volume of his own sermons, metrical translations of many psalms, original hymns for Emanu-El's prayer service, and a translation of the fourth volume of Heinrich Graetz's *History of the Jews* for the short-lived American Jewish Publication Society. Nevertheless, life in New York was apparently less than satisfying. In 1870 his friends and admirers in New Orleans established a new Reform congregation called Temple Sinai and, just as soon as its structure was completed in 1872, Gutheim accepted their invitation to become the temple's first rabbi—a post he held until his death in 1886.[25]

Gutheim's stint in New York provided him with the opportunity to experience the benefits that came from the regular association with colleagues. In New York and other large cities, Jewish ministers frequently worked together on projects relating to Jewish communal welfare. The relatively large number of Jewish religious leaders in a city like New York made it possible for Jewish ministers to work collectively, sensing that, like any other group, they would wield more influence if they joined together as a guild. Gutheim may very well have carried this lesson with him when he returned to New Orleans.[26]

It is also interesting to note that with the four principal objectives set down during the first session of the new Southern Conference—though a bit more specific than those articulated by the Eastern Conference— the founding members avoided placing matters of religious faith and practice on their organizational agenda:

1) The interchange of opinions and views on all subjects appertaining to the functions of the rabbinical office.
2) The fostering and promoting of literary work relating to Judaism and its history.
3) The promoting of "fraternal feelings" among the members of the Conference.
4) The organizing and administration of congregational religious schools "in accordance with approved methods."[27]

These objectives suggest that, in this early stage at least, some in the Northeast *and* in the South hoped that the two regional groups would work closely together, perhaps even amalgamate as one. There are other intimations that close cooperation was the goal of some members of both associations.

First, it is clear that each conference knew what the other was doing. When the Southern Conference opened on Tuesday morning, April 14, 1885, the following telegram dated April 13 was read aloud and received with applause: "The Rabbinical Conference now in session send the Southern Rabbinical Conference this fraternal greeting with best wishes for success. [signed] Dr. K. Kohler."[28]

The Southerners wasted no time in responding to Kohler with a telegram of their own: "The Southern Conference, just organized, heartily reciprocates the good wishes expressed." And they affixed a noteworthy postscript: "Our motto," the Southern rabbis declared, "is union, peace and progress."[29]

That Kohler's name was appended to the telegram is a fascinating curiosity. Though he was an active and prominent member of the Eastern Conference, Kohler was *not* the secretary of the association. In fact, Kohler was not even a member of the executive committee. The significance of this peculiarity becomes even more apparent when Kohler wired a second dispatch read to the Southerners on the opening day of their second conference, held December 29–30, 1885. In his rejoinder to the Southern Conference's communication to the Easterners, Kohler—apparently speaking for himself and not, as we shall see, for the Eastern Conference—significantly repeated their thought: "Fraternal greetings to your conference; best success; union and progress is our common motto." "Union and progress," undoubtedly referred to the reformist hope that unity and progress were indeed obtainable.[30]

That the Southerners also received an "official" message from the president and officers of the Eastern Conference—with contents that differed significantly from that of Kohler's—lends further weight to the conjecture that Kohler drafted these notes on his own initiative. Gottheil's telegram expressed the wish that "under God their labors may redound to the preservation of our common faith and the religious welfare of our people. [signed] G. Gottheil, President and F. de Sola Mendes, secretary."[31]

Additional evidence lends credence to the theory that the two events were, at the very least, informally connected. On April 15, 1885, the second day of the Southerners' first convention, they adopted two resolutions indicating that (a) they had already obtained rather extensive information as to what had transpired during the meeting of the Eastern

Conference the preceding January, and (b) they had decided to establish contact officially with their colleagues in the Eastern Conference. First, the Southerners ratified a resolution in which they pledged their "support and sympathy" for the purposes of the Alliance Israélite Universelle—a discussion of which had occupied the Easterners during their first conference. Second, they voted to have the conference's secretary "enter into correspondence with the secretary of the Eastern Conference, requesting an interchange of views and opinions."[32]

To whatever extent the hope existed that these two regional associations could work in tandem, such a cooperative venture never got off the ground. In fact, the last six months of 1885 witnessed a series of events that not only subverted the nascent effort to link the two regional rabbinical associations but led to the establishment of a Reform-dominated Central Conference and, ultimately, to a permanent division between the so-called radicals and conservatives.

A Watershed Platform in Pittsburgh

When the 18 rabbis who had gathered in Pittsburgh on November 16 to 18, 1885, sat down to deliberate the now-famous platform Kaufmann Kohler placed before them, Isaac M. Wise—serving as chair—opened the debate with his often-quoted query: "Gentlemen, what are we going to do with this Declaration of Independence?" Although Wise may have simply been asking whether the group was going to adopt the platform, his question actually prefigured the document's historic impact, for in the aftermath of Pittsburgh, the long-sought-after dream of a united American Judaism was supplanted by the reality of a unified Reform Jewish movement. The establishment of the Central Conference of American Rabbis three years after the promulgation of the platform gave institutional substance to the independence the reformers had wrought in Pittsburgh.[33]

Several factors conjoined during the first half of 1885 to pave the road to Pittsburgh. First of all, those loyal to Wise, HUC and a more radical approach to religious reform sensed that their day was about to dawn.[34] Already in 1884 Wise himself predicted that before too long a coalition of HUC graduates and the other liberal colleagues would be capable of forming a viable and permanent national rabbinical association. The first official gathering of the newly organized Hebrew Union College Alumni Association, which took place in St. Louis in July, 1885, made Wise's claim that much more credible.[35]

In addition to the increased strength of the so-called radicals' camp, an intensification of hostilities between radicals and conservatives during the first half of 1885 may very well have impelled Kohler to convene the legendary conference that met in Pittsburgh. As we have seen, tensions between these two factions had waxed and waned for many years, and the hard feelings flared up once again in May 1885 when Alexander Kohut (1842–1894), the newly installed rabbi of New York's Ahavat Chesed (Lovers of Mercy) congregation, began preaching a series of sermons attacking Reform Judaism. Kohut's discourses incensed Kohler who took up the gauntlet in June 1885 by delivering a series of five lectures that ardently championed the validity of religious reform.[36] In a letter to his congregation's Board of Trustees, Kohler explained why he decided to spar so publicly with his traditionally minded colleague: "We want Union. We want co-operation in all matters pertaining to the common interests of Judaism in America and world over. But we cannot allow any interference with our religious progress by Rabbinical anathemas."[37]

Speaking before the CCAR in 1935, on the fiftieth anniversary of the Pittsburgh conference, David Philipson insisted that the disputation between Kohut and Kohler was "the real cause for the calling of the Pittsburgh conference by Dr. Kohler." Philipson may have been overstating for effect, but there can be little doubt that the Kohut/Kohler controversy of 1885 inflamed an ideological sore that had festered for many years.

The Kohut/Kohler conflict attracted widespread attention. This clash of the intellectual titans stimulated rekindled interest in the ideological debate about Judaism's future. Traditionalists in the East began calling for the establishment of a seminary that would compete with HUC and educate rabbis to serve conservative and orthodox pulpits. Simultaneously, Kohler concluded that unity with the conservatives was no longer a viable option. According to Philipson it was this realization that prompted Kohler to write to rabbis throughout the country and invite all those who believed in "Reform and Progress" to join him in Pittsburgh "for the purpose of discussing the present state of American Judaism, its pending issues and its requirements, and of uniting upon such plans and practical measures as are demanded by the hour."[38]

Kohler's religious conviction, his sense of urgency and, possibly, his impatience with the affairs of the Eastern Conference may be discerned in a personal note he appended to David Philipson's invitation to Pittsburgh: "Let us concentrate our forces and *accomplish* something *creditable* and worthy of a Conference of Rabbis! We must have you, and I wish you would prepare or suggest something in the way of *practical* reform!"[39]

Three members of the Eastern Conference—Kohler, Max Schlesinger (1837–1919),[40] and Philipson—attended the Pittsburgh Conference (approximately 8% of the Eastern Conference's membership). Two others, Max Landsberg (1845–1928) and Leopold Wintner (d. 1923), sent letters of support. No one from the Southern Rabbinical Conference came to Pittsburgh, but six members—Henry Berkowitz, Henry M. Bien (d. 1895), James K. Gutheim, Sigmund Hecht, Joseph Silverman, and Joseph Stolz (approximately 35 percent of the Southern Conference's membership)—sent Kohler letters and telegrams lamenting their inability to attend and wishing their colleagues success in their meeting.[41]

In Pittsburgh Kohler told his colleagues that it was "high time to rally our forces to *consolidate,* to build." Without doubt, the Pittsburgh Platform provoked consolidation. The conferees had framed, in eight concise paragraphs, a statement that defined what were then the core values of American Reform Judaism. In its promulgation, the platform earned strong reaction—both positive and negative; no one remained indifferent. Many extolled the document as an elegant expression of the religious sentiments they cherished. Others excoriated the platform's abandonment of traditional rite and practice.[42]

Consequently, the fact that the two regional rabbinical conferences reacted to the platform in profoundly different ways should come as no surprise. When the members of the Eastern Conference reconvened in May 1886, the liberal and conservative elements of the organization showed unmistakable signs of heightened polarization as a result of Pittsburgh. The group's president, Gottheil, pleaded for tolerance and forbearance among his colleagues: "Brethren—if the bond that holds us together were, indeed, so brittle that the least shock or friction could shatter it and drive us apart, little would it matter what I said today . . . Our doom would be sealed."[43]

Despite Gottheil's plea for equanimity, the more conservative members of the group viewed the Pittsburgh meeting as a calamity. An unsigned editorial in the *American Hebrew* wondered whether conservative congregations ought to continue supporting the UAHC and the HUC. These attacks incited pro-Reform members of the Eastern Conference, who charged that the underlying goal of their opponents was obviously "the disruption of the Union of American Hebrew Congregations and the destruction of the Hebrew Union College."[44] Wise himself, never one to shy away from a fight, subsequently declared that the Reformers were the true American orthodox and that the conservative elements in American Judaism constituted "an anachronism."[45]

Gottheil assured those assembled that the Eastern Conference would neither adopt nor be swayed by any one doctrine or tenet. As he put it, "membership in this Association carries with it no responsibility for an associate's opinions; we do not attempt to convert one another." The purpose of their organization, Gottheil maintained, was merely to provide a forum for united efforts in the fields of charity and Jewish education. Membership in the association did not, he insisted, bind members to any action or stance. Just gathering together for open discussion and dialogue was sufficient justification for their meeting; "even if no tangible result could be attained . . . we do not come together in vain." Nevertheless, tensions in the Eastern Conference had flared to such an extent that by the end of 1886 Gottheil wondered whether the Jewish Ministers Association would be adjourning for the usual period of six months—or indefinitely![46]

Prior to the conclusion of its first meeting in April 1885, the Southern Conference agreed to reconvene the following October in New Orleans, probably because the Eastern Conference had planned to meet and did in fact meet October 26–27, 1885. The Southerners *did* meet again in New Orleans, but not in October. They gathered two months later, in December. Although no explicit reason for the two-month delay survives in the conference documents, it is possible that the Southern Conference's October meeting was postponed in deference to the Pittsburgh conference that had unexpectedly been scheduled for mid-November.[47]

In any event, the text of the Pittsburgh Platform circulated quickly throughout the Jewish community. In contrast to the Easterners, those in the Southern Conference evidenced much greater accord with one another and with the controversial principles adopted in Pittsburgh. The platform spoke to Southerners, who had become accustomed to living as a distinct minority far from any center of Jewish life and culture. Furthermore, many of Wise's rabbinical allies—his students and former students—served congregations in the Midwest and South. Wise's personal endorsement of the platform obviously carried weight with disciples who served in these regions. The degree to which the platform spoke to the Southerners may be seen in the fact that their conference officially endorsed the declaration (although the membership did reserve the right, individually and collectively, "to dissent from any practical deductions that may be drawn from [it]").[48]

When the Southern Conference reconvened on December 30, 1885, the group easily succeeded in ratifying several resolutions, any one of which would have been much too controversial for the Eastern Conference to debate:

1. They appointed a committee to discuss how their group could best achieve "uniformity in textbooks and prayerbooks" for their synagogues and schools.
2. Recognizing the success of the Hebrew Union College and the "able, unselfish and faithful labor of its President and faculty," they passed a resolution pledging themselves to a "full measure" of "moral support to the Union of American Hebrew Congregations and the HUC."[49]
3. The Southerners "subjected the principles enunciated by the Pittsburgh Conference to an anxious and rigorous examination" and decided that "they are in harmony with the spirit of Progressive Judaism and must be regarded as the inferences made by Jewish teachers from the oldest conceptions of our faith."[50]

The ability of the Southern Conference to adopt these resolutions bespoke the ideological unity of its members. Even as the impact of the Pittsburgh Platform consolidated the Southern rabbinical conference, it fractured the tenuous spirit of accord that still survived in the rabbinical association of the East.

Over the next three years the Eastern Conference assiduously avoided issues related to ritual or communal uniformity. As Gustav Gottheil pointedly remarked, "the *unity* which has until now been represented by the identity of faith and practice, may still be preserved despite the diversity of opinion and the differences of ritual now obtaining." He reminded his colleagues that all previous attempts to establish permanent rabbinical conferences had failed, "perhaps [because] the synodical character given to these assemblies proved fatal to them."[51]

Gottheil's remark served as a warning to his colleagues; whenever rabbis created a synod-like conference that tried to legislate or enact religious policy, the inevitable result was dissension and disunity. To avoid the problem, rabbis should join together in a professional association that would facilitate the more benign goal of fruitful dialogue. Between

1886–1888 the Easterners dealt almost exclusively with "theoretical questions, and fostering of united work."[52]

The committee structure of the Eastern Conference reflected the areas upon which they could agree to work together: the committee on "Moral Instruction in Public Schools" debated the advantages and disadvantages of universal education. The committee on the "Home Prayer-Book" concerned itself with prayers for "daily use and occasional devotions of a domestic nature." A committee on "Marriages" dealt primarily with the group's concern over the laxity of some secular laws regulating marriages and divorce that were construed to be "detrimental to the sanctity of the home life." In addition, the Easterners listened to numerous learned papers written by conference members, and they issued joint statements lamenting the death of prominent individuals, such as Henry Ward Beecher and Emma Lazarus. Despite the fact that the Eastern Conference's leadership tried to steer the group's agenda away from ideological disputations, the schism between the conference's reformists and conservatives grew. After 1886 the so-called radicals—men like Philipson and Kohler—apparently stopped participating in the Eastern Conference.[53]

Here again the Southerners followed a distinctly different path. The religious consensus that typified their region influenced the organizational character of the Southern Conference. Evidently, the rabbis who belonged to the Southern Conference had no trouble agreeing on common goals and a shared ideology. As early as 1886 the Southerners began working toward uniform ritual and communal practices. The structure of the Southern Conference included committees on "Uniformity of Text-Books in our Schools and Prayer-Books in our Synagogues"; liturgical committees on "Confirmation," "Marriage," and "Burial"; and even a committee for the preservation of the "History of Jews in the Southern States." When HUC ordinees Maximilian Heller (1860–1929), class of 1884, and Moses P. Jacobson (1864–1945), class of 1886, joined the Southern Conference in 1887, the reformist/Cincinnati tradition quickly consolidated and dominated the spirit of the Southern Conference. The Southerners resolved to openly champion the advancement of the Hebrew Union College.[54]

The Advent of The CCAR

In his memoirs, David Philipson claimed that late in March 1889 Wise told him the large class of rabbis he was about to ordain would provide him with enough rabbinical disciples of his own to guarantee the organization of a national rabbinical organization. At the conclusion of the Union of American Hebrew Congregations meeting held in Detroit in July of that same year, the rabbis in attendance convened to organize "a Central Conference of American Rabbis." Predictably, the newly established Central Conference garnered most of its support from the Midwest, the West and the South. The universalist message of the Pittsburgh Platform made good religious sense to the smaller, more isolated Jewish communities that struggled to endure in these three regions of the country. Furthermore, almost all of Wise's "boys" (i.e., HUC alumni ordained during the years 1883 to 1889) were serving pulpits in these regions. Six former members of the Southern Conference became charter members of the newly established Central Conference. By comparison, only two former Eastern Conference members joined: Lippman Mayer (1841–1904) of Pittsburgh and David Philipson, who in 1888 left Baltimore to return to Cincinnati. Although there is no record of the Southern Conference having been formally disbanded, by 1893 virtually every one of the 26 names on the roster of the Southern Conference had joined the CCAR. For all intents and purposes the Central Conference absorbed the membership of the Southern Conference, creating a rabbinical association with a national constituency.[55]

The Eastern Conference, on the other hand, avoided any such merger. A number of Eastern rabbis belonged to both the Eastern Conference *and* the CCAR in the early 1890s. HUC alumnus Joseph Silverman, who came to New York's Congregation Emanu-El in 1888, brought fraternal greetings from the Eastern Conference to the second meeting (July 1891) of the Central Conference. The gesture sparked "an extended discussion of the true intent and significance of the message," and Silverman, Joseph Leucht (1840–1920) and Lippman Mayer (all members of the Eastern Conference at that time) were instructed on motion to "formulate the sentiments and attitude of the Central Conference toward the Jewish Ministers' Association." If formulated, these sentiments were never recorded. One thing is certain: the CCAR flourished and rapidly attracted a national constituency. The Eastern Conference, on the other hand, soon recast itself as a local Board of Jewish Ministers.[56]

At the first annual CCAR convention held in Cleveland, Ohio, on Sunday, July 13, 1890, Wise outlined a conference agenda that must have been familiar to the rabbis who had been members of the now defunct Conference of Rabbis of Southern Congregations:

1. The united rabbis of America have a right and duty to produce a uniform form of worship for all our houses of worship.
2. The united rabbis have the duty to provide a catechism for the Sabbath-schools on the same principle with the ritual.
3. The united rabbis should give fresh impulses to the study of the literature of Israel.
4. Whatever the individual could not or should not do, and yet ought to be done in support of Israel's mission . . . the Conference could and should do.[57]

Wise reminded his colleagues that "the main duty of a rabbi in Israel is to preserve, develop and exalt Judaism in strict adherence to its own spirit and a conscientious appreciation of the just demands of time and place." This, Wise insisted, was the essence of a modern, "progressive" Judaism. According to Wise, this ideological solidarity must be a foundational principle—"the *conditio sine qua non*"—for all those who wish to join the Central Conference: "The so-called orthodox or conservative men may be of a different opinion in regard to the rights of time, place and circumstances, contrary even to the admissions of the Talmud. In this association and conference no difference of opinion on this point can justly prevail [and this is] the basis on which the development of Judaism shall be continued."[58]

So from the very inception of the CCAR, membership became synonymous with a commitment to the principles of religious reform, a tacit affirmation of the Pittsburgh declaration. The key to the new rabbinical association's success was indeed ideological homogeneity. By 1890 it was clear that only one of the two regional conferences which preceded the establishment of the CCAR could abide by this axiom. The Eastern Conference, beset as it was by impassioned ideologists of every persuasion and the complexities of an ever-expanding immigrant metropolis, eventually evolved into the New York Board of Jewish Ministers. The board adopted the organizational model of a council or league in which participants with ideological differences joined together for study and cooperation on noncontroversial matters of common concern. The Board eschewed ruling on matters of ritual or ideological policy that might engender controversy or provoke schism.

On the other hand, the principles of Reform as set forth in the Pittsburgh Platform constituted a modus vivendi congruous with Jewish life in the South. The Southern rabbis needed a rabbinical organization in which they could work collectively to survive in their modern American environment. As Wise would later say, rabbis must respond to "the just demands of time and place." The Southerners wanted to address the exigencies of modern life by adopting principles, prescribing curricula, and developing liturgical uniformity that befitted their day and age. These initiatives offered those who lived in smaller Jewish communities a viable stratagem (as Wise put it) "to preserve, develop and exalt" a Judaism that had planted its roots in a vast, non-Jewish landscape. Ultimately, it was this same spirit of ideological unity—a perception that the newly established Central Conference was comprised of colleagues who believed in the same religious values and shared a common vision for contemporary Judaism—that imbued the fledgling CCAR with its genuine vitality.

In his reminiscences about the beginning of the CCAR, Wise explained that those attending the rabbinical association's first meeting selected the name "Central Conference" because two regional rabbinical organizations (Eastern and Southern) were already in existence. "It was supposed," Wise said, "that members would come, aside from alumni and faculty of the Hebrew Union College, from the Central States." For the sake of historical drama, Wise may very well have been minimizing his original ambitions for the Conference. After all, he had been the primary advocate of a national rabbinical body from his earliest days in America, and it is difficult to imagine that the great architect of American Judaism would have been satisfied with the concept of three independent, regional bodies. It is important to remember that, in its very first official act, the new Central Conference cast itself as the historical heir of "all modern Rabbinical Conferences held from Braunschweig in 1844, and including all like assemblages held since." This new conference was not to be merely a regional association without doctrine. To the contrary, it was to be, as Wise would say, "the lawful authority in all matters of form."[59]

By 1893 Wise could justifiably pronounce, with characteristic panache, the four-year-old CCAR a "phenomenal success." With a membership in excess of 120, the Conference attracted not simply those from the central states but "the rabbis of the largest and most prominent congregations in the land, East and West, North and South, and the entire faculty of the Hebrew Union College." The organization had indeed become "truly national." Wise's observation was a confirmation of the fact that the Southern Conference had, in an apparently seamless fashion, folded itself into the Central Conference. The Southern Conference's ideological commitment to Reform made it, in essence, a regional prototype for the national rabbinical conference it would ultimately help to form. This convenient collaboration altered, in effect, the geographical meaning of the words "Central Conference," for the new national rabbinical organization had indeed become central, but *not* in reference to location alone. As the first national rabbinical organization to attract "the learning and the working ability of American Judaism," the *Central* Conference had quickly become the *leading* association of American rabbis.[60]

Notes

1. *CCAR Yearbook* 1 (1891):3–4.

2. The Cleveland Conference was not exclusively a rabbinical conference since a few laymen also attended.

3. Rabbi Max Lilienthal (1815–1882) established the Rabbinical Literary Association in 1879. This organization provided rabbis and some laity with a forum for intellectual discussion and exchange of views. See Jacob Rader Marcus, *United States Jewry* (Detroit, 1993) 3:125, 529.

4. *CCAR Yearbook* 1 (1891):13–16.

5. On the early history of the CCAR, see Sidney L. Regner, "The History of the Conference," in *Retrospect and Prospect: Essays in Commemoration of the Seventy-Fifth Anniversary of the Founding of the Central Conference of American Rabbis, 1889–1964* (New York, 1965), 1–19. For a summary of Wise's explanation on the failure of previous conferences see Regner, 3.

6. Marcus, *United States Jewry* 3:125–26. See also Michael A. Meyer, *Response to Modernity: A History of the Reform Movement in Judaism* (New York, 1988), 276.

7. Marcus, *United States Jewry* 3:126.

8. *CCAR Yearbook* 1 (1891):123, and Marcus, *United States Jewry,* 3:58–59.

9. The rabbis of Chicago, for example, began meeting locally as early as 1873. See Marcus, *United States Jewry* 3:529.

10. Malcolm H. Stern, "The Philadelphia Board of Rabbis: 125th Anniversary Address" (unpublished address in possession of author, June 8, 1988), 1–3.

11. *Jewish Conference Papers (1886) Together with Reports of the Meetings of the Jewish Ministers' Association of America* (New York, 1887), 39.

12. There is some evidence to suggest that the invitation was issued by a small group of New York Jewish ministers who had, a few years earlier, organized themselves into The New York Board of Jewish Ministers. See David de Sola Pool, "The New York Board of Jewish Ministers," in *The Jewish Communal Register of New York City, 1917–1918* (New York, [1918?]), 294.

13. The Jewish Ministers' Association of America is referred to exclusively as the "Eastern Conference" in the minutes book of the Conference of Rabbis of Southern Congregations.

14. Wise described this controversy in great detail. See his first presidential address to the CCAR in *CCAR Yearbook* 1 (1891):13–17. Michael A. Meyer used the phrase "an ephemeral broad unity" in describing the Union of American Hebrew Congregations (UAHC) during the first decade of its existence, see *idem, Response to Modernity,* 260.

15. Marcus, *United States Jewry* 3:135–37. See also Michael A. Meyer, *A Centennial History of Hebrew Union College-Jewish Institute of Religion, 1875–1975* (Cincinnati, 1993), 38–43.

16. Arthur Kiron has recently published an insightful essay on the life of Sabato Morais. See "'Dust and Ashes': The Funeral and Forgetting of Sabato Morais," *American Jewish History* 84 (September 1996):155–88. On Leeser see Lance J. Sussman, *Isaac Leeser and the Making of American Judaism* (Detroit, 1995).

17. Meyer, *A Centennial History,* 42–43.

18. *Jewish Conference Papers (1886),* 39.

19. Meyer, *A Centennial History,* 38, 41. On Gottheil's professional associations and attitudes toward colleagues, see Richard Gottheil, *The Life of Gustav Gottheil: Memoir of a Priest In Israel* (Williamsport, Pa., 1936), 97–145.

20. *Jewish Conference Papers (1886),* 40.

21. Little has been written about the Conference of Rabbis of Southern Congregations despite the fact that the manuscript minutes of its meetings (hereafter cited as "Minutes") have survived and are now located in the American Jewish Archives, Cincinnati, Ohio, in the Conference of Rabbis of Southern Congregations File. Also, a small portion of these minutes was published in the *CCAR Yearbook* 2 (1892):57–65. Unless noted to the contrary, all references to "Minutes" refer to the original manuscript.

22. Like its Eastern counterpart, the Conference of Rabbis of Southern Congregations was comprised of several individuals who were destined for careers of prominence in the American rabbinate: Jacob Voorsanger (1852–1908), then the rabbi of Houston's Beth Israel Congregation, went on to become a distinguished minister at Congregation Emanu-El of San Francisco, and Max Samfield (1844?–1915), a founding member of the CCAR, served Congregation B'nai Israel of Memphis for nearly 45 years. Significantly, the three recent ordinees from the fledgling rabbinical college in Cincinnati who attended the historic gathering later distinguished themselves in the American rabbinate: Henry Berkowitz eventually assumed the pulpit of Rodeph Shalom Congregation in Philadelphia and was the founder and chancellor of the Jewish Chautauqua Society. Ordained in 1884, Joseph Silverman became the rabbi of Congregation Emanu-El, New York City. Joseph Stolz was ultimately called to Chicago's Isaiah Temple, where he served for more than three decades.

23. *The Occident* 1 (1843–1844):554–55.

24. Gutheim's departure from the South may have come as a surprise at the time. His decision to leave New Orleans in May 1963 rather than take the Oath of Allegiance required by the Union military made Gutheim a bona fide Confederate hero. In his *Jubilee Souvenir of Temple Sinai, 1872–1922* (New Orleans, 1912), II, Rabbi Max Heller (Gutheim's successor) noted Gutheim's loyalty to the region by his "refusing to take the oath of loyalty" and retreating "with his family to the privations of 'the Confederacy,'" before being lured to New York. For more on Gutheim's voluntary exile from New Orleans, see Bertram W. Korn, *American Jewry and the Civil War* (Philadelphia, 1951), 47–51.

25. For more biographical information on Gutheim, see Gary P. Zola, "James Koppel Gutheim," *American National Biography* (1999).

26. In November 1853 Isaac Leeser attended the cornerstone laying ceremonies for the Jews' Hospital in New York, where he encountered "no less than fourteen" of his fellow Jewish clergymen. Leeser, who came from a relatively substantial Jewish community in Philadelphia, was so taken by the phenomenon that he later remarked that the gathering consisted of "more Jewish ministers than we ever saw at one time." See Jacob Rader Marcus, *Memoirs of American Jews* (New York, 1974), 2:85.

27. "Minutes," 3–5.

28. Ibid., 2.

29. Ibid.

30. Ibid., 12.

31. Ibid., 20.

32. Ibid., 11.

33. For the quote see the "Proceedings of the Pittsburgh Rabbinical Conference, 1885" in Walter Jacob, ed., *The Pittsburgh Platform in Retrospect* (Pittsburgh, 1985), 109.

34. David Philipson, "The Pittsburgh Rabbinical Conference," *CCAR Yearbook* 45 (1935): 193–97.

35. Max B. May, *Isaac Mayer Wise: A Biography* (New York, 1916), 336.

36. Robert W. Ross, "The Pittsburgh Platform of 1885: One Hundred Years Old," in Jacob, *The Pittsburgh Platform,* 55–62.

37. Ibid., 195.

38. David Philipson, "The Pittsburgh Rabbinical Conference," 195–196.

39. Ibid., 197.

40. On Schlesinger, see *CCAR Yearbook* 30 (1920):211–14.

41. From "Authentic Report of the Proceedings of the Rabbinical Conference Held at Pittsburg, Nov. 16, 17, 18, 1885" (hereafter noted as "Authentic Report") as quoted by Jacob, *The Pittsburgh Platform in Retrospect,* 91.

42. Cf. Meyer, *Response to Modernity,* 265–70.

43. *Jewish Conference Papers (1886)*, 43.

44. Meyer, *Response to Modernity,* 266–70. For quote *see Jewish Conference Papers (1886)*, 46.

45. *CCAR Yearbook* 3 (1893):6–7.

46. Ibid., 45, 47.

47. *CCAR Yearbook* 2 (1892):60, and "Authentic Report" in Jacob, *The Pittsburgh Platform*, 91.

48. It appears that the Conference of Rabbis of Southern Congregations was the only rabbinical organization to *specifically* endorse the renowned Pittsburgh Platform. Although the platform was generally considered the unofficial statement of American Reform Judaism, the Central Conference of American Rabbis never officially adopted the famed principles. It did, however, cite the Pittsburgh resolutions when it officially incorporated all of the resolutions and decisions of earlier rabbinical assemblies. See *CCAR Yearbook* 1 (1891):14.

49. *CCAR Yearbook* 2 (1891):62.

50. Ibid., 63.

51. *Jewish Conference Papers,* 50.

52. Ibid.

53. Ibid., 51–53, and *Jewish Conference Papers* (1887), 61–68. Philipson stopped attending in 1886, Kohler stopped attending in 1887.

54. "Minutes," 26. Heller succeeded Gutheim at Temple Sinai of New Orleans. Jacobson served the congregation in Macon, Georgia.

55. HUC ordained 21 rabbis from 1883 to 1889. The vast majority of the members of this group were serving congregations in the Midwest, West, and South. The six Southern rabbis who became charter members of the CCAR were Henry Berkowitz, Sigmund Hecht, Maximillian Heller, Max Samfield, Joseph Silverman, and Joseph Stolz. The fact that the minutes of the Conference of Rabbis of Southern Congregations from the year 1885 were published in the second volume of the *CCAR Yearbook* lends further evidence to the contention that the Southern Conference voluntarily (though unofficially) merged into the Central Conference. See *CCAR Yearbook* 2 (1892):57–65.

56. *CCAR Yearbook* 2 (1892):12. In 1886 the Eastern Conference had 52 names on its membership roster. By 1894, 23 of these names appeared on the roster of the CCAR:

Victor Caro
Joseph H. M. Chumaceiro
O. J. Cohen
E. Eppstein
Gustav Gottheil

A. Guttman
Maurice Harris
Leon Harrison
Kaufmann Kohler
Max Landsberg
Joseph Leucht
David Levi
William Lowenberg
David Philipson
Adolph Radin
Leo Reich
Max Schlesinger
M. Sessler
S. Sparger
L. Stern
M. Ungerleider
Leopold Wintner
Aaron Wise

57. Ibid., 19–21.
58. *CCAR Yearbook* 1 (1891): 16. The Latin quote is from *CCAR Yearbook* 4 (1894):70.
59. *CCAR Yearbook* 1 (1891):4, 19.
60. *CCAR Yearbook* 4 (1894):25–26, 69.

3
The Mixers

The Role of Rabbis Deep in the Heart of Texas
Hollace Ava Weiner

Wanted: Rabbi. Young man, native of America or England, that is a good lecturer who can make himself agreeable with either Orthodox or Reform Congregation. In other words, we want a MIXER. We pay $1,500 a year.[1]

Rabbi Samuel Rosinger was uncertain whether Beaumont's Temple Emanuel wanted a rabbi or a bartender. Intrigued by the Texas mystique and charmed by the colloquial ad, the Midwestern rabbi was among a handful of clergy who responded to the synagogue's search in 1910. Other rabbis who answered the call were more educated and experienced than Rosinger, a 32-year-old with only two years in a pulpit. Yet only Rosinger was invited to deliver a trial sermon in the Texas oil town. After a weekend of preaching in his thick Hungarian accent, the darkly handsome Rosinger signed a two-year contract that stretched into a lifetime.

Months after he was hired the rabbi asked temple President Hyman Perlstein, "What made you decide to invite me?" Perlstein replied, "I liked your beautiful handwriting."[2]

Forget theology. Forget philosophy. Forget erudition. Forget credentials. During Texas' post-frontier, turn-of-the-century years, the Lone Star State's remote Jewish congregations wanted their rabbis to be mixers—ethnic brokers who could "bridge the gap between different cultures," ambassadors-at-large to the gentiles, envoys who would mix and blend and make a good first impression.[3] They wanted men with personality and presence, leaders able to stand shoulder to shoulder with the pastors at the First Baptist Church and the Catholic priests of the plains. A rabbi's views, ritual practices, oratorical style, scholarship, and piety were secondary to human relations. Small in numbers, Texas Jews sought not spiritual guidance but role models who could dispel unvoiced prejudices and act as representatives to the larger community. In the opinion of Rabbi David Rosenbaum, leader at Austin's Congregation Beth Israel from 1911 to 1922, Texas Jews had grown self-conscious about Judaism and wanted each rabbi to be "the Honorable Ambassador and Minister Plenipotentiary of the Synagog [*sic*]." Writing for *The Jewish Monitor*, the rabbi added: "We no longer live in the Ghetto world of our own. . . . The Christians' favorable view of the rabbi is of paramount importance to us."[4]

Given such scant selection criteria, rabbis who gravitated to Texas were generally not at the top of their rabbinical classes, if indeed they had attended a seminary. Many were "free-lancers," never ordained.[5] They tended to be mavericks. Some, particularly those from Europe, wished to break with religious traditions and believed it possible in a place with little Jewish history. Others had no better pulpit offers. Many reluctantly came to a state that seemed virtual exile with its dirt roads and dearth of Jews. Ironically, rabbis who remained any appreciable length of time excelled in the face of challenge. In a young state with little hierarchy or caste, they stepped into a leadership vacuum and left footprints that helped shape twentieth-century Texas.

Texas was Bible Belt territory where assimilated Jews called themselves Hebrews and were respected as people of the Book. Rabbis, no matter how small their flocks, often achieved the eminence of bishops as they moved to meet the basic human and communal needs in the sparsely populated state. Their Old Testament roots gave them a "degree of prestige" as leaders of the chosen people.[6] Schooled outside the region, rabbis represented erudition and an exotic addition to the frontier. Having assumed a seat at the table, rabbis became community leaders whose opinions mattered. Elsewhere they may have been perceived as mediocre or parochial, but in Texas these clergy had moral clout. A rabbi's sense of social justice, honed through centuries of Jewish thought, gave him sway in a dominion where most Christian clergy emphasized salvation in the next world rather than on earthly turf.

From the start, Texas proudly distinguished itself from the Deep South and the rest of the nation. Its history harks back to 1836 and a war for independence from Mexico, not England. During the Civil War, Texas was the only Confederate state to remain unscathed by major land battles. Yet mentally and physically, war fronts helped define Texas. Savage Indian raids continued through 1875, while in settled areas they had ceased by 1860. Mexican border incursions flared until 1916. "The reverberations of this warfare spread far beyond the . . . frontier, affecting both attitudes and organization," observes a current historian.[7] Texans prized individualism, not conformity. The Texas constitution vested less power in its elected officials than any other state except California.[8] Early Texas legislators were reluctant to act or tax in response to communal needs. Rabbis often filled the voids.

One rabbi spearheaded statewide prison reform. Another founded a hospital that treated blacks and whites in a segregated era. A third sat on the University of Texas Board of Regents and became a symbol of academic freedom. Rabbis launched charity networks in Houston, Dallas, Fort Worth, San Antonio, and El Paso, fledgling social institutions that grew into the Community Chest and United Way. In Houston, Rabbi Henry Barnstein gathered part-time musicians into an ensemble that became the nucleus of the city's symphony. In Corpus Christi the symphony evolved from a Sunday afternoon group that listened to Rabbi Sidney Wolf's classical records. In Dallas a rabbi organized the city's "first free school" in the 1870s.[9] Another Dallas rabbi, William Greenburg, was the catalyst behind formation of the humane society, the art league, and the Critic Club, a think tank for civic improvements.[10] Rabbi G. George Fox used his position as chairman of the Fort Worth Charity Commission to organize a Texas Welfare Conference that evaluated indigents' needs.[11] Fox published a Jewish weekly that circulated in four states and editorialized against the Ku Klux Klan. Other rabbis defended unpopular issues such as evolution, minimum-wage legislation, and an end to the poll tax. Instinctively rabbis formed ecumenical alliances with Christian clergy. Like pastors elsewhere in the South and the Far West, they initiated municipal Thanksgiving services that gained national notice.

Not only did these rabbis reach out to the community but across the miles to one another. In the 1880s five rabbis carved the state into circuit-riding territories—nearly a decade before this became a topic of concern among national Jewish rabbinical councils.[12] The Texas rabbis set up Sabbath schools and supervised new congregations in the countryside. The circuit-riding model continued for decades after the original quintet of rabbis departed.

The Texas tradition of rabbinic cooperation expanded in 1927 with creation of a Kallah, a unique annual symposium where Reform, Conservative, and Orthodox rabbis discoursed on theological topics.[13] A dozen rabbis met in Houston for the first "Kallah convention" to "transplant" some of the learning acquired in Northern institutions "into the land of the South," according to Abraham Schechter, a traditional rabbi and the Kallah's founder.[14] A byproduct of the Kallah was what Rabbi David Lefkowitz Sr. of Dallas termed "this fine comradeship."[15]

Rabbis traveled together to the meetings, which lasted from Sunday through Wednesday. Most presented academic papers or led discussions. "It was the only place for exchange of rabbinic fellowship and scholarship. It was scholarly without being profound," recalled Houston's Rabbi Robert I. Kahn, who attended this singular institution from 1935 until the 1980s, when it was supplanted by an array of rabbinic conferences.[16] The Lone Star Kallah was but one instance in which Texas' isolation fostered accomplishments, fellowship, and unexpected rewards.[17]

Despite the welcome rabbis received from one another and from the Christian community, a Texas pulpit was no prize. "It was distinctly . . . small town in atmosphere with no particularly progressive ideas," Rabbi Greenburg wrote of Dallas circa 1902.[18] The Texas terrain was rugged with a climate to match—parched, 100-degree summers in West Texas, hurricanes along the Gulf Coast, sudden hailstorms throughout Texas' central corridor, a swath that Indian nations dubbed Tornado Alley.

Rabbi Hyman Saft, from 1887 to 1889 the first spiritual leader in the East Texas town of Marshall, stretched mosquito netting over the windows of his house to keep at bay lizards, bats, and snakes.[19] Yellow fever epidemics were common. A "pestilence" in 1867 killed the Reverend Dr. L. Steiner, a 30-year-old rabbi from Bohemia who had served only months in Houston.[20] "I suppose a good many people . . . think that Texas is an entirely wild country, for they hear of so many rough things happening," Galveston's spiritual leader, Dr. Abraham Blum, wrote in 1878.[21] In Waco, Rabbi Aron Suhler "was pretty scared up" one night in 1884 when a bullet shattered a windowpane in his study. "It was a close call for the rabbi," reported the *Dallas Weekly Herald.*[22] When Rabbi Henry Barnstein, an Englishman, told New York immigration authorities he was headed for Texas in 1900, customs officials suggested he pack a gun. The rabbi recalled that advice several months later when a horseback rider galloped by and shot the man seated next to him on a hotel porch.[23] Barnstein never bought a pistol, but he did invest in boots. "Those boots weren't very dignified gear for a rabbi," he told the *Houston Press,* "but Houston was a sea of mud."[24]

Early Texas Jews

In 1836 the Republic of Texas had 39,000 inhabitants residing between its pine-forested eastern flank that borders the Deep South and its parched western deserts.[25] Two hundred scattered Jews lived under the Lone Star flag, including three who fought with General Sam Houston at the decisive Battle of San Jacinto.[26] Another Jewish soldier, A. Wolf of England, died defending the Alamo.[27] In that year of Texas Independence, this expansive territory that stretches 801 miles north to south (from the Panhandle to the Gulf of Mexico) and 770 miles east to west (from Texarkana to El Paso) had no Jewish institutions. When Texas became part of the United States a decade later it still lacked Jewish institutions. A Hebrew cemetery was consecrated in Galveston in 1852 by a visiting rabbi. Two years later, Houston Jews dedicated a cemetery and, in 1859, incorporated Beth Israel, the "pioneer congregation of Texas," and dedicated a synagogue.[28] The pattern of Jewish communities deeding land to bury their dead before coalescing into other communal institutions followed an ancient blueprint replicated in Europe's Old World Jewish communities and across the American frontier.[29] The pattern was repeated in Galveston (1855 with a cemetery and 1868 with a synagogue), in San Antonio (1854 and 1874), Austin (1866 and 1876), and Dallas (1872 and 1874).[30]

The notion of the Lone Star State as a land of Jewish opportunity did not begin to permeate the general immigrant consciousness until a decade after the Civil War—a conflict in which over 200 Texas Jews fought mostly for the South.[31] Spared the devastation the war brought the rest of the Confederacy, Texas became a postwar destination for thousands of refugees who nailed "Gone To Texas" or "GTT" signs on their porches and migrated west. Texas was still cut off from the rest of the country. America's major rail routes traversed the nation from coast to coast, bypassing Texas, which had 400 miles of track. In 1873 the Legislature rammed through, over opposition from the governor, a constitutional amendment permitting land grants to railroads. Construction of track began in earnest.[32]

By 1877, 3,300 Jews resided in Texas—0.3 percent of the state population.[33] Texas was the area of second settlement for these Jews. Most hailed from Germany and had lived elsewhere in the South or Northeast. They were part of a wave of German migration that had begun around 1820 and eventually brought 5 million ethnic Germans to the US, including 200,000 Jews.[34] An intense German migration to Texas began in 1844, and by 1846 more than 7,000 German Protestants had settled in the Hill Country region north of San Antonio.[35] The Jewish Germans who came to Texas filtered in singly or in family groups. They opened stores and, with the growth of Texas rail routes, encouraged overseas relatives to follow. In Palestine [Pal-es-teen], a forested East Texas county seat that had previously counted a handful of Jews, the new rail routes brought five Jewish families and 10 young bachelors, enough to foster joint celebrations of Jewish holidays and a visit from a circuit-riding rabbi. By 1879 their numbers had increased to 11 families, and Palestine's Jews included a "city father" and a volunteer firefighter.[36] In Denison, a North Texas prairie town where the minuscule Jewish popu-lace swelled to 12 families after the arrival of the railroad, local Jews in 1873 organized the Mount Sinai Sabbath School. More than 25 young-sters, age eight and younger, met weekly in private homes to read chap-ters chronologically from the Old Testament.[37]

Waller County, a watermelon capital 50 miles northwest of Houston, attracted no Jews until after the Civil War, when a chain migration began from Kempen, a town in the Prussian province of Posen. Kempen-born Gabriel Schwarz and his brother Sam, a wounded Confederate veteran, journeyed from Charleston, South Carolina, to Hempstead, drawn there by a rail depot. They opened emporiums and sent for overseas nephews and friends. By 1873 they persuaded their brother, Rabbi Heinrich (Chayim) Schwarz, then 49, to pack his Torah scroll and join the family.

Rabbi Schwarz had served in small-town Prussian pulpits in Reichen-bach, Allenstein, and Gumbinnen. In his handwritten notebook he re-marked that a multitude of Jews was leaving the Prussian provinces for the big cities of Europe and the fabled cities of America. Few of the re-maining Jewish youngsters were interested in the scholarship he tried to impart. He was weary of slaughtering sheep and chickens and raising money for dwindling congregations. He longed for a scholarly life. Moreover, he saw few marital prospects for his daughters. He read the *American Israelite*, the weekly newspaper published in Cincinnati and mailed to him by his Texas relatives. He realized that Hempstead was no New York, but the Texas branch of his family made a comfortable living. America had no "cruel laws" barring Jews from occupations and univer-sities. Across the Atlantic his offspring could achieve "the cultivation of all their faculties."[38]

Rabbi Schwarz and his wife Julia (Gittel) Nathan emigrated with their youngest sons and daughters, arriving in Texas in the spring of 1873 in time for Shavuot. By 1888 the Schwarzes had constructed a backyard chapel, a Protestant-style edifice with white clapboard exterior and arched, Gothic windows with yellow stained-glass panes. Here Rabbi Schwarz led a congregation comprised of 30 to 50 Jews, mainly relatives and *landsleit*. They named their synagogue *Cheychal Chayim*—a play on words that means Heinrich's Temple and Temple of Life.[39]

Schwarz was the first ordained rabbi to lead a Texas congregation, according to the late dean of American Jewish historians, Dr. Jacob Rader Marcus.[40] Other spiritual leaders had served, but their credentials are questionable or lacking. Schwarz wrote scholarly articles and poetry for *Die Deborah,* the German-Jewish weekly published in Cincinnati by the same editorial staff as the *American Israelite*.[41] He was invited to Dallas and Houston when congregations consecrated new synagogues. An elder in Texas' far-flung religious community, Schwarz became mentor to Houston's Jacob Voorsanger, a self-trained rabbi who left Texas in 1886 for San Francisco's Emanu-El Congregation, where he gained a reputation as the "foremost rabbi on the West Coast."[42] Voorsanger wrote to the *American Israelite* as follows:

> The Rabbi H. Schwarz is, in your correspondent's humble opinion, one of the best Jewish scholars in the country and, were it not for his comparative ignorance of English, would grace the highest position in the land. His memory . . . is wonderful and the constant flow of wisdom that proceeds from his lips is of exceeding benefit to his visitors. . . . Your correspondent, with gratitude, chronicles the pleasure he has derived from his . . . visits to the congenial home of this modest scholar. Still vigorous and in the enjoyment of health, though occasionally ailing, he is of incalculable benefit within his present limited sphere.[43]

Rabbi Schwarz presided over the family pulpit until his death in 1900.

Before Schwarz's arrival in Texas, synagogues had been served by a variety of clergy who generally used the title "reverend," a term borrowed from the British to describe a pastor who was not ordained.[44] The first of these Jewish spiritual leaders called to Texas was the Reverend Zacharias Emmich, a religious man from Baden who answered an 1859 ad from Houston's Congregation Beth Israel. The synagogue advertised for a "hazan, shohet and mohel," a person trained to chant the Hebrew liturgy, slaughter animals according to kosher ritual, perform circumcisions on eight-day-old Jewish males, and read from the Torah.[45] When Emmich's contract was not renewed in February 1862, he left full-time religious work for the business world, advertising himself as a "dealer in Glassware, Crockery, Cutlery and Groceries."[46] He still participated in the life of the congregation as a teacher and pulpit substitute. His experience became a familiar pattern as a succession of individuals spent brief stints serving synagogues in Dallas, Houston, Waco, and other embryonic Texas congregations before switching to other pursuits or moving out of state. Waco's first rabbi, the Reverend Mayer May, hallucinated one Sabbath eve in March 1882, alarming congregants when he spoke about spiritual messages from his mother. The next morning he lined up his students outdoors to lecture them on Jesus Christ. A local physician deemed the rabbi insane.[47] Waco's next rabbi, Aron Suhler, left the full-time pulpit to sell insurance and teach in order to earn enough money to feed his family of nine children.[48] The Waco congregation had paid him with chickens and eggs. Suhler continued to serve Temple Rodef Sholom as a board member and substitute rabbi. Max Heller, one of the first rabbis ordained at Hebrew Union College, was called to Houston as a young man in 1886 after serving briefly in a Chicago pulpit. At Houston's Beth Israel he instituted "Rules of Order" in an attempt to silence chattering congregants who wandered in late and walked out during his sermons.[49] Heller stayed in Texas six months before vaulting to New Orleans' Temple Sinai in February 1887.[50] Houston's Beth Israel Congregation hired 14 rabbis before the turn of the century, including one who was fired after a month in the pulpit. In 1915 the *Texas Jewish Herald* lamented the rapid turnover of Lone Star spiritual leaders whose stays averaged three or four years. "It requires at least five or six years of study to learn to know all the members of the average congregation," the *Herald* observed.[51]

Texarkana, a town that straddles the Texas-Arkansas state line, was founded in 1873 and had a Jewish population exceeding a minyan within three years. But Mount Sinai Congregation lacked a rabbi. According to the *Jewish South*, Texarkana did have an "apostate" rabbi, a Jewish scholar who had converted to Christianity and wore the cloth of a Cumberland Presbyterian minister.[52] That clergyman was the Reverend Charles Goldberg. The son of a Polish rabbi, Goldberg emigrated to the United States in the 1840s. While working as a peddler in Missouri he fell gravely ill. He was nursed back to health and apparently born again in the home of a minister who converted him in 1847. Goldberg served as a Confederate chaplain then preached throughout Texas and Arkansas until he was called to the Cumberland Presbyterian Church of Texarkana. When the town's Jews recruited him at the High Holidays, he accommodated them. His Rosh Hashanah and Yom Kippur sermons delivered in Yiddish and English won praise from Jews and Christians. Subsequently "he tutored a number of Jewish boys in Hebrew to help them prepare for their Bar Mitsva [*sic*] ceremony."[53] He never proselytized his Jewish friends. Nonetheless, a skeptical correspondent from the Atlanta-based *Jewish South* excoriated the reverend as a hypocrite, a "snake," and a phony "without sincerity and with false pretenses, sailing under the colors of assumed Christian piety."[54]

Despite such outside criticism, gentile and Jew worked together in the emerging state. Frontier egalitarianism was generally the rule.[55] The Hebrew Benevolent Association marched in Houston's 1856 Fourth of July parade.[56] Jews were elected to early city councils in El Paso, to the first school board in Corpus Christi, and to the state legislature where Galveston's Rabbi Blum delivered an opening prayer in 1874.[57] Another Jew, Texas war veteran David Spangler Kaufman, was Speaker of the Texas Assembly and among Texas' first delegation to Congress, where he served from 1846 until his death in 1851.[58]

As in small towns throughout the South and the Far West, Jewish-owned storefronts were prominent on town squares. Haberdasher, dry goods merchant, and tobacconist were among the chief occupations of Texas Jews but not their sole pursuits. The first editions of the turn-of-the-century *Jewish Encyclopedia* singled out the Lone Star State for its "unusually large number of Jewish citizens prominent in public life and in the learned professions."[59] In 1878 and 1879, the *Jewish South* marveled at the number of millionaire Jewish merchants in Galveston, Houston, and Austin and at the prevalence of Jewish professionals in the big cities: "Galveston . . . boasts of Jewish notaries, lawyers, bankers, and gentlemen of other high standing."[60]

Jewish doctors were present from the earliest days of the Texas Republic. Among them were Jacob Henry and Isaac Lyons, Surgeon-Generals in Texas' war for independence, and Moses Albert Levy, surgeon in chief to General Sam Houston's victorious army.[61] Levy also served on the first Texas Board of Medical Examiners. Another Jewish doctor, Arthur S. Wolff, was appointed Brownsville's quarantine officer in 1867.[62] Rabbi Abraham Blum enrolled at Galveston's Texas Medical College, and within a year earned a medical degree and the twin title of "Reverend Doctor."[63]

Other professions had a sprinkling of prominent Jews. Educator Olga Bernstein Kohlberg of El Paso started the state's first free public kindergarten in 1892.[64] Among the state's earliest artists and performers was opera singer Isabella Offenbach Maas of Cologne, who moved to Texas in 1844 after marrying a Galveston man.[65] Houston journalist Leah Cohen Harby wrote for *Harper's* and *Ladies Home Journal* and penned the lyrics to *Flag Song of Texas,* an honor that netted her a $100 award from the Daughters of the Republic of Texas.[66] Arriving in Nacogdoches in 1826, Adolphus Sterne, a lawyer, merchant, linguist, and financier, was among the earliest Jewish settlers and soldiers in Texas (although he adopted his wife's Catholicism).[67] Philadelphia born Simon Mussina, an attorney and a Jew of Dutch ancestry, laid out the town of Brownsville.[68]

Some Jews achieved notoriety. Actress Adah Isaacs Menken, saluted as the Naked Lady from Nacogdoches, toured America and Europe performing in *Mazeppa* in a flesh-colored body stocking. She married Texan Alexander Isaacs in 1856.[69] Gambler Abe Rothschild was tried twice for the 1879 murder of his wife, Diamond Bessie, whose dance hall jewels were missing when Marion County sheriff's deputies found her dead body at the site of the pair's last picnic.[70]

Jews fit into all walks of life. Anti-Semitism was unremarkable in frontier Texas. Throughout the Southwest, Jews' small numbers did not call much notice to their religious differences, according to a turn-of-the-century Jewish chronicler.[71] Latent prejudice was overridden by curiosity toward Hebrews and concern with pressing day-to-day tasks.[72] Few pioneers cared about lineage, much less liturgy. Similar to their cohorts in neighboring states and across the Far West, Texas Jews rose to leadership posts in fraternal lodges and auxiliaries of the Masons, Rotary, Shriners, and other lodges where application involved a vote or veto of the membership. Certainly bigotry existed in Texas. Texans openly discriminated against Mexican Americans and African Americans. Racial minorities resided in poor, segregated enclaves. Custom usually restricted them to menial jobs and allowed them no role in government except along the lower Rio Grande, where Latinos were a majority.[73] Texans' racial prejudices were exacerbated by the wars against the Indians, the Mexicans, and the Union.[74] But Texans had no historical conflict with the Jews, nor were Jewish people as discernible as racial minorities. The frontier ethic judged Jews as individuals and gave them a chance to prove their mettle. Beginning in 1877, when a Jewish banker was turned away from a posh upstate New York hotel, Jews in the Northeast were excluded from resorts, but at that very time Texas was creating social institutions and welcoming new blood.[75] Also, the social stereotype of Jews as brash and crass differed little from the image of the crude, boastful Texan in the days of the cattle drives and the oil booms. When anti-Semitism did surface in the form of name-calling and stereotyping, Texas rabbis reacted with rebukes and education. In Dallas, Rabbi Greenburg addressed the Dallas Pastors Association on "Misunderstandings between Jew and Christian" and "Prejudices."[76] Vaudeville acts that mocked the Jews led Rabbi Barnstein to deliver a series of sermons in 1909 about "The Jew in English Drama."[77] The Jew "is always a paradigm of virtue or a monster

of inequity," the rabbi observed. "He is shamefully caricatured, griev-
ously wrought. This is inflicted not through prejudice, but ignorance,
partly . . . to court popularity, giving the playgoers the Jew they wish to
see."[78] When an offensive act was booked on the state's vaudeville circuit, rabbis alerted one another by telegram. Before curtain time Rabbi
Lefkowitz in Dallas and Rabbi Rosenbaum in Austin lobbied theater
managers to censor insulting jokes.[79] In 1921, Rosenbaum wrote a colleague, "A committee in Austin watched a dress rehearsal and discussed
. . . what to eliminate."[80]

In Beaumont, Rabbi Rosinger's first exposure to American anti-Semitism came through the eyes of his son, a six-year-old taunted as a "Jew-
baby" on his first day of school in 1914.[81] The rabbi described his dismay and disappointment in the *Texas Jewish Herald*. Fort Worth's Rabbi
George Fox, writing in the *Jewish Monitor,* decried a similar slander after
Christian children harassed Hebrew school students with cries of "dirty
Jews" and "Jew noses."[82] Later, when a Dallas wholesale clerk denigrated a Fort Worth clothier as "the Jew," Fox wrote a blistering editorial that
elicited a written apology from the owner of the offending business.[83]

Houston's Rabbi Barnstein changed the spelling of his name to Barnston in 1920. The new spelling had nothing to do with anti-Semitism but
everything to do with lingering anti-German sentiment. However, his
family roots were not German but Dutch, and the family surname was
originally spelled Barnstijn.[84]

Rabbis Organize

In the 1870s an assortment of itinerant Jewish clergy drifted in and out
of Texas billing themselves as scholarly speakers. Some were charlatans
who displayed false letters attesting to religious credentials. They took
advantage of home hospitality, absconded with cash and jewelry, and
swindled small Jewish communities out of funds.[85] This ministerial
plague stirred legitimate spiritual leaders to action. Using the pen name
Koppel Von Bloomborg, Houston's Rabbi Voorsanger wrote in the *American Israelite* in October 1880: "Texas is successfully rid of the *ministres am-
bulants* [wandering preachers] who infested her cities like an army of
grasshoppers; . . . the minds of our brethren here are no longer poisoned and prejudiced on account of several disgraceful *soi-disant* clergymen, who indulged in all sorts of vices, making themselves a shame and
a by-word and the religion they professed to serve a reproach; since then,
the Texas ministers who remained, and those who came subsequently

have made every effort to promote the cause of Judaism."[86] On 6 October 1880 Voorsanger and the state's four other active rabbis—Blum of Galveston; H. M. Bien of Dallas; Isadore Lowenthal of San Antonio; and J. W. Sophar, recently arrived from Mississippi—met in Houston to divide Texas into circuit-riding territories. The rabbis' missionary tasks involved setting up religious schools, establishing uniform text books and lessons, introduction of children's services, talking lay leaders into assuming teaching roles, and encouraging Jews to charter congregations.[87] The rabbis met with rural Jews in private homes and Masonic halls and urged observance of Jewish rituals in the home. They preached an end to indifference toward Judaism and decried the "desecration of the Sabbath . . . a general fact in Texas."[88] A circular issued to the "Israelites of Texas" by the five circuit-riding rabbis exhorted: *"Remember the Sabbath day to keep it holy. . . .* Our dear children suffer from the sad examples that are constantly being placed before them."[89] Religious observance among Texas' early Jews—and among coreligionists throughout the Far West—was generally lax, particularly in small towns. Merchants kept their shops open on Saturdays, the Jewish Sabbath, when most farmers and ranchers traveled to town. Voorsanger complained that Jewish families neglected to light the traditional pair of candles to usher in the Sabbath.

Dutch-born Voorsanger, based at Houston's Beth Israel Congregation from 1878 to 1886, had been on the circuit prior to 1880, teaching and preaching in farm towns such as Calvert and Navasota. He followed the example set by Blum, whom the *Jewish South* credited with "doing a vast deal of good by establishing Sunday Schools in the country places, where there are no ministers."[90] Blum was "known from one end of Texas to the other, and oftentimes expose[d] himself to the severity of the climate and the dangers of the sea in his journeys to distant communities in behalf of the cause."[91] Blum organized religious schools in Brenham, Waco, Fort Worth, Corsicana, and Brownsville. In Mexico he started a Jewish Sabbath school in Matamoros and journeyed to Nuevo Laredo to circumcise an infant.[92]

Historian Louis Schmier considers the concept of circuit-riding rabbis revolutionary, noting that it was not until the late 1880s that the Union of American Hebrew Congregations began examining the issue and not until 1895 that the Union's Committee on Circuit-Preaching endeavored to implement a comprehensive plan.[93] As late as 1931, the Arkansas Religious Assembly contemplated the need for circuit-riding rabbis but abandoned the idea after a Jewish census concluded there were far fewer Jews than previously estimated.[94]

Exactly how the quintet of Texas rabbis divided up the Lone Star State is unclear, but the principles they established were followed for decades by their successors. Waco's second rabbi, Aron Suhler, left his Waco pulpit in mid-week in 1883 to set up Hebrew classes in Fort Worth, 90 miles distant. Rabbi G. George Fox, leader at Fort Worth's Temple Beth-El from 1910 to 1922, considered himself a "missionary" to the Jews of rural Texas. Fox reveled in trips to the Oklahoma frontier where, in Ardmore, he helped turn a vacant church into a synagogue, and to Wichita Falls, Texas, where he persuaded a frustrated Orthodox lay leader to experiment with the less observant brand of Reform. In Gainesville, on the Texas side of the Oklahoma state line, the rabbi revived a defunct congregation that lasted "until the Jewish population there melted away." And in the Panhandle, where he journeyed twice a month, Fox helped a handful of Amarillo Jews start a congregation and Sunday school "until they got someone on a regular basis." In the tiny oil town of Drumwright, Oklahoma, he helped the handful of Jewish families organize High Holy Day services.[95]

With This Ring . . .

When Rabbi Henry Barnstein was searching for a pulpit in the United States, he received offers from Lincoln, Nebraska, and Houston, Texas. He chose Texas because the board of directors at Beth Israel wrote him that a dozen couples were awaiting the arrival of a rabbi to get married.[96] He responded to the need. Most of the frontier's early Hebrew settlers were conscious of Jewish continuity and sought Jewish spouses for themselves and their offspring, according to Western historians Harriet and Fred Rochlin. They write that the Jewish culture "viewed a bachelor as 'no man at all,' and one who married outside the faith as dead."[97] Some eligible Jewish men, like Rabbi Schwarz's son, Leo, traveled back to Europe for a bride. On a trip to Germany in 1884 he married Selma Weinbaum, also a descendant of a rabbinical family.[98] Leo spoke so highly of his Texas family that Selma wore white gloves for her first meeting with the Hempstead relatives. She never got over the disappointment of finding the rest of the women in aprons.[99]

Many of Texas' Jewish merchants traveled across the country to buy and distribute wares, all the while staying alert for marital prospects. El

Paso clothing manufacturer Haymon Krupp, whose later success as an oilfield wildcatter on state-owned land would enrich the University of Texas, married New Yorker Leah Silverman in 1899.[100] Jacob Calisher, a German Jewish merchant who moved to El Paso in 1881, met his future wife, Ada Fleishman, when he was doing business in Richmond, Virginia. The resourceful bride turned their Texas home into a boarding house.[101] Samuel "Little Sam" Kaufman, whose dry goods business was in Indian territory just north of Texas' Red River, married Julia Weitzenhoffer of Lexington, Kentucky. Their wedding, 17 January 1899, in Purcell, an outpost of the Chickasaw Nation, drew guests from El Paso and Kansas City. At Kaufman's bachelor party in Purcell's Clifton Hotel, 125 guests ate oysters on the half shell. Texas Rabbi H. Friedman of Gainesville officiated at the wedding, which was followed by a lavish party where guests puffed cigars and danced to Hungarian folk music.[102]

Rabbis remained on the alert for prospective Jewish mates for themselves, their offspring, and their acquaintances. When Rabbi Schwarz traveled to Dallas in 1876 for the dedication of Temple Emanu-El, his daughter Clara accompanied him.[103] Five months later she married Temple Emanu-El's rabbi, Aron Suhler, a widower and an 1866 graduate of the Jewish Seminary in Wurzburg.[104] Rabbi G. George Fox came to the attention of Hortense Jannette Lewis when she spotted his photo in the newspaper the week he arrived in Fort Worth. She told her sister that she planned to marry the new rabbi. Nine months later, three other rabbis attended their nuptials.[105]

When Sidney Wolf, the first rabbi to serve Corpus Christi, lost his wife to childbirth and pneumonia in 1936, he counted 42 other bachelors in his congregation. To ease his loneliness and theirs, he launched a "bachelors club" for the purpose of "pooling our problems, hopefully to attract the attention of eligible young ladies."[106] They met with success: Jewish girls came by train from San Antonio for weekend picnics and dances. The young adults gradually paired off. Wolf, however, remained single. A Cleveland rabbi who had grown up with Wolf then turned matchmaker, suggesting he correspond with Bertha "Bebé" Rosenthal, a native of France living in Lafayette, Louisiana. After an initial exchange of letters the rabbi took a night train 450 miles to meet this blind date. A five-month courtship and a 46-year marriage followed.

Judging from historical evidence, intermarriage was controversial but not uncommon. Mixed marriages were bound to occur in a region where minority Jews mingled easily with their neighbors. Pioneer surveyor, publisher, and politician Jacob de Cordova was fluent in Hebrew and led some of the state's earliest Jewish services. An advocate of religious freedom, he married a Baptist, Rebecca Sterling, in a ceremony performed by a Presbyterian minister. He advised settlers to bring a Bible to Texas because "this was not a land of milk and honey."[107] Physician soldier Moses Albert Levy married a non-Jewish woman, had his children baptized, and was not buried in a Jewish cemetery.[108] Simon Mussina, the Jewish settler who laid out the streets of Brownsville, never married, but his sister wed a Galveston Presbyterian minister.

Tyler's Congregation Beth El, chartered in 1887, stipulated in its bylaws that members who married outside the faith would be expelled: "No applicant shall be qualified for membership who is . . . united in marriage contrary to the ordinances of the Jewish religion and any member marrying out of the pale of Judaism shall thereby forfeit his membership."[109] But views toward mixed marriages softened. In July 1900, one month after the congregation's rabbi, the Reverend Isaac Kaiser, resigned and moved to Texarkana, Tyler's board repealed the bylaws that pertained to mixed marriages. The amended section stated: "All Israelites that are honorable shall have the right to join this congregation if elected."[110] The temple's next rabbi, Maurice Faber, did not perform mixed marriages, but his son Edwin married a gentile woman from Colorado who did not convert. She moved to Tyler, participated in Jewish life there, and is buried in Tyler's Hebrew cemetery. In Brownsville the bylaws governing the Jewish cemetery allowed for interment of non-Jewish spouses so long as no Christian ritual accompanied the burial.[111] In Beaumont, Rabbi Rosinger's board of trustees insisted that a non-Jewish spouse long active in the congregation be buried in the temple cemetery. Rosinger's Solomonic solution was to place a strand of wire fencing inside the perimeters of the man's grave. Technically, the deceased was laid to rest in a separate cemetery.[112]

Intermarriage was a reality. Still, it was a rare rabbi who performed marriage rites between a Christian and a Jew. Galveston's Rabbi Blum insisted that conversion of the gentile partner precede the marriage vows. In 1874 wedding guests in Galveston witnessed the conversion to Judaism of Theodosia Rushing. Following the conversion ceremony the bride and groom advanced to the *chuppa*.[113] Rabbi Henry Cohen did "not like intermarriage," but occasionally found it "necessary" if a young couple "eloped" and lived together "as man and wife" for several months. During his six decades in Texas, Cohen performed approximately 20 interfaith wedding ceremonies. Nearly all of these couples joined his synagogue and enrolled their offspring in Jewish religious schools.[114]

Rabbi Sidney Wolf publicly protested mixed marriages. "Marriage is in itself such a complex relationship that different religions merely contribute to the problems of adjustment. . . . A couple who has a mixed marriage is welcome to participate in the affairs of the temple," Wolf told a local newspaper reporter in 1972.[115] Wolf, similar to his colleague Henry Cohen, performed an occasional intermarriage. San Antonio native Allen Goldsmith said that Wolf married him and his Episcopalian bride, Priscilla Crea, in 1953, then surprised the couple with a wedding gift—dinner for two at the Dragon Grill, a swanky but illegal gambling club. The couple had previously, three months before, been joined by a Unitarian minister. The rabbi had put a Jewish stamp of approval on the union.[116]

Another rabbi who joined couples of mixed backgrounds was San Antonio's Ephraim Frisch, a Lithuanian-born, Minnesota-reared rabbi who served the Alamo city's Temple Beth El from 1923 to 1942. He married an interfaith couple on 19 May 1929, at the First Presbyterian Church in Gonzales, Texas, according to his Record Book of Ministerial Functions.[117] "On inter-marriage, I have performed several and find it increasingly difficult to refuse them," he wrote a New York colleague who asked him to counsel a soldier stationed in Texas and engaged to a Christian girl from Austin. "Invariably refusal means an antagonism towards Judaism on the part of the couple. . . . I have never exacted a promise on the part of the couple. I have never exacted a promise on the part of the non-Jew that the children, if any, be reared as Jews. Personally, I don't consider this a fair request."[118] Frisch's record book covering his tenure in San Antonio lists eight conversions—"inductions into the Jewish faith," he called them. At least two were young women who planned to marry Jewish men. Two others, a man and a woman, converted after several years of marriage to a Jewish spouse.

Texas' Jewish newspapers devoted countless columns to Jewish marriages and the flurry of parties surrounding them. Each issue described at least three weddings, engagements, or showers per week, down to the room decorations. Abundant press coverage indicates that Texas Jews intended to perpetuate their religious identity even as their ties to Europe declined and their assimilation as Americans increased.

The Second Migration

Also receiving constant coverage in the local Jewish press was the proliferation of Jewish institutions. Groups such as the Workman's Circle, Hebrew Free Loan Associations, and Yiddish literary clubs reflected a new tide of Jewish arrivals. After 1881, oppressive decrees enacted in czarist Russia forced Jews to flee persecution in Eastern Europe. A second wave of Jewish immigrants, far larger than the earlier German tide, began reaching the United States. Between 1881 and the early 1920s, when restrictive immigration quotas were enacted, 2 million Eastern European Jews entered the United States. Some filtered into Texas, with the tide peaking from 1907 to 1914 when 1,500 Jews a year entered through the port of Galveston.[119] Unlike earlier Jewish settlers, these newcomers were not soldiers of fortune, hardy adventurers, or risk-taking entrepreneurs following new rail lines into Texas. Survival as Jews rather than wanderlust fueled their journeys. These new arrivals had lived in insulated Jewish enclaves practicing a tradition-steeped Judaism that they sought to transplant. They were accustomed to prayer shawls and skullcaps—worship garb that most assimilated German Jews had discarded. They clung to the dietary laws, resisted mixed seating of men and women at synagogue, and opposed the trend toward English-language prayer books. Strife inevitably followed.

In Tyler, a cluster of traditional worshippers broke away from Congregation Beth El in 1897. They celebrated the Sabbath in the Woodmen of the World lodge. By the summer of 1903 the faction had chartered a new synagogue, Ahavath Achim. From Poland they recruited the Reverend S. Greenberg, a scholar who served as cantor, *shochet,* and *mohel.*[120]

In Houston, the arrival of *Ost Juden*—East European Jews—led to a "cleavage" in 1887, according to the minutes of Congregation Beth Israel. Throughout the previous three decades the temple had gradually shifted from traditional to Reform Jewish practices. Arguments over the liturgy surfaced as early as 1868, when the Reverend Zacharias Emmich made a successful motion to switch to an American prayerbook. A year later a faction could not muster the votes to repeal the measure. Soon thereafter the temple was burglarized and the books stolen. They apparently were not recovered. In 1874 Beth Israel officially joined the Reform movement's Union of American Hebrew Congregations. In the mid-1880s the congregation debated a series of motions that barred guests who wore yarmulkes, a slap at recent arrivals. With tension mounting, the traditional contingent bolted Beth Israel in 1889 and organized Houston's first traditional synagogue, Adath Yeshurun.[121]

Most small Texas towns accommodated a range of traditions and observances. They had little choice but cooperation. In Texarkana, for example, the East European Jews who preferred traditional worship conducted a separate service under the same roof as the Reform Jews but at different times or in separate rooms. If the more religious group lacked the necessary 10 adult men to convene a service, a Reform Jew on call would oblige.[122] In Brenham a Reform Jew donated the land on which a traditional synagogue, B'nai Abraham, was constructed in 1892 replete with a *mikvah,* a ritual bath.[123] In San Antonio, when a new rabbi was installed at Congregation Beth-El in 1923, a joint service of the city's three synagogues welcomed the new leader.[124]

In Fort Worth many families maintained dual memberships at Ahavath Sholom, the traditional synagogue founded in 1892, and Reform Congregation Beth-El, begun in 1902. Working together, Fort Worth's Jews created a B'nai B'rith chapter in 1902, a Hebrew Relief Society in 1902, a Hebrew Free Loan Society in 1907, a Hebrew School in 1908, and a Hebrew Institute that helped acculturate adults "just off the boat." The Galveston Movement directed eight immigrants a month to Fort Worth —a trickle compared with immigration in the north. The small number of "greenhorns" kept tensions between Jews minimal.[125]

At the turn of the century Texas remained a state with a low concentration of Jews—15,000, a mere 0.5 percent of the state's population. (That compared with Ohio's 50,000 Jews, one percent of its population, and New York's 400,000 Jews, or five percent of its residents.)[126] By 1900 Texas had 25 Jewish congregations, most without rabbis. Those with vacant pulpits included Austin's Congregation Beth Israel with 25 families and 50 students; Gainesville's United Hebrew Congregation with 28 families; and Palestine's Beth Israel, still so small that congregants convened in private homes. In 1900 Rabbi Maurice Faber arrived in Tyler to lead a temple of 43 families, a position he held until his death in 1934.[127] At the turn of the century Martin Zielonka left Waco's Temple Rodef Sholom, which had 48 families and 110 students, for El Paso's smaller Temple Mount Sinai, which listed 45 families and 30 school-age youngsters.[128] He, too, relinquished the pulpit only with his death in 1938. Houston's Temple Beth Israel counted 92 families and 103 students when it hired its fifteenth rabbi, Henry Barnstein, in 1900. Barnstein attained emeritus status in 1943. In Galveston Rabbi Henry Cohen's Reform Temple B'nai Israel was the state's largest, with 162 families and 200 students.[129]

Rabbis took root in Texas around the turn of the century. Where 20 years before five rabbis had carved the state into circuit-riding routes, now there were 15 rabbis and Jewish institutions in 40 towns.[130] The rabbis who stayed made their marks. Simultaneously, the Lone Star State was undergoing a transition from a frontier, cattle, and cotton economy into a more stable place with new jobs in logging, shipping, and petrochemical industries. Rabbis witnessed the transition.

Galveston's Henry Cohen

In all the State of Texas,
From Fort Worth to San Anton'
There's not a man who hasn't heard
Of Rabbi Henry Cohen.[131]

The archetype of the successful Lone Star rabbi was Henry Cohen, the legendary "Man who Stayed in Texas." He served as Galveston's spiritual leader for 64 years from 1888 until his death in 1952. Cohen became the dean of Texas rabbis, an example to clergy of all faiths, and an adviser at all levels of government. He served on the prison board and successfully lobbied the Legislature to raise the age of consent for statutory rape from 10 to 18, separate first offenders from long-time criminals, and place debtors and other nonviolent felons on supervised probation. On the national level Cohen was appointed to refugee relief committees, and he advised the artist painting biblical symbols on murals inside the Library of Congress.[132]

Cohen failed to impress everyone during his first visit to Galveston to deliver a trial sermon. Two teenage girls laughed at his manner of speech because this short rabbi with starched white cuffs, cutaway coat, and British accent stuttered. Yet the synagogue leadership recognized Cohen as a dynamic, worldly rabbi with the moxie to thrive in their teeming town. Temple B'nai Israel President Leo N. Levi told the young ladies snickering at the rabbi's speech impediment, "He'll get over it, and if he doesn't we'll get used to it."[133] Besides, Cohen could stutter comfortably in eleven languages, and Galveston's port was a veritable Tower of Babel.

An island town 50 miles south of Houston and two miles off the Texas mainland, Galveston and its Gulf Coast beaches were a vacation destination for hordes of tourists before air conditioning and air travel. The island's opposite shore was a marshland, a breeding ground for alligators, rattlesnakes, and mosquitoes. Further plaguing the island were hurricanes and soupy fog reminiscent of Henry Cohen's British homeland.

Blessing the isle was the state's deepest harbor, which in the late nineteenth century made Galveston a banking capital and bustling port that shipped most of the state's pecans and cotton. By the turn of the century this "gateway to Texas" had become the fifth largest cotton exporter in the United States. With 2.2 million bales shipped per year, Galveston produced one-eighth of Texas' state tax revenue. Its ostentatious Victorian homes built by merchant princes, its state medical college campus, and its flourishing vice district made Galveston the state's most cosmopolitan city, the Manhattan of Texas.[134] And with 1,000 Jews among its 22,000 residents, it was Texas' Jewish capital for decades. Henry Cohen's past included adventures as interpreter for the British military in South Africa and a pulpit in Kingston, Jamaica. He had found a bit too sedate his previous three years as rabbi in Woodville, Mississippi, an Old South town still rehashing the Civil War. The 25-year-old rabbi fell in step with the Galveston mix. As his son and daughter-in-law wrote: "Texas reminded him somewhat of South Africa. Here he was in young country again—country that you could see growing—vigorous and a little rowdy, . . . a city looking ahead, not backward, and the residents did not date things 'before the War.'"[135]

Cohen became the first historian of the Texas Jewish community, using his circuit-riding time to interview descendants of Hebrew pioneers. It was Cohen who in 1894 penned "Jews of Texas" for the second volume of the American Jewish Historical Society's scholarly journal. In 1901 and 1906 he wrote articles on Texas for the first editions of the *Jewish Encyclopedia*.[136] Cohen's research incorrectly determined that a Frenchman, Henri Castro, who had "mounted the first organized emigration to Texas from a foreign country," was a Jew. Between 1843 and 1846 Castro encouraged 5,000 Europeans to make the young republic their home. Cohen documented the narrative of Jamaican-born Jew Jacob de Cordova, who introduced the Order of the Odd Fellows to Texas, served on Houston's first Chamber of Commerce, was elected to the 1847 Legislature, laid out the city of Waco, and mapped and sold acreage across the state. Cohen also noted many less prominent Jews who helped place Texas on the map.

A natural catastrophe catapulted Cohen to national acclaim. On 8 September 1900 a cataclysmic hurricane swept a tidal wave over Galveston Island, making rubble of 3,600 homes and killing more than 6,000 inhabitants, a death toll that stands as the nation's worst in a natural disaster. Nine days later Red Cross founder Clara Barton arrived on the scene. Barton mustered headlines and a national relief effort that funneled money, clothing, and food to an island falling prey to dysentery, yellow fever, and despair.[137] Looting was rampant, even ghoulish, as thieves cut fingers off corpses to plunder rings. Rabbi Cohen led relief efforts with a shotgun stuck lopsidedly under his arm.[138]

Cohen's partner in the wake of the hurricane was the Right Reverend James Martin Kirwin, an Ohioan assigned to Galveston in 1896. Residents grew accustomed to seeing "the rabbi and Father Kirwin of the Catholic Diocese dash down the street together," one of Cohen's congregants wrote. "Father Kirwin [was] tall, muscular, handsome; the rabbi short, energetic, forceful. The city knew the two were fast friends who helped one another in congregational needs. They were an example for all to follow."[139]

Cohen and Kirwin watched anxiously when the Ku Klux Klan organized across Texas. The KKK began to gain a foothold in Texas on 9 October 1920 when white-robed visitors from Georgia marched in a Confederate veterans' parade in Houston. Starting with Klavern No. 1 in Houston, the Klan spread rapidly. Galveston's Klan, established five weeks later, was Klavern No. 36.[140] Although the Klan's rhetoric harped on Catholics with dual allegiances and Jews with shrewd business practices, the Texas Klan, unlike chapters in Northern and Southern cities, did not light crosses in front of Catholic churches or synagogues. In Texas, Klan vigilantism and violence took the form of whippings, abductions, and tarring and feathering of victims, mostly blacks but often white men branded "wayward husbands" or bootleggers.[141]

In Galveston hooded Klansmen interrupted a revival at the First Baptist Church to announce an upcoming initiation and present a $100 offering to the church, a common KKK practice designed to gain Protestant recruits. The Galveston Klan's initiation ceremony was staged under a cross lit with red electric lights. But when Klansmen filed for a parade permit in 1922, Kirwin and Cohen together went to the City Council to object. The clout of the clergymen proved so effective that a Klan parade was not staged in Galveston. Due to the efforts of Cohen and Kirwin and the general tolerance of Galveston's diverse community, the Klan never established a strong presence there as it did in Austin, Houston, Beaumont, Dallas, and Fort Worth, where Klan slates were swept into office in the elections of 1922.[142]

In September of 1922 Klan delegates took over the state Democratic convention. The Texas electorate also sent Klan candidate Earle B. Mayfield to the US Senate. Beyond Texas the Klan elected county and state officials in Arkansas, Georgia, Louisiana, Oklahoma, and Oregon.

Pushing itself as a superpatriotic organization, the Texas Klan recruited members from lodges, police departments, and the judiciary. Not until the presidential election year of 1924 was the Klan soundly repudiated in Texas.[143]

Cohen had solidified his humanitarian reputation during the seven years prior to World War I. During that time, he helped implement New York philanthropist Jacob Schiff's Galveston Plan, a scheme to divert European immigrants from New York harbor to the American Southwest. Rabbi Cohen greeted all immigrants at the dock in their native tongues. He made certain they bathed, ate, and received any mail awaiting them. The Jewish Immigrants Information Bureau, which opened in Galveston in the spring of 1907, helped place each individual in a job in the Southwest or Midwest. Cohen also activated the network of Texas rabbis to find jobs and lodgings for the Jews who remained in the state. An estimated 10,000 European Jews entered the United States via the Galveston Movement—far fewer than the 2,500 a year Jacob Schiff projected and a drop in the bucket compared with the numbers arriving in New York but a significant addition to the underpopulated Southwest.[144] In his role as greeter and immigrant advocate the rabbi did not confine his efforts to Jews. He persuaded President Taft to overrule the pending deportation of a Greek-Catholic stowaway.[145] President Wilson dubbed the rabbi the "first citizen of Texas."[146]

In Cohen's later years Northern congregations and institutions put out feelers to lure this energetic rabbi out of Texas. He turned these offers down, including the presidency of Hebrew Union College in Cincinnati, in part because his wife Mollie preferred her hometown.[147] But in Cohen's formative years, it was Texas, the state that wanted "good mixers," that went after this rabbi who rode a bicycle to temple and sermonized with a stutter that would have precluded him from most established pulpits.[148] That voice was heeded.

El Paso's Martin Zielonka

"We have always said that good positions are made—not found," wrote a reporter in 1915 for the *Texas Jewish Herald*.[149] The weekly was referring to El Paso Rabbi Martin Zielonka, who had just signed a five-year contract extension with Temple Mount Sinai. Zielonka had come to Texas in 1899 fresh from ordination at Cincinnati's Hebrew Union College.[150] His mother had relatives in Waco, a central Texas river town sometimes called Six-Shooter Junction. Congregation Rodef Sholom, which had seen eight rabbis come and go since 1882, invited the young rabbi to lead. Zielonka, born in Berlin and raised in Cincinnati, had not traveled beyond the Ohio River Valley during his schooling. In Texas he became a circuit rider, journeying by stagecoach and train to Austin, Taylor, Fort Worth, and Victoria to perform rabbinical functions.[151] The rabbi met his bride-to-be, Dora Schatzky, "at a dance to which young Jewish ladies came from great distances," according to a letter written by the couple's son.[152] She was from San Antonio, the daughter of a Russian-Jewish traveling salesman and a mother descended from a line of antebellum Louisiana merchants.

In 1900 the couple accepted a call from Temple Mount Sinai in El Paso, a border town flavored by neighboring Mexico and the Indian cultures of the Santa Fe Trail. Twenty-three-year-old Zielonka became the sole Jewish clergyman between Chihuahua and California. Dubbed the "Reform Rabbi of the West," he had a rabbinical circuit that spanned a 600-mile radius that encompassed Albuquerque, Tucson, Phoenix, Santa Fe, Alamogordo, Tucumcari, Big Spring, Mexico City, and even Los Angeles if the need for a Jewish officiant arose.[153]

Opportunity abounded in this Wild West crossroads where alligators swam in the downtown fountain. Among its 15,906 inhabitants could be found gunslingers, trappers, traders, temperance leaders, and 45 Jewish families.[154] Zielonka served on the city planning commission, becoming a self-taught authority. He spoke at Rotary conventions throughout the West on such advances as paved streets, trolley cars, and parks. Zielonka organized El Paso's first charities and pitched in to raise money to construct buildings for the Salvation Army and the YMCA. He spoke out on behalf of children of Hispanic indigents and "flayed" the school board in sermons, "charging it with ignoring the obvious needs of Mexican children."[155] On call on both sides of the border, Zielonka negotiated with the bandit Pancho Villa for the release of prisoners and watched, terrified, as the revolutionary leader shot the lock off a jail cell door.[156] Zielonka witnessed a murder one Sunday morning in 1910 when a drunken gambler barged into Ernst Kohlberg's cigar store and shot the owner.[157] Another time the rabbi was roused in the middle of the night to officiate at a real shotgun wedding.

Zielonka made repeated forays into Mexico and reported to the Central Conference of American Rabbis about the status of the country's 1,500 to 2,000 scattered Jews.[158] When illegal European Jewish immigrants began stealing across the border from Mexico in 1921, this rabbi called an urgent meeting of his rabbinic colleagues along the coast. Their cities, too, had witnessed increasing arrests of Jewish stowaways hidden on commercial ships that docked in their ports.[159] The bulk of these immigrants, with passports forged in Berlin and one-way steamship tickets as far as Veracruz, had been lured to Mexico by rumors of easy access to the United States. Instead, border guards enforcing strict immigration laws arrested the refugees and triggered deportation proceedings. Zielonka, with backing from his fellow Texas rabbis, worked with B'nai B'rith to resettle 8,164 illegal European Jews south of the border.[160] B'nai B'rith opened a Mexico City Bureau that functioned for a decade as settlement house, infirmary, language school, and free loan association. Immigrants were put to work as peddlers. This wave of East European Jewish immigrants laid the foundation for Mexico's contemporary Jewish community.[161]

His congregants recall Zielonka as a moralizing pastor, an accomplished public servant, and a disdainful spiritual leader. He harangued families for going "automobiling" rather than attending services where he delivered tedious sermons. He snapped at students who giggled during Hebrew class, expelling at least one from religious school. He touted his German origins, even denigrating his wife's descent from a Russian line.[162] For years Zielonka snubbed Hungarian-born Rabbi Joseph Roth, a graduate of the Jewish Theological Seminary who served at El Paso's Congregation B'nai Zion from 1923 to 1953.[163] His attitude seemed at odds with his decade of work resettling Eastern European immigrants in Mexico. Years later, when those immigrant Jews from south of the border migrated to El Paso, many rejected Zielonka's congregation because the rabbi had a cold demeanor and had stripped his temple of the traditions with which they were comfortable.[164]

El Paso's second synagogue, a *shul* organized in 1912, attracted these East European Jews. Animosity between the new synagogue, Congregation B'nai Zion, and Zielonka's Temple Mount Sinai mounted over the issue of Zionism. Zielonka believed in the Diaspora, the dispersion of Jews and the spread of Jewish ideas around the world. While Zielonka pushed for Mexican resettlement, others pushed for Palestine. He was convinced that a Jewish nation in the Middle East would exacerbate tensions between Jews and Muslims and that Jewish nationalism would pervert the religion's moral ideals. His thinking was consistent with that of most of his Reform colleagues. Writing in his personal notebook in February 1937 he explained: "I can see no difference between the nationalism of Germany, Poland, Romania and . . . Jewish nationalism. Groups usually act alike. We know what misery has been caused by these. [There is] no reason to feel that Jewish nationalism would act different." The rabbi feared that Zionism had already stirred animosity between Arabs and Jews. "Palestine is not an uninhabited region. We occupied it for a comparatively short time. . . . There has been no so-called anti-Semitism between Mohammedans and Jews. We are creating it. Nationalism of Arabs has been aroused. [We] don't want peace at a British bayonet's edge. . . . For me Zionism is not a way out for Weltschmerz of Jewry."[165]

In line with his anti-Zionism, Zielonka attacked Hadassah, a women's group that fostered medical training and research in Israel. The rabbi argued that Hadassah's agenda was pure nationalism and that it spouted "propaganda."[166] Hadassah founder Henrietta Szold visited Texas in 1912, 1914, and 1919 to foster interest in Zionism and organize local chapters.[167] Early chapters were established in Houston, Wharton, Waco, Austin, Dallas, Fort Worth, and San Antonio, but not El Paso.

El Paso women made three futile attempts—in 1928, 1936, and 1937—to organize Hadassah.[168] "I felt we had enough women's organizations," Rabbi Zielonka snapped at Tamar de Sola Pool when she queried him on the subject in 1937.[169] Mrs. Pool, three-time national president of Hadassah, and her husband David, rabbi of New York's Spanish and Portuguese Synagogue Shearith Israel, visited El Paso to help launch a chapter. Zielonka's clout meant that Jewish women in El Paso did not join the Hadassah network until 1943, five years after his death. Barbara Goodman Ettinger, whose mother founded that Hadassah chapter, reflected that Zielonka's power mirrored the strength of El Paso's early German families who, socially and economically, were the backbone of the Jewish community.[170]

Zielonka did work cordially with the local chapter of the Council of Jewish Women, chartered in 1917 and rooted in Reform movement principles of social service. The Council of Jewish Women took food baskets to Jewish immigrants stranded in Mexico and escorted Jewish children in Juarez across the border to attend Sunday school.[171] Zielonka also mixed in the general community. He recruited a temple youth basketball squad and stiffly posed for team photos when his boys beat the YMCA; he spent his Sunday mornings kibitzing with the regulars at a tobacco store, puffing on his pipe.[172] Although some found him haughty, he was well respected, and on his death was eulogized in a front-page obituary that cast him as a humanitarian. In Mexico, B'nai B'rith's 1993 centennial was marked with publication of a book about the Jewish migration to that country, a volume dedicated to Martin Zielonka.[173]

Tyler's Maurice Faber

Zielonka's El Paso years parallel the Texas career of Rabbi Maurice Faber. Faber arrived in the summer of 1900, invited by a congregation impressed with reports of a patriotic speech he had delivered to a Midwest gathering on the US Constitution. Born in Hungary in 1854, Faber often remarked that "he was more of an American than those who chanced to be born here because he was 'an American by choice.'"[174] Faber, the descendant of a long line of rabbis, rejected the orthodoxy of his forebears. Although his father had no use for the movement, the younger rabbi embraced Reform Judaism. The ideological break between father and son proved irreparable. Ordained in 1873, Faber departed Hungary in 1879 for the United States. He found a part-time pulpit in Titusville, Pennsylvania, at Congregation B'nai Zion, a Reform synagogue with a dozen families. In 1898 he moved to Keokuk, Iowa, a Mississippi River congregation with a grandiose Reform synagogue founded in 1856 and a proud history as Iowa's oldest Jewish congregation. Unfortunately, Keokuk, which called itself Iowa's Gate City, was past its prime. Steamboats were outmoded; the railroad had bypassed the town; the congregation, with 21 families, including 13 students, was drying up.[175] When Tyler, Texas, advertised for a rabbi two years later, Faber eagerly applied.

Tyler's legacy and landscape evoked not the Western cowboy but the Deep South. Seventy-five miles from Louisiana, Tyler had served as a supply base for the Confederacy because of its bountiful harvests and natural forests that produced mints, berries, sweetgum, sassafras and a wealth of pharmaceutical ingredients.[176] The countryside's rolling, sandy-loam hills later made it a rose-growing capital with annual flower pageants, parades, Southern belles, and balls. By 1900 three colorful governors and one US senator had hailed from Tyler, a county seat with 30,000 inhabitants and about 100 Jews, many of them retailers in business around the town square.[177] Faber, with his bellowing voice and strong opinions, fit into the political mix. He chaired town hall meetings, snared land and funds for a Carnegie public library and raised money to feed handicapped children at home and to purchase matzoh for an impoverished Talmudic academy in Prague.[178] When Faber delivered a high school commencement address for 95 graduating seniors, 1,200 people jammed the auditorium to savor his words.[179]

Faber was chaplain at Tyler's St. John's Masonic lodge, which dated to 1849. When Ku Klux Klansmen infiltrated the 500-member lodge in 1925 they insisted that new Masonic lodge members apply simultaneously for membership in the Klan. The rabbi led a faction of lodge members in opposition. The dispute led to a state Masonic investigation and a 10-month suspension of the St. John's charter. Over the next several months, a breakaway lodge of 65 men formed with Rabbi Faber installed as chaplain and listed among the officers. With the agreement of the new lodge, the St. John's charter was restored. A decade later, during hard economic times, a resolution to merge the two bodies failed.[180]

A decade before the Masonic split, Faber's bearing and prestige led a local politician to recommend that the governor appoint the rabbi to the University of Texas Board of Regents. Faber, the first clergyman to sit on that board and its second Jew, was amused when the certificate naming him a regent identified him as "Father Faber." The governor, James "Pa" Ferguson, was a school dropout and a Methodist preacher's son with little inkling of Judaism. A populist elected by "the boys at the forks of the creeks," the governor likewise had no hint of the rabbi's intellectual independence.[181] Accustomed to selling prison pardons and dispatching state employees to buy cattle for his ranch, the governor also maneuvered to run the university. He targeted for dismissal six faculty and one staff member who had criticized his administration or become involved in political crusades with which he disagreed. One of the objectionable professors, the head of the journalism department, owned a newspaper that "skinned the governor from hell to breakfast."[182] Another, a physicist, crusaded against the state capital's red-light district, focusing disrepute on the capital city of Austin. A third, famed folklorist, John A. Lomax, published cowboy song lyrics the governor derided as too lowbrow for an academician. ("When I die, don't bury me at all. Just pickle my bones, in alcohol.")[183] Some of the faculty appeared to have overcharged the university for mileage expenses. Ferguson branded the whole lot of them "butterfly chasers."[184] He wrote the rabbi expecting his vote to oust them. The rabbi balked. In September, 1916, Faber wrote the governor: "I never dreamed that . . . the appointee is expected to be a mere marionette to move and act as and when the Chief Executive pushes the button or pulls the string . . . I cannot pledge myself to follow the arbitrary will of any person, no matter how high and exalted, without being convinced of the justice of his demands. In my humble opinion such course will disorganize and disrupt the University, the just pride of the people of Texas."[185] The governor responded, threatening to remove Faber from the board: "I do not care to bandy words with you further. . . . I shall not hesitate to repair the wrong which I have done in appointing you. . . . You are defying your friends and proving yourself culpably disloyal by aligning yourself with a political ring in the University who, if permitted to continue, will cause the people sooner or later to rise up and disown the whole affair."[186]

The pair's peppery correspondence—printed in Texas newspapers and introduced into evidence during the governor's impeachment trial in July 1917—turned Faber into an icon of academic freedom. Letter writers lauded Faber as an "American citizen and patriot who understands the genius of our government and reveres its institutions." The governor was reviled as an "ass," prone to braying in public and private.[187] Wrote Austin's Episcopal Reverend Y. H. Kinsolving of the rabbi: "King Agrippa said to St. Paul: Almost thou persuadest me to be a Christian. I say to you: Almost thou persuadest me to be a Hebrew."[188]

Beaumont's Henry Rosinger

The course of Texas history changed overnight in January 1901, when a rumbling emanated from beneath the ground in Beaumont. A gusher of oil erupted that could not be capped for a week. Beaumont, begun as a lumber town during Texas' second year of independence and named for a man who won a wager, soared from obscurity to history. As 75,000 barrels a day flowed from the depths of the Spindletop field, the city burgeoned from a few thousand inhabitants to a boomtown. Bars, bordellos, and brawls thrived in the following decade. Mostly men populated the town. Business deals were struck that matured into international oil companies, among them Gulf, Mobil, and Texaco. The timber industry grew to accommodate housing needs. The nearby Gulf port took on tonnage. Gradually, women and families came. Needs changed, and religion grew more relevant. A succession of clergy came and went for close to a decade, not just in the Jewish community but also among Christians. It took time for organized religion to gain a foothold. Several dozen Jewish families had lived in Beaumont before the oil strike. Scores more Jewish merchants followed. The town's Jewish congregation, established in 1887 and chartered in 1900, held services in members' stores until they erected their first building the same year the oil boom began.[189]

Beaumont was ripening into a stable city when Samuel Rosinger responded to Temple Emanuel's advertised call for a "mixer." For the previous two years the rabbi had held a pulpit in Toledo, Ohio. Texas, 1,200 miles south of Toledo, seemed worthy of Rosinger's wanderlust. A new movie genre, the Western, was catching on with the release of Texan Tom Mix's first cowboy film. Oil discoveries fueled the Lone Star state's mythology. Beaumont did not disappoint Rosinger and his wife, New Yorker Gertrude Kaelter. Rosinger unabashedly "caught the contagion of bragging" about the state.[190] Beaumont had the raw ingredients and potential for adventure and growth, but the town had its share of problems endemic to the oil that lubricated its boom.

The gravest need Rosinger perceived in his new community was health care. Tuberculosis victims lived quarantined in tents. Rosinger enlisted community-wide help to provide medical care. He created a Red Cross chapter. He headed the county tuberculosis association. He spearheaded a successful $50,000 county bond election in 1922—during the height of Ku Klux Klan activity—that financed construction of the Jefferson County Tuberculosis Hospital. The institution treated both whites and blacks—albeit in facilities eight miles apart. Earmarking county funds for African Americans during the segregated Jim Crow era was a feat attempted by few public figures.[191]

In the rapidly growing community, Rosinger took the lead in other areas as well. He saw the need for parental involvement in the schools and was elected president of the high school PTA. To project his views, he became lead editorial writer for the *Texas Jewish Herald*. He used his paper pulpit to encourage observance of Jewish dietary laws, reasoning that they fostered moderation, hygiene and a "religious atmosphere in the home."[192] He railed against intermarriage, in a three-part series of columns, terming it a cancer, a disease tantamount to "religious suicide."[193] He recommended new juvenile literature aimed at Jewish youngsters.[194] He backed prohibition, arguing that vodka had spurred Russian pogroms against the Jews.[195] He used Louis Brandeis' appointment to the US Supreme Court to editorialize in favor of Zionism: "No one doubted [Brandeis'] patriotism because of his Zionist activity. . . . This shows that the incompatibility of Zionism with Americanism is [untrue]."[196] While Rosinger found himself at odds with his Reform colleagues on the issue of Zionism, this apparently created no divisions within the Kallah of Texas rabbis, which was regularly attended by Zielonka, Cohen, and the other anti-Zionist Reform rabbis.

Rosinger had a knack for bridging differences. Born in the foothills of Hungary's Carpathian Mountains, he left his native village of Tibolddarocz at age nine to study religion under a series of Hungarian scholars. Educational opportunities drew him to universities in Budapest, Bern, and finally to Berlin, where he received his undergraduate degree. In 1904 Rosinger migrated to New York, where he simultaneously studied for a master's degree at Columbia University and ordination as a Conservative rabbi at the Jewish Theological Seminary. Rosinger's spiritual mentor was Solomon Schechter, founder of the Conservative movement and president of its seminary. His academic mentor was Dr.

Joseph Jacobs, the seminary's registrar, who taught English to foreign-born rabbinic students and helped turn Rosinger into a prolific editorial writer. Rosinger had found his niche in Beaumont, an environment foreign to his upbringing yet suited to his independence. He delighted in retelling the story about a visiting lecturer from the North who incredulously asked him, "What heinous sin have you committed that in expiation you have buried yourself in this hole?" The rabbi replied, "I told him that, far from being buried, I was very much alive."[197]

A Look Back and Forward

Texas' wide open spaces, undeveloped terrain, and embryonic institutions proved fertile territory for energetic rabbis. Despite the paucity of Jews and the dearth of academic outlets, rabbis who stayed in Texas accomplished far more than if they had served cosmopolitan pulpits elsewhere. Texas rabbis did not have the luxury of focusing on one field. Conditions compelled them to fill many voids, participate in an array of endeavors, and become civic leaders comfortable in all aspects of their social culture. Cohen, Faber, Zielonka, and Rosinger are early twentieth-century examples.

The same case can probably be made for remote pulpits in other states, particularly in the Far West and Southwest, where the tasks outnumbered the people and newcomers and innovation were welcome. *Western States Jewish Historical Quarterly* has published detailed biographical articles on a number of colorful California rabbis who fit the role of mixer and humanitarian. These include Voorsanger and Blum, who launched the circuit-riding concept in Texas and continued their roles as ethnic brokers when they moved to West Coast pulpits.[198] Jewish histories that focus on Montana, New Mexico, and Arkansas, however, do not highlight many activist rabbis, at least not on the scale shown in Texas.[199] More study is suggested in this area, because conditions similar to frontier Texas existed throughout the West. Harriet and Fred Rochlin, in *Pioneer Jews*, state that during the initial settlement, many rabbis drawn to the western frontier were misfits running from personal problems. "The most desirable [rabbis] were snapped up by congregations east of the Rockies or by the few affluent synagogues on the West Coast."[200] When Hebrew Union College, founded in 1875, and the Jewish Theological Seminary, established in 1887, began educating American-born rabbis, more spiritual leaders moved west. They largely thrived, providing "models of exemplary Jews to the public at large and [stimulating] interest in human betterment, education and aid to the needy."[201] In 1907 British-born San Francisco Rabbi Jacob Nieto told a

reporter from London's *Jewish Chronicle*, "Speaking of the Western states
. . . the rabbis occupy a high position. They are in every sense, the representatives of the Jewish community. . . . They are looked up to as representatives, not only by Christians but—what is more important—by
the Jewish community itself."[202]

Historian Deborah Dash Moore has explored a similar phenomenon
among rabbis and congregants who built new Jewish communities in
post–World War II Miami and Los Angeles. "In a community where old-
timers are people who have lived there more than five years, new leaders spring up every day. . . . Unconnected to old routines [and] . . . without long established hierarchies," Jews in new frontiers have the freedom
to innovate, rebel against their parents' orthodoxy, and leave traditional paths behind."[203]

When Jews first formed religious institutions in Texas in the nineteenth century, they wanted leaders well versed in ritual. They advertised
for ministers who were Torah readers, kosher butchers, and circumcis-
ers. As Texas Jews assimilated into American culture and discarded
ancient traditions, these early "reverends" became irrelevant to their
needs. What Texas Jews realized they truly needed were "mixers" who
would help integrate them into the fabric of their towns. They desired
modern, polished representatives of their faith. The old-style "reverends" performed an array of functions *inside* the Jewish community.
As congregations matured, the rabbi's role changed into that of someone who performed an array of tasks *beyond* the Jewish community.

The pattern of rabbinic civic involvement begun during Texas' frontier period continued beyond the turn of the century into the present
era, particularly in young suburbs like Arlington, a town between Dallas
and Fort Worth, which hired its first rabbi a decade ago, and remote
cities such as Lubbock, where modern-day rabbis became cultural leaders.[204] From Fort Worth to Texarkana, rabbis' names appear on corner-
stones and above doorways at modern medical institutions, museums,
and social service facilities. Texas' Jewish community hovers at 0.6 percent of the population. Where there is a leadership vacuum, rabbis become high-profile civic figures.

Notes

1. *American Israelite*, 7 April 1910, 2.

2. Samuel Rosinger, "Deep in the Heart of Texas," in *Lives and Voices: A Collection of American Jewish Memoirs*, ed. Stanley F. Chyet (Philadelphia, 1972), 134;
Edwin Gale, interview with author, 21 January 1995.

3. Mark K. Bauman and Arnold Shankman, "The Rabbi as Ethnic Broker: The Case of David Marx," *Journal of American Ethnic History* 2 (Spring 1983): 51.

4. David Rosenbaum, "The Rabbi as Ambassador to the Gentiles. Chips from a Rabbinical Workshop," in David Rosenbaum papers, box 1, folder 1, Spertus College Archives, Chicago.

5. Jacob Rader Marcus, interview with author, 13 December 1992.

6. David Goldberg, rabbi in Corsicana, Tex., in 1916 writes, "Christianity is based on Old Testament. . . . This circumstance alone is sufficient to keep the Jews in considerable prominence before the non-Jew." *Texas Jewish Herald*, 18 May 1916; Hasia Diner, *A Time for Gathering: the Second Migration, 1820–1880* (Baltimore, 1992), 225.

7. T. R. Fehrenbach, *Lone Star: A History of Texas and the Texans* (New York, 1968), 280.

8. Ibid., 434–47.

9. *Dallas Daily Herald*, 30 May 1876.

10. Michael V. Hazel, "The Critic Club, Sixty Years of Quiet Leadership," *Legacies: A History Journal for Dallas and North Central Texas* (Fall 1990): 9–17; William H. Greenburg, "Autobiographical Sketch of William H. Greenburg," 29 March 1948, Critic Club collection, A6354, Dallas Historical Society.

11. G. George Fox, "The End of an Era," in *Lives and Voices*, 279.

12. Louis Schmier, *Reflections of Southern Jewry: The Letters of Charles Wessolowsky, 1878–1879* (Macon, Ga., 1982), 81.

13. "Unique in American Jewry is the Kallah of the Texas Rabbinical Association, founded at Houston . . . for the discussion of religious and rabbinical questions. The Association took its name from the popular academic courses given in two months of each year in Babylonia," writes Henry Cohen in "Texas," *Universal Jewish Encyclopedia* (New York, 1943), 10:205; *Kallah* is Hebrew for bride, an allusion to the Torah as the bride of God. "It is also an acrostic: An Assembly of Students of Torah. *K'neseth Lom'de Ha-Torah*. This derivation gives it the same root as the English word *college,*" writes Austin Rabbi Samuel Halevi Baron in "What the Kallah Is," *Kallah 5696 Yearbook. Tenth Anniversary. Kallah of Texas Rabbis* (Houston, 1937), 1.

14. Abraham I. Schechter, "Report of the President," and "Message of the President to the First Annual Kallah Convention of Texas Rabbis," *The Kallah. An Annual Convention of Texas Rabbis. March 1927 to March 1928, Volume I. Yearbook* (Houston, 1928), 8, 11–12.

15. David Lefkowitz, "Greeting of the President to the Third Annual Kallah Convention of American Rabbis," *The Kallah. An Annual Convention of Texas Rabbis. Adar 5689 to 5690. March 1929 to March 1930. Volume III. Year Book, 5690* (Dallas, 1929), 5.

16. Robert I. Kahn, interview with author, 4 March 1997.

17. In Arkansas another unique institution fostered by isolation was called the Kehillah, or the Arkansas Jewish Assembly. This voluntary federation of Jewish communities, including lay people and clergy, met from 1931 to 1951. Its focus was communal, not philosophical. Three hundred people attended the first meeting, called by Rabbi A. B. Rhine of Hot Springs. Carolyn Gray Lemaster, *A Corner of the Tapestry: A History of the Jewish Experience in Arkansas 1820s–1990s* (Little Rock, 1994), 309–15.

18. Greenburg, "Autobiographical Sketch."

19. Audrey Daniels Kariel, "Memories of Marshall, Texas," *Western States Jewish Historical Quarterly* 14 (April 1982): 200.

20. Steiner arrived sometime before Passover and died in September 1867. *American Israelite*, 22 January 1869, 2.

21. *San Francisco Jewish Progress*, 10 June 1878, from Texas Jewish Historical Society Collection, Galveston folder, Center for American History, University of Texas at Austin; William M. Kramer and Reva Clar, "Rabbi Abraham Blum: From Alsace to New York by Way of Texas and California," *Western States Jewish Historical Quarterly* 11 (October 1979): 73–88.

22. "The chief of police thinks someone standing near the house fired a pistol accidentally and the ball penetrated the window." *Dallas Weekly Herald,* 30 October 1884.

23. Jack Barnston, telephone interview with author, 14 April 1997.

24. *Houston Press,* 1 June 1943.

25. Of these inhabitants, 30,000 were Caucasian, 4,000 were Mexican, and 5,000 were African American. Fehrenbach, *Lone Star,* 287; Mike Kingston, ed. *Texas Almanac and State Industrial Guide* (Dallas, 1993), 109.

26. Mordecai Podet, *Pioneer Jews of Waco* (Waco, 1986), 6.

27. "One of the Alamo's martyrs, A. Wolf, was a Jew," writes Rabbis Henry Cohen, Ephraim Frisch, and David Lefkowitz in "One Hundred Years of Jewry in Texas, the Original Researches of Dr. Henry Cohen," Jewish Advisory Committee for the Texas Centennial Religious Program, 1936, collection of the Texas/Dallas History and Archives Division, Dallas Public Library; Simon Wolf lists this fighter in his roster of Jewish soldiers, writing, "A. Wolf, killed at the storming of the Alamo, in the Texan War, December, 1835." Simon Wolf, *The American Jew as Patriot, Soldier and Citizen* (Philadelphia, 1895), 75.

28. *Occident,* 8 September 1859.

29. "Jewish life began with the first burial," writes Hasia Diner. A committee was formed to prepare and bury the dead according to traditional rituals. Next followed an organization to maintain the cemetery. The descendants and the community shared this age-old responsibility. Diner, *A Time for Gathering,* 92–93,

125; Elaine H. Maas, *The Jews of Houston, An Ethnographic Study* (New York, 1989), 11, 13.

30. Henry Cohen, "Texas," *Jewish Encyclopedia* (New York and London, 1906), 12:121–22; Henry Cohen, "Settlement of the Jews in Texas," in *Publications of the American Jewish Historical Society* 2 (1894): 139–156; Henry Barnston, "The Jews of Houston," Congregation Beth Israel Archives, Houston Metropolitan Research Center, Houston Public Library.

31. Wolf, *American Jew as Patriot, Soldier and Citizen*, 424; Frances Kallison, "100 Years of Jewry in San Antonio," thesis, Trinity University, 1977.

32. Seymour V. Connor, *Texas: A History* (New York, 1971), 269–71.

33. The US Jewish population in 1877 was 229,000. *American Jewish Yearbook, 1914–15* (Philadelphia, 1914), 352. Texas' total population in 1870 was 818,000. It doubled by 1880 to 1.6 million. *Population of States and Counties of the U.S.: 1790–1996* (Washington, D.C., 1996).

34. Diner, *A Time for Gathering*, 35; Maas, *Jews of Houston*, 12.

35. Fehrenbach, *Lone Star*, 292–96.

36. "Up to twelve months ago, only two Jewish families lived here, but since then we have been progressing wonderfully and been connected on the east, west and south by railroads with the rest of the civilized world and five more Jewish families besides some eight or ten young men have found their way hither. They now constitute the bone and sinew of the county, all being among our first class merchants. Without any exception they are all well to do." *American Israelite*, 18 April 1873; Schmier, *Reflections of Southern Jewry*, 104–06.

37. *American Israelite*, 17 October 1873.

38. Heinrich Schwarz, from his handwritten notebooks, private collection of his great-grandson William Roddy, Waco, translated for the author by Alex Rofe, Department of Bible, Faculty of Humanities, Hebrew University of Jerusalem. Rabbi Schwarz was the great-grandfather of Robert Schwarz Strauss, former chairman of the Democratic Party and ambassador to Russia. Robert Strauss, interview with author, 10 July 1995.

39. The temple building no longer exists, although the rabbi's descendants still operate the Schwarz store, the state's oldest, continuous family retail enterprise. Hollace Weiner, "The Big Store: The family-owned Schwarz retail emporium, founded in Hempstead in 1871 by an immigrant, has lasted into the age of Wal-Mart, and it's still going strong," *Fort Worth Star-Telegram*, 24 January 1995; "Jews in Texas," *Texas Jewish Herald*, 26 November 1914; Gale interview.

40. Arriving 6 weeks before Schwarz, Rabbi Sam Sanger, a Waco merchant, filled the Rodef Sholom pulpit only occasionally. Jacob Rader Marcus concluded that Schwarz was the first ordained rabbi to hold a pulpit in Texas. Marcus dismissed other spiritual leaders as free-lancers and poseurs (Marcus interview).

Another early spiritual leader, Abraham Blum, was colorful and accomplished but not scholarly like Schwarz and other rabbis who achieved ordination in Europe during this period. For further reading on Blum see William M. Kramer and Reva Clar, "Rabbi Abraham Blum: From Alsace to New York by Way of Texas and California," *Western States Jewish Historical Quarterly,* 11 (January 1980): 170–84; (April 1980): 266–81.

41. Heinrich Schwarz's articles in *Die Deborah* include: "On the New Year Festival 5637," 15 September 1872; "Wine, a Rabbinic Legend," 18 May 1877; "On the Year 5639," 27 September 1878; "Elegy for the Day of Jerusalem, Tisha Beab Poem," 4 August 1892; "Poem: New Year's Eve 5653," 22 September 1892; "Moses Mendelssohn: Sketch Found by Local Pastor in Posthumous Papers of His," 25 May 1893, 1 June 1893, 8 June 1893; "Elegy on the Day of Jerusalem," 9 September 1897; "Translation: A Wonderful Deliverance from Shebet Yehudah of R. Solomon Aben Veega, 15th Century Spain," 16 August 1898; "The Oldest Source Known for the Three Rings in Jewish Literature," 1 September 1898; "At the Turn of the Year," 11 September 1898; "Humoresque from Talmud and Midrash," 15 September 1898; "Rashi," 15 September 1898; "Our Abodah," 29 September 1898; "General Charity among our Ancestors," 1 December 1898; "Strength of Character," 22 December 1898; "Memorable Days of Death from the Literary Remains of Dr. Leopold Zunz," 29 December 1898 (Zunz was a leader of modern Jewish scholarship in western Europe); "The Holy Scripture," 19 January 1899.

42. Kenneth Zwerin and Norton Stern, "Jacob Voorsanger: From Cantor to Rabbi," *Western States Jewish Historical Quarterly,* 15 (April 1983): 195–202; "Jacob Voorsanger," in *Encyclopaedia Judaica* (Jerusalem, 1972), 16: 223.

43. [Koppel Von Bloomborg, pseud.] Jacob Voorsanger, "Lone Star Flashes," *American Israelite,* 19 October 1880.

44. Jay Henry Moses, "Henry A. Henry: The Life and Work of an American Rabbi, 1849–1864" (Rabbinical diss., Hebrew Union College-Jewish Institute of Religion, 1997), 10.

45. "Wanted at Houston, Texas—The Hebrew Congregation Beth Israel is desirous of engaging a gentleman who is capable to act as Chazan, Shohet, Mohel and Bangal Korney [*Ba'al Korhey* or Torah reader]; one who is able to deliver occasionally a discussion will be preferred. Fixed salary $1,000 per annum besides perquisites which, if he be a mohel, will reach a considerable amount as there is no mohel in the country. Applications in person or in writing with necessary testimonials must be directed to the president M. A. Levy or O. Davidson." *American Israelite,* 18 November 1859; Emmich was educated in Frankfurt am Main, had lived for a time in Cincinnati, and had previously led services in Lafayette, Ind. *Occident,* 15 March 1860, 306; Anne Nathan Cohen, *The Cente-*

nary History of Congregation Beth Israel of Houston, Texas, 1854–1954 (Houston, 1954), 3.

46. *Houston City Directory of 1866,* xiii, quoted in Helena Frenkil Schlam, "The Early Jews of Houston" (master's thesis, Ohio State University, 1971); Ruthe Winegarten and Cathy Schechter, *Deep in the Heart: The Lives and Legends of Texas Jews, a Photographic History* (Austin, 1990), 21.

47. *Dallas Weekly Herald,* 16 March 1882; "The Rev. Mr. M. May . . . has become insane and has been placed under the care of physicians," Podet writes, quoting the March 1882 Rodef Sholom newsletter in *Pioneer Jews of Waco,* 24. May's previous pulpits included Congregation Beth Israel in Portland, Ore., where he was accused of "libertine behavior, of impugning the virtue of women congregants, and of lack of faith." He fired a pistol during a street corner fistfight with an Oregon congregant who pounced on him and tore his coat. The bullets missed. Harriet and Fred Rochlin, *Pioneer Jews: A New Life in the Far West* (Boston, 1984), 207; Norton B. Stern and William M. Kramer, "Mayer May: Pioneer Portland Rabbi," *Western States Jewish Historical Quarterly* 21 (January 1989): 103–13.

48. William Suhler, series of telephone and personal interviews with author, July, 1995.

49. "Rules of Order. . . . Everyone entering the Temple must repair to his seat in a noiseless and becoming manner. . . . Conversation is strictly prohibited. . . . Everyone must endeavor to be in his place in the Temple before the commencement of the service and there remain until its conclusion. . . . Persons entering . . . during the sermon, while the choir is singing, or the congregation is standing, shall remain near the door and not repair to their seats until the respective exercise is ended. . . . Every person must conform strictly to the regulations, as to the time when the congregation is standing or sitting. . . . It is strictly forbidden to gather together in the vestibule or near the Temple, prior to, during or after divine service. . . . Children under the age of six years are not permitted to be brought into the Temple." Cohen, *Centenary History,* 30–31.

50. Barbara S. Malone, "Reform and Dissent: The Americanization of Max Heller, 1860–1898" (master's thesis, Tulane University, 1990), 52–59.

51. *Texas Jewish Herald,* 21 January 1915; Jay Moses describes the rabbinate as an "embryonic profession" in nineteenth-century America. Within congregations, tradition faced modernity, and rapid turnover on the pulpit "illustrates how volatile the rabbinate was at that stage of American Jewish history." Moses, "Henry A. Henry," 49.

52. Schmier, *Reflections of Southern Jewry,* 123; LeMaster, *A Corner of the Tapestry,* 71–72.

53. David Max Eichhorn, *Evangelizing the American Jew* (Middle Village, N.Y., 1978), 117–18; *American Israelite,* 6 October 1876.

54. Schmier, *Reflections of Southern Jewry,* 123.

55. "On the edge of civilization, all men started equal," Fehrenbach observes in *Lone Star,* 322.

56. Maas, *Jews of Houston,* 26–34.

57. Kramer, "Rabbi Abraham Blum," 85.

58. Winegarten and Schecter, *Deep in the Heart,* 9; James Lee Kessler, "B. O. I.: A History of Congregation B'nai Israel, Galveston, Texas," (doctoral dissertation, Hebrew Union College, 1988), 12; Wolf, *American Jew as Patriot,* 74.

59. "Texas, in proportion to her Jewish population, has had an unusually large number of Jewish citizens prominent in public life and in the learned professions. . . . Jews played a very considerable part in the settlement and development of Texas." "America," *Jewish Encyclopedia* (1906), 1: 499.

60. Schmier, *Reflections of Southern Jewry,* 80–83.

61. Wolf, *American Jew as Patriot,* 72–75; Kessler, "B. O. I.," 12; Moses Albert Levy, a Dutch immigrant, graduated from medical school in 1832 and practiced in Richmond, Va. He was a widower when he moved to Texas in 1835 to fight for its independence. Personal papers from collection of Louis Lechenger, Houston. For detailed biography see Daniel N. Leeson, "In Search of the History of the Texas Patriot Moses A. Levy, Part I, Part II," *Western States Jewish Historical Quarterly* 21 (July 1989): 291–306, 22 (October 1989): 22–37.

62. Natalie Ornish, *Pioneer Jewish Texans* (Dallas, 1989), 246.

63. His surgeries were probably still restricted to circumcisions, says biographer William Kramer. Kramer, telephone interview with author, 18 April 1997; Kramer, "Rabbi Abraham Blum," 82.

64. Ornish, *Pioneer Jewish Texans,* 217–19. Further information on the Kohlbergs is in Floyd S. Fierman, "Insights and Hindsights of Some El Paso Jewish Families," *El Paso Jewish Historical Review* (Spring 1983): 152–55.

65. Ibid., 231–32.

66. Ibid., 241.

67. *The Jewish Texans* (San Antonio, 1974), 2.

68. Ibid.; Ornish, *Pioneer Jewish Texans,* 263–64.

69. "La belle Menken," an actress, dancer, poet, vocalist and superstar, was born near New Orleans and embraced as a local star by audiences in every state where she resided: Texas, Louisiana, California and Ohio. She is buried in Paris, France. Max Heller, *Jubilee Souvenir of Temple Sinai, 1872–1922,* 23–24; Ornish, *Pioneer Jewish Texans,* 132–33; Rochlin, *Pioneer Jews,* 173–74.

70. Kessler, 12–13; Winegarten and Schecter, *Deep in the Heart: Lives and Legends of Texas Jews,* 66.

71. Max J. Kohler, "Some Jewish Factors in the Settlement of the West," *Publications of the American Jewish Historical Society* 16 (1907): 23; see also Norton B.

Stern and William M. Kramer, "Anti-Semitism and the Jewish Image in the Early West," *Western States Jewish Historical Quarterly* 4 (January 1973): 129–40.

72. Generalizing about the southwestern frontier, Henry Tobias writes: "On the frontier people have to rely on one another. . . . Jews get heavily involved in new institutions. . . . An infinitesimal part of the population, clearly they have to adapt." Their involvement in Masons and Rotary shows their acceptance in the emerging social networks. He adds that immigrants and accented people were common in the West. Tobias, *A History of the Jews of New Mexico* (Albuquerque, 1990), 44.

73. For information on Hispanic involvement in Brownsville see Louise Ann Fisch, *All Rise: Reynaldo G. Garza, The First Mexican-American Federal Judge* (College Station, 1996).

74. "The Texan attitude toward colored races, probably, was closer to the Nazi view of eastern Europeans, who seemed to provide a ready-made laboring mass. Anti-Semitism was far less a Texan than a Northern American trait, which, much evidence shows, was given impetus by European immigration. No mobs in Texas ever attacked a Jew. . . . The Texas violence toward blacks, which at times could be very violent, was provoked and condoned not by any desire to wipe Negroes off the earth but to keep them conquered and in their appointed place. Anti-Semitism, historically, often was provoked by a very real superiority, in certain things, shown by Jews, as well as the obvious religious intolerance of many ages." Fehrenbach, *Lone Star,* 654.

75. Howard Sachar, *History of the Jews in America* (New York, 1992), 98–101.

76. Greenburg, "Autobiographical Sketch."

77. "The Jew in English Drama," Rabbi Henry Barnston collection, sermon 294, box 5, folder 6, Houston Metropolitan Research Center, City of Houston, Houston Public Library.

78. Ibid.

79. David Lefkowitz to Henry Cohen, 25 November 1921, Henry Cohen Papers, box 3M239, correspondence 1921–1922, Center for American History, University of Texas at Austin; David Rosenbaum to Henry Cohen, 27 November 1921, Henry Cohen Papers.

80. David Rosenbaum to Henry Cohen, 2 December 1921, Henry Cohen Papers; "[The comedian] has been playing this sketch from coast to coast and gets held up in 'wild Texas,' " writes J. K. Hexter to Henry Cohen, 25 November 1921, Henry Cohen papers.

81. Samuel Rosinger, "Public School Troubles," *Texas Jewish Herald,* 31 December 1914.

82. Editorial, *Jewish Monitor,* 8 July 1915.

83. "Merchants, Please Notice," *Jewish Monitor,* 26 March 1920.

84. Jack Barnston interview; Barnston, Genealogies file, American Jewish Archives.

85. Voorsanger, "Lone Star Flashes," *American Israelite*, 29 October 1880; Kramer, "Rabbi Abraham Blum," 86–87.

86. Voorsanger, "Lone Star Flashes," *American Israelite*.

87. Kramer, "Rabbi Abraham Blum," 84.

88. Voorsanger, "Lone Star Flashes."

89. Ibid.

90. Schmier, *Reflections of Southern Jewry*, 81, 113; "Calvert Texas: Two Views—1880," *Western States Jewish Historical Quarterly* 14 (January 1982): 118–22.

91. Voorsanger, "Lone Star Flashes," *American Israelite*.

92. Kramer, "Rabbi Abraham Blum," 82–84.

93. Steven Fox, "On the Road to Unity: The Union of American Hebrew Congregations and American Jewry, 1873–1903," *American Jewish Archives* 32 (November 1980): 186–88; Schmier, *Reflections of Southern Jewry*, 81.

94. LeMaster, *A Corner of the Tapestry*, 320–21.

95. Fox, "End of an Era," 278–79.

96. Barnston interview.

97. Rochlin, *Pioneer Jews*, 83–105.

98. Selma Schwarz, "Statement made to me in Fort Worth, Texas, April 10, 1939." From the Texas box in the collection of the late Rabbi Jacob Rader Marcus.

99. Bernice Davis (granddaughter of Selma Weinbaum Schwarz), interview with author, 19 June 1995.

100. Floyd S. Fierman, "Insights and Hindsights of Some El Paso Jewish Families," 168–69.

101. "Calisher," Floyd Fierman Collection, Leona G. and David A. Bloom Southwest Jewish Archives, University of Arizona, Tucson.

102. *Purcell [Indian Territory] Register,* 20 January 1899, Floyd Fierman Collection, Bloom Southwest Jewish Archives.

103. "The Jewish Synagogue. The Dedication Ceremonies—Solemn and Impressive Ritual 'The Lord is in His Holy Temple'—Addresses and Sermon," *Dallas Daily Herald,* 30 May 1876.

104. "The Herald acknowledges the receipt of a handsome invitation from Rev. and Mrs. B [*sic*] Schwarz to attend the marriage ceremony of their daughter Clara to Rev. A. Suhler, the rabbi of our Jewish synagogue. The felicitous event takes place on the 10th of next month when we will be on hand to congratulate the happy couple if business will permit a trip to Hempstead where the ceremony will take place." *Dallas Weekly Herald,* 2 September 1876; "Stroke of Paralysis Fatal for Dr. Suhler," *Waco Daily Tribune,* 1 March 1916; Suhler interviews.

105. "Fox-Lewis," *Fort Worth Star-Telegram,* 27 November 1910.

106. Sidney A. Wolf, "My Life and Career: Rabbi Sidney Wolf, June 13, 1972," in *Our Golden Years. A History of Temple Beth El, Corpus Christi, Texas,* ed. Helen K. Wilk (Corpus Christi, 1984), 77.

107. Mrs. J. W. (La Una de Cordova) Skinner, granddaughter of Jacob de Cordova, to The [Texas] Board of Control, 30 March 1953, de Cordova Family Collection, No. 99, box 7 folder 2, American Jewish Archives; Schlam, "Early Jews of Houston," 5–6; Maas, *Jews of Houston,* 28; Ornish, *Pioneer Jewish Texans,* 58–66, 164.

108. Leeson, "In Search of the History of the Texas Patriot Moses A. Levy, Part I, Part II," *Western States Jewish Historical Quarterly* 21 (July 1989): 329–406, (October 1989) 22–37.

109. "Reflections on One Hundred Years of Temple Beth El," Temple Beth El collection, Tyler, Texas.

110. *Congregation Beth El Temple Minute Book 1895,* Temple Beth El Collection, Tyler, Texas.

111. "A non-Jewish spouse may be buried here but no religious ceremony or prayers except Jewish or non-sectarian prayers are permitted within the walls of the cemetery." Ruben Edelstein, "The History of the Brownsville Hebrew Cemetery," Ruben Edelstein Collection, Brownsville, Texas.

112. Lawrence Blum, interview with author, 10 July 1997; Shirley Alter, interview with author, 11 July 1997.

113. Kramer, "Rabbi Abraham Blum," 84–85.

114. "Questionnaire on Intermarriage," Henry Cohen II papers, Philadelphia.

115. Margaret Ramage, "Retirement only a Beginning School, Civic Work Beckons Rabbi Sidney Wolf," *Corpus Christi Caller-Times,* 18 June 1972.

116. Allen Goldsmith, interview with author, 4 April 1997.

117. *Record Book of Ministerial Functions, Dec. 1923–Oct. 30, 1938,* Ephraim Frisch papers, American Jewish Archives.

118. Ephraim Frisch to Rabbi B. A. Tintner, 18 March 1940, Ephraim Frisch Nearprint files, American Jewish Archives.

119. Sachar, *A History of the Jews in America,* 117, 300.

120. Harvey E. Wessel, "A History of the Jews of Tyler and Smith County, Texas," in *Tyler and Smith County, Texas: An Historical Survey,* ed. Robert W. Glover and Linda Brown Cross (Tyler, 1976), 201–55; "Reflections on 100 Years of Temple Beth El"; "Seventy-Fifth Anniversary of Ahavath Achim Congregation," Texas Jewish Historical Society Collection, Tyler vertical file, Center for American History; Greenberg's descendants, using his wife Jenny's seasoning recipe, launched a smoked kosher turkey business that is still in operation. Hollace Weiner, "A Tale of Turkeys," *Fort Worth Star-Telegram,* 28 November 1996.

121. Cohen, *The Centenary History,* 8–11, 23, 30; Maas, *Jews of Houston,* 34–39.

122. LeMaster, *A Corner of the Tapestry,* 72, 89–90.

123. Robert A. Davis, "Virtual Restoration of Small-town Synagogues in Texas." Internet, www.neosoft.com/~TJHS/identity.html.

124. *San Antonio Express,* 8 December 1923.

125. Flora Schiff, "History of Fort Worth Jews," *Reform Advocate,* 24 January 1914.

126. "Statistics of Jews," *American Jewish Yearbook 1911–12,* 268.

127. "Dr. Faber to Quit, He Has a Fine Position in the State of Texas," *The Gate City [Iowa],* 28 August 1900, Lipstate collection.

128. Fanny Sattinger Goodman, "In the Beginning: The Jewish Community of El Paso, Texas," 1970, El Paso file, American Jewish Archives.

129. Beaumont: Temple Emanuel, Rabbi Aaron Levy, 43 families, 40 pupils, four classes, three teachers; Brenham: Congregation B'nai Abraham, Rabbi S. Rabbinowitz, 25 families, 12 pupils, three classes, one teacher; Hempstead: Congregation Heychal Chayim, Rabbi Chayim Schwarz, 27 active members, 14 honorary out of town members; Austin: Congregation Beth Israel, no rabbi, 25 families, 50 students; Corsicana: 25 families, Rabbi Solomon Solomons; Dallas: Congregation Emanu-El, Rabbi George Kohut, 100 families, 10 students, seven classes and confirmation; Dallas: Congregation Shaareth Israel, Rabbi B. Lurie, 55 members, 53 students; Dallas: Congregation Tifferet Israel, Rabbi Greenstein, 33 families, 25 students; Fort Worth: Ahavath Sholom, 32 families, a reader but no rabbi; Gainesville: United Hebrew Congregation, 28 families and a pulpit recently vacated by Rabbi H. Friedman; Galveston: Ahavas Israel, Rabbi Jacob Geller, membership figures not listed; Houston: Beth Israel, Rabbi Henry Barnston, 103 families, 92 students; Houston: Adath Yeshurun, Rabbis M. Epstein and J. Hurwitz, 45 families, 85 students; San Antonio: Agudath Achim, Rabbi Solomon Rubin, 30 families, 50 students; San Antonio: Temple Beth El, Rabbi Samuel Marks, 82 families; Waco: Agudath Jacob, Rabbi Dr. S. Levy, 40 families, 20 students; and Waco: Temple Rodef Sholom, Rabbi Harry Weis (resigned), 48 families, 110 students, six classes, six teachers. Congregations listed without rabbinical leaders are Palestine's Congregation Beth Israel; Victoria's B'nai Israel (supervised by Galveston's Henry Cohen), Marshall's Congregation Moses Montefiore Adath Israel. List compiled from "Local Organizations," *American Jewish Yearbook, 1900,* 256–623, and *American Jewish Yearbook, 1900–01,* 463–75.

130. This census counted 694 rabbis and cantors in America. *American Jewish Yearbook 1903–04,* 40.

131. The country western ballad opened a television special about Cohen on NBC's Religious Hour series. Irve Tunick, "An America Ballad," Frontiers of Faith series, NBC Television, 15 May 1955, reprinted in *Henry Cohen, Messenger of the Lord,* ed. A. Stanley Dreyfus (New York, 1963), 77.

132. Henry Cohen, "Portrait of a Rabbi," in Dreyfus, ed., *Henry Cohen*, 3–65. (The writer, a Philadelphia rabbi, is the Galveston rabbi's grandson.); Ornish, *Pioneer Jewish Texans*, 119–30.

133. Cohen, "Portrait of a Rabbi," 13.

134. David G. McComb, *Galveston: A History* (Austin, 1986), 170–71.

135. Anne Nathan and Harry I. Cohen, *The Man Who Stayed in Texas: The Life of Rabbi Henry Cohen* (York, Pa., 1941), 61.

136. Henry Cohen, "Settlement of the Jews in Texas," *Publications of the American Jewish Historical Society*, 2 (1894): 139–56; Henry Cohen, "Texas," *Jewish Encyclopedia* (New York and London, 1906), 12:121.

137. McComb, *Galveston: A History*, 133; Paul Lester, *The Great Galveston Disaster* (Philadelphia, 1900), ii, vii, 99.

138. Haley, *Texas: From Spindletop through World War II*, 137.

139. Marguerite Meyer Marks, "Memories of Rabbi Henry Cohen As I Knew Him," *Western States Jewish Historical Quarterly* 18 (January 1986): 120–25.

140. Charles C. Alexander, *Crusade for Conformity: The Ku Klux Klan in Texas, 1920–1930* (Houston, 1962), 1–14.

141. Ibid.

142. Haley, *Texas: From Spindletop through World War II*, 137; McComb, *Galveston: A History*, 170, 211; Alexander, *Crusade for Conformity*, 5, 12; For additional reading on the Klan in Texas see Norman D. Brown, *Hood, Bonnet, and Little Brown Jug: Texas Politics, 1921–1928* (College Station, 1984).

143. Alexander, *Crusade for Conformity*, 43–55. On Klan election wins in other states in 1922 see "Klan Victories in Oregon and Texas," *Literary Digest* 75 (25 November 1922): 12; Norman F. Weaver, "Knights of the Ku Klux Klan in Wisconsin, Indiana, Ohio, and Michigan" (Ph.D. diss., University of Wisconsin, 1954); Frank Bohn, "The Ku Klux Klan Interpreted," *American Journal of Sociology* 50 (January 1925): 385–407; Guy B. Johnson, "A Sociological Interpretation of the New Ku Klux Movement," *Social Forces* (May 1923): 440–45.

144. Henry Cohen, "The Galveston Movement: Its First Year," reprinted from 16 April 1909 edition of *B'nai B'rith Messenger of Los Angeles* in *Western States Jewish Historical Quarterly* 18 (January 1986): 114–19.

145. Webb Waldron, "First Citizen of Texas," *Readers Digest* (February 1939): 97–98, condensed from *Rotarian*.

146. Cohen, "Portrait of a Rabbi," 16.

147. "Cohen had pizzazz," said historian Jacob Rader Marcus. "... he was a personality. . . . He was something of a poseur—small, dressed with a Prince Albert jacket. He called it a 'Prince Isaac' coat. He had big white cuffs. Made notes on his cuffs. It was maybe an English custom. The story I hear is he didn't get a salary but he could go to the Kempner bank and draw anything he wanted. Nev-

er withdrew much. They would take care of him as long as he lived. He was highly respected by the gentiles." Marcus interview.

148. Editors at the *American Jewish Yearbook* sent questionnaires in 1901 to rabbis in the United States asking for biographical information. Many rabbis describe in detail the institution of their ordination or state the name of the European rabbi who conferred on them a "rabbinical diploma." Cohen's listing omits such mention. His entry reads as follows: "Henry Cohen—born April 7, 1863. Son of David Cohen. Educated at London in Jews Hospital under Rev. John Chapman; Jews College Evening Classes under Dr. Friedlander; Beth Hamedrash, under Dayan Spiers." Cyrus Adler, ed. "Biographical Sketches of Rabbis, 1902," *American Jewish Yearbook* (Philadelphia, 1902), 40–108; Galveston rabbi and historian James Kessler concurs with this conclusion; Kessler interview.

149. *Texas Jewish Herald*, 2 April 1915.

150. Podet, *Pioneer Jews of Waco*, 86.

151. Zielonka mentions that he is acquainted with Jews in Sherman, Denison, Taylor, Tyler, Austin, Hillsboro, Fort Worth, Victoria, Longview, Marshall, Dallas, and San Antonio. Martin Zielonka to Rabbi Max Heller, 26 May 1900, in "Correspondence, diaries, reports and sermons, 1876–1932," Max Heller Collection, American Jewish Archives.

152. Rabbi David Leopold Zielonka, 1937, untitled manuscript, Carl Zielonka collection, Tampa, Fla.; Hazel Friedlander Weisman (niece of Dora Schatzky Zielonka), telephone interview with author, 20 August 1994.

153. On the occasion of a testimonial dinner for Zielonka in 1935, Jews from synagogues in Arizona, New Mexico, and Los Angeles wrote letters outlining the rabbi's role in launching their congregations. Herman Lefkowitz to Harry Barnett, 18 November 1935; Joshua Bloch, Chief, Jewish Division of the New York Public Library, to Temple Mount Sinai, 21 November 1935, Carl Zielonka collection; Evelyn Rosing Rosen, "Martin Zielonka: Rabbi and Civic Leader in El Paso," *El Paso Jewish Historical Review* (September 1982): 5–12; David L. Zielonka, son of Martin Zielonka, 1937, untitled manuscript.

154. Fanny Sattinger Goodman, "In the Beginning: The Jewish Community of El Paso, Texas," 1970, El Paso file, American Jewish Archives; Mangan, *El Paso in Pictures*, 38–47; *El Paso Times*, 25 May 1934.

155. Rosen, "Martin Zielonka," 5–12.

156. David L. Zielonka, untitled manuscript.

157. Ibid.; Floyd S. Fierman, "Insights and Hindsights of Some El Paso Jewish Families," *El Paso Jewish Historical Review* (Spring 1983): 152–55.

158. "All in all, there were not more than 1500 or 2000 scattered over the entire country," writes Martin Zielonka in "Romance of the Jew in Mexico," Mexico Bureau Collection, B'nai B'rith Archives, Washington, D.C.

159. "Report of Rabbi Zielonka's Trip to N.Y. March 23rd, 1921," Martin Zielonka file, American Jewish Archives; Martin Zielonka to Adolf Kraus, telegram, 27 May 1921, Mexico Bureau Collection, B'nai B'rith Archives; Martin Zielonka to Felix Warburg, telegram, 6 March 1921, Felix Warburg collection, box 195, file 15, American Jewish Archives.

160. Hannah Sinauer, "A Report of the History and Activities of the B'nai B'rith Mexican Bureau (1921–1931)," B'nai B'rith Archives, Washington, D.C.

161. Alicia Gojman de Backal, *Memorias de un Desafío* (Mexico City, 1993), 65–100; Martin Zielonka, "The Jew in Mexico," in *Central Conference of American Rabbis 34th Annual Convention, June 27–July 2, 1923, Cape May, N.J.*, 33:425–43.

162. Carl Zielonka, telephone interview with author, 20 September 1993; David M. Zielonka, grandson of Martin Zielonka, telephone interview with author, 15 September 1993.

163. Paso Del Norte Jewish Historical Society Meeting, El Paso, group discussion with author, 29 October 1995.

164. Sally Rosen, telephone interview with author, 8 April 1994.

165. Martin Zielonka, 2 February 1937, in "Sermons, Lectures and newspaper clippings dealing with his career, material on Mexico City Jewish community, and necrologies, and resolutions of sorrow. El Paso, Texas. 1900–1938," Microfilm 484, American Jewish Periodical Center, Klau Library, Hebrew Union College-Jewish Institute of Religion, Cincinnati.

166. Ibid.

167. Beaumont's Rabbi Rosinger, who had attended classes with Szold at the Jewish Theological Seminary, extended a welcome and endorsed her efforts. Rosinger, "Deep in the Heart of Texas," 126.

168. Fanny Sattinger Goodman, "Beginning of the El Paso Chapter of Hadassah," notes from April 1974 speech, collection of Barbara Goodman Ettinger, El Paso.

169. "My strictures apply to Zionism, whether its officials be men or women. The Hadassah movement is the Women's Zionist Organization. I told Mrs. Poole [*sic*] that I felt we had enough women's organizations." Microfilm 494; Tamar de Sola Pool, Israel-born lecturer and language teacher, was national president of Hadassah. *Who's Who in American Jewry 1938–1939*, 3:821.

170. Barbara Ettinger, e-mail, 18 March 1997.

171. Paso Del Norte Jewish Historical Society meeting.

172. Floyd S. Fierman, "Insights and Hindsights of Some El Paso Jewish Families," *El Paso Jewish Historical Review* (Spring 1983): 152; David L. Zielonka, untitled manuscript.

173. Backal, *Memorias de un Desafío*, 108–09.

174. "Rabbi M. Faber of Tyler Dies Today," *Tyler Daily Courier Times*, 17 September 1934.

175. *American Jewish Yearbook, 1900*, 254; see also Simon Glazer, *The Jews of Iowa: A Complete History and Accurate Account of Their Religious, Social, Economical and Educational Progress in This State* (Des Moines, 1904), 303–07; Jack Wolfe, *A Century of Iowa Jewry: As Complete a History As Could Be Obtained of Iowa Jewry from 1833 through 1940* (Des Moines, 1941), 278.

176. Vicki Betts, *Smith County Texas in the Civil War* (Tyler, Texas, 1978), 38.

177. *Jewish Monitor,* 5 May 1922.

178. "Annually, Rabbi Faber solicited his friends for their Passover contributions to the Prague seminary," states the introduction to a memorial book distributed in January 1935, a month after Faber's death. "For a number of years, as the Feast of Passover approached, he would address a modest but earnest appeal to his Rabbinical friends that they should urge their Religious Schools to allot some of their charity funds for the purchase of the required Unleavened Bread by impoverished students of a Talmudic Academy with whose plight Rabbi Faber had become personally acquainted during visits in Prague, Czechoslovakia," writes Rabbi Samuel Halevi Baron of Austin in *In Memoriam: Rabbi Maurice Faber, His Memory for Blessing* (Tyler, Texas, 1935), Lipstate collection.

179. Maurice Faber, Miscellaneous file, American Jewish Archives.

180. Pete Martinez, "A History of Tyler Masonic Lodge No. 1233," *Chronicles of Smith County Texas* 35 (Summer 1996): 22–27; Eugene Lipstate, grandson of Rabbi Faber, telephone interview with author 18 July 1996; "The Klan grew rapidly among Masons and Shriners," writes Brown. "So many Masons joined the Klan that in some communities the Masonic lodge became simply an adjunct of the local Klan chapter. 'It's the fun making, social side of the Masons,' an Austin newspaperman was told." Brown, *Hood, Bonnet, and Little Brown Jug, Texas Politics, 1921–1928*, 52–53.

181. For a detailed summation of Ferguson's life see Brown, *Hood, Bonnet, and Little Brown Jug*, 95–97; Bruce Rutherford, *The Impeachment of Jim Ferguson* (Austin, 1983); Ouida Ferguson Nalle, *The Fergusons of Texas, or "Two Governors for the Price of One"* (San Antonio, 1946).

182. Testimony from the governor's impeachment proceedings states, "His complaint against Mr. Mayes was that his paper had skinned the governor from hell to breakfast." *Journal of the Senate, State of Texas, Second Called Session, Thirty-Fifth Legislature, Convened in the City of Austin, August 1, 1917, and Adjourned without Day August 30*, 634.

183. John A. Lomax and Alan Lomax, eds., "Rye Whiskey" in *Best Loved American Folksongs* (New York: 1947), 198–99; *Dallas Morning News*, 10 August 1917, 2.

184. Rutherford, *Impeachment of Jim Ferguson*, 8.

185. Faber to Ferguson, 20 September 1916. The complete Ferguson-Faber correspondence is in Lipstate collection; *San Antonio Express*, 17 December 1916; R. L. Batts papers, W. L. Hogg papers, and Texas Jewish Historical Society collection, Center for American History, University of Texas at Austin.

186. Ferguson to Faber, 25 September 1916.

187. Hal Lattimore to Maurice Faber, 19 December 1916, W. L. Hogg papers; Tom E. Hogg to Maurice Faber, 18 December 1916, Lipstate collection.

188. Y. H. Kinsolving to Maurice Faber, 17 November 1916, Lipstate collection.

189. Lorecia East, *History and Progress of Jefferson County* (Dallas, 1961), 47; Florence Stratton, *The Story of Beaumont* (Houston, 1925); Connor, *Texas. A History*, 318; *Golden Anniversary, 1900–1950: A History of Congregation Temple Emanuel* (Beaumont, Texas, 1950).

190. Rosinger, "Deep in the Heart of Texas," 114–53.

191. The vote was 540 to 160 in favor of the $50,000 hospital bond package. Jefferson County Commissioners Court election records 10 October 1922; *Beaumont Daily Journal*, 11 October 1922.

192. Samuel Rosinger, *Jewish Herald*, 29 June 1916.

193. Samuel Rosinger, *Jewish Herald*, 16 August 1917; 30 August 1917; 6 September 1917.

194. Samuel Rosinger, *Jewish Herald*, 31 May 1917.

195. Rosinger, *Jewish Herald*, 9 August 1917.

196. Samuel Rosinger, *Jewish Herald*, 8 June 1916.

197. Rosinger, "Deep in the Heart of Texas," 127–33.

198. See *Western States Jewish Historical Quarterly:* Norton B. Stern and William M. Kramer, "Jewish Padre to the Pueblo," 2 (July 1971): 193–226; William M. Kramer and Reva Clar, "Emanuel Schreiber, Los Angeles' First Reform Rabbi," 10 (July 1977): 354–70, (October 1977): 38–55; Kramer and Clar, "Sigmund Hecht: A Man who Bridged the Centuries," 7 (July 1975): 356–75, (October 1975): 79–90, 8 (January 1976): 169–86; Kramer and Clar, "Rabbi Abraham Blum: From Alsace to New York by Way of Texas and California," 12 (January 1980): 170–84, 13 (April 1980): 266–81.

199. The Montana history focuses on the development of communities and congregations, not their spiritual leaders, who did not stay long and were often student rabbis. Julie L. Coleman, *Golden Opportunities: A Biographical History of Montana's Jewish Communities* (Helena, 1994); Tobias provides a helpful ethnographic study with information on population figures and commercial enterprises in *History of the Jews of New Mexico;* LeMaster describes the work of Rabbi A. B. Rhine of Hot Springs and Rabbi Ira Sanders, who founded a school of so-

cial work at the state university. LeMaster, *A Corner of the Tapestry*, 64–65; Rochlin, *Pioneer Jews*, 310–11.

200. Rochlin, *Pioneer Jews*, 212–14.

201. Ibid.

202. "Congregations and the Rabbis in the West Compared with Those in England—1907," *Western States Jewish Historical Quarterly*, 11 (July 1980): 345.

203. Deborah Dash Moore, *To the Golden Cities, Pursuing the American Jewish Dream in Miami and L.A.* (New York, 1994), 77, 95–110.

204. Matthew Brady, "Popular Arlington rabbi resigns," *Fort Worth Star-Telegram, 31 October 1996;* Rabbi Keith Stern, interview with author, 18 February 1997; Hollace Weiner, "A Reverence for Art in Lubbock," *Fort Worth Star-Telegram*, 22 August 1993.

II
SMALL-TOWN LIFE

INTRODUCTION

American Jewish history is often viewed from an urban perspective, partly because of the large number of people who made homes in New York and other cities, and partly because of the institutional dominance of the metropolitan areas. Yet many Jews found economic opportunity and possibly greater tolerance in small communities scattered throughout the country. When juxtaposed to the national historical literature, southern Jewish history writing emphasizes the small-town experience. The articles here take the story beyond nostalgia to sophisticated analysis and explore both the positives and negatives of small-town life. Taken together they illustrate the give and take of tradition and adaptation as well as geographic and economic mobility.

Whether the place of origin was Bavaria, Posen, or Alsace-Lorraine for earlier immigrants or the Russian Pale of Settlement, or the Isle of Rhodes for those arriving after 1881, Jews in Europe and the Ottoman Empire typically lived in small towns and made ends meet in skilled or semi-skilled occupations, selling goods, or acting as go-betweens in rural economies. Entering America's heartland was thus a natural step especially for the more adventuresome willing to live apart from larger Jewish enclaves.

From the beginning into the early nineteenth century, those who ventured away from core Jewish communities were usually single men who traveled conducting business. Settlement came as a town demonstrated economic viability. Nonetheless this stage in the town's development did not end Jewish mobility.

A viable Jewish core population was necessary for a cemetery, benevolent society, and minyan (traditionally a quorum of ten men required for formal services). Jewish men brought wives and children or found Jewish spouses, business partners, and employers. Following the chain migration model, many towns hosted viable Jewish populations composed of a few extended families with neighbors originating from the same European community. Links to surrounding towns supported Jewish institutions and traditions, and links of family, business, and Jewish institutions to cities with larger Jewish populations were also common.

If the town benefited from good transportation corridors and its hinterland flourished, both the town and its Jewish community could also grow. Jews typically lived near each other in a pattern described as ethnic clustering. If the town grew into a city and the city expanded, the cluster and Jewish institutions tended to move to emerging suburbs.

Although some moved to towns lacking Jews, many Eastern European Jews settled where Central European Jews previously lived or where a small contingent of old-timers remained. Those communities that survived experienced such in- and out-migration every few decades. Economic opportunity drew the newcomers with the added benefit of an already extant Jewish presence. In turn, the newcomers offered a larger Jewish core to support and reinvigorate institutions. However, friction could ensue over ritual observance, power, and ways of relating to the general community.

Not all migrants came independently. Jewish agricultural labor and settlement away from northern industrial cities to ameliorate potential antisemitism were encouraged. The Industrial Removal Office, the Galveston Movement, and the Hebrew Immigrant Aid Society employed local agents to supervise relocation efforts in places willing to accept immigrants, although they met with mixed success.

Lee Shai Weissbach's article brings alive many of these as well as additional patterns. His and others' research emphasizes the importance of East Europeans in sometimes creating and at others reinvigorating small-town Jewish communities. Whereas earlier research emphasized German American Reform Judaism and anti- or non-Zionism, the new work uncovers Eastern European Orthodoxy and Zionism. Southern Jewish history now looks less divergent from that of the history in similar environments elsewhere. Weissbach explains the rise and decline of these Jewish communities, and, in the process, explicates many survival mechanisms.

Deborah R. Weiner studies the lives of Jews in the Appalachian coal towns. She finds close parallels with Jews in Rocky Mountain communities. Her article traces the importance of women in filling important economic and religious niches and as "guardians of tradition." Weiner discusses the significance of "family economy" in a boom and bust environment, and how women were continuing their East European economic roles while expanding their boundaries in terms of Jewish institution building. The women's role in the latter was critical albeit often behind the scenes. Although synagogue board representation did not come easily, a "feminization" of Judaism among these new immigrants paralleled that which took place during the nineteenth century among Reform Jews and within many Protestant denominations. How much of this process was the result of economics—women's ability to raise funds for congregations—and how much the result of men leaving the pews for the marketplace and thus providing a void which the women filled? Weiner points to survival mechanisms but also to what may be called a schizoid factor in which Jews joined Protestant organizations and otherwise adopted Christian practices even as they attempted to maintain tradition. Her work illustrates a recurring theme: how Jews accommodated to the local environment and conditions in a fashion directly related to their cultural background. Obviously other immigrant groups did the same, but this does not negate the question of why a groups' cultural baggage can exert such influence.

Both Weiner and Weissbach discuss the rise and decline of small-town Jewish communities, a common topic that Ira Sheskin treats from the perspective of the human geographer. Some of the reasons for both phenomena are Jewish-specific while others were common to all Americans. Still, Sheskin argues that the Jewish South is atypical of the region and stresses an internal migration process as part of the reason.

Ironically, Jews resided in towns partly because of an apparent greater degree of tolerance and acceptance, and many left because of a sense of alienation and the desire to live in more viable Jewish communities. Furthermore, Jews contributed disproportionately economically, educationally, politically, and culturally to these towns, although frequently their children and ultimately they departed because of limitations in these very areas. Today, low taxes, the rise of retirement and vacation havens, and military, educational, research, and medical facilities are contributing to another renaissance of small-town Jewish life. The movement from snowbelt to sunbelt is being reenacted for small towns as well as for prosperous cities.

4
East European Immigrants and the Image of Jews in the Small-Town South

Lee Shai Weissbach

In accounts of the Jewish experience in the smaller cities and towns of the South, the story of immigrants from Eastern Europe has received far less attention than it deserves. Rather, it has been the story of Jewish pioneers from the states of Central Europe that has figured most prominently in shaping the image of small-town Southern Jewry. To some extent, this is understandable, for it was the so-called German Jews who founded the best-known smaller Jewish communities of the South in the mid-nineteenth century, and it was they who constituted almost the entire population of these communities for several decades. To cite but one example, in 1880 individuals from Central European places of birth such as Bavaria, Prussia, or Alsace headed 33 of the 43 identifiable Jewish households in Alexandria, Louisiana, while American-born children of Central European parents headed another six. By contrast, Russian-born Jews headed only three of Alexandria's identifiable Jewish households, while a Sephardic Jew from the island of St. Thomas headed another.[1]

German Jews have dominated the image of small-town Southern Jewry not only because they arrived early but also because, sensing that they could be highly integrated into American society without totally abandoning their Judaism, they eagerly adopted an Americanized lifestyle and moved into the mainstream of local activity. Throughout the late nineteenth century and well into the twentieth, Jews of Central European background were playing prominent roles in the public life of small towns throughout the South, even as Jews from Eastern Europe, steeped in the culture of the shtetl, were beginning to arrive in their midst. In Lexington, Kentucky, for example, German Jews headed both chambers of the city council at one point in the 1880s, and in 1890 the

Munich-born president of congregation Beth Tefilloh in Brunswick, Georgia, also presided over the city's Board of Alderman. In 1900 Jacob Trieber, who was born near Breslau in Germany and settled in Helena, Arkansas, became the first Jew appointed to a federal judgeship, and by the turn of the century Mississippi had seen at least seven different Jewish mayors of small towns, all undoubtedly of Central European origin. By 1917 two members of the German-Jewish congregation Anshe Emeth in Pine Bluff, Arkansas, had been elected mayor of their town.[2]

In business, also, German Jews achieved a high profile. In the late nineteenth and early twentieth centuries, department stores founded by Jews from Central Europe were among the most important mercantile establishments in one small Southern town after another. Examples include S. Waxelbaum and Son in Macon, Georgia; J. Weisman and Company in Marshall, Texas; Weil Brothers and Bauer in Alexandria, Louisiana; Heinemann's Department Store in Jonesboro, Arkansas; M. M. Ullman and Company in Natchez, Mississippi; Simon Switzer's The Valley in Vicksburg; and Winner and Klein in Meridian.[3]

Just as the stories of German-Jewish pioneers and notables have been fundamental in shaping the image of small-town Southern Jewry, so too has the Reform movement. This is because the oldest congregations in the South's small communities tended to adopt Reform Judaism quite early in the movement's history and because these congregations, founded and supported by rapidly acculturating Central Europeans, frequently dominated local Jewish life for many decades.

The ubiquity of Reform congregations in the small towns of the South around the turn of the century is indeed quite striking. A survey of the 81 towns in the South that had total populations of under 50,000 and Jewish populations of at least 100 but less than 1,000 around 1907 reveals that in 44 of these towns there was a synagogue affiliated with the Union of American Hebrew Congregations (since 1873 the umbrella organization of Reform Judaism) and that in another 15 towns there was an unaffiliated synagogue that can be identified with Reform on the basis of its practices or its name (the Greensboro Hebrew Reformed Congregation in North Carolina, for example).[4] In other words, around the turn of the century Reform congregations were present in 73 percent of the South's most significant small-town Jewish centers. Furthermore, even as East European Jews were arriving in the small towns of the South and beginning to organize their own institutions, in over half of the triple-digit Jewish communities of the region, the local Reform congregation was the only one in town.

In some states of the Deep South, Reform Judaism dominated even more dramatically. In Alabama, for instance, there were seven communities in the first decade of the twentieth century with Jewish populations of at least 100 but less than 1,000. Each of these communities was reported to have only a single congregation, and in six of them it was Reform. In the same period, every one of the seven triple-digit Jewish communities in Louisiana and every one of the eight in Mississippi had a Reform congregation, while only one triple-digit community in each of these states also had another congregation. The close association of small-town Southern Jewry with Reform was further reinforced by the very high proportion of Southern assemblies that constituted the Union of American Hebrew Congregations in the early decades of its existence; in 1907, when only about 14 percent of all American Jewish congregations were in the South, a full 41 percent of the congregations affiliated with the UAHC were in that region of the country.[5]

Still, the importance for small-town Southern Jewry of its German-Jewish pioneers and public figures, of its early Reform congregations, and of the highly Americanized lifestyle that these individuals and institutions have come to represent should not completely overshadow the fact that the arrival of East European immigrants in the small towns of the South had a great many consequences. The time has now come to examine the experience of these immigrants more fully and to consider the relationship of that experience to the image of small-town Jewish life in the South.

Among the most noticeable effects of the arrival of East European Jews was the growth of many of the South's smaller Jewish centers. In a few cases, the influx of East Europeans was so great that it raised the local Jewish population beyond the 1,000 mark and edged it into the ranks of what might be considered midsize Jewish centers. As Table 4.1 indicates, there were 14 Jewish communities in the South where the reported Jewish population was in triple digits in the late 1870s, just before the era of mass migration from Eastern Europe began, but where it had exceeded 1,000 by 1927. Generally speaking, the small communities that were transformed into more substantial Jewish centers were in cities that were themselves evolving into important urban hubs. On average the Jewish population of the towns listed in Table 4.1 increased almost twelvefold in the half century after 1880, to a mean of over 5,000 souls, while the total population of these towns grew almost eightfold.[6]

The significance of East European immigration for those Southern communities that attained Jewish populations of 1,000 or more in the early decades of the twentieth century has been recognized in accounts

Table 4.1. Cities of the South with Triple-Digit Jewish Populations, ca. 1878 and Jewish Populations over 1,000 in 1927

		Jewish Pop. c. 1878	Total Pop. 1880	Jewish Pop. 1927	Total Pop. 1930
CITY	ST.				
Montgomery	AL	600	16,713	3,000	66,079
Little Rock	AK	655	13,138	3,000	81,679
Jacksonville	FL	130	7,650	4,000	129,549
Atlanta	GA	525	37,409	11,000	270,366
Savannah	GA	603	30,709	3,800	85,024
Shreveport	LA	900	8,009	2,000	76,655
Charleston	SC	700	49,984	2,100	62,265
Chattanooga	TN	178	12,892	3,385	119,798
Dallas	TX	260	10,358	7,500	260,475
Ft. Worth	TX	116	6,663	2,100	163,447
Houston	TX	461	16,513	11,000	292,352
San Antonio	TX	302	20,550	8,000	231,542
Waco	TX	158	7,295	1,500	52,848
Norfolk	VA	500	21,966	7,800	129,710
AVERAGES		435	18,561	5,013	144,414

Sources: For Jewish population c. 1878: Union of American Hebrew Congregations, *Statistics of the Jews of the United States* (Philadelphia, 1880), *passim.* For Jewish population, 1927: *American Jewish Year Book* 30 (1928–29), pp. 180–96. For total population, 1880: United States Census Office, *Compendium of The Tenth Census* (June 1, 1880) (1883; rpt. New York, 1976), part I, 380–405. For total population, 1930: United States Bureau of the Census, *Abstract of the Fifteenth Census of the United States* (1933; rpt. New York, 1976), 26–33.

of their histories, as has the important role of East Europeans in the development of those Southern communities that were already major Jewish centers even before 1880 (Baltimore, Richmond, Louisville, Memphis, and New Orleans, for example).[7] Less often noticed, however, and much more significant for this discussion, is the fact that even in those Southern Jewish communities that remained quite modest in size well into the twentieth century, the coming of East Europeans often meant notable growth. To take but a few examples, the Jewish populations of Charlotte, North Carolina, and of Monroe, Louisiana, each stood at

about 100 before the start of East European migration, but by 1927 Charlotte's Jewish population had risen to 400 and Monroe's to 500. In the
same period the Jewish community of Augusta, Georgia, grew from 240
to 970, and that of Wheeling, West Virginia, grew from 300 to 750.

The available census materials reveal perhaps most accurately the
exact role of East European immigrants in the demographic profiles
of those Southern Jewish communities that remained relatively small
throughout the first half of the twentieth century. In Lexington, Kentucky, for example, the Jewish population rose from 140 around 1878 to
about 750 in 1927, and the manuscript census returns for the town show
that by 1920 East European immigrants or their children headed the vast
majority of Jewish households there. Of the 98 Jewish heads of household in Lexington for whom information is available, 15 were immigrants from Central Europe and another 16 were the American-born
descendants of Central European Jews, while fully 63 heads of Jewish
households were immigrants from Eastern Europe and another four
were the children of East Europeans.[8] In Alexandria, Louisiana, where
the Jewish population increased from about 200 around 1878 to about
560 in 1927, census returns reveal that in 1920 two out of every five identifiable Jewish households were headed by individuals of East European
background. Of the 109 Jewish households identifiable in the records,
24 were headed by individuals born in Central Europe and 42 were headed by American-born children of Central Europeans. At the same time,
37 of Alexandria's Jewish households were headed by East Europeans
born abroad and another six were headed by American-born children
of East Europeans.[9]

It was not only in those small communities that experienced growth,
however, that the arrival of East European immigrants was so vital, for
even those small-town communities that did not expand noticeably in
the decades after 1880 often depended on East European migration simply to sustain themselves. For example, the total Jewish population of
Vicksburg, Mississippi, was about 500 in the late 1920s, just as it had been
in the late 1870s, but in 1920 individuals born in Russia or Poland headed at least a dozen Jewish households in the city, and immigrants from
Austrian Galicia headed at least two others.[10] Conversely, those small-
town communities that attracted few if any East European Jews were the
ones that failed to thrive in the early decades of the twentieth century
and often died out. Eufaula, Alabama, and Port Gibson, Mississippi, each
had over 100 Jews in the late 1870s, and Owensboro, Kentucky, was home
to over 200 Jews in that period, but a half century later all three of these
towns had Jewish populations of under 50.

At least as significant as the contribution of East European immigrants to the growth or preservation of older small-town communities was their role as founders of new Jewish centers during the final years of the nineteenth century and in the early years of the twentieth. Indeed, by the time mass migration from Eastern Europe was ended by the restrictive legislation of the 1920s, the vast majority of triple-digit Jewish communities in the South were relatively new centers in places where no Jews at all, or only a handful, had lived before 1880.

In 1927 there were 104 communities in Southern towns with total populations under 100,000 that were home to at least 100 Jews but less than 1,000 (the average total population of these towns was about 25,000 in 1930). These triple-digit centers, listed in Table 4.2, might be consid-

Table 4.2. The Triple-Digit Jewish Communities of the South in 1927 with Selected Population Data

CITY	ST.	Jewish Pop. c. 1878	Pop. c. 1907	Jewish Pop. 1927	Total Pop. 1930
Anniston	AL		250	125	22,345
Bessemer	AL		100	in	20,721
Demopolis	AL		124	150	4,037
Gadsden	AL			116	24,042
Mobile	AL	530	1,000	950	68,202
Selma	AL	200	315	281	18,012
Tuscaloosa	AL	22	106	208	20,659
El Dorado	AK			124	16,421
Fort Smith	AK	66	200	420	31,429
Helena	AK	180	160	400	8,316
Hot Springs	AK		225	250	20,238
N. Little Rock	AK			500	19,418
Pine Bluff	AK	250	463	400	20,760
Texarkana	AK	44	175	200	10,764
Daytona	FL			250	16,598
Orlando	FL			290	27,330
St. Augustine	FL			300	12,111
St. Petersburg	FL			100	40,425
W. Palm Beach	FL			600	26,610
Albany	GA	100	238	275	14,507

(*continued*)

Table 4.2. Continued

CITY	ST.	Jewish Pop. c. 1878	Pop. c. 1907	Jewish Pop. 1927	Total Pop. 1930
Athens	GA	100	139	185	18,192
Augusta	GA	240	313	970	60,342
Bainbridge	GA			220	6,141
Brunswick	GA		200	120	14,022
Columbus	GA	275	543	700	43,131
Macon	GA	350	550	650	53,829
Rome	GA	46	102	225	21,843
Ashland	KY			170	29,074
Covington	KY			500	65,252
Lexington	KY	140	238	750	45,736
Newport	KY			600	29,744
Paducah	KY	203	247	800	33,541
Alexandria	LA	206	600	560	23,025
Baton Rouge	LA	94	50	750	30,729
Bogalusa	LA			100	14,029
Lafayette	LA		57	100	14,635
Lake Charles	LA		125	320	15,791
Monroe	LA	128	200	500	26,028
Plaquemine	LA	61	125	132	5,124
Annapolis	MD		150	see note	12,531
Cumberland	MD	140	200	720	37,747
Frederick	MD			102	14,434
Hagerstown	MD	42	231	650	30,861
Canton	MS	150	100	108	4,725
Clarksdale	MS			200	10,043
Greenville	MS	320	500	375	14,807
Greenwood	MS		125	250	11,123
Hattiesburg	MS			148	18,601
Jackson	MS	88	108	169	48,282
Meridian	MS	160	394	575	31,954
Natchez	MS	220	513	151	13,422
Vicksburg	MS	520	688	467	22,943
Asheville	NC		100	700	50,193
Charlotte	NC		104	400	82,675
Durham	NC		200	375	52,037

(continued)

Table 4.2. Continued

CITY	ST.	Jewish Pop. c. 1878	Pop. c. 1907	Jewish Pop. 1927	Total Pop. 1930
Fayetteville	NC			116	13,049
Goldsboro	NC	147	188	120	14,985
Greensboro	NC		150	400	53,569
Henderson	NC			190	6,345
Hendersonville	NC			115	5,070
High Point	NC			101	36,745
Raleigh	NC		39	150	37,379
Wilmington	NC	200	200	390	32,270
Wilson	NC			140	12,613
Winston-Salem	NC			325	75,274
Beaufort	SC	29	123	see note	2,776
Camden	SC			108	5,183
Columbia	SC	see note	150	590	51,581
Georgetown	SC			135	5,082
Greenville	SC			195	29,154
Sumpter	SC	89	158	200	11,780
Bristol	TN		110	108	12,005
Brownsville	TN		74	100	3,204
Jackson	TN			188	22,172
Austin	TX		213	490	53,120
Corpus Christi	TX		60	200	27,741
Corsicana	TX	90	380	330	15,202
Laredo	TX			128	32,618
Marshall	TX	113	200	170	16,203
Mercedes	TX			250	6,608
Palestine	TX			120	11,445
Port Arthur	TX			173	50,902
Texarkana	TX		125	175	16,602
Tyler	TX		257	500	17,113
Wichita Falls	TX			505	43,690
Alexandria	VA		116	140	24,149
Charlottesville	VA	100	91	112	15,245
Danville	VA	68	114	180	22,247
Hampton	VA		110	144	6,382
Harrisonburg	VA	67	116	105	7,232

(*continued*)

Table 4.2. Continued

CITY	ST.	Jewish Pop. c. 1878	Pop. c. 1907	Jewish Pop. 1927	Total Pop. 1930
Lynchburg	VA	100	250	425	40,661
Petersburg	VA	163	61	705	28,564
Roanoke	VA		175	455	69,206
Staunton	VA	66	43	108	11,990
Suffolk	VA			114	10,271
Bluefield	WV			220	19,339
Clarksburg	WV			235	28,866
Fairmount	WV			140	23,159
Logan	WV			116	4,396
Martinsburg	WV			304	14,857
Morgantown	WV			250	16,186
Parkersburg	WV		100	392	29,623
Wheeling	WV	300	475	750	61,659
Williamson	WV			128	9,410
AVERAGES		64	137	307	25,139

Sources: For Jewish population c. 1878: Union of American Hebrew Congregations, *Statistics of the Jews of the United States* (Philadelphia, 1880), *passim* [see note 9 to the text]. For Jewish population c. 1907: *The Jewish Encyclopedia* (New York, 1901–16), 12:371–74, and *American Jewish Year Book* 9 (1907–08): 123–430 [see note 4 to the text]. For Jewish population, 1927: *American Jewish Year Book* 30 (1928–29): 180–96. For total population, 1930: United States Bureau of the Census, *Abstract of the Fifteenth Census of the United States* (1933; rpt. New York, 1976), 26–33.

Note: Columbia, S.C., is listed in the *Statistics of the Jews* with no population figure but the town undoubtedly had a Jewish population of 100 or more around 1878. Annapolis, Md., and Beaufort, S.C., were each reported to have triple-digit Jewish populations both c. 1907 and in 1937, so these towns have been included in this table. Columbia's Jewish population has been estimated at 100 in calculating average Jewish population c. 1878; Annapolis's Jewish population has been estimated at 300 and Beaufort's at 100 in calculating average Jewish population in 1927.

ered the quintessential small-town Jewish communities of the early twentieth-century South and, as the table indicates, 62 of them had no Jewish population at all on the eve of mass migration from Eastern Europe,
or at least not enough of a Jewish population to be noticed in the late
1870s, when the first serious attempt was made to count the number of
Jews in the United States. In addition, 14 of the small communities of
1927 had reported Jewish populations of less than 100 in the late 1870s,
and only three of these (Baton Rouge, Louisiana; Jackson, Mississippi;
and Harrisonburg, Virginia) had established congregations at that time.
In other words, only about 27 percent of the triple-digit Southern Jewish communities of the late 1920s had substantial Jewish populations before the era of East European migration began. Of course, not all the
Jewish settlers who moved into towns that were essentially devoid of Jews
before 1880 came from Eastern Europe, but there is no doubt that viable Jewish communities could not have been established in such places
without East European immigrants.

East European Jews arrived in smaller cities and towns in the South
for much the same reasons that they came to all sorts of other places
throughout the United States in the decades after 1880. As in every other region of the country, stories abound in the South of individuals who
ended up in one small town or another more or less by chance. Simon
Schiffman settled in Greensboro, North Carolina, in 1892 because he
had come upon a jewelry store for sale there while he was changing
trains on his way to Asheville. David Kusin, with the $3,000 in his pock-
et he had won at poker aboard a troop ship on his way home from military service during World War I, decided to settle in Texarkana, Texas,
because he was impressed with the place when his train from Monroe,
Louisiana, made a lunch stop there.[11]

Other East Europeans arrived in various Southern towns because they
were sent by the Industrial Removal Office, the organization created in
1901 by the Baron de Hirsch Fund to resettle immigrants in locations beyond the major cities of the Atlantic seaboard. The goal of the IRO was
to relieve the density of the Jewish population in the big cities of the East,
especially New York. In order to carry out its mission, the organization
had representatives in many of America's more substantial Jewish communities, including several in the South, where it hoped to relocate immigrants. But the IRO also had agents in scores of smaller cities and
towns throughout the country, and during the roughly two decades of
its activity it dispatched individuals and families to dozens of small towns
in the South, many with no more than a handful of Jewish residents. One

indication of the scope of the IRO's efforts is that in the first 10 years of its work the organization placed individuals in all but 11 of the 81 triple-digit Jewish communities identifiable in the smaller towns of the South at the time.[12]

To be sure, not all the immigrants relocated by the IRO remained in the towns to which they were sent. Many became uncomfortable far from their families and from the opportunities that big cities offered, while others were simply misfits who lasted only a few days in their new environments. The local IRO representative in Macon, Georgia, referred to one potential transplant as "a *dead beat* not worthy the waste of a minute's consideration," and the agent in Lake Charles, Louisiana, once protested about "a rascal" sent by the IRO who committed theft, contracted debts, and then skipped town. "The people here are thoroughly disgusted with the whole proposition" the Lake Charles agent grumbled, "and they blame me for having induced them to import Russian immigrants." Moreover, even where placements eventually succeeded, new immigrants often had difficulty adjusting. In June 1904 the IRO's local contact in Vicksburg, Mississippi, wrote concerning a tinsmith and a locksmith who had been sent there: "I have [only] by perseverance kept these two men in our city," he reported, complaining that one of them "can not and seems unwilling to speak English."[13]

On the other hand, many stories of immigrants dispatched from New York recount how they settled into their new small-town surroundings with relative ease. Late in 1905, for instance, the IRO agent in Fort Smith, Arkansas, advised the organization's head office that "Benjamin Hoberman is doing nicely here . . . He worked a few weeks as an elevator boy, then he left the department store where he was working and began to peddle in town and vicinity. He is now self-supporting and satisfied."[14]

Of course, it was neither serendipity nor placement by the IRO that brought most of the East Europeans who came to various towns in the South but rather information about economic opportunities there, often conveyed by relatives or acquaintances. For instance, Max Marx settled in Bogalusa, Louisiana, in 1906 because the Great Southern Lumber Company had just opened a mill there and its establishment signalled economic expansion. Marx opened a hardware business in Bogalusa, ran it together with his seven children, and convinced a number of his friends and relatives to settle in the town as well. Jacob Berman, who was born in Lithuania in 1887 and came to the United States by way of Copenhagen and Montreal, settled in Clarksburg, West Virginia, in

1908 because the brother of someone he had met in Baltimore offered him a position managing a store. Maurice Cohen arrived in Pine Bluff, Arkansas, in 1924 because he was given a job there by a man his mother had nursed back to health in a boarding house in Minneapolis several years earlier. Eventually Cohen bought the store he had come to oversee.[15]

One result of the patterns of migration that operated in the South (as elsewhere) was that many small-town Jewish communities had large contingents of East Europeans who were related to each other in one way or another. In 1908, for example, the Brith Achim congregation organized by East European Jews in Petersburg, Virginia, had 37 members, but these 37 represented only 19 families, with three families supplying 16 of the congregants. In recounting his community's history in the 1960s, the rabbi of Temple Beth Israel in Clarksdale, Mississippi, explained that many of the families in his congregation were of Lithuanian origin, and he made a statement that could have applied in dozens of other towns as well: "Relatives helped relatives immigrate, and a large number of our congregation are related to one another."[16]

Data from the manuscript census records of 1920 help illustrate the interrelationship among East European Jewish households in the small-town South. Among the Russian-born heads of Jewish households in 1920 Alexandria, Louisiana, for example, were two each named Caplan, Goldberg, Posner, Rubin, and Walder. Among the Russian-born heads of Jewish households in 1920 Lexington, Kentucky, were two each named Ades, Kaplan, Kravitz, Levin, Paritz, Rosen, and Wides. Also living in Lexington were three Russian-born heads of household named Grossman, four named Rosenberg, and five named Levy. To be sure, some individuals with the same last names may not have been related to each other, but there were certainly also related household heads in Alexandria and Lexington who had different surnames, especially if their connection was through marriage. Hyman Berkowitz, who arrived in Lexington about 1925, had relatives in town with the surnames Goller, Herman, Gordon, and Levy.[17]

Of course, the impact of East European Jews on the small-town South was by no means purely demographic, for wherever these settlers constituted a collection of more than just a few families they constructed their own East European Jewish communities, creating their own set of communal institutions and their own social milieu. In those small towns where older communities of German Jews already existed, what the East Europeans constructed were essentially separate subcommunities, for a

sort of uneasiness and even antagonism defined the relationship between the two groups, much as in larger Jewish centers.

Certainly the most fundamental Jewish institutions created by East European immigrants in the small towns of the South were congregations
established along Orthodox lines. In those places where organized Jewish life was based primarily on the coming of East Europeans, it was
common in the early twentieth century to find only a single congregation, Orthodox in practice. Such was the case in Hampton, Virginia,
where immigrants founded B'nai Israel in 1899, and in Annapolis, Maryland, where East Europeans established Keneseth Israel in 1906.

In those towns where organized Jewish life predated the arrival of East
European Jews the pattern differed. Here the newly arrived East Europeans frequently organized congregations that functioned alongside
preexisting assemblies, for the immigrants were uncomfortable in these
older congregations, which had almost invariably adopted Reform practice by the end of the nineteenth century. Examples are legion. In Petersburg, Virginia, the East Europeans' Brith Achim was founded in 1896
to function independently of Rodef Sholem, organized by German Jews
as early as 1858. In Wilmington, North Carolina, where the Temple of
Israel congregation had been founded in 1867, the Orthodox Bnai Yisroel was established in 1906. In Columbia, South Carolina, where Etz
Hayyim had been serving the community as a Reform congregation
since the end of the nineteenth century, the Orthodox Beth Sholem was
organized in 1908. In Macon, Georgia, Sherah Israel was chartered in
1904 to satisfy the needs of East European immigrants in a town that had
had a German-Jewish congregation since 1859, and in Brunswick, Georgia, where the Reform Beth Tefilloh had been present since 1885, the
Orthodox Agudath Israel was founded in 1919. In Pine Bluff, Arkansas,
East European Jews established the Orthodox B'nai Israel in 1907 because they were not comfortable at the Reform Anshe Emeth, which dated back to 1866. Fort Smith's Orthodox congregation, also named B'nai
Israel, began functioning in 1913 alongside the United Hebrew Congregation, which had been in existence since the 1880s.[18]

Nor were synagogues the only elements of the infrastructure of small-
town Jewish life that East Europeans maintained for themselves in accordance with Orthodox practice. They often made provision for a supply of kosher meat, for example, and they tried to be certain that a
mikvah (ritual bath) was available. In many places the new immigrants
established their own cemeteries, separate from the burial places administered by local Reform congregations. In Macon, Georgia, for in-

stance, the local German Jews had acquired a burial ground within the city's Rose Hill cemetery as early as 1845, and the Reform Temple Beth Israel had expanded it in 1879. At the beginning of the twentieth century, however, Sherah Israel established its own separate section in Rose Hill. In Wilmington, North Carolina, the Temple of Israel controlled the True Brothers cemetery, established in 1852, so the Orthodox Bnai Yisroel bought its own burial ground. In Alexandria, Louisiana, the principal Jewish cemetery was laid out across the Red River in Pineville in 1861, but the city's Orthodox Jews declined to make use of it and in 1914 established their own burial place on the eastern outskirts of Pineville.[19]

All this is not to say, however, that the East Europeans who settled in the small towns of the South always maintained a strictly Orthodox lifestyle. From the very beginning, they made compromises in personal observance. It seems that most East European merchants opened their stores on Saturday, for example, and that practical concerns made it difficult for many of those who were inclined to observe kashruth to do so. A student rabbi visiting Beckley, West Virginia, in 1935 noted that none of the East European Jews in that town used kosher food because "conditions don't allow it," and another student rabbi visiting New Bern, North Carolina, in the same year observed that "none [of the local Jewish families] seem to keep strictly kosher, though some few observe certain dietary rules."[20] Years later a resident of Williamson, West Virginia, recalled that "my grandfather kept kosher, but [discovered] it's too hard to keep kosher in a small town," and another reported that "when we moved to Williamson [in the interwar period] . . . mother realized she couldn't keep a kosher home [but] she still would not mix milk and meat."[21]

Besides the existence of Jewish institutions guided by Orthodox principles and the carryover of traditional practices such as observing elements of kashruth, there were other factors that helped maintain a distinctly East European subculture in many small towns in the South. Certainly one such factor was the tendency of East European immigrants to live and work near each other. One woman who arrived in Georgia in 1921 remembered that "all the Jewish merchants in Augusta were on one block of Broad Street," and that "the localism for the Jewish neighborhood was Kugel Avenue, which in reality was Ellis Street." A man who grew up in Arkansas before World War II recalled his father "sending him down Pine Bluff's Main Street to notify various Jewish businessmen that a minyan . . . was needed."[22]

The historian Louis Schmier has observed that in Valdosta, Georgia, where the population of East European Jews seems to have hovered just below 100 in the interwar period, residential patterns not only reflected a certain cohesiveness among the Jews but also reinforced the estrangement from gentile society that East European immigrants felt in many small towns. "Hill Avenue was the only really acceptable street on which to live," Schmier reports, but Troup Street, which the locals often called "Jew Street," was "at the lower end of the scale." Similarly, "Patterson Street was the only 'proper' commercial street . . . [while] Ashley Street, where the Jews located their stores, was degradingly known as 'Nigger Street' because on it were located the saloons and stores where blacks traded."[23]

An even more important factor in perpetuating an East European Jewish subculture was the pervasive use of Yiddish as the language of daily life. Unfortunately, the enumerators employed by the United States Census Bureau in the early twentieth century were not always careful about how they ascertained and recorded the mother tongues of the individuals they listed, so even though information on language is included in some census documents, it is difficult to discover exactly how many small-town Jews in the South considered Yiddish their vernacular. Because many of those recorded as having Russian or Hebrew or some other language as their mother tongue were likely to have spoken Yiddish on a daily basis, the number of Yiddish speakers in the census is certainly under-reported. Still, it is striking how often Yiddish does appear as the native tongue of small-town Jews. In Lexington, Kentucky, for example, 29 heads of household are listed as having Yiddish as their native language, and 23 more are listed as having Hebrew.[24]

Furthermore, a wealth of anecdotal evidence attests to the persistence of Yiddish among Jewish immigrants in the small-town South. From turn-of-the-century Durham, North Carolina, for example, comes the story of two East European immigrants who went before a local judge in a dispute involving contested ownership, business rivalry and intimations of wife swapping, and argued out the entire case in Yiddish with the court supplying a translator.[25] And from Lexington, Kentucky, comes the tale of the highly regarded Yiddish poet I. J. Schwartz, who lived and wrote in the heart of the Bluegrass region for over a decade just after World War I. More to the point, Schwartz found in Lexington an entire Yiddish-speaking microcosm. Myer Godhelff, who grew up there in the 1920s and '30s, reported that the people with whom his parents associated "all spoke Yiddish in person and on the telephone." Although they knew Russian, Godhelff's parents seldom used it, and they were reticent about conversing in English as well. "Only at home in our circle of Jewish friends and at the synagogue did they speak all out," he recalled, "and it was always Yiddish."[26]

That newspapers in Yiddish circulated among East European Jews throughout the small towns of the South also attests to the centrality of that language. The Grossmans, one of the most important Jewish families in turn-of-the-century Corpus Christi, Texas, subscribed to the Yiddish-language *Tageblatt* in the years before World War I. In the period before World War II, Hyman Berkowitz of Lexington "was a regular subscriber to *Der Tog* . . . as well as a reader of the *Forward,* borrowed from his brother-in-law."[27] The fact that many of the institutions established by East Europeans conducted their business in Yiddish also indicates its pervasiveness and its role in preserving a traditional culture. Congregants of Brith Achim in Petersburg, Virginia, kept minutes in Yiddish during the 1920s, and the rabbi preached Yiddish sermons in the synagogue during the interwar period. The Orthodox *chevra kadisha* (burial society) of Petersburg kept minutes in Yiddish until 1946. In Macon, Georgia, a chapter of the Yiddish cultural and socialist-oriented mutual aid organization, the Workman's Circle, existed during the World War I era, and an adult Bible class offered at the city's Sherah Israel synagogue in the 1930s was "conducted entirely in Yiddish."[28]

The appearance of Zionist societies in small towns throughout the South also reflects the presence there of East European Jews with a strong ethnic identity, for in the decades before World War II the more acculturated German-Jewish families of the South were unlikely to support the concept of Jewish nationalism.[29] As early as 1907 the *American Jewish Year Book* noted the existence of Zionist groups in small towns such as Austin and Tyler, Texas; Vicksburg, Mississippi; Newport, Kentucky; and Hagerstown, Maryland; and other Zionist societies continued to appear in small communities to which East European immigrants were attracted. In Texarkana, straddling the Arkansas and Texas border, Zionists formed an association during 1917, for example, and by 1919 individuals from Petersburg, Virginia, were traveling to Zionist conventions, although they did not formally establish a local Zionist organization until 15 years later. The East European Jews of Durham, North Carolina, were so immersed in Zionist activity that by the early 1940s the town even had chapters of factional groups, such as the religious Zionist organization Mizrachi and the Labor Zionist youth movement Habonim.[30]

Perhaps the most visible of all American Zionist societies in the interwar period (as today) was the women's organization Hadassah, founded by Henrietta Szold in 1912 to raise funds for health care and other projects in Palestine and to promote Jewish education in the United States. Thus, in the years before midcentury, the presence of a Hadassah chapter in a town was a very good indicator of Zionist activism at the local level. It is significant, therefore, that in the period before World War II Hadassah chapters sprang up not only in the principal cities of the South but also in many of the small towns to which East European immigrants had moved. By 1937, aside from chapters in substantial urban centers such as New Orleans, Birmingham, Atlanta, Memphis, Louisville, Richmond and Norfolk, Hadassah also had chapters in two dozen places in the South with total populations under 100,000 and Jewish populations under 1,000 (often substantially so). A list of these chapters is presented in Table 4.3. Moreover, although Hadassah seems to have ceased publishing comprehensive lists of its local groups after 1937, other sources suggest that the number of its chapters in the small-town South continued to grow considerably in subsequent years. In 1939, for example, new Hadassah chapters were organized in three different small cities in Mississippi: Clarksdale, Hattiesburg, and Jackson. Roanoke, Virginia, had a Hadassah group by 1943, and by then the Roanoke community was also supporting a chapter of the Zionist Organization of America and a branch of the Zionist youth group Young Judaea.[31]

If it is true, then, that East European immigrants constituted such a distinctive element in so many of the small cities and towns of the South in the decades before midcentury, why is it that their presence has had so little influence on the standard image of small-town Southern Jewry? One reason is that popular accounts of local Jewish history, which are often designed to demonstrate the long association of Jews with a particular place and to build a sense of pride and belonging within the contemporary Jewish community, tend to highlight early settlers and public figures (German Jews in the best-known small towns) and to emphasize Jewish acculturation. Moreover, the stories of the various small Jewish communities of the South often have been told by writers with an integrationist perspective who are inclined to stress the influence of Reform Judaism. Indeed, in many small-town Jewish histories the story of local Jewish life is inexorably intertwined with that of the local Reform temple.[32] Significant as well is the fact that the two contemporary institutions most devoted to preserving the legacy of the small Jewish communities of the South, the American Jewish Archives in Cincinnati and the Museum of the Southern Jewish Experience in Utica, Mississippi, are both affiliated with the Reform movement.

Table 4.3. Hadassah Chapters in Southern Towns of under 100,000 Total Population and under 1,000 Jewish Population, 1936–37

Location of Chapter	St.	Hadassah Members 1936–37	Jewish Pop. 1937	Total Population 1930	Total Population 1940
Columbus	GA	15	735	43,131	53,280
Cumberland	MD	30	820	37,747	39,483
Asheville	NC	25	950	50,193	51,310
Burlington	NC	12	41	9,737	12,198
Charlotte	NC	51	720	82,675	100,899
Durham	NC	46	360	52,037	60,195
Fayetteville	NC	39	148	13,049	17,428
Goldsboro	NC	24	143	14,985	17,274
Kinston	NC	29	130	11,362	15,388
Raleigh	NC	21	334	37,379	46,897
Wilmington	NC	62	330	32,270	33,407
Austin	TX	23	575	53,120	87,930
Breckenridge	TX	19	80	7,569	5,826
Corpus Christi	TX	51	645	27,741	57,301
Corsicana	TX	40	360	15,202	15,232
Richmond-Rosenberg (see note)	TX	34	145	29,718	32,963
Overton	TX	19	55	426	2,313
Tyler	TX	79	650	17,113	28,279
Wharton	TX	40	89	2,691	4,386
Danville	VA	28	290	22,247	32,749
Hampton-Phoebus	VA	24	208	9,338	9,401
Petersburg	VA	51	393	28,564	30,631
Bluefield	WV	36	210	19,339	20,641
Weirton	WV	37	350		2,476
Averages		35	365	25,735	32,412

Sources: For data on Hadassah chapters: *Hadassah Year Book* (1937), 106–14. For Jewish population, 1937: *American Jewish Year Book* 42 (1940–41): 239–64. For total population, 1930: United States Bureau of the Census, *Abstract of the Fifteenth Census of the United States* (1933; rpt. New York, 1976), 26–33. For total population, 1940: United States Bureau of the Census, *Sixteenth Census of the United States—1940, Volume 1: Population* (Washington, D.C., 1942), *passim.*

Note: The Hadassah chapter of Richmond and Rosenberg, Texas, was designated the Fort Bend chapter after the county in which these towns were located. All population figures associated with this chapter are given for the county as a whole. All Hadassah chapters were likely to have drawn members not only from the towns in which they were located but from surrounding towns as well.

Also coloring perceptions of small-town Southern Jewry are current discussions of Jewish life in the South that emphasize the high level of acculturation among Jews in small communities. A report on a recent documentation project, for example, suggests that the way to "best interpret the Southern Jewish experience" is through statements such as that of the woman from Hot Springs, Arkansas, who characterized her mother's Judaism by relating that "she didn't eat bacon on Saturday," or that of the congregant from Cleveland, Mississippi, who lauded the idea of early temple services on Friday evenings "because kids can come before they go to football games."[33]

But there are other reasons as well that the arrival of East European immigrants has had a relatively limited impact on the way small-town Southern Jewry has been depicted. One of these is that the appearance of East European Jews in the South's smaller Jewish centers did not call attention to itself by altering the fundamentally entrepreneurial character of those communities. Many of the East European Jews who settled in the small-town South probably began as peddlers, and most became merchants, small-scale business owners, and clerks, very much like their German-Jewish predecessors.

Unlike the case in major Jewish centers such as New York and Baltimore, or even in midsize centers such as Louisville and Memphis, it was truly exceptional for a significant working-class element to appear in one of the South's triple-digit Jewish communities. Quite anomalous, for instance, was the presence in the late nineteenth century of a hundred or more Jewish cigarette rollers from Russia and Poland in Durham, North Carolina. These workers, recruited from New York in the 1880s by the budding tobacco magnate James Duke and by his competitor W. T. Blackwell, congregated in one section of town, conducted their lives in Yiddish, and may even have established their own place of worship. But even in Durham a coherent Jewish working-class culture existed for only a short time. As cigarette-making machinery became more reliable and as cigarette manufacturers began to prefer more docile local laborers, the Jewish cigarette rollers of Durham were driven out of work and nearly all left town, taking up peddling or other pursuits in the South or returning to New York.[34]

Much more typical of the occupational patterns of East European Jews in the small-town South was that prevailing in Lexington, Kentucky, where the 53 Russian- or Polish-born Jewish heads of household identifiable in the 1920 census included 11 dry-goods merchants, 10 clothing merchants, seven proprietors of tailor shops, and three owners of grocery or produce firms. Only a handful of the 53 Russian or Polish household heads in Lexington's Jewish community were employed in what might be considered atypical jobs for small-town Jews: one was a barber, one a radiator repairman, one a mail clerk, and one a simple laborer.[35]

Of the 31 Russian-born Jewish heads of household in Alexandria, Louisiana, in 1920, at least 22 were merchants of one sort or another, half of them in the dry goods business. Among the other Russian-born Jewish householders in Alexandria were a miller, a junk dealer, a buyer of hides and furs, a watchmaker, a traveling salesman, and two shoemakers. The dozen or so East European heads of Jewish households in 1920 Vicksburg included a shoe store owner, a furniture store owner, a clothing store owner, two dry goods merchants, and three junk or hide dealers, but only one wage earner, a tailor. In Durham even Moses Gladstein, the tobacco worker who had been James Duke's main contact in New York when he was recruiting cigarette rollers, soon became the proprietor of a clothing store.[36]

An even more important reason that the arrival of East European immigrants did not profoundly transform the standard picture of small-town Southern Jewry is that the highly distinctive subculture these newcomers established was a relatively short-lived phenomenon. One indication of this is the fact that in towns where the pre–World War II Jewish population did not rise above 1,000, the Orthodox congregations founded by East Europeans frequently died out within a few decades of their establishment, and some did not even make it that long. In Vicksburg, Mississippi, for example, the Orthodox congregation Ahavas Achim lasted only from 1900 until 1906, and in Jonesboro, Arkansas, the Orthodox congregation, organized in 1892, was disbanded by 1927 when its remaining members joined the town's older congregation, the Reform Temple Israel. In Pine Bluff the East Europeans' B'nai Israel found that it could support a full-time rabbi for only about 10 years after its establishment in 1907, and by the 1930s the congregation was barely functioning. The Orthodox B'nai Israel of Fort Smith disbanded completely in the 1930s; years later a member of the Reform congregation in town recalled the poignant moment when "several Orthodox men brought B'nai Israel's two [Torah] scrolls to the temple, . . . joining their lot with the Reform."[37]

Indeed, in some small towns in the South, Reform congregations that predated the arrival of East Europeans consciously attempted to accommodate more traditional Jews and thus to hasten the demise of local Orthodox congregations or to forestall their creation in the first place. It is likely that these established congregations were motivated less by doctrinal fervor than by the fear that the Jews of their towns could not support more than one place of worship and the realization that their temples had to attract new members to survive. As early as 1895 the minutes of the Reform congregation Oheb Sholom in Goldsboro, North Carolina, noted that "certain Israelites were holding services outside the Temple," and to these individuals, who were almost certainly East Europeans, it extended a welcome to join the congregation. In 1927 Temple Beth Tefilloh in Brunswick, Georgia, enticed a group of East European immigrants to merge with their established Reform congregation, after the newcomers had been holding Orthodox High Holiday services in a rented hall for some 20 years.[38]

In Vicksburg, Sol Kory, rabbi from 1903 until 1936 of the local Reform temple, Anshe Chesed, seems to have made the integration of East European families into his congregation a very high priority. Although Reform Jews at the time were often quite hostile to the trappings and ceremonies of more traditional Jews, Rabbi Kory allowed head coverings at Anshe Chesed for many years, and he occasionally would get old timers to attend traditional minyanim. The temple also kept traditional burial shrouds on hand for those who wanted to make use of them. Rabbi Stanley Brav, Kory's successor, wrote that "Rabbi Kory must have gone out of his way . . . to enarm [sic] in welcome every new Jewish family, as it arrived in the city; at the time making that family feel 'at home' in Anshe Chesed [as much] as humanly possible, and guaranteeing that whatever traditionalist needs they may personally feel, he would assist them to fulfill." In much the same vein, Carolyn Gray LeMaster, the historian of Arkansas Jewry, reports that through the 1930s in Texarkana, East European Jews who preferred a traditional liturgy met early on Saturday mornings at the Reform synagogue, Mount Sinai, while "members of the Temple cooperated by filling in the needed number for a minyan."[39]

The philosophy of outreach to East Europeans adopted by many Reform congregations in the small-town South was articulated perhaps most frankly in a World War II–era pamphlet prepared by Jacob Weinstein of the Union of American Hebrew Congregations' Department of Synagogue and School Extension. Weinstein argued that in order to function in small communities, the Reform movement had to gain "the confidence of men who think they have extremely different theological notions" and work to maintain in these communities rabbinic leadership that was "modern in every way" but still possessed of "a sympathetic understanding of all of orthodox life and customs." He marvelled at "how far the recently orthodox will travel on the road to religious liberalism, provided he is certain that his guide is not temperamentally a stranger" and he asserted cynically that observant Orthodox Jews "will listen respectfully to the most heretical opinions" as long as they are "expressed in Yiddish."[40]

Of course, not all small-town congregations founded in accordance with Orthodox practice at the turn of the century disappeared completely from the scene, but those that did survive almost never maintained their Orthodox identities past the middle of the twentieth century. Over the decades they altered their characters substantially, first transforming themselves into bodies that could serve a wide range of religious philosophies and ultimately abandoning Orthodoxy completely. In Petersburg, Virginia, Brith Achim began moving from Orthodoxy toward Conservative practice as early as 1927 in order to prevent members (as their minutes said) "from drifting away altogether to competitive synagogues and temples," and in 1939 the Orthodox Tree of Life Congregation, established around 1917 by Russian immigrants to Clarksburg, West Virginia, entered into an uneasy merger with the town's Reform congregation, Temple Emanuel, and it too moved in the direction of Conservatism. In North Carolina, Durham's Beth El signaled its changing character when it hired a Conservative rabbi in place of an Orthodox leader for the first time in 1947, and in Georgia, Macon's Sherah Israel made the move from Orthodoxy to Conservatism at about the same time, adopting a new prayerbook and affiliating with the Conservative movement's United Synagogue.[41]

Some turn-of-the-century Orthodox congregations had made the journey all the way to Reform by the 1950s. In Ashland, Kentucky, East European immigrants had organized Agudath Achim as an Orthodox assembly in the 1890s, but it had already adopted Reform practices by the era of World War I, and in the early 1920s it became a member of the Union of American Hebrew Congregations. In Bluefield, West Virginia, Ahavath Sholom had come into being as an Orthodox body in 1904, but in the period before World War II it went through a Conservative phase, and by 1945 it too was Reform, affiliating with the UAHC in 1947.[42]

Yet another example of philosophical transformation comes from Clarksdale, Mississippi, where the Beth Israel congregation established by Lithuanian immigrants in the mid-1890s dominated local Jewish life throughout the twentieth century (a second Clarksdale congregation, Kahelas Jakef, was absorbed by Beth Israel after only a few years of in-

dependent operation just before World War I). When Beth Israel erected its first synagogue in 1910, the services conducted in the building
were Orthodox, and those people in the community who wished an al-
ternative met outside its confines. When Beth Israel constructed a new
synagogue in 1929, however, it became home to a wide variety of religious activities. By 1940 Reform, Conservative, and Orthodox services
were all being held in the building; "all three denominations of the Jewish faith . . . find free expression under one roof," reported one observer at the time. After World War II Beth Israel's character continued to
evolve. "As younger people moved up to high office," the synagogue's
rabbi recalled in the 1960s, "Reform became dominant, an organ was installed . . . and the congregation joined . . . the Union of American Hebrew Congregations." In 1963 separate Orthodox services were abolished completely and a new "universally satisfying" liturgy was adopted,
one that was "Reform with a Conservative tinge."[43]

All these examples of changing congregational identity are drawn
from the South's more visible small Jewish communities, those centers
of at least 100 but less than 1,000 Jews that are the main focus of this
study. Not surprisingly, however, the pattern of Orthodox congregations
shifting their identities could be observed in the South's very smallest
Jewish communities as well. In Laurel, Mississippi, for example, Congregation Kenneseth Israel was established as an Orthodox body in
1906, but as early as 1931 one of its members was already reporting that
"the existence of a tendency towards reformation is strongly felt in the
congregation." Less than a decade later Kenneseth Israel left the Union
of Orthodox Hebrew Congregations and joined the Reform Union of
American Hebrew Congregations instead.[44]

By the time the first generation of East European immigrants to the
small towns of the South had died out, the extinction of Orthodox Judaism in that environment was essentially complete. As the twentieth
century entered its final decade, Orthodox congregations of one sort or
another could be found flourishing in and around major Southern metropolises such as Memphis, Atlanta, and Miami, and also in a few of the
South's mid-size Jewish communities (Little Rock, Arkansas, and Charlotte, North Carolina, for example), but congregations that identified
themselves as Orthodox were reported to be functioning in only two of
the South's truly small Jewish communities: Vidalia, Georgia, and Greenwood, Mississippi. Moreover, neither of these communities represented
a significant presence; neither had a resident rabbi and neither had a
Jewish population of more than 100.

The demise or at least the transformation of virtually all the Orthodox congregations established in the small towns of the South, and the
waning of traditional culture there more generally, was no doubt accelerated by the fact that already at the turn of the century it was not uncommon for families to abandon small-town life if Orthodox religious
practice and a traditional lifestyle were extremely important to them.
Nathan Blecker's biography provides a case in point. Blecker arrived in
Jonesboro, Arkansas, around 1890 and established a dry goods business
there that soon had branches in several other towns as well. He craved a
more intensively Jewish environment for his family, however, but he did
not want to give up his thriving commercial enterprise, so he moved his
wife and children from Jonesboro to Memphis and made arrangements
to be with them on each sabbath. Blecker preferred to live apart from
his family all week long rather than have his children reared in a community with only a limited Jewish infrastructure. The life story of Julius
Friedland is illustrative here as well. Friedland came from Minsk, Russia,
to serve as a rabbi, *mohel* and *shochet* in Meridian, Mississippi, around
1904. Later he and his family moved to Tyler, Texas, but before long they
transplanted themselves once again, this time to New York, "where they
felt they would be more comfortable among their *landsmen*."[45]

Those East European immigrants who did remain in small towns despite their attachment to traditional Judaism found it extremely difficult
to pass on their outlook and practices to a second generation. For one
thing, small-town Jewish communities could seldom provide the extensive educational opportunities available (if not always utilized) in larger
cities. In 1919 the *American Jewish Year Book* published data on Jewish education in the various communities of the United States which is very
useful for gauging the availability of Jewish schooling in the small-town
South. For 45 of the 104 towns listed in Table 4.2, no information on
schooling is provided in the *Year Book* survey at all, and it is safe to assume that in most or all of these towns no formal Jewish education was
available whatsoever in the period just after World War I. Furthermore,
in the remaining 59 towns of Table 4.2, where schooling was available, it
was not very intensive. In 38 of these 59 towns, Jewish education was provided only one day a week (presumably Sunday), and in another 12 formal education was available but two or three days a week. In only nine
of the towns was formal Jewish education provided on a daily basis.[46]

Although Jewish educational opportunities may have been provided
in some small communities on a more informal basis, and the situation
might have improved in some places after 1919, it is nonetheless clear

that four decades into the era of mass migration from Eastern Europe the picture of formal Jewish schooling in the small-town South was rather bleak. Not only was Jewish education often unavailable, but when classes were offered they were not necessarily of high quality. One man who grew up in Williamson, West Virginia, before World War II reported that "our religious school was a farce—I learned nothing." Another recalled that his bar mitzvah ceremony "was a sham . . . We were growing up in a Christian world [and] we ourselves knew so little about Judaism."[47]

The inability of the immigrant generation to pass on its attitudes and knowledge meant that the children of East European settlers in the small-town South invariably came to adopt a way of life that was far less intensively Jewish than that of their mothers and fathers. Speaking of the time when the children of Durham's immigrant Orthodox families first began to stray from the ways of their parents, the local historian Leonard Rogoff observes that "the young girls giggled when they passed the mikvah, and boys more interested in baseball and football had no interest in swinging chickens around their head to expiate sin." The author Eli Evans describes the sons of the Orthodox founders of Durham's Beth El synagogue as men less concerned with maintaining tradition than with "attracting new membership, building a new building, driving to services in a new car, and streamlining the service." He speaks of the older members of the congregation in the era of World War II as attempting "to talk across the chasm to another generation already lost to Orthodoxy."[48]

Typical of the life stories of second-generation East European Jews in the small-town South is that of Joseph Dave, who grew up in Durham just before World War I. He described his Lithuanian-born father and his mother as "devoted to Orthodoxy" and recalled that they "always thought of Zionism." Dave's Jewish education in Durham was "Orthodox" and "included reading of Hebrew," but his Jewish schooling ended when he became bar mitzvah, and by the time he was a young adult his religious ties were exclusively with Reform congregations, first in Cincinnati where he was a student and later in Asheville, North Carolina, where he settled in 1923 and became an active member of Temple Beth ha-Tephila.[49]

Of course, the third generation of small-town Jews was even less likely than the second to be steeped in the traditions of the immigrants who first came to America. Yetta Brandt, whose parents spent their early years in Augusta, Georgia, and Durham, North Carolina, explained it this way: "My parents did not really know a lot about the Jewish religion themselves. They could not possibly pass on to us what they did not know . . . I guess their parents, my grandparents, never taught them to be Jewish the way that they had learned in Europe."[50] And just as a familiarity with traditional religious observance invariably diminished from one generation to another, so too did other aspects of East European culture, including the use of Yiddish. As Myer Godhelff, the Lexington resident who reported on his parents' circle of Yiddish-speaking friends, recalled, "I understood Yiddish very well but hardly spoke it, as I now was learning English and being educated through the Lex[ington] school system and later at U.K. [the University of Kentucky]."[51]

East Europeans of the immigrant generation must have had mixed feelings about the way their children and grandchildren were drifting away from traditional culture, and occasionally outside observers offered assessments of the attitudes of this older generation. Samuel M. Silver, a student rabbi in Logan, West Virginia, in the 1930s recognized that the East European Jews he encountered remained somewhat ambivalent about the shift toward Reform in their congregation. Most of the people in the congregation "having Orthodox background, miss the warmth of old-fashioned services," he reported. "On reflection, however, most of them realize HUC [the Hebrew Union College and its influence] will keep religion in their children." Years later an older East European Jew in Williamson, West Virginia, echoed these sentiments: "What turned me toward Reform was that my son liked Reform so much."[52]

On the other hand, at about the same time that Samuel Silver was commenting on the reluctant willingness of first-generation small-town Jews to embrace Reform, the UAHC's Jacob Weinstein offered a somewhat different assessment. "These dyed-in-the-wool orthodox are not worried about their children," he wrote with his characteristic bluntness. "The evidence of their ignorance of Jewish life and the indifference and apostasy in the wake of such ignorance only confirms the elders in their own stiff-necked righteousness."[53]

Clearly, the small Jewish communities of the South were not alone in witnessing a decline in religious observance and the abandonment of Yiddish among the children of East European immigrants raised in America. These changes were underway all over the United States, and, if anything, they may even have proceeded somewhat more slowly in smaller Jewish communities.[54] But what is most significant here is that the transformation of the East European lifestyle was much more complete in the South's smaller Jewish centers than it was in the larger cities of the region (or in larger cities in general), because after a very few decades no critical mass remained in the small-town environment to allow for the survival of any sort of religiously observant or intensively ethnic Jewish subcommunity. Those few families that might have tried to rear their children in a highly traditional lifestyle found themselves struggling to do so in nearly total isolation. The author Melissa Fay Greene has described the early years of Rachel Shilsky, a rabbi's daughter who endured not only a dysfunctional family but also an Orthodox upbringing in the racist and often anti-Semitic environment of pre–World War II Suffolk, Virginia, as an "ugly duckling childhood" because Rachel, "raised so far from the swans of Jewish New York, . . . scarcely [knew] that the possibility existed for undespised Jewish life."[55]

As the middle of the twentieth century approached and the East European Jews of the small-town South retreated from the highly religious and ethnic character of their Jewishness, they began moving toward the kind of Southernness that distinguished the well-established German Jews of the region. Although in many places the chilly relationship between German Jews and East Europeans was not mitigated until well after midcentury, as early as 1935 student rabbi Louis Josephson reported that in New Bern, North Carolina, there was "no distinct cleavage" between the German and East European segments of the local Jewish community. "They belong to [the] same congregation and social club," he reported, and "socially and in religious practice there is little difference between them." Similarly, one study of an unnamed small-town Jewish community in the South in the 1950s and '60s divided "new Jews" (those that reflected the influences of the immigrant experience and of the North) from "old Jews" (those identified with the South) not on the basis of the German or East European places of origin of their families but rather on the strength of their identification with a kind of de-ethnicized Southern Jewish society, whether that connection went back three or four generations or only one or two.[56]

The dilution of ideology in the small-town South (as elsewhere in America) also advanced the disappearance of a distinctive East European culture after midcentury. As Zionism became less ideological and as a generalized support for Israel became the norm among American Jews in the decades after the establishment of the state in 1948, a commitment to Zionism no longer remained the preserve of those grounded in the nationalist doctrines of East European Jewry. Similarly, as Reform Judaism left behind the militant assimilationism of its Classic phase, Jews of East European background became even more comfortable with Reform and more inclined to accept it as the philosophy of their congregations. Indeed, by the end of the twentieth century Reform Judaism seemed to be as pervasive in the small-town South as it had been at the end of the nineteenth. In the early 1990s in Mississippi, for example, 12 towns were reported to have only a single Jewish congregation, and in nine of these towns that congregation was Reform. In all five of the single-congregation towns in Alabama the local congregation was Reform, and in seven of the nine towns in Georgia with only a single Jewish house of worship the synagogue was affiliated with Reform. In West Virginia, Reform temples were present in five of the seven towns with only one congregation, and in Texas in the early 1990s Reform congregations were the ones functioning in 10 of the 12 towns where only one synagogue was reported.[57]

Moreover, after the middle of the twentieth century the distinctiveness of small-town Jewish life in the South itself became a less significant matter, for as the century progressed a great many of the quintessential small communities of the pre–World War II era lost their old character, either because they developed into more substantial Jewish centers or because they went into decline. Of the 104 triple-digit Jewish centers identifiable in 1927, 19 had been transformed by the early 1980s into more significant communities with populations above 1,000 and expanded Jewish infrastructures (this was the case, for example, in Orlando and St. Petersburg, Florida; in Lexington, Kentucky; in Charlotte and Raleigh, North Carolina; in Columbia, South Carolina; in Austin, Texas; and in Roanoke, Virginia). On the other hand, in the same period about one-third of the triple-digit communities of 1927 had seen their Jewish populations drop below 100.

Furthermore, of the 51 triple-digit Jewish communities of 1927 that still had between 100 and 1,000 Jews five or six decades later, about half had diminished in size. In Mississippi, for instance, Greenwood's Jewish population dropped from about 250 in 1927 to about 100 in 1983, while the reported Jewish population of Meridian fell from 575 to 135, and that of Vicksburg fell from 467 to 260. In Maryland the reported Jewish population of Cumberland went from 720 to 265 between 1927 and 1983, while that of Hagerstown went from 650 to 275. As a brochure distributed in the early 1990s by the Museum of the Southern Jewish Experience observes, "in many small towns, the story of [the Southern Jewish] experience survives only as a cherished memory."[58]

To be sure, triple-digit Jewish communities have continued to play a role in the Jewish geography of the South, but this is in large part because a number of new communities of that size have developed in the region, often in expanding industrial centers. A case in point is the community of Dalton, Georgia. Just before World War II Dalton had a reported Jewish population of only 40 individuals and there was no organized Jewish life in the town. In the years after 1940, however, Dalton began developing into one of the world's foremost carpet manufacturing centers, and the Jewish population of the town increased rapidly. In 1983 Dalton's Jewish population was reported to be 235, and its synagogue was beginning its fifth decade of operation.[59] Similarly, in Spartanburg, South Carolina, the Jewish population never surpassed 100 in the pre–World War II era, but in the decades after the war, Spartanburg blossomed as one of the South's major textile centers, and by the early 1980s its Jewish population approached 300.

The growth of educational institutions in some of the South's smaller cities also stimulated the development of new triple-digit communities. Chapel Hill, a town dominated by the University of North Carolina, was reported to have only 32 Jews in 1937 but 230 by 1968. Fayetteville, home of the University of Arkansas, had no reported Jewish population at all before the middle of the century, but by 1983 it was home to 120 Jews.

Still, the new triple-digit Jewish communities that appeared in the South in the decades after World War II were quite different in character from the region's earlier small-town Jewish centers, for these new communities depended heavily on the arrival of Northern Jews, for whom the culture of the South was quite alien. Communities built by transplanted business executives, cosmopolitan scholars and teachers, and retirees from big cities are quite distinct from the classic small Jewish communities of the pre–World War II South. Moreover, the unique character even of those long-established small communities that have survived into the latter part of the twentieth century has been diluted as the result of several developments, including advances in transportation and technology that have facilitated the outreach programs of organizations such as B'nai B'rith and the UAHC and have allowed small communities to maintain much closer ties with midsize and larger Jewish centers.

It is perhaps inevitable that the image of small-town Southern Jewry will be forever dominated by the personae of German-Jewish pioneers, business magnates, and civic leaders, and by the Americanized lifestyle and the institutions that have come to be associated with these early settlers. The portrayal of the small-town Southern Jew as religiously liberal, highly acculturated, and fiercely loyal to the South is hallowed because of its nineteenth-century origins and it endures because of the brevity of the period during which an essentially Orthodox and manifestly ethnic East European Jewish subculture was maintained in the South's smaller Jewish communities. Moreover, the historical periods that seem to fascinate students of the South most, the eras of the Civil War and Reconstruction in the nineteenth century and of the Civil Rights movement in the twentieth, are periods that do not overlap with the time when East European Jewish culture was most clearly in evidence in the smaller cities and towns of the region. Nonetheless, any account of the history of small-town Southern Jewry cannot be complete if it neglects the distinctively East European subculture that materialized in many corners of the South around the turn of the century and that lingered there for a while in the decades before World War II.

Notes

The research for this article was supported in part by a fellowship from the National Endowment for the Humanities and by grants from the Lucius Littauer Foundation and the Arts and Sciences Research Committee of the University of Louisville. I wish to thank Leonard Rogoff for sharing his unpublished paper "Small-Town Orthodoxy, Southern Style," which touches briefly on some of the themes developed here.

1. Manuscript returns of the United States Census [hereafter Ms. Census], Alexandria, Rapides Parish, Louisiana, 1880.

2. See "Jewish Citizens Play Prominent Part in All Affairs of City," *Lexington Herald*, April 15, 1917; "Seventy Fifth Anniversary: Temple Beth Tefilloh" (Brunswick, Ga., 1961); Carolyn Gray LeMaster, *A Corner of the Tapestry: A History of the Jewish Experience in Arkansas, 1820s–1990s* (Fayetteville, Ark., 1994), 166–67; Leo E. Turitz and Evelyn Turitz, *Jews in Early Mississippi* (Jackson, Miss., 1983), xiv; Ralph Goldenstein, ed., "History and Activities of Congregation Anshe-Emeth, Pine Bluff, Arkansas, 1867–1917" ([Pine Bluff?], 1917), 34.

3. See "$300,000 in Dry Goods: S. Waxelbaum & Son," *A Picture of Macon, Georgia: Macon Evening News, Industrial Issue* (1889); Ruthe Winegarten and Cathy Schechter, *Deep in the Heart: The Lives and Legends of Texas Jews* (Austin, Texas, 1990), 44; Melanie Torbett, "Building a Downtown," *CENLA: The Magazine of Central Louisiana* (May/June 1993), 10; LeMaster, *Corner of the Tapestry*, 153; Turitz and Turitz, *Jews in Early Mississippi*, 20–21, 53, 103.

4. In this study the states of the South are considered to be those of the South Atlantic, East South Central, and West South Central regions of the United States as defined by the US Bureau of the Census in the early twentieth centu-

ry. These states are Alabama, Arkansas, Delaware, Florida, Georgia, Kentucky, Louisiana, Maryland, Mississippi, North Carolina, Oklahoma, South Carolina, Tennessee, Texas, Virginia, and West Virginia. Throughout this article, Jewish population figures for c. 1907 are based on data in *The Jewish Encyclopedia* (New York, 1901–1916), 12:371–74, and in the *American Jewish Year Book* [hereafter *AJYB*] 9 (1907–1908): 123–430. In cases where these sources give different population data for the same town, the two figures have been averaged. For a fuller discussion of the two sources used here, see Lee Shai Weissbach, "Small Jewish Communities in the Era of Mass Migration: The American Experience," in *Patterns of Migration, 1850–1914,* ed. Aubrey Newman and Stephen W. Massil (London, 1996), 159–61. Information on the congregations of the South in 1907 is also from *AJYB* 9 (1907–1908): 123–430. General population figures for c. 1907 are based on data for the nearest census year, 1910, as given in United States Bureau of the Census, *Thirteenth Census of the United States Taken in the Year 1910, Volume 1: Population* (Washington, D.C., 1913), 87–97.

5. A list of UAHC congregations in 1907 is in *AJYB* 9 (1907–1908): 115–18. On the total number of congregations in the US in 1906, see Uriah Zvi Engelman, "Jewish Statistics in the U.S. Census of Religious Bodies," *Jewish Social Studies* 9 (April 1947), table VI.

6. Throughout this article, Jewish population data for c. 1878 is from Union of American Hebrew Congregations, *Statistics of the Jews of the United States* (Philadelphia, 1880), and Jewish population data for 1927 is from *AJYB* 30 (1928–1929): 180–96. General population data for 1880 is from United States Census Office, *Compendium of the Tenth Census (June 1, 1880)* (1883; rpt. New York, 1976), part I, 380–405. General population data for 1930 is from United States Bureau of the Census, *Abstract of the Fifteenth Census of the United States* (1933; rpt. New York, 1976), 26–33. For a fuller discussion of the *Statistics of the Jews,* see Lee Shai Weissbach, "The Jewish Communities of the United States on the Eve of Mass Migration: Some Comments on Geography and Bibliography," *American Jewish History* 78 (September 1988): 79–91. On turn-of-the century urban growth in the South, see John B. Boles, *The South through Time: A History of an American Region* (Englewood Cliffs, N.J., 1995), 382 ff.

7. See, for example, Steven Hertzberg, *Strangers within the Gate City: The Jews of Atlanta, 1845–1915* (Philadelphia, 1978); Charles Reznikoff and Uriah Z. Engelman, *The Jews of Charleston: A History of an American Jewish Community* (Philadelphia, 1950); Elaine H. Maas, *The Jews of Houston: An Ethnographic Study* (New York, 1989); Isaac M. Fein, *The Making of an American Jewish Community: The History of Baltimore Jewry from 1773 to 1920* (Philadelphia, 1971); Myron Berman, *Richmond's Jewry, 1769–1976: Shabbat in Shockoe* (Charlottesville, Va., 1979); and

Herman Landau, *Adath Louisville: The Story of a Jewish Community* (Louisville, 1981).

8. Ms. Census, Lexington, Fayette County, Kentucky, 1920.

9. Ms. Census, Alexandria, Rapides Parish, Louisiana, 1920.

10. Ms. Census, Vicksburg, Warren Country, Mississippi, 1920.

11. Karen R. Goody, "The Greensboro Jewish Community: Keeping the Memories under Glass" (master's thesis, Wake Forest University, 1984), 17; Winegarten and Schechter, *Deep in the Heart,* 127.

12. On the identifiable communities of the first decade of the twentieth century, see note 4. On IRO placements, see *Tenth Annual Report of the Industrial Removal Office for the Year Nineteen Hundred and Ten* (New York, 1911), table 1.

13. Communications in the IRO Collection (*I-91), American Jewish Historical Society, Waltham, Mass.: from Macon, Nov. 4, 1912, Box 17; from Lake Charles, Nov. 30, 1905, Box 15; from Vicksburg, June 30, 1904, Box 15.

14. Communication in the IRO Collection, American Jewish Historical Society: from Fort Smith, Oct. 10, 1905, Box 15.

15. See Michael S. Arnold, "Fading Tradition: Bogalusa Losing Jewish Presence," *New Orleans Times Picayune,* November 24, 1995; Debra Weiner, "The Jews of Clarksburg: Community Adaptation and Survival, 1900–1960," *Southern Jewish Historical Society Newsletter* (March 1995): 4–5; and LeMaster, *Corner of the Tapestry,* 283.

16. See Louis Ginsberg, *History of the Jews of Petersburg,* 1789–1950 (Petersburg, Va., 1954), 67–68; and "Beth Israel's 75th Year to be Celebrated," *Clarksdale Press Register,* October 10, 1969.

17. Ms. Census, Alexandria, 1920; Ms. Census, Lexington, 1920; and questionnaire completed by Bernard Wolf Barron, 1993, in the possession of the author.

18. On Petersburg, see Ginsberg, *History of the Jews of Petersburg,* 65–66; and *AJYB* 9 (1907–1908): 420. On Wilmington, see "North Carolina," *The Universal Jewish Encyclopedia* (New York, [1948?]) [hereafter *UJE*], 8:238. On Columbia, see "South Carolina," *UJE,* 9:664. On Macon, see "History of our Congregation" (leaflet, Macon, Ga., [1987?]), 1; and "The Way It Was: Macon's Temple Beth Israel Celebrates 125th," *The Southern Israelite,* May 4, 1984, 7. On Brunswick, see "Georgia," *UJE,* 4:538. On Pine Bluff and Fort Smith, see LeMaster, *Corner of the Tapestry,* 84, 87.

19. On Macon, see "History of our Congregation," 1; "The Way It Was," 7; and John C. Butler, *Historical Record of Macon and Central Georgia* (1879; rpt. Macon, 1958), 325. On Wilmington, see *AJYB* 9 (1907–1908): 348; and "North Carolina," *UJE,* 8:238. On Alexandria, see "Jewish Cemetery" and "B'nai Israel Jew-

ish Cemetery," in Mary Parker Partain, *Gone But Not Forgotten: Cemetery Inscriptions of Rapides Parish* (Pineville, La., [1992?]).

20. Questionnaires completed by Morton Applebaum and Louis Josephson, 1935, in "Student Survey 1935–1936" (Manuscript Collection #5), American Jewish Archives, Cincinnati [hereafter AJA].

21. See Jerome Paul David, "Jewish Consciousness in the Small Town" (rabbinic thesis, Hebrew Union College, 1974), 34.

22. See Myrna Katz Frommer and Harvey Frommer, *Growing up Jewish in America: An Oral History* (New York, 1995), 44–45; and LeMaster, *Corner of the Tapestry,* 84.

23. Louis Schmier, "Jews and Gentiles in a South Georgia Town," *in Jews of the South: Selected Essays from the Southern Jewish Historical Society,* ed. Samuel Proctor and Louis Schmier with Malcolm Stern (Macon, Ga., 1984), 12.

24. Ms. Census, Lexington, 1920.

25. See Leonard Rogoff, "Small-Town Orthodoxy, Southern Style" (paper presented at the annual meeting of the Southern Jewish Historical Society, New Orleans, La., 1995), 11.

26. See Gertrude W. Dubrovsky, introduction to I. J. Schwartz, *Kentucky,* trans. Gertrude W. Dubrovsky (Tuscaloosa, Ala., 1990); and questionnaire completed by Myer B. Godhelff, 1996, in the possession of the author.

27. Winegarten and Schechter, *Deep in the Heart,* 129; Barron questionnaire.

28. See Ginsberg, *History of the Jews of Petersburg,* 80–83; Newton J. Friedman, "A History of Temple Beth Israel of Macon, Georgia" (Doctor of Theology diss., Burton Seminary of Colorado, 1955), 69; and "History of our Congregation," 1.

29. On the hostility of Reform Jews in the South to Zionism as late as the 1940s, see Eli N. Evans, *The Provincials: A Personal History of the Jews in the South* (New York, 1973), 99 ff.

30. See *AJYB* 9 (1907–1908): 37–44; LeMaster, *Corner of the Tapestry,* 72; Ginsberg, *History of the Jews of Petersburg,* 79–80; and "North Carolina," *UJE,* 8:238.

31. On Mississippi, see Mississippi Historical Records Survey Project, "Inventory of the Church and Synagogue Archives of Mississippi: Jewish Congregations and Organizations" (Jackson, Miss., 1940), 13. On Roanoke, see "Virginia," *UJE,* 10:428.

32. See, for example, Goldenstein, "History and Activities of Congregation Anshe-Emeth;" Gertrude Philippsborn, *The History of the Jewish Community of Vicksburg (from 1820 to 1968)* (mimeographed booklet, Vicksburg, 1969); Helen Kohn Hennig, *The Tree of Life: Fifty Years of Congregational Life at the Tree of Life Synagogue, Columbia, S.C.* (Columbia, S.C, [1946?]); and Martin I. Hinchin, *Fourscore and Eleven: A History of the Jews of Rapides Parish, 1818–1919* ([Alexandria, La.?], 1984).

33. Marcie C. Ferris, "The Southern Jewish Experience," in "Jewish Life in Wilkinson County, 1820–1920: Views of a Vanished Community," ed. Marsha Oates (exhibition brochure, Woodville, Miss., 1995), 9.

34. See Leonard Rogoff, "Jewish Proletarians in the New South: The Durham Cigarette Rollers," *American Jewish History* 82:1–4 ([1994–1995]): 141–57; and Evans, *The Provincials*, 15–17.

35. Ms. Census, Lexington, 1920.

36. Ms. Census, Alexandria, 1920; Ms. Census, Vicksburg, 1920; and Evans, *The Provincials*, 17.

37. See Mississippi Records Survey, "Inventory," 23–24; and LeMaster, *Corner of the Tapestry*, 80–81, 84, 87.

38. See "Digest of the Minutes of Oheb Sholom Congregation [Goldsboro, N.C.], 1883–1958," Histories File, AJA, 5–6; and "Seventy Fifth Anniversary: Temple Beth Tefilloh."

39. Philippsborn, *Jewish Community of Vicksburg*, 43–44; Lemaster, *Corner of the Tapestry*, 89–90.

40. Jacob J. Weinstein, "The Religious Situation among Small Town Jewries" (n.p., n.d.), 11.

41. See Ginsberg, *History of the Jews of Petersburg*, 81–82; Weiner, "Jews of Clarksburg," 4–5; Rogoff, "Small-Town Orthodoxy," 13; and "History of Our Congregation," 1–2.

42. See Lee Shai Weissbach, *The Synagogues of Kentucky: Architecture and History* (Lexington, Ky., 1995), 18; and Abraham I. Shinedling, *West Virginia Jewry: Origins and History, 1850–1958* (Philadelphia, 1963), xxix, 370–71.

43. "Beth Israel's 75th Year." See also Mississippi Records Survey, "Inventory," 21–22, 24.

44. See David B. Marcus, "Historical Aspect of the First Thirty Years of Laurel [Mississippi] Jewry" (typescript, 1931), Histories File, AJA; and "Mississippi," *UJE*, 7:588.

45. LeMaster, *Corner of the Tapestry*, 80–81; Winegarten and Schechter, *Deep in the Heart*, 89.

46. See *AJYB* 21 (1919–20): 330–583.

47. See David, "Jewish Consciousness," 16–17.

48. Rogoff, "Small-Town Orthodoxy," 9–10; Evans, *The Provincials*, 117–18.

49. Questionnaire completed by Joseph Dave, c. 1975, AJA.

50. See Rogoff, "Small-Town Orthodoxy," 12.

51. Godhelff questionnaire.

52. See questionnaire completed by Samuel Silver, 1935, in "Student Survey 1935–1936" (Manuscript Collection #5), AJA; and David, "Jewish Consciousness," 15.

53. Weinstein, "Religious Situation," 8.

54. See Ewa Morawska, *Insecure Prosperity: Small-Town Jews in Industrial America, 1890–1940* (Princeton, N.J., 1996).

55. Melissa Fay Greene, "In Search of a New Vocabulary," *CommonQuest* (Fall 1996): 58. Greene's essay is a review of James McBride, *The Color of Water* (New York, 1996), of which Rachel Shilsky is the subject.

56. See Josephson questionnaire; and Theodore Lowi, "Southern Jews: The Two Communities," in *Jews in the South,* ed. Leonard Dinnerstein and Mary Dale Palsson (Baton Rouge, La., 1973), esp. 270. Lowi's essay also appears in Abraham D. Lavender, *A Coat of Many Colors: Jewish Subcommunities in the United States* (Westport, Conn., 1977).

57. See Ellen Chernofsky, ed., *Traveling Jewish in America* (Lodi, N.J., 1991).

58. See "Welcome to the Museum of the Southern Jewish Experience" (brochure, n.p., [1993?]). Jewish population data for 1937 is available in *AJYB* 42 (1940–41), for 1968 in *AJYB* 70 (1969), and for 1983 in *AJYB* 84 (1984).

59. See "Temple Beth El, Dalton, Georgia, 1940–1980" (anniversary booklet, n.p., 1980).

5
Jewish Women in the Central Appalachian Coal Fields, 1890–1960

From Breadwinners to Community Builders

Deborah R. Weiner

When Bessie Zaltzman died in 1949, she left most of her estate to her son Louis. This was not a trifling amount, because entirely through her own efforts she had amassed a small fortune worth $84,000. Starting out fifty years earlier with nothing but a shiftless husband whom she divorced around 1905, she managed to acquire a cow and scraped together a living for herself and her three small children, selling butter and milk. Eventually she had a few cows, a small shop to sell her wares, and then some real estate. She became a landlady, owning small residential properties and overcoming crises that included floods, fires, and lawsuits. Not only was she a determined businesswoman, she was also determined until the end of her life to maintain her commitment to Orthodox Judaism. Of her two surviving children, she left only a token amount to her son Abe, who had disaffiliated with the Jewish community. She did, however, instruct Louis to make sure that Abe was never in economic distress and established a Kaddish fund to ensure that her errant son would be properly mourned after his death. She also left money to Jewish charities and three synagogues: one in Jerusalem and the others in Bluefield and Keystone, West Virginia, in the coal fields where she had spent her entire adult life after emigrating from Russia as a teenager.[1]

Bessie Zaltzman was a woman of strong will, as her business enterprise and her frequent clashes with other members of Keystone's Jewish community show. The outlines of her life represent a somewhat unusual, but by no means implausible, trajectory for an East European Jewish woman of her day. Although it is tempting to dwell in detail on the life of this fascinating woman, she is cited here as just one telling example of the role played by Jewish women in the coal fields of central Appalachia. From the late 1890s and well into the post–World War II era, women were essential to the creation and maintenance of numerous, small, Jewish coal field communities. Their economic contributions allowed their households to survive and prosper within a notoriously unstable local economy, while their concern with creating a Jewish environment for themselves and their families led them to become the driving force behind Jewish communal organization. Not only did their efforts enable Jewish communities to flourish deep in the mountains of central Appalachia, their commitment to transmitting their heritage to their children under less-than-ideal conditions demonstrates how women in small-town America ensured the maintenance of Jewish continuity for future generations.

The Great Migration of East European Jews to America coincided with the development of the nation's southern coal fields, which began in earnest in the early 1880s and peaked during World War I. In just a few short years, the coal industry transformed a thinly populated region of Appalachian Mountain farm families to a rural-industrial society controlled by large companies, with a growing work force and a pressing need for commercial services to support the new industrial activity. Newcomers from a variety of ethnic groups flocked to central Appalachia, attracted by the opportunities of a booming economy. Most of them— African Americans from other parts of the South and immigrants from Southern and Eastern Europe—went to work in the coal mines. But others, especially Jewish immigrants, sought to provide retail services to a growing population. The Jews who came to the region followed a pattern exhibited by a significant minority of East European Jewish immigrants; as many as 30 percent of the migration stream chose not to settle in New York and other major port cities, but rather to search for opportunities for self-employment in smaller cities and towns across the nation. In the coal fields, their success in constructing a niche within the small commercial sector of an overwhelmingly industrial economy enabled them to establish their own small yet vital communities. Between the 1890s and 1930s, Jews from Eastern Europe founded congregations in nine small coal field towns in southern West Virginia, southeastern Kentucky, and southwestern Virginia.[2]

The survival of these Jewish coal field communities depended on three requirements. First, like everyone else in the region, Jewish families had to provide for themselves within the confines of the coal economy. Second, they had to feel comfortable enough with their social environment to make the commitment to stay. Third, they couldn't become so comfortable as to completely assimilate into the surrounding culture. An internal desire to maintain their distinct identity, their religion, and at least some version of their cultural practices had to motivate them. As many historians of small-town Jewry have noted, maintenance of Jewish identity was especially difficult for Jews who lived far from the centers of American Jewry as tiny minorities in the midst of an overwhelmingly Christian population. In all of these dimensions—economic, social, and cultural—Jewish women played a crucial role in sustaining their families and communities.[3]

Despite the opportunities of a growing economy, members of the region's commercial sector faced daunting challenges. The boom-and-bust nature of the coal industry caused frequent periods of wage cuts and layoffs that shriveled the purchasing power of the local work force. Strikes and other forms of labor conflict, endemic to the coal fields, also severely affected local merchants. National downturns, such as the Great Depression, hit coal fields even harder than other places because of the reliance on a single industry. Many local businesses faced the experience of losing everything and starting again from scratch, with bankruptcies not uncommon. Meanwhile, during the good times, payday Saturdays would find the stores crowded with shoppers and their owners would have to scramble to meet the demand.[4]

Like other groups in the U.S. and in the coal fields, Jews devised strategies based on their old country traditions and experiences to overcome adverse economic conditions. One major strategy was a reliance on the family economy. Small Jewish businesses in America were true family businesses, with wives and children working alongside husbands and fathers to help make ends meet. Daughters as well as sons helped in the store from an early age. In the coal fields, young women as well as men not only worked for their parents, but also took jobs as sales clerks at other stores in order to contribute to the household income. Many coal field families in the early years took in boarders, a responsibility that fell entirely on the wives. Jews who grew up in the region during the 1920s and 1930s recalled that at the very least, their mothers "helped out" in the family store during busy times. But "helping out," though it was the accepted term to describe a wide range of women's economic activities, greatly understates the contributions to the household economy made by many of these women.[5]

Motivated by varying combinations of family need and personal fulfillment, Jewish coal field women often took on significant responsibilities in the family business. Some wives acted as their husband's business partner in decision making and division of labor, if not in a legal or financial sense. The division was often based on personality, with the more outgoing partner serving customers and the more reserved one handling behind-the-scenes tasks such as bookkeeping. If the family owned more than one store, the wife sometimes managed a store. One man related that after his father went bankrupt in the Depression, his mother went to work in the family's next business venture out of necessity. Yet she remained active once conditions improved, which suggests that she was too important, or enjoyed it too much, to quit. One woman remarked that for her mother, the store "was her life." She liked working and would spend most days at the store. Of course, this did not absolve her from domestic chores, and she could often be found cleaning the house at 2:00 a.m. Another woman recalled that her mother did just about everything in their small, family, dry goods store, from serving customers to altering clothing to traveling with her husband to New York on buying trips. In many ways this was a hardship for the family; as the daughter stated, "We were latchkey kids." Yet she saw her mother as a role model of strength and ability, proudly calling her a "tremendous buyer." Meanwhile, her mother had "no social life," torn between work and home duties. But she looked forward to the New York trips, where she and her husband would splurge on the opera.[6]

Many immigrant groups of the era had a history of married women helping to earn income for the family, mostly by working in the home or in a family business. For Jewish women, religious custom made it even more acceptable to play a major economic role. Since the cultural ideal for Jewish men in Eastern Europe was a life devoted to religious study, a woman who could operate a business to support the family while her husband pursued his scholarship earned respect and praise. Although Eastern Europe's economic realities made this ideal possible for very few families, the concept of a married woman as breadwinner was ingrained in traditional culture. Jews who grew up in the coal fields recounted many instances of grandmothers owning or operating small shops in Eastern Europe, New York, or Baltimore, and their daughters who came to the region simply built on their example.[7]

Coal field census records and business directories from 1900 to 1920 listed married Jewish women as owners of clothing stores, dry goods stores, and confectionaries. In later years they owned pharmacies, jewelry stores, and even one auto supply business. Some of these women had husbands who operated their own separate businesses, such as

Blanche Sohn, who owned a confectionary and then a dry goods store while her husband, Eli, operated a saloon and later a clothing store from around 1904 to 1920. When the couple went into business together, she did the buying, according to a 1920 local newspaper item that informed readers, "Mrs. Eli Sohn is in the markets purchasing spring millinery. She will buy largely for the approaching season. Mr. Eli Sohn is painting the front of his store building in a very handsome style." A few women entrepreneurs, such as Bessie Zaltzman, had husbands who either could not or would not support them. More common were widows who took over their late husband's business or started one after his death, sometimes in partnership with grown sons. Mollie Gaskell, widowed in 1912 at age twenty-seven, became one of Williamson, West Virginia's most respected merchants and a Jewish community leader as proprietor of the Williamson Bargain House (under the name M. V. Gaskell). Ethel Catzen Cohen inherited and managed her father's extensive business interests in Northfork, West Virginia, where he had been the chief real estate developer.[8]

Despite the respect local Jewish communities showed to most of these women, Bessie's story reveals it was possible to overstep the boundaries of accepted female behavior. As early as 1902 she became embroiled in a number of legal battles against Jewish businessmen which blazed in the local courts for years. One man tried to take advantage of her weak position as a divorced woman by holding her liable for a loan he had made to her ex-husband. His motivation may have been purely economic, but there is a hint of moral disapproval on the part of her opponents as well. Before her divorce, this man had spread rumors that she was having an affair—rumors that were probably true. Some years later, another Jewish man, whom she had sued over a sick cow she had purchased from him, advised her that she needed to get herself a husband. Her retort: "I don't have to have no husband. I have got good children and I have got good property."[9]

Certainly the Jewish tradition of female entrepreneurship contradicted the modern, middle-class ideal that a woman's place was in the home. After the immigrant generation passed away, it became less common for women to be heavily involved in the family business—or operate their own business—except out of necessity. One woman interviewed for this article acted as her husband's business partner into the 1970s because she enjoyed it and because she had grown up in her parents' family business. Yet she saw herself as an exception. More typical in the post–World War II era was a woman described by her son as "99 percent a homemaker," a woman whose ambition "was to be a good hausfrau." Since she had been forced to quit school in the sixth grade in Baltimore to help her struggling family by working in the needle trade, the middle-class ideal probably came as welcome relief from a life of toil. Nevertheless, in many Jewish coal field families, single daughters continued to work as teachers, stenographers, nurses, and even manager of a local radio station, while a few married women remained active in the family business into the third generation, long after economic security had been achieved. Once a family business became successful, women who did choose to stay involved often had their household duties relieved by a live-in maid (a common presence in middle- and upper-middle-class households in the coal fields and throughout the South).[10]

Interviews with Jews who grew up in the region, men and women now in their seventies and eighties, reveal a sense of pride in their mother's strength, capability, and resourcefulness, as demonstrated to their children by their economic activities. As one man said approvingly, "my mother had a good business head on her." Another remembered his mother as a "bright, feisty little woman" who pragmatically chose to work as a saleslady in another family's dress shop as the best way to earn an income after her husband's early death. This same combination of determination and confidence in helping to meet their families' economic needs would also characterize the efforts of Jewish coal field women to meet the religious and cultural needs of their small communities.[11]

While women's economic activities built on East European customary practices and went against the tide of middle-class American life, their actions in the communal arena would be at odds with Jewish tradition and well in keeping with modern American religious and social trends. Jewish women in Eastern Europe may have been accepted as breadwinners in the marketplace, but their religious role was strictly confined to home and family. Their responsibilities were not trivial; since much of Jewish ritual takes place within the home, women's religious duties were recognized as significant. Nevertheless, their role was clearly subservient to that of men, who carried out the supreme command to study the sacred texts and who went daily to the synagogue to pray. As feminist historians have noted, one of those prayers provides a telling view of the female position in traditional Judaism, as the men expressed their thanks to God for not making them women.[12]

A variety of factors converged to lead Jewish coal field women into the traditionally male communal realm. In the first place, somewhat paradoxically, Jewish immigrant women who settled in the region were more likely than their male counterparts to remain loyal to their traditional upbringing. After all, it was usually their husbands, fathers, and brothers who had made the choice to follow business opportunities rather than remain in the sheltering embrace of Jewish neighborhoods in the cities. Women were often reluctant, or at least had reservations, about leaving their families behind to move to an area where few Jews lived and where it would not be easy to maintain a traditional Jewish life. As one woman said in an interview, "I can't tell you how my mother reacted coming from Brooklyn, New York, to Scarbro, West Virginia." Her mother in fact exclaimed to her husband, "You brought me to a wilderness!"[13]

Economic imperatives would continue to drive the men. Though many of them were attached to the traditions themselves, they were willing to make sacrifices because making a living had to come first. The first ritual to go, of course, was observance of the Sabbath, since Saturdays were the busiest shopping days at the coal fields. Spending the day in prayer, study, and rest was completely out of the question. The men also found it impossible to hold daily prayer services. Also, as Williamson Jewish leader Ida Bank stated in a 1926 speech reviewing the progress of her local congregation, "petty business jealousies" had prevented the men from coming together to address communal needs. Some men did take on religious and communal responsibilities, from merchants who acted as lay rabbis and community leaders to ordained rabbis imported by the local congregations. But women soon became the prime movers in attempts to maintain Jewish identity and practice both within and outside the home.[14]

Their efforts began in the home, where women observed as many rituals as possible. They continued to light candles on the Sabbath and tried to follow the dietary practices of Orthodox Judaism. Difficulties in obtaining kosher meat and other kosher foods led most of them to gradually abandon strict observance, but they continued to prepare traditional meals, especially on the holidays. Some of their strategies were clearly ineffective, if sincere: one man recalls that his mother brought her own knives to the local (non-Jewish) butcher and asked him to use them to carve her cuts of meat. Jews who grew up in the coal fields remember the strenuous attempts their mothers made to keep a Jewish home. Even if the women eventually had to give up various traditions, the effort in itself made a strong impression on their children and went a long way toward reinforcing a Jewish identity. With fathers consumed by work and rarely home, almost all the people interviewed for this article pointed to their mother's influence as being decisive. As one woman typically remarked," [M]y mother instilled a lot of Judaism into us."[15]

The piety of an individual woman inspired one town's Jewish population to take its first steps toward communal organization. Sana Moskovitch Pickus came from Russia to join her three grown sons in Beckley, West Virginia, in 1921, and the small Jewish community held its first religious services in honor of her arrival. The following year, the town's Jewish women organized a religious school for the children, which they operated for more than ten years before the congregation itself was officially founded. Their action was highly typical of Jewish women in other small American towns, both in the coal fields and beyond.[16]

As their concern with maintaining a Jewish way of life in the home spilled into the communal realm, women in small towns often organized religious groups or activities well in advance of the formal establishment of congregations. For example, the Jewish Ladies Guild of Williamson convened in 1913 as the town's first Jewish organization. As one of its early leaders wrote, the Ladies Guild "was organized for social reasons and also to take care of the needy Jewish traveling poor who were very numerous at that time." The three motives that caused Jewish women in the coal fields to come together—to educate their children, to meet charitable needs, and to improve their social life—also typified the objectives that caused Jewish women in other American small towns to coalesce. Mutual aid and organized charity to the Jewish poor were deep-rooted concepts in religious and communal life. Traditionally, men oversaw these functions, but women in small-town America often took them over when the men failed to act. The activities of most of the coal field ladies aid societies started with assistance to transient Jews who were as much of an embarrassment to the Jewish community as anything else; generally, charity took the form of money for a meal and a train ticket out of town. The women also made donations or small loans to local families, Jewish and non-Jewish, that had fallen on hard times. In the context of providing charity, the women could also enjoy social gatherings with other Jewish women—a considerable incentive.[17]

As the women became more organized and expanded their fund raising, their activities reveal stronger assertions of Jewish identity. As a typical example, in the early 1920s the annual beneficiaries of the Hebrew Ladies Aid Society of Welch, West Virginia, included an orphan asylum in Palestine, the Orthodox Jewish Home for the Aged in Cincinnati, and the matzo funds of New York and Baltimore. The women also raised money to help destitute rabbis and other poverty-stricken Jews in the old country, including the "hunger-suffering" sister of Keystone's rabbi. In later years, support for Zionist groups such as Hadassah became prevalent. Contributing to Jewish causes in faraway places, from Baltimore to Israel, kept the women in touch with the currents of modern Jewry and enabled them to keep from feeling isolated in their coal field homes.[18]

But the women recognized that these coal field homes deserved their attention as well and that there were local Jewish issues that desperately needed to be addressed. They soon turned their attention to the critical goal of passing their heritage on to their children. In Beckley this goal provided the motivating force to organize, and other coal field women's groups also considered it a key priority. The Williamson Ladies Guild founded a religious school in 1916—still several years before the congregation officially came into existence. In her 1926 speech, Ida Bank recalled that there were "five children who attended our first Sabbath School and I was their teacher, with no experience in this work, with no instructions, only with the will and ambition to do something for the children along religious lines and to help them on the path to Judaism." Another leader, Ida Nabe, identified the three main functions of the group: "First, religious instruction of our children; second, the support of our charities and institutions; third, helpful in all things congregational." A Jewish man who grew up in Logan, West Virginia, recalled that "the little [religious] education we had" was provided by women and the occasional visiting rabbi. The Welch congregation had a local rabbi to instruct their children, but he needed the occasional assistance of the women, whose role was "to make the children be good."[19]

Ida Nabe's phrase, "helpful in all things congregational," is misleading, since it sounds more like a supportive than a leading role. In actuality, after seeing to their children's education, the coal field women's groups embarked on an ambitious agenda to promote full-fledged Jewish congregations with regular religious services, programs, and, most important, places of worship. The women poured their energy into raising funds to build synagogues. They also organized and cooked for the religious/social events that held communities together: Hanukkah parties, Purim festivals, community seders. They organized trips to large cities to buy kosher and holiday foods. They made sure that the single men in their midst had a family to go to during Jewish holidays and they hosted visiting rabbis in their homes. When new Jewish families moved into town, they immediately visited the wives and applied peer pressure if necessary to get them to join in. They were not above a little arm twisting in their efforts to maintain group cohesion; members who missed meetings without a valid excuse received a fine.[20]

The progression from an initial concern with charity to religious education of the children to congregational development—in other words, the evolution from Ladies Aid Society to Temple Sisterhood—was the common pattern of American Jewish women's groups of the first half of the twentieth century. Some historians, such as Jenna Weissman Joselit and William Toll, downplay the sisterhood role as being essentially auxiliary, while others, such as Jacob Rader Marcus and Sherry Blanton, recognize it as crucial to the very existence of Jewish communities in small towns. Beth Wenger notes that the role of Jewish women in congregational development was indeed significant but often masked because it took place offstage. She points out that Jewish women served as "unseen caretakers of communal needs. . . . It was not uncommon for women's groups to raise money and then allow male-dominated synagogue boards to allocate the funds."[21]

Research from the coal fields supports the view that women's role in communal organization was critical, not merely auxiliary, yet, as Wenger suggests, often hidden. As elsewhere, men were the ones who actually incorporated Jewish institutions, spoke at dedication ceremonies for the newly built synagogues, and served on the boards. Certainly, some men did play a strong role in organizing religious activities and raising funds. But they often needed considerable prodding, and women were a necessary behind-the-scenes force. For example, in Welch the men had a mutual aid society of their own. Yet the ladies, in a 1919 meeting, voted to help the men "in making their meetings more interesting and get the members to attend the meetings better." As might be guessed, this mostly involved serving meals. The men's society revived but eventually disbanded. Later, after the synagogue was built, the newly named Welch Sisterhood kept things together, since, as one woman put it at the time, the men "have had no real organization, only a few men taking any interest in Temple matters at all."[22]

So out of necessity, with the same pragmatism that guided their economic behavior, women moved their religious activities out of the home and into the communal realm previously denied them by tradition. With men spending most of their time on their businesses, Jewish coal field women began to see themselves as the guardians of religion, and the men were hard-pressed to disagree. The women were participating in what Wenger has termed a "new, gender-based reorganization of Jewish communal life" that signified a "radical" alteration in women's traditional role. Yet in the coal fields, as elsewhere, this reorganization was not particularly controversial. For one thing, as long as women did not demand public recognition for their leadership, they did not overtly disturb preexisting notions about the proper communal power structure. Their new responsibilities could be seen simply as an extension of their customary task as nurturers and therefore, according to Joselit, "did not challenge prevailing assumptions."[23]

More important, women's new role conformed to prevailing American social patterns. In society at large, men had mostly abdicated religious leadership in their full-time pursuit of capitalist success. Their abdication was accompanied by what historians such as Paula Hyman have referred to as the "feminization" of religious life in America and other industrial societies. Religion now fell into the domestic sphere where women reigned. Thus, for Jewish men and women anxious to Americanize without abandoning their religion and identity, the emergence of women's communal role was a natural and welcome occurrence.[24]

Accompanying this development was a shift away from Orthodox Judaism and toward Reform Judaism, with its much less restrictive view of women. Almost all of the coal field congregations moved from Orthodox to Reform during the 1920s, and the expanded activities of women certainly influenced this process. Yet even while breaking new ground, women clung to tenets of traditional Judaism that felt right to them. The Williamson Sisterhood, for example, sponsored an annual religious service in the 1920s which was led entirely by women. This surely would have been considered ridiculous in Eastern Europe, if not dangerously revolutionary. Yet the same women focused their education efforts on boys to make sure they were prepared for the traditional bar mitzvah. Many of them still tried their best to keep a kosher home, a practice considered obsolete by most followers of Reform Judaism at that time. In 1922 the Welch Sisterhood decided against affiliating with the Reform Movement's Federation of Temple Sisterhoods, instead opting to join the Women's League of the United Synagogue of America because "this league is Orthodox to its utmost." The following year the women changed their minds and joined the Reform group. Pragmatism had won out; the Federation had a West Virginia state affiliate that offered more in the way of resources and support.[25]

Such contradictory and ambivalent behavior suggests that the process of change was not completely free of conflict. And despite societal support for women's increased communal involvement, some tension did occur along gender lines. In Logan controversy erupted when women tried to move their role from behind the scenes to the forefront, asking to be recognized as members of the congregation and entitled to seats on the board. The February 1925 minutes of the congregation, kept by Secretary Harry Stern, read as follows: "[The Sisterhood ladies said they] wanted to become members of our congregation and assist us in our work. They could not state how they could benefit us. This brought up considerable discussion pro and con with the result that it was decided to table this matter . . . until the Sisterhood could bring someone here who would be able to tell us more clearly the benefits of having the ladies of the Jewish community as active members of the B'nai El Congregation." The men's response shows not only that there were boundaries women still would not be permitted to cross, but that their previous contributions, although critical, had gone unrecognized. The women knew what to do about this, however. The following month the minutes note that the community seder normally held every year had been canceled, since "it would work a hardship on the ladies." After that the minutes record increased consultation with the sisterhood on matters such as taking care of a visiting rabbi and renting a permanent space to hold services. The men still would not accept the official membership of women, but voted to have joint meetings with the sisterhood board on "matters of importance."[26]

Communal activities helped immigrant Jewish women adjust to a coal field environment that many of them had found alien on first arrival. The opportunity to socialize with women of similar background and to engage in cultural expressions that were important to them mitigated the consequences of living far from the centers of Jewish life and contributed to their willingness to remain in the region. Their daughters, who grew up in the coal fields, participated in Jewish women's groups on reaching adulthood. Communal involvement helped them maintain an identity that had been instilled by their parents. This generational continuity was necessary for Jewish communities to continue to thrive in the face of Americanization and integration into coal field society.

Assimilatory pressures beckoned because, despite the feelings of displacement that new arrivals may have experienced, Jews were far from unwelcome in their new surroundings. The emerging middle class of coal field merchants and professionals was too small to reject any potential members. They saw Jewish families as fellow contributors to the development of the region—people who brought skills and networks that were needed to progress. Indeed, Jewish families were among the founders of several coal field towns. Jewish men joined other merchants as small-town boosters and contributed to town development through their commercial and civic activities. And yet their religious and cultural distinctiveness in an area of devout Christianity meant that Jews could never be complete "insiders," even if they wanted to be. Torn between assimilating into middle-class society and maintaining their separate identity—and aware that by remaining religiously and culturally different, they would always be viewed by their neighbors as not quite fitting in—coal field Jews developed strategies to negotiate the subtle terrain between difference and belonging. Their communal organizations represented one key strategy: the congregations, the B'nai B'rith lodges, and the women's groups helped to mediate between the Jewish collective and the surrounding society.[27]

The ladies aid societies and sisterhoods enabled Jewish coal field women to express their separate identity, yet in ways that were similar and acceptable to their middle-class Christian counterparts, since women's church groups were extremely popular at the time. Without their own organizations they found themselves assimilating perhaps further than they intended: Jewish women in Welch first belonged to the Women's Missionary Society of the Methodist Episcopal Church before organizing the Welch Hebrew Ladies Aid Society in 1915. With their own communal groups facilitating their interaction, Jewish women could freely and respectably join with other middle-class women in social clubs and charity work. Their organizational activities extended beyond their own community, for example to Salvation Army rummage sales, Red Cross flood relief efforts, and distributing annual Christmas baskets to the poor during the Depression. They also held events to promote Jewish-Christian understanding and to educate their neighbors, who often showed considerable ignorance about Judaism. The Williamson Sisterhood held an annual "Neighbor Night," when each member invited one of their Christian friends to Friday night services. The Welch Sisterhood participated in the Welch United Council of Churches in the late 1940s and early 1950s, although the Williamson Sisterhood bowed out of their local branch in 1947, having decided, according to one leader, that "we have no place in this organization."[28]

Despite this hint that interfaith relations were not always pleasant, the coal field version of Jewish women's religious articulation could take some rather ecumenical forms. In the 1920s, before the Beckley congregation acquired its own building, the sisterhood "aided in the holding of religious services . . . at the Beckley Presbyterian Church, with a non-Jewish choir, and with a student rabbi from the Hebrew Union Col-

lege." In preparing to furnish their new temple in 1922, Welch Sisterhood members visited some of the town's newer churches to see how
Christian women had furnished *their* places of worship. Things got a little ridiculous in 1935 when the Williamson Sisterhood minutes saw fit to
report that "the flowers in the temple on Easter Sunday were sent by Mr.
Hammond of the Mark Russell Seed Co."[29]

While most socializing occurred within their own group, among people they felt entirely at ease with, Jewish women did not remain sheltered
behind their ethnic associations. Indeed, some Gentiles became full-
fledged sisterhood members; the *History of the Beckley Jewish Community*
acknowledges the active contributions of women "who had married Jewish men, either with or without becoming formally attached [through
conversion] to Judaism." Most Jewish women mixed easily with other residents of coal field towns, and those from pioneering families were ac-
corded particular respect. In a 1920 eulogy of one such woman, the
Welch newspaper stated: "Mrs. [Pauline] Josephy was one of the most
popular ladies of the city and enjoyed a broad friendship. She was active
in business and charitable circles and her untimely death caused a shadow of sincere sorrow to sweep the entire city. . . . She had been a resident
of Welch for a number of years and assisted her husband in the conduct
of a flourishing store here." Mrs. Josephy's friends in the Methodist
women's society (of which she had formerly been a member) passed a
resolution expressing its "love for and appreciation of [her] life and
beautiful character." Local newspapers also noted the contributions of
Jewish women to civic life and what passed for "high society" in these
rugged little towns. In 1922 the Welch newspaper praised the "delight-
ful" dinner served by the Welch Sisterhood at a Chamber of Commerce
meeting. (On the menu: chicken fricassee, string beans, mashed pota-
toes, celery, liver salad, pickles, hot rolls, and French pudding with wine
sauce.) A 1933 society column item called a sisterhood event "the most
brilliant social affair to be held in Welch this season."[30]

Certainly this congenial atmosphere helped Jewish women become
comfortable with their lives in the coal fields. For some, however, interaction with non-Jews had its dangers. One woman who grew up in the
region admitted that her mother did not want her to have gentile
friends, and especially discouraged her friendship with boys, fearing that
it would lead to intermarriage. Another woman stopped speaking to her
daughter for several years after she married a local non-Jewish man.
Eventually intermarriage became a fact of life that the older generation

was forced to accept although their efforts to deter it were at least partly successful. Many second-generation coal field Jews stated in interviews that despite their friendships with non-Jews, their parents had passed on to them a strong aversion to intermarriage that caused them to make special efforts to find Jewish mates.[31]

For at least three generations of Jewish women, communal work helped resolve the tension between the urge to fit in and Americanize, and the urge to preserve their cultural heritage and lead a Jewish life. Communal activities served as both expressions of Jewish values and ways to interact with non-Jews. Their organizations were in perfect social conformity with those of the churchwomen around them, thus allowing them to retain a distinct identity and blend in at the same time. Indeed, as many historians of small-town American Jewry have pointed out, forming their own religious groups helped legitimate the Jewish population in the eyes of the larger society, especially in the religion-soaked atmosphere of the South. That motivation no doubt pertained to the coal fields as well; the interfaith activities of Jewish women's groups reveal a desire to interact with gentile women on equal terms. Alternatively, women's communal activities enabled them to enter into larger coal field society, have social intercourse with others, yet have a familiar base to return to. This base provided a refuge not just from assimilation, but also from undercurrents of anti-Semitism which were certainly not absent and were occasionally felt by Jews who grew up in the region. Communal solidarity also helped assuage whatever underlying discomfort may have been caused by a ubiquitous Christianity that in some of its forms could be alienating or even threatening.[32]

Despite Jewish women's successful efforts to foster community, factors undermined Jewish community life. Women who grew up in the region often went away to college (partly motivated by the desire to find Jewish husbands), and most of them did not return. They were replaced, in a demographic sense, when local Jewish men who went off to college brought wives back with them when they came home to enter the family business. Ultimately, however, economic conditions would prove fatal to Jewish life in the coal fields. Starting in the mid-1950s, a drastic and sustained decline in the coal field economy caused local businesses to suffer and led young people to make their lives elsewhere. Of the nine coal field congregations, most disappeared by the 1980s, though two still remain today. But for the first half of the century, Jewish women's communal, economic, and social activities helped carve out a place for Jewish communities in the coal fields. Their efforts advanced the cause of Jewish continuity by instilling a Jewish identity that persists in their descendants, wherever they may live.[33]

Notes

Research for this article was funded in part by a Starkoff Fellowship from the American Jewish Archives, Cincinnati, Ohio, and a West Virginia Humanities Council Fellowship.

1. Will Book 6, 496, Deed Books 36, 79, 92, 93, 101, 102, 105, 112, 132, 159, Circuit Court records 1909–1910, McDowell County Courthouse, Welch, W.Va.; U.S. Census Bureau, Manuscript Census, McDowell County, W.Va., 1900; Louis Zaltzman, letter to Abraham I. Shinedling, reprinted in Abraham I. Shinedling, *West Virginia Jewry: Origins and History, 1850–1958* (Philadelphia: Maurice Jacobs, Inc., 1963), 986.

2. On the history of central Appalachia and the development of its coal fields, see Mary Beth Pudup, Dwight Billings, and Altina Waller, eds., *Appalachia in the Making: The Mountain South in the Nineteenth Century* (Chapel Hill: University of North Carolina Press, 1995); Ronald D. Eller, *Miners, Millhands, and Mountaineers: Industrialization of the Appalachian South, 1880–1930* (Knoxville: University of Tennessee Press, 1982); Randall G. Lawrence, "Appalachian Metamorphosis: Industrializing Society on the Central Appalachian Plateau, 1860–1913" (Ph.D. diss. Duke University, 1983); Jerry Bruce Thomas, "Coal Country: The Rise of the Southern Smokeless Coal Industry and its Effect on Area Development, 1872–1910" (Ph.D. diss., University of North Carolina, 1971). On the tendency of some East European Jewish immigrants to journey beyond America's large metropolitan areas, see for example Joel Perlmann, "Beyond New York: The Occupations of Russian Jewish Immigrants in Providence, R.I. and Other Small Jewish Communities, 1900–1915," *American Jewish History* 72 (March 1983): 369–94; Ewa Morawska, *Insecure Prosperity: Small-Town Jews in Industrial America, 1890–1940* (Princeton: Princeton University Press, 1996). On the economic niche constructed by coal field Jews, see Deborah R. Weiner,"Middlemen of the Coalfields: The Role of Jews in the Economy of Southern West Virginia Coal Towns, 1890–1950," *Journal of Appalachian Studies* 4 (Spring 1998): 29–56. The nine coal field congregations were located in Beckley, Keystone, Kimball, Logan, Welch, and Williamson, West Virginia; Harlan and Middlesboro, Kentucky; and Pocahontas, Virginia. A tenth congregation was located on the edge of the coal fields in the regional center of Bluefield, West Virginia. Shinedling, *West Virginia Jewry;* Harlan, Kentucky, Congregation B'nai Sholom Records (includes congregation, sisterhood, and B'nai B'rith), Small Collections, The Ja-

cob Rader Marcus Center of the American Jewish Archives, Cincinnati, Ohio (hereafter AJA);"Student Rabbi Survey, 1935–1936," Hebrew Union College Collection (AJA).

3. On the maintenance of Jewish identity in small-town America, see Lee Shai Weissbach, "East European Immigrants and the Image of Jews in the Small Town South," *American Jewish History* 85 (September 1997): 231–62; Leonard Rogoff, "Synagogue and Jewish Church: A Congregational History of North Carolina," *Southern Jewish History* 1 (1998): 43–81; Abraham Karp, *Haven and Home: A History of the Jews in America* (New York: Schocken Books, 1985); Marshall Sklare, *America's Jews* (New York: Random House, 1971); Abraham D. Lavender, ed., *A Coat of Many Colors: Jewish Subcommunities in the United States* (Westport, Conn.: Greenwood Press, 1977). On Jewish identity in the coal fields, see Frank Anthony Fear, "The Quest for Saliency: Patterns of Jewish Communal Organization in Three Appalachian Small Towns," (master's thesis, West Virginia University, 1972); and Jerome Paul David, "Jewish Consciousness in the Small Town: A Sociological Study of Jewish Identification," (master's thesis, Hebrew Union College, 1974).

4. On the economic conditions faced by coal field merchants, see Weiner, "Middlemen of the Coalfields."

5. John Bodnar, *The Transplanted: A History of Immigrants in Urban America* (Bloomington: Indiana University Press, 1985); Judith E. Smith, *Family Connections: A History of Italian and Jewish Immigrant Lives in Providence, Rhode Island, 1900–1940* (Albany: SUNY Press, 1985); Charlotte Baum, Paula Hyman, and Sonya Michel, *The Jewish Woman in America* (New York: Dial Press, 1976); Morawska, *Insecure Prosperity*. On the economic activities of Jewish family members in the coal fields, see U.S. Census Bureau, Manuscript Census, Fayette, Logan, McDowell, Mingo Counties, W.Va., and Tazewell County, Va., 1900, 1910, 1920; *Beckley City Directory 1932* (Pittsburgh: R. L. Polk & Co., 1932); Williamson, *West Virginia, City Directory, 1952* (Chillicothe, Ohio: Mullin-Kille Co.) and *Williamson Daily News*, 1952; Shinedling, *West Virginia Jewry*, 512.

6. Martha Albert, interview with author, Williamson, W.Va., November 8, 1996; Gail Bank, phone interview with author, September 28 and October 4, 1998; Sidney Fink, interview with author, Beckley, W.Va., October 12, 1996; Bernard Gottlieb, interview with author, Clarksburg, W.Va., November 5, 1996; Reva Totz Hecker, interview with author, Baltimore, Md., November 5, 1998; Emanuel Katzen, interview with author and Maryanne Reed, Princeton, W.Va., May 30, 1996; Lou Mankoff, interview with author and Maryanne Reed, Williamson, W.Va., March 1996; Ira and Mary Jo Sopher, interview with author, Beckley, W.Va., October 13, 1996; Jean Abrams Wein, interview with author, Beckley, W.Va., October 13, 1996; Sam and Harvey Weiner, interview with au-

thor, Logan, W.Va., November 8, 1996; Milton Koslow, interview with author, Charleston, W.Va., May 13, 1998; Irving Alexander, "Wilcoe: People of a Coal Town," *Goldenseal* 16 (Spring 1990): 28–35; U.S. Census Bureau, Manuscript Census, McDowell and Logan Counties, W.Va., Tazewell County, Va., 1920; *Beckley City Directory 1940* (Pittsburgh: R. L. Polk & Co., 1940). Manuel Pickus, interview with author, Charleston, W.Va., May 18, 1998; Betty Ofsa Rosen, interview with author and Maryanne Reed, Williamson, W.Va., May 28, 1996; Betty Schuchat Gottlieb, interview with author, Parkersburg, W.Va., December 18, 1997.

7. Bodnar, *The Transplanted;* Smith, *Family Connections;* Thomas Kessner and Betty Boyd Caroli, "New Immigrant Women at Work: Italians and Jews in New York City, 1880–1905," *Journal of Ethnic Studies* 5, no. 4 (Winter 1978): 19–31; Marc Zborowski and Elisabeth Herzog, *Life Is with People: The Jewish Little-Town of Eastern Europe* (New York: International Universities Press, 1952); Baum, et al., *The Jewish Woman in America;* Paula E. Hyman, *Gender and Assimilation in Modern Jewish History* (Seattle: University of Washington Press, 1995); Irene D. Neu, "The Jewish Businesswoman in America," *American Jewish Historical Quarterly* 66 (1976–1977): 137–54.

8. U.S. Census Bureau, Manuscript Census, McDowell and Mingo Counties, 1910, 1920; *Beckley City Directory, 1932, 1940;* Kitts City and Coalfield Directory, 1904 (Bluefield, W.Va.: City Directory Co., 1904); *Bluefield City Directory, 1910–1911* (Pittsburgh: R. L. Polk & Co., 1910); *Bluefield City Directory, 1915–1916* (Pittsburgh: R. L. Polk & Co., 1914); *West Virginia State Gazetteer and Business Directory, 1900–1901, 1904–1905, 1910–1911, 1914–1915* (Pittsburgh: R. L. Polk & Co.); *Williamson Daily News,* February 6, 1920, p. 4; Shinedling, *West Virginia Jewry,* 803, 1102, 1302; Abraham I. Shinedling and Manuel Pickus, *History of the Beckley Jewish Community* (Beckley, W. Va.: Biggs-Johnston-Withrow, 1955), 20, 44, 56; Martha Albert interview.

9. In 1902 Sam Katzen sued Jake Shore for slander for spreading the rumor that he and Bessie (separated from her husband but not yet divorced) were living together. Bessie and Jake were already engaged in a property dispute by that time. Sam eventually dropped his suit and paid all court costs, which suggests that there was some truth behind the rumors. One lawsuit that Bessie was involved in ended up in the West Virginia Supreme Court, which overturned a decision against her and sent the matter back for retrial. While the outcome of most of her court battles could not be ascertained, it appears that at least one case was settled out of court after many years, perhaps because of the weariness of all concerned. Circuit Court records 1902, 1909, 1910, Deed Book 102, McDowell County Courthouse; "Zolsman vs. Totz," *West Virginia Supreme Court of Appeals Book* 74 (June 1914): 604–06.

10. Baum, et al., *The Jewish Woman in America;* Hyman, *Gender and Assimilation in Modern Jewish History;* Smith, *Family Connections;* Neu, "The Jewish Businesswoman in America"; Eli Evans, *The Provincials: A Personal History of Jews in the South* (New York: Simon & Schuster, 1997), 255–62; Martha Albert interview; Sidney Fink interview; Milton Koslow interview; Betty Ofsa Rosen interview; Shinedling, *West Virginia Jewry,* 1007, 1294; Rose Marino, *Welch and Its People* (Marceline, Mo.: Walsworth Press, 1985); Shinedling and Pickus, *History of the Beckley Jewish Community,* 20, 51, 64, 67; *Beckley City Directory, 1940; Williamson, West Virginia, City Directory, 1952.*

11. Bernard Gottlieb interview; Milton Koslow interview.

12. Zborowski and Herzog, *Life Is with People;* Baum, et al., *The Jewish Woman in America;* Hyman, *Gender and Assimilation in Modern Jewish History;* Jenna Weissman Joselit, "The Special Sphere of the Middle-Class American Jewish Woman: The Synagogue Sisterhood, 1890–1940," in *The American Synagogue: A Sanctuary Transformed,* Jack Wertheimer, ed. (New York: Cambridge University Press, 1987), 206–30.

13. Jean Abrams Wein interview. In her memoir *The Jew Store* (Chapel Hill: Algonquin Books, 1998), Stella Suberman offers an eloquent description of her mother's reservations about leaving behind family and the Jewish community to accompany her husband to western Tennessee, where he opened a store.

14. Williamson, West Virginia, B'nai Israel Sisterhood Records, 1913–1953, Microfilm Reel 348–49, AJA; Harlan congregation records; Shinedling and Pickus, *History of the Beckley Jewish Community;* Shinedling, *West Virginia Jewry.* As East European Jews adapted to American work patterns, the cessation of Sabbath observance of course became a widespread phenomenon throughout the country, but especially in small towns where no internal Jewish economy existed. See Gerald Sorin, *A Time for Building: The Third Migration, 1880–1920* (Baltimore: Johns Hopkins University Press, 1992), 180–81; Morawska, *Insecure Prosperity,* 155–56.

15. Early on a few coal field towns had Orthodox rabbis who served as *schochets.* One or two Jewish merchants trained in *kashrut* took on the job of slaughtering chickens, but not all families had access to these sources of kosher meat. Some families tried ordering meat from Cincinnati, Ohio, or Charleston, West Virginia, but it often arrived spoiled. Lou Mankoff interview; Bernard Gottlieb interview; Milton Koslow interview; Jean Abrams Wein interview; Manuel Pickus interview; Sidney Fink interview; Reva Totz Hecker interview. The phenomenon of "kitchen Judaism" as an important component of ethnic identity has been commented upon by many authors. See for example Morawska, *Insecure Prosperity,* 158.

16. Shinedling and Pickus, *History of the Beckley Jewish Community,* 81–86.

17. Williamson Sisterhood records; Harlan Sisterhood records; Welch, West Virginia, Congregation Emanuel records (includes Hebrew Ladies Aid Society, sisterhood, and B'nai B'rith records), Manuscript Collection, Box 379, AJA; Logan, West Virginia, Congregation B'nai El records (includes congregation, sisterhood, and B'nai B'rith records), Microfilm Reel 2125, AJA; Shinedling and Pickus, *History of the Beckley Jewish Community*, 127–28; Marino, *Welch and Its People*; Sherry Blanton, "Lives of Quiet Affirmation: The Jewish Women of Early Anniston, Alabama," *Southern Jewish History* 2 (1999): 25–53; William Toll "A Quiet Revolution: Jewish Women's Clubs and the Widening Female Sphere, 1870–1920," *American Jewish Archives* 41 (Spring/Summer 1989): 7–26; Jacob Rader Marcus, *The American Jewish Woman: A Documentary History* (New York: Ktav, 1981); Hyman, *Gender and Assimilation in Modern Jewish History*.

18. Sisterhood records, Williamson, Welch, Logan, Harlan; Shinedling and Pickus, *History of the Beckley Jewish Community*, 127.

19. Shinedling and Pickus, *History of the Beckley Jewish Community*, 86; Sisterhood records, Welch and Williamson; Sam Weiner interview.

20. Sisterhood records, Williamson, Welch, Logan, Harlan.

21. Joselit, "The Special Sphere"; Toll, "A Quiet Revolution"; Blanton, "Lives of Quiet Affirmation"; Beth S. Wenger, "Jewish Women and Voluntarism: Beyond the Myth of Enablers," *American Jewish History* 79 (1989–1990): 16–36. Marcus asserts, "it cannot be overemphasized: the synagogue—the Jewish community, too—was, and still is, dependent upon women." (*The American Jewish Woman: A Documentary History*, 777).

22. Sisterhood records, Williamson, Welch, Logan, and Harlan; Shinedling and Pickus, *History of the Beckley Jewish Community;* Shinedling, *West Virginia Jewry*.

23. Wenger, "Jewish Women and Voluntarism," 17, 21; Joselit, "The Special Sphere," 223; Toll, "A Quiet Revolution." One clue that women did not realize the radical nature of their foray into new gender territory was that they continued to refer to themselves by their husband's name in all their organizational records. For the historian, some detective work is needed to discover that "Mrs. Hyman Bank" was really Ida. Sherry Blanton notes the same phenomenon in her study of the women of Anniston, Alabama.

24. Hyman, *Gender and Assimilation in Modern Jewish History;* Wenger, "Jewish Women and Voluntarism"; Joselit, "The Special Sphere"; Toll, "A Quiet Revolution." Hyman analyzes the paradox of Jewish women as "guardians of religion," pointing out how the role was at the same time tradition-centered and modern, both assimilatory and nonassimilatory. By upholding tradition in the home, women conformed to family-centered notions of modern bourgeois religion; by their communal activities they attempted to preserve Jewish distinctiveness and

Jewish culture while participating in larger American trends that ran counter to longstanding Jewish practice (see pages 26–31).

25. "Jewish Women Hold Services," *Mingo Republican,* December 3, 1926; Shinedling and Pickus, *History of the Beckley Jewish Community;* congregation records, Logan, Harlan, Welch.

26. Logan congregation minutes, 1925.

27. See Mary Beth Pudup, "Town and Country in the Transformation of Appalachian Kentucky," in Pudup, Billings, and Waller, eds., *Appalachia in the Making: The Mountain South in the Nineteenth Century,* 270–96, on the welcoming attitude that coal field local elites showed to newcomers whom they considered to be fellow boosters. An investigation of coal field newspapers from the first three decades of the century uncovered numerous articles praising the commercial and civic endeavors of local Jewish merchants. See Weiner, "Middlemen of the Coalfields." Almost all of the people interviewed for this article expressed some version of the "insider-outsider" dichotomy. Many dismissed it as relatively unimportant to their lives, but for others it resulted in an ambivalence that emerged as they struggled to explain the subtle contradictions involved in their relations with non-Jews. Immigration historians have discussed how ethnic-based organizations, far from isolating their members and promoting separatism, actually aid in the assimilation process by mediating between old and new environments and helping immigrants adapt to their new homes. See for example Bodnar, *The Transplanted.*

28. Sisterhood records, Logan, Welch, Williamson. On Jewish communal groups mirroring middle-class Christian groups, see Toll, "A Quiet Revolution"; Hyman, *Gender and Assimilation in Modern Jewish History;* Rogoff, "Synagogue and Jewish Church."

29. Shinedling and Pickus, *History of the Beckley Jewish Community,* 127; Sisterhood records, Welch and Williamson. Evidently, the non-Jewish choir was not a particular innovation of Beckley Jews; according to Sherry Blanton, the Anniston temple choir "has been exclusively composed of Christians." ("Lives of Quiet Affirmation," 46).

30. Shinedling and Pickus, *History of the Beckley Jewish Community,* 130; *McDowell Recorder,* September 3 and 24, 1920; *McDowell Recorder,* January 20, 1922; *Welch Daily News,* October 24, 1933.

31. Jean Abrams Wein interview; Reva Totz Hecker interview; Betty Gottlieb interview; Bernard Gottlieb interview; Sam and Harvey Weiner interview; Gail Bank interview; Sidney Fink interview. An undetermined percentage of coal field Jews did discontinue their association with Judaism and the Jewish community, either because of intermarriage or for other reasons. Interviewees could name several individuals and families who, for all practical purposes, had

"stopped being Jews." However, their number was far too small to threaten the existence of coal field Jewish communities.

32. On Jewish communal organization as a path to legitimacy in small-town society, see Evans, *The Provincials*, 93; Toll,"A Quiet Revolution"; Rogoff, "Synagogue and Jewish Church." Interviews with coal field Jews reveal an overall attitude that denied the existence of anti-Semitism yet acknowledged that Jews could be made to feel different by the larger society, sometimes uncomfortably so. Also, local Christian radio shows, attempts to impose prayer in the public schools, and other manifestations of aggressive Christianity occasionally disturbed members of the Jewish coal field population.

33. For details on the decline of Jewish coal field communities, see Shinedling, *West Virginia Jewry*, and Weiner, "Middlemen of the Coalfields."

6

The Dixie Diaspora

The "Loss" of the Small Southern Jewish Community[1]

Ira M. Sheskin

The major purpose of this chapter is to describe recent changes in the geographic distribution of the Jewish population of the U.S. South and to discuss competing theories as to why small southern Jewish communities have been declining over the past few decades. First, this chapter discusses the increase in Jewish population of the South Census Division, from 330,000 in 1937 to 1,264,000 in 1997. However, when one defines a "Jewish South," omitting Florida and Maryland/DC, the increase is not nearly as striking, and most of it is spatially concentrated in Atlanta, Dallas, Houston, and northern Virginia. Second, this chapter examines the geographic distribution of the Jewish population in the South in 1997. At the MSA scale, Southeast Florida (507,000) and the Washington/Baltimore corridor (244,000) are the two largest centers. Atlanta (77,000), Dallas (45,000), and Houston (42,000) can be seen as secondary centers. Third, this chapter discusses the significant gains made by some larger metropolitan areas and the loss of small southern Jewish communities. By 1997, 44 southern Jewish communities that had existed in 1960 had ceased to exist, or had dropped below 100 members. More than 20 other small (100–499 person) Jewish communities lost population during this period. Only six small Jewish communities (three in Florida) showed significant growth. Finally, the chapter examines the history of anti-Semitism in the South, the changing occupational structure of southern Jews, the intermarriage and assimilation of the southern Jewish population, and the general population decline of small southern towns. All these factors help provide explanation for the decline of the Jewish population in small southern towns.

Introduction

American Jewish history is often said to commence with the migration of 23 Jews from Brazil to New Amsterdam in 1654. Yet much of the early history of Jews in America is not a history of the Northeast, but of the South. The first known Jew in North America was Joachim Gaunse, a mining technologist from Prague, who settled for one year (1585) at Roanoke Island, Virginia, to serve as a metallurgist in the colony founded by Sir Walter Raleigh. The earliest synagogues were to be found not only in New Amsterdam, Newport (RI), and Philadelphia, but also in Savannah, New Orleans, and Charleston. (Congregation Kahal Kadosh Beth Elohim was founded in 1749 and is the second oldest congregation in the country.)

The earliest Jewish settlers in the South were mostly of Sephardic origin. Sephardic Jews are those whose ancestors came from Spain and were expelled in 1492 during the Spanish Inquisition. Many Sephardic Jews migrated to the Ottoman Empire, whose Sultan welcomed Jews expelled from Spain. In contrast, Ashkenazic Jews are those who trace their heritage to other parts of Europe, particularly Eastern Europe. Some differences exist in customs and in the worship service between the two major groups. While friction has existed between the two groups at various times and in various places, such friction is relatively rare in 20th century America.

The first Jewish settlers in the South were a group of 42 who came from London's Sephardic community in 1733 to settle in Georgia, although this settlement had dissipated by 1740. During the first decade of the 1800s, Charleston, South Carolina, had a Jewish population of about 500 and was the largest, wealthiest, and most cultured Jewish community in the United States (Gribetz, 1993). One of the earliest examples of an American Jewish self-help group was the Hebrew Orphan Society of Charleston, organized in 1801. It was also in Charleston in 1824 that the first attempt occurred to establish a Reform Jewish congregation, an experiment that lasted only until 1833. In Baltimore, in 1842, the country's first enduring Reform congregation was established.

It was not until the middle of the 1800s that German (Ashkenazi) Jews arrived in the South, mostly in connection with the cotton industry (Glanz, 1974). When the large migration of Eastern European Jews to the United States began, the vast majority of the 2,326,458 Jewish migrants to the United States from 1881–1924 settled in the Northeast. Thus, the percentage of American Jews living in the South declined rapidly. It was not until after World War II that Jews originally from Eastern Europe (Ashkenazi Jews) migrated in large numbers from the Northeast and Midwest to major southern cities as part of the general movement of Americans to the Sunbelt, leading to the significant expansion of the Jewish population discussed in this chapter (Sheskin, 2000a).

In an introduction to five articles on Jews in the South, Lavender (1977) noted that little sociological and historical attention has been paid to southern Jewry. Classic works on the topic include Dinnerstein and Pallson (1973), Golden (1974), Kagonoff and Urofsky (1979), and Procter, Schmier, and Stern (1984). This situation has improved somewhat in the past two decades, particularly with the republication of Evans' (1997) history of southern Jewry. Some additional interest has been shown by the building of Jewish museums in such places as Atlanta, Miami, Jackson (MS), and Utica (MS).

Geographers have generally ignored southern Jews. Perhaps this is because Jews are such a small percentage of southerners (1.4%) and because, at least until recently, southern Jews were a small percentage of all American Jews. No references to southern Jews could be found in the past 20 volumes of the *Southeastern Geographer*. Even Heatwole's (1985) article on the "Unchurched in the Southeast, 1980" fails to connect the fact that a number of counties with high percentages of unchurched persons also have a high percentage of Jews. (Jews tend to join synagogues at lower rates than Christians join churches.) A number of articles on migration to Florida fail to mention the fact that a good percentage of that migration has been Jewish. Even Hartshorn's (1997) "The Changed South, 1947–1997," which discusses ethnic changes in the South, fails to mention the significant growth of the Jewish population. The only known geographic works on Jews in the South are the 14 demographic studies of southern Jewish communities, mostly of Florida communities, by Sheskin (1982, 1987, 1992, 1993b, 1994a, 1994c, 1995a, 1995b, 1997a, 1997b, 1999b; Sheskin, Ukeles, and Miller, 1996a, 1996b; Tobin and Sheskin, 1991).

Data Sources

Due in part to the doctrine of the separation of church and state, data on religious preference have not been collected by the Census Bureau since 1957. Thus, unlike most other ethnic groups, a number of different techniques, all of which have significant drawbacks, have been used to derive recent estimates of the Jewish population in medium and large urban areas. These include procedures involving absences from public school on major Jewish holidays, death-rate methods, the use of surrogate census variables (such as percentage Russian/Polish origin), random-digit-dialing survey techniques, and methods using Distinctive Jewish Names (DJNs) (Sheskin, 1998b). An extensive discussion of the counting of Jewish populations may be found in Kosmin, Ritterband, and Scheckner (1988). A discussion of random-digit-dialing (RDD) telephone surveys as a method of estimating the size of Jewish populations may be found in Varady and Mantel (1982).

For smaller Jewish communities, use of such sophisticated techniques as RDD would be cost prohibitive. Rather, the Research Department of the United Jewish Communities (the central coordinating body of the organized Jewish community, formed in 1999 by the merger of the Council of Jewish Federations, the United Jewish Appeal, and the United Israel Appeal) simply sends a form to a rabbi, professional, or lay leader in each community. This person then makes a "guesstimate" of the Jewish population based upon the number of Jewish households who are affiliated in some way with the community and an estimate of the number who are not. These numbers are published annually in the *American Jewish Year Book*.

Because many Jews define themselves as Jewish by ethnicity (such is the case for about 20% of American Jews), or think of themselves as Jewish by both ethnicity and religion but do not belong to a synagogue or a Jewish Community Center (JCC), counting Jews is much more difficult than counting other religious groups. Also, during the period examined in this chapter (1960–1997), Reform Judaism officially changed the definition of being Jewish to include the children of a Jewish father, if those children are being raised Jewish.[2] Note that this expanded definition has had, in the opinion of this author, relatively little impact upon the population figures used in this chapter, but, if anything, this changing definition would act to increase the numbers of Jews in small Jewish communities. Thus, without this changing definition, we *might* find an even more significant loss of such communities. Thus, some caution should be used when examining Jewish population estimates and changes in these estimates. Small changes may or may not reflect reality.

Much of this chapter examines changes in southern Jewish communities from 1960 to 1997. Why 1960? Many lives were disrupted during World War II. Some younger southern Jews who fought in this war resettled in their home towns after the war and stayed. Others moved out after a brief return. Since 1960 is 14 years after the end of World War II, the chosen period is unaffected by changes engendered by the War. The latest data available at the time of this writing were for 1997.

While extant geographic studies of U.S. religious groups have been completed at the county level (Halvorson and Newman, 1994; Zelinsky, 1961), this chapter examines changing Jewish population size at the "community" level. Some communities include only one small town, whereas others include several counties. Communities in this chapter are defined in accordance with the *American Jewish Year Book.* In areas that have a Jewish Federation (a central fund-raising and coordinating body), the community is the area served by that federation. In Palm Beach County, two Jewish communities are defined because the area is served by two federations, while in Atlanta one federation services four counties. In some instances, a community consists of one isolated town. In other cases, several small towns in relatively close proximity may share various Jewish institutions. In such cases, because the Jewish population in these towns think of themselves as one community, the *American Jewish Year Book* treats them as one community.

The *Year Book* individually identifies any Jewish community in the United States of 100 or more individuals.[3] Although other smaller concentrations exist, the maintenance of any type of real "community" structure is extremely difficult with fewer than 50 families present. With fewer than 50 families, it is difficult to maintain the institutions that are necessary to sustain a Jewish community, such as a cemetery, a synagogue, and a religious school.[4] Weissbach (1998), in examining the history of small Jewish communities, also uses 100 persons as the threshold for indicating that a viable Jewish community exists.

The Changing Size of the Jewish Population in the South

Table 6.1 shows the changes in the Jewish population of the South Census Division over the past 60 years. During this period, the Jewish population dramatically increased from 330,000 to 1,264,000, an increase of 282%. During this same period, the overall population of the South increased by only 123%. Thus, the Jewish population share in the South increased from 0.8% to 1.4%.

The national share of Jews who live in the South Census Division also has increased significantly over the six decades. In 1937, only 7% of American Jews lived in the South. This percentage shows a continuous increase to 21% in 1997. Thus, more American Jews now live in the

Table 6.1. Changes in the Regional Distribution
of the Jewish Population

Census Division	1937	1960	1972	1984	1997
Northeast	69%	67%	63%	54%	48%
Midwest	19%	14%	12%	11%	12%
South	7%	9%	12%	18%	21%
West	5%	11%	13%	16%	19%
Total	100%	100%	100%	100%	100%
Total South Jewish population	330,110	486,200	722,325	1,072,780	1,264,000
Florida	21,000	112,000	270,000	559,000	620,000
Maryland/DC	95,000	133,000	202,000	223,000	240,000
Atlanta	12,000	14,500	18,000	33,500	77,300

The Jewish South (South minus FL, MD, and DC)

Percentage of U.S. Jews	4%	4%	4%	4%	7%
Jewish population	214,360	215,700	250,595	290,260	382,500

Sources: Calculated by author from the *American Jewish Year Book, 1938, 1961, 1973, 1985,* and *1998.*

South than in either the West or the Midwest. The Northeast, however, has more than double the Jewish population of the South (Sheskin, 1998a).

But these numbers are actually quite misleading, if the object is to speak about changes in the Jewish population of the South, because, from a Jewish demographic perspective, the "South Census Division" has little meaning. Two areas of the South Census Division are not "South" for Jews. First, in Maryland/D.C., 98% of the Jewish population lives in the Washington/Baltimore Corridor. This area is really a part of the Northeastern megalopolis and not part of the South. Second, in Florida, more than 90% of Jews live in communities, mostly in Southeast Florida, that contain large numbers of elderly retirees from the Northeast, and to a much lesser extent, the Midwest (Sheskin, 1982, 1987, 1991, 1993a, 1994c, 1995b, 1997a, 1999a, 2000b). In many ways, Southeast Florida is an exurb of New York and is not a "Southern Jewish community." In fact, Southeast Florida may be the only place in the United States where one looks north to find the South.

United Jewish Communities recognized this special "Jewish geography" when they established their regional offices: Maryland and D.C. (and Virginia and Delaware) are considered to be Northeastern states, and Southeast Florida was separated from the remainder of the South and given its own separate regional office.

Most important, the greatest growth in the Jewish population of the South Census Division is due to the increase in Florida. In 1937, 21,000 Jews lived in Florida. This number increased to 620,000 by 1997 (Table 6.1). Thus, of the increase of 934,000 in the South's Jewish population, 66% was in Florida. Another 16% occurred in Maryland/D.C. Therefore, more than 80% of the reported growth in the South's Jewish population occurred in areas atypical of the South.

A very different picture emerges for the "Jewish South" (which omits Florida and Maryland/D.C.) than for the South Census Division. From 1937 to 1984, only 4% of American Jews lived in the Jewish South. During this period, the number of Jews in the Jewish South increased from 214,000 to 290,000, a modest increase of 35% in almost five decades. From 1984 to 1997, the percentage of American Jews in the Jewish South increased from 4% to 7%, from 290,000 to 382,000, an increase of 92,000. Even this increase is spatially concentrated, with 46% in Georgia (almost all of which was in Atlanta) (Sheskin, Ukeles, and Miller, 1996b), 37% in Texas (mostly Dallas and Houston), and 15% in Virginia (Sheskin, 1995a) (mostly in northern Virginia). (The latter area could also be viewed as part of the Baltimore/Washington corridor.)

The significant increase in the Jewish population of these southern areas is clearly related to migration from the Northeast to the South. Between 1972 to 1997, a significant shift occurred in American Jewish geography, with the Jewish population of New York declining by 890,000, Pennsylvania by 125,000, and Ohio by 31,000. During this same period, Florida increased by 375,000 (exclusive of part-year residents), Georgia by 56,000, Texas by 42,000, and Virginia by 32,000. Much of this migration to the Jewish South was driven by skilled employment opportunities in these Sunbelt cities.

The Current Geographic Distribution of Jews in the South Census Division

The current distribution of Jews in the South at the state level is shown in Table 6.2. The dominance of Florida is clearly demonstrated, with secondary concentrations in Maryland, Texas, Georgia, and Virginia. Only

Table 6.2. Changes in the Jewish Population of the South
Census Division

State	1960	1997	Increase (decrease)	Percentage change
Alabama	10,000	9,000	(1,000)	−10.0
Arkansas	3,400	1,700	(1,700)	−50.0
Delaware	8,500	13,500	5,000	58.8
Florida[a]	112,100	620,000	507,900	453.1
Georgia	24,800	84,500	59,700	240.7
Kentucky	11,000	11,000	0	0.0
Louisiana	16,100	16,500	400	2.5
Maryland	118,100	214,000	95,900	81.2
Mississippi	4,000	1,400	(2,600)	−65.0
North Carolina	10,300	23,500	13,200	128.2
Oklahoma	6,400	5,200	(1,200)	−18.8
South Carolina	7,100	9,000	1,900	26.8
Tennessee	16,800	18,000	1,200	7.1
Texas	60,900	124,000	63,100	103.6
Virginia	31,200	75,500	44,300	142.0
Washington DC	40,300	25,500	(14,800)	−36.7
West Virginia	5,200	2,400	(2,800)	−53.8

[a]Excludes large numbers of part-year residents.

Sources: Calculated by author from the *American Jewish Year Book, 1961* and *1998.*

small numbers of Jews are found in Mississippi, Arkansas, and West Virginia. The index of dissimilarity between Jews and non-Jews in the South Census Division is 48%, indicating that the geographic distribution of Jews is very different from non-Jews. The Jewish population is significantly more clustered than the general population and this clustering has increased over time. In 1960, 75% of Jews lived in the top five states for Jewish population in the South. This increased to 90% in 1997.

Jews are an overwhelmingly urban population, with only about 3% of American Jews living in rural areas (Goldstein and Goldstein, 1996). Thus, if one examines the distribution of Jews in the South at the metropolitan area scale, it becomes obvious that examining the distribution of Jews at the state level is somewhat misleading. At the MSA scale, Southeast Florida (507,000) and the Washington/Baltimore corridor (244,000) are evident as the two largest centers. Atlanta (77,000), Dallas

(45,000), and Houston (42,000) can be seen as secondary centers. Of the ten other MSAs with 10,000–24,000 Jews, four (Pinellas County, Orlando, Sarasota, and Tampa) are in Florida.

The 1998 *American Jewish Year Book* identifies 140 Jewish communities in the South. Recall that the *Year Book* individually identifies any Jewish community in the United States of 100 or more individuals. Twenty-six small Jewish communities may be found in Florida and 23 in Texas. Other southern states have very few Jewish communities: Oklahoma (2), Arkansas (3), Kentucky (3), Delaware (3), and Mississippi (4).[5] Table 6.3 shows that most Jewish communities are small: 44% of the communities contain only 100–499 persons; 10% have 500–999; and 23%, have 1,000–4,999. Thus, more than three-fourths of the communities contain fewer than 5,000 persons. Only 7% are large communities of 25,000 and over.

Losses and Gains of Southern Jewish Communities

In recent decades, a number of writers have noticed the disappearance of small southern Jewish communities. Applebome (1991) reported the demise of the Jewish communities of Port Gibson and Natchez, Mississippi, where today non-Jews are restoring the old synagogue and preserving the history. Garrison (1999), White (1991) and *The State* (1991) also reported similar trends. Epstein (1997) provided a series of interviews with Jews from small southern towns. The following discussion represents the first attempt to quantify the loss of Southern Jewish communities.

Table 6.3 shows the manner in which Jewish community-size distribution has changed over the past 37 years. The most striking result is the decline in the number of small communities, from 98 to 62, a decline of 37%. Forty-four communities that existed in 1960, ranging in size from 455 in Pine Bluff (AK) and 350 in Clarksdale (MS) to only 100 persons, have now dropped below the 100-person threshold. Thus, 44 existing southern Jewish communities have ceased to exist in the sense that they either are totally devoid of members, or have dropped below the level of a "functioning" community. Note, however, that 25 of these communities still have a synagogue that functions on at least a part-time basis (Chernofsky, 1997). Many only have religious services once or twice a month and do not have a rabbi. More than 20 other small (100–499 person) Jewish communities lost population in this period. Only six small communities (three in Florida) showed significant growth.

In the 500–999 community size range, a loss of seven communities

Table 6.3. Changes in Community-Size Distribution of the Jewish
Population of the South Census Division

Community Size	1960	1997	Increase (decrease)
25,000 +	4	11	7
10,000–24,999	4	11	7
5,000–9,999	9	10	1
1,000–4,999	31	33	2
500–999	21	14	(7)
100–499	98	62	(36)
Total number of communities	167	141	−26

Sources: Calculated by author from the *American Jewish Year Book, 1961* and *1998.*

may be noted, and ten communities within this population range lost population. Each of the community-size categories of 1,000 and over gained communities over the period. The communities with the greatest absolute growth include Broward County (FL) (213,000), South Palm Beach County (FL) (86,000), Montgomery and Prince Georges County (MD) (70,000), Palm Beach County (FL) (64,000), Atlanta (GA) (63,000), and Miami (FL) (54,000). Of these communities, only Atlanta is in the "Jewish South."

Seventeen Jewish communities that did not exist in 1960 came into existence at some point during the past 37 years. Eight of the 17 are retirement communities located in Florida: South Palm Beach, Naples, Stuart/Port St. Lucie, Port Charlotte/Punta Gorda, Ocala-Marion County, Winter Haven, Vero Beach, and Crystal River. South Palm Beach County (FL) has increased from fewer than 100 to 86,000; Naples (FL) from fewer than 100 to 3,500; and Stuart/Port St. Lucie, from fewer than 100 to 3,000.

Five new small communities have been established in university towns: Fayetteville (AK, University of Arkansas), Greenville (NC, East Carolina University), Rock Hill (SC, Winthrop), College Station-Bryan (TX, Texas A&M), and Blacksburg (VA, Virginia Polytechnic Institute). In fact, many small Jewish communities in the United States are maintained in university towns. According to Silberman (1985, p. 99), "by 1969 Jews constituted 9% of the faculty of American colleges and universities as a whole and 20% of the faculties of elite institutions." Thus, we find Jewish communities in some areas because the university faculty and students (more than 90% of young Jews go to college; see Kosmin, et al., 1991) help to create the community in college towns.

Consistent with the observations of Zelinsky (1961) about the Jewish tendency to move to resort towns, two new small communities have developed in resort areas: Ocean City (MD) and Myrtle Beach (SC). Two communities, which were small suburbs of larger communities, have developed their own identities: Howard County (MD), with about 10,000 Jews, and Covington/Newport (KY), with about 500 Jews. The fastest-growing and the fastest-decreasing Jewish communities, in terms of percentage growth during this time period (excluding the 17 Jewish communities which did not exist in 1960) are shown in Table 6.4. Of the top 15 communities in terms of percentage increase in Jewish population, nine are in Florida and two are in North Carolina.

Of the 12 communities with the greatest percentage decrease in Jewish population, five are in Texas and three are in West Virginia. That Galveston has been losing Jewish population is interesting, in light of the Galveston movement, an attempt during the early part of this century to divert European Jewish immigration from New York to the South, via the port of Galveston. Jews in places like New York were afraid that if the Jewish population increased any further in the Northeast, an anti-Semitic backlash might occur. About 5,000 Jews were diverted to Galveston, but the project ended as World War I began.

Note that some of the communities that have gained significant numbers are today among the larger Jewish communities in the South. However, the places with the largest percentage decreases are all small places that have simply grown smaller.

Reasons for the Increase in Large Jewish Communities

The growth in Jewish communities may be attributed to two factors. First, much of the growth in Florida Jewish communities is based upon retirement migration. Many of the children of the large Eastern European migration (1881–1924) gained middle-class- to upper-middle-class status. At retirement, through a chain migration process, they moved to the South, particularly to Miami-Dade, Broward, and Palm Beach counties in southeast Florida (Sheskin, 1991). Second, Jews took part in the migration of Americans to the Sunbelt at an even faster pace than the American population in general (Sheskin, 1998a). Because of the generally high socioeconomic status of the American Jewish population (Kosmin, et al., 1991), Jews were attracted to white-collar employment in the burgeoning suburban service industries of southern cities. For example, in Atlanta, 16% of Jews are employed in retail, 14% in the medical field, 10% in finance, insurance, and real estate, 9% in business ser-

Table 6.4. Greatest Percentage Increases and Decreases
in Community Size

Greatest percentage increases/decreases	1960	1997	Absolute change	Percentage change
INCREASES				
Broward County FL	6,975	220,000	213,025	3054.1
Palm Beach County FL	3,000	67,000	64,000	2133.3
Raleigh NC	490	5,500	5,010	1022.4
Ft. Myers FL	525	5,000	4,475	852.4
Brevard County FL	525	5,000	4,475	852.4
Orlando FL	2,500	21,000	18,500	740.0
Sarasota FL	2,100	17,000	14,900	709.5
Austin TX	1,300	10,000	8,700	669.2
Gainesville FL	210	1,600	1,390	661.9
Chapel Hill-Durham NC	425	3,100	2,675	629.4
Pinellas FL	3,330	24,200	20,870	626.7
Charlotteville VA	140	1,000	860	614.3
Alexandria-Arlington-Fairfax VA	6,400	35,100	28,700	448.4
Atlanta GA	14,200	77,000	62,800	442.3
Tallahassee FL	315	1,640	1,325	420.6
DECREASES				
Galveston TX	2,000	800	(1,200)	(60.0)
Port Arthur TX	260	100	(160)	(61.5)
Amarillo TX	420	150	(270)	(64.3)
Greenville MS	450	160	(290)	(64.4)
Wheeling WV	800	275	(525)	(65.6)
Shreveport LA	3,400	1,070	(2,330)	(68.5)
Sumter SC	520	160	(360)	(69.2)
Wharton TX	330	100	(230)	(69.7)
Clarksburg-Fairmont WV	365	110	(255)	(69.9)
Huntington WV	925	250	(675)	(73.0)
Waco TX	1,250	300	(950)	(76.0)
Hot Springs AR	550	130	(420)	(76.4)

Sources: Calculated by author from the *American Jewish Year Book, 1961* and *1998*, and Sheskin (1992, 1993b, 1994a, 1994b).

vices, and 9% in education. Fully 47% are employed in a professional position (Sheskin, Ukeles, and Miller, 1996b).

Reasons for the Decline in Small Southern Jewish Communities

Four different theories may be postulated to explain the decline of small southern Jewish communities. First, as with other parts of the United States, anti-Semitism has existed, to varying degrees, in various parts of the South. Thus, the possibility exists that Jewish communities disappeared or declined because of out-migration caused by the fact that Jews found themselves unwelcome in certain areas. Second, Jewish communities may have disappeared or declined as a result of outmigration caused by changes in employment opportunities. Third, the possibility exists that Jewish communities have disappeared or declined because of the intermarriage and assimilation of their members. To some extent, this theory may be viewed as the opposite of the anti-Semitism theory, because it implies that non-Jews were willing to marry Jews and to accept into their communities those Jews who were willing to assimilate. Fourth, the possibility exists that those Jewish communities that were lost existed in areas where the general population also declined, that is, the loss in Jews is commensurate with a general downturn in an area. These theories may be termed the anti-Semitism theory, the employment theory, the assimilation theory, and the general decline theory.

The Anti-Semitism Theory

Anti-Semitism in the South has varied significantly both spatially and temporally. Both anecdotal evidence and evidence from scientific surveys support its existence at a level commensurate with the idea that many Jews have left the South because of its existence. But note that researchers have differed on the seriousness of southern anti-Semitism.

Four major outbreaks of anti-Semitism in the South deserve special mention. First, in 1913, Leo Frank, a northern Jewish manager of a pencil factory in Atlanta, was accused of murdering a 14-year-old employee, Mary Phagan. The prosecutor stated in his summation that the Jews "rise to heights sublime, but they also sink to the lowest depths of degradation." (The prosecutor, Hugh M. Dorsey, was elected governor of Georgia in 1916.) The crowd outside the courtroom chanted "hang the Jew, hang the Jew." Frank was convicted. As the appeal process continued, anti-Semitism showed itself throughout many areas of the rural South.

In Marietta (GA), for example, notices were distributed to Jewish merchants ordering them to leave. Twenty-five men, including a clergyman, two former superior court justices, and a former sheriff, abducted Frank from his prison cell and hung him. In 1986, a witness statement led to the exoneration of Leo Frank (Sachar, 1992).

Second, after Rabbi Rothschild of Atlanta's oldest synagogue, The Temple, spoke out in favor of civil rights in 1958, neo-Nazi extremists bombed The Temple (Greene, 1996). This incident was meant as a warning to Rabbi Rothschild, who, in sermon after sermon, addressed his congregation forcefully to fulfill the call for justice by supporting integration. This incident illustrates well the problem that southern Jews faced during the civil rights era. While many may have supported integration, and certainly the tenets of the Jewish faith did, as a small minority with a history of persecution, they were often reluctant to speak out for fear of retribution.

Third, after World War II, Miami Beach was a predominantly Christian community, with signs that indicated "No Jews Wanted," "Christians Only," and "Restricted Clientele" (Moore, 1994, p. 154; Green and Zerivitz, 1991). And from April to December 1951, 16 bombings occurred in the Miami area and eight were against Jewish centers and synagogues.

Fourth, a series of bombings occurred in 1957–1958, with Jewish support for integration as the motivation. In November 1957, a bomb was discovered outside Temple Beth El in Charlotte, North Carolina. And in February 1958 a similar incident occurred at the entrance to Temple Emanu-El in Gastonia, a satellite city of Charlotte. In March, a bomb caused extensive damage to Miami's Temple Beth-El, with an anonymous caller threatening similar bombings against other advocates of integration. On the same day, the Jewish Community Center in Nashville also was damaged. In April, bombs damaged the Jewish Community Center in Jacksonville and Birmingham's Temple Beth El (Gribetz, 1993).

Examples abound as well of insensitivity to the Jewish population, as when, in 1844, the governor of South Carolina issued a Thanksgiving message calling for special prayers to Jesus Christ. During the Civil War, the Jews of Paducah (KY) were briefly expelled from their homes in accordance with an order from General Grant. Also during the Civil War, the citizens of Thomasville (GA) passed a resolution banning Jews from the town. In 1862, as food shortages and inflation were hampering the Confederate cause, the *Richmond Examiner* referred to Jews as the worst "speculators" and "extortioners." Maryland restricted Jews from holding public office until 1826, as did North Carolina until 1868 (Gribitz, 1993).

Until 1872, the Tennessee state constitution had a provision requiring a "Christian" minister to open the legislative sessions. In 1969, Sam Massell, the first Jew to be elected mayor of Atlanta, charged some of his opponents with anti-Semitism. Reporters had referred to him as the "Jewish liberal" from the "synagogue district" of the city. Even the title of Eli Evans' (1993) classic work on southern Jewry, *The Lonely Days Were Sundays,* implied that many Jews felt like outsiders in the South.

The continuing existence of anti-Semitism in the South since the mid-1980s is seen in two questions asked on a number of demographic studies of local southern Jewish populations (Sheskin, 2000b). First, 14 studies of southern Jewish communities asked respondents if they had personally experienced anti-Semitism in their local community within the previous year (Table 6.5). The results vary from 11% having experienced anti-Semitism in Broward and South Palm Beach to 31% responding in the affirmative in Orlando.

Second, on a scale of "a great deal, a moderate amount, a little, or none at all," large percentages see a great deal or a moderate amount of anti-Semitism in their local community. Table 6.5 shows that this result varies from 45% in Charlotte to 73% in Miami. Thus, southern cities do have high percentages of Jews who have experienced anti-Semitism or who feel that a significant degree exists in their area, although t-tests show no difference in the values on either variable between southern and nonsouthern communities. On average, in southern communities, 18.6% experienced anti-Semitism, compared to 21.5% in nonsouthern communities (t = 1.274, α = .215). On average in southern communities, 57.3% reported a great deal or a moderate amount of anti-Semitism, compared to 58.4% in nonsouthern communities (t = .2750, α = .785). Note that these comparisons are between the perceptions of Jews in the South about anti-Semitism in the South and perceptions of Jews in the non-South about perceptions of anti-Semitism in the non-South. Whether Jews in the South felt that if they moved to Northern cities they would be moving to areas of less anti-Semitism is unknown.

Note, however, that those cities with the anti-Semitic incidents mentioned above, and those cities noted in the paragraphs just above, are all cities that have shown significant *increases* in their Jewish populations. Many observers of the southern Jewish scene comment that, while mostly covert anti-Semitism did exist, in general the South was an amenable locale for Jews. Many religious fundamentalists in the rural South were respectful of Jews, or even philo-Semitic, viewing Jews as the "People of the Book" (Golden, 1955). In fact, the first Jew to hold elective office in

Table 6.5. Perception of and Experience with Anti-Semitism
in the Local Community

Community	Year of study	Perceive a great deal or moderate amount of anti-Semitism in local community[a]	Personal experience with anti-Semitism in past year in local community[a]
Southern communities			
Baltimore	1985	70	22
Broward	1997	54	11
Charlotte	1997	45	22
Dallas	1988	70	22
Miami	1994	73	14
Orlando	1993	63	31
Richmond	1994	50	23
Sarasota	1992	47	13
South Palm Beach	1995	51	11
South Broward	1990	63	12
St. Petersburg	1994	56	22
Tidewater	1988	NA	17
Washington, D.C.	1983	57	28
West Palm Beach	1999	46	12
Nonsouthern communities			
Atlantic City	1985	53	24
Cleveland	1996	67	22
Columbus	1989	57	NA
Essex-Morris	1986	NA	17
Harrisburg	1994	57	21
Las Vegas	1996	66	NA
Milwaukee	1996	58	24
Monmouth	1997	41	13
Rochester	1986	53	23
St. Louis	1994	73	30
SF Bay Area	1988	44	17
Toronto	1991	71	NA
Worcester	1986	50	22
York	1999	69	24

[a]In percentages.
  Sources: Sheshkin, 2000b.

the United States was Frances Salvador, who, in 1775 and 1776, was elected as a delegate to the South Carolina Provincial Congress. Florida elected the first Jewish senator (David Levy Yulee) in 1845. Martin Behrman served as mayor of New Orleans from 1904 to 1920.

Kaganoff and Urofsky (1979, p. xiii) warned that we must "distinguish between the Jew as a symbol and the Jew as a real, flesh and blood neighbor. The southern white may have hated the alleged international Jewish banking conspiracy headed by the Rothschilds, but he rarely connected the sinister Rothschild with Sam Cohen, who ran the dry-goods store down the street and was practically a "good ole boy."

Another important point is that anti-Semitism has historically acted to reinforce Jewish identity. That is, in areas with moderate amounts of anti-Semitism, the sense of attack from the outside acts in a way that causes the Jewish community to "circle the wagons." In situations where Christians act favorably toward Jews, Jews are more inclined to intermarry and assimilate. Thus, anti-Semitism and insensitivity no doubt played a significant role in the outmigration of Jews from some areas of the South, but it was probably not the major reason for the outmigration of Jews in many areas.

The Employment Theory

Not having been allowed to own land in most European countries, Jews did not develop farming skills. Many were involved in retail activity in Europe and brought those skills to the United States. Thus, in small southern towns, it was common for a large percentage of the peddlers and merchants to be Jewish (Suberman, 1998). Morris Rich, a Hungarian Jew, opened (in 1867) M. Rich, a retail store in Atlanta, which became the first chain of department stores in the South known for good labor relations and liberal credit terms. In places like Miami and Hendersonville (NC), almost all of the early retail activity was owned by Jews.

But, "the story of Jews in the South, at least a major part of it, is the story of fathers who built businesses for their sons who did not want them," stated Eli Evans in Applebome (1991, p. 17). About 51% of American Jewish adults have a four-year college degree or more, compared to about 26% of all Americans. Many southern Jewish children attended colleges (often outside the South) in areas with large Jewish communities. They achieved educational levels that prepared them for professional occupations, not for managing a retail outlet. In other cases, they simply experienced what it was like to live in a large Jewish community and no longer wished to return to being a tiny minority in a small town.

Another aspect of the change in occupational structure was clearly caused by the change in the nature of retail activity in the United States. Over the period examined in this chapter (1960–1997), small stores on downtown main streets have increasingly been replaced by large, chain discount stores (such as Kmart and Wal-Mart) (Posey, 1994) and by large, big-box retailers (Home Depot, Office Depot, and ToysRUs). In small southern cities, it was often small Jewish-owned retail activity that was replaced. There is no question that much Jewish outmigration from the area occurred as a result of occupational shifts in the Jewish population and changes in the nature of retail properties.

The Assimilation Theory

Dinnerstein and Palsson (1973, p. 14) noted that "the Jews adapted readily to the southern environment. Wherever they settled, they contributed to the development of the community. Most of the literature demonstrates that they considered assimilation of great importance, and consequently intermarriages between Jews and Gentiles were frequent. Jewish politicians served as Southerners first, and as American citizens second." But even before the beginning of the period examined in this chapter, Kaplan (1957) had already noted that a lack of Jewish mates— particularly in the small towns—had encouraged a high rate of intermarriage and loss of one's children as part of the Jewish community through assimilation. More recent data to support the decline resulting from the assimilation of Jews into Christian southern culture are shown clearly in Table 6.6, where 33% of households interviewed in the 1990 National Jewish Population Survey (Kosmin et al., 1991) included persons of Jewish descent who claim they are no longer Jewish, either in a religious or an ethnic sense. The 33% is significantly higher than the 26% in the Midwest, the 16% in the West, and the 9% in the Northeast. That another 29% of households in the South contain both core Jews and non-Jews, mostly due to intermarriages, shows that this process of assimilation continues. Thus, in only 38% of households of Jewish heritage in the South is everyone Jewish. That this has happened not only supports the assimilation theory, but lends credence to the general lack of anti-Semitism: non-Jewish southerners have been willing to marry Jewish Southerners. Applebome (1991), in examining the loss of Jewish communities in Mississippi, also noted that it is difficult to maintain small Jewish communities over the generations as children either intermarry or migrate to larger communities.

Kaganoff and Urofsky (1979, p. xii) observed that in places like New York "the large Jewish population had a major impact on the culture and

Table 6.6. Jewish Identity Household Types, 1980, in Percent

	Jewish identity household types			
Geographic area	No core Jews households[a]	Mixed Jewish households[b]	Core Jewish households[c]	Total percentage
Northest	9	26	65	100
Midwest	26	25	49	100
South[d]	33	29	38	100
West	16	32	52	100
United States	16	27	57	100

[a]Households in which no member currently identifies as Jewish, but some (or all) household members are of Jewish descent.
[b]Households in which some members are part of the Core Jewish population (people who consider themselves secular Jews or religious Jews or are converts to Judaism) and some, mostly through inter-marriage, are not.
[c]Households in which all members are part of the Core Jewish population.
[d]The Jewish South, except Florida and Maryland.
Sources: Kosmin et al., 1991, and author.

lifestyle of that city. . . . But the Jews in the South always remained a minority, at times an almost invisible minority. They did not affect the South as much as they imbibed its value and became part of it." And a number of anecdotal reports show the problems facing those southern Jews who desperately wanted to maintain a Jewish identity for their children. We can note two examples almost 200 years apart. In 1791, Chyet (1979) referenced letters from a Jewish woman living in Virginia to her parents in Germany that "here they [her children] cannot become anything else [but Gentiles]. Jewishness is pushed aside here . . . My children cannot learn anything here, nothing Jewish." More recently, the volume by Suberman (1998) *(The Jew Store)* relates the story of her family, who felt forced to leave the business her father had built in a small Tennessee town. They moved to New York when the children reached a certain age, so that they could develop a Jewish identity. The 1990 National Jewish Population Survey data confirm that many Jews who did not leave the South have become so much a part of it that their Jewish heritage has been lost.

The General Decline Theory

In some cases, the decline in Jewish population parallels a decline in the general population of the area. In fact, in 20 of the 44 cases in which the

Jewish population of a community has dropped below the 100 threshold, a significant decline has also occurred in the general population. In only seven cases has the Jewish population declined in the face of an increase of 10,000 or more in the overall population of a city.

It is clear from the above discussion that all four of the theories of decline in the Jewish population of small southern cities contribute to an explanation for the significant decline in small southern cities.

Finally, note that during the 1960–1997 period, the U.S. as a whole lost 115 Jewish communities and gained 85. Thirty-eight percent of the lost communities have been in the South, 33% in the Northeast, 29% in the Midwest, and 0% in the West. Of the 85 communities that have been added, 51% have been added in the West, 20% in the South, 19% in the Northeast, and 11% in the Midwest. No doubt the reasons for the losses and gains of Jewish communities in other parts of the U.S. are similar to the reasons postulated for the South.

Summary and Conclusion

While Jews continue to be concentrated in the Northeast, recent decades have seen significant growth in the Jewish population in the South, particularly in Florida and the Washington/Baltimore corridor. Secondary areas of growth have included Atlanta, Houston, and Dallas. Yet, even in the midst of this growth, many small southern Jewish communities have been lost. Just since 1960, 44 small Jewish communities (which had populations of 100–499 in 1960) have basically disappeared, due to anti-Semitism in the South, the changing occupational structure of southern Jews, the intermarriage and assimilation of the southern Jewish population, and the general population decline of small southern towns. All of these factors help to provide explanation for the decline of the Jewish population in small southern towns, although the relative importance of these factors remains a subject for further research. Another is the possible effect of the Internet on maintaining ethnic ties when one lives outside an ethnic enclave (Romm, 1996; Zakar and Kaufmann, 1998). The creation of new communities in retirement, university, and resort towns has not offset the loss of the small, traditional southern Jewish communities. With the demise of these small Jewish communities goes a piece of Southern geography and history.

While it is likely that Jewish communities will continue to exist throughout the South, the trend toward greater spatial concentration is the most likely scenario. The forces of assimilation for those living in small, southern Jewish communities are probably too significant to be overcome by other factors. As Jews become more concentrated in the urban South, it is likely that these Jewish communities will have increasing impact on the politics and economics of southern cities.

Notes

1. "Diaspora" is a Greek word meaning "dispersion." Historically, this term has been used to describe the spread of Jews around the world after the destruction of the Second Temple by the Romans. As evidenced by Chaliand and Rageau (1995), this term is now applied to a myriad of ethnic groups (including Armenians, Chinese, Lebanese, and Vietnamese). A diaspora is defined by Chaliand and Rageau (1995, pp. xiv–xvi) as an ethnic or religious group that has undergone a collective, forced dispersion, that maintains a collective memory, and that transmits this heritage from generation to generation. The term is used here to describe Jews in the South, who are part of the overall Jewish diaspora, and, while identifying as southerners, also feel connected to Jews throughout the world.

2. Traditionally, only the children of a Jewish mother were considered to be Jewish.

3. The *American Jewish Year Book* does collect information on Jewish "communities" of less than 100 and includes them in the state totals. It does not report them individually.

4. *The Commercial Appeal* (Memphis) recently reported on Blytheville, Arkansas, one of the lost Jewish communities identified in this chapter (September 11, 1999). Blytheville was listed in the *American Jewish Year Book* as a community of 100 Jews in 1960 and is no longer listed. Fifty-two-year-old Temple Israel now has a membership of about two dozen adults. The stained glass windows, memorial plaques, and Torah are being given to a Memphis synagogue. Plans are being made to sell the building. Some of the members who now live in Memphis return to Blytheville for a once-per-month service. They project that the High Holidays in 1999 will probably be the last. The leaders of Temple Israel indicate that many of their members went to college in larger cities and never returned.

5. A table showing the size of each southern Jewish community in 1960 and in 1997, as well as the absolute and percentage change in the Jewish population from 1960–1997, is available from the author.

Literature Cited

American Jewish Committee. Various years. *American Jewish Year Book*.

Applebome, P. 1991. "Small-Town South Clings to Jewish History," *New York Times,* September 29, 1991, pp. 1, 17.

Chaliand, G. and Rageau, J-P. 1995. *The Penguin Atlas of Diasporas* (New York: Viking).

Chernofsky, E. 1997. *Traveling Jewish in America* (Lodi, NJ: Wandering You Press).

Chyet, S. F. 1979. "Reflections on Southern-Jewish Historiography," in N. M. Kaganoff and M. I. Urofsky, eds. *Turn to the South: Essays on Southern Jewry* (Charlottesville: University Press of Virginia) pp. 13–20.

Dinnerstein, L. and Pallson, M., eds. 1973. *Jews in the South* (Baton Rouge: Louisiana State University Press).

Epstein, H. 1997. *Jews in Small Towns* (Santa Rosa, CA: Vision Books International).

Evans, E. N. 1993. *The Lonely Days Were Sundays* (Jackson: University Press of Mississippi).

Evans, E. N. 1997. *The Provincials: A Personal History of Jews in the South. Rev. Ed.* (New York: Free Press).

Garrison, G. 1999. "Small-town Synagogue, Temple Beth-El, Jewish Community Helped Shape Anniston," *The Birmingham News* April 16, pp. 1H, 3H.

Glanz, R. 1974. "The Spread of Jewish Communities Through America Before the Civil War," *YIVO Annual of Jewish Social Science,* Vol. 15, p. 38.

Golden, H. 1955. "Jew and Gentile in the New South, Segregation at Sundown," *Commentary,* Vol. 20, pp. 403–04.

Golden, H. 1974. *Our Southern Landsman* (New York: G.P. Putnam's Sons).

Goldstein, S., and Goldstein, A. 1996. *Jews on the Move: Implications for Jewish Identity* (New York: State University of New York Press).

Green, H. A., and Zerivitz, M. K. 1991. *Jewish Life in Florida* (Miami: Hallmark Press).

Greene, M. F. 1996. *The Temple Bombing* (New York: Perseus Press).

Gribetz, J. 1993. *The Timetables of Jewish History* (New York: Simon and Schuster).

Halvorson, P. L. and Newman, W. M. 1994. *Atlas of Religious Change in America.* (Atlanta: Glenmary Research Center).

Hartshorn, T. A. 1997. "The Changed South, 1947–1997," *Southeastern Geographer,* Vol. 37, pp. 122–39.

Heatwole, C. A. 1985. "The Unchurched in the Southeast," *Southeastern Geographer,* Vol. 25, pp. 1–15.

Kaganoff, N. M., and Urofsky, M. I., eds. 1979. *Turn to the South: Essays on Southern Jewry* (Charlottesville: University Press of Virginia).

Kaplan, B. 1957. *The Eternal Stranger: A Study of Jewish Life in the Small Community* (New York: Bookman Associates).

Kosmin, B., Ritterband, P., and Scheckner J. 1988. "Counting Jewish Populations: Methods and Problems," *American Jewish Year Book* (New York: American Jewish Committee and the Jewish Publication Society) pp. 204–41.

Kosmin, B., et al., 1991. *Highlights of the CJF 1990 National Jewish Population Survey* (New York: The Council of Jewish Federations).

Lavender, A., 1977. *A Coat of Many Colors, Jewish Subcommunities in the United States* (Westport, Greenwood Press).

Moore, D. D. 1994. *To the Golden Cities, Pursuing the American Dream in Miami and L.A.* (New York: The Free Press).

Posey, A. S. 1994. "Grocery Retail Location and Function in Columbia, South Carolina," *Southeastern Geographer,* Vol. 34, pp. 92–107.

Proctor, S., Schmier, L., and Stern, M., eds. 1984. *Jews of the South: Selected Essays from the Southern Jewish Historical Society* (Macon, GA: Mercer University Press).

Romm, D. 1996. *The Jewish Guide to the Internet* (Northvale, NJ: Aronson).

Sachar, H. M. 1992. *A History of the Jews in America* (New York: Alfred A. Knopf).

Sheskin, I. M. 1982. *Population Study of the Greater Miami Jewish Community* (Miami: Greater Miami Jewish Federation).

Sheskin, I. M. 1987. *Jewish Demographic Study* (West Palm Beach: The Jewish Federation of Palm Beach County).

Sheskin, I. M. 1991. "The Jews of South Florida," in T. D. Boswell, ed., *South Florida, Winds of Change* (Washington, D.C.: Association of American Geographers) pp. 163–80.

Sheskin, I. M. 1992. *The Sarasota-Manatee Jewish Federation Community Study* (Sarasota: The Sarasota-Manatee Jewish Federation).

Sheskin, I. M. 1993a. "Jewish Ethnic Homelands in the United States," *Journal of Cultural Geography,* Vol. 13, pp. 119–32.

Sheskin, I. M. 1993b. *The Jewish Federation of Greater Orlando Community Study* (Orlando: The Jewish Federation of Greater Orlando).

Sheskin, I. M. 1994a. *The Jewish Federation of Pinellas County Community Study* (Clearwater, FL: The Jewish Federation of Pinellas County).

Sheskin, I. M. 1994b. "Jewish Identity in the Sunbelt: The Jewish Population of Orlando, Florida," *Contemporary Jewry,* Vol. 15, pp. 26–38.

Sheskin, I. M. 1994c. *The 1994 Jewish Demographic Study of Dade County* (Miami: Greater Miami Jewish Federation).

Sheskin, I. M. 1995a. *The Jewish Community Federation of Richmond Community Study* (Richmond: The Jewish Community Federation of Richmond).

Sheskin, I. M. 1995b. *1995 Jewish Community Study of South Palm Beach County* (Boca Raton, Florida: The Jewish Federation of South Palm Beach County).

Sheskin, I. M. 1997a. *The Jewish Federation of Broward County Community Study* (Fort Lauderdale: The Jewish Federation of Broward County).

Sheskin, I. M. 1997b. *The Jewish Federation of Greater Charlotte Community Study* (Charlotte: The Jewish Federation of Greater Charlotte).

Sheskin, I. M. 1998a. "The Changing Spatial Distribution of American Jews," in

H. Brodsky, ed., *Land and Community: Geography in Jewish Studies* (Bethesda, MD: University Press of Maryland) pp. 287–95.

Sheskin, I. M. 1998b "A Methodology for Examining the Changing Size and Spatial Distribution of a Jewish Population: A Miami Case Study," in *Shofar, Special Issue: Studies in Jewish Geography,* Vol. 17, pp. 97–116.

Sheskin, I. M. 1999a. "The Demography of Tradition," in *Responses to an Aging Florida,* (Spring) pp. 18–21.

Sheskin, I. M. 1999b. *The Jewish Federation of Palm Beach County Community Study* (West Palm Beach: The Jewish Federation of Palm Beach County).

Sheskin, I. M. 2000a. "American Jews," *Contemporary Ethnic America,* J. O. McKee, ed. (Lanham, MD: Rowman and Littlefield), in press.

Sheskin, I. M. 2000b, *How Jewish Communities Differ: Variations in the Findings of Local Jewish Demographic Studies* (New York: City University of New York, Mandell L. Berman Institute, North American Jewish Data Bank), in press. Sheskin, I. M., Ukeles J., and Miller R. 1996a. *Jewish Population Study of Delaware* (Wilmington, DE: The Jewish Federation of Delaware).

Sheskin, I. M., Ukeles, J., and Miller R. 1996b. *The 1996 Jewish Population Study of Atlanta* (Atlanta: The Atlanta Jewish Federation).

Silberman, C. E. 1985. *A Certain People, American Jews and their Lives Today* (New York: Summit Books).

Suberman, S. 1998. *The Jew Store* (Chapel Hill, NC: Algonquin Books of Chapel Hill).

The State, 1991. "An Era Passes: Jewish Communities Dying in Dixie," Columbia, SC. September 29.

Tobin, G., and Sheskin, I. M. 1991. *The Jewish Federation of South Broward Community Study* (Hollywood, FL: The Jewish Federation of South Broward).

Varady, D. P., and Mantel, Jr., S. J. 1982. "Estimating the Size of Jewish Communities Using Random Telephone Surveys," *Journal of Jewish Communal Service,* pp. 225–34.

Weissbach, L. S. 1998. "Unexplored Terrain: The History of Small Jewish Communities," *Shofar,* Vol. 17, pp. 59–71.

White, G. 1991. "The Dwindling-Empty Stores, Silent Temples: The Rural South's Jewish Culture Is Dying," *Atlanta Journal/Constitution.* March 31.

Zakar, S. M. and Kaufmann, D. Y. B. 1998. *Judaism Online* (Northvale, NJ: Aronson).

Zelinsky, W. 1961. "An Approach to the Religious Geography of the United States: Patterns of Church Membership in 1952." *Annals of the Association of American Geographers,* Vol. 51, pp. 139–67.

III
BUSINESS AND GOVERNANCE

INTRODUCTION

In large part Jews succeeded in America because their European experiences prepared them to fill economic niches few others entered. As they rose economically and enjoyed relative tolerance, they contributed to civic affairs. The individual stories in this section provide flesh and bone to the broad outlines of success. They also illustrate dynamic interaction within and between groups on the local, regional, national, and even international levels. Neither isolated nor provincial, Jews in the South benefited from numerous networks.

Those who fled the Inquisition departed Spain and Portugal with few possessions. Some started in Dutch or Spanish colonies and then moved to Louisiana, Florida, or South Carolina having already begun their economic ascent. At Georgia's inception in 1733, prominent members of London's Spanish and Portuguese congregation sent Jews to Savannah, prompting protest from British trustees. However, in a time of epidemic, a Jewish doctor among the immigrants led colony leader James Oglethorpe to defend their presence. In their ranks too was a Portuguese vintner, and wine was a critical mercantile objective. Thus the provision of needed services fostered rights and opportunities.

Individuals adapted to port and frontier environments as merchants and brokers. Willingness to move or try again when a venture failed and experience in foreign languages contributed to success in this international marketplace. A few served as translators of and brokers with Native Americans. In the early 1800s Jews traveled to inland transportation/commercial centers.

Elliott Ashkenazi's article demonstrates many factors for success during this age of the Jewish peddler. Like their colonial predecessors, the Seligmans and Lehmans filled economic niches and knew few boundaries of section or country. Examples illustrate mobility, complex business exchanges, technological innovations, adaptation to changing conditions, and kin, business, and friendship networks. Although agriculture dominated the southern economy, intolerance had limited Jewish landholding in Europe and consequently few Jews farmed. As merchants and providers of credit, however, they helped make production rational and profitable. Children and grandchildren started schools and entered professions.

Reflecting their economic position and acceptance, Jews joined elite charity societies and supported their adopted land in wars. They also served in elected and appointed positions on the local level and in congress where many advocated secession and supported slavery (positions discussed in Part 4).

Congregations wrote Washington and Jefferson offering allegiance and successfully soliciting opinions favorable to separation of church and state and religious toleration. They also protested the Damascus incident (in which Jews were wrongfully accused of killing Christians), an American treaty with Switzerland in the face of the latter's antisemitic policies, and the Mortara case. Participation in such lobbying reflected a Jewish identity and an international outlook that separated Jews from other southerners.

The Civil War delayed economic momentum only temporarily. To Canter Brown Jr., the Dzialynski brothers embody the shared Jewish and New South values of business success and civic uplift, and their activities illustrate Jewish contributions to the rebuilding of Florida. Morris and Philip Dzialynski experienced ups and downs in business and moved repeatedly to locate opportunity. In additional to economic development ventures, Philip concentrated on general stores while Morris found success as a wagon and carriage merchant. Active in the Jewish community, they formed bridges between the two worlds.

As discussed in Part 5, some historians contend that adaptation to southern mores and practices by Jews led to acceptance and election to public offices. Brown provides evidence both in favor of and challenging this thesis. Supporting the Confederacy and serving in its military eased acceptance and offered networking ties. Nonetheless for the Dzialynski brothers, personal attributes, important roles in economic reconstruction, and other contributions outweighed their support for the South in explaining political preferment. That by the 1880s Jews who moved south from the North achieved similar success demonstrates this conclusion. Moreover, Philip Dzialynski may have been viewed as a war profiteer.

During the late 19th century and into the 20th, many economic and political patterns continued, and new ones emerged. Jews served as city councilmen, school board members, and mayors, sponsoring business-progressive programs. Yet such activities seemingly declined with the lynching of Leo Frank in 1915 and the rise of antisemitism. Eastern European Jews again started as peddlers and opened scrap metal yards, pawn broker shops, and liquor stores. Sephardim concentrated on delicatessens, clothing and hat cleaning establishments, and shoemaking and repair businesses. Besides relying on Jewish wholesalers and family and landsleit networks, these groups obtained financing through free loan associations and Morris Plan banks through which a person lacking collateral could obtain a loan if two people vouched for him. Shopkeepers lived above their stores and purchased investment properties. Immigrants' children expanded family businesses, became professionals, or entered government employ.

When conflict and cooperation marked the interaction between Jews of central and eastern European descent, ethnic brokers facilitated cooperation. As my article suggests, these individuals negotiated among diverse constituencies and occasionally challenged behavioral boundaries. Business success was virtually a prerequisite for acceptance across national and denominational lines. The ethnic brokers and mediating agencies, including federations of Jewish charities, acted as internal political instruments of adaptation and the maintenance of tradition.

America's open door to immigrants closed during the 1920s, a decade of economic expansion. These dual factors hastened acculturation and the rise of the new immigrants and their children into the middle class. The Great Depression and World War II temporarily delayed these advances. In small towns, Jewish communities rose and fell according to local economic factors. The introduction of a new industry, the presence of a military installation, the growth of a college, or later emergence as a retirement, recreation, or research haven could translate into renewal for an area. Conversely, a stagnant economy, the building of suburban malls, national credit cards, and civil rights demonstrations could doom small towns as well as urban businesses. Before and after World War II, Jews in growth-oriented cities started chains mirroring nineteenth century satellite stores. Yet consolidation in the last quarter of the twentieth century doomed the family department store. The occupational profile of Jews in the region became more diverse, and spread to business, medicine, academia, and other professions.

Before the Civil War, some Jewish women ran businesses as sole traders. Besides supporting troops, one headed nursing activities at a Confederate hospital. They actively participated in and even led Lost Cause/Confederate memorial activities. Jewish women took in boarders, and worked as buyers, salespeople, and bookkeepers for husbands or in their own right. Many middle and upper class women worked in congregational and charity activities which led them into affiliation with federations of women's clubs and political lobbying, especially under the auspices of the National Council of Jewish Women. Serving virtually every immigrant group since the 1890s, NCJW sections have been in the forefront in resettlement and Americanization efforts. Jewish women actively supported the League of Women Voters and the passage of the Nineteenth Amendment. In the years between the world wars, many advocated peace and disarmament. Positions opened in education, social work, law, and government.

Aid expanded for Jewish causes such as Jewish war sufferers during and after World War I, Jews in Palestine and Hitler's Germany, refugees, and Israel. Demonstrations for Russian refuseniks marked another turning point in activism. Southern Jews joined with Jews throughout America in all of the efforts.

As business people, office holders and civic boosters, Jews contributed disproportionately in relation to their size and percentage of population. In a region of the country often characterized as parochial and anti-intellectual, Jews advocated culture, the arts, and education. Why were these things so, and what do they imply about the relationship between acculturation and continuity of a broadly defined "Jewishkeit"?

7
Jewish Commercial Interests Between North and South

The Case of the Lehmans and the Seligmans

Elliott Ashkenazi

It is becoming increasingly apparent that the regional economies of nineteenth-century America had numerous interconnections. The cotton trade between southern and northern ports and the return shipment of textiles and other manufactured goods of domestic and European origin have long been seen as fundamental to national economic development during most of the last century.[1] It is also clear that such development did not occur in a vacuum, or in a jar of statistics. Human beings generated the energy needed to open a store, send merchandise from one place to another, and participate in other aspects of American trade and commerce. As we rehumanize business history, we learn anew that personal factors like religion and ethnic origin not only affected the kinds of economic activities pursued and the ways they were pursued, but also intertwined social and economic relationships to such an extent that each provided a foundation for the other.

The Jewish business community of nineteenth-century America provides an excellent example. Initially engaged in trade, and later in investment banking and finance, immigrant Jews adapted to America by taking advantage of their common religious, geographic, and ethnic backgrounds. In so doing Jews created ties among the various regions of the country during an era that we are accustomed to regard as one of sectional strife, war, and a divisive postwar period known as Reconstruction.

As goods, people, and capital moved between North and South, self-help among Jews who lived for longer or shorter periods in the South, and contacts with fellow Jews in the North, helped make the South economically and socially (the two must be considered together) attractive for Jews. Southern economic successes eventually helped Jews participate in the more rarified world of underwriting and investment banking that developed around Wall Street during the latter part of the century. The Jewish financiers of late-nineteenth-century New York, among whom were members of the Lehman and Seligman families, dealt primarily with each other (in part from necessity), and presented a classic case of the reciprocal importance of social matters and business enterprise.

The Lehmans and the Seligmans were from small towns in Bavaria. The first members of each family to arrive in America began their careers by selling dry goods and general merchandise as peddlers and storekeepers in antebellum Alabama. The paths of the two famiies also crossed in Manhattan, at Temple Emanu-El on Fifth Avenue and in the Jewish clubs uptown, and of course on Wall Street. The families eventually became related by marriage, in classical "Our Crowd" fashion, when grandchildren of the immigrant generation joined hands in matrimony and cemented financial bonds. These stories, however, have much to do with southern Jewish life and North-South contacts.

Our focus on Jewish merchants and bankers does not mean that only Jews performed in the manner of the Lehmans and Seligmans. The emphasis on family members as business partners and on business affairs as instigators of social relationships is one that has its roots in the very beginnings of trade, and can be found in Renaissance Italy, sixteenth-century Germany, colonial America, and among the Yankee traders of the nineteenth-century United States.[2] In many other instances, at many different times and in many different locations, minority groups performed particular economic functions that were not performed adequately by others in the larger society. In the context of southern society before and after the Civil War, however, the Jewish experience provides a recent example of the role of a minority group in the economic development of an agricultural region, performing functions that were not so readily performed by many others.[3]

Merchandising in the South and West

The first of the Seligmans, Joseph, came to the United States in 1837, at age seventeen; Henry Lehman, the first of three brothers, arrived in 1844, twenty-two years old. Neither came with much money or many connections, although Joseph Seligman left his hometown, Bayersdorf, in the company of several other of its residents.

For the Seligmans, and for many others at this time, emigration was something of a communal decision. Not so, apparently, for Henry Lehman, who peddled through the Alabama countryside until he managed to open a general store in Montgomery in 1847, the year that town became the state capital. By 1848, brothers Emanuel and Mayer were with him in Alabama.[4]

Joseph Seligman also started his American career as a peddler, but in Pennsylvania. William and James joined him after two years. The South initially attracted only James, who thought peddling would be less competitive there. He did well enough to persuade his brothers, who then numbered four, to come to Mobile in 1841. They serviced the towns and plantations of the Alabama countryside, first from one store in Selma and then from three others, all in rural locations. James made regular trips to New York to buy inventory for the country stores and for those of his brothers who remained peddlers.[5]

The Seligmans continued this line of business for about seven years, until 1848, while their younger brothers and sisters came over from Bavaria after their mother died in 1842. The newcomers did not stay in New York City, however. Jesse took young Henry with him to upstate New York to open a dry goods and clothing store, an outlet for J. Seligman & Bros., the importing firm organized by Joseph, the oldest brother, in New York City, with the profits from the successful years of trading in Alabama. Jesse and Henry met Mexican War hero Ulysses S. Grant in Watertown, near their store, and began a friendship that was to continue for many years and provide crucial support for the Seligman brothers in Republican circles during the Civil War and after. William and his sister Babette's husband, Max Stettheimer, moved to St. Louis to open another clothing store.[6]

With the discovery of gold in the West, Jesse took another younger brother, Leopold, to San Francisco to open a general store. They hoped to meet the demands of the '49ers, and rented space in the first brick building built there. When Jesse left to handle some of the growing firm's European banking business, William took his place in the lucrative San Francisco market.

But the Seligmans had more than shopkeeping in mind for themselves. While the San Francisco store sold merchandise to the growing population of the area, it also bought gold to hedge the firm's currency transactions and to sell in the European market. When Joseph reluctantly closed the store in 1867 it was the last Seligman office to be involved in merchandising. Too much money was tied up there, money that could be used more effectively in banking and currency transactions.

There can be little doubt that some of the Seligmans, at least, met and competed with Henry Lehman, a fellow Bavarian peddling in the same unlikely part of the United States and whose dry goods store in Montgomery, fifty miles to the east of the Seligmans' store in Selma, opened the year before the Seligmans sold their southern business and went to New York. The distances between towns in the Deep South were substantial; peddlers were among the few who braved the poor roads that linked the plantations and villages of the agricultural South. One can imagine these enterprising German-speaking Jews meeting at a wayside and comparing notes.

The Cotton Trade

Cotton transactions lay at the foundation of the southern economy. Sales by grower to factor or grower to merchant were ultimately paid for with drafts drawn on New York agents or exporters. The drafts were of a certain duration or were drawn at sight for immediate payment or acceptance. When foreign buyers were involved, the sellers drew bills of exchange in pounds or francs on English or French spinners or their agents. Both drafts and bills could be discounted and converted to cash or credit in New York. Whether a cotton sale was profitable could easily depend on the outcome of the currency transactions.

When the Seligmans imported merchandise, as they did in the 1850s, they depended on bills of exchange to generate the English pounds or French francs used to pay for their purchases abroad. The Lehman brothers, for their part, had become so active in the cotton trade from Alabama to New York that they opened an office in New York to handle their own exchange transactions in 1858, about ten years after that of the Seligmans.

The Civil War and Its Aftermath

The two families spent the Civil War years in different ways. There had been no Seligman living in the South for many years; the Lehmans were divided between North and South. Emanuel Lehman, but for a trip to England, spent the war in New York. Mayer, his only surviving brother (Henry having succumbed earlier to yellow fever in New Orleans) and a southern patriot, moved from Alabama to New Orleans, a city under

Union control since April 1862.[7] They hoped to protect their southern assets and concentrate their funds in the South to await the end of fighting.

The Seligmans did what they could to aid the Union cause. At the very outset of the war they obtained contracts to provide troops with uniforms. They also used their European contacts to help finance the Union war effort. Henry went to Frankfurt in 1862, a time when Union fortunes were low, the outcome of the war in doubt, and the position of some European powers equally so. He and his family successfully sold American bonds to the Europeans through the new Frankfurt office and generated important diplomatic support for Lincoln.

At the end of the war the Seligmans were able to regard themselves more as bankers and less as merchants, and naturally felt allied to the government in Washington, among whose principal postbellum concerns were the integration of the South into the rest of the country and the return of the nation's finances to a peacetime footing. With these ends in mind the Seligmans opened a New Orleans office in the fall of 1865, managed by Jesse's brother-in-law Max Hellman and named Seligman, Hellman & Co. In 1868 Max's brother Theodore, married to Joseph Seligman's daughter Frances (the family interconnections are endless), took over the management of the New Orleans office and remained there until 1880. Max then returned to Europe, as he had always wanted to do, to take charge of the family's Paris firm.

Joseph Seligman, self-appointed chairman of the various family enterprises and working with brother William as J. & W. Seligman & Co. in New York, proceeded quite cautiously in generating business for the office in New Orleans. Correspondence from Joseph in New York to Max Hellman during 1866 and 1867 illustrates many of the difficulties even a successful and well-connected group of businessmen faced in the South immediately after the Civil War.[8] Joseph's unwavering desire was to use the New Orleans office for banking purposes, for clearing the drafts and bills generated by the cotton trade, not for buying and selling the commodity itself, as the Lehmans did. Profit depended on two factors: the careful selection of bills and drafts for purchase, to minimize the risk that American or European cotton buyers, or those who endorsed the bills or drafts in the regular course of business, would be unable to meet their obligations if business soured; and successful currency transactions involving the buying and selling of exchange, greenbacks, and gold.[9]

The first postbellum cotton season was a time of uncertainty for all.

The Seligmans were rightly concerned about the state of communications and transportation in the South. In January 1866, soon after it opened, the New Orleans office asked for $100,000 in currency, and continued to make similar requests on a regular basis.

Joseph was careful to divide greenback shipments into parcels of no more than $50,000, so the money would not all be on one vessel or train. Insurance could not always be obtained for currency shipments in larger amounts because of the number of robberies. Trains were as unsafe as ships. On Max Hellman's return from a summer trip to Europe, he left New York for New Orleans on the Louisville & Nashville Railway, only a few days before a train on the same route was demolished by robbers.[10] The Seligmans stayed out of a proposed bullion business in Utah because shipments from there would be so subject to robbery. They also knew enough to protect the value of their regular currency shipments by selling gold in New York at the same time they sent greenbacks to New Orleans, thereby avoiding the risk of currency fluctuations.

It took time to figure out how to make best use of the telegraph lines between the two cities. Joseph Seligman advised Hellman to play up to the "telegraphic people," who according to Joseph gave friends the earliest information on changes in the New York gold rates. Joseph also cautioned on the importance of the wording of telegrams, realizing that the abbreviated method of communication could easily lead to misinterpretations. The importance of technological innovations in communications no longer stopped at the nation's borders, for the transatlantic cable began to function late in 1866, putting spinners in Europe and England in closer touch with price changes for their raw material in the United States.

Cotton, Currency, and Commercial Paper

Joseph refused to allow New Orleans to take any steps that might expose that office (and hence New York) to the risks of the cotton market, for cotton had been kept at an artificially high price by wartime disruptions. There was no telling how far the price would drop; indeed, whether it would drop at all. Hellman's purpose in New Orleans was to buy bills and drafts drawn on buyers of cotton for resale in New York. As long as the endorsements on them were reliable, the bills and drafts circulated freely. A banker in Seligman's position in New York offered them for sale to those in need of funds.

Seligman hoped to sell the drafts and bills from New Orleans without putting his firm's endorsement on them, even if it meant losing one half to three quarters of a point on the sale. Their own endorsement, said Joseph correctly, would make the firm liable should the drafts not be paid at maturity. At first Joseph instructed Hellman to endorse the commercial paper not to the New York firm but to the name of an individual employee in the New York office, so afraid was he of seeing his firm's name appear. Soon the paper came to New York without any endorsement, and Joseph sold what he could at the lower price but without the Seligman endorsement and without the potential exposure an endorsement would create.

Joseph's conservative approach to their first season in business did indeed protect them from substantial liabilities. While the firm could safely endorse as much as 100,000 of cotton bills and make a good profit on their resale, Joseph did not want to take such risks in their first go at the commercial banking business in a climate of unstable prices. His judgment proved correct.[11]

The Seligmans withstood periodic swings in the cotton and currency markets because their domestic and European branches worked together to offset troubles in any one market. As long as gold was available and its price did not drop precipitously the Seligmans were able to hedge their currency transactions.[12] European offices were always potential buyers and sellers of gold, and themselves dealt in exchange. If American markets were disturbed, the European firms could and did provide what America needed, be it a buyer or seller of gold or currency. Conversely, when the Bank of England experienced a fiscal crisis in 1866 after a large commercial bank collapsed, the central bank having to increase its gold reserves instantaneously, the Seligmans were able to arrange for the transfer of $20,000,000 in gold to the Bank of England.[13]

In two months' time business between Seligman, Hellman & Co. in New Orleans and J. & W. Seligman & Co. in New York appeared to have stabilized, with New York making a profit on all the bills sent from New Orleans. Older firms began to complain that it was difficult to make a profit in New Orleans anymore because so many new competitors had appeared after the war. Joseph Seligman agreed, and was happy to be one of the new competitors. The decline of premiums on gold and exchange was the problem in this business, not the buying and selling of drafts and bills.[14]

Joseph became bolder during the Seligmans' second cotton season, but he still appeared conservative in the face of numerous suggestions from Max Hellman to expand into direct cotton buying and other riski-

er propositions. Joseph encouraged Max, rather, to work together with
J. H. Schroeder & Co., a respected Liverpool financer of cotton. They
would have to share the profit in New Orleans, but good representation
in Liverpool would be worth it. He also wanted Hellman to increase his
business with American spinners, some of which was done through drafts
on Boston rather than New York. Even though a draft on Boston was
worth from one- to two-sixteenths less than one on New York, Joseph
wanted the business because of the volume, and brother William went
to Boston in November 1866 to find clients for New Orleans.

Finance and Banking

Banking and currency transactions necessarily enmeshed the Seligmans
in all the issues of finance and banking raised by the end of hostilities,
among them the withdrawal of greenbacks and return to the gold standard, the national banking system itself, and the government's position
as a debtor on the national and international scene.[15] They functioned
less dramatically as a source of funds for the Deep South at a time when
cash was not readily available, helping the regional economy function.

Existing records indicate, furthermore, that Seligman, Hellman &
Co., from its inception, made some of its funds available to the many Jewish merchants involved in the cotton trade in New Orleans. Jewish cotton traders in New Orleans were able to draw on the Seligmans, even if
the Seligmans did not purchase cotton directly, and even if Joseph in
New York preferred to develop a strictly banking presence for New Orleans.

Another unspectacular part of the Seligmans' business in New York
was to act as agents for their London and Frankfurt offices in collecting
payments from American importers on behalf of European sellers who
sold under letters of credit issued in Europe. The existing records indicate that the percentage of Jewish merchants at both ends of these transactions was high. Because of the use of letters of credit, this part of the
banking business did not cause the Seligmans difficulties. Of less interest to the Seligmans were the frequent requests coming from Europe for
American merchants to pay or accept the drafts of European sellers without letters of credit. Again the parties on both sides were usually Jewish.

The Seligmans tested the waters of banking and bullion trading after
the Civil War, and liked what they saw. The New York office, importers of
clothing before and during the war, engaged solely in banking once the

war ended. They were considered Jewish bankers working for the Jewish business community in their various locales, but not exclusively so.

As we have seen, the Seligmans were able to participate in public as well as private financing, and continued to do so into the twentieth century. Their interests in the South, begun in the peddling days of the 1840s, changed as circumstances changed, but proved to be of long standing.[16] Their genius lay in linking the defeated Confederacy to other regions that could supply something the South lacked, a functioning fiscal and monetary structure. All participants in the southern economic framework benefitted from the northern, western, and European connections of one family, the Seligmans, whose members did indeed help rebuild the financial structure of the South, and of the nation, after the war.

The Lehmans of Alabama

If Joseph Seligman preferred to make money in the Deep South after the war without becoming a cotton or sugar merchant, Emanuel and Mayer Lehman had taken a different approach. They intended to revive business in Montgomery, Alabama, when possible, the basis for which had been the maintenance of large warehouses for the storage of cotton used by the Lehmans as collateral for deposits given them in the same way that customers deposit money in a bank. Mostly destroyed in the war by retreating Confederate troops, the warehouses were rebuilt by the Lehmans. At the same time they came to the aid of the postbellum state government of Alabama. The Lehmans lent it $100,000 when the state desperately needed money, and as thanks were made state fiscal agents, much in the way the Seligmans had acted on a larger scale during the war for the national government.

Tangible Lehman assets in Alabama grew to about $1,500,000 in the 1870s, about 20 percent of that in the form of real estate. Lehman holdings came to include plantations, factories (particularly the Tallassee Textile Mill and the Indian Hill Factory), and urban property. Lehman Bros. in New York also invested some of its own money in southern real estate but more often in railway securities and southern municipal bonds as the stock market began to come into its own. They did not shy away from long-term investments.

Equally important were funds generated by the Lehmans to link southern growers of cotton to the end users in England. Lehman warehouses allowed the firm to buy cotton directly from growers and store it until prices justified sale. Their inland facilities in Montgomery led the way in eliminating the middlemen located at the port cities, Mobile and New Orleans. Family ties in England assured the Lehmans of buyers. Lehman Bros. in New York regularly bought cotton from its southern offices and sold it the next day at a profit to Newgass, Rosenheim & Co, in Liverpool, their English agents and relatives.

To make funds available for New Orleans the Lehmans dissolved their existing firm in New York and transferred over $500,000 to a relatively new office in the midst of the defeated Confederacy. Mayer moved permanently to New York, and brother-in-law Benjamin Newgass ran the daily operations in New Orleans until 1872, when Henry Abraham, from the Jewish community that had started life in Alabama in the early 1850s, replaced him. The firm then took on the name Lehman, Abraham & Co. The Lehmans soon became so dominant in the cotton trade that when 132 cotton merchants met to form the New York Cotton Exchange in 1870, Mayer Lehman was not only one of them, but also on its first board of governors and head of its first finance committee.

The Lehmans never expected their New Orleans office to engage in a retail banking operation similar to that in Montgomery. They did expect to buy and sell cotton and supply urban and rural merchants with merchandise and financing for their cotton transactions. After the war various methods of sharecropping or share-renting came into use for arranging economic relationships between landowners and former slaves or others who did not own land. These relationships served to diffuse control over the disposition of a substantial portion of the crop. The landowner could lay claim only to whatever portion of a crop was due under share arrangements and no longer controlled the purchase and distribution of food, clothing, and supplies, as under the slave system.

With some exceptions, planters did not succeed in running general stores that could have captured the business of the sharecroppers. Those working the land became customers of "furnishing merchants" (many of them Jewish) who supplied merchandise in exchange for promises, secured by crop liens, to deliver cotton to the storekeeper. Country merchants became cotton traders and would have become speculators but for the support of the Lehmans and others like them.

The Lehman firm in New Orleans played a major role in the postbellum economy by (1) supplying cotton growers directly with merchandise; (2) supplying the "furnishing merchants" who traded with the growers; and (3) using funds from New York to buy cotton on the open market in New Orleans or from inland points in Louisiana, Mississippi, Texas, or Arkansas. In all three situations the Lehmans supported the business of those with whom they dealt by offering to buy cotton from those who grew it or, more frequently, from those who themselves acquired it in the course of their retail trade.

By the mid-1870s the value of the cotton coming through the New Orleans firm was in the range of $5,000,000. The list of merchants and storekeepers who sold cotton to the Lehmans from offices in New Orleans or from rural locations is noteworthy for the significant number of Jews on it. These merchants may have looked to Lehman, Abraham & Co. to supply merchandise for their stores, but the Lehman firm played a more important role by buying whatever cotton the merchants themselves acquired.

The Lehmans provided a secure outlet for cotton to untold numbers of Jewish merchants throughout the region who therefore could stabilize their own businesses. Records of Lehman Bros. also show that the New Orleans firm bought up numerous plantations and country stores, sometimes when their owners could not meet their obligations. Those in trouble were generally allowed to remain in possession and work to pay off their debts.

The Lehmans lived in the South, either Montgomery or New Orleans, for less than twenty years. But they expanded their business interests there for another thirty years. The number of Jews with whom they dealt, and to whom they offered services rarely available to southern merchants or cotton growers, let alone Jews, is too great to ignore when considering Jewish community development in the South in the period following the Civil War.

Overview

The years of Reconstruction in the South offered unusual economic opportunities that could be exploited because of the presence of people like the Lehmans and the Seligmans. In turn, these families laid the foundation for their own participation in the New York securities market and ultimately in the investment banking world of New York, which included a distinctive group of closely knit Jewish families of German origin like themselves.[17]

This sketch of the Seligmans and Lehmans as immigrant American entrepreneurs living in or working with the South is not only one of business and finance, is not defined by periods of residence, and is not lim-

ited to the family members here discussed. It is, rather, bound up with
the social and economic development of communities, Jewish and non-
Jewish, and with the individual lives of many above and below the Mason-Dixon Line.

At a time when the emphasis on pride in a particular locale and on
ethnic history as a living organism encourages us to take a microscopic
view of things, it is helpful to recognize at the same time that the South
was and is part of a nation. The southern economy in the nineteenth
century had important regional aspects, to be sure, but even then part
of our story is the development of a national economy.

The activities of the Lehmans and the Seligmans, however, ought to
make clear the extent of the interconnections between a regional economy and the economies of other sections of the country, particularly
New York. They indicate, as well, that religious identification was an important connection. The ways in which infusions of capital and other
forms of help from the North could transform and sustain not just a business but groups of Jewish individuals living in the South have communal
as well as commercial implications. As we uncover more and more information on commercial and financial relationships connecting Jews
in the South with those in the North, especially New York, we bring to
life a unifying factor in the face of assumed separation and southern isolation. We also do a service by adding another piece to the mosaic of
nineteenth-century United States history. We do not concern ourselves
only with one of many ethnic histories, fascinating though they may be.
We are dealing with American history.

Notes

An earlier version of this chapter was read at the 1990 annual meeting of the Organization of American Historians.

1. Still the best account is that of Robert G. Albion, *The Rise of New York Port,
1815–1816* (New York: Scribner's, 1939).

2. See Barry E. Supple, "A Business Elite: German-Jewish Financiers in Nineteenth-Century New York," *Business History Review* 31 (1957): 143–78. For a
good example of marriage and business in the antebellum plantation social
setting, see Morton Rothstein, "Sugar and Secession: A New York Firm in Antebellum Louisiana," *Explorations in Entrepreneurial History,* 2nd ser. 5 (1968): 115–
31. Members of the Leverich family, New York merchants, moved South and became related by marriage to, among other prominent landowners, William Mi-

nor and Stephen Duncan, two of the largest planter/capitalists in Mississippi and Louisiana.

3. As general background on this question and for the paper in general, see the author's *The Business of Jews in Louisiana, 1840–1875* (Tuscaloosa: University of Alabama Press, 1988).

4. The disappearance of the Lehman Bros. investment firm as an independent entity in the past few years may say something about the current investment banking climate, but does not detract from the influence of the firm throughout its history and of many family members in political and philanthropic matters. What it does mean is that any unknown Lehman business records from the nineteenth century will be virtually impossible to track down. I was fortunate enough to have contacted the firm, then known as Lehman Bros. Kuhn, Loeb Inc., several years ago at a time when a move to new, ever more opulent offices had unearthed a forgotten fireproof storage box containing business records and correspondence covering 1866 to 1881. Much of the information on the Lehmans in this paper comes from those documents.

5. Two manuscript articles on the Seligmans, dating from the 1930s and 1940s, have been at the New York Historical Society for some time. Written by Linton Wells and George Seligman Hellman, respectively, they are both helpful. Of greater moment are the copies of some of the business records and correspondence of the various Seligman firms and family members from the nineteenth and early twentieth centuries, recently donated by J. & W Seligman & Co, to the Bass Collection of the Bizzell Memorial Library at the University of Oklahoma in Norman. Most of the material here presented relating to the Seligmans comes from those records, known as the Seligman Archives. I wish to express my appreciation to Professor Daniel Wren and Mrs. Sidney Baraff, who were so helpful in organizing this large collection and helping me make most efficient use of an all-too-brief visit.

6. The physical mobility of the brothers, extraordinary in the case of the Seligmans, was characteristic of the mid-nineteenth-century Jewish immigrants who relied on peddling and trade to give them their start in America.

7. He provided more evidence of the importance of family ties to business matters. He there married Babette Newgass, member of the English family who represented the Lehmans in Liverpool when selling cotton to mill-owners. When the Lehmans opened their office in New Orleans, their first partner would be Babette's brother Benjamin, and the firm name would be Lehman, Newgass & Co.

8. Inland Letter Book 1, Seligman Archives, Bass Collection, University of Oklahoma, Norman, Oklahoma, has, among other correspondence, copies of the

New York office letters to both New Orleans and San Francisco but overwhelmingly to New Orleans, for these years.

9. For an excellent study of the framework within which the Seligmans conducted their banking business, see Edwin J. Perkins, *Financing Anglo-American Trade: The House of Brown, 1800–1880* (Cambridge: Harvard University Press, 1975).

10. Seligman to Hellman, 15 November 1866, Inland Book I, Seligman Archives.

11. Seligman to Hellman, 29 January 1866, Inland Book I, Seligman Archives.

12. The government steadily undermined the Seligmans' arbitrage activities by regularly selling gold and keeping its price down during the early part of 1866. War in Europe between Austria and Prussia brought gold to Europe and lifted the price at home.

13. Joseph Seligman to Hugh McCulloch, Secretary of Treasury, 26 May 1866, Inland Book I, Seligman Archives.

14. Joseph Seligman to Hellman, 17 March 1866, Inland Book I, Seligman Archives.

15. The background on the nation's financial situation at the end of the Civil War can be found in Robert P. Sharkey's classic *Money, Class, and Party* (Baltimore: Johns Hopkins Press, 1959, paperback ed., 1967), particularly chaps. 2, 3, and 6.

16. Theodore Hellman and his wife Frances Seligman, who lived in New Orleans until 1880, occupied central positions within the New Orleans Jewish community, part of a story yet to be told.

17. See Supple, "A Business Elite." Not only did the group marry among themselves, cementing or creating business affiliations, but they went to great lengths to find business partners among family. Until 1924, for example, all eleven partners in Lehman Bros. bore the surname Lehman.

8
Philip and Morris Dzialynski

Jewish Contributions to the Rebuilding of the South

Canter Brown Jr.

"What can we not say of Morris Dzialynski?" asked Rabbi Pizer Jacobs of Congregation Ahavath Chesed in Jacksonville, Florida, as he began to eulogize the distinguished community leader on May 8, 1907. As the rabbi spoke, "a steady down pour of rain" fell outside and, according to the *Jacksonville Florida Times-Union,* "those who could not find room in the Temple took refuge in the piazzas of the neighboring houses." Within the synagogue "the whole people of the city were represented." The *Times-Union* proclaimed, "Never before has there been such general expression of sorrow and regret over the death of any person."[1]

Over a lifetime of service, Morris Dzialynski had earned the respect of his fellow citizens while endeavoring against difficult odds to build a life of security and comfort for his loved ones, just as had other members of his family, particularly his brother Philip. "[Morris] came a boy to this country," recalled Rabbi Jacobs of Jacksonville's late mayor and municipal judge, "and though starting from a very humble beginning, he ascended, step by step, from the healthy work of nature's fields to the lofty position of city magistrate." The rabbi continued: "Like many noble men his character was a gradual progression through bitter experience. He showed he had the making of a noble character."[2]

The story of Morris and Philip Dzialynski, and of their family, offers a fascinating study of lives founded in an honorable pursuit of the American Dream. It reflects as well the history of hundreds, if not thousands, of Jewish immigrants to the United States in the wake of the European revolutions of 1848. Perhaps most importantly, the Dzialynskis typify those individuals of initiative and character who helped to revive the economic, cultural, political, and religious life of the South in the Civil War's aftermath.

The study of the roles filled by Jewish men and women during the Reconstruction era remains in its infancy. As interest in the subject grows, one aspect of the topic deserves special attention: the part played by Jewish businessmen such as the Dzialynski brothers in the development of Southern communities. The importance of examining this issue lies not only in an interest in Jewish history but also in a broader interest in understanding how the South managed, economically and socially, to struggle to its feet as well as it did, even when the reality of its recovery placed the region at a distinct disadvantage to the rest of the country.[3]

The creation and growth of numerous small towns and villages also stand out as a principal element of the post-Civil War Southern revival. The large-scale plantation economy lay in ruins, as did the factorage system by which the plantations had been supplied with goods and supplies. Instead, wholesale merchants operating out of larger commercial centers came to service general stores located eventually "at almost every crossroad in the South." Many individuals at both ends of this new system of mercantile organization, including Philip and Morris Dzialynski, were Jews. Thus, an understanding of the lives and experiences of the Dzialynski brothers provides broader insight into this additional and important facet of Southern history.[4]

The Brothers Settle in Florida

Philip and Morris Dzialynski were born in Prussian Poland. The sons of Abraham Samuel Dzialynski and his wife Rosalie Diamond ("Rachin") Dzialynski, Philip came into the world on June 15, 1833 in Posen, and Morris followed on July 14, 1841. The family eventually included at least three other brothers, John, Jacob, and Henry, and four sisters, Dora, Hannah, Helena, and Augusta. Little information has survived about the boys' early years in Prussia, save for a single sentence of reminiscence by Philip's eldest son, "Philip D." (George I. P. Dzialynski), who recorded, "fought in the Polish Rev. in '48 with Jacobi and Schultz." After the revolt, perhaps because he had participated on the losing side, fifteen-year-old Philip emigrated from Prussia and settled in New York City. By 1853 he had prospered sufficiently to send for the rest of the family.[5]

George Dzialynski recalled that the family's crossing of the Atlantic took fifty-seven days, but their first stop after the voyage proved a temporary one. Mother Rachin died within three months of landing in New

York, perhaps from the rigors of the crossing. The family lingered in the city until January 21, 1854, when sister Helena married Robert S. Williams, also a native of Prussian Poland. Soon after the nuptials Abraham relocated the family to Jacksonville, Duval County, Florida, while Robert and Helena resettled nearby in Hamilton County. It may be that Philip had visited the area previously "as a peddler."[6]

In those years just prior to the Civil War, Florida remained mostly remote and sparsely settled. The Jacksonville that greeted the Dzialynskis in 1854 was not far from being a frontier town. Its population amounted to less than fifteen hundred, diminished slightly from the previous year due to a smallpox outbreak. Still, the community was one of the state's larger towns, and optimism about its future swirled in the air. The recent erection of several steam-powered sawmills had spurred growth of the local lumber industry, and efforts to develop the town's potential as a port through railroad construction were ongoing.[7]

In Jacksonville the Dzialynskis began to accustom themselves to their new home and to build the family's future. The younger children, including Morris, attended the town's common schools, while Philip and his father supported the family, likely by peddling. On August 11, 1856, Philip married fellow Prussian émigré Ida Ehrlick in Suwannee Shoals, a trading center in Columbia County on the south side of the Suwannee River located not far from the Williamses' Hamilton County home. On June 8, 1857, Ida gave birth to a son, George, in their Jacksonville home. Daughter Regina (or "Jennie") followed within two years. Philip's sisters Hannah and Dora also married during the family's early years in Jacksonville, if not earlier. Tragedy struck, however, in the fall of 1857 when a yellow fever outbreak took the lives of father Abraham and brothers Jacob and Henry. Theirs were among the first burials in Jacksonville's Old Jewish Cemetery, believed to be the first Jewish cemetery in Florida.[8]

Philip in Madison

In 1860, Jacksonville's long-awaited rail connection with the interior of the state was completed, and that opened for Philip Dzialynski the opportunity to establish himself as a businessman. Philip moved the family a little more than one hundred miles due west of Jacksonville to Madison, the seat of Madison County. The village of five hundred or so white residents and perhaps as many black slaves looked forward to a future filled with great prospects. It formed a part of the plantation region known as Middle Florida that lay between the Apalachicola and Suwannee Rivers, and the community already benefited from cotton prosperity. The railroad's arrival seemed likely to encourage even more growth. By the time the first train arrived there on July 4, 1860, Philip already had opened a general merchandise store.[9]

The Dzialynskis found little time to establish themselves at Madison. Within a few months the presidential election of 1860 had taken place, and, in its aftermath, secessionist sentiments raged throughout the South, including in plantation-dominated Madison County. When news of Florida's secession reached the town in January 1861, the reaction among most whites was one of joy. "This place was settled by natives of South Carolina," a local woman explained, "and no doubt we imbibed our fire eating propensities from that State." She added, "We believed in the doctrines of John C. Calhoun."[10]

Madison's residents quickly set about organizing Confederate volunteer companies, which affected the Dzialynski family almost immediately. One of the companies was Company G of the Third Florida Infantry, known as the Madison Gray Eagles. Twenty-year-old Morris Dzialynski was among the first to enlist in its ranks. By summer 1862, Dzialynski and the Gray Eagles had been ordered north to join the Army of Tennessee.[11]

In Morris's absence, Philip remained in Madison to support the family and to tend to his mercantile business. Wartime life was not without its opportunities. "Madison County's job was to provide supplies for the fighting men," a local historian commented, "and to be a refugee center for those who fled areas taken over by the Union Army, such as Fernandina, Jacksonville and St. Augustine." The town eventually emerged as a Confederate commissary center. Dzialynski, accordingly, capitalized on the commercial possibilities this situation afforded.[12]

Fortunately for the family, Madison escaped direct armed conflict during the war. It served, however, as a staging point for Confederate efforts to eliminate bands of deserters and Union sympathizers in nearby Taylor and Levy Counties. The greatest threat to the town came from the ill-fated Union initiative in February 1864 that culminated in the Battle of Olustee, ten miles east of Lake City. Even then the Union forces were repelled at a point well over sixty miles to the east of the Dzialynski home.[13]

Though Madison escaped military threat, Philip nonetheless found himself assailed by personal tragedy. On January 16, 1864, his wife Ida died while giving birth to a son, Rudolph. Shortly thereafter Philip relocated the family, including his own three children and siblings John and Augusta, to Savannah, Georgia. From all indications, the five or so years he would spend there would prove at once the most painful and the most fulfilling of his life.[14]

Before examining the Dzialynski family's Savannah experiences, though, one additional point should be considered about their wartime life in Madison. No specific evidence points to why Philip moved the family. He may have done it simply for a better business opportunity or because of a desire to provide for his children through an early remarriage. Anti-Semitism, however, may have provided the motivation.

As Bertram Wallace Korn has described, the Civil War unleashed intense prejudices in certain areas of the South, some Southerners finding in Jews the perfect scapegoats for Southern reverses on the battlefield. One such incident occurred at Thomasville, Georgia, which lies some forty miles northwest of Madison. There, on August 30, 1862, local citizens denounced the "unpatriotic conduct" of "German Jews" and, reportedly, banished them from the town. Reports then in circulation also suggested that "denunciations of Jewish merchants were frequent in the area, and that the habit had spread from town to town throughout the state." Mark I. Greenberg has questioned whether the Thomasville event carried quite the dire connotations previously suggested, but the possibility remains that Madison witnessed some similar experience. Unfortunately, since most Florida newspapers of the era have not survived, no solid evidence exists to answer the question one way or the other. The principal objections raised against the Thomasville action were voiced at a public meeting held in Savannah, which may have tipped the scales in Savannah's favor when Philip decided to relocate.[15]

Philip in Savannah

Philip apparently found business opportunities in Savannah without too much trouble. Specifically, he entered into a partnership with young Prussian émigré Julius Slager in 1865. Their dry goods store was located first at 70 Saint Julian Street. When the partnership dissolved in early 1866, Philip continued for a time, as the *Savannah Daily Herald* reported on March 6, to operate from "the old stand." In that early postwar era Savannah enjoyed a commercial revival, and Philip managed to benefit from it. Soon he operated as a "commission merchant" for all of southern Georgia and northern Florida, with branch offices in Madison and Quitman, Georgia, not far to the north.[16]

As early as October 1866 the Dzialynski name had begun to carry substantial weight in the business circles of Florida and south Georgia. "The immense mercantile establishment of Philip Dzialynski, at 103 Bryant St., Savannah, Ga., deserves to be patronized by Floridians," declared the *Tallahassee Sentinel.* "In the first place, goods can be bought as cheaply there, as in any Northern City; and then, Mr. D. has done business in Florida for fifteen years and is thoroughly acquainted with the wants of our people," the article continued. "He advertises as he does business, on a large and liberal scale," it concluded. "Look at his fine double column advertisement in this paper and remember where his house may be found when you go to Savannah."[17]

In Savannah Philip also established a new family. On May 28, 1865, he married Prussian-born Mary Cohen, sister to Savannah merchant Jacob R. Cohen. The couple's first child, a daughter they named Esther, arrived in April 1866. Sadly, the infant passed away in December 1867. The loss compounded the grief that the family already felt from the March 1865 death of Philip's infant son Rudolph.[18]

Despite Philip's anguish over the children's deaths, the happiness that he otherwise felt in his life prevailed. George Dzialynski remembered his father as a "Hebrew scholar," and during the Savannah years Philip, for the only time in his adult life, found himself fully able to pursue his interest in and love for Jewish culture and religion. He assumed, for example, a leadership role in the affairs of Savannah's B'nai Berith Jacob Congregation. In May 1866 he participated in the solicitation of bids for the design and construction of the congregation's synagogue. Upon the occasion of its consecration, he served as a "special marshal" for the ceremonies. He also acted as the congregation's representative in the organization of the Savannah Hebrew Collegiate Institute, and, when the institute opened in November 1867, he served on its first permanent council. This love for education and his Jewish heritage would reassert itself later in Philip's life, but it would do so under far less refined circumstances.[19]

Morris at War and in Jacksonville

Morris Dzialynski shared Philip's pride in his Jewishness, although some time would pass before Morris could act upon it. In his first battle as a Confederate soldier, at Perryville, Kentucky, Morris suffered a severe wound. Following a period of convalescence, he fought at Murphreesboro but, according to Florida's Confederate cavalry hero J. J. Dickison, "his wound unfitted him to remain in the field, and he was detailed in the blockade running service between Indian River [Florida] and Nassau." Dickison claimed that Morris made "five [blockade running] trips successfully before the end of the war." Rerick's *Memoirs of Florida,* written about the same time, noted, "The particular attempts at blockade running in which he was engaged, were . . . not successful, but through no fault of the brave men who made the attempt."[20]

As brother Philip established himself in Savannah, Morris returned with the peace to a war-devastated Jacksonville. He shortly thereafter married Rosa Slager, the eighteen-year-old German-born daughter of Charles Slager, known locally as "the merchant prince of Jacksonville," and niece of Philip's Savannah friend and business partner Julius Slager. Within one year their only child, Rosalie, had entered the world.[21] The family thereafter settled into an increasingly prosperous life in Jacksonville, which quickly became Florda's most dynamic and important city.

Great similarities emerged in Philip and Morris Dzialynski's lives after the Civil War's end. Both participated actively in the commercial, social, and political lives of their communities. Both applied habits of industry and tenacity, combined with a sense of humor and humility. And both remained close to their Jewish heritage.

Despite these many similarities, their lives also differed significantly. First and foremost, Morris contentedly accepted his good fortune in the fast-growing city of Jacksonville while Philip found himself compelled to leave Savannah and pursue his fortune on the rough southwest Florida cattle frontier. With one exception that will be discussed shortly, Morris' life mostly proceeded in a gentle progression, slowly but uniformly upward—at least until the incapacitation and later death of his wife in 1905. Philip's life, on the other hand, evolved as a roller-coaster ride that combined elements of boom and bust, violence, satisfaction, and despair. His experience, as it turned out, typified frontier life itself.

The Southwest Florida Frontier

As was true for his reasons for moving to Savannah, Philip's motivations for leaving can only be surmised. Crop failures in 1866 and 1867 undermined the city's prosperity in the years that followed. The development of rail transportation and the accompanying growth of cotton farming in upland regions brought, in Eric Foner's words, "a wholesale shift in regional economic power." Port cities such as Savannah steadily lost economic ground to inland hubs such as Atlanta. In the process, many Savannah "commission merchants" endured bankruptcy and, by decade's end, Philip likely stood among them.[22]

Whatever the reason, in the early months of 1870 Philip's family moved to Palatka, Florida, a country town and budding resort located up the St. Johns River from Jacksonville. Included in the party were two new daughters, Fanny (born in 1868) and Helena (1870).[23] The Dzia-lynskis lived in Palatka with Philip's brother-in-law Jacob R. Cohen, who also had just relocated from Savannah to open a store. Philip briefly worked for Cohen at Palatka, but Jacob soon would pass along a better opportunity. He had entered into a partnership with cattleman Julius C. Rockner to open a series of general stores along the southwest Florida frontier (southeast Florida was then virtually uninhabited save for a few hundred Seminole Indians). In the post-Civil War era this frontier ran roughly down the Peace River; in modern terms, from just south of to-day's Lakeland in Polk County (approximately thirty-five miles east of Tampa) to a Gulf of Mexico outflow at Punta Gorda and Charlotte Har-bor in today's Charlotte County. No towns of consequence yet had ap-peared in the area. The 1850s military post at Fort Meade offered the c-losest thing to a village in the vicinity. Polk County's seat lay ten miles to the north in Bartow, and cattlemen had begun settling and trading six-ty miles south of there at Fort Ogden. These were the locations at which Cohen and Rockner planned to operate their stores.[24]

The opportunity afforded by entering into the mercantile business on the Peace River frontier was greater than it might have appeared. Al-though the area remained an isolated, underpopulated expanse of cat-tle range, plans then in motion aimed to open up the region for settle-ment and exploitation. In June 1869 Republican Governor Harrison Reed had publicly committed his administration to supporting a rail-road to Charlotte Harbor. At its next regular session in February 1870, the Florida legislature also sanctioned the creation of a corporation to clear the Peace River for light-draft steamboat navigation from Charlotte Harbor to as far north as Fort Meade. Finally, the southwest Florida cat-tle industry had begun to prosper when the demand for cattle in Span-ish Cuba exploded after an insurrection in the island's cattle-producing locales. Optimism ran high along the Peace River.[25]

Philip in Bartow

The optimism of 1870, it thus may be seen, drew Philip south on the dif-ficult and time-consuming trail to the frontier. When he opened the Bartow store in September, though, he must have questioned just what he had brought upon himself. As one pioneer recorded of the Polk County seat, "It looked liked an open field covered with dog fennel six feet high in those days, with just a few buildings scattered here and there." Trouble with finding customers in the vicinity soon turned to trouble between the owners, further complicating Philip's task. By the spring of 1871, Jacob Cohen and Julius Rockner had dissolved their partnership. As a result, Rockner took complete control of the more-prosperous Fort Meade and Fort Ogden stores, while Cohen retained the one in Bartow and kept Philip in charge of it.[26]

When Philip first arrived in Bartow, it was so small that it could barely even be called a village. That the community existed at all had stemmed from the generosity of cattleman Jacob Summerlin, who had moved away several years previously. Still, Bartow had pride of place as Polk's county seat, and, as the county's fortunes swelled with the cattle trade, Bartow's presumably would swell as well. Unfortunately for Philip and others, time's passage proved otherwise. "The business of the county is meager," a local man recorded in the mid-1870s, "so much so that the county cannot afford business for two lawyers (not a single case, either civil or criminal, on the docket); one has to *cow-drive* and the other is an *accountant* in a mercantile house to make a genteel livelihood."[27]

Despite the modest nature of his new home, Philip quickly plunged into the village's affairs. Within a few months after his arrival, for example, he had helped to organize a Bartow chapter of Royal Arch Masonry with assistance from Charles Slager, who long had occupied leadership positions within Florida Masonry. Philip's selection as a chapter officer signaled his acceptance by the townspeople. The merchant's growing popularity and his interest in civic matters was attested to the following year when Republican Governor Reed appointed Dzialynski, a Democrat, as a Polk County commissioner. Again, Slager may have assisted. A wartime Union loyalist who had helped to found the Florida Republican party at Jacksonville in 1867, Slager held local offices in Jacksonville until he relocated to Tampa in late 1870. There Slager served as postmaster and, beginning in 1871 (thanks to a Reed appointment), as Hillsborough County sheriff.[28]

Dzialynski's social and civic life might have been on the rise, but his business prospects had taken a tumble by the time of his appointment to the county commission. Late in 1870, Francis Vose, a disgruntled investor in prewar Florida railroad bonds, obtained a federal court injunction against the state that essentially forbade it from granting public lands for internal improvements until its obligations to him were discharged. Since the state's financial conditions prohibited it from satisfying Vose's claim, projects such as the railroad to Charlotte Harbor and the clearing of the Peace River, both of which depended upon land grants for their financing, abruptly came to a halt.[29]

Philip in Orlando and Fort Meade

The rapid expansion of his Bartow business forestalled, Philip Dzialynski first strove unsuccessfully to make a go of things before turning his gaze to greener pastures. Particularly, he urgently attempted to collect old accounts in order to satisfy his own obligations. By spring 1874, however, circumstances forced him to retrench by relocating to the less isolated, though tiny town of Orlando, near the navigable St. Johns River. Jacob R. Cohen had invested in the area, which cattleman Jacob Summerlin was attempting to develop as a community and as a railhead for the cattle industry. Ossian B. Hart, a childhood friend of Summerlin's who became governor in January 1873, strove to assist by reaching an accommodation on the Vose Injunction, but Hart's untimely death in March 1874 effectively killed the plans. Under the circumstances, Summerlin immediately put his Orlando store up for sale on advantageous terms. Mary Cohen Dzialynski thereupon purchased it for her husband.[30]

By all accounts, though, Philip never abandoned the possibilities of the Peace River frontier. Although the Vose Injunction had halted development projects, it had not damaged the flourishing Cuban cattle trade. By 1876 Spanish gold doubloons received from cattle sales provided the area with most of its circulating money. According to the reminiscence of one area pioneer, doubloons were so plentiful that "in many of our country log houses may be found an iron 'gopher'—a Hall Warmer, or Butler—in which the wily farmer or rancher secretes the frolicsome doubloon."[31]

Mostly, Philip looked toward Fort Meade. The capital of Florida's cattle kingdom during the mid-1870s, the town earned $400,000 annually from cattle sales by 1874, while local merchants did a very considerable business of about $100,000 per year. A local man described the village as a "flourishing, busy, and bustling little town, on a beautiful bluff on the left bank of Peace creek." His report continued, "The health and water is fine, and society refined and orderly." How refined society could have been on that violent frontier is open to question, but, to the extent that any society existed in the area, it existed at Fort Meade. In 1877, a second local man added descriptive detail. "Some five or six stores are established here, and it is a place of considerable business," he observed. "Most of the trading is with the stock men and the stock raisers, who handle more money, as a general thing, than any other class in South Florida."[32]

The lure of Fort Meade's prosperity proved irresistible to Philip. In spring 1876 he and Mary bought Julius Rockner's general store and established a home that they were to maintain, with one short interruption, for the next thirteen years. They slowly began to rebuild their finances. While plagued by earlier debts, Philip achieved a breakthrough late in the decade when he entered into a partnership with the area's physician and druggist Dr. Charles L. Mitchell, brother to future governor Henry L. Mitchell. Dzialynski, Mitchell & Co. became one of the leading commercial establishments on Fort Meade's Wire Street and grew with the affluence of the cattle trade.[33]

Whereas postwar Savannah had offered Philip an opportunity to satisfy his cultural and religious needs, during the late 1870s and through the 1880s Fort Meade provided him a forum for utilizing his talents as an entrepreneur, businessman, and civic leader. The list of projects in which he involved himself from 1876 to 1889 runs long, and it may fairly be said that he furnished influence and effort behind most early attempts of significance to open up southwest Florida to immigration and development. For example, he helped to organize the Tampa, Peace Creek and St. Johns Railroad (eventually the South Florida Railroad), the planned- but never-built Fort Meade, Keystone and Walk-in-the-Water Railroad, the Tampa and Fort Meade Hack Line, and the Tampa and Fort Meade Telegraph Company.[34]

There was much more. Philip stood out as one of the first individuals to subdivide and sell lots at Fort Meade, and he emerged as one of south Florida's first real estate agents and brokers. With Mary, he opened a hotel, the Dzialynski House, and augmented its income with that of a livery stable. He invested in citrus groves, helping to pioneer their development in the area. He exported exotic bird plumes and alligator skins to Paris, served again as a county commissioner, and—when Fort Meade incorporated in 1885—sat as chairman of its first board of aldermen. The same year, he and two other men built the town's first substantial school building. Earlier he had served on the building committee of the Methodist church. In short, Philip Dzialynski participated in nearly every aspect of the town's life.[35]

His many business, civic, and social interests notwithstanding, Philip never lost touch with his heritage or religion, and, at times, he managed to bring a sample of Jewish culture to the frontier. An early example involved the 1877 marriage of his daughter Jennie to Louis Herzog of Baltimore. Townspeople celebrated the wedding as a community event. A justice of the peace administered the legal aspects of the occasion while Philip "performed the Jewish part of the ceremony." As late as 1890 the "Hebrew scholar" was traveling to Tallahassee to conduct services for Yom Kippur. It can be no accident that Philip visited his brother Morris in Jacksonville within days of the 1882 dedication of the town's Ahavath Chesed synagogue.[36]

Beyond his commitment to his heritage, Dzialynski also devoted himself to the cause of temperance, and this may be seen a resolve not wholly alien to the frontier world in which he lived. A lodge of Good Templars organized at Fort Meade in 1877 with Philip participating. Within a few years he had convinced most of the town's leading citizens to sign a pledge "that not a foot of ground should be leased, sold or given away whereon might be built a drinking saloon of any kind where intoxicating beverages are sold." Shortly thereafter fire consumed the community's only saloon, an event that local citizens saw as "evidently the work of an incendiary." When funds became available to rebuild the bar, culprits mysteriously broke into the post office and stole the money. The guilty party or parties escaped apprehension.[37]

The direct action taken to win Fort Meade for the temperance cause illustrates the southwest Florida frontier's violent nature, and, most assuredly, Philip was no stranger to violence. In 1877 he witnessed firsthand Julius Rockner being ambushed and shot down by cattle baron William W. "Bill Ham" Willingham. During the brief period in the early 1880s when he operated a store in Tampa, Dzialynski looked on as one of the town's leading citizens gunned down one of the area's few physicians.[38]

By 1878 the violence approached more closely and personally. That year south Florida's most famous bandit, John W. "Hub" Williams—known as the "Robin Hood of South Florida"—accosted Dzialynski. When Philip encountered the outlaw, however, it turned out that Williams had met his match. A Tampa newspaper reported the engagement:

> Last Saturday afternoon a desperado named John Williams made an assault on Mr. Philip Dzialynski in his store with a drawn pistol and demanded $200. Mr. Dzialynski of course refused to comply with his

demand, when the man Williams made several efforts to shoot him, but fortunately the pistol failed to fire. Mr. Dzialynski, being alone, finally made his escape from the store and locked Williams up inside while he went for assistance. Williams being unable to get into the safe, broke out before Mr. Dzialynski returned. After Williams escaped from Dzialynski, another Fort Meade man shot the desperado but he made his getaway.[39]

Through all of these years and adventures, Philip Dzialynski's actions and contributions created immense good will for him among his fellow frontier-dwellers. The details of Fort Meade's 1878 Fourth of July celebration provide a glimpse of the position he had come to occupy within his community. "On the 3d the town was full of arrivals," an onlooker related in a Tampa newspaper, "but it was the morning of the 4th that the stream began to pour in from every quarter. Buggies, wagons, horses, ox-teams and mules came in one extended procession." Guests found seats under a pavilion erected on the Peace River's west bank, as well as tables two hundred feet long piled high with food. After dining, they heard speeches and delighted in singing. Then came the special moment. "At the close came more singing," the onlooker declared, "and—a pistol shot had a startling effect upon the gathering, especially when some shouted 'the Indians are coming' . . . and now came a weird troupe of mounted figures dressed in most fantastic costumes." He continued: "They came up in procession and filed in around the pavilion, and a representative of the fatherland (German) ascended the steps and delivered an oration on 'The fort of Ghuly' in true Teutonic style, eliciting a large amount of laughter." Philip's participation helped to ensure the occasion's success, and it became an annual event for the region thereafter.[40]

Morris in Jacksonville

In contrast with his brother Philip's frontier life, Morris Dzialynski lived in relative peace and quiet. The only incident hinting at the same kind of excitement occurred in 1870, when, as a result of a business dispute, a Chatham County, Georgia, grand jury indicted him for "obtaining goods under false pretenses." When an officer arrived at Jacksonville to return Morris to Savannah for trial, however, a kind of frontier justice intervened. "The arrest having been made," the *Savannah Daily Republican* reported, "officer Phillips started for the depot for the purpose of proceeding to Savannah on the evening train, but found his way impeded in such a manner by Messrs. M. Rosenberg, H. Berlack and a number of other friends of Mr. Dzialynski, that he was unable to reach the train before its departure."[41]

Morris never caught that train to the trial, but the event did interrupt his Jacksonville life temporarily. He departed the town for elsewhere, possibly either New Orleans or Galveston, Texas, where his father-in-law Charles Slager also had relocated. In 1873, after the Chatham County authorities dropped the charges against the exile, he returned to Florida. "We are pleased to see on our streets the familiar face of Morris Dzialynski," Jacksonville's *Tri-Weekly Florida Union* informed its readers in April 1874. "[He] is glad to return home to those who extend him a hearty welcome back."[42]

The incident with Officer Phillips demonstrates the personal popularity that still-young Morris enjoyed in Jacksonville. For the remainder of his life, that popularity stood him in good stead and, far more than his brother Philip did, Morris utilized it for political purposes. Before examining his political career, though, a mention of the similarities in the approaches Philip and Morris took to life and their communities might be useful.

As was true for many Jews in Florida and the South, the Dzialynski brothers relied upon merchandising for their livelihood. Philip operated general stores on the frontier. Morris specialized in the sale of carriages, buggies, and wagons in Jacksonville, the state's largest mainland city, where he was also the leading auctioneer. Morris, in fact, stood out as the first early Jacksonville merchant to specialize in vehicle sales, and the innovation brought him a certain statewide renown. "In the extent, variety, and character of his stock, the taste and judgment displayed in its make and finish, and the acknowledged style and durability of his vehicles," an 1885 report observed, "Mr. Dzialynski has won for himself a well-deserved reputation with the trade which enables him to a front rank among dealers in this line of goods." Morris's approach to merchandising would prove far more economically reliable over time than would Philip's.[43]

Both men gained entrées into their communities through active involvement in fraternal organizations. In Savannah, Philip served as an officer of the Joseph Lodge of the Independent Order of B'nai B'rith. In southwest Florida, he helped organize lodges of the Royal Arch Masons and the Good Templars.

Morris, meanwhile, helped to lead Masonry in Jacksonville. In late

1867 he won election as an officer of Solomon Lodge No. 20, F. & A. M. ("Free and Accepted Mason"), and the following spring he helped to organize Duval Lodge U-D. The relationships both men formed through these fraternal activities proved useful to their business and civic careers.[44]

Finally, both men chose to remain close to their Jewish roots. To some extent Morris enjoyed an advantage over Philip in that Jacksonville hosted a small but thriving Jewish community. In July 1867 its members met at Charles Slager's residence and "organized a society for the worship of God." Morris took on responsibilities as the group's treasurer. The town not being large enough yet to support a synagogue, its modest goals were "to worship by reading of prayers and Canticles on the Sabbath and by holding Sunday schools in both the Hebrew and English on every Sunday." Holiday services and activities were held in private houses and later in the Masonic Temple. In 1882 the town's leading Jews gathered under Morris's presidency to found Congregation Ahavath Chesed, the second oldest congregation in the state. Dzialynski family members then closely involved themselves in the construction of a sanctuary on the corner of Laura and Union Streets.[45]

Morris as Politician

Building upon family connections and fraternal, religious, and business relationships, Morris launched himself early into the politics of Jacksonville and Duval County. Despite the Republican political hegemony there in Reconstruction's early years, he won election in 1868 to the city's governing authority as a Democrat (referred to at the time as a "Conservative"). "It afforded me great pleasure to meet here my friend, M. A. Dzialynski, who now is deservedly one of the most popular and reliable merchants in Florida," a visitor observed to the *Savannah Daily Republican* in February 1869. He continued: "I have known him for fifteen years, and when the cruel war commenced . . . he cheerfully buckled on his arms and volunteered to battle for the South, and nobly and gallantly did he demean himself while in the Confederate army. In proof of his high regard and [respect] which the people here entertain for him, he not only enjoys the advantage and profits of a large trade, but anxious to show their appreciation of true worth, the people in October last elected him one of the aldermen of this city by complimentary vote." The visitor concluded, "If all Germans were like this man, we would have a better state of things in mercantile matters throughout this country."[46]

Although Morris eventually had a long and distinguished career in politics and government, including nine years on the city council, his earliest attempt to rise further than the town council met with frustration in the highly partisan politics of the town. In 1875 black Republican Thomas Lancaster defeated Dzialynski for the position of city assessor by a lopsided vote, but the following year saw a different result. In a campaign filled with charges of Republican corruption and Democratic intimidation, Democrats captured control of Jacksonville's government, and Morris took the office.[47]

With the "Redemption" of Florida by the Democrats in 1877 came more openings for political involvement. Within days of taking office, Governor George F. Drew appointed Morris the treasurer of Duval County. He went on to serve four two-year terms in the position. Soon, he also had ascended to the presidency of the city council.[48]

Then came the Jacksonville mayoral election of 1881. The Democrats were not expected to do well that year. Some reaction to Bourbon (Conservative Democratic) control of the state had set in, and the city's Republican organization had offered as its candidate the chairman of the party's state executive committee. The Democrats, yearning for a strong candidate, turned to Morris. The campaign proved short but intense, with the key issue becoming Morris's pledge to enforce Sunday closing laws. When the votes were counted, he had triumphed narrowly. "As the result was unexpected," one observer commented, "[the Republicans'] surprise was as great as their mortification."[49]

The next year Mayor Dzialynski ran for reelection. He had earned credentials as a "law and order" man who gave support to the business community's interests, although he had broken his key 1881 campaign pledge by permitting certain saloons "to operate more or less openly on Sundays." The new campaign soon centered on the question of the open saloons, and Morris quickly ordered Sunday closings. As added insurance, and as he also had done the previous year, he ran not on the Democratic but rather on the People's ticket (a device to attract some Republican votes). His decision proved its worth for, on election day, he again won by a small majority, this time of eighty-seven votes.[50]

The 1882 election offered a true test of Morris's political popularity among Democrats and independents. From the little information available, it seems that William Ledwith, the Republican in the race, probably could have bested just about any opponent other than Dzialynski. Accounting for a good deal of Morris's political strength were qualities of personality that made him so likable. Like Philip, Morris did not seem to take himself too seriously. On certain moral issues both brothers held firm commitments, but Morris proved the more equable and easygoing of the two.

The brothers also shared a great sense of humor, which, according to the *Jacksonville Florida Times*, Morris displayed to his advantage during the 1882 campaign:

> A TIMES reporter emerged from a group of excited politicians near Rice's grain store, and walking a few steps away came upon the two opposing candidates for the Mayoralty in calm and friendly conversation.
>
> "I was saying," said Mr. Dzialynski, grasping the reporter by the arm, "that this has been, so far, the pleasantest campaign ever had in this city, and I have just told General Ledwith that if by any chance he should beat me, which no one knows better than he that he can't do, I shall, when I swear him in, make the best, and the longest speech ever made by a retiring Mayor. I will put him through in first-class style."
>
> "Yes, said the General, "I know you will do that, Morris, and it is one of the things that gives me the greatest pleasure in defeating you."
>
> "Enjoy it," said Morris, "it is a pleasure that cannot last."[51]

Mayor Dzialynski declined to run for a third term, but he remained active in state and local affairs. In 1884 he sat as an alternate delegate to the Democratic National Convention in Chicago, where he supported Grover Cleveland's nomination. In Jacksonville, he joined the board of trade; organized one of the town's first baseball clubs; served as a port warden, volunteer fire captain, and fraternal leader; and involved himself in a myriad of other social and civic activities. In 1895 a group of conservative Democratic businessmen asked him to run for municipal judge on a Citizens ticket, and he won easily. Morris retained that office until his death.[52]

The Brothers' Last Years

As Morris was enjoying his business and political careers in Jacksonville in the late 1880s, Philip's fortunes had taken a turn for the worse. The exact circumstances remain unclear, but the Fort Meade area's perennial boom-and-bust cycle apparently had undermined his financial security. By late in 1889 he had moved the family ten miles north to Bartow, where he had lived two decades earlier. There, Philip undertook to manage the Orange Grove Hotel with Mary's help, but his health declined. *The Bartow Polk County News* related, "The many friends of Mr. Philip Dzialynski . . . are glad to see his genial face on the streets again after his severe illness."[53]

Despite an 1892 announcement by Philip that he was moving the family to South Carolina, they remained in Bartow until 1895,[54] and then their destination was Jacksonville instead. Philip died there on January 16, 1896, in Morris's home. "Mr. Dzialynski was a kind and genial gentleman," the *Jacksonville Florida Times-Union* reflected, "and had a large circle of friends all over the state."[55]

Following Philip's death, Morris and Rosa Dzialynski continued to live in Jacksonville while Morris presided as municipal judge. When Rosa passed away suddenly on June 12, 1905, the *Jacksonville Florida Times-Union* described her as "a Lady known and Beloved in Jacksonville." When Morris succumbed to a stroke on May 5, 1907, the same paper declared that "the taking away of his life partner, to whom he was perfectly devoted, was a blow from which he never recovered." His body lay in state in the council chamber of Jacksonville's city hall. Of his funeral service at the synagogue he had helped to build, a reporter for the *Times-Union* wrote: "The Temple was filled to its utmost capacity. Men and women from every walk of life were there. Jews and Gentiles were there to attend the ceremonies over the body of their beloved friend. Never before in Jacksonville has there been such a scene." Morris Dzialynski was buried not far from the body of the brother who had brought him to America.[56]

The Dzialynski brothers left revolutionary strife to come to the United States and built for themselves and their families successful lives that earned them the respect of almost all who knew them. From the ruins of the Civil War, they helped rebuild their communities and their state. In the process, they never lost sight of their faith or their Jewish heritage. In their lives can been seen the lives of other Jews who put down their roots in the South before and in the aftermath of the war. They played a key role in helping to feed, clothe, house, and comfort a defeated, impoverished, and exhausted people, and they extended the hand of support that helped to permit the region eventually to emerge from despair. As Philip Dzialynski's obituary read, theirs certainly were "long and useful" lives.[57]

Notes

The author expresses his appreciation for the encouragement, support, and assistance of Professor Samuel Proctor of the University of Florida.

1. *Jacksonville Florida Times-Union,* May 6, 1907.

2. Ibid.

3. On the revolutions of 1848 and Jewish involvement in them, see, for example, Priscilla Robertson, *Revolutions of 1848, A Social History* (Princeton, N.J.: Princeton University Press, 1952); Rudolf Glantz, "The German-Jewish Mass Emigration, 1820–1880," *American Jewish Archives* 22 (April 1970). As to the roles filled by Jewish businessmen in post–Civil War Southern economic life, see, for instance, Elliot Ashkenazi, *The Business of Jews in Louisiana, 1840–1875* (Tuscaloosa: University of Alabama Press, 1988); Stephen J. Whitfield, "Commercial Passions: The Southern Jew as Businessman," *American Jewish History* 71 (March 1982): 342–57; Mark I. Greenberg, "Creating Ethnic Identity in Dixie: The Jews of Savannah, Georgia, 1830–1900" (Ph.D. dissertation, University of Florida, 1996); idem, "Tampa Mayor Herman Glogowski: Jewish Leadership in Gilded Age Florida" in *Florida's Heritage of Diversity: Essays in Honor of Samuel Proctor,* ed. Mark I. Greenberg, William Warren Rogers, and Canter Brown Jr. (Tallahassee: Sentry Press, 1997).

4. Thomas D. Clark, *Pills, Petticoats and Plows: The Southern Country Store* (Indianapolis: Bobbs-Merrill, 1944); idem, "The Post–Civil War Economy in the South" in *Jews in the South,* ed. Leonard Dinnerstein and Mary Dale Palsson (Baton Rouge: Louisiana State University Press, 1973), 21.

5. Ruth Hope Leon, "The History of the Dzialynski Family," 1–2 (typescript, Jacksonville Historical Society Archives, Jacksonville); "Helena Dzialynski Williams" (typescript, n.d.), 1–2 (original in collection of Rabbi Stanley Garfein, Tallahassee; xerographic copy in collection of the author); Rowland H. Rerick, *Memoirs of Florida, Embracing a General History of the Province, Territory and State; and Special Chapters Devoted to Finances and Banking, the Bench and Bar, Medical Profession, Railways and Navigation, and Industrial Interests,* 2 vols. (Atlanta: Southern Historical Association, 1902), 1:520. A later biographical article on George I. P. Dzialynski, as well as family tradition, asserts that George's grandfather Abraham, rather than father Philip, joined the Polish revolt in 1848 and that Philip arrived in the United States as early as 1845. Biographical questionnaire of George I. P. Dzialynski in "Dzialynski Family File" (Haydon Burns Public Library, Jacksonville, n.d.); Pleasant Daniel Gold, *History of Duval County Florida* (St. Augustine: Record Co., 1928), 344–45; Bertha Zadek Dzialynski, "Within My Heart" (typescript, Jacksonville, 1944), 63–64 (original in collection of Perry Coleman,

Jacksonville; xerographic copy in collection of the author). The portion of Bertha Zadek Dzialynski's memoir that concerned her life in Fort Meade during 1882–90 has been published. See Canter Brown Jr., ed., "A Prussian-born Jewish Woman on the Florida Frontier: Excerpts from the Memoir of Bertha Zadek Dzialynski," *Southern Jewish History* 7 (2004): 109–54.

6. "Helena Dzialynski Williams," 1; Gold, *History of Duval County,* 345; Rerick, *Memoirs,* 1:520. Before arriving in Jacksonville, the Dzialynski family may have stayed for a short time with or near the Williamses at Suwannee Shoals, north of Lake City on the Suwannee River. No Dzialynski is recorded as paying a state or county tax in Duval County until 1857. Leon, "History of the Dzialynski Family," 1; *Jacksonville Florida Times-Union,* January 16, 1896; Duval County, Florida, tax books, 1854–1857 (available on microfilm at Florida State Archives and State Library of Florida, Tallahassee).

7. *Jacksonville Tri-Weekly Florida Sun,* January 22, 1876; Thomas Frederick Davis, *History of Early Jacksonville, Florida* (Jacksonville: H. and W. B. Drew, 1911), 117–18; Canter Brown Jr., "The Florida, Atlantic and Gulf Central Railroad, 1851–1868," *Florida Historical Quarterly* 69 (April 1991): 411–20. On Florida's Jewish heritage generally, see Henry Alan Green and Marcia Kerstein Zerivitz, *Mosaic: Jewish Life in Florida, A Documentary Exhibit from 1763 to the Present* (Coral Gables: MOSAIC, Inc., 1991).

8. The Dzialynski home in Jacksonville was located at the corner of Adams and Ocean streets. George I. P. Dzialynski is thought to have been the first Jewish babe born in the town. Dora Dzialynski married Jacob Burkeim, while Hannah wed Harris Berlack. At their deaths, Abraham was fifty-two years of age; Henry, nineteen; and Jacob, twelve. Gold, *History of Duval County,* 345; Rerick, *Memoirs,* 1:520; Natalie H. Glickstein, *That Ye May Remember: Congregation Ahavath Chesed 1882–1982, 5642* (Jacksonville: Congregation Ahavath Chesed, 1982), 18; manuscript returns, Eighth United States Decennial Census, Madison County, Florida (population schedule); Leon, "History of the Dzialynski Family," 1; *Jacksonville Florida Times-Union,* January 16, 1896; Dzialynski family tombstones, Old City Cemetery, Jacksonville.

9. Jacksonville's rail line was the Florida Atlantic and Gulf Central Railroad, whose president in 1860 was Jacksonville lawyer and businessman John P. Sanderson. Scraps of information suggest a business association between Philip Dzialynski and Sanderson, but its nature remains unclear. The FA&GC ran westward from Jacksonville to Lake City, where it linked with the Pensacola and Georgia Railroad. That line carried the rails further westward to Madison, Tallahassee, and beyond. Brown, "Florida, Atlantic and Gulf Central Railroad," 420–23; Paul E. Fenlon, "The Florida, Atlantic and Gulf Central Railroad," *Flori-*

da Historical Quarterly 32 (October 1953): 79–80; Elizabeth II. Sims, *A History of Madison County, Florida* (Madison: Madison County Historical Society, 1986), 56; manuscript returns, Eighth United States Decennial Census, Madison County, Florida (population schedule); Francis A. Walker, *Ninth Census—Volume I: The Statistics of the Population of the United States* (Washington, D.C.: Government Printing Office, 1872), 98; Larry E. Rivers, *Slavery in Florida, Territorial Days to Emancipation* (Gainesville: University Press of Florida, 2001), 16–46; Philip Dzialynski and others to President Andrew Johnson, July 1, 1865, in John P. Sanderson file, U.S. Adjutant General's Office, Case Files of Applications from Former Confederates for Presidential Pardons, 1865–1867, record group 94, microcopy M-1003, roll 15, National Archives; Philip Dzialynski to E. M. L'Engle, January 16, 1873, E. M. L'Engle Papers, folder 67, Southern Historical Collection, University of North Carolina, Chapel Hill.

10. Sims, *History of Madison County,* 64.

11. Ibid., 65; John J. Dickison, "Military History of Florida" in *Confederate Military History,* ed. Clement Anselm Evans, 12 vols. (Atlanta: Confederate Publishing Co., 1899; reprint ed., Secaucus, N.J.: Blue & Gray Press, 1962), 11:257–58; David W. Hartman and David J. Coles, comps., *Biographical Rosters of Florida's Confederate and Union Soldiers, 1861–1865,* 6 vols. (Wilmington, N.C.: Broadfoot Publishing Co., 1995), 1:324–36. On Jewish contributions to the Confederate cause, see Robert N. Rosen, *The Jewish Confederates* (Columbia: University of South Carolina Press, 2000).

12. Sims, *History of Madison County,* 69; Sylvanus Masters Hankins, Sr., "My Recollections of the Confederate War" (typescript, n.d.), n.p. (xerographic copy in collection of Leland M. Hawes, Tampa, and in the collection of the author); Philip Dzialynski file, Confederate Papers Relating to Citizens or Business Firms, record group 109, microcopy M-346, roll 269, National Archives.

13. John E. Johns, *Florida During the Civil War* (Gainesville: University of Florida Press, 1963; reprint ed., Macclenny, Fla.: Richard J. Ferry, 1989), 165–66, 190; Canter Brown Jr., "The Civil War, 1861–1865," 240–43, in *The New History of Florida,* ed. Michael Gannon (Gainesville: University Press of Florida, 1996).

14. Biographical questionnaire of George I. P. Dzialynski; Leon, "History of the Dzialynski Family," 2; Gold, *History of Duval County,* 345.

15. Bertram Wallace Korn, "American Judaeophobia: Confederate Version" in Dinnerstein and Palsson, *Jews in the South,* 141, 150; Louis Schmier, "Notes and Documents on the 1862 expulsion of Jews from Thomasville, Georgia," *American Jewish Archives* 32 (April 1980): 9–22; Mark I. Greenberg, "Ambivalent Relations: Acceptance and Anti-Semitism in Confederate Thomasville, Georgia," *American Jewish Archives* 45 (spring/summer 1993).

16. By 1870 Julius Slager had moved to Jacksonville where he engaged in the insurance business. *Purse's Directory of the City of Savannah, Together with a Mercantile and Business Directory* (Savannah, 1866), 188; *Savannah City Directory for 1867* (Savannah: N. J. Darrell & Co., 1867), 83; *Savannah Daily Herald,* February 10, 1866; *Savannah Daily Advertiser,* November 23, 1868; manuscript returns, Ninth United States Decennial Census, Duval County, Florida (population schedule); Kenneth Coleman, ed., *A History of Georgia* (Athens: University of Georgia Press, 1977), 233. On the Savannah Jewish community generally, see, for example, Greenberg, "Creating Ethnic Identity in Dixie"; and Saul Jacob Rubin, *Third to None: The Saga of Savannah Jewry, 1733–1983* (Savannah: Congregation Mickve Israel, 1983).

17. *Tallahassee Sentinel,* October 30, 1866.

18. Mary Cohen's relationship to the various Cohen families of Savannah remains somewhat hazy. Chatham County records do not contain a record of Mary and Philip's marriage. *Savannah Daily News and Herald,* April 25, 1866; Leon, "History of the Dzialynski Family," 2; telephone interview, Rabbi Saul Jacob Rubin, Savannah, by the author, March 21, 1990 (notes in collection of the author); Chatham County marriage license records, Office of the Clerk, Chatham County Courthouse, Savannah; *Purse's Directory,* 29; *Directory of the City of Savannah for 1870* (Savannah: J. H. Estill, 1870), 37.

19. Savannah's B'nai Berith Jacob asserts that it is the South's oldest continuously Orthodox congregation. Biographical questionnaire of George I. P. Dzialynski; *Savannah Daily News and Herald,* May 8, 1866; Rubin, *Third to None,* 146, 148, 158–59.

20. Dickison, "Military History," 258; Rerick, *Memoirs,* 1:520.

21. Rosalie Dzialynski later married Solomon Iseman of Jacksonville. *Jacksonville Tri-Weekly Florida Union,* April 23, 1874; *Jacksonville Florida Times-Union,* June 13, 1905.

22. Eric Foner, *Reconstruction: America's Unfinished Revolution, 1863–1877* (New York: Harper & Row, 1988), 141, 395; *Savannah Morning News,* October 31, 1868; Philip Dzialynski to L'Engle, January 16, 1873, L'Engle Papers, folder 7; Protest of the Cashier of the Merchants National Bank of Savannah, June 15, 1869, John P. Sanderson probate file, Duval County probate records, Duval County courthouse, Jacksonville.

23. Not included in the family move to Palatka in 1870 were brother John, by then twenty-three years of age, and sister Augusta, twenty-two. Either by 1870 or shortly thereafter both had married; John to Annie Jones, and Augusta to Sol Hertz "of New York." After his marriage John lived in New York for a time, and his first child Henry was born there about 1875. Within two years he had returned to Jacksonville, where he made a living as a cigar maker. By the century's

turn John was engaged in business as a tobacco buyer with headquarters in Quincy, Florida. *Savannah Morning News,* October 25, 1871; manuscript returns, Ninth United States Decennial Census, Putnam County, Florida, and Chatham County, Georgia, and Tenth United States Decennial Census, Duval County, Florida (population schedules); biographical questionnaire of George I. P. Dzialynski; Leon, "History of the Dzialynski Family," 1; *Jacksonville Florida Times-Union,* January 16, 1896; *New York Tobacco Leaf,* July 21, 1897.

24. Manuscript returns, Ninth United States Census, Putnam County, Florida (population schedule); *Tampa Florida Peninsular,* June 7, 1871; Canter Brown Jr., *Jewish Pioneers of the Tampa Bay Frontier* (Tampa: Tampa Bay History Center, 1999), 32–35; idem, *Florida's Peace River Frontier* (Orlando: University of Central Florida Press, 1991), 195–200; idem, *Fort Meade, 1849–1900* (Tuscaloosa: University of Alabama Press, 1995), 52–61.

25. Jerrell H. Shofner, *Nor Is It Over Yet: Florida in the Era of Reconstruction, 1863–1877* (Gainesville: University of Florida Press, 1974), 209; Brown, *Jewish Pioneers,* 32–35; idem, *Florida's Peace River Frontier,* 195–200; *Florida Laws (1870),* 98–99; *Tampa Sunland Tribune,* July 21, 1877.

26. *Tampa Florida Peninsular,* June 7, 1871; *Lakeland Ledger,* June 3, 1951; Canter Brown Jr., *In the Midst of All That Makes Life Worth Living: Polk County, Florida, to 1940* (Tallahassee: Sentry Press, 2001), 114, 119–21; idem, *Jewish Pioneers,* 34–35.

27. Louise Frisbie, *Peace River Pioneers* (Miami: E. A. Seemann Publishing, 1974), 31–34; Dennis Eagan, *Sixth Annual Report of the Commissioner of Lands and Immigration of the State of Florida for the Year Ending December 31, 1874* (Tallahassee: State of Florida, 1874), 190.

28. *Tampa Florida Peninsular,* July 8, 1871; record of commissioned officers, vol. 1871–1879, n.p., record group 156, series 259, Florida State Archives; Canter Brown Jr., *Tampa In Civil War and Reconstruction* (Tampa: University of Tampa Press, 2000), 153–55.

29. Shofner, *Nor Is It Over Yet,* 251; Canter Brown Jr., *Ossian Bingley Hart, Florida's Loyalist Reconstruction Governor* (Baton Rouge: Louisiana State University Press, 1997), 245–47.

30. Jacob R. Cohen participated as secretary of the meeting at which an incorporation election for Orlando was called on June 23, 1875. He was elected an alderman that year and reelected two years later. In 1877 he married Rachel Williams, the daughter of Tallahassee merchant Robert S. and Helena Dzialynski Williams and niece of Philip and Morris Dzialynski. Cohen soon relocated to Tallahassee, where he died on November 5, 1901. Dzialynski to L'Engle, January 16, 1873; *Kissimmee Osceola Sun,* September 18, 1975; H. L. Mitchell to E. M. L'Engle, April 28, 1874, L'Engle Papers, folder 75; Brown, *Ossian Bingley Hart,*

277–79; idem, *Jewish Pioneers,* 53–54; Orange County deed records, Book H-2, 309–313, Orange County Courthouse, Orlando; Eve Bacon, *Orlando: A Centennial History* (Chuluota: Mickler House Publishers, 1975), 59, 61, 68–69; *Jacksonville Florida Times-Union,* November 6, 1901.

31. Joe A. Akerman Jr., *Florida Cowman: A History of Florida Cattle Raising* (Kissimmee: Florida Cattlemen's Association, 1976), 104–06; *Jacksonville Florida Times-Union,* October 24, 1884.

32. James W. Covington, *The Story of Southwestern Florida,* 3 vols. (New York: Lewis Historical Publishing Co., 1957), 1:161; Eagan, *Sixth Annual Report,* 189, George W. Wells, *Facts for Immigrants: Comprising a Truthful Account of the Five Following Counties of South Florida; To-Wit: Hernando, Hillsboro, Polk, Manatee and Monroe* (Jacksonville: Press Book and Job Office, 1877), 23; Brown, *Fort Meade,* 56–68.

33. Wire Street, Fort Meade's principal commercial district, was so named because the International Ocean Telegraph Company's line ran down its length to a crossing of the Peace River. The one interlude during which the Dzialynskis lived elsewhere than Fort Meade commenced in November 1879 when Philip moved his family to Tampa, where he opened a store. His partnership with C. L. Mitchell continued, however, and by March 1881 he and the family had returned to Fort Meade. Polk County deed records, Book B, 413–15; *Jacksonville Florida Times-Union,* November 3, 1889; *Tampa Sunland Tribune,* April 20, 1878, November 13, 1879, April 1, 1880, March 26, 1881; Theodore Hartridge to L'Engle, February 12, 1878, Sanderson probate file; Canter Brown Jr., "The International Ocean Telegraph," *Florida Historical Quarterly* 68 (October 1989), 149–50, 158–59. On the early Jewish presence in Tampa, see Brown, *Jewish Pioneers,* 6–33; Richard E. Sapon-White, "A Polish Jew on the Florida Frontier and in Occupied Tennessee: Excerpts from the Memoirs of Max White," *Southern Jewish History* 4 (2001): 93–122.

34. *Tampa Sunland Tribune,* July 21, November 24, December 8, 1877; *Laws of Florida (1883),* 123.

35. Sherman Adams, *Homeland: A Description of the Climate, Productions, Resources, Topography, Soil, Opportunities, Attractions, Developments and General Characteristics of Polk County, Florida* (Bartow: Tigner, Tatum, 1885), 70; George W. Hendry, *Polk County, Florida: Its Lands and Products* (Jacksonville: Ashmead Brothers, 1883), 50; *Bartow Informant,* August 25, 1881; *Tampa Sunland Tribune,* July 10, 1881, October 26, 1882; record of commissioned officers, vol. 1871–1879, n.p.; Polk County mortgage records, Book A, 297–99; *Jacksonville Florida Times-Union,* September 5, 1885.

36. Biographical questionnaire of George I. P. Dzialynski; Leon, "History of

the Dzialynski Family," 2; *Tampa Sunland Tribune*, November 24, 1877; *Bartow Polk County News*, October 10, 1890; *Jacksonville Florida Daily Times*, September 21, 1882.

37. The International Order of Good Templars, founded in 1851, was dedicated to "temperance, peace, and brotherhood with emphasis on personal abstinence from intoxicating drink." *Tampa Sunland Tribune*, January 5, 1878, April 2, 1881, October 26, 1882; *Bartow Informant*, September 16, 1882.

38. *Tampa Sunland Tribune*, August 4, 1877, June 10, 1880; *Tampa Sunday Tribune*, October 28, 1951.

39. *Tampa Sunland Tribune*, October 19, 1878.

40. Ibid., July 13, 1878; Brown, *Fort Meade*, 73–75.

41. *Jacksonville Florida Union*, December 20, 1870, quoted in *Savannah Daily Republican*, December 22, 1870.

42. Charles Slager died in Texas either in late 1873 or early 1874. *Jacksonville Tri-Weekly Florida Union*, April 23, 1874; *Savannah Morning News*, February 19, 1873.

43. Wanton S. Webb, *Webb's Historical, Industrial and Biographical Florida* (New York: W. S. Webb & Co., 1885), pt. 1, p. 141.

44. *Savannah Morning News*, December 24, 1868; *Jacksonville Florida Union*, December 21, 1867; *Jacksonville East Floridian*, March 5, 1868.

45. Pensacola hosted Florida's first Jewish congregation. Other offices of the Jacksonville congregation in 1867 were: Charles Slager, president; F. Edrehi, vice president; S. Felner, secretary; E. Robinson, P. Halle, and I. Grunthall, trustees. *Jacksonville Florida Union*, July 13, 1867; Glickstein, *That Ye May Remember*, 19–21; T. Frederick Davis, *History of Jacksonville, Florida and Vicinity: 1513 to 1924* (Jacksonville: Florida Historical Society, 1925; reprint ed., Jacksonville: San Marco Bookstore, 1990), 410.

46. *Savannah Daily Republican*, February 12, 1869.

47. Rerick, *Memoirs*, 1:520; Barbara Ann Richardson, "A History of Blacks in Jacksonville, Florida, 1860–1895: A Socio-Economic and Political Study" (Ph.D. dissertation, Carnegie-Mellon University, 1975), 192, 195; Davis, *History of Jacksonville*, 296–97; Canter Brown Jr., *Florida's Black Public Officials, 1867–1924* (Tuscaloosa: University of Alabama Press, 1998), 103.

48. Two weeks after Drew appointed Morris Dzialynski Duval County treasurer, he also appointed Philip to the Polk County board of commissioners. Since both were fervent Democrats, it may be assumed that they participated actively in Drew's campaign. Record of commissioned officers, vol. 1871–1879, n.p.; Rerick, *Memoirs*, 1:520.

49. The 1881 mayoralty election's final vote saw 559 ballots cast for Dzialyn-

ski and 529 for opponent Horatio Jenkins, Jr. *Savannah Morning News*, March 23, April 3, 8, 1881; Richard A. Martin, *The City Makers* (Jacksonville: Convention Press, 1972), 138; Davis, *History of Jacksonville*, 198.

50. Following his 1882 reelection, Morris placed the issue of Sunday closing in the hands of the city council. Controversy flared, and, for the remainder of his term, stalemate ensued. Martin, *City Makers*, 138–40; Davis, *History of Jacksonville*, 198; *Jacksonville Florida Times*, April 4, 1882.

51. *Jacksonville Florida Times*, April 2, 1882.

52. Rerick, *Memoirs*, 1:520; *Jacksonville Florida Times-Union*, June 27, 1884, May 31, June 19, 1895, May 6, 1907.

53. Philip's daughter-in-law Bertha Zadek Dzialynski, wife of George, attributed the decline of his prosperity to the effects of the hard freezes of December 1885 and January 1886 and to a yellow fever scare in 1887. Dzialynski, "Within My Heart," 109–10; *Jacksonville Florida Times-Union*, November 11, 1889; *Bartow Polk County News*, September 19, 1890.

54. Philip's daughter Fannie had married Myer Greenfield of Beaufort, South Carolina, in May 1888, and he may have been planning to join them. After Fannie's birth in 1868 and Helena's in 1870, the Dzialynskis had either four or five additional children: Miriam or Minnie in 1871; Gertrude on October 17, 1874; Abraham Samuel in 1877; and Etta in 1878. An infant, "Little Eva," is buried near Philip and Mary, and may have been their daughter. She was born October 1, 1875, and died April 9, 1877. *Jacksonville Florida Times-Union*, February 9, 1892; *Bartow Advance Courier*, May 30, 1888; manuscript returns, Tenth United States Census, Hillsborough County, Florida (population schedule); Leon, "History of the Dzialynski Family," 2; tombstone inscription, Little Eva Dzialynski, Old City Cemetery, Jacksonville.

55. After Philip's death, Mary moved first to Tallahassee and then to Gainesville. She served in the latter community as manager of the Commercial Hotel. Her daughter Etta married Louis E. Cohen of Tallahassee there on March 19, 1902. Not long thereafter Mary returned to Tallahassee and lived with the Cohens. She passed away in 1935 and was buried with Philip in the Old City Cemetery, Jacksonville. Near Mary in 1910 lived her son Abe and his wife Ellain, who had married in 1899. Son George married Bertha Zadek in Gainesville on May 7, 1882. Gertrude, who later served on the faculty of Gainesville's East Florida Seminary as well as in numerous governmental positions, including personal secretary to Florida governor Napoleon Broward of Jacksonville and deputy collector of U.S. Internal Revenue for the District of Florida, married John Archibald Corbet in Jacksonville on September 15, 1915. Reportedly having attained the distinction of being one of Florida's first two women lawyers and having chaired the organizational session of the Florida State League of Women

Voters, Gertrude passed away in Jacksonville on January 24, 1931. *Jacksonville Florida Times-Union,* January 16, 1896; *Tallahassee Weekly Floridian,* March 21, 1902; manuscript returns, Thirteenth United States Census, Leon County, Florida (population schedule); tombstone inscription for Mary Cohen Dzialynski, Old City Cemetery, Jacksonville; Leon, "History of the Dzialynski Family"; Wendy S. Loquasto, ed., *150:Celebrating Florida's First 150 Women Lawyers* (Charlottesville, Va.: LEXIS Publishing, 2000), 17–18.

56. *Jacksonville Florida Times-Union,* June 13, 1905, May 6, 9, 1907; James B. Crooks, "Jacksonville Jewry After the Fire: 1901–1919," *Northeast Florida History* 1 (1992):77.

57. *Jacksonville Florida Times-Union,* January 16, 1896.

9
Role Theory and History

The Illustration of Ethnic Brokerage
in the Atlanta Jewish Community
in an Era of Transition and Conflict

Mark K. Bauman

In given situations, individual behavior tends to conform to specific patterns accepted and reinforced by the society or social circle. Social scientists label these patterns of behavior "roles."[1] Still, individuals may alter roles or deviate somewhat from the norm, and expected behavior can change. Understanding these processes and classifying roles can help us comprehend group dynamics, individual actions and adaptation of ethnic groups to each other and society. This case study will focus on Atlanta Jewry at a critical period of change to illustrate how a particular need was met by individuals who conformed to the role of "ethnic broker," and thus facilitated the process of adaptation.

The General Setting

The outline of American history from the last decade of the nineteenth century through the first third of the twentieth century is generally agreed upon by historians. The country underwent a series of often traumatic, sometimes contradictory and frequently inter-related movements. The industrial revolution was attaining a plateau in which the factories and industries came to symbolize the American economy. They drew peasants from rural Southern and Eastern Europe as well as from the American farms and small towns into the cities, the bastions of commerce. The associated transportation and communications revolutions brought people, ideas and markets together.

Moving from an age of innocence, various movements arose attempting to deal with the newly emerging realities. Populists, labor unions, socialists, muckrakers—even "boss" politicians—tried to force the political-economic structure open to diverse interests, and the chamber of commerce-type business reformers attempted to bring business efficiency and good management techniques to bear on government and the inner cities. The social sciences were delineated and "professionalized" as the "scientific" views of the academy tried to clarify issues and systematize utilitarian knowledge. The religious community debated Christian socialism, the social gospel and revivalism as it would fundamentalism and modernism during the 1920s. From the late 1890s into the 1920s the disparate movement (really a variety of movements amidst an underlying desire for action) called Progressivism seemed to nurture hope to an insecure society. With World War I and especially the Depression, much of the optimism would be displaced with pessimism. The era included the rise of lynching, Jim Crow laws and the re-birth of the Ku Klux Klan, and the formation of the National Association for the Advancement of Colored People, xenophobia and the closing of America's door to open immigration, and a massive influx of newcomers.

The South experienced its own variations of the national trends. Gradually moving toward business and commercial interests, the 1880s brought an ambivalent acceptance of the "New South" creed, if not the reality. While metropolises like Birmingham and Atlanta throve, agriculture continued to dominate without flourishing. Desirous of obtaining a labor supply, immigration was encouraged, albeit with comparatively meager results. Populism found a home in the South as did conservative religion and revivalism. Progressivism, too, developed although with clearly more demagogic and racist characteristics.

The city of Atlanta, like its urban counterparts elsewhere in the South, came to epitomize the New South even as it appeared somewhat un-Southern. Beginning as a small village in the 1830s, a key decision to join five railroads at one terminus led to its rapid expansion by the eve of the Civil War. The railroads made Atlanta into a commercial hub and a primary target for General William T. Sherman's march to the sea. The growing retail businesses and educational system kept pace with the population. Streetcars allowed the population to move outward in a suburban configuration. The trend during the first three decades of the twentieth century was toward what Howard Preston has called the "autopolis." While Atlanta boasted of its own New South spokesman, Henry Grady, it also developed a local brand of boosterism, "the Atlanta Spirit." Stunned by corruption and inefficient management, perhaps its leading businessman and citizen, Asa G. Candler, took time away from his duties running the Coca-Cola Company to serve as a "Progressive" mayor in 1917. Conservative Protestantism was the dominant ethos and the city, led by its mayor, welcomed Billy Sunday for an extended revival in that year.[2]

Perhaps unique in the South, Atlanta attracted a largely middle class black community. The black colleges in the city formed the center of the intellectual circle while the businesses along "Sweet Auburn" offered economic opportunity. The general acceptance did not prevent a major race riot in 1906 or the establishment of the Klan headquarters in the city.[3]

The Atlanta Jewish Community

The first Jews came to Atlanta in 1845 while it was still called Marthasville. Peddlers and small shopkeepers originally from Germany, they moved in and out of the little town. While some adapted to the new society, occasionally sold slaves and fought for the Confederacy, others opposed slavery and left rather than fight in behalf of an institution they opposed. Religious institutions were formed with a benevolent society established in 1860 to provide burial assistance, and services conducted informally from 1852. Gemilath Chesed, the Hebrew Benevolent Congregation ("The Temple"), was organized in 1867.[4]

After the Civil War the town rapidly expanded. The economic opportunity and the already extant Jewish community proved to be a magnet for other German Jewish immigrants. By 1880 there were an estimated 600 Jews in a total population of 37,409. Most of these moved into the manufacturing and retail sales areas and became visible as their names appeared on the facades of major department stores. They were accepted also into political and civic activities, with several serving as aldermen, city councilmen, state legislators and mayors pro tempore, and with Victor Kriegshaber elected president of the chamber of commerce in 1916.[5]

Largely welcomed, although not into social circles, the German Jewish community was also accomodating. A struggle was waged in the congregation in the late nineteenth century between those who favored the traditional Orthodox beliefs and practices and the practitioners of the "Americanized" Reform mode. The latter finally claimed victory in 1895 with the election of Rabbi David Marx, a disciple of the leader of the Reform movement in America, Isaac Mayer Wise, and a recent graduate of Hebrew Union College. The changes Marx instituted along Classical Reform lines and his close relationship with the city's Protestant clergy and community leaders eased The Temple membership's path toward secularism, but also (to Marx' chagrin) away from religiosity.[6]

Coincident with the declining commitment of the German Jewish community, two major events challenged this group's complacency. The most dramatic of these was the lynching of Leo Frank amidst an outpouring of anti-Semitic venom. Frank was a young Jewish factory manager from New York called by his uncle, a longtime respected citizen of the city, to Atlanta. Frank quickly became a part of The Temple community, married well and was elected president of the local B'nai B'rith lodge. When in 1913 Mary Phagan, a thirteen-year-old employee of his factory, was found brutally murdered, he was accused and convicted on only scanty evidence and contradictory testimony as throngs of people made anti-Semitic remarks from the windows of the courthouse and Tom Watson's *Jeffersonian* unleashed a vituperative attack. His death sentence later commuted to life imprisonment by the state governor, John M. Slaton, Frank was taken from the Atlanta Penitentiary to the young girl's home of Marietta and lynched. The Knights of Mary Phagan, a hate group established in her memory, became the forerunner of the modern Ku Klux Klan.[7]

While other minor anti-Semitic incidents and insensitive actions occurred before and after this event, none equalled it in its impact upon the German Jewish community. Their acceptance would now be viewed as fragile and tenuous. Some departed the city and still others refused to discuss the case even seventy years later. The second event was less traumatic, but more far reaching. This was the arrival of new immigrant groups which transformed the community.

In the wake of Russian pogroms in the early 1880s a wave of East European Jews migrated to America, reaching a peak in the decade before the First World War. A contingent of this group came to Atlanta and overwhelmed the German Jews numerically. By 1910 there were approximately 1,250 Jews of West European origin compared to 2,250 East Europeans. The newcomers spoke Yiddish, were Orthodox in their practices and beliefs, and began, as did most immigrant groups, at the bottom ranks of the economic order. In Atlanta, they tended to live together and to work as peddlers, small retail merchants (particularly of grocery stores in which they could also live), salesmen and tailors.[8]

The East Europeans met with acceptance by the German Jewish community until their numbers and distinctiveness became more pronounced. Within a short period of time, however, the differences between the two became almost as important as the unifying factors. The East Europeans were viewed as socially, economically and culturally inferior and their language, customs and religious traditions were perceived as Old Worldly. The Temple members as a whole treated the immigrants with condescension, as objects of charity in need of Americanization. They did not accept them into membership in The Temple, or the Standard Club, the German Jewish social organization. Tellingly for our discussion of role theory, they did not find the behavior of their co-religionists acceptable.[9]

The East Europeans, for their part, resented the "Deutsche" Jews with their sense of superiority. The new immigrants developed their own institutions, Congregations Ahavath Achim, Shearith Israel and Orthodox/Hasidic Anshe S'fard, and the Progressive Club for socializing. They created their own self help agencies and generally went their own way. They perceived the German Jews as deceiving themselves with the illusion that they were accepted and that the process of assimilation was good and desirable. With the images of pogrom and persecution fresh in their memories, these Jews continued to emphasize identity and tradition, and to look down upon the West Europeans. They thought of Rabbi Marx as an individual leading his flock out of Judaism and did not find the behavior of their co-religionists to be acceptable.

Nonetheless, the two groups were joined by religion and history and were linked by the broader non-Jewish community. Out of their sense of *tzedakah* (charity) and a desire to raise the level (viz., facilitate assimilation) of the East Europeans, the German Jews transformed and expanded their social service agencies to accommodate their Orthodox brethren. Rapid assimilation could also improve the image of the Jew in the Gentile mind. The East Europeans accepted the leadership and financing because they frequently could not afford to provide the services themselves. While clearly divided over the issue of Zionism and a Jewish national homeland, the two groups also cooperated in relief efforts for Jewish refugees in Europe and the Middle East.[10]

Another sub-community brought different needs and characteristics to Atlanta. Sephardic Jews from the Turkish empire began arriving in the city in 1906. These Jews left their native lands seeking economic opportunity rather than to flee substantial persecution. Approximately one hundred Levantine Jews lived in Atlanta in 1912, the third largest number in an American city. There were sixty-five families by 1924. These mostly young people included in their cultural baggage experience as shopkeepers and artisans, secular and religious educations, and strong bonds to their old world communities. They spoke Ladino, a mixture of Hebrew and Spanish, and conducted their rituals with different pronunciation and forms than both the East and West European Jews. Clannish by background and circumstance, the Sephardim conducted their own services beginning in 1907 and organized a congregation, self help and social organizations. Small in number and generally amicable in their dealings with others, they were not perceived as a challenge to either East or West European power or image. The German Jews, at first doubting if they were Jews at all, assisted them in the process of Americanization through educational and cultural programs conducted by Temple women, and provided limited financing, stepping in with guidance as financial planning seemed to be lacking. The East Europeans, themselves busily adapting, remained removed although they did sell the newest Atlanta Jews burial plots.[11]

The Role of the Ethnic Broker

Essentially the description of Atlanta is that of concentric social circles. On one level Jews and non-Jews interacted. On a second level three Jewish sub-communities interacted. The relation between any two of these groups affected the other relationships. While the German Jews were well on their way toward assimilation, they continued to seek security and acceptance from the non-Jewish community, who, for its part, found interaction with these Jews to be rewarding and desirable albeit not necessarily on a plane of total equality. East European and Sephardic Jews may be seen as individuals in a stage of transition. Some of the East Europeans were rapidly assimilating and yet retained a distinct sense of pride in uniqueness and identity, while others remained largely tradition-oriented. The Sephardim were closer to the latter, but, less conspicuous, they were allowed to adjust gradually and with less friction.

None of these groups would benefit from isolation. Each could profit from liaison with the other. Thus a major need could be provided by mediating agencies. Some of these were institutionalized; the development of the Atlanta community chest with Jewish involvement in the mid 1920s, East and West Europeans forming a federation of Jewish charities, The Temple's Rabbi Marx initiating a Unity Club with Christian ministers, and Jewish clergy gathering at congregation cornerstone laying ceremonies and at meetings to raise funds for Jewish refugees overseas. In each of these and other instances, individuals were needed who were known and accepted to at least some degree by the interacting groups.

Their behavior had to conform to a pattern congenial to both their constituency and the interacting group. They fulfilled the role of the ethnic broker.

The ethnic broker is a communicator who is respected by his group and acts as a spokesman in intergroup relations.[12] The functions of the role include bridging the gap between cultures, interpreting and communicating group needs and facilitating the transition to the new society. Brokers may be traditionalist or assimilationist in their emphasis, but they are united in their conscious, or unconscious tasks of assisting people in finding a place within the general society.

Some brokers qualify for the role by physical attributes, occupation or achievement valued by the society. The captain of the football team may "break the ice" with the head of the cheerleaders for the other players. The strongest or smartest leads the street gang in negotiations with a rival group, or city police. The clergyman or congregation president is invited to speak before a church of another faith. The professional social worker, or ward boss, acts as broker for one ethnic community to another. These brokers are generally selected formally or informally by their social circle, while others are singled out by the outside group seeking contact. Booker T. Washington is an outstanding example of the latter. His speaking ability, educational accomplishments and especially his ideology and conformity to expected behavior made of him an outstanding ethnic broker for the white society. Economic, educational, political or social attainments might bring others to the attention of the broader society.

Attainments, physical attributes, and/or specific abilities might be enough to stimulate initial contact, but they are insufficient unless behavior patterns are acceptable to both groups. The successful broker must retain contact and the respect of his community while developing a working relationship through behavior patterns acceptable to the outside circle. This duality may lead to role conflict if behavior acceptable to one group is unacceptable to the other.

The Ethnic Broker in Atlanta's Jewish Community

To illustrate the concept of ethnic broker three individuals have been identified who acted out that model in Atlanta in this transition era from 1890 through the 1930s. They represent three different origins, became brokers based upon different factors, and frequently interacted with each other in the broker role. A fourth individual has been identified as one who could have become an ethnic broker, but was rejected and, in fact, rejected the role in response to a role conflict which resulted in what one circle perceived as unacceptable behavior.

The German Jews were clearly in the position of leadership vis-à-vis the other social circles which composed the Atlanta Jewish community. Their leadership included liaison with the non-Jewish community and outreach to the East European and Sephardic Jews. Harold Hirsch (1881–1939) assumed these brokerage functions, conformed to acceptable behavioral patterns and was rewarded for his service.

After Victor Kriegshaber and David Marx,[13] Harold Hirsch became the foremost spokesman for The Temple community. Born in Atlanta, Hirsch was the son of merchant Henry Hirsch, who had migrated to America from Ginsheim, Germany, and Lola Hutzler of Richmond, Virginia. He received his early education in the Atlanta public schools, graduating from Boys' High School in 1898. He received a Bachelor of Arts degree from the University of Georgia and the LL.B. degree from Columbia University Law School in 1904. Upon graduation, Hirsch returned to Atlanta where he entered the firm of Candler and Thomson. Two years later he became a founding member of Candler, Thomson and Hirsch, a partnership continued for the next twenty-two years. John S. Candler, the senior member of the firm, was a retired justice of the Supreme Court of Georgia and brother of Coca-Cola magnate Asa Candler.[14]

Hirsch gained prominence as the general counsel and, after 1923, vice president of the Coca-Cola Company. In a series of cases argued through to the United States Supreme Court, he won landmark decisions in the areas of trademark and unfair competition practices that brought him recognition as an international expert in the field of corporate law. Hirsch organized the Coca-Cola Bottlers' Association and obtained a favorable ruling concerning franchise rights. Appointments to numerous committees and corporate directorates came in recognition of his abilities and accomplishments. He was elected to the United States Trademark Association, the Committee on the Juristic Center for the Association of American Law Schools (forerunner of the American Law Institute), and Associate Attorney of the Inheritance Tax Attorneys Association. Hirsch was appointed to the Federal Board of Tax Appeals and served as vice president of the National Manufacturers and Stores Corporation, the Lichens Company, Bobbs Mortgage and Investment Company, president of the Scripto Manufacturing Company and three oil companies, and director of three banks and several other corporations.

In 1930 he was considered for a position on the U.S. District Court for the Northern District of Georgia, but declined the honor. The University of Georgia awarded him a Doctor of Laws degree honoris causa in 1927. He had been elected to Phi Beta Kappa upon the incorporation of a chapter at that university in 1917.

Business success could come as a result of scholarship, ability and hard work. Elective and appointment positions and financial rewards were positive reinforcements. True success and acceptance as a valued member of the community, however, required a wider pattern of behavior of another sort and out of the board room. Contemporaries writing about Hirsch emphasized "his soundness of judgment," his generosity and wide interests, his "many talents and many sympathies," "forgetful[ness] of himself," and "his enthusiasm." He was "devoted to his friends," "warmhearted," wise and able, loyal and devoted. Hirsch "lived simply and without ostentation," used his wealth "wisely and charitably," "remembered his obligations to his community," "never wavered in his confidence," and encouraged and inspired others.[15] Recurring themes include loyalty, devotion, optimism, fairness, toleration, and service beyond those chores which would obtain personal remuneration.

It was in the latter area that Hirsch excelled and was able to communicate to the non-Jewish community an image of his co-religionists as community builders. His interests centered around education and social welfare programs. Hirsch's concern for young people was quite evident. He provided annual scholarships for Boys' High School graduates to attend the University of Georgia and financed other boys and girls on an individual basis. He helped organize the Emory University Law School and taught equity there for six years, contributing his salary to the library for the purchase of books. In 1924 he was selected to the Advisory Board of the Georgia College Placement Bureau, which was formed to classify individual student achievement which could be used by employers for placement. He also served as chairman of the Collegiate Association, designed to improve higher education in the state, the Commission to Study Atlanta's [Educational] Needs, the Citizens Advisory Committee and the Georgia Citizen Educational Movement. His greatest efforts were reserved for the University of Georgia. He led several alumni campaigns and spearheaded the drive to build a new stadium. He headed both the city and state alumni associations and served as chairman of the Board of Managers of the alumni association. In 1928 he procured funds for the establishment of a Bureau of Business Research as part of the Georgia School of Commerce to survey the state tax system. At one point

Hirsch's name was mentioned for the chancellorship of the university, but he declined to be considered. The law school building was named for him in 1932 in a campaign in which he was not allowed to donate funds. Hirsch was called the school's "most loyal living alumnus," and made an honorary life member of the Gridiron Club. It was one thing for a wealthy alumnus to donate money and head financial campaigns; it was another for him to give of himself. The recurring theme in the comments about Hirsch's concern with youth was that he took a genuine interest. When he brought young attorneys into his firm, for example, he encouraged them by stating that they did a better job in a case than he could have done.[16]

In the field of social welfare, Hirsch served as membership chairman and secretary of the executive committee of the Atlanta Community Chest and supervised the raising of over $600,000 in one week in 1923. The Family Welfare Society of Atlanta, the Georgia Association of Workers for the Blind and the American Foundation for the Blind listed him among their boards. In an era in which lay leadership was called upon for fund raising and guidance as opposed to hands-on management, Hirsch epitomized the commitment to involved service.[17]

Hirsch was accepted as much as any Atlanta Jew could be into the Gentile society.[18] As he was perceived by members of the Jewish community, he "had everything": "money," "position," and "standing." When he spoke before the Kiwanis Club upon his return from Europe in 1922, he was introduced by his boyhood friend, influential businessman, Henry C. Heinz. When he helped lead the Atlanta phase of the Y.M.C.A. drive during World War I to raise money for facilities for American servicemen, he joined the city's wealthiest and most powerful citizens. Besides the honors and appointments already alluded to, Governor Nathaniel Harris named him the lawyer member of the state board of accountants. He even purchased the Atlanta Crackers baseball team in conjunction with Walter Candler, Robert ("Bobby") Jones, George Woodruff and H.Y. McCord, men whose names were synonymous with wealth, power, service and standing.[19] From the perspective of role theory, he was receiving the positive reinforcements for a particular behavior pattern. As an ethnic broker, Hirsch was representing what a Jew could do and how a Jew could behave. Essentially he was emanating a positive ethnic image which served to overcome negative stereotypes and foster coexistence.

Harold Hirsch could not have performed as a legitimate ethnic broker had he severed his ties to his religious social circle. Had he gone too far in the direction of assimilation, his behavior would have been rejected by the Jewish community and the non-Jewish community would not have viewed him as a representative ethnic figure. Hirsch conformed to the broker model by retaining his ethnic identity and providing a leadership role in the Jewish community parallel to that in the Gentile community.

Within the German Jewish community Harold Hirsch became the outstanding spokesman for growth and development. Besides serving on numerous Temple committees, he was elected successively to the Board of Trustees (1919–1923), the second vice presidency (1924–1927), first vice presidency (1927–1930), and presidency (1930–1934). He was the major force behind a new edifice on Peachtree Street begun in 1928, and helped keep the congregation afloat financially during the Depression years. Wealth and power notwithstanding, Hirsch conducted youth and High Holiday services periodically.[20]

For Hirsch, The Temple was a base for liaison with the larger Jewish community. Especially was he active in the Union of American Hebrew Congregations (U.A.H.C.), the coordinating arm of the Reform movement in America. He was elected chairman of the executive committee of the South Eastern Conference of the Union, to the national directorate, and the Department of Synagogue and School Extension. He served also on the executive committee of the American Jewish Committee, the pioneer human rights organization. Hirsch gave unstintingly of his time and energy for the relief of Jewish war sufferers in Europe and the Middle East, ultimately participating in the reorganization of the Joint Distribution Committee in 1930.[21]

Bringing people and efforts together for education or relief was a major thrust of Progressivism during the first decades of the twentieth century which carried over and fit naturally with the career of businessmen like Hirsch.[22] He brought order to community projects much as he did to the Coca-Cola Company and the Trust Company Bank. Order was equated with efficiency and sound management. It was also a means of subduing conflict and friction.

There was little question of a German-American Jew of Hirsch's stature reaching out to either the Gentile or national and international Jewish communities. This was acceptable, rewarding behavior. To seek out ties with the East European Jewish community in Atlanta took more dedication and indicated continuity in ethnic brokerage functions. Hirsch worked closely with the newer immigrants in behalf of overseas relief and through the Federation of Jewish Charities. His crowning achievement was the unification of the various overseas and local Jewish charities' fundraising campaigns into the Jewish Welfare Fund in 1936. He travelled from pulpit to pulpit in Atlanta pleading for harmony, typically emphasizing, "All Israel are brethren."[23]

Harold Hirsch, in many ways, emulated members of the non-Jewish community in his behavioral pattern of economic success and service. He sought ways to assist people and use his acumen to build the community into one unit. Other ethnic brokers may be chosen out of necessity rather than through their desire to function in that role. Such was the case with Ezra Tourial (1885–1941), whom the German Jewish community enlisted as a liaison with the Sephardic community. The latter wanted to help the Sephardim and did so educationally and financially. But when it came to individual aid and direct personal relations, the cultural gap proved to be wide. Thus a person whose behavioral patterns could be understood and accepted by both groups was needed to fill the void.

Ezra Tourial was born in Bodrum, Turkey, and migrated to America about 1905. After a short stay in Montgomery, Alabama, he became one of the first two Sephardim to move to Atlanta (1906). Beginning with the Majestic Shoe Repair business and a clothing cleaning and pressing company, by the early 1920s Tourial had become a leather goods wholesale dealer and a prosperous man. Many Sephardim had brought their expertise in shoemaking and leather crafts with them from the Ottoman Empire, but they lacked the capital to start in business. Tourial assisted many of these individuals by providing credit and loans. He was thus acting as an ethnic broker by easing the entry of his brethren into the American economic system.[24]

The small number of Sephardic families (actually mostly bachelors) began meeting in each others' homes for services in 1907. By 1910 they formed Congregation Ahavath Shalom. Within two years, however, virtually one half of the members (22) split away to establish Congregation Or Ahayim. Members of two slightly different Sephardic sub-cultures had been drawn together by background, but then had separated over differences. There were variations in *minhag* (ritual) between those from the mainland and those from the Isle of Rhodes and the mainlanders may have been more provincial. The latter elected Ezra Tourial the president of their new congregation. A small, close knit community reasonably isolated from other groups in the city, the Sephardim quickly saw the impracticality of separation and reunited in 1914. Tourial and Rabeno Galanti, who had facilitated the merger, formed a free loan association with the funds remaining from Or Ahayim. This association provided money to help Sephardim start businesses and relocate to other cities for better economic opportunity. Tourial was elected president of the united and renamed Congregation Or VeShalom in 1916. Remaining dedicated and involved, he donated a Torah, paid the rabbi's salary for a year during the Depression, and was the first congregant to leave the synagogue a substantial amount of money in his will.[25]

Most of the Jewish charities of a city-wide nature in Atlanta had been organized by members of The Temple. By the early twentieth century they were geared toward assistance for the East European Jews who had also started self-help societies. By the 1920s, direction of three organizations was shared. Typically, people seeking aid would be known to either the members of the board or their friends, and investigation of needs and conditions was not difficult. Contact with the Sephardic congregation was made through Ezra Tourial. His wealth, standing and influence amongst the Sephardic Jews and relative assimilation into American life and customs made him the natural selection. Because he responded in a "responsible, business-like" fashion, one assignment led to another. He served on the board of the Hebrew Orphans' Home from 1924 to 1930 as the first member from the Sephardic community, and on the board of the Federation of Jewish Charities in 1927 and from 1934 to 1935. When a Sephardic family requested assistance from the Montefiore Relief Association, the suggestion was made that "a prominent member of the Sephardic community be invited to serve on the Board as regards the problems affecting families of their community." Besides the president of Or VeShalom, they specifically requested Ezra Tourial.[26]

While relations between Turkish Jews and German Jews remained cordial, the East European and German Jews of Atlanta had a far more ambivalent relationship. A broker like Harold Hirsch could remain aloof from conflict because the friction, while not to his liking, probably would not involve him personally. An East European broker could not enjoy that luxury. Maintaining identity and acceptable behavior within his subcommunity could lead to conflict with the Reform Jews and role breakdown for the potential broker. The parallel experiences of two individuals will be used to illustrate this theme and highlight the narrow line separating acceptable and unacceptable (deviant) behavior.

Morris Lichtenstein (1868–1926) was born in Bawske, Kurland, Russia to J.B. and Hindy Lichtenstein. He arrived in America in 1890, settling in Baltimore. Two years later he moved to Atlanta where he worked first in a wholesale dry goods house and then opened a similar business in his home. By 1913 he had accumulated sufficient capital to organize the Mutual Savings Company for insurance and business loans. This was renamed Morris Lichtenstein and Company six years later.[27]

Leon Eplan (1861–1923), a close friend and frequent collaborator with Morris Lichtenstein, was born Leon Herman in Odessa, Russia. He became a baker, but was drafted into the Russian army. He deserted the army and fled Russia in 1881 because he refused to fight for a country which would allow the anti-Semitic Kishinev massacres to occur. On his way to the port of embarkation at Le Havre, France, his traveling companion died of a heart attack. Since this man had a passport and he did not, Leon took the document and assumed his friend's last name. Leon Eplan's journey took him to New York, Philadelphia and Nashville before he accepted the advice of a man he met on the ship crossing the Atlantic and settled in Atlanta in 1882. Thus he became one of the earliest East European Jews to settle in the city, and, at first, maintained a cordial relationship with the German Jews.[28]

Eplan obtained a wagon load of merchandise on credit from Hyman Mendel and started to peddle his wares to surrounding towns during the week and returned to Atlanta for the Sabbath. After a period of several months, he was able to accumulate enough money to open a wholesale clothing store. He gradually amassed substantial resources after opening three pawn shops and auxiliary businesses and investing in real estate. Much of his trade was centered in the poor Jewish and black district of the south side of the city. He helped others get started and brought his wife, son and nine other relatives over from Russia. Eplan was a fighter and a survivor.

Recognizing the difficulties the East European Jews had in obtaining credit with their meager collateral, Eplan became involved with the Atlanta Loan and Savings Company. This was the second institution begun in America along the lines of the "Morris Plan." Arthur J. Morris had realized that many people were capable and "of sound character," but lacked the resources to qualify for a loan to begin a business. His plan allowed people to borrow money if they could demonstrate consistent earning power and obtain the signatures of two guarantors. Leon Eplan joined the board of the Atlanta company in 1913, two years after its founding and later became vice president. Eplan, as well as Lichtenstein and Tourial, frequently served as a sponsor in this way, and Lichtenstein's short term banking venture borrowed from the Morris Plan concept.[29]

By the late 1880s, as the number of East European Jews increased and lines of division were drawn, the work of Eplan and Lichtenstein was instrumental in the creation of separate religious and benevolent societies. An Orthodox congregation, Ahavath Achim, opened its doors in 1887 and Eplan served as its first or second president. Lichtenstein joined somewhat later, but quickly emerged as the "Jewish mayor for the Russian Jews" and the most respected leader of the congregation. He, too, was elected president. Eplan helped found, and for two years presided over, the Progressive Club, a social club for East Europeans who were not accepted into the German Jewish Standard Club.[30] Lichtenstein and Eplan petitioned for a charter for a Young Mens' Hebrew Association to "promote the cause of the Jewish religion, social intercourse and the intellectual development of its members." The Y.M.H.A. emphasized literary, dramatic and athletic activities as well as Americanization. The two men organized and led an Independent Citizens' Club to raise the political consciousness of the Russian immigrants, facilitate naturalization, and actuate interest group voting.[31] Participation in overseas relief efforts and protests against anti-Semitic outbursts followed naturally given the background of both individuals. Both were also involved in Zionism. When organizing the American Jewish Congress in 1916 to bring together all American Jewish agencies under one umbrella, Eplan served as chairman of the state organizing committee and Lichtenstein was a participant in the referendum meeting.[32]

The work of the two in social service agencies was virtually inseparable. They organized the Montefiore Relief Association which offered financial assistance to those in need. The Free Loan Branch, an auxiliary agency later named for Lichtenstein, provided small loans without interest to withstand immediate hardship. Typical was the record for 1915. $2,223 in loans were given to needy families to be paid back at the rate of $1 per week and $4,029 were distributed as direct charity. The total administrative cost was $6. Leon Eplan was re-elected president of the parent body over his objections, and Lichtenstein acted as chairman of the lending affiliate. Eplan presided over the Atlanta Federation of Jewish Charities for five years and served on its board for fifteen years. He was a director of the Hebrew Orphans' Home for over a decade. Lichtenstein was president of the Jewish Education Alliance and vice president of the Federation for many years. Both men worked for organizations providing social and religious outlets for Jewish soldiers stationed at Camp Gordon during World War I.[33]

The nature of the involvement of these men in these agencies was two-

fold. First, they were serving their East European co-religionists by providing charity, educational and social opportunities, and interpersonal
contact. Ethnic brokers, they assisted in the process of adjustment by
communicating the ways of and easing the accommodation to the dominant society. The Alliance, for example, became the center of communal life. It was the meeting place for debates, cultural programs, athletic events and dances. The Federation unified the fundraising efforts and
administrative machinery of four benevolent societies in 1906 which
were joined by three others six years later. It was in the forefront of modernization efforts in the social service realm nationally which emphasized sound, efficient business management supervised by a professionally trained, clinically oriented staff. The Hebrew Orphans' Home, the
regional facility of the B'nai B'rith, stressed help for families so that they
could keep their households together in times of economic hardship. It
disbanded when the most up-to-date theory emphasized placing orphans in foster homes. It was considered a model of its kind. During
their years of service, Eplan and Lichtenstein facilitated the transition
from lay to professional staffing and took real interest in particular cases
and in establishing policy.[34]

Secondly, Eplan and Lichtenstein were fostering bonds of mutual cooperation between the East and West European Jewish sub-communities
in Atlanta. The Federation, Alliance, and Home were jointly managed
by the two groups and created a platform for understanding. Lichtenstein, in particular, was viewed as the link for the Russian Jews to their
German counterparts.[35] They could work together and learn to respect
each other. Selection for positions on these boards and as presidents of
these organizations testified to the prestige Eplan and Lichtenstein had
within one community and the acceptance they achieved from another
as a result of ability. As ethnic brokers, they narrowed the gap between
groups.

No two individuals are entirely alike and each performs according to
slightly different behavioral expectations. When the behavior of one of
these people deviated sufficiently from the norm allowable by the German Jewish community, he was ultimately rejected. His behavior, too, was
a reflection of his rejection of German Jewish treatment.

Besides cooperating with the German Jews, Eplan and Lichtenstein
occasionally became resentful of the treatment afforded their social circle and protested. The German Jews, with their relative wealth and level of accommodation, felt they could and should criticize the newcom-

ers. Their tone was often condescending. The East Europeans were in a stage of transition in which their tradition, pride and identity were at stake. Their natural reaction was defensive and aggressive.

The behavior patterns were bound to clash and did noticeably on three separate and significant occasions. In 1896 the editor of the Atlanta *Jewish Tribune,* George W. Markens, commented upon the activities of the Council of Jewish Women and the Hebrew Ladies Benevolent Society. The Council had opened a Sabbath school and the Ladies Society, a bathhouse, allegedly in response to public school teachers' complaints concerning the East European children's cleanliness and the feeling the German Jews had that these Orthodox young people knew little about their religion. Markens' disdain was obvious. Eplan and Lichtenstein responded by closing the school and complaining about the public attack. They recognized past assistance with appreciation, but held that the aid should be offered without disrespect. Their brethren would achieve prosperity and adjust to American citizenship. Markens followed his initial attack with another outburst. This one was launched against the Independent Citizens' Club organized by Eplan and Lichtenstein to encourage naturalization and voting. The club had held a meeting to endorse candidates at Congregation Ahavath Achim. To the editor, this was mixing politics and religion in an un-American fashion. He asserted: "A more undignified proceeding has never been recorded in the annals of progressive Judaism, and . . . we bow our heads with shame." Eplan maintained that his activities made the immigrants more respected members of the community and encouraged pride in America.[36]

The third incident involved only Leon Eplan directly. In 1914 in the midst of Tom Watson's attack on Leo Frank, a Civic Educational League was established joining the Jewish community together for defense and security. At a Sunday afternoon meeting, Rabbi David Marx, spiritual leader of The Temple, alluded to his beliefs that the presence of the unassimilated and lower class East Europeans had negatively affected the image the Jews had within the Gentile community. The immigrants' arrival had thus contributed to the rising tide of anti-Semitism, and they were thus partly responsible for Frank's conviction. On the Thursday after this meeting Leon Eplan responded with a scathing attack on Marx and his attitude vis-à-vis the East European Jewish community. A special meeting of the Board of Trustees of the Federation of Jewish Charities was called to consider Eplan's behavior. The minutes of the board denounce Eplan for making "an incendiary speech, arraying the classes in our community against each other, [and] calculating to counteract the efforts of the League to reunite our people." Eplan thereupon resigned his vice presidency and a committee was called upon for a "draft resolution repudiating and condemning similar occurrences." The resolution finally adopted emphasized the continued need for the "good fellowship and brotherly spirit" which had previously characterized Federation efforts and concluded: "Therefore we refuse to tolerate any attempt of any man or any set of men to disturb the harmony and happiness of our organization. We stand for one religion and as American citizens we know no difference in Judaism regardless of ancestry. We pledge our best efforts for the best results for the uplift of Judaism and America."[37] Just as Markens had assumed that "Svengali" Eplan had placed Morris Lichtenstein, a gentleman, "under [his] magic spell,"[38] and was the real culprit of the earlier friction, Eplan had been singled out for his behavior without even a note concerning Marx's unfounded statements.

The special meeting, resignation and statement were actually symbolic gestures defining the ever-changing boundaries between two groups in transition. The established group was in the position to mark the cut-off point for legitimate behavior and define its own actions as the rightful position. The final resolution was designed to vent frustrations and thus create a tighter bond. The concentric social circles could disagree, but not to the extent of personal attack against a major leader of the group with most direct contact to the larger society and particularly the individual whose function it was to create the clerical image of the Jews to the Gentile society.[39]

What characteristics had made Morris Lichtenstein's behavior acceptable and defined Eplan's as deviant? What personality traits had allowed the former to emerge as a true ethnic broker, while the latter had chosen the path of an in-group spokesman? Lichtenstein was essentially a compromiser. He would note differences, but not to the point of an open break with either his East European constituency, or the German Jews whom he tried to relate to and emulate. He was consulted concerning personal problems within his congregation and called upon to settle minor disputes. According to Kenneth Stein, the historian of his congregation, his "leadership had the effect of reducing tensions between the Congregation and the German Jewish community." Lichtenstein, more than Eplan, sought to go outward, fit in and be accepted. A frequent worker in behalf of the Atlanta Community Chest, that organization's board passed a resolution upon Lichtenstein's death emphasizing his "spirit of optimism and determination . . . his genial personality and untiring efforts," and his inspiration. Eplan, too, was credited with being deeply involved with "upbuilding movement[s]" and with throwing himself into such efforts "wholeheartedly, unselfishly and effectively," but he clearly chose the path of the proud, unflinching maverick even within his own smaller social circle.[40]

In 1905 a group of people split off from Congregation Ahavath Achim. These individuals were more Americanized than the East Europeans who had followed them to Atlanta. They were afraid that their children would be lost to Judaism because of the continued reliance on Hebrew and especially Yiddish in the services, and they were leaving behind the Orthodoxy of their youth. Rising in economic status, they lived in the neighborhood of The Temple and had actually requested membership in the latter and been rejected. The new congregation was named Beth Israel and considered itself Conservative. It was led by Leon Eplan. Beth Israel gradually declined and was disbanded. The members blamed the hostility of Ahavath Achim congregants (who viewed them as leaving Judaism) for their failure. Leon Eplan, according to the memory of his son, refused to rejoin the parent congregation.[41]

Leon Eplan had been one of the first East European Jews to come to Atlanta. By the time this group expanded into significant size, he was well on his way toward adaptation and success. His behavior no longer reflected the traits of a "greenhorn." He knew the newcomers would adapt quickly and easily into American society, and that they only required initial assistance. He wanted that assistance to be rendered with dignity. He resented the disrespect displayed by the German Jewish group and expressed his emotions in an outspoken fashion which actually emulated the demeanor of the latter toward those they considered below them. The German Jews felt it to be their duty to express themselves in that fashion in their role of Americanizer. It was their right not to have the same behavior enacted against them. Leon Eplan was recognized as a fighter. He refused to accept subservient status.[42]

Ultimately East European and German Jews were inexorably united in their own minds and in the minds of the broader society. The boundaries were not designed to keep individuals out; just to clarify suitable behavior patterns. Leon Eplan continued to serve on the board of the Federation and the other agencies. He gained the grudging respect of the German Jewish community. Rabbi Marx and Abraham Hirmes, rabbi of Ahavath Achim, officiated at his funeral. Many years later, Marx remarked that he had disagreed with Eplan, but had respected him and thought of him as a fine gentleman.[43]

Conclusions

Various behavior patterns were expected from members of different social circles within the Atlanta Jewish community and between the Jewish and non-Jewish communities. One could act in a certain fashion within this group, but similar behavior would not be acceptable outside of that group. The concentric social circles considered it advantageous to interact. Interaction would stimulate conformity and mutual well-being. To facilitate interaction, individuals who would conform to behavior at least partly acceptable to other social circles came forward, or, as was the case with Ezra Tourial, were called upon to act as ethnic brokers. The ethnic brokers chosen had first to prove themselves to their own sub-communities and earn the respect and esteem associated with leadership. As intermediaries, they fulfilled the additional responsibility of the ethnic broker of easing the transition to the adoptive environment.

The description of the Atlanta Jewish community is probably more typical than unique. The general pattern of sub-communities at various stages of adjustment parallels that of other Jewish centers and of ethnic and minority communities throughout the United States. Neither are the actions or behavior patterns of Harold Hirsch, Ezra Tourial, Morris Lichtenstein or Leon Eplan solely illustrative of the Atlanta experience. The intermediary role of the ethnic broker, in fact, may be as important for many interest groups as for the particularized ethnic enclave.

The underlying purpose of this paper has been to encourage the use of role theory in ethnic studies. The following are some of the questions which need to be addressed. Are there communities which function without ethnic brokers? If so, why are they required in some communities and not in others? Does more conflict arise when they are not present? Do communities require an ethnic broker at one point in their development and not another? Do the expected functions of ethnic brokers change according to community factors? What factors effectuate the transformation? Comparative studies on roles in various ethnic communities should clarify the similarities and differences vis-à-vis culture, group change, and individual actions. What other roles can be identified which aid the historian in understanding group dynamics? What about the club joiner, the sisterhood president, housewife/volunteer, or the synagogue president? Both longitudinal and latitudinal studies are required to begin to come to grips with these questions.

Notes

The author would like to express his appreciation for helpful insights and assistance to Professors Charles Strickland and Chris Unger, Ms. Elise Eplan, Mrs. Ruby Eplan Goldstein, the late Max Gettinger, the staff of the Coca-Cola Archives and Ms. Vivian Chandler, formerly of the InterLibrary Loan Department, Atlanta Metropolitan College Library.

1. Helpful general surveys of role theory include Bruce J. Biddle, *Role Theory: Expectations, Identities and Behaviors* (New York: 1979) and Florian Znaniecki, *Social Relations and Social Roles* (San Francisco: 1965). An insightful use of role theory in history is Kai T. Erikson, *Wayward Puritans: A Study in the Sociology of Deviance* (New York: 1966).

2. The histories of Atlanta include Franklin M. Garrett, *Atlanta and Environs: A Chronicle of its People and Events* (Athens: 1969); James M. Russell, "Atlanta, Gate City of the South, 1847 to 1885" (Ph.D. dissertation, Princeton University, 1971); Thomas M. Deaton, "Atlanta During the Progressive Era" (Ph.D. dissertation, University of Georgia, 1969); Richard J. Hopkins, "Patterns of Persistence and Occupational Mobility in a Southern City: Atlanta, 1870–1920" (Ph.D. dissertation, Emory University, 1972); Howard L. Preston, *Automobile Age Atlanta: The Making of a Southern Metropolis, 1900–1935* (Athens: 1979); Charles Howard Candler, *Asa Griggs Candler* (Georgia; 1950); Jean Martin, "Mule to MARTA, Volume 1," *Atlanta Historical Bulletin,* XIX (1975), 1–112; *idem,* "Mule to MARTA, Volume II," *Atlanta Historical Bulletin,* XX (Winter, 1976), 1–208.

3. On Atlanta's black community see the special "A Salute to Atlanta's Black Heritage," issue of the *Atlanta Historical Bulletin,* XXI (Spring, 1977); Dewey W. Grantham, Jr., *Hoke Smith and the Politics of the New South* (Baton Rouge; 1958); John Dittmer, *Black Georgia in the Progressive Era* (Urbana: 1977); Charles C. Crowe, "Racial Violence and Social Reform—Origins of the Atlanta: Race Riot of 1906," *Journal of Negro History,* LII (July, 1968), 234–56; *idem,* "Racial Massacre in Atlanta," ibid , LIV (April, 1969), 150–73; David M. Chalmers, *Hooded Americanism* (New York: 1965).

4. Steven Hertzberg, *Strangers in the Gate City: Jews of Atlanta, 1845–1915* (Philadelphia: 1978): *idem,* "Unsettled Jews: Geographic Mobility in a Nineteenth Century City," *American Jewish Historical Quarterly,* 67 (December, 1977), 125–39; *idem,* "The Jewish Community of Atlanta From the End of the Civil War Until the Eve of the Leo Frank Case," ibid., 62 (March, 1973), 250–85; Janice O. Rothschild, *As But a Day: The First Hundred Years, 1867–1967* (Atlanta: 1967); *idem,* "Pre-1867 Atlanta Jewry," *American Jewish Historical Quarterly,* 62 (March, 1973), 242–49.

5. Hertzberg, *Strangers,* pp. 232, 235–37; Solomon Sutker, "The Jews of At-

lanta, Their Social Structure and Leadership Patterns" (Ph.D. dissertation, University of North Carolina, 1950), pp. 73, 79; Hertzberg, "Jewish Community," p. 267; Mark K. Bauman, "Victor H. Kriegshaber, Community Builder" *American Jewish History* 79 (Autumn 1989): 94–110.

6. Rothschild, *As But A Day;* Bauman and Shankman, "Rabbi as Ethnic Broker."

7. The standard source on the Leo Frank case is Leonard Dinnerstein, *The Leo Frank Case* (New York: 1968). See also Harry Golden, *A Little Girl is Dead* (Cleveland: 1965); Rothschild, *As But a Day;* Mark K. Bauman and Arnold Shankman, "The Rabbi as Ethnic Broker: The Case of David Marx," *Journal of American Ethnic History,* 2, 2 (Spring, 1983), 51–68.

8. For statistics, see Hertzberg, "Jewish Community," pp. 260–65; on the East European immigrants, see Irving Howe, *World of Our Fathers* (New York: 1976); Glazer, *American Judiasm;* Kenneth W. Stein, *A History of the Ahavath Achim Congregation, 1887–1977* (Atlanta: 1978); *idem,* "A History of Ahavath Achim Congregation, 1887–1927," *Atlanta Historical Journal,* XXIII (Fall, 1979), 107–18; Arnold Shankman, "Atlanta Jewry, 1900–1930," *American Jewish Archives* (November, 1973), 131–55; Mark K. Bauman, "Centripetal and Centrifugal Forces Facing the People of Many Communities: Atlanta Jewry from the Frank Case to the Great Depression," *Atlanta Historical Journal,* XXIII (Fall, 1979), 25–54.

9. For this and the following paragraph see sources cited in n. 8, above, and interview with Mr. and Mrs. Robert Zimmerman, 27 September 1978; interview of Samuel Eplan conducted by Dennis Meir, 11 February 1976 (Atlanta Chapter, American Jewish Committee Oral History Project, deposited at Emory University) (hereafter cited as AJC Project); interview of Sadie Saul Jacobs conducted by Nancy Saul, 17 February 1976, AJC Project; interview of David Marx, Jr., conducted by Richard Flexnor, 4 May 1978, AJC Project; Rothschild, *As But a Day.*

10. Mark K. Bauman, "The Emergence of Jewish Social Service Agencies in Atlanta," Georgia Historical Quarterly 69 (Winter 1985) 488–508; Board of Trustees Minutes, Jewish Education Alliance, microfilm box 242, reel 53, Georgia Department of Archives and History (GDAH); Minutes, Executive Committee, Federation of Jewish Charities, microfilm box 242, reel 54, GDAH; Minutes, Board of Directors, Federation of Jewish Charities, microfilm box 242, reel 55, GDAH; Minutes, Board of Trustees, Montefiore Relief Association, microfilm box 242, reel 55, GDAH; Bauman and Shankman, "Rabbi as Ethnic Broker."

11. On Sephardic history in Atlanta, see Sol Beton, ed., *Sephardim and a History of Congregation Or Veshalom* (Atlanta: 1981); Joseph I. Cohen, "Congregation Or VeShalom, The Formative Years, 1906–1937," in Beton, *Sephardim,* pp. 102 (for census), 101, 129; Hertzberg, *Strangers,* p. 96 (for comparative figures);

Isaac N. Habif, "Or VeShalom: The Sephardic Congregation of Atlanta," *The American Sephardi*, 2 (1969).

12. On ethnic broker, Marilyn A. Trueblood, "The Melting Pot and Ethnic Revitalization," in *Ethnic Encounters*, George L. Hicks and Philip E. Leis eds., (Belmont, Calif.; 1977), 153–67; Jonathan D. Sarna, "The Spectrum of Jewish Leadership in Ante-Bellum America," *Journal of American Ethnic History*, 1, 2 (Spring, 1982), 59–67; Bauman and Shankman, "Rabbi as Ethnic Broker," pp. 51–52.

13. Victor H. Kriegshaber and David Marx have been described as ethnic brokers in Bauman, "Kriegshaber;" and *idem* and Shankman, "Rabbi as Ethnic Broker." There was a symbolic transition during the 1920's as Kriegshaber often served as regional head of fund raising for Jewish overseas relief with Hirsch as city or state chairman. (Atlanta *Journal*, 2 December 1918, 23 February 1920; Atlanta *Constitution*, 19 February 1922). By the time Kriegshaber died in retirement in 1934, the mantel of prestige as probably the most influential and admired Jew in Atlanta had passed to Hirsch. Shankman, "Atlanta Jewry," 147.

14. Atlanta *Journal* (19 June 1919) reported the death of Henry Hirsch at the age of 82. He was a Confederate veteran and "prominent" businessman (Hirsch Brothers) active in community programs. David Marx, "Harold Hirsch, *"American Jewish Year Book*, 42, 164–72; Walter G. Cooper, "Harold Hirsch," *The Story of Georgia*, 4 (New York: 1938), 522–23; Mrs. J.B. Weil, "Harold Hirsch, Organizer of the Coca-Cola Bottlers' Association," *The Coca-Cola Bottler* (April 1959), 138–39, 190; Atlanta *Constitution*, 14 June 1928, 26 September 1937, 27 September 1937; Atlanta *Journal*, 27 September 1939; Minutes, Board of Directors, Trust Company of Georgia, 14 November 1939 (copy furnished by Coca-Cola Archives); *The Southern Israelite*, 1 April 1933, 6 October 1939; James Harvey Young, "Three Southern Food and Drug Cases," *Journal of Southern History*, XLIX (February, 1983), 3–36; "Harold Hirsch," *Who Was Who in America*, I (Chicago; 1934), 569.

15. Written memorials are a difficult source to deal with since they are a form of public adulation. Yet, if they are taken as an exposition of behavior lauded by the given audience and are reinforced by repetition from other audiences, they become a useful gauge of expected behavior and of how well an individual conforms to the role model. Cooper, "Harold Hirsch;" Atlanta *Constitution*, 26 September 1939, 27 September 1939; Atlanta *Journal*, 27 September 1939; Minutes, Board of Trustees, Trust Company of Georgia; 14 November 1939; Weil, "Harold Hirsch," p. 139; *Red and Black* (University of Georgia student newspaper), 29 October 1939.

16. *The Southern Israelite*, 1 April 1933; Atlanta *Constitution*, 26 September 1939; Atlanta *Journal*, 13 November 1921, 27 September 1939; Marx, "Harold

Hirsch," p. 169; *Red and Black*, 29 October 1932 (quote); Weil, "Harold Hirsch." Hirsch was also deeply involved in the arts. He served as a director and/or officer of the Atlanta Symphony Orchestra Association, the opera association, the art association, the Music Festival Association, and the Stone Mountain Memorial Association. Atlanta *Constitution*, 14 June 1928; Atlanta *Journal*, 17 March 1925.

17. Atlanta *Constitution*, 26 September 1939. On the professionalization of social work and the delegation of responsibility for fund raising to laymen see Roy Lubove, *The Professional Altruist: The Emergence of Social Work as a Career, 1880– 1930* (Cambridge, Mass.: 1965).

18. It has been widely held that Jews could be accepted into economic and government circles in Atlanta, but did not mix with non-Jews "after 5 o'clock." Interview with David Marx, Jr.

19. Interview with Rebecca Gershon, 26 September 1978; Atlanta *Constitution*, 19 December 1922, 19 November 1917, 21 October 1916; Atlanta *Journal*, 5 November 1929.

20. The Hebrew Benevolent Congregation Collection, box 4, file 133, Atlanta Historical Society; Marx, "Harold Hirsch," pp. 171–72; Atlanta *Constitution*, 26 September 1939; Hebrew Benevolent Congregation Records, American Jewish Archives, microfilm 552 (hereafter cited as microfilm 552), notes on Temple meeting addressed by Hirsch, 27 March 1928 (he was initially the largest single donor, pledging $11,500), Board of Trustees Minutes 1929, Rabbi Marx's calendar, 14 January 1917, November 1920, 10 November 1924, Rabbi's annual report, 9 October 1923.

21. Marx, "Harold Hirsch," pp. 171–72; Atlanta *Journal*, 28 November 1918, 6 December 1925, 7 December 1925; Atlanta *Constitution*, 26 September 1939; *The Southern Israelite*, 29 March 1929, 4 November 1930; Marx's calendar, 6 December 1925, microfilm 552.

22. Robert Wiebe, *Search for Order, 1877–1920* (New York: 1967) and *idem, Businessmen and Reform: A Study of the Progressive Movement* (Cambridge, Mass.: 1962).

23. Minutes, Board of Trustees, Federation of Jewish Charities, GDAH; Rothschild, *As But a Day*, p. 80; "The Transformation of Jewish Social Services in Atlanta," American Jewish Archives Journal 53 (2001): 83–111; Marx, "Harold Hirsch," (quote); interview with Josephine Joel Heyman conducted by Judith Cole, n.d. (May, 1983), AJC Project.

24. On this and the following paragraph, see interview with Ralph Tourial (Ezra was his uncle, business partner and the man who raised him), 21 March 1983; interview with Sol Beton, 12 February 1979; Beton, *Sephardim*, pp. 101, 138–39; *idem,* "Sephardim-Atlanta," *Atlanta Historical Journal*, XXIII (Fall, 1979),

119–27; Cohen, "Congregation Or VeShalom," p. 129; Atlanta *Journal,* 19 October 1941.

25. Hertzberg, *Strangers,* p. 96; Beton, *Sephardim,* pp. 252, 137–39.

26. Bauman, "Transformation"; Bauman, "Centripetal and Centrifugal;" Sutker, "Jews of Atlanta;" Minutes, Board of Trustees, Montefiore Relief Association, 12 August 1929, 23 August 1929; Beton, *Sephardim,* p. 138.

27. Lucian, *History of Fulton County, Georgia* (Atlanta: 1930), 482–84; interview with Jack Lichtenstein (Morris Lichtenstein's son); 21 March 1983.

28. On this and following paragraph, see Eplan interview; Samuel L. Eplan, "Biography of the Eplan Family and Side Lights of Early Atlanta," 1971 typescript graciously provided by Mrs. Rubye Eplan Goldstein. Eplan joined the German-dominated Schiller Lodge No. 71 of the Independent Order of Odd Fellows and served as noble grand leader. Hertzberg, *Strangers,* p. 168.

29. Eplan, "Biography;" Joseph Earle Birnie, *The History of the National Bank of Georgia* (Atlanta: 1978), pp. 1, 7–8, 17, 21. The Atlanta Loan and Savings Company was the forerunner of the National Bank of Georgia. Lichtenstein interview; Tourial interview.

30. Eplan, "Biography," p. 5; Stein, *Ahavath Achim,* pp. 7, 28–29, 76; *Ahavath Achim Sisterhood Souvenir Journal* (Atlanta: 1953); Atlanta *Journal,* 26 February 1916.

31. Hertzberg, *Strangers,* pp. 124 (quote), 159; Stein, "History of Ahavath Achim," p. 116; Atlanta *Journal,* 13 July 1923.

32. Atlanta *Journal,* 10 June 1919, 27 January 1916, 13 February 1918, 15 February 1918; Atlanta *Constitution,* 8, 14–17 May 1920, 19 July 1920, 26 August 1922, 29 August 1922, 6 September 1916; Elise R. Eplan (Leon Eplan's great-granddaughter), "The Early Years of the Atlanta Jewish Community: The Ordeal of Settlement" (Honors thesis, Brandeis University, 1982), p. 55.

33. Knight, *History of Fulton County,* p. 484; Eplan, "Biography," p. 4; *The Jewish Outlook,* 1 (1913), 9; Atlanta *Journal,* 10 February 1915, 15 February 1915, 13 July 1923, 31 March 1918, 23 April 1918; Atlanta *Constitution,* 13 July 1923, 19 November 1917; minutes of organizations cited in n. 30, above.

34. For this and following paragraph, see Hertzberg, *Strangers,* pp. 136–37; H. Joseph Hyman, "The Jewish Education Alliance," *The Jewish Outlook,* 1 (1913), 5–9; Bauman, "Emergence"; Stein, *Ahavath Achim,* p. 28. The Hebrew Relief Society, the Free Kindergarten and Social Settlement, the Council of Jewish Women and the Central Immigration Committee united in 1906 and were joined in 1912 with the Jewish Education Alliance, the Montefiore Relief Association, and the Free Loan Assocation.

35. In his official capacity, Lichtenstein often associated with and gained the recognition of the Sephardic community. Joseph I. Cohen, "Condensed Histo-

ry of Congregation Or VeShalom," undated (1935) typescript translated by Alan Cohen, Rebecca Selber, Joseph D. Franco, graciously provided by Sol Beton.

36. Hertzberg, *Strangers,* pp. 128–31 (Markens quoted on p. 130).

37. Ibid., p. 212; Minutes, Executive Committee, Federation of Jewish Charities, 31 October 1915 (quotations), GDAH; Solomon Sutker, "Social Service in the Jewish Community of Atlanta," unpublished manuscript (1983), p. 8.

38. Hertzberg, *Strangers,* pp. 129–30.

39. See Biddle, *Role Theory,* p. 213, on legitimate and illegitimate behavior; and especially Erikson, *Wayward Puritans,* Chapter 1 and passim. On Marx as the liaison with the non-Jewish community, see Bauman and Shankman, "Rabbi as Ethnic Broker."

40. Stein, *Ahavath Achim,* pp. 28–29; Atlanta *Journal,* 20 August 1926, 13 July 1923.

41. Stein, *Ahavath Achim,* pp. 13–14; Hertzberg, *Strangers,* pp. 93–94; Eplan, "Biography," p. 4.

42. Interview with Mrs. Rubye Eplan Goldstein (Leon Eplan's daughter), 11 April 1983 (for Eplan as a fighter).

43. Atlanta *Journal,* 13 July 1923; ibid.

IV
INTERACTION

INTRODUCTION

Jews were influenced by and influenced others in every aspect of life. This part highlights interaction using the spectrum from acceptance to persecution, and black/Jewish relations in particular. The "yes, but" approach highlights ambiguity.

Colonial America was fraught with de jure bigotry. Because of the Inquisition, Jews avoided Spanish and Portuguese territories, or lived in them while practicing their religion secretly. The *Code Noir*, known for its relative humanity to slaves, banned Jews from French territory. England believed in established churches and, at best, limited toleration. Yet the need for workers and harmony among people with varied beliefs led to de facto acceptance.

South Carolina's charter welcomed dissenters, including Jews, and its Fundamental Constitutions proclaimed toleration. Jews and Huguenots successfully petitioned for citizenship rights, and Jews voted. In Anglican Virginia, Jews could not exercise citizenship rights, employ Christian indentured servants, or attend the College of William and Mary. Nonetheless they purchased land and were parties in court cases. In Maryland's 1649 act of religious toleration, the Catholic proprietor granted toleration only to those believing in Jesus Christ, but legal disabilities did not halt Jewish residence as long as they did not flaunt their differences with Christianity. In Georgia, Oglethorpe challenged the trustees' exclusionary policies. Again formal political disabilities paled in relation to actual rights.

Bills of rights in state constitutions separated church and state. The Virginia of Jefferson and Madison led the way, its statute of 1786 granting religious toleration. Jews prospered, joined fraternities, and won elective office. Businesses were often labeled "Jew stores," a long-used designation that separated them and their implied business practices from others, but when Moses Sheftall was black-balled from a dance society in 1807 Georgia, he felt sufficiently confident of his dual identity as Jew and citizen to protest in the press, providing for scholars an illustration of the "yes, but" approach to history. While Maryland's Jews achieved success, the "Jew Bill" (which gave Jews the right to participate fully in politics) required years of effort before final passage in 1824. North Carolina failed to grant similar rights until its 1868 constitution; only in New Hampshire did the battle take longer. Yet Jacob Henry won election to the state legislature and defended his right to serve before the elimination of a test oath.

Howard N. Rabinowitz synthesizes the dual story of acceptance versus antisemitism. He and others contend that Jews found greater hospitality in the South than Jews in the North and Europe, or African Americans in the region. Structural and non-structural factors were at work. Though small in population, early residency provided Jewish communities a southern pedigree. Blacks and Catholics bore the brunt of discrimination and thus warded off antisemitism. Jews also blended into the landscape to survive in a hostile environment, and, by doing so, paid a high price for tolerance. Neither like other southerners nor northern Jews, marginal status kept them on their best behavior.

Following John Higham, Rabinowitz argues that "modern, systematic anti-Semitism" rose in the late 1800s when racialism and social discrimination ran rampant. A key event is the murder conviction and lynching of Leo Frank. The Frank case has been viewed as an anxiety response to movements from rural to urban and agricultural to industrial America, as a proto-Populist reflection of sex and class biases, and as part of labor issues, dislocation, and politics.

Was the case aberrant or a virulent outbreak of endemic prejudice? Anti-Semitism appeared especially during the appeals process, and the lynching is distinctive. Nonetheless Frank was not the only Jew who confronted the violent South. Jewish men lost their lives in Reconstruction Tennessee and Florida, and a Jew was later castrated in North Carolina. Like the Frank case, these incidents took place at times of intense violence against African Americans and close association with the latter was involved. Still they were immediate and direct, whereas the Frank case unfolded over three years and affected the formation of both the modern Ku Klux Klan and the Anti-Defamation League.

History provides perspective. Southern Jewish participation in the Civil War is perhaps the best example of Jews' accepting southern values and contributing to the prevailing society in order to be accepted. Acceptance is marked by Jews who attained cabinet positions and served as officers. Robert Rosen finds little if any formal discrimination against Jews by the Confederate government, in contrast to the North. Nonetheless Judah P. Benjamin, highest ranking Jew by birth in the Confederacy, had to defend himself against bigotry although he married a Catholic and did not affiliate with Jewish organizations. Thus Benjamin's case illustrates accommodation, acceptance, and prejudice. A Thomasville, Georgia, resolution gave Jewish residents ten days to depart and banned future settlement. Neighboring Talbotton's grand jury issued a present-ment against Jewish businesses for unpatriotic conduct. Both examples illustrate resentment against profiteering and counterfeiting, actions not limited to Jews. That Jews were singled out reflected stereotypes and a motif of Jews as aliens. Nonetheless only one Jewish family left Thomas-ville, and the actions apparently exerted negligible overt impact.

During the 1890s Jews were subject to discrimination by whitecappers in a pattern of antagonism to Jews and blacks continuing with the sec-ond KKK Yet how much the Populists or Klan actually attacked Jews be-yond stereotypical pronouncements is debatable. With some exceptions, Jonathan Sarna's distinction between the mythical Jew to be hated and the Jew next door who was a person of the Bible and one with whom an individual did business seemed to be the norm. Nonetheless Jews were banned from social clubs and mardi gras associations, organizations pre-viously welcoming them, and college admissions quotas took root on several campuses. In towns Jews felt more vulnerable but probably ex-perienced less discrimination. They were not perceived as the same threat as they were in places where Jews were associated with industrial dislocation.

Little changed between the 1930s and 1960s. From William Dudley Pelley's Fascist Silver Shirts in Ashville, North Carolina, to the Colum-bians and supporters of George Lincoln Rockwell, the path opened to hatemongers who bombed synagogues during the civil rights era. Only in the last decades has discrimination abated.

What about daily experiences and feelings? Jews generally enjoyed business, civic, and political access. Social acceptance proved problem-atic and varied according to the era, the size and nature of Jewish and gentile populations, and how many generations Jews had resided in a lo-cale. Jews interviewed during the last decades typically deny the exis-tence of bigotry. But when pressed they recall name-calling, childhood fights, the five-o'clock limit on social interaction (in which Jews would interact with non-Jews in business or on behalf of civic projects, but their social lives would not mix), and the rise of Jewish clubs in response to exclusionary policies. Individuals express perceptions from acceptance to marginality and alienation regardless of attempts to conform. They felt accepted and vulnerable simultaneously.

Black/Jewish history is again informed by the "yes, but" interpreta-tion. Jews owned slaves roughly in the same proportion as others in their socio-economic bracket and location, and bought and sold slaves as part of trade. Slaves worked in businesses and on the few plantations owned by Jews, although the majority served in the homes of urban Jews. Jewish opinions concerning slavery and secession did not vary from their Christian counterparts. Yet Jews were never a substantial percentage of either the slaveholding or selling population. In fact, African Americans owned more slaves than Jews did in Charleston during the 1800s.

Still, Joshua D. Rothman's article entices the appetite for more complex studies. Rothman depicts the story of a Jewish man and African American woman who tested the limits of discrimination in nineteenth century Virginia. The couple manipulated an irrational system to protect the economic well being of the woman and their progeny. David Isaacs was not the only Jew to marry or have a long term relationship with a black paramour. Scattered examples of this and manumission appear in many histories although these actions have not been quantified or compared with those of white Christians.

Jewish peddlers often sold goods to black customers. When Jews settled and opened stores, the customer/businessperson relationship continued and, for the poor Jewish immigrant, African Americans remained important customers. Contrary to regional mores, Jews offered goods at low prices, on credit, or bargained, addressed African Americans in respectful fashion, and employed them. Yet Jews profited from such actions.

To borrow Arnold Shankman's phrase, the two were "ambivalent friends." Black perceptions of Jews and their practices were mixed. Jews were to be emulated and were admired as the people of the Bible. Nonetheless some African Americans shared white Christian stereotypes of Jews and protested business practices that negatively affected them. Many Jews shared racist beliefs with other whites but such prejudice was often mitigated by a sense of historical persecution shared with African Americans and the Prophetic social justice mission. Some Jews viewed the struggle for black rights as a means to expand rights for themselves, although others eschewed the cause as a lightning rod for antisemitism.

Clive Webb's article shows that Jews were both highly acculturated and vulnerable in cities like Montgomery. Some adhered to southern racial mores while fear silenced moderates. In his book *Fight Against Fear: Southern Jews and Black Civil Rights* (2001), Webb examines the few Jews who championed segregation as well as an important minority advocating black rights.

The beginning, end, and even existence of a black-Jewish coalition or alliance are hotly debated. What do the terms imply? Was a formal arrangement between the two or participation of a majority of each required? Are these reasonable expectations? If only a minority of Jews participated but they represented a disproportionate number of whites, what weight does this have? Was the arrangement equal, and if not, how and why was it different? How and why did the relationship change over time? How many southern Jews supported various positions and to what degree did they influence events? Some Jews believed that acquiescence to or acceptance of southern mores fostered their acceptance while others believed that the fight for black rights advanced the liberties of Jews as well. Were either or both correct? If prejudice against blacks shielded Jews from persecution, why did eras of acute racism and antisemitism coincide? Given the historical experience of Jews, why did not more speak out? Even the most articulate in the South refrained from marches and encouraged northerners to modulate protest methods. The more fearful or racist denounced national Jewish organizations. To what degree were these reactions the result of acculturation, the consequence of justifiable fear, or different perspectives on the potential for gradual change? Responses varied between Jews of long residence versus regional newcomers; between Reform, Orthodox, and Conservative; between those of central, eastern European, or Sephardic origin; between those in towns and cities, the Deep South or more moderate areas. Many blacks and Jews who supported civil rights were branded communists. How should this factor into the equation? During the last twenty-five years black-Jewish coalition organizations emerged in cities including Atlanta. Sometimes Jews supported blacks candidates or related issues, and other times worked in opposition. Blacks have done the same in terms of Jews and what are viewed as Jewish issues. How and why has the relationship changed since the heyday of the civil rights movement?

These questions reflect the complexity and ambiguity of inter-group relations, the subject of the three articles in this section. The authors depict the tenuous, although generally positive, relationship between Jews and the white Protestant majority as well as the tools Jews used to navigate their survival and success as a minority group. In each article, African Americans play pivotal roles. In Rabinowitz's study, Jews benefit from the presence of a larger, more despised group. Jews and blacks are brought together by Rothman as they use cracks in the system to prosper. Like Rabinowitz, Webb illustrates how some Jews sought acceptance by adapting majority mores, yet even in Montgomery the attitudes of individual Jews toward black civil rights, reflecting distinctive values and their own minority status, diverged from the white norm. Clearly Jewish history cannot be isolated from that of other groups.

10

Nativism, Bigotry and Anti-Semitism in the South

Howard N. Rabinowitz

The December 1986 issue of *American Jewish History* reflected the growing interest in the study of American anti-Semitism.[1] There are many reasons for this new attention to a neglected topic. Some of the interest has to do with the growing sophistication of Jewish history that has begun to transcend its filiopietistic origins and celebration of the openness of American society. There is also the increasing awareness among historians of the similarities and differences between the experiences of Jewish and non-Jewish immigrants. Finally, Jews, in general, have become more sensitive to this issue in recent years due to the alleged rise of anti-Semitism among blacks. Yet while covering a wide range of subjects, the *AJH*'s special issue also represents a current trend by neglecting the study of anti-Semitism in the South.[2]

Any study of Southern anti-Semitism would also have to assess the impact of bigotry and nativism in general. For some people, of course this would be a straightforward subject. On the one hand, conservatives might simply dismiss any evidence to the contrary and proclaim the absence of discrimination in the land of freedom, equality, and opportunity. Radicals, on the other hand, would condemn the entire nation and especially the South for a long history of prejudice, racism and oppression directed against all outsiders. However, since I am a liberal, an academic and a Jew, nothing is ever simple. In fact, this is truly a complicated subject because it relies so much on one's frame of reference. That is, questions about bigotry, nativism and anti-Semitism have meaning only in terms of "compared to what?"

This article, therefore, will briefly chronicle the history of nativism, bigotry and anti-Semitism in the nation as a whole and then assess the degree to which the South shared in this national pattern of behavior and examine the reasons for the similarities and differences. I make no claim to new research in primary sources. Instead I have drawn primarily on a number of articles, most of them conveniently gathered in a few anthologies, and the handful of monographs that consider aspects of Southern Judaism. Several of these secondary sources have been only recently published and have not been included in previous analyses of anti-Semitism. More importantly, in using these and other sources, I have often imposed my own perspective. Thus, in accounting for the degree of Southern anti-Semitism, I will emphasize a previously unrecognized blend of structural and nonstructural factors that centers on the critical role of Jewish Southerners' acceptance of racial discrimination and a special set of historical circumstances that made Southern Jews different from both other Jews and other Southerners.

Before doing so, however, it is necessary to make clear my basic point of departure. Whatever our assessment of the nature and extent of anti-Semitism in the nation and region, the fact is that American anti-Semitism pales next to that practiced elsewhere, whether in the past or present. Here we will find no equivalent of Russia's settlement laws, pogroms, Doctor's Purge or current bars against emigration; France's Dreyfus Case; Spain's Inquisition; or England's Parliamentary religious test; to say nothing of the Nazi horror or the rich Germanic intellectual anti-Semitism that nurtured it. This, of course, does not lessen the suffering of the victims of anti-Semitism in America, but it does enable us to keep that suffering within the proper perspective.

To begin with, it is important to remember that America historically has had the most generous emigration and immigration policy in the world. Throughout most of our history people have been free to enter and leave this country in unprecedented fashion. Even the late 18th century Alien and Sedition Acts and the mid-19th century Know Nothing Movement did not challenge our tradition of unrestricted immigration and with the exception of Chinese and Japanese exclusion in the late 19th and early 20th centuries, that policy remained in force until the institution of quotas aimed primarily at southern and eastern European immigrants in the 1920s.

Yet despite the image symbolized by the Statue of Liberty of America as a refuge for the world's tired and poor, Americans have always been ambivalent about being a Nation of Immigrants. The negative reaction to recent Asian, Mexican, Haitian and Cuban migration is nothing new.

Significant numbers of Americans reacted the same way to the influx of the Irish in the 1840s and 1850s and to Jews and Italians and other so-called New Immigrants in the late 19th and early 20th centuries. American nativism and bigotry toward such outsiders or aliens has flourished especially during times of crisis, in which old line Americans felt threatened by rapid economic and social change linked to industrialization and urbanization. The three most significant eras for such concerns were the 1840s and 1850s, 1880s and 1890s; and the 1920s. During all of these periods the rural, capitalist, democratic and Anglo-Protestant values upon which the nation was allegedly founded were seen as under attack. As a result of the defensive nationalism we call nativism, immigrants were viewed sometimes as threatening because of their allegedly radical ideas, at other times because of different religious values and at still other times for alleged racial differences. At all times, however, both justified and unjustified economic fears, whether from people at the top, middle or bottom of society magnified the nature of the alien threat.[3]

Sometimes Jews were a primary target of this nativism, at other times only secondary targets and at still other times not singled out but part of the general nativist thrust. In the 1850s, for example, Irish Catholics were the chief enemies of the Know Nothings who in New York actually ran a Jewish candidate for Governor. Jews, however, were clearly a prime target of the nativists during the restrictionist movement of the early twentieth century.

Indeed, it would seem that until the late nineteenth century this country was remarkably free, at least relatively, of anti-Semitism. It is true as Martin Borden has recently noted in *Jews, Turks and Infidels* that unlike the federal constitution, almost all of the original state constitutions required office holders to affirm their beliefs in Protestantism or Christianity and that numerous efforts were made to amend the Constitution to indicate that the U.S. was a Christian nation. Yet the office-holding provisions for the most part were soon eliminated or not enforced and the Christian nation efforts failed.[4] Similarly, Rabbi Bertram Korn was correct to note the marked increase in anti-Semitism during the Civil War aimed at alleged Jewish profiteering, capped by General Grant's infamous but widely supported 1863 order expelling all Jews "as a class" from the Department of the Tennessee within twenty-four hours.[5] But that proved to be a temporary outbreak and the birth of modern, systematic anti-Semitism in this country clearly dates from the late nineteenth century.

Three groups were in the forefront of this wave of modern anti-Semitism: Northeastern and primarily New England intellectuals such as Henry and Brooks Adams; Southern and Midwestern rural radicals; and urban masses, themselves often of immigrant backgrounds. This anti-Semitism took primarily four forms: verbal or written criticisms of Jews that included the dissemination of vicious stereotypes; calls for laws restricting Jewish immigration or influence; violence against individual Jews; and de facto social and economic discrimination.[6]

It is important to note here as historian John Higham reminds us, that anti-Semitic statements or beliefs did not necessarily result in anti-Semitic actions and that the range of those actions could vary. In any event the years from 1880 to 1930 brought a broad range attack on Jews that included, in addition to immigration restriction, harangues by New England intellectuals and Populist speakers; social discrimination that included exclusion of Jews from resorts where they had previously enjoyed unrestricted access, the opening of restricted country clubs and residential districts, and the establishment of quotas at the nation's major universities; economic discrimination by leading law firms and large corporations; and even frequent physical harassment such as the attack of Irish workers and police on the funeral procession of Rabbi Jacob Joseph in New York City in 1902.[7]

Given this general pattern in the nation's response to its Jewish citizens, what can we say about the extent to which the South shared in this experience?

On the one hand, there is much support for the contention that while no worse than the rest of the country, the South at the least did not depart from the national pattern. After all, with the exception of Jefferson's Virginia (thanks to the Statute on Religious Liberty), all the original southern states joined their northern counterparts in having religious tests for voting or state officeholding that excluded Jews.[8] Several strongly resisted removing those restrictions, including North Carolina which didn't do so until enactment of the Radical Republican constitution during Reconstruction in 1868. And even in Jefferson's Virginia, it took seven years to approve the Statute on Religious Liberty, and it was at his university that America's first Jewish professor, the English mathematician James Joseph Sylvester, was hounded out of his position in 1842, less than five months after his appointment. A physical assault by two anti-Semitic students was the direct cause of his departure but further hastening it was a hostile environment in which the organ of the Presbyterian church could state that "The great body of people in this Commonwealth are by profession Christians and not heathen, nor musselmen, nor Jews, nor Atheists, nor Infidels. They are also Protestants and not Papists." As such, the paper continued, they had the right to require their professors to be adherents to a "pure morality based upon Christian principles," though, it added in a nice touch, "without fanaticism." After Sylvester's departure no foreign scholar was appointed for the remainder of this century, thus undermining Jefferson's dream for a cosmopolitan university, expressed in the composition of the first faculty that included four Britons, one German, three Southerners and only one native of Virginia.[9]

Such insular thinking was reflected on a region-wide basis during the Civil War. As Rabbi Korn notes, Southerners joined their northern counterparts in their suspicion and condemnation of Jews for their alleged profiteering, corruption and disloyalty, an antagonism that focused in the South on the powerful Confederate cabinet member Judah P. Benjamin of Louisiana and led among other things to the expulsion of German Jews from Thomasville, Georgia in 1862. Thus one Jew could write to the *Richmond Sentinel* in 1864, "I have marked with sorrow and dismay the growing propensity in the Confederacy to denounce the Jew on all occasions and in all places. The press, the pulpit, and grave legislators, who have the destiny of a nation committed to their charge, all unite in this unholy and unjust denunciation."[10]

As elsewhere, anti-Semitism diminished with the end of the war, but the economic crisis of the late nineteenth century led many southern farmers to focus on international Jewish bankers and northern Jews as scapegoats for their problems and helped launch the Populist movement. Former Populists like Tom Watson of Georgia carried such thinking into the twentieth century, as he railed against Jews as editor of the ironically named *The Jeffersonian* and eventually as a United States Senator. And his words could lead to deeds, as in his stirring up passions that led in 1915 to the most dramatic expression of southern anti-Semitic feeling—the lynching for the murder of little Mary Phagan of northern-born pencil factory superintendent Leo Frank near Atlanta. Typically, Watson defended the lynching by claiming that, "all over this broad land there are millions of good people, not duped by Jew money, and lies, that enthusiastically greet the triumph of law in Georgia."[11]

Meanwhile southern resorts and country clubs joined their northern counterparts in exchanging Jews, leading to the profusion of Jewish clubs and resorts in the South. As late as the 1870s, when Richmond's most fashionable club, the Westmoreland, was organized, membership included several Jews and once elected a Jewish president. Yet one study published in 1949 revealed that not only did the Westmoreland now exclude Jews, but so too did the Commonwealth Club, Country Club of Virginia, the Hermitage Country Club, the Junior League, and the most fashionable women's groups. It is not clear when this shift occurred, but it was likely around the turn of the century, as witnessed by the fact that the Richmond YMCA still accepted Jews as members in 1910 but not as lodgers.[12] The YMCA's policy might have reflected more concern about visiting rather than local Jews. If so, then it was echoed by the region's universities and colleges which, like the University of Virginia, established quotas for Jewish students aimed primarily at non-residents. As late as 1961, the dean of Emory Dental School, who had cut off admission of Jewish but not Gentile applicants from New Jersey, New York, and Connecticut, still required students on the application form to indicate their "race"—Caucasian, Jew or Other. Exposed by the Atlanta Anti-Defamation League, the dean resigned but subsequently served as dean of the Medical University of South Carolina from 1964–1971.[13]

Southern politicians like Mississippi Governor and Senator Theodore Bilbo and Congressman John E. Rankin added their voices to the forces of the anti-Semitic tide. Rankin, for example, viewed Jews as dragging the nation into World War II and during the Cold War summed up the issue facing America as "Yiddish Communism versus Christian civilization." For Rankin, as well as Bilbo, however, the real threat from Jews came in the area of civil rights. And though the chief enemy was the northern Jew, whom Bilbo referred to as "New York Jew 'Kikes' that are fraternizing and socializing with Negroes for selfish and political reasons," all Jews might suffer as a result of their actions.[14] And again such words led to deeds first in the marches of the KKK during the 1920s and the revived Klan and White Citizen Council attacks on Jews and Jewish institutions in the 1950s and 1960s that included cemetery desecrations, attempted economic boycotts, and synagogue bombings.

Yet despite such examples, those few historians who have looked at this subject, and especially Southern Jews themselves, claim that in fact the South has been more receptive to Jews and has exhibited less anti-Semitism than the nation as a whole, and certainly less than the East and Midwest.[15] And indeed there is much evidence to suggest that aside from the West, the South has been the least anti-Semitic region in the country. Harry Golden, the late editor of the *Carolina Israelite*, wrote in 1955 that "There is very little real anti-Semitism in the South. There is even a solid tradition of philo-Semitism, the explanation of which lies in the very character of Southern Protestantism itself—in the Anglo-Calvinist devotion to the Old Testament and the Hebrew prophets and the lack of emphasis on the Easter story which has been so closely connected with European anti-Semitism." Golden, of course, was writing before the wave of synagogue bombings, and even he acknowledged what he called the social apartheid that existed between Gentile and Jew when the sun went down, especially in the largest cities, but the record provides much support for Golden's contention if not for the widespread existence of philo-Semitism, then at least for the relatively lesser amount of anti-Semitism.[16]

The tolerance of Jews has been especially evident in politics. The first Jew elected to the U.S. Senate was David L. Yulee (born Levy) who was instrumental in achieving statehood for Florida and was sent to the Senate in 1845. As was true of the second Jewish senator and future Confederate cabinet member, Judah P. Benjamin, Yulee married outside the faith and was not a practicing Jew, but both men were identified in the press and by voters as Jews and elected nonetheless.[17] On the state level, during the early 20th century Charles Jacobson was the second most powerful man in Arkansas state government as a result of his close association with the Redneck governor Jeff Davis.[18] Jews were especially successful on the local level. Many Richmonders are familiar with the careers of the multi-term antebellum councilman Gustavus Myers and the postbellum state legislator William Lovenstein.[19] Elsewhere, Montgomery, Alabama, in 1875 was perhaps the only city in American history where both the Republican and Democratic candidates for mayor were Jewish and by the 1870s there was already a Jewish seat on Atlanta's board of education.[20] And although there seems to have been a decline in the frequency of Jewish office holding in the aftermath of the Frank lynching, much of it seems to have been at least partially voluntary on the part of Jews, as the Watsons, Bilbos, and Rankins of the South were always repudiated by the "respectable folk." Similarly, and as surprising as it might seem in today's environment, the 19th century efforts to publicly proclaim the U.S. a Christian nation were centered in the Midwest and not in the South.[21]

Economic discrimination against Jews seemed to be much less than in the North, except perhaps in places such as Birmingham, Alabama, where northern corporate influence was especially pronounced.[22] No doubt individual Jews were denied jobs because of their religion but there was little systematic discrimination. Jews did suffer from so-called blue laws or Sunday closing laws but no more than in the rest of the country. In this area Richmond was especially enlightened, as during the

1840s Jewish merchant opposition to the state's Revolutionary Era Sunday closing law and similar new city ordinances aimed at slaves and free Negroes led future Major Joseph Mayo to have the first law amended and the second rescinded.[23] Social discrimination, while present to a greater degree than commonly acknowledged, seems to have been less extensive than in the North, especially in the case of social relations in smaller towns and in the area of college admissions.

What we have then is a good deal of conflicting evidence about the relative importance of anti-Semitism in the South. Allowing, however, for the variety of experience within the South and indeed within all regions, it seems that with the possible exception of the use of violence, the South and Southerners can justifiably claim to have exhibited less anti-Semitism and even nativism than certainly the East and Midwest. Perhaps Virginius Dabney's assessment in his introduction to Rabbi Myron Berman's *Richmond Jewry* holds for other communities as well: "relations between the Jewish and gentile communities of Richmond are as cordial as can be found anywhere. The Ku Klux Klan has never been able to get a firm foothold here, and anti-Semitism is at a minimum."[24]

But if this is so, the important question still to be asked is: Why? After all, contrary to Harry Golden's claim, the South's commitment to evangelical Protestantism might have just as logically led to anti-Semitism and the small town and rural nature of southern life which supported it might have been expected to produce heightened parochialism and suspicion of outsiders. We should not forget the writer to the *Richmond Enquirer* in 1864 who believed it blasphemous for a Jew to hold so high an office as Secretary of State and thought the prayers of the Confederacy would have more effect if Judah Benjamin were dismissed from the Cabinet.[25] Even more troubling have been figures such as President W.W. Thornton of the University of Virginia, who in 1890 told the editors of the *American Hebrew:* "All intelligent Christians deplore the fact that the historical evidences of Christianity have so little weight with your people." To him anti-Semitism could be explained by the "mere fact of difference."[26]

Although one cannot do justice to this complicated issue in a brief essay, there are three general reasons why the South, if not the least anti-Semitic region in the nation, can at least lay claim to being no worse than the norm. The first has to do with structural factors; the second with the presence of other targets for prejudice; and third, the conscious actions of Southern Jews themselves.

The structural factors are relatively clear cut. There were simply not

as many Jews in the South as elsewhere and a larger percentage settled
in rural areas. More than that, they tended to arrive early in the region's
major cities such as Charleston, Richmond, and Savannah, early enough,
indeed, to be among some of the South's first families. In addition to arriving early, they filled a needed economic role, not only in the major
towns, but as Golden notes, in the small towns of the back country. It is
also worth emphasizing, however, that these early migrants tended to be
Sephardic or German Jews and that for the most part the late 19th century influx of Eastern European Jews had much less of an impact on the
South, thus keeping Southern Jewish communities relatively settled and
stable. Where the new immigrants did have an impact as in Richmond
and Atlanta, it was still less than in New York, Philadelphia and Chicago
and the resulting discrimination was therefore less. But more important
than the origins or timing of the Jewish migration were the kinds of pursuits the Southern Jews engaged in. They were less likely than their
northern counterparts to try to enter the professions or large corporations and challenge already entrenched Gentile interests. Whether consciously or unconsciously they were more likely to stay in the family business, usually mercantile, and thus pose less of a threat to their Gentile
fellow residents.[27]

But even if Southern Jews had been more threatening in terms of
their numbers, origins, or aspirations, their white southern contemporaries might still have not singled them out for special discrimination
due to the presence of other, more threatening groups. As the Mississippi editor Hodding Carter put it, "it takes perseverance to hate Jews
and Negroes and Catholics all at the same time." Protestant Southerners had always feared Catholics even more than Jews. Alabama Senator
Tom Heflin relished running against the Pope, the man Tom Watson
called a "fat old dago." And of course, no one needs to be reminded of
the nature of black-white relations in the South. As North Carolina journalist Jonathan Daniels wrote in 1938, "In most Southern towns, except
where many Jews have recently come in, the direction of racial prejudice
at the Negro frees the Jews from prejudice altogether—or nearly altogether."[28]

But potential white Southern antagonism toward Jews would not have
been deflected by their concentration on blacks had Jews not accepted
the Southern racial climate as it was. And here we get to the basic source
of the relative acceptance of Jews in the South. For conscious decisions
by Southern Jews together with the less conscious structural factors already noted have enabled them to assimilate, not completely, but to a

greater degree than their northern brethren. One Richmonder caught this desire to assimilate or blend in, noting that the city's "old Jews" believed "they ought to be as quiet and unostentatious as possible."[29] And nowhere have the effects of this assimilation been more evident than in the matter of race relations. It is not clear whether or not the Southern Jew's public behavior reflects his private feelings but publicly he has chosen implicitly or explicitly to support the status quo. This tendency was already present prior to the Civil War as Southern Jews reacted to the institution of slavery in the same way as did their Gentile contemporaries. Not only were Jews slaveholders, but politicians such as David Yulee and Judah P. Benjamin strongly opposed abolition and helped lead their states out of the Union.[30]

In recent years, slavery, of course, was not the issue. But civil rights was and here Southern Jews sought to keep a low profile. Some went so far as to join the White Citizens Councils (something which helps explain why some Councils were not more anti-Semitic), but as other Southerners had come to expect, most simply chose to remain silent. Those who were visible tended to apologize for the actions of their more civil rights-oriented Northern brethren and to make clear that the latters' views were not those of Southern Jews. Thus, when a group of Northern rabbis was arrested in Birmingham for their racial protests, they were visited by a delegation of local Jews who urged them to go home; otherwise reprisals would follow against Birmingham Jews.[31] In Richmond, Jewish leaders, on similar grounds, in 1958 implored the young, aggressive Northern-born head of the city's Anti-Defamation League office not to publicly challenge a threatening and perhaps anti-Semitic editorial directed at the ADL's support for desegregation by *Richmond News Leader* editor James J. Kilpatrick.[32] By taking such actions, Southern Jews helped encourage a long standing tradition in which even purveyors of anti-Semitism could distinguish between what John Higham has called the evil Jew far away, and the Jew next door.

Such incidents reveal two important points. First, they show that Southern Jews realized the linkage between acceptance and conformity to Southern values, particularly regarding blacks. Such conformity, of course, transcended race. Jews had for some time been trying to blend in. As Rabbi David Marx of Atlanta told his congregation in 1900, "In isolated instances there is no prejudice entertained for individual Jews, but there exists widespread and deep seated prejudice against Jews as an entire people."[33] In part to defuse such feelings, Reform rabbis such as Marx and Richmond's Edward N. Calisch abolished skull caps, initiated

Sunday morning services, minimized Hebrew in the liturgy, and stressed close relations with their Christian counterparts. In the effort to disavow what made Jews, in Calisch's words "aliens in occidental climes," Jewish services became more Christianized; through a similar process, Jewish attitudes on race became more Southernized.[34]

It must be emphasized, however, that the meshing of Southern Jewish and Gentile attitudes was never complete in any area including race. Yet Southern Jews were still different from those in the North. Indeed Southern Jews are classically marginal men. In the fragmentary survey data comparing Southern Jewish attitudes with those of their Gentile contemporaries and Northern Jews, they end up somewhere in the middle—that is, more liberal than Gentile white Southerners but less so than Northern Jews.[35]

What helps account for this middle position is a second point about the Southern Jewish reaction to the civil rights movement. For the linkage between the acceptance of Jews and racial conformity reflected an appreciation of the region's penchant for violence and the frightening potential for latent anti-Semitism to become blatant. As one Mississippian put it: "We have to work quietly, secretly. We have to play ball. Anti-Semitism is always right around the corner. . . . We don't want to have our temple bombed. If we said out loud in Temple what most of us really think and believe, there just wouldn't be a Temple here anymore. They [the Gentile neighbors] let it alone because it seems to them like just another Mississippi church. And if it ever stops seeming like that, we won't have a Temple. We have to at least pretend to go along with things as they are."[36]

Synagogue bombings elsewhere in the South were not necessarily anti-Semitic in nature; the real targets were often the forces of change in Southern race relations. But most Jews did not make such fine distinctions, and while some courageous rabbis like Jacob Rothschild of Atlanta, Norfolk native Charles Mantinband who served in Alabama, Mississippi and Texas, and Emmet Frank of Alexandria, Virginia, spoke out against segregation, most, like their congregants, kept their mouths shut despite whatever reservations they had.[37]

The lesson then is that Southern Jews have paid a price for whatever greater acceptance they might have achieved. Jews, like blacks, had to know their place. This is, of course, easy for a northern or now western Jew to say, but it is not meant as criticism. After all, Southern Jews despite their environment, have had as a group more enlightened views on race relations than their Gentile neighbors and were right to fear the outrage of their fellow whites. And one can expect the differences between Northern and Southern Jews to be reduced in the coming years as regional characteristics in general continue to weaken. Northern Jews became more conservative; Jewish newcomers to the South bring a heightened ethnic awareness with them and race becomes less important to Southern whites. Until this happens, however, the situation of Southern Jews will remain special and any attempt to assess the nature of nativism, bigotry and anti-Semitism in the South will have to take into account the fear of reprisal as the foundation of the region's allegedly cordial Jewish-Gentile relations.

Notes

1. See, for example, John Higham, *Send These to Me: Jews and Other Immigrants in Urban America* (New York: 1975); David A. Gerber (ed.), *Anti-Semitism in American History* (Urbana: 1986); Leonard Dinnerstein, *Uneasy at Home: Antisemitism and the American Jewish Experience* (New York: 1987). Among still useful older works are Carey McWilliams, *A Mask for Privilege: Anti-Semitism in America* (Boston: 1949) and Leonard Dinnerstein (ed.), *Antisemitism in the United States* (New York: 1971).

2. I have referred to the "alleged rise" of anti-Semitism among blacks because it is not clear to me, despite extensive publicity, just how widespread or deep-seated that anti-Semitism is or how different it might be from less visible past beliefs. For rare examples of interest in southern anti-Semitism, see some of the essays in *American Jewish Historical Quarterly,* 62 (March 1973) which is a special issue devoted to "Jews in the South" and others in two collections of essays: Leonard Dinnerstein and Mary Dale Palsson (eds.), *Jews in the South* (Baton Rouge: 1973) and Nathan M. Kaganoff and Melvin I. Urofsky (eds.) *Turn to the South: Essays on Southern Jewry* (Charlottesville: 1979).

3. The work of John Higham remains the best introduction to the history of nativism in America. See especially his *Strangers in the Land: Patterns of American Nativism 1860–1925* (1955; paperback reprint; New York: 1963) and *Send These to Me.*

4. Morton Borden, *Jews, Turks, and Infidels* (Chapel Hill: 1984), pp. 11–52, 58–74.

5. Bertram Wallace Korn, "American Judaeophobia: Confederate Version," in Dinnerstein and Palsson, *Jews in the South,* pp. 153–69.

6. Higham, *Send These to Me,* Chaps. 7–8.

7. Ibid., Chaps. 7–9. On the funeral riot, see also Leonard Dinnerstein, "The Funeral of Rabbi Jacob Joseph," in Gerber, *Anti-Semitism in American History,* pp. 275–301.

8. Borden, *Jews, Turks and Infidels*, pp. 36–50.

9. Ibid., 13–15; Lewis S. Feuer, "America's First Jewish Professor: James Joseph Sylvester at the University of Virginia," *American Jewish Archives*, 36 (November, 1984), 152–201, quote 156.

10. Korn, "American Judaeophobia," *passim*, quote 143.

11. C. Vann Woodward, *Tom Watson: Agrarian Rebel* (Galaxy Book Edition; New York: 1963), pp. 434–49, quote 445; Leonard Dinnerstein, *The Leo Frank Case* (New York: 1968). Despite his well-earned reputation for Jew-baiting, in 1901 Watson, using very different rhetoric, had successfully defended a Jewish merchant unjustly charged with murder. See, Louis E. Schmier, "No Jew Can Murder: Memories of Tom Watson and the Lichtenstein Murder Case of 1901," *Georgia Historical Quarterly*, 70 (Fall, 1986), 433–55.

12. David and Adele Bernstein, "Slow Revolution in Richmond, Va.: A New Pattern in the Making," *Commentary*, 8 (December 1949), 539–46; for YMCA policy, see Arnold Shankman, "Friend or Foe? Southern Blacks View the Jew 1880–1935," in Kaganoff and Urofsky, *Turn to the South*, pp. 118, 191.

13. Marcia Graham Synnott, "Anti-Semitism and American Universities: Did Quotas Follow the Jews?," in Gerber, *Anti-Semitism*, pp. 262–63.

14. Edward S. Shapiro, "Anti-Semitism Mississippi Style," ibid., pp. 129–51, quotes 135, 140.

15. See, for example, Higham, *Send These to Me*, pp. 162–64 and most of the essays in Kaganoff and Urofsky, *Turn to the South*.

16. Harry L. Golden, "Jew and Gentile in the New South: Segregation at Sundown," *Commentary*, 20 (November 1955), 403–12, quote 403.

17. Leon Hühner, "David L. Yulee, Florida's First Senator," in Dinnerstein and Palsson, *Jews in the South*, pp. 52–74; Benjamin Kaplan, "Judah Philip Benjamin," ibid., pp. 75–88.

18. Raymond Arsenault, "Charles Jacobson of Arkansas: A Jewish Politician in the Land of the Razorbacks, 1891–1915," in Kaganoff and Urofsky, *Turn to the South*, pp. 55–75.

19. Myron Berman, *Richmond's Jewry—Shabbat in Shockoe, 1769–1976* (Charlottesville: 1979), pp. 127–29, 235–36.

20. *Montgomery Alabama State Journal*, April 8, 1875; *Atlanta Constitution*, May 6, 1890. Savannah was another southern city in which Jews were prominent office-holders. Herman Myers, for example, served as Mayor from 1895 to 1897 and 1899–1907. David J. Goldberg, "The Administration of Herman Myers as Mayor of Savannah, Georgia 1895–1897 and 1899–1907," (M.A. thesis, University of North Carolina, Chapel Hill, 1978).

21. Arsenault, "Charles Jacobson," p. 67; Borden, *Jews, Turks, and Infidels*, pp. 58–74. The case for the South's relative lack of interest in proclaiming the

U.S. a Christian nation is even stronger than Borden suggests since he ignores what Southerners did when they wrote their own constitution. The preamble to the Confederate Constitution merely invokes "the favor and guidance of Almighty God" (not Jesus) and Article 6, Section 4 bars religious tests for qualifications for office or public trust under the Confederate States, "The Constitution of the Confederate States of America, March 11, 1861," in *Documents of American History*, ed. Henry Steele Commager (8th ed.: New York: 1968), pp. 376, 384.

22. Mark Lowett, "Rabbi Morris Newfield and the Social Gospel: Theology and Societal Reform in the South," *American Jewish Archives*, 34 (April 1982), 68.

23. Borden, *Jews, Turks, and Infidels*, pp. 118–21.

24. Berman, *Richmond's Jewry*, p. xiii.

25. Korn, "American Judaeophobia," pp. 137–38.

26. Quoted in Stephen J. Whitfield, "Jews and Other Southerners: Counterpoint and Paradox," in Kaganoff and Urofsky, *Turn to the South*, p. 86. Whitfield's extremely well-written and witty essay is the only previous scholarly attempt to engage the broad sweep of southern anti-Semitism; however, the author chose to alternate examples of positive and negative attitudes toward southern Jews without arriving at a firm conclusion about the extent, in either absolute or relative terms, of the region's anti-Semitism.

27. See, for example, Berman, *Richmond's Jewry*; Steven Hertzberg, *Strangers Within the Gate City: the Jews of Atlanta 1845–1915* (Philadelphia: 1978).

28. Quoted in Whitfield, "Jews and Other Southerners," pp. 86, 87.

29. Bernstein, "Slow Revolution in Richmond," p. 542.

30. Bertram Wallace Kora, *Jews and Negro Slavery in the Old South 1789–1865* (Elkins Park, Pa.: 1961); Hühner, "David L. Yulee"; Kaplan, "Judah Philip Benjamin."

31. Lecture of Rabbi Richard Rubenstein, USS Waterman, June 1963. For similar reaction throughout the South see P. Allen Krause, "Rabbis and Negro Rights in the South, 1954–1967," in Dinnerstein and Palsson, *Jews in the South*, pp. 360–85 and Leonard Dinnerstein, "Southern Jewry and Desegregation 1954–1970," *American Jewish Historical Quarterly*, 62 (March 1973), 231–41.

32. Murray Friedman, "One Episode in Southern Jewry's Response to Desegregation: An Historical Memoir," *American Jewish Archives*, 33 (November 1981), 170–83.

33. Quoted in Whitfield, "Jews and Other Southerners," p. 82.

34. Ibid., pp. 89–90; Berman, *Richmond's Jewry*, Chap. 8, quote 250.

35. Alfred O. Hero, Jr., "Southern Jews," in Dinnerstein and Palsson, in *Jews in the South*, pp. 217–50; Hero, "Southern Jews and Public Policy," in Kaganoff and Urofsky, *Turn to the South*, pp. 143–50; Abraham D. Lavender, "Jewish Val-

ues in the Southern Milieu," ibid., pp. 124–34; John Shelton Reed, "Ethnicity in the South: Some Observations on the Acculturation of Southern Jews," *Ethnicity,* 6 (March 1979), 97–106.

36. Quoted in Marvin Braiterman, "Mississippi Marranos," in Dinnerstein and Palsson, *Jews in the South,* p. 356.

37. See, for example, Krause, "Rabbis and Negro Rights," *passim;* Malcolm H. Stern, "The Role of the Rabbi in the South," in Kaganoff and Urofsky, *Turn to the South,* pp. 30–32.

11

"Notorious in the Neighborhood"

An Interracial Family in Early National and Antebellum Virginia

Joshua D. Rothman

On September 6, 1796, Thomas West, aware of the illness that would kill him just a few months later, wrote his last will and testament. West, a white blacksmith, owned land in both Amherst and Albemarle Counties, including ten half-acre lots in the town of Charlottesville, which amounted roughly to one-fifth of the town at the time of his death. In his will, West named two of his children—James Henry West and Nancy West— as heirs. Both children were free people of color born of a relationship between the elder West and a woman named Priscilla, who at one point in her life had belonged to her children's father. West left all of his land, livestock, and furniture, as well as his eight slaves, to James Henry West and his family. His fourteen-year-old daughter Nancy West was left only the annual interest on forty pounds held by her guardian, local merchant Thomas Bell, until she turned twenty-one, at which time she would receive the principal.[1]

Among the witnesses to Thomas West's will was David Isaacs, another local merchant. Isaacs, born in 1760 in Frankfurt-am-Main, Germany, had immigrated to the United States and moved to Charlottesville sometime in the early 1790s from Richmond, where he and his brother Isaiah had been traders in Cohen and Isaacs, one of the city's largest mercantile firms. Both Jewish, the Isaacses were also among the founders of Beth Shalome, the capital's first synagogue. In Charlottesville, the brothers lived downtown on land rented from Thomas West.[2] While David Isaacs had a direct economic relationship with Thomas West for the few years that he lived in Charlottesville before West's death, he had an even more significant, lasting, and unusual relationship with West's daughter Nancy.

Between 1796 and 1817, David Isaacs and Nancy West had seven children together. By the time of David Isaacs's death in 1837 he and Nancy West (who occasionally, though rarely, used Isaacs's last name) had maintained a familial relationship for over forty years and had lived in a single household for seventeen of those years in downtown Charlottesville, where Isaacs owned a mercantile business and West ran a bakery. Between them the couple amassed substantial wealth, and by 1850 Nancy West owned real property valued at $7,000, enough to make her the richest non-white person in Albemarle County.[3]

Interracial sex *per se* was not illegal in early national and antebellum Virginia, but laws prohibiting interracial marriages had been in place since the colonial era and anti-fornication laws punished all offenders having sex outside of marriage whether or not it crossed the color line.[4] In this legal environment, a stable, successful, and familiar couple like David Isaacs and Nancy West—a relationship that, to us, might seem improbable if not impossible for that era—nonetheless thrived. An investigation of their financial dealings, land transactions, and courtroom encounters provides a rare glimpse at how an interracial couple operated and even prospered within the legal and social boundaries of a Virginia that discouraged their sexual activities and frowned upon their family, but which lacked either the motivation or the power to end their relationship. Examining the lives of exceptional couples at the margins like Isaacs and West is essential to understanding the rules of race, sex, gender, and class in the South before the Civil War—and to appreciating that unusual circumstances like theirs came with rules all their own.

The example of West and Isaacs also reinforces arguments made in the work of recent historians, who have complicated our understandings of racial and sexual relations in the early national and antebellum South with studies of multiracial families, coerced and consensual interracial sex involving both free people and slaves, and the lives of free people of color. Collectively, these scholars have demonstrated that there were significant gaps between the ideals white southerners often projected about themselves and their world and the experience of life on the ground in their society.[5] The story of David Isaacs and Nancy West adds valuable details to this evolving historical portrait of multiracial families and their peculiar positions in early national and antebellum southern communities. In particular, it reveals how intricately and inextricably connected the couple's domestic and financial arrangements were, and how their economic position influenced precisely when members of the white community in Charlottesville chose to revoke the toleration they usually demonstrated for West and Isaacs's relationship. Additionally, West and Isaacs's story shows their ingenious ability to turn laws of race, gender, marriage, and property designed primarily for legally married white couples to their distinct pecuniary advantage. What stands out most about Isaacs and West's sexual association is that, relative to the law, it was less directly oppositional than it was startlingly ambiguous. For example, when the couple altered their domestic arrangements around 1820, they threatened both the moral sensibilities and the economic interests of some whites. When they were subsequently accused of violating Virginia's laws against illicit sex, however, not even the highest court in the state would find them susceptible to criminal prosecution. Cautiously, at some risk, but with a consistent strategy, David Isaacs and Nancy West exploited their unique status by sneaking through legal loopholes, thus ensuring both their own economic stability and the financial futures of their children.

Still, no matter how financially successful they became, nearly being branded as criminals reminded them that they were perpetually vulnerable to legal harassment by whites. Although West and Isaacs never faced the possibility of criminal charges again, the same kinds of jealousy and resentment toward the couple's economic stature that provoked their original legal troubles seethed well into the 1840s. They learned that there would always be some whites who would try to take advantage of the idiosyncrasies of the couple's relationship in pursuit of their own economic gain. Rather than indicating the strength of interracial families in Virginia before the Civil War and the protections afforded to them, the experience of Nancy West and David Isaacs actually highlights the ultimate fragility and tenuousness of their status. That the couple managed to evade each obstacle placed before them is a testament not only to their shrewdness, intelligence, and foresight, but also to their enormous luck. Property and wealth can bring power, stability, and security. They can also provoke envy, greed, and hostility. For Nancy West and David Isaacs, they brought both.

On October 11, 1822, the grand jury sitting at the Albemarle County Court, on evidence provided by two witnesses, presented David Isaacs and Nancy West for "umbraging the decency of society and violating the laws of the land by cohabitating together in a state of illicit commerce as man and wife."[6] There are no extant descriptions of the testimony that brought about the presentment, but presumably the most germane facts were simply that the couple lived in the same house and acted as a married couple. Nineteen months later, on May 13, 1824, the court found the facts of the evidence against Isaacs and West to be true and asked the couple to show cause why Jonathan Boucher Carr, the local commonwealth's prosecuting attorney, should not bring an indictment against them for the crime of fornication. West and Isaacs's lawyer argued that, even conceding the facts in the presentment, the language used by the Grand Jury failed to accuse the couple of violating any particular statute, and he questioned whether the state could prosecute them on a fornication charge at common law. This legal strategy baffled the county court. Uncertain "whether, admitting the facts presented by the Grand Jury to be true, an Information will lie for the said offence at the suit of the Commonwealth," the court determined the case had to be sent to the General Court in Richmond for decision. West and Isaacs objected, probably because they hoped the county court would dismiss the case on the spot, but were overruled.[7] In November 1826 their case finally worked its way onto the docket of the General Court in Richmond, where the justices ruled that the state of Virginia could not prosecute David Isaacs and Nancy West on any charge as presented by the grand jury.[8] On May 8, 1827, nearly five years after the original presentment, the Albemarle County Court dismissed all cases against Isaacs and West.[9]

The two witnesses who appeared before the grand jury in 1822 would have had to have been white, because David Isaacs was not black and Virginia law only allowed the testimony of people of color against other people of color. A fire in 1865 burned nearly all the original case papers of the General Court, precluding any precise knowledge of the witnesses' identities, but even without such specific information it seems extraordinarily curious that anyone would air a sexual grievance against Isaacs and Nancy West in 1822. Charlottesville was a small town with just 260 residents in 1810, and it had grown little by the early 1820s. Much of the town's population lived within a few blocks of the couple.[10] By 1822 a significant percentage of Charlottesville's residents must have known that David Isaacs and Nancy West were carrying on a long-term sexual relationship. The couple had already had all seven of their children, the oldest of whom (their daughter Jane) was twenty-six years old. Clearly Isaacs and West were in long-standing violation of anti-fornication laws that prohibited sexual intercourse between unmarried persons, yet for more than twenty-five years no one had chosen to do anything about it. David Isaacs's own economic clout, along with that of his network of business colleagues (many of whom were also prominent in local social and legal circles), might have prompted hesitation among people tempted to complain publicly about his relationship with West. Isaacs was a successful merchant and an esteemed member of the local business community. Among his associates were merchants John Kelly, John Winn, Twyman Wayt, James and Samuel Leitch, and John R. Jones, all of whom had been appointed by the county court during the 1810s to assist him in his capacity as executor of the will of his brother Isaiah, who had died in 1806.[11] Kelly, "a man of sterling integrity and a decided Christian gentleman," was a founder of the town Presbyterian church in the 1820s. Winn owned the enormous Belmont estate, traded in real estate, and served for a time as town postmaster, a position in which he was succeeded by Twyman Wayt. John Jones, who was later noted for his exceptionally "energetic and industrious life," served as a county magistrate beginning in 1819, acted as the financial agent for numerous local planters, and eventually became the first president of the Albemarle branch of the Farmers' Bank of Virginia.[12]

David Isaacs also counted Opie Norris and Alexander Garrett among his close friends in town, naming both as co-executors of his own will.[13] Norris drew especial respect from Charlottesville residents, one of whom wrote after his death that he was "a man of mark . . . as useful and beneficial to this community as any man that ever lived here." A merchant who also served as a county magistrate, Norris was a town trustee for many years, secretary-treasurer of a local turnpike company, and at one point in his life the owner of a blacksmith shop as well as a popular tavern. Garrett, meanwhile, dealt in real estate and spent most of his life in public office, serving as deputy sheriff and then as clerk for both the county and circuit courts. He also became the first bursar of the University of Virginia, married the daughter of one of Thomas Jefferson's nephews, and was named an executor of Jefferson's estate in 1826.[14] In addition to having influential friends in town, Isaacs had prominent customers throughout Albemarle County, not the least of whom was Jefferson himself, who bought all sorts of items from Isaacs ranging from meat, butter, and cheese to books and a horse. Jefferson's nephew, Dabney Carr Jr., had been friends with Isaiah Isaacs, serving as a witness to a codicil of his will. Thomas Jefferson also made purchases from many other local merchants, but the long-standing patronage of prominent planters like him helped establish David Isaacs as a worthy, reputable, and respectable businessman.[15]

As a Jewish immigrant, however, David Isaacs would always be somewhat of an oddity in Charlottesville. Around 2,700 Jews lived in the United States in 1820 out of a total population nearing ten million, and only 300 or so lived in Virginia. A few Jews other than David Isaacs lived in

Charlottesville in the early nineteenth century, including merchant Isaac Raphael and lawyer Nathaniel Wolfe, but two-thirds of Virginia's Jewish population lived in Richmond.[16] Being a Jew in antebellum America meant numerical near-insignificance but also often entailed cultural marginality and social prejudice. The anti-Semitism that Jews faced in the antebellum United States paled in comparison to that confronted by Jews in Europe and was tempered by political, economic, and religious tolerance. Nevertheless, bigotry was widespread in America. Throughout the country the word "Jew" was used both as a generic pejorative and specifically as a synonym for a cheat. Overt hostility and violence toward Jews was rare, but white Christian churches consistently preached that Judaism was an inferior religion. Jews were unusual and therefore exotic and interesting, but most gentiles also viewed Jews suspiciously and stereotypically as untrustworthy and avaricious. As historian Jacob Marcus writes, early-nineteenth-century Americans were ambivalent toward Jews, and tolerance and acceptance frequently coexisted with rejection and a strong sense of Jewish difference. No matter the precise position of Jews, though, they "resigned themselves to the inevitable; there would always be a dividing line between Jews and Christians."[17]

David Isaacs's position as an outsider among white Christian society may have made his relationship with Nancy West—who, as a free woman of color, was also an outsider—less offensive to other whites than had her partner been a white gentile. In the 1820s most Americans believed Jews were probably racially white, and they were treated as white under Virginia law, but the racial position of Jews was never entirely fixed due to centuries-old European folklore and stereotypes about distinct Jewish physiognomy.[18] In addition, Isaacs's religion certainly distanced him from many of his white Christian neighbors. They might not have expected him to adhere to as high a moral standard as that to which they believed they held themselves. If a distinction of faith helped at all in keeping David Isaacs and Nancy West out of a courtroom, however, such a distinction also meant that regardless of his economic standing, Isaacs could never fully integrate himself into Charlottesville's business and legal communities, which were held together as much by familial as by financial links. Samuel and James Leitch were brothers. John R. Jones's brother-in-law and his first business partner was Nimrod Bramham, another merchant and a man who later became legally entangled with David Isaacs. After parting ways with Jones, Bramham joined fortunes with his son-in-law, William Bibb. John Kelly's son-in-law was none other than Opie Norris, while John Winn and Twyman Wayt were not only partners but had also married two sisters from the same family. John Winn's oldest son Benjamin would grow up to marry the daughter of Ira Garrett, Alexander Garrett's brother.[19] Without access to these sorts of connections, David Isaacs could be deeply immersed in Charlottesville's mercantile world, yet he would never be entirely of it.

It seems most likely, in fact, that one or more of Isaacs's fellow merchants instigated court proceedings against him and Nancy West in 1822. While changes that the couple made to their relationship in 1819 and 1820 may have prompted some complaints to be made on the basis of moral concerns, a closer look at the accusations brought against them suggests that economic interests probably played a significant role as well. Nancy West's economic position suddenly and dramatically improved beginning in 1819. Members of the merchant class frequently shared the same economic concerns, but they were also in competition with one another, which could breed jealousy and vindictiveness, especially when finances got tight. In the wake of the Panic of 1819, merchants who found it very difficult to collect debts owed them even as they tried to pay off debts of their own would have felt particularly vulnerable. Certainly it is not hard to imagine their antagonism toward the economic success of a free woman of color at such a time, especially when they perceived her as having procured that success in large part through an illegal sexual relationship with a white man. Perhaps the local mercantile elite felt that it was time to remind the couple that they lived free of social and legal harassment mostly at the behest of the white community, and that there were limits to what they could and could not do.[20]

During most of the first two decades of the nineteenth century, Isaacs and West carried on their relationship and continued to have children while living in separate homes and owning their own independent businesses. In 1799 Nancy West turned seventeen. Able to convince Thomas Bell to forward the forty pounds left to her by her father, she purchased a half-acre of land—lot number 46 near Charlottesville's southern boundary—from her brother, James Henry West. She probably took up regular residence there around the time she turned twenty-one in 1803 and began raising her family and establishing herself professionally as a baker.[21] Isaacs himself lived just one block north and one block west on his own land on Main Street, lot 36, which he had purchased in 1802. A two-story wooden building on the property served both as his home and his mercantile store.[22] On the 1810 census, Nancy West and David Isaacs are listed as heads of different households. Isaacs lived alone, and West lived with five other free people of color, four of whom were probably the children she and Isaacs had at the time—Jane, Thomas, Hays, and Tucker.[23]

This arrangement began to change late in 1819. In December Nancy West put the land she lived on up for sale.[24] Six months later she purchased the bulk of lot 33, which was on Main Street just a few lots east of where David Isaacs lived, and she began renting out the property to assorted businesses.[25] In addition, the 1820 census reveals that Nancy West was no longer the head of a household, but that David Isaacs suddenly had ten free people of color living in his home. As many as eight of these individuals were Nancy West and the couple's children, who now totaled seven after the births of Frederick, Julia Ann, and Agness between 1812 and 1817. West began running her bakery out of this building as well, next to David Isaacs's storefront.[26] Less than two years later, the grand jury brought its presentment against the couple. For more than twenty years after they had their first child together, then, David Isaacs and Nancy West had maintained separate households; technically, they even lived in separate parishes of Albemarle County.[27] It seems that so long as the couple kept their relationship a strictly illicit one and pretended that it did not exist, Charlottesville's white community was willing to let it go unchallenged. Only when the couple started living together as a single family unit did some members of the community find their arrangement unacceptable. Throughout the early national and antebellum periods, interracial sexual activity, especially between a slaveowner and his female property but also between free people, could generally be tolerated so long as certain proprieties were observed, one of which was never to flaunt such relationships as if they were legitimate. West and Isaacs's sudden public pretense to being a family thus probably played a role in provoking the charges against them. When the grand jury presented Isaacs and West, it also presented two other couples (at least one of which was also interracial and cohabitating) for fornication charges, which suggests that their case may have been part of a small crusade by whites intent on rooting out sexual relationships that represented, in the words of Albemarle County judge Archibald Stuart, offenses "against good morals."[28]

Probably not coincidentally, the other interracial couple, Joshua Grady and Betsy Ann Farly, lived on lot 26, property owned by David Isaacs just two blocks west of where he lived with Nancy West. Grady was a white blacksmith and Betsy Ann Farly was a free woman of color whose father was Daniel Farly, a free man of color. Daniel Farly resided at the east end of Main Street and was himself the oldest son of Mary Hemings,

Sally Hemings's older sister. Mary Hemings lived across the street and half a block west of West and Isaacs in a house on lot 23 she had shared with Thomas Bell (formerly Nancy West's legal guardian) from the late 1780s until Bell's death in 1800. Bell had purchased Mary Hemings and her two children by him (Daniel Farly not among them) from Thomas Jefferson at her request in 1792 and informally freed her. By 1822 Mary Hemings also lived with her and Bell's daughter Sally Jefferson Bell and Sally's husband Jesse Scott, a man descended from whites and Native Americans. A number of Isaacs and West's children would later marry into the Hemings family as well. When Isaacs and West began living together, then, they not only presented themselves to Charlottesville as a legitimate family, but they also bolstered an interracial community on Main Street that had been growing since the eighteenth century. Their presence may have brought the size of that community to a critical mass that finally provoked one or more Charlottesville whites to take action against it by striking at its newest and therefore most vulnerable members.[29]

It is impossible, however, to discount the significance of Nancy West's improved economic position, which was coterminous with her new living arrangements. Before 1819 she had been marginalized within the Charlottesville community spatially, socially, and economically. West was a free woman of color who owned property and a business, and who carried on a sexual relationship with a white man, but at least she was peripheral to the public gaze. She may have lived just a few blocks from David Isaacs, but her land sat at the edge of town. As late as 1820 her original property, including the structures on it, was valued at only $400, at a time when most lots nearer the courthouse, even those just a block closer, were worth at least three times that amount. Before 1820 Nancy West posed no serious or visible threat, literally or figuratively, to the economic standing of other members of the white community. After that year, however, she not only lived openly as the wife of a white man, but she was accumulating capital and occupying valuable, centrally located real estate alongside other whites. The lot Nancy West purchased on Main Street in 1820 was practically across the street from her original location, but it was worth nearly $1,900, which represented economic strength on a completely different scale than that she had previously enjoyed.[30]

For some Charlottesville residents, then, Nancy West and David Isaacs had crossed the boundaries of acceptability in numerous ways—not least of which was economic—and it was time to call them to account for it.

The Albemarle County grand jury, however, seemed confused as to how to proceed against West and Isaacs, a confusion that was especially apparent in their failure to specify the precise nature of the charges they wanted the court to bring against the couple. The language of the presentment alleged that the couple violated "the laws of the land," but it contained what appeared to be contradictory accusations. On the one hand, Isaacs and West supposedly had committed the crime of engaging in the "illicit commerce" of a sexual relationship outside of marriage, with the legal implication that they were in violation of anti-fornication statutes. Yet simultaneously, according to the presentment, the offensiveness of their relationship lay in their "cohabitation as man and wife"; that is, acting as if they were married. Given their respective races, this phrasing could be interpreted as an accusation of another crime altogether, namely that of racial intermarriage.

In its opinion on West and Isaacs's case delivered in November 1826, the General Court refused to entertain such vagaries of the presentment. In a case it had only recently decided, the court held that a single act of fornication could not be prosecuted at common law without other circumstances which in and of themselves would qualify as misdemeanors.[31] If, for example, a couple had sexual intercourse in public, the court argued that it "would be indeed an enormous indecency, and so grossly offensive and shocking to the feelings of society, as to entitle it to severe legal animadversion." Such circumstances, though, did not attend to West and Isaacs's case, and the Albemarle County grand jury never claimed that they had. The General Court suspected that the grand jury had included language about the couple living together to intimate that by sharing a household, the couple made their offense against society particularly outrageous. The grand jury presumably meant to imply that, insofar as the nature of their relationship had become so obvious, West and Isaacs had "aggravate[d] its malignity." For their part, however, the justices of the General Court felt that the facts that the couple "occupied the same chamber, ate the same board, and discharged towards each other the numerous common offices of husband and wife" were "in themselves harmless and inoffensive." In short, the court determined that a couple living together as husband and wife could not be said to be acting contrary to public morals. At least at common law, anti-fornication statutes could be used to punish flagrant and public acts of sexual indiscretion, but not (regardless of a lack of formal validation from the state) a marriage-style relationship. If the Albemarle County grand jury wanted to try and charge Nancy West and David Isaacs with violating the state law against fornication, which technically had nothing to do with the egregiousness of the circumstances surrounding the sexual behavior, it could try. Under the presentment before the court, however, the justices ruled that the couple had committed no recognizable crime.[32]

In part, the leniency shown to West and Isaacs can be explained by the specifics of their case as it related to the judicial interpretation of the common law, the principles of which easily gave the General Court a defensible rationale for not punishing an interracial couple guiltless of either flagrantly fornicating or of being legally married. The Albemarle County grand jury badly bungled its presentment against the couple, partially because the white community as a whole had failed to do anything about West and Isaacs for so long. Whites in Charlottesville had allowed the couple to carry on their relationship unchallenged so long as the couple did not pretend it was legitimate. Once Isaacs and West did suggest legitimacy by their new living arrangement, however, it was too late to find a court that would do anything about it. Also, while the presentment ostensibly attacked violations of both racial and sexual mores, it effectively attacked neither. To claim there had been a criminal violation of the racial order meant acknowledging the semblance of marriage in which West and Isaacs lived, but to attack the violation of the sexual order required challenging that very acknowledgment. In other words, Nancy West and David Isaacs either could be married or could be fornicators, but they could not be both. The General Court, presented with this legal and social conundrum, chose to leave the relationship as it was.

Still, even though the General Court rejected the validity of the charge against West and Isaacs on reasonable grounds, the couple had escaped mostly on a technicality. In other cases involving interracial sex, high courts across the South did sometimes demonstrate a willingness to override common law traditions to express their own or the community's disgust. Had sex across the color line truly appalled the justices of the General Court, surely they could have broadened the interpretation of common law to envelop the Charlottesville case and thereby closed the loophole that enabled even the most thinly veiled interracial sexual relationships to go unchecked. That they refused to do so in part suggests a judicial lack of motivation to take action against sexual activity between white men and black women in Virginia, especially when conducted entirely in private. More specifically, there were relationships like that of Isaacs and West all across Virginia, some of which surely involved more prominent individuals than a Jewish merchant from a small hinterland town. Had the justices deemed interracial sex behind closed doors susceptible to prosecution in this instance, no one could predict how many other white men might be exposed to similar charges.[33]

The decision of the General Court still begs the question of why the grand jury did not present the couple as being in violation of some specific statute. Surely a statutory case, either for fornication or for interracial marriage, might have had a better chance of success. Prosecuting the couple for violating the statute against interracial marriage would have done the most severe damage to West, Isaacs, and their family together. In 1822 the white party to an interracial marriage faced six months in jail and a $30 fine, and any member of the clergy performing a marriage ceremony between people of different races had to pay a fine of $250.[34] But proving a charge of interracial marriage here probably would have proved exceedingly difficult. There is no evidence West and Isaacs ever married, and given the potentially severe legal repercussions of such an act it would have been foolish for them to have done so. Additionally, their marriage would have been a violation not only of state law but of Jewish law as well, since Nancy West was not Jewish.

It is worth observing that, even if the couple had been married, ambiguities surrounding Nancy West's status might have made it difficult to bring a case of a racial nature against her and Isaacs. To be defined as mulatto under Virginia law in 1822, a person had to have at least "one-quarter" African ancestry.[35] Nancy West's father, Thomas West, was white. To use the fractional language of the time, his daughter therefore would have been, at most, "half-black." But perhaps she was even less than that. Whites in her community certainly appear to have known her ancestry, and in numerous documents she is described as a "free mulatto woman." Yet when she registered as a free person of color with the county court in 1837, she was described as being of "light complexion."[36] Her brother James legally married a white woman, Susannah Harlow, in Albemarle County in 1794, suggesting that his (and Nancy's) mother's racial ancestry may have been mixed enough for her children with a white man to become legally white.[37] Had a case of interracial marriage been brought against West and Isaacs, then, proving conclusively that West fell within the guidelines of the racial definition statute making her a mulatto, while possible, might have been complicated. Once the "blood" aspect of her racial identity became an admissible legal question, then how the white community treated her would have played a role in further determining her status. At least two of her children were educated with white children in local schools, and one local man testified in a separate lawsuit that her nieces and nephews were "esteemed, received and accepted as white men, were educated with white children and required to perform and did perform Militia and other duties, required only of white men, and allowed to intermarry without objection on the score of blood, with white women."[38] Perhaps a case could be made that Nancy West, too, was effectively a white woman. In antebellum Virginia, race may have been fixed according to law, but it was far more malleable in practice. It has become a standard trope of historical treatments of race that the category itself is a fiction, constructed and reconstructed socially, legally, culturally, economically, and in a multitude of other ways. While the limitations of the public record make it difficult to speculate about how Nancy West and her family envisioned their own racial identities, West's color, ancestry, and local standing all would have complicated the possibility of using race against her in a prosecution for racial intermarriage.[39]

Proving a statutory case of fornication, on the other hand, should have been relatively easy and straightforward. That the couple had had sexual intercourse was evident, and even the General Court conceded that, given the evidence presented by the grand jury, "the existence of a statutory offence may be inferred."[40] It is not entirely clear why the Albemarle County grand jury chose not to pursue a charge based on the infraction of the anti-fornication statute. Possibly it was just a tactical legal mistake, but perhaps the grand jury wanted to use its presentment to express a broader sense of moral outrage than was suggested by the language of the fornication statute, which included nothing specifically about race. From this perspective, trying to bring West and Isaacs up on charges was less about punishing them than about publicly rebuking and humiliating them with a reminder that although they might consider their family legitimate, the white community did not.

Ultimately, even if West and Isaacs had been found guilty of violating anti-fornication laws, their punishment would have been mild, just a ten-dollar fine.[41] Despite the revulsion that white Virginians expressed publicly toward sex across the color line, there was very little the law could do to stop it. Since West and Isaacs were not married and there were no laws specifying penalties for interracial sexual acts of any sort, no one really could prevent the couple from living together and building a family—unless the community was literally willing to run them out of town. When confronted with interracial sexual relationships, however, whites in Charlottesville, like whites in general across the state before the Civil War, seem to have had no inclination to take such extreme action.[42]

Even if some people were so inclined, West and Isaacs probably had enough support from other members of the white community to prevent it. More than anything else, the charges against Nancy West and David Isaacs demonstrate that their family was always vulnerable to legal harassment and that its legitimacy could always at least be called into question. The case brought against them was mostly a psychological ploy, intended to anger and instill insecurity precisely at a time when West, Isaacs, and their children were trying to build a new sense of familial intimacy by sharing a household. Ironically, with its decision the General Court effectively, if not legally, recognized the relationship of David Isaacs and Nancy West as what we might call a common-law marriage. No statutory case of fornication was ever made against them, but living under the duress of pending criminal charges for nearly five years may well have wrought psychological damage against the couple and their family nonetheless.

Surely David Isaacs and Nancy West knew that attempting to live together and establish adjacent businesses openly as husband and wife might arouse the hostility of some of their neighbors and possibly even invite criminal prosecution. The question remains why they made such a move despite this awareness. Certainly Isaacs and West wanted to live together with their children because they were a family. Moreover, immediate practical concerns may have played a role, since David Isaacs's house was much bigger than Nancy West's, which may have been very cramped with so many children—at least two of whom, Jane and Thomas, were themselves actually adults—trying to live in it along with their mother. In fact, between 1802 and 1833, David Isaacs added one-story wings onto either side of his home, no doubt in part to make room for the increasing number of residents.[43] Yet it is clear that the couple also had long-term concerns about their family's economic stability and security, concerns that could be alleviated considerably through their new arrangement. Solidifying their relationship as domestic partners was part of a conscious effort to strengthen the security of their respective—and subsequently, their collective—finances. That they did so successfully solely because of the illegality of their relationship could only have antagonized their white accusers even more.

By 1820, if David Isaacs's economic position was established, it was not necessarily stable. As a merchant, if he were smart and careful he could prosper, but the assumption of debt and extensions of credit that accompanied his enterprise also entailed a great deal of risk. Misfortune or carelessness could produce financial ruin. David Isaacs was very familiar with the vagaries of the market, having sued at least seven different people for debt between 1810 and 1822 alone.[44] However, in addition to the uncertainties inherent to his business, David Isaacs faced other potential threats to his financial stability. When his brother Isaiah died in 1806, he had left behind not only his estate of real and personal property but also four young children, for whom David Isaacs took primary responsibility. Although two of Isaiah's children had died by the early 1820s, David Isaacs's entanglement of his own financial affairs with those of his deceased brother and his surviving niece and nephew made his economic situation even more precarious than that of other merchants.[45] With no bankruptcy laws in Virginia in the 1820s, what a man in David Isaacs's position needed perhaps more than anything else was a form of insurance—some sort of knowledge that he had somewhere to turn for support and assistance should catastrophe befall him.

As a free person of color, Nancy West also needed security above anything else. In some ways, by 1819 she was fortunate. Both capital and land were typically beyond the reach of free blacks in Virginia, most of whom lived in dire poverty at the very bottom of the socioeconomic ladder. Free women of color in particular confronted severely restricted employment opportunities, but throughout her life, Nancy West had been able to rely on white male patrons—her father, Thomas Bell, David Isaacs—to help shield her from trying economic circumstances. Still, her relationship with Isaacs was tenuous to the extent that it was not recognized by law, meaning that she could be assured of Isaacs's protection only so long as he lived. Despite having some of her own resources, had David Isaacs died anytime before 1819, Nancy West would have been left very heavily dependent on his estate for survival. The debts inevitably accrued by Isaacs as a merchant and as an executor would have to be paid in the event of his death. There was therefore no guarantee that West could rely on inheritance for financial stability.[46]

Nancy West's financial interests, in turn, were inextricable from those of her children, for if she could not survive economically, neither could they. Free women of color frequently had to rear their families alone, since they generally outnumbered free black men and were usually too poor to purchase enslaved spouses. Again, West was in a privileged position in this regard so long as David Isaacs lived, but in 1819 he was nearly sixty years old and had five children with West who were still under age thirteen. Jane Isaacs, the couple's oldest daughter, was twenty-three and a milliner, enabling her to assist her mother both financially and as a secondary caregiver if necessary, but without Isaacs's support the entire family would have to struggle like so many other free families of color.[47] In addition to their individual interests, then, David Isaacs and Nancy West shared collective concerns regarding their children. Together they faced the anxieties of continuing to support their offspring until they all reached maturity, as well as of guaranteeing the security of their children's futures as they came of age.[48]

The structure of Isaacs and West's relationship after 1819 nicely served their mutual financial interests and concerns. For David Isaacs, having Nancy West by his side both domestically and economically meant that he had some financial security should disaster strike. He could rely on her as an outside source of capital to vouch for him, provide security in case of debt, and even support him if he went completely bankrupt. Living, working, and owning land alongside David Isaacs, meanwhile, operated to Nancy West's distinct advantage as well. She not only gained access to greater wealth and potential income, but, more significantly, to some degree of independence. If anything were to happen to David Isaacs after these maneuvers, Nancy West was now assured of having sufficient means to support herself. This improved financial relationship also served the interests of the couple's children. If Isaacs lost his money or died or both, West was in a better position to support the couple's children as they grew, and by helping her to increase her wealth and landholdings over time, it allowed West to pass some or all of that property on to her children as they got older and needed financial footholds of their own.

Throughout her life Nancy West always acquired land from members of her own family or that of David Isaacs, and Isaacs himself repeatedly facilitated West's economic mobility by actively helping to ensure that she had significant resources independent of his own wealth. The lot West bought in downtown Charlottesville in 1820 was, like the property she procured in 1803, land that had originally belonged to her father. Thomas West had rented the lot to Isaiah Isaacs during his lifetime and bequeathed it in his will to James Henry West's four children, each of whom held one-quarter interest. Between 1817 and 1819 David Isaacs purchased three-quarters of the lot from Nancy West's nieces and nephews. Just over a year later, Isaacs sold his entire share to Nancy West for $600, who herself purchased the final quarter from her niece Susannah in 1823.[49] By the time West bought Isaacs's portion of the property in 1820, she had sold her land on the outskirts of town to a free man of color named William Spinner for exactly $600, but there had been legal complications in the exchange. Consequently, she had not yet received any payment for that land, and would not until 1829.[50] She was earning her own money as a baker, but it still seems unlikely that West would have had $600 saved from her own income alone to pay Isaacs for the land. Instead, it appears that David Isaacs purchased most of the land in pieces, specifically for the purpose of then transferring it to Nancy West, with her purchase money then either given or loaned by him. At the very least, it was an unusual exchange, one made much easier for West by Isaacs's intervention. In his will, despite the fact that he had already sold the land legally to West, Isaacs made a specific point of relinquishing "all the right, title, interest, claim or demand" he had in the plot. Presumably this was to be certain that no one would question the land transfer or suggest that Nancy West's land was in reality still owned in any way by Isaacs or paid for with his funds. It was important that anyone who asked know that this property belonged exclusively and entirely to Nancy West.[51]

In 1824 West paid $400 for the northern half of another lot, number 19, directly across the street from the land she had bought in 1820. By this time it is certainly possible that she had enough money saved both from her business and from rents and profits collected on her property to conduct the transaction entirely on her own accord.[52] Still, David Isaacs mediated this exchange as well, since the seller was his nephew Hays Isaacs, for whom David continued to be partially responsible as executor of his brother's will.[53] David Isaacs no longer needed to be a financial backer for West, but this familial connection gave her privileged access to a land purchase she might not have had otherwise. Finally, in 1827 West purchased another Charlottesville property, lot 25, directly from Isaacs, who had bought it from a member of the Taliaferro family, who had purchased it from the estate of Thomas West.[54] David Isaacs did not have to sell land to Nancy West at all. But the couple astutely realized that dividing accumulated wealth between them ultimately was more stable and secure than simply aggrandizing Isaacs's estate. The only other time Nancy West ever came into land ownership was when David Isaacs bequeathed her in his will partial interest in his property, some of which she eventually purchased outright from his estate.[55]

Obviously, every free family, white or black, worried about the state of its finances, and many of both races kept property ownership within their extended families. In this respect there was nothing especially unusual about David Isaacs and Nancy West.[56] The couple was unusual, however, because even as antebellum Virginia law deprived them of an official marriage, they were not only effectively married but the law gave them an ability to stabilize their finances and hedge against economic peril that few white couples could ever have. In most Virginia families, married women had practically no authority to hold or dispose of property until 1877. Instead, by law every wife became a *femme covert*, meaning that upon marriage a woman surrendered ownership of all her personal and real property to her husband. A husband could not sell his wife's real estate entirely at will, but he was entitled to use it as he chose and keep all profits derived from it. That same property, though, could then be lost by both parties to a marriage in the event that creditors came calling. One of the few ways for a married woman to retain any property rights was to have a trust established for her in equity by someone else (usually by her father)—but almost invariably a trust came with conditions that precluded the full range of its use. The legalities of trusts were so complicated that, over time, the equity system yielded increased litigation.[57]

Yet because of the unusual nature of their relationship, Nancy West and David Isaacs effectively circumvented and subverted the restrictions of the Virginia property laws. West could never claim a dower right in Isaacs's estate as a legally married woman might, but since she and Isaacs were not married she eluded the restrictions of coverture. Even more valuable than a dowry, perhaps, she could own her own property outright without interference or conditions on its use and thus did not need the protection for women that a dowry provided. Race and gender barriers in antebellum Virginia may have limited Nancy West's ability to accumulate real estate and other forms of wealth, but, with regard to property rights, Virginia law actually made Nancy West's position stronger precisely by the means it attempted to restrict her. She was a free woman of color who, specifically because she was "married" (in fact but not in law) to a white man, had more economic independence, strength, and mobility than nearly any married white woman. Furthermore, while white families could protect a married woman's property from creditors through equity, the delimited conditions of its use restricted the free flow of capital both for families and the larger society, and almost always precluded strategies of cooperation that might otherwise maximize a couple's and their family's economic potential through more flexible and collective uses of capital. Nancy West and David Isaacs were not bound by any such fetters. Many white couples, in fact, may have wished they could have enjoyed the economic dynamics of this relationship. In fact, it may have been especially galling to them that West and Isaacs could structure their financial lives so advantageously even as (and, ironically, because) they lived and worked together but stayed unmarried.[58]

West and Isaacs's financial arrangements would be put to the test even before the General Court handed down its opinion in the state's case against the couple. In the spring of 1826 a number of Charlottesville merchants sued Isaacs for debts they believed he owed them in his capacity as executor of his brother's will. By the mid-1830s over half a dozen Charlottesville business owners sued Isaacs in three different lawsuits that dragged on through the courts for twenty years, past the time of Isaacs's death. As the suits progressed, the various plaintiffs demonstrated their willingness to use West and Isaacs's relationship against them in order to head off their defense. That they tried at all demonstrates again how white men in conflict might use evidence of an interracial sexual relationship instrumentally, as a means of attack in pursuit of a larger goal. That they failed reinforces the notion that while whites might have some success in harassing an interracial couple by using the law, they had greater difficulty in using it to produce more tangible consequences.

When David Isaacs's nephew Hays Isaacs turned twenty-one in February 1824, he came into his full inheritance from his father Isaiah. It seems he celebrated by going on a spending spree, mostly in Charlottesville. Local merchants and tradesmen familiar with both the young man and his financial situation willingly extended him credit, and Hays accumulated debts at numerous establishments totaling well over $1,000. Unfortunately, Hays was a financially inexperienced and irresponsible young man, more comfortable with buying and spending than with saving and accounting. By the end of 1824 some of the Charlottesville merchants tried to collect, only to have Hays refuse to pay, claiming he had no money. Nimrod Bramham and William Bibb consequently sued him for debt in Richmond, where he had also purchased some items from that branch of Bramham and Bibb's mercantile firm. In March 1826 a court in Henrico County ruled in favor of the plaintiff, at which point Hays Isaacs promptly left Virginia and never returned.[59]

Just a month later Joel Yancey, another Charlottesville merchant, filed suit in chancery in Albemarle County against David Isaacs. Yancey believed that David Isaacs, as the executor of Isaiah Isaacs's estate, still held a large sum of money for Hays Isaacs. Since Hays owed Yancey more than $400 but was unable or unwilling to pay his debts (and for that matter, could not even be located), Yancey's suit maintained that David Isaacs ought to be held responsible for paying his nephew's creditors. In June 1826 the merchant John R. Jones, who owned a store directly across the street from Isaacs and Nancy West, filed a lawsuit similar to Yancey's, and their cases were eventually joined together. In 1830 Bramham and Bibb, along with five other men to whom Hays owed money, sued David Isaacs as well.[60]

John R. Jones filed a statement that detailed his individual claims but also spoke to the complaints all the creditors had about how Isaacs had administered his nephew's inheritance. Hays Isaacs had signed away to David Isaacs all claims to his inheritance very soon after he came of age. Jones argued, however, that Isaacs had hurried his nephew—who in any event was "totally without experience" in analyzing financial accounts—through the release process, even paying an attorney $100 just to get Hays's signature quickly. David Isaacs, Jones alleged, had mishandled the accounting for his brother's estate and wanted to procure his nephew's release "for the purpose of closing the door to any investigation" into the accounts. Furthermore, Jones claimed that David Isaacs knew that Hays had amassed substantial debts. By getting Hays to relinquish his rights the elder Isaacs hoped to avoid having to fulfill his nephew's obligations and instead keep what remained of Hays's inheritance himself. Jones demanded that Hays's debts to him be paid from David Isaacs's accounts.[61]

Isaacs responded in March 1827. First, he argued that he had never wanted to be his brother's executor at all. The other men named as executors had "declined incurring the trouble and responsibility." As Isaiah's only brother and closest relative David Isaacs felt a "sacred duty" to take the job on himself, but he claimed he "indulged no hope or expectation" that it would be "either safe or profitable to him." Isaacs further claimed that he had never cheated his nephew out of what rightfully belonged to him. He explained that Hays "was and had been unsettled and itenerant [sic]" and was considering leaving Virginia when he turned twenty-one. In addition, the accounts of Hays's inheritance suggested to both uncle and nephew that when Hays came of age, the amount being held for him would be roughly equivalent to bills that still had to be paid and to money owed David Isaacs in his capacity as executor. Consequently, they had mutually agreed that Hays would release his claims and let his uncle work out the details. David Isaacs insisted that the $100 paid to his attorney was for services accumulated over time and not merely to obtain Hays's signature, as Jones's suit alleged. Furthermore, he had wanted to make a final settlement of Hays's accounts because he feared he might become responsible for the young man's future entanglements and possibly suffer "loss and, probably, great injustice." Rather than using any "undue means" to procure Hays's release, trying to swindle his nephew, or avoid investigation, David Isaacs contended that he had tried to end his financial connection to Hays precisely so he would never have to face the kind of lawsuit he now confronted. So far as he was concerned, his dealings with Hays Isaacs and his inheritance were complete, and he maintained that he could not be held responsible for any additional debts Hays had incurred.[62]

Witness testimony in the case centered on two issues. The first was Hays Isaacs's alleged incompetence concerning financial matters. V. W. Southall, David Isaacs's lawyer, testified that Hays had seemed satisfied with his uncle's handling of his accounts. Although he did not know Hays very well, Southall believed Hays seemed capable of making his own financial decisions, but he conceded that Hays did not "take time to examine the items composing the account." The merchant Isaac Raphael testified that Hays would not do blindly whatever David Isaacs told him to, but that Hays was also not "capable of investigating complicated accounts and of making judicious contracts about his property." Daniel Keith, Charlottesville's constable, lived one block from David Isaacs and was asked whether he thought Hays capable of handling money or property. Keith answered, "I knew him well. And think him incapable of managing either." Keith also found him generally to be "foolishly extravagant."[63]

As the plaintiffs' lawyer probed these white community members for their assessments of Hays Isaacs, he also hammered away at David Isaacs's relationship with Nancy West and their daughter Jane. Opie Norris was asked if Nancy West and Jane Isaacs were "both members of the family" of David Isaacs, "the first in the character of wife, and the second as daughter." Norris, giving an honest but disingenuous answer, probably in an effort to protect his friends, replied that Nancy and Jane lived in Isaacs's house but that he did not know for certain "that Nancy West is the wife of the defendant Isaacs or Jane Isaacs the daughter—only from public rumor." Daniel Keith, meanwhile, said that he knew Nancy and Jane and that "Nancy lives with [David Isaacs] as wife and Jane is called the daughter." Keith, Norris, and Isaac Raphael all also testified that they believed that around the time Hays turned twenty-one Nancy West had purchased his house and land in Charlottesville and that both she and Jane might have received some slaves from him.[64]

David Isaacs and Nancy West had had their fornication charge dismissed just six months prior to the witness testimony in the Yancey and

Jones lawsuit, only to find themselves confronted with an antebellum catch-22. Their original legal troubles had them trying to answer the accusation that they were not a legitimate family. Now Yancey and Jones argued that Isaacs's financial transactions were of questionable legality because he and Nancy West *were* in fact a family. The point of clarifying that David Isaacs's relationship with Nancy West was one of husband and wife was never overtly made in the case papers, but the implication was obvious: David Isaacs had taken advantage of his unusual relationship with Nancy West to acquire real and personal property from his nephew for himself. By making West the purchaser, the argument went, Isaacs was trying to avoid the obvious charge of a conflict of interest that might arise had he purchased the property directly, but since West was effectively if not legally Isaacs's wife he could still enjoy the benefits from its use. Similarly, while Jane Isaacs nominally owned some of the slaves once belonging to Hays Isaacs, in reality David Isaacs had merely boosted his own holdings through his daughter's ownership. These transparent ruses, Yancey and Jones suggested, were clear abuses of David Isaacs's power as executor of Isaiah Isaacs's estate. He had exploited his inexperienced nephew's finances for his own personal aggrandizement.

It is impossible to know how well or how poorly Hays Isaacs understood his financial affairs or, for that matter, how much of an effort David Isaacs made to keep his nephew informed. At the very least, numerous aspects of the situation looked suspicious. David Isaacs's own lawyer admitted that Hays hardly looked over his uncle's accounts before relinquishing his claims. That Nancy West and Jane Isaacs purchased land and may have procured slaves from Hays in December 1824, just as Bramham and Bibb were filing a suit against the young man in Richmond, suggests perhaps that David Isaacs and Nancy West indeed colluded to protect Hays's assets from being lost to pay off his debts. These transactions were certainly a conflict of interest for David Isaacs, since even if they were undertaken at some level to protect Hays, any economic improvements in the lives of Nancy West and Jane Isaacs represented improvements in David Isaacs's life as well. Jones and Yancey had a point when they drew attention to the peculiarities of the Isaacs-West family finances.[65]

David Isaacs's own defense offered only weak responses to the accusations made against him. Undoubtedly, he was being honest when he said he wanted to be rid of any financial responsibility for his nephew. Hays's reckless spending placed David Isaacs at enormous risk, and we have already seen how greatly the elder Isaacs valued security. Ultimate-

ly, though, David Isaacs's only substantive response to the charges of
Hays's creditors was a demand that the letter of the law be upheld. Re-
gardless of what others might think of Hays's fiscal capacities, David
Isaacs argued, he had never coerced Hays into signing anything. He and
Hays Isaacs had a legally binding agreement between them, and no third
party ought to have the authority to challenge its legitimacy. As David
Isaacs pointed out in his response to Bramham and Bibb's lawsuit against
him, elaborating on an argument made in his response to Yancey and
Jones, Hays had never attempted to retract his agreement to the arrangement between them, nor had Hays ever intimated that he believed he
might have made a mistake. Consequently, David Isaacs claimed he
could not "see the principle of equity which authorizes other and third
persons to impugn or question the right and authority of a legatee or
distributee . . . after their arrival to age, upon considerations sufficient
to themselves, to release and acquit an executor or guardian of any
claim."[66]

The Albemarle County Circuit Superior Court of Law and Chancery
ruled against David Isaacs on May 16, 1834. Based on its own readings of
Isaacs's accounts, the court found that he still owed Hays over $2,500 of
his inheritance from Isaiah Isaacs. It ordered that the young man's debts
be paid from this sum and that David Isaacs turn over to Hays directly
what remained. Essentially, the court accepted the claims of Yancey,
Jones, Bramham and Bibb, and Hays's other creditors, all of whose cases
the court ruled on together. Hays Isaacs's release to his uncle was technically legal, but the court ruled it could not be construed to have a negative impact on any parties aside from David and Hays. David Isaacs, the
court agreed, had procured his nephew's release "as a protection against
the claims of the creditors." Additionally, the court took David Isaacs to
task for his handling of his nephew's estate, suggesting he had done an
injustice to his nephew for his own convenience and probably his own
gain. David was not guilty of any criminal activity, but the court asserted
that Hays's release was "not founded on an actual settlement, in which
every thing is explained; but obtained, as it would seem, with the view of
preventing the necessity of such a settlement." The court mentioned
nothing about David Isaacs's relationship with Nancy West or the financial transactions between her and Hays Isaacs.[67]

David Isaacs immediately looked to appeal the court's verdict. In order to do so, however, he had to have someone post security equivalent
to at least double the amount of the judgment issued against him. If
Isaacs lost his appeal and then had insufficient funds to fulfill the court's

decision, whoever posted security for him would be obliged to pay. Nancy West was available to assist, as was Jane, who now went by Jane West after having married her cousin Nathaniel H. West in 1832. On June 27, 1834, Nancy, Jane, and Nathaniel West all entered into a bond with David Isaacs, Hays Isaacs, and his creditors. The Wests collectively pledged over $7,000 as security, the entirety of their estates. Once again, David Isaacs and Nancy West proved their relationship provided them with financial strength and a degree of mutual reliance unavailable to others. Yet because they derived their strength only from being inextricably connected to one another, their fortunes still rose and fell together. Here, the Wests' gesture entailed enormous risk.[68]

The same day that Isaacs filed his appeal, Hays Isaacs's creditors jointly filed a bill of exceptions with the Albemarle court claiming that the security posted by the Wests was invalid. First, they argued that Nancy West, though a "woman of colour," was "the wife *de facto* of David Isaacs . . . now living, and for many years having lived with the said David Isaacs as his wife, and which connection is notorious in the neighborhood in which they reside." Second, they claimed that any property West claimed to own in reality belonged to Isaacs. She may have purchased the land herself, but they alleged she did so entirely "with the *funds* of the said David Isaacs." The creditors further tacked on the assertions that Jane West could not enter into a valid contract because she was *a femme covert* as a result of her marriage to Nathaniel West, and that Nathaniel West, in turn, was himself "notoriously insolvent" and owned no property at all. Taken as a whole, the intent of these objections was to head off David Isaacs's appeal of the judgment against him altogether by accusing him of trying to post security for himself, since all the pledged money really belonged to him. Being from Charlottesville, Hays's creditors knew that David Isaacs's most realistic sources of sufficient security lay in his own family. If they could demonstrate a reason for the court to reject the legitimacy of the Wests' security, David might well be unable to find another person to put up any money in their place. He would have to start paying off his nephew's debts immediately.[69]

Nathaniel and Jane West paid no land taxes in Charlottesville in 1834 and could have only contributed little to David Isaacs's security. The crux of the matter, then, was whether Nancy West actually had any estate legally distinct from that of David Isaacs. The objections specifically addressing her shared the claim that she did not. In the first, the creditors claimed that Isaacs and West lived as husband and wife, and while their relationship could not be recognized in law as a marriage because it crossed the color line, in this instance it ought to be treated as if it were a legitimate union. If Nancy West was therefore a married woman, she could not possibly post security for David Isaacs because her estate was legally his estate. Realizing that these grounds for objection might carry little weight with any court, since the fact remained that the couple could not be and was not legally married, the creditors filed their second objection. Here, they claimed that any property Nancy West appeared to own was merely an illusion designed to conceal David Isaacs's holdings.[70]

Hays Isaacs's creditors had good reason for wanting their money quickly. Whether or not Nancy West actually owned her own property, they had seen how David Isaacs relied on her whenever he got into financial trouble or looked for some economic advantage. What would happen if Isaacs got into additional legal difficulties while he appealed the judgment against him in this case? By the time a court ruled on the creditors' lawsuit, Isaacs and West could lose both their fortunes, leaving the men to whom Hays Isaacs owed money no possibility of collection, at least not without additional legal proceedings. Each of the objections to Nancy West's posting of security was logically sound, and they reflected the effort by Hays's creditors to object on every possible ground. When placed together in a single document, however, the objections were logically inconsistent. In the first objection the creditors asked the court to acknowledge the legitimacy of West and Isaacs's domestic partnership on equal footing with a legal marriage, thereby invalidating Nancy West's property ownership. In the second objection, meanwhile, it was taken for granted that the relationship could not be legally recognized. The point here was not that Nancy West could not own property, but that in fact she did not. In the same document, then, Nancy West was both married to a white man and not married to a white man. She both owned property and yet could not own property. Having all these claims be true was impossible, but the creditors cannot be blamed for trying. The failure of state law to define the relationship of West and Isaacs effectively meant that any attempt to confront the couple legally would be absurdly slippery. Nancy West and David Isaacs fell through the cracks between the laws and exploited them. Without explanation, the Albemarle court rejected the bill of exception, the Wests' posted security was accepted, and the appeal proceeded. Just as the General Court had determined seven years earlier, little could be done about David Isaacs and Nancy West without addressing a host of other difficult legal issues.

David Isaacs died in 1837. In his will, he provided that Nancy West could continue to reside in the house in which his family lived and worked for as long as she lived, and he directed that it be sold upon her death and the proceeds divided into seven portions for the couple's children. He allowed Nancy to select any items of personal property from the estate she wished to keep and ordered that most of the remainder then be sold at public auction, with the proceeds to be given to a charity selected by his executors. She chose some cooking utensils, a few tables and a dozen chairs, a bureau, a bed and bedstead, an expensive metal clock, and David Isaacs's sleeve buttons and watch chain. At public auction in April 1837, Isaacs's son Tucker purchased some mugs, bowls, and other kitchen accessories, and his daughter Julia Ann's husband Eston Hemings—a son of Thomas Jefferson and Sally Hemings—bought some similar items. Numerous members of the Scott family, who were neighbors, family friends, and distant relatives by marriage, also made some purchases, including Isaacs's copy of the writings of Thomas Jefferson.[71] Little if any of the proceeds from the estate sale went to charity. David Isaacs's estate had a fair number of debts, no doubt compounded by the Panic of 1837. Isaacs's administrator, Egbert R. Watson (Isaacs's chosen executors had failed to qualify), spent more than a decade slowly paying off his liabilities, mostly by collecting debts still owed Isaacs and through rents, profits, and sales of property owned by his estate.[72]

In some ways, the late 1830s and early 1840s were years of great success for Nancy West. David Isaacs's death undoubtedly was painful and there were financial difficulties attendant to settling his estate. West, though, was also able to sell and transfer property to the couple's children and their families, bringing to fruition what had likely been her and Isaacs's long-term goal of insuring self-sufficiency in adulthood for their offspring. As David Isaacs neared the end of his life and then passed away, and as West entered her later years—she was fifty-five by the time of Isaacs's death—this goal became increasingly imperative. In 1836 Nancy West gave a portion of lot 33 to Jane "in consideration of the natural love and affection which she bears to the said Jane West."[73] Nancy probably lived with her daughter for a number of years on this spot as well, since in September 1837 she arranged for a five-year rental of the house she and David Isaacs had lived in, most likely to help pay off Isaacs's debts. Although Isaacs had "loaned" West the property, rental fees accrued to his estate, which technically continued to own the property.[74] Back in her own house in 1842, Nancy West sold the property next door (lot 35) to Eston Hemings, and the following year Tucker Isaacs purchased a small piece of land on lot 33 from his mother next to his sister Jane.[75] By the end of 1843, Nancy West still lived in the house she had shared with David Isaacs and paid taxes on the land, but because Isaacs's estate still retained control over the property she no longer owned anything outright.[76]

Whatever pride came from being able to foster her children's independence, Nancy West still had her own lingering fiscal responsibilities. In early 1846 the Richmond Court of Appeals rejected David Isaacs's appeal from the Albemarle chancery court, but by this point the assets held by Isaacs's estate were not nearly enough to cover the sums owed to Hays and to the numerous merchants of Charlottesville. With accumulated interest and inflation over more than a decade, the debts now totaled around $5,000. It was only a matter of time until Egbert Watson let Nancy West know he had no other option but to ask her to auction off her house. In June 1846 she consented to the sale, but given her own pledge to pay Hays's debts if David Isaacs could not, she really had very little choice. Reluctant to relinquish her family home, however, she bought most of the property back herself for $2,300, while Tucker, who was also acting by this year as his mother's financial agent, bought a small piece of the property for himself.[77] As the time drew near for her to make her first payment for this purchase, however, Nancy West found herself low on funds. If she could not pay for the property, it would be resold, and if the purchase price failed to cover the debts owed by Isaacs, West could still be held accountable to pay what remained.

Even as the decree of the Court of Appeals placed Nancy West in a vulnerable position yet again, it simultaneously provided her with the means to overcome it. The court ordered David Isaacs's estate to pay all of Hays Isaacs's debts, and in keeping with Hays's apparent tendency to borrow money from nearly everyone he knew and not pay it back, he had still had an unpaid loan from Nancy West. In November 1846 Nancy West sued Hays Isaacs in chancery. The story she told in her deposition to the court went back to her land purchase from Hays in the 1820s. As discussed earlier, Hays had sold West half of lot 19 in Charlottesville in 1824. The other half of the lot belonged to Isaiah Isaacs's living daughter, Fanny. In 1825 or 1826, West recalled, Hays offered to buy out his sister's interest and sell the rest of the property to West, but he needed to borrow some money to make the purchase. West loaned him $200, but he never made the purchase, never returned her money, and left the state. West believed at the time of her statement that he lived in Arkansas, leaving her no prospect of collecting directly from him.[78]

With more than twenty years of accumulated interest added to the $200 Hays owed Nancy West, his debt would go a long way toward helping her cover the price of her home, and she practically begged the court to grant her lawsuit. It was her only chance to recover her money. The Albemarle chancery court granted the case, and West and Egbert Watson (who, as administrator of David Isaacs's estate, also administered Hays's accounts) settled out of court in 1850. Finally, David Isaacs's debts were paid, and Nancy West kept her home—barely.[79]

Undoubtedly, Nancy West felt somewhat desperate when she filed her plea to the court in 1846. She herself very nearly crashed financially right along with her deceased husband, and her personal holdings were always at least partially conditional on his financial circumstances. But while she would have had to move from her home had she been unable to scrape together the money to pay for it, it is unlikely that Nancy West would have been relegated to the poorhouse. David Isaacs assisted her in procuring assets independent of his own both so that she could survive financially without him and so that he might depend on her if he needed to. Nancy West implemented precisely the same strategy in the next generation. Because she had already transferred so much of her own wealth to her children, by the 1840s West had established a safety net both for them and for herself. A blend of insecurity and stability thus inhered to Nancy West's position throughout her life in Charlottesville, both domestically and financially. She was effectively married and raised a large family, but the legality of that marriage and consequently the legitimacy of that family was never certain. She managed to attain wealth and pass significant amounts of that wealth on to her children, but her personal fortunes were dependent upon the financial strength of David Isaacs, which in the end was unsure. The dynamics that obtained in the domestic and the financial always overlapped and were integrally related.

In 1850 Nancy West sold almost all the land she still owned in Charlottesville and shortly thereafter moved to Chillicothe, a town in Ross County, Ohio, and the home of numerous communities of free people of color emigrating from Virginia. She died there late in 1856.[80] For much of her life, her economic stature and domestic relationship with David Isaacs seem to have meant that the legal and social hostility facing free people of color in Virginia did not greatly affect her desire to remain where she had been born. In 1832, for example, even as the Virginia legislature passed a series of restrictive laws against free blacks and slaves, she and her son Frederick started and ran a newspaper known as the Charlottesville *Chronicle* from a building she owned. If Nancy West ever thought about leaving Virginia before David Isaacs died, her actions do not indicate that she had any intention of doing so, and at least for some years after his death her transfer of property to her children implies that she assumed they would stay in Charlottesville as well.[81]

Surely the changing political, legal, and social environments for free people of color in Virginia in the late 1840s influenced her departure. Amidst growing sectional tensions, the General Assembly passed new legislation further constraining the activities and movements of free people of color. These new restrictions included a tax on free blacks to pay for their own colonization to Liberia (which both Frederick and Tucker Isaacs paid in 1850), and a renewed effort to uphold the 1806 removal law, which forced slaves freed after that year to leave the state unless they received explicit permission to remain. Despite her long tenure in her community and having been born a free woman, in 1850 Nancy West found herself before the Albemarle County court along with dozens of other free people of color and asked to prove she was born free and a legal resident of Virginia. Having to make this appearance must have been humiliating, and Nancy West may have chosen to heed Virginia's clear invitation to leave the state.[82]

More than the generally hostile legal environment, the migration of Nancy West's children probably played the greatest role in her decision to move. Eston and Julia Ann Hemings had lived in Ohio at least part of the time since the late 1830s, joining Eston's brother Madison, who had moved there after Sally Hemings died in 1835. By the late 1840s Virginia law stripped free people of color of the right to return to the state if they left, clinching Eston and Julia Ann's decision to remove to Ohio permanently, which they had done in any event by 1845. Since the early 1840s Tucker Isaacs and his wife Betsy-Ann had also sometimes lived in southern Ohio with her parents, former Monticello slaves Joe Fossett (who was also a son of Mary Hemings) and his wife Edy. While Nancy West successfully demonstrated her right to remain in Virginia in 1850, Betsy-Ann Isaacs was not so fortunate. Born a slave, manumitted in 1837, but never having received permission from the legislature to remain, she was required to leave the state; she and Tucker departed Virginia permanently shortly thereafter. Agness Isaacs, Nancy West's youngest daughter, moved to Ohio in the early 1850s along with her husband Jerman Evans, a free man of color from Charlottesville whom she had married in 1836. Agness received her mother's home and property in Chillicothe as an inheritance. By the end of 1850 Nancy West was nearly seventy years old. Her husband had long since died and his accounts were finally settled. Three of her children had departed a Virginia that obviously no longer wanted their presence, and she too decided to live out her days elsewhere.[83]

In the end Nancy West and David Isaacs had achieved much. They had maneuvered through the labyrinths of their local community and of Virginia law to build and maintain successfully a forty-year relationship that should have been impossible. They established themselves as landowners, businesspeople, and parents, and utilized their own success to place their children, whose lifetimes would traverse the Civil War and Reconstruction, in positions where they too might succeed. But each in turn would have to do so on different terms and in different circumstances and social environments than their parents, and they each chose to follow different paths. Among David Isaacs's and Nancy West's children, only Jane West remained in Charlottesville by the onset of the Civil War, where she died a wealthy woman in 1869. Thomas Isaacs's whereabouts for much of his life are unknown. Hays Isaacs, the couple's second son (not Isaiah Isaacs's heir), died a young man in 1839. Frederick Isaacs removed to Wythe County in southwestern Virginia, where he had such difficulties with debts in the late 1830s that he ended up in jail before finally filing in 1837 for bankruptcy under recently passed Virginia laws. Agness Isaacs lived out her life in Ohio, as did Tucker Isaacs, whose house, according to family oral history, served as a station on the Underground Railroad. Tucker Isaacs would also bring suit against an Ohio hotel after the Civil War for refusing to rent him a room. Julia Ann Isaacs moved to Wisconsin with Eston Hemings in the early 1850s. The couple changed their last name to Jefferson and became white persons.[84]

Notes

1. Albemarle County Will Book 3, pp. 302–03; Albemarle County Will Book 4, pp. 18–19. Unless otherwise stated, all Albemarle County records are held at the Albemarle County Courthouse, Charlottesville. James Henry West, "the son [of] Perscilla," was born into slavery, but Thomas West had sold him his freedom for five shillings in 1785; see Albemarle County Deed Book 9, p. 177. Nancy West was born a free person in 1782, which suggests that her mother must have been freed sometime after James's birth. Priscilla, with or without Thomas West, may also have had a third child named Penelope. David Isaacs left some

money in his will to Penelope, a free woman of color and the "daughter of old Ciller." Albemarle County Will Book 12, p. 367. Thomas West's land in Amherst County, to which James Henry West moved sometime shortly before 1800, currently lies within the borders of Nelson County along the Rockfish River.

The author would like to acknowledge Peter S. Onuf, Cinder Stanton, Edward L. Ayers, Annette Gordon-Reed, Robert Vernon, and the anonymous readers for the *Journal of Southern History* for their assistance, comments, and useful criticisms.

2. Jacob Rader Marcus, *United States Jewry, 1776–1985* (4 vols.; Detroit, 1989–1993), I, 149–50; Myron Berman, *Richmond's Jewry, 1769–1976: Shabbat in Shockoe* (Charlottesville, 1979), 2–3 and 7–9; Herbert T. Ezekiel and Gaston Lichtenstein, *The History of the Jews of Richmond from 1796 to 1917* (Richmond, 1917), 13–16, 240; Carol Ely, Jeffrey Hantman, and Phyllis Leffler, *To Seek the Peace of the City: Jewish Life in Charlottesville* (Charlottesville, 1994), 2; Nancy E. Willner, "A Brief History of the Jewish Community in Charlottesville and Albemarle," *Magazine of Albemarle County History*, XL (1982), 2; Albemarle County Deed Book 20, p. 436; and Albemarle County Will Book 4, pp. 18–19. Cohen and Isaacs dissolved their partnership in 1792. Isaiah Isaacs first appears on the personal property tax lists in Albemarle County in 1792, and David Isaacs appears first in 1793; Albemarle County Personal Property Tax Books, 1792, 1793, MSS 5145-d, microfilm supplement reel A-1, Special Collections, Alderman Library, University of Virginia [hereinafter cited as ACPPTB].

3. Manuscript Census Returns, Seventh Census of the United States, 1850, Albemarle County, Virginia (hereinafter cited as Manuscript Census, [year], Albemarle County), National Archives Microfilm Series (hereinafter cited as NAMS) M-432, reel 932, frame 203. In fact, this made her one of the richest free women of color in the entire upper South. According to Loren Schweninger, in 1850 just four free black women in the upper South owned $5,000 or more in real estate. Loren Schweninger, "Property-Owning Free African American Women in the South, 1800–1870," *Journal of Women's History*, I (Winter 1990), 34.

4. Virginia's colonial legislature explicitly forbade interracial marriage for the first time in 1691. In 1662 the body had addressed the question of interracial sex specifically, imposing a double fine on extramarital relations involving black and white partners. The anti-fornication laws in place by the end of the eighteenth century, however, levied no such additional penalty for interracial sex. W. W. Hening, ed., *The Statutes at Large; Being a Collection of All the Laws of Virginia from the First Session of the Legislature in 1619* (13 vols., Richmond, New York, and Philadelphia, 1809–1823), II, 170 (1662, Act 12), and III, 86–88 (1691, Act 16); *A Collection of All Such Acts of the General Assembly of Virginia, of a*

Public and Permanent Nature, As Are Now in Force (Richmond, 1794), Chap. 138, sec. 6; and *The Revised Code of the Laws of Virginia* (2 vols.; Richmond, 1819), I, Chap. 141, sec. 6, pp. 555–56. See also A. Leon Higginbotham Jr., and Barbara K. Kopytoff, "Interracial Sex and Racial Purity in Colonial and Antebellum Virginia," *Georgetown Law Journal,* LXXVII (1989), 1967–2029; and Peter W. Bardaglio, "'Shamefull Matches': The Regulation of Interracial Sex and Marriage in the South before 1900," in Martha Hodes, ed., *Sex, Love, Race: Crossing Boundaries in North American History* (New York and London, 1999), 112–38, esp. 113–21.

5. Important studies of these subjects include but are not limited to Martha Hodes, *White Women, Black Men: Illicit Sex in the Nineteenth-Century South* (New Haven and London, 1997); Michael P. Johnson and James L. Roark, *Black Masters: A Free Family of Color in the Old South* (New York and London, 1984); Melton A. McLaurin, *Celia, A Slave* (Athens, Ga., and London, 1991); Thelma Jennings, "'Us Colored Women Had to Go Through A Plenty': Sexual Exploitation of African American Slave Women," *Journal of Women's History,* I (Winter 1990), 45–74; Kent Anderson Leslie, *Woman of Color, Daughter of Privilege: Amanda America Dickson, 1849–1893* (Athens, Ga., and London, 1995); Cynthia Kennedy-Haflett, "'Moral Marriage': A Mixed-Race Relationship in Nineteenth-Century Charleston, South Carolina," *South Carolina Historical Magazine,* XCVII (July 1996), 206–26; Henry Wiencek, *The Hairstons: An American Family in Black and White* (New York, 1999); Carolyn J. Powell, "In Remembrance of Mira: Reflections on the Death of a Slave Woman," in Patricia Morton, ed., *Discovering the Women in Slavery: Emancipating Perspectives on the American Past* (Athens, Ga., and London, 1996), 47–60; Adele Logan Alexander, *Ambiguous Lives: Free Women of Color in Rural Georgia, 1789–1879* (Fayetteville, Ark., 1991); T. O. Madden Jr. with Ann L. Miller, *We Were Always Free: The Maddens of Culpeper County, Virginia, A 200-Year Family History* (New York and London, 1992); and Diane Miller Sommerville, "The Rape Myth in the Old South Reconsidered," *Journal of Southern History,* LXI (August 1995), 481–518. Other works on these topics are cited where appropriate throughout the notes below.

6. Albemarle County Law Order Book, 1822–1831, October 11, 1822, p. 51.

7. It is unclear whether West and Isaacs even made an effort to deny the charges against them, but it would have been both futile and perjurious to do so. The Albemarle County Court indicted Nancy West's nephew, Nathaniel West, for perjury the same day the court sent his aunt's case to Richmond. Found not guilty many years later, the timing of Nathaniel West's legal trouble suggests that he may have lied in an effort to protect family members from prosecution. Albemarle County Law Order Book, 1822–1831, May 13, 1824, pp. 129 and 131; and Albemarle County Law Order Book 1831–1837, October 11, 1832, p. 87.

8. *Commonwealth* v. *David Isaacs and Nancy West*, 5 Rand. 634 (Va. 1826).

9. Albemarle County Law Order Book, 1822–1831, May 8, 1827, p. 246.

10. Manuscript Census, 1810, Population Schedule, Albemarle County, NAMS M-252, reel 66, frame 217. Unlike the 1810 census, in subsequent years the population of Charlottesville was not separated from county totals, which makes it extraordinarily difficult to chart the town's growth with specificity. The population of Albemarle County as a whole, however, grew slowly between 1810 and 1850, from just 18,268 in 1810 to 19,750 in 1820, 22,618 in 1830, 22,924 in 1840, and 25,800 in 1850; census figures cited in John Hammond Moore, *Albemarle: Jefferson's County, 1727–1976* (Charlottesville, 1976), 115–16. Even allowing for a generous population increase in the town, by 1822 Charlottesville seems unlikely to have comprised more than three to four hundred people. There were 25 free people of color living in Charlottesville in 1810.

11. Albemarle County Law Order Book, 1809–1821, May 15, 1812 and May 12, 1818, pp. 137 and 328; and Albemarle County Will Book 1, pp. 25–29.

12. Mary Rawlings, ed., *Early Charlottesville: Recollections of James Alexander, 1828–1874* (Charlottesville, 1942), 20–21, 30–31, and 34 (first quotation on p. 34); and Rev. Edgar Woods, *Albemarle County in Virginia* (Charlottesville, 1901), 239–40 (second quotation on p. 239), 242–43, 341, and 346–47.

13. Albemarle County Will Book 12, p. 370.

14. Rawlings, ed., *Early Charlottesville*, 11, 12, 35 n. 11, 49 n. 5, and 65 (quotation on p. 35); Woods, *Albemarle County in Virginia*, 201–3, 243–44; and James A. Bear Jr. and Lucia C. Stanton, eds., *Jefferson's Memorandum Books: Accounts, with Legal Records and Miscellany, 1767–1826*, The Papers of Thomas Jefferson, 2d ser. (2 vols.; Princeton, 1997), II, 947 n. 71.

15. Jefferson was also at least an acquaintance of Nancy West's father, Thomas. David Isaacs sent Jefferson unsolicited books on Judaism and thought enough of the former president to be one of the earliest contributors to the proposed University of Virginia. Ely, Hantman, and Leffler, *To Seek the Peace*, 3–4; Albemarle County Will Book 1, pp. 25–29; Marcus, *United States Jewry*, I, 361; and Bear and Stanton, eds., *Jefferson's Memorandum Books* (see its index for mentions of Thomas West, as well as for numerous notations of payments made to David Isaacs and other Charlottesville merchants).

16. Ira Rosenswaike, "The Jewish Population of the United States as Estimated from the Census of 1820," in Abraham J. Karp, ed., *The Jewish Experience in America* (5 vols.; Waltham, Mass., 1969), II, 2, 8–9, and 19C; Ely, Hantman, and Leffler, *To Seek the Peace*, 3; and Willner, "A Brief History," 2–3.

17. Marcus, *United States Jewry*, I, Chaps. 14–15 (quotation on p. 553). See also Frederic Cople Jaher, *A Scapegoat in the New Wilderness: The Origins and Rise of Anti-Semitism in America* (Cambridge, Mass., and London, 1994), esp. Chap. 4;

and Howard N. Rabinowitz, "Nativism, Bigotry and Anti-Semitism in the South," *American Jewish History,* LXXVII (March 1988), 437–51. That typical contemporary forms of anti-Semitic prejudice also pervaded Charlottesville in this era is suggested by an 1820 editorial reprinted in the Charlottesville *Central Gazette* that, while not hostile toward Jews, stereotyped British Jews as "great bankers" whose value to the United States as potential immigrants would lie primarily in their talents with money. Charlottesville *Central Gazette,* February 4, 1820, p. 4.

18. The racial status of Jews was a matter of some inconclusive debate in the United States as the language of "racial science" became the widespread means by which Americans discussed racial difference by the 1850s. Before midcentury Americans discussed the racial position of Jews very little and generally accepted Jews as whites, albeit a distinct class of whites. Most importantly for David Isaacs's story, "[t]he Jewish racial question was not a social or political issue in the antebellum South: whatever anti-Semitism Southern Jews encountered was primarily economic or religious." Leonard Rogoff, "Is the Jew White?: The Racial Place of the Southern Jew," *American Jewish History,* LXXXV (September 1997), 195–230 (quotation on p. 201). See also Sander Gilman, *The Jew's Body* (New York and London, 1991), Chap. 7, and Jaher, *Scapegoat in the New Wilderness,* Chap. 5. Karen Brodkin discusses the racial position of Jews in the United States after the 1880s in *How Jews Became White Folks and What That Says about Race in America* (New Brunswick, N.J., and London, 1998).

19. Woods, *Albemarle County in Virginia,* 143, 147, 239–40, 243, and 346–47.

20. While there is no direct evidence to implicate him, John R. Jones seems an especially likely candidate to have brought Isaacs and West to the attention of the Albemarle criminal justice system. Not only was his mercantile business located on property directly across the street from David Isaacs's, but (as discussed below) he would act extraordinarily antagonistically toward him in lawsuits beginning in the mid-1820s. Jones also served as a member of the grand jury that presented Isaacs and West in 1822. Albemarle County Law Order Book, 1822–1831, October 7, 1822, p. 31.

21. Albemarle County Deed Book 1, p. 162. Nancy West paid taxes on this land in 1800, but did not in 1801, 1802, or 1803, which suggests that someone else (someone other than Thomas Bell, who paid James West for the land but who died in 1800) probably took legal responsibility for the land and its taxes. In addition, Nancy West exchanged a small piece of the property in 1803 to have some fences built, further indicating that she probably did not reside regularly on the property before that year. Albemarle County Land Tax Books, 1800–1804, MSS 5145-b, microfilm supplemental reel 2, Special Collections, Alderman Library, University of Virginia (hereinafter cited as ACLTB); and Albemarle County Deed Book 14, pp. 263–64.

22. Albemarle County Deed Book 1, pp. 158–59; and Declaration 619, April 1802, microfilm 5794, reel 2, vol. 15, Mutual Assurance Society of Virginia Declarations, Alderman Library (hereinafter cited as Mutual Assurance Society).

23. Manuscript Census, 1810, Population Schedules, Albemarle County, NAMS M-252, reel 66, frame 179; Rawlings, ed., *Early Charlottesville*, 74, 79; and Albemarle County Will Book 12, p. 368.

24. Albemarle County Deed Book 22, pp. 46–47.

25. Ibid., 177–78. In 1828, for example, the land was occupied by one Mr. Schroff, a tinner; see Rawlings, ed., *Early Charlottesville*, 72.

26. Manuscript Census, 1820, Population Schedule, Albemarle County, NAMS M-33, reel 130, frame 75.

27. Until 1832, although most of the town of Charlottesville lay in Fredericksville Parish, the outskirts of town, including the plot on which Nancy West originally lived, were part of neighboring St. Anne's Parish; see ACLTB, 1833, supplemental reel 4.

28. Albemarle County Law Order Book, 1822–1831, May 13, 1824, p. 131. Two petitions to the General Assembly from Albemarle County in the decade or so before Isaacs and West were charged indicate that Charlottesville residents also had broader concerns beyond interracial sex about immorality and disorder in their midst. In 1815, for example, twenty-five men asked the state legislature to extend the jurisdiction of town trustees one mile beyond Charlottesville's borders, enabling them to suppress "riots" at "some houses of ill fame within a few feet of the town." The legislature refused this entreaty, only to receive another petition in 1818 making a similar request. This time, the thirty-three signatories complained about large Sunday gatherings of blacks at "tipling-shops" just beyond the town's boundaries, activities that were "inimical to sober habits and morals" and "contrary to good policy and our own safety." It is unclear to what extent the changing evangelical culture of early-nineteenth-century Virginia might have played a role in these protests. By 1850 Charlottesville had forty-five churches, but no denomination had a church building in town at all until 1826. In addition, prominent among the signatories to both petitions were many members of the merchant community, including David Isaacs, suggesting that concerns about drinking and prostitution may have been economic as much as, if not more than, moral. Legislative Petitions—Albemarle County, #6459, December 8, 1815, and #7213, December 14, 1818, Library of Virginia, Richmond; and Moore, *Albemarle: Jefferson's County*, 77–81, 155.

29. Census records indicate that Joshua Grady and Betsy Ann Farly almost certainly lived together by 1820 and continued to do so until at least the 1830s. The third couple brought before the court in 1822 was Andrew McKee, a white man and a hatter who was later a party to a lawsuit filed against David Isaacs, and

Matsy Cannon, whom I have been unable to locate elsewhere in the public record. Andrew McKee had no free people of color sharing his household in either 1820 or 1830, but a white woman between the ages of 26 and 45 did live with him in 1820. Manuscript Census, 1820, Population Schedule, Albemarle County, NAMS M-33, reel 130, frames 71 and 80; Manuscript Census, 1830, Population Schedule, Albemarle County, NAMS M-19, reel 197, frames 254 and 274; Rawlings, ed., *Early Charlottesville,* 89; Lucia Stanton, "Monticello to Main Street: The Hemings Family and Charlottesville," *Magazine of Albemarle County History,* LV (1997), 97–100, 109–10; and Ervin L. Jordan Jr., "'A Just and True Account': Two 1833 Parish Censuses of Albemarle County Free Blacks," *Magazine of Albemarle County History,* LIII (1995), 136.

30. Nancy West's original property, lot 46, was valued at just $300, with her house adding an additional $100. By contrast, the land she purchased in 1820, lot 33, was worth $1000, while the buildings on it were valued at an additional $880. ACLTB, 1820–1821, supplemental reel 3.

31. *Samuel Anderson v. Commonwealth,* 5 Rand. 627 (Va. 1826).

32. *Commonwealth v. Isaacs and West* (quotations at 635).

33. On the judicial handling of cases involving interracial sex and interracial marriages in the antebellum South, see Peter W. Bardaglio, *Reconstructing the Household: Families, Sex, and the Law in the Nineteenth-Century South* (Chapel Hill and London, 1995), 48–64, and 260 n. 112. On Virginia see also Peter Wallenstein, "Race, Marriage, and the Law of Freedom: Alabama and Virginia, 1860s–1960s," *Chicago-Kent Law Review,* LXX (1994), 371–437, esp. 389–94.

34. *Revised Code of the Laws of Virginia* (Richmond, 1819), Chap. 106, secs. 22–23, p. 401.

35. Hening, ed., *Statutes at Large,* XII, 184 (1785, Chap. 78).

36. Since 1793 free people of color in antebellum Virginia had been required by law to register with their county court. When Nancy West registered as Nancy Isaacs in 1837 (the earliest registration for her that I was able to locate), she was described as "aged 56 years, 5 feet 1 inch high, light complexion, a scar upon the left cheek, a mole upon the left side of the nose no other scars or marks perceivable." Albemarle County Minute Book, 1836–1838, Oct. 2, 1837, p. 263.

37. Albemarle County Marriage Register, 1780–1868, August 29, 1794.

38. Rawlings, ed., *Early Charlottesville,* 73, 79; and testimony of Benjamin Wheeler, *Hays v. Hays,* [1836?], Albemarle County Ended Chancery Causes (Circuit Superior Court), Case 354 (Library of Virginia, Richmond).

39. Barbara J. Fields's famous pair of essays are useful places to begin a historical investigation of the concept of race as a constructed category in the United States, though a scholarly understanding of race as a fiction goes back at least to the work of W. E. B. Du Bois; see Barbara Jeanne Fields, "Ideology and Race

in American History," in J. Morgan Kousser and James M. McPherson, eds., *Region, Race, and Reconstruction: Essays in Honor of C. Vann Woodward* (New York, 1982), 143–77; and Fields, "Slavery, Race, and Ideology in the United States of America," *New Left Review,* CLXXXI (May/June 1990), 95–118. In the spirit of "critical race theory," whose foundational premise is the examination of racial categories, works discussing the construction of "whiteness" have become increasingly numerous of late; important recent works include Grace Elizabeth Hale, *Making Whiteness: The Culture of Segregation in the South, 1890–1940* (New York, 1998); Eric Lott, *Love and Theft: Blackface Minstrelsy and the American Working Class* (New York, 1993); and David R. Roediger, *The Wages of Whiteness: Race and the Making of the American Working Class* (London and New York, 1991). On cases involving people of ambiguous race and the process of making racial determinations about them in the nineteenth century, see Ariela Gross, "Litigating Whiteness: Trials of Racial Determination in the Nineteenth Century South," *Yale Law Journal,* CVIII (October 1998), 109–88; and Hodes, *White Women, Black Men,* Chap. 5. On the origins of race and racism in colonial America see Winthrop D. Jordan, *White Over Black: American Attitudes Toward the Negro, 1550–1812* (Chapel Hill, 1968); Kathleen M. Brown, *Good Wives, Nasty Wenches, and Anxious Patriarchs: Gender, Race, and Power in Colonial Virginia* (Chapel Hill and London, 1996); Edmund S. Morgan, *American Slavery, American Freedom: The Ordeal of Colonial Virginia* (New York, 1975), esp. Chap. 15; and Theodore W. Allen, *The Invention of the White Race.* Vol. Two: *The Origin of Racial Oppression in Anglo-America* (London and New York, 1997).

40. *Commonwealth v. Isaacs and West,* at 635.

41. *Revised Code of the Laws of Virginia,* I, Chap. 141, sec. 6, pp. 555–56 (passed 1792).

42. Generally, a sort of practical white apathy in Virginia seems to have held even in cases where a white woman became involved with a black man. The Nansemond County census for 1830, for example, listed at least nine free men of color with white wives, while a divorce case from Campbell County in 1816 involved a free man of color and his white wife who were considered married in their community but not in law. They do not seem to have faced any sort of legal persecution. The lack of effort by whites to take action against interracial couples may have pervaded many other parts of the South as well, as suggested by a study of antebellum Alabama indicating the existence of many stable familial relationships between free black men and white women. Other studies of antebellum South Carolina and Louisiana point to similar phenomena, though the instances discussed involved enslaved women, and it could be argued whites in these places had somewhat different understandings of racial hierarchy than Virginians. On toleration for sexual intercourse between white women and

black men in the South, see Hodes, *White Women, Black Men,* Chap. 1. See also James Hugo Johnston, *Race Relations in Virginia and Miscegenation in the South, 1776–1860* (Amherst, Mass., 1970), Chap. 10, esp. 265–66; Thomas E. Buckley, S.J., "Unfixing Race: Class, Power, and Identity in an Interracial Family," *Virginia Magazine of History and Biography,* CII (July 1994), 349–80; Joshua D. Rothman, "'to be freed from thate curs and let at liberty': Interracial Adultery and Divorce and Antebellum Virginia," *Virginia Magazine of History and Biography,* CVI (Fall 1998), 443–81; Gary B. Mills, "Miscegenation and the Free Negro in Antebellum 'Anglo' Alabama: A Reexamination of Southern Race Relations," *Journal of American History,* LXVIII (June 1981), 16–34; Kennedy-Haflett, "'Moral Marriage'"; and Judith Kelleher Schafer, *Slavery, the Civil Law, and the Supreme Court of Louisiana* (Baton Rouge and London, 1994), Chap. 7.

43. Isaacs built a one-story wing onto the west side of his home between 1802 and 1806, and tax records suggest he made this addition in 1803. A small boost in the rental value of the property between 1815 and 1816 may indicate the second wing was built in one of those years, but insurance records indicate its existence by 1833. ACLTB, 1803–1804, 1815–1816, supplemental reels 2 and 3; and Declarations 5201 (1806) and 8233 (1833), reel 8, vol. 63, and reel 14, vol. 94, Mutual Assurance Society.

44. Albemarle County Law Order Books, 1810–1811, pp. 49, 475; 1811–1813, pp. 134–35, 333; 1813–1815, p. 372; and 1821–1822, pp. 163, 363.

45. At the time of his death, Isaiah Isaacs had four children by his wife Hetty Hays, who had also died by 1806—Fanny, Hays, Patsy, and David. By 1824 only Fanny, who married a man named Abraham Block and moved away from Charlottesville, and Hays, who seems to have moved between Charlottesville and Richmond, were still alive. Albemarle County Will Book 1, pp. 25–29; and Albemarle County Deed Book 24, pp. 316–17.

46. Although the Virginia legislature had passed a liberal manumission act in 1782, white Virginians expressed increasing discomfort with the growing free black population in its wake. Legally, the 1806 removal act provided that unless they successfully petitioned the legislature, all freed slaves now had to leave the state within one year of being manumitted or be reenslaved. Other restrictive legislation followed over the course of the antebellum period, including a wave of laws in the early 1830s and in the late 1840s and early 1850s. Socially, whites generally disliked the very presence of people who were of African descent but were not enslaved and treated them with disdain. Economically, while there were greater opportunities for work in urban areas, most free men of color worked as rural agricultural laborers or as tenant farmers living in a perpetual cycle of debt that prefigured the postbellum status of many freedmen. Free black women most commonly worked where they were allowed to, especially as

washerwomen or seamstresses, and faced astounding poverty. That some free people of color, including a significant number of women, were able to thrive in Virginia and the South as a whole was the result of great struggle, mutual support forged by communities, families, and institutions, and the occasional ability to form patronage relationships with whites, both sexual and otherwise. The classic study of free blacks remains Ira Berlin, *Slaves Without Masters: The Free Negro in the Antebellum South* (New York, 1974). Other important general studies include Loren Schweninger, *Black Property Owners in the South, 1790 1915* (Urbana and Chicago, 1990), Chaps. 1–4; Johnson and Roark, *Black Masters;* Leonard P. Curry, *The Free Black in Urban America, 1800–1850: The Shadow of the Dream* (Chicago, 1981); and Eugene D. Genovese, "The Slave States of North America," in David W. Cohen and Jack P. Greene, eds., *Neither Slave nor Free: The Freedman of African Descent in the Slave Societies of the New World* (Baltimore and London, 1972), 258–77. Studies of free blacks in individual states abound, but those on Virginia in particular include Tommy L. Bogger, *Free Blacks in Norfolk, Virginia, 1790–1860: The Darker Side of Freedom* (Charlottesville and London, 1997); Madden, *We Were Always Free;* A. Leon Higginbotham Jr. and Greer C. Bosworth, "'Rather Than the Free': Free Blacks in Colonial and Antebellum Virginia," *Harvard Civil Rights-Civil Liberties Law Review,* XXVI (Winter 1991), 17–66; Suzanne Lebsock, *The Free Women of Petersburg: Status and Culture in a Southern Town, 1784–1860* (New York and London, 1984), Chap. 4; Luther Porter Jackson, *Free Negro Labor and Property Holding in Virginia, 1830–1860* (New York and London, 1942); and John H. Russell, *The Free Negro in Virginia, 1619–1865,* Johns Hopkins University Studies in Historical and Political Science, Series XXXI, No. 3 (Baltimore, 1913). For a study of one free black family in Albemarle County see Kirt von Daacke, "Slaves Without Masters? The Butler Family of Albemarle County, 1780–1860," *Magazine of Albemarle County History,* LV (1997), 38–59.

47. West and Isaacs's oldest son, Thomas Isaacs, perhaps could have assisted his mother as well. David Isaacs mentioned Thomas in his will and left him an inheritance, meaning Thomas was still alive as late as 1837, but nothing else is known about him, including his whereabouts at that point.

48. On free women of color and familial concerns see Lebsock, *Free Women of Petersburg,* Chap. 4; cf. Michael P. Johnson and James L. Roark, "Strategies of Survival: Free Negro Families and the Problem of Slavery," in Carol Bleser, ed., *In Joy and In Sorrow: Women, Family, and Marriage in the Victorian South, 1830–1900* (New York and Oxford, 1991), 88–102. See also Whittington B. Johnson, "Free African American Women in Savannah, 1800–1860: Affluence and Autonomy Amid Adversity," *Georgia Historical Quarterly,* LXXVI (Summer 1992), 260–83; Virginia Meacham Gould, ed., *Chained to the Rock of Adversity: To Be Free, Black, and Female in the Old South* (Athens, Ga., and London, 1998); Alexander,

Ambiguous Lives; and Schweninger, "Property-Owning Free African American Women."

49. Isaacs began purchasing the land in 1817, the same year West gave birth to the couple's last child, which may suggest that Isaacs and West planned her move closer downtown a number of years before it actually occurred. Albemarle County Deed Books 20, pp. 436–37, 449; No. 21, pp. 380, 408–09; No. 22, pp. 177–78; and No. 23, pp. 255–56.

50. The original deed of sale to Spinner in 1819 conveyed him a specifically measured piece of lot 46, when in fact West should have conveyed the entirety of her remaining interest, which was slightly more than the 1819 deed provided. The consequent legal haggling meant the deed had to be redone in 1829. Until the land exchange was finally completed in 1832, Nancy West technically continued to own and pay annual land taxes on the property, and she received no payment for the land's sale until after the second deed was signed. Albemarle County Deed Books 22, pp. 46–47; No. 28, pp. 169–70; and ACLTB, 1819–1833, supplemental reels 3 and 4.

51. Albemarle County Will Book 12, p. 367.

52. Between 1820 and 1824 the estimated annual rent on lot 33 was $100. ACLTB, 1820–1824, supplemental reel 3.

53. Albemarle County Deed Book 24, pp. 316–17.

54. Albemarle County Deed Books 13, pp. 315–17; No. 19, pp. 361–62; and No. 26, p. 379.

55. Albemarle County Will Book 12, pp. 366–70; Albemarle County Deed Books 39, p. 232; No. 41, pp. 318–19; and No. 47, pp. 12–13. Nancy West's purchases from relatives and intimates may also be suggestive of the role race and gender played in economic exchange in Charlottesville. It may simply have been easier to buy land from those one knew or were related to, but the pattern of people from whom West purchased her property might also indicate an awareness on her part that others were reluctant to sell land to free people of color or to women. West's economic elevation, then, was not only easier to do through her family, but perhaps she could only do it through her family.

56. As Luther P. Jackson has suggested about free black property accumulation, for example: "Free Negro ownership of property involved a variety of interests and motives. . . . One of the strongest of these interests was the maintenance and perpetuation of the family. The ownership of property welded the family together and enabled the holder to share his possessions with his family circle." Jackson, *Free Negro Labor and Property Holding,* 164.

57. If a trust in equity was established for a married woman, it was often undertaken by a father for his daughter as both a means for her security and/or as insurance against a careless or exploitative husband, or by a husband wishing

to protect property from loss. Whatever the motivation, a trust was an option generally available only to relatively wealthy women. On the legal rights of married women in the antebellum era generally, see Elizabeth Bowles Warbasse, *The Changing Legal Rights of Married Women 1800–1861* (New York, 1987). On the legal rights of married women in Virginia up to and through the passage of the Married Women's Property Act in 1877, see Joan R. Gundersen and Gwen Victor Gampel, "Married Women's Legal Status in Eighteenth-Century New York and Virginia," *William and Mary Quarterly*, 3d ser., XXXIX (January 1982), 114–34; Suzanne D. Lebsock, "Radical Reconstruction and the Property Rights of Southern Women," *Journal of Southern History*, XLIII (May 1977), 195–216; Sara Frances Ketchum, "Married Women's Property Law in Nineteenth-Century Virginia," (M.A. thesis, University of Virginia, 1985); and Cynthia Gianakos, "Virginia and the Married Women's Property Acts," (M.A. thesis, University of Virginia, 1982). On equity, the multiple motivations that lay behind an estate's establishment, and the complications and restrictions that accompanied equity, see Lebsock, *Free Women of Petersburg*, Chap. 3.

58. In some ways West and Isaacs's relationship prefigured the effects of the Married Women's Property Act of 1877. For women, as one author writes, that law's "main purpose was to protect the wife's property from being lost to her husband's creditors. . . . A married woman in Virginia could now own, manage, and dispose of her separate property as if a *femme sole*"; Gianakos, "Virginia and the Married Women's Property Acts," 37. In the same vein, historian Suzanne Lebsock argues that laws protecting married women's property offered protection to men as well, since "a man who was about to lose his own holdings could rest in the knowledge that in the future his wife's property would be secure." Just so with David Isaacs and Nancy West. Lebsock, "Radical Reconstruction and the Property Rights of Southern Women," 203.

59. *Bramham & Bibb v. Isaacs*, Albemarle County Ended Chancery Causes (Circuit Superior Court), Case 58; *Yancey v. Isaacs*, Albemarle County Ended Chancery Causes (Circuit Superior Court), Case 46, both in Library of Virginia, Richmond; and Albemarle County Chancery Order Book, 1831–1842, May 16, 1834, pp. 97–99. The third case was *John R. Jones v. Isaacs*, Case 55, but the papers for both Yancey's and Jones's lawsuits are archived together in folders under Yancey's name.

60. Albemarle County Chancery Order Book 1831–1842, pp. 21, 32, 45, 50, 96, and 97. The other plaintiffs were Samuel Leitch, Andrew McKee, James Saunders, Fountain Wells, and George Toole. McKee was a hatter, Saunders a lawyer, and Toole a tailor who lived and worked in a house owned by Wells.

61. Statement filed by Rice Wood on behalf of John Jones, June 28, 1826, *Yancey v. Isaacs*.

62. Reply of David Isaacs, March 20, 1827, *Yancey v. Isaacs.* Hays Isaacs's release, dated a few months after his twenty-first birthday, relieved David Isaacs of responsibility for "all and every claim and demand of whatever character or description which . . . I possibbly [*sic*] may have against him . . . it being doubtful upon a full and fair settlement, which of us may be debtor to the other." Release of Hays Isaacs, June 22, 1824, *Bramham & Bibb v. Isaacs.*

63. Testimony of V. W. Southall, Isaac Raphael, and Daniel Keith, November 1827, *Yancey v. Isaacs.*

64. Testimony of Opie Norris, Isaac Raphael, and Daniel Keith, November 1827, *Yancey v. Isaacs.* Hays put the slaves he had inherited from his father in trust in December 1824 to be sold in the event he could not pay off debts he had to Jane, Nancy West, and Fountain Wells. It is not clear whether Jane or Nancy ever actually owned any of these slaves outright—although some of their neighbors believed they did—or even if the sale was necessary. In any case, under a provision of his father's will, eventually Hays Isaacs was legally obligated to free all the slaves that he had inherited. On his death, Isaiah Isaacs, "being of the opinion that all men are by Nature equally free," manumitted a number of slaves outright in addition to devising a plan to free others. Deed of Trust between Hays Isaacs, Daniel Keith, Nancy West, Jane Isaacs, and Fountain Wells, in *Yancey v. Isaacs* (a copy also appears in Albemarle County Deed Book 25, pp. 75–77); and Albemarle County Will Book 1, pp. 25–29. According to property tax records, Nancy West, Jane Isaacs, and David Isaacs (who, like many merchants, probably had customers who sometimes settled their debts with slaves rather than cash) all periodically owned slaves, but never more than a few at once and apparently not for very long at a time. Neither Isaacs nor West owned any upon their deaths in 1837 and 1856, respectively; their eldest child, Jane Isaacs, owned seven slaves at the outbreak of the Civil War. It is unclear if, when, or how either Nancy West or David Isaacs used, sold, or manumitted their slaves when they did own them. Thousands of African Americans purchased slaves throughout the South before the Civil War, sometimes for purposes of economic exploitation and sometimes to keep families together. Since Virginia's removal law of 1806 forced emancipated slaves to leave the state, many slaveowning people of color in Virginia actually possessed relatives who likely would have had to move away if manumitted. Given the intertwined nature of enslaved, free black, Native American, and white ancestries in the extended West-Isaacs-Hemings families, it seems probable that at least some slave ownership by Nancy West and David Isaacs involved protecting family members. We know for certain that some other members of their extended family acted with such a motive. At the estate sale of many of Thomas Jefferson's slaves, for example, Jesse Scott purchased his brother-in-law Joe Fossett's wife and two of the Fossetts' children to keep them

from being sold to others. Albemarle County Deed Book 25, pp. 75–77; ACPPTB, 1815–1836, supplemental reels A-3 through A-6; Manuscript Census, 1860, Albemarle County, Slave Population Schedule, NAMS M-653, reel 303, frame 34, p. 4; Stanton, "Monticello to Main Street," esp. 101–02; and Rawlings, ed., *Early Charlottesville,* 74. On free black slave ownership see Johnson and Roark, "Strategies of Survival"; Philip J. Schwarz, "Emancipators, Protectors, and Anomalies: Free Black Slaveowners in Virginia," *Virginia Magazine of History and Biography,* XCV (July 1987), 317–38; Larry Koger, *Black Slaveowners: Free Black Slave Masters in South Carolina, 1790–1860* (Jefferson, N.C., and London, 1985); Jackson, *Free Negro Labor and Property Holding,* Chap. 7; Carter G. Woodson, "Free Negro Owners of Slaves in the United States in 1830," *Journal of Negro History,* IX (July 1924), 41–85; and John H. Russell, "Colored Freemen as Slave Owners in Virginia," *Journal of Negro History,* I (July 1916), 233–42.

65. If David Isaacs ever engaged in some creative accounting or exploited his position as his brother's executor, John Jones himself undoubtedly tried to exercise some shady prerogatives of his own. Jones had been a commissioner appointed by the Albemarle County Court in 1823 to help settle David Isaacs's accounts as Isaiah's executor. According to Jones, once Hays Isaacs owed him money, he could no longer act objectively and he excused himself in 1825. He objected to all previous work he had done as a commissioner, which effectively suspended any settlement of accounts. David Isaacs never appealed to the court for new commissioners, which Jones used to accuse him of concealing malfeasance. Jones neglected to mention, however, that after he excused himself he arranged for Hays to sell him all his real estate, which included land in Richmond, two hundred acres in Louisa County, and another seventy-two acres in Henrico County in addition to the land in Charlottesville, if he could not pay a debt of just $254.94. This exchange, of course, was illegal, since Hays had already sold his land in Charlottesville to Nancy West a year earlier, which Jones must have known, having been a commissioner at the time of the sale (Hays had also sold the interest in his inheritance to a man from Lynchburg in exchange for "a valuable consideration" two weeks before he made his deal with Jones. Hays Isaacs thus sold Charlottesville lot 19 three different times, indicating that he was either very stupid, very criminal, or both). As David Isaacs pointed out in his defense, Jones's dealings also pointed directly to his own efforts to cheat Hays Isaacs and to his own abuse of inside knowledge of Hays's affair, since Jones knew the cumulative value of Hays's land far exceeded any debts Hays owed to Jones. In addition, David Isaacs pointed out that it was somewhat illogical and astoundingly duplicitous for Jones to assert that Hays Isaacs was incompetent to make financial decisions while Jones was so obviously willing to take the young man's land at a fraction of its value. Statement filed by Rice Wood on behalf of

John Jones, June 28, 1826; Reply of David Isaacs, March 20, 1827; Deed in trust from Hays Isaacs to Rice Wood for John Jones, May 21, 1825; Release of Hays Isaacs to Timothy Fletcher, May 5, 1825, all in *Yancey v. Isaacs;* and Albemarle County Deed Book 25, pp. 223–24, 231.

66. Reply of David Isaacs, February 5, 1831, *Bramham & Bibb v. Isaacs.*

67. Albemarle County Chancery Order Book, 1831–1842, pp. 97–99; and Opinion of the Court, May 16, 1834, *Yancey and others v. Isaacs.* The court also found that John Jones had not acted at all improperly in his dealings with Hays Isaacs.

68. Bond between David Isaacs *et al.,* and John R. Jones *et al.,* June 27, 1834, *Yancey v. Isaacs;* and Albemarle County Marriage Register, March 27, 1832.

69. Bill of exceptions filed by *Jones and others v. Isaacs et al.,* June 27, 1834, *Yancey v. Isaacs.*

70. Nathaniel West paid personal property taxes in 1834 on just four slaves and three horses. Jane West paid no taxes of her own and there is no record of a separate estate created for her before her marriage. When Nathaniel West died later in 1834, his estate was valued at just over $ 1,200. Just over half that sum came from two slaves and a carriage, with the remainder mostly tied up in household goods. In 1835 Jane West paid taxes on one slave, and she paid no land taxes at all until 1838. ACPPTB, 1834, 1835, supplemental reel A-4; ACLTB, 1834–1838, supplemental reels 4 and 5; and Inventory and Appraisement of the Estate of Nathaniel H. West, Albemarle County Will Book 12, pp. 31–32.

71. Albemarle County Will Book 12, pp. 366–70 and 396–401. Ironically, as county magistrates, Nimrod Bramham and Andrew McKee were among those who appraised David Isaacs's estate in 1837.

72. A complete settlement of David Isaacs's estate was not made until 1850. See Albemarle County Will Books 13, pp. 172–73; No. 14, pp. 85–86; No. 15, pp. 210–13; No. 17, pp. 67–69; No. 18, pp. 477–82; No. 20, pp. 291–93; and Albemarle County Deed Book 41, p. 238.

73. Albemarle County Deed Book 35, p. 340. Jane and Nathaniel West and Eston and Julia Ann Hemings probably lived in houses next door to one another on lot 33 from as early as 1832, when both couples married. In 1837 Nancy West sold a portion of the lot on which the Hemings' home sat to Thomas Grady and Anderson Shiflett. Grady and Shiflett agreed also to buy out Julia Ann's dower claim, even though it was not entirely clear that she had one since, as the deed recorded, the property was "given, but never conveyed" to her and Eston by Nancy West. Jane West's home sat on the portion of the land given to her by her mother in 1836, and she held it until 1850, when she moved to a part of lot 36. Albemarle County Deed Book 35, pp. 264–67; No. 48, pp. 16–17, 429–30; Albe-

marle County Marriage Register, March 27 and June 14, 1832; and Declaration 8597 (1837), reel 14, vol. 95, Mutual Assurance Society.

74. Albemarle County Deed Book 35, pp. 205–08. An insurance policy for the property indicates that Nancy West did not live in the house in 1840. Declaration 11186 (1840), reel 16, vol. 103, Mutual Assurance Society.

75. Albemarle County Deed Books 39, p. 232; and No. 41, pp. 267, 319.

76. ACLTB, 1844, supplemental reel 5.

77. Albemarle County Deed Book 47, pp. 12–13. Also in 1846, and also with Nancy West's consent, Watson sold lot 26, the only other piece of property Isaacs's estate still owned, in an effort to raise money to fulfill the Court of Appeals' decree, but this lot was in a swampy and low-lying area and brought in just a few hundred dollars. Albemarle County Deed Book 44, pp. 145–46.

78. Nancy West also indicated she believed Hays had first been in New Orleans before appearing in Arkansas, and she may have been correct on both counts, given the whereabouts of Hays's sister, Fanny, who lived in Arkansas with her husband Abraham Block in the 1840s and through at least 1855, when Hays formally released any claim he had left in his sister's half of lot 19. Abraham Block was instrumental in founding a synagogue in New Orleans in 1827. In the 1980s, archaeologists excavated a trash pit behind the Block house in Washington, Arkansas. Albemarle County Deed Book 54, p. 37; and Leslie C. Stewart-Abernathy and Barbara L. Ruff, "A Good Man in Israel: Zooarchaeology and Assimilation in Antebellum Washington, [Arkansas]," *Historical Archaeology*, XXIII (1989), 96–110.

79. There is no record of the exact terms of the settlement, but presumably Watson agreed to pay Hays Isaacs's debt to Nancy West rather than deal with the hassles of yet another lawsuit involving David Isaacs's estate. *West v. Isaacs,* Albemarle County Ended Chancery Causes (Circuit Superior Court), Case 370, Library of Virginia, Richmond; and Albemarle County Chancery Order Book, 1849–1854, p. 78.

80. It is not clear precisely when Nancy West moved to Ohio, though it was probably sometime in 1851 or 1852. She was still in Virginia in December 1850 and bought land from Eston Hemings in Ohio in 1852. By 1854, when she finally sold the last piece of property she held in Virginia, she is referred to in Albemarle County records as Nancy West of Chillicothe, Ohio. Albemarle County Deed Books 48, pp. 428–29; No. 49, pp. 197–98; No. 53, p. 260; Albemarle County Will Book 25, pp. 156–59; Albemarle County Minute Book, 1850–1854, p. 6; and Judith P. Justus, *Down From the Mountain: The Oral History of the Hemings Family: Are They the Black Descendants of Thomas Jefferson?* (Perry, Ohio, 1990), 111.

81. Nothing is known about the Charlottesville *Chronicle,* which was published

only in 1832 and 1833 from a site on lot 33, other than James Alexander's recollection that it was a "*quasi* democratic sheet." Rawlings, ed., *Early Charlottesville,* 72–73; see also Elizabeth Copeland Norfleet, "Newspapers in Charlottesville and Albemarle County," *Magazine of Albemarle County History,* L (1992), 75–76.

82. ACPPTB, 1850, supplemental reel A-8; Albemarle County Minute Book, 1850–1854, p. 6; *Acts of the General Assembly of Virginia, 1847–1848,* Chap. 10, secs. 34–37, pp. 118–19; Chap. 13, p. 126; Chap. 26, pp. 162–64; *Acts of the General Assembly of Virginia, 1849–1850,* Chap. 6, pp. 7–8; *Revised Code of the Laws of Virginia* (Richmond, 1849), Chap. 107, pp. 465–68, Chap. 198, secs. 22–23, pp. 745–48, and Chap. 212, pp. 786–89. Ira Berlin documents the increasingly hostile legislation against free people of color in Virginia and across the South in the 1850s in *Slaves Without Masters,* Chap. 11. Tommy Bogger documents the hostile social environment for Norfolk's free people of color in the 1850s in *Free Blacks in Norfolk, Virginia,* Chap. 7.

83. Stanton, "Monticello to Main Street," esp. 111–20; Albemarle County Deed Books 35, pp. 388–89; No. 42, pp. 282–83; Albemarle County Minute Book, 1850–1854, p. 13; Albemarle County Marriage Register, October 20, 1836; and Albemarle County Will Book 25, pp. 156–59. Before leaving Virginia for good, Tucker Isaacs had earned a reputation in Charlottesville as a painter and builder. He also seems to have picked up the skills of a forger, perhaps from his brother Frederick, who was known for his talent of perfectly replicating the signatures of every signer of the Declaration of Independence. In 1850 Tucker Isaacs went on trial for forging a free pass for his still-enslaved brother-in-law Peter Fossett, who at the time belonged to none other than John R. Jones. Perhaps Jones's underhanded dealings with his parents gave Tucker Isaacs some extra motivation to free his wife's brother. Isaacs successfully pleaded not guilty to the charge. Rawlings, ed., *Early Charlottesville,* 79–80; and Albemarle County Minute Book, 1848–1850, February 5 and 6, 1850, pp. 308–10.

84. According to the 1860 census, Jane West was worth over fourteen thousand dollars. Manuscript Census, 1860, Population Schedules, Albemarle County, NAMS Reel M-653, p. 367; Justus, *Down From the Mountain,* 108, 111; Stanton, "Monticello to Main Street," 119–20; West-Isaacs family Bible records, privately held; Albemarle County Will Book 28, p. 207; Albemarle County Deed Books 34, pp. 510–12; and No. 35, pp. 47–49, 51–52.

12
Closing Ranks

Montgomery Jews and Civil Rights,
1954–1960

Clive Webb

The arrest of Rosa Parks on December 1, 1955, provided the spark which ignited the long smoldering resentments of black Montgomerians. For 381 days they waged a boycott of the city bus lines, frustrating the opposition of white authorities and financially crippling the local transit company. More profoundly it resulted in a Supreme Court decision outlawing segregation on public transportation. Equally momentous was the emergence of the man who would serve as the spiritual figurehead of the civil rights movement: Dr. Martin Luther King Jr.

In the wake of the Montgomery bus boycott, one national black newspaper acclaimed King as "Alabama's Modern Moses." Since the darkest days of slavery African Americans had sought spiritual salvation by comparing their own condition to that of God's Chosen People, the Israelites of the Old Testament. Throughout their years of enslavement they prayed for the Moses who would deliver them from their suffering unto the Promised Land. During the boycott, the black citizens of Montgomery had similarly sustained their morale by singing the old slave spirituals, raising their voices at the nightly mass meetings in rousing renditions of "Go Down Moses, Way Down in Egypt Land." "As sure as Moses got the children of Israel across the Red Sea," King exhorted the black community, "we can stick together and win." Others too drew the analogy between the historical experience of Jews and the contemporary predicament of African Americans. Looking back on the boycott, white liberal activist Virginia Durr evoked the specter of Nazi Germany in describing the strength of racist opposition.[1]

Ironically the parallel between the centuries of suffering endured by

African Americans and Jews was lost on one group of people. During the long, bitter struggle against segregation, the Jewish community in Montgomery acquiesced with the authorities in opposing the boycott. "Montgomery Jews want to bury their heads," asserted King, "and repeat that it is not a Jewish problem. I want to go on record, and agree that it is not a Jewish problem, but it is a fight between the forces of justice and injustice. I want them to join with us on the side of justice."[2]

King expressed disappointment with the response of whites in general. He was however especially frustrated at the failure of Jews to assist the cause. Jews had suffered untold discrimination across the globe and down through the centuries. Their perseverance in the face of extreme prejudice had served as an inspiration to blacks suffering under the Jim Crow system. It was expected that they would show more sensitivity than other whites toward the boycott. As noted by the National Jewish Community Relations Advisory Council, "Negroes see Jews in the South as part of the hostile white community, yet as members of a minority group, from whom a measure of support for Negro aspirations should consequently be forthcoming. Because such support is less than expected, the hostility toward all whites is augmented in the case of Jews by an added measure of resentment." Some of this resentment was expressed by King himself. As he wrote to one Jewish activist: "I think we all have to admit, that there are Jews in the South who have gone out of their way to consort with the perpetrators of the status quo. I saw this in both Montgomery, Alabama and Albany, Georgia."[3]

How then do we account for the hostility of Montgomery Jews? The historian David Chappell has recently analyzed white reaction to the bus boycott. His study reveals that despite initial uncertainty the white community soon stood in collective opposition to desegregation. The small minority of dissenters were silenced by fear of the majority.[4] It is the intention of this article to assess whether or not Jews were among the liberal faction forced under duress to dissociate themselves from the boycott. A specific case study of Montgomery reveals that the Jewish community was indeed concerned more with self-preservation than with the morality of the boycott. As will be seen, however, it also reveals some more unpleasant truths.

These truths provide a further dimension to the continuing debate about the relationship between African Americans and Jews. Since the 1960s, scholars have produced a substantial literature on this subject. The overwhelming concern of such studies has been to trace the formation and eventual fracturing of a supposed political alliance between the two peoples. This alliance is alleged to have reached its apotheosis during the civil rights demonstrations of the early- to mid-1960s, but to have collapsed under the strain of the black separatist movement in the latter part of that decade.[5]

In recent years, revisionist historians have challenged conventional notions about the relationship between African Americans and Jews. Serious doubts have been cast upon the strength and cohesion of the alliance. In particular, questions have been asked as to whether those Jews who immersed themselves in the civil rights struggle drew their motivation from their distinctive ethnic and religious identity or were simply part of a broader white liberal movement.[6]

This article offers a further dimension to the revisionist argument. The existing studies on the relationship between African Americans and Jews have focused almost entirely upon cosmopolitan northern cities such as New York and Chicago. The interaction between the two peoples in the southern states has, in contrast, received relatively little attention.[7] This has been a crucial omission. Closer scrutiny of the response of southern Jews to the desegregation crisis provides a contrasting perspective to the prevailing orthodoxy on black–Jewish relations. "The Jew in the South does not consider this problem on the simple basis of being either for or against the elimination of racial segregation," once observed the journalist Harry Golden. "In fact the Jew in the South rarely thinks at all in terms of the Negro."[8] An examination of events in Montgomery not only challenges assumptions about the character of the political alliance between the two peoples, but questions its very existence.

Jews first settled in Montgomery during the early nineteenth century. Not until June 1852 were there sufficient numbers to organize a formal congregation, Kahl Montgomery. It was a further eleven years before construction work was completed on Temple Beth-Or. During the late nineteenth and early twentieth centuries, the Jewish community in Montgomery grew and diversified. By the 1950s, there were three different congregations. In addition to those who worshipped at the Reform temple Beth-Or were the Conservative congregation Agudath Israel and the smaller Sephardic congregation Etz Ayahem. Together these congregations included 1200 individuals in a city with an overall population of 130,000.[9]

Despite the paucity of their numbers, Jews exerted a considerable influence in Montgomery, especially in economic affairs. Jewish names such as Weil, Cohen, and Klein figured prominently on the shop fronts in the downtown area. The president of the Chamber of Commerce,

Max Baum, was also Jewish. Baum was but the latest Jew to hold high office in Montgomery; as early as the 1870s, Mordecai Moses had been
elected mayor of the city.[10] Such accomplishments reflected the sound
relationship between Jews and Gentiles in the city. In 1952 Congregation
Kahl Montgomery had celebrated its hundredth anniversary. The event
elicited warm congratulations from such dignitaries as Mayor William
Gayle and Governor Gordon Persons.

The outbreak of the bus boycott only three years later suddenly threatened to destabilize the Jewish community. Although Montgomery Jews
refrained from any involvement in the escalating struggle over civil
rights, they were alarmed at the actions of their co-religionists in other
parts of the country. Northern Jews had played a conspicuous role in the
civil rights movement ever since the establishment of the National Association for the Advancement of Colored People in 1910. Among the
signatories of the original NAACP charter were a number of elite German Jews: Dr. Henry Moskowitz, Mrs. Lilian Wald, and Rabbis Emil
Hirsch and Stephen S. Wise. Five years after the formation of the
NAACP, another Jew, Dr. Joel E. Spingarn, was elected chairman of the
Board of Directors. Although originally established with the singular
purpose of protecting the civil liberties of American Jews, defense agencies such as the Anti-Defamation League and American Jewish Committee had by the 1940s also begun to lend their active support to the black
cause.[11]

It was therefore little surprise that Jewish civic, religious, and political
organizations throughout the North should have championed the
Supreme Court decision of May 1954. Evidence of the psychological
damage suffered by black children in segregated schools was provided
by both the American Jewish Committee and American Jewish Congress.
The Anti-Defamation League had acted as a friend of the court in support of the NAACP. After the court had upheld the plaintiffs' case, an
ecstatic Henry Schultz, national chairman of the ADL, informed reporters that the decision "will wipe out the anachronistic 'separate but
equal' doctrine that has been nothing more than a legal cover for the
imposition of second-class status on millions of Negro citizens. The people of the South, white and Negro, will be the better for it."[12]

The Montgomery bus boycott received equally enthusiastic support
from northern Jews. Jews made significant donations to the MIA.[13] Their
public expressions of sympathy emphasized the morality of the black
cause and the dignity and determination of the boycotters themselves.
This was never more true than during the Passover festivities of 1956.

Passover commemorates the emancipation of the ancient Hebrews from their enforced servitude in Egypt. In the words of one rabbi, it is "a celebration of the spiritual idea of freedom." In the minds of many national Jewish leaders, the bus boycott in Montgomery was a potent expression of the struggle for human liberty. Mrs. Moise Cahn, president of the National Council of Jewish Women, urged greater effort on the part of every citizen to "ensure equal justice" for African Americans. In an effort to destroy the morale of the boycotters the Montgomery police had resorted to tactics of intimidation and unfair arrest. On 16 January, Martin Luther King had himself been imprisoned after an alleged speeding offence. In his Passover address, Rabbi William Rosenblum of New York asserted that the conviction of the MIA president "emphasizes some of the amazing contradictions upon which the American people and the world should ponder." After the bomb attacks on the homes of both King and fellow MIA activist E. D. Nixon, the Chicago Rabbinical Association similarly issued a resolution denouncing as "treasonable" any act of violence intended to undermine the integration process. The Association proclaimed 28 March a day of prayer for "the harassed Negroes of Montgomery, Ala."[14]

Montgomery Jews responded with extreme indignation to the intervention of their northern co-religionists in the integration struggle. Harsh reprisals were exacted against the defense agencies. Membership subscriptions were cancelled. Donations dried up. The Jewish Federation of Montgomery in particular resorted to financial blackmail, threatening the cancellation of its annual financial contribution to its national organization, in an effort to silence public support of desegregation. According to the sociologist Joshua Fishman, the Anti-Defamation League was similarly "plagued" with "resignations and protests."[15]

Nor were Montgomery Jews alone in expressing their concern at the involvement of the organization in the racial crisis. One weekend in late October 1957, members of the ADL national executive committee met with representatives from five Alabama cities in an effort to address their escalating alarm. The opinions of the Alabama officials carried sufficient weight that a compromise proposal was agreed: "Whenever any public action shall be contemplated by the ADL affecting a regional constituency, such action shall be taken only after consultation with such regional constituency; in any public action by the ADL, full consideration be given to the welfare and best interest of all Jews throughout the country, including those who reside in the region affected."[16]

Similar turmoil was suffered by the American Jewish Committee. In

1958 the organization called an emergency meeting to discuss its role in the civil rights movement. The meeting had been forced upon the Committee by the actions of the Montgomery Jewish Federation. Its members had the previous year threatened to shut off all funds to their parent organization unless the AJC reconsidered its involvement in the integration struggle. The AJC had initially attempted to call the bluff of their blackmailers. The Federation, however, was not bluffing. In May 1957 its members proceeded to cancel their annual financial allocation to the Committee. Tempers had not subsided by the time AJC delegates met in New Orleans. Montgomery businessman Leonel Weil seized the occasion to castigate the national executive for its failure to consult openly with southern members. Concerned to end the internecine squabbling, AJC officials agreed in similar terms to the ADL compromise that they would seek the opinions of their southern members before engaging in any future civil rights activity.[17]

What provoked such hostility towards the national defense agencies? The answer was more than a minor dispute over the unilateral manner in which northern officials determined tactics. Indeed the determining factor was fear. The involvement of Jewish organizations in the integration struggle had fueled the fevered imaginations of conspiracy theorists across the American South. Racial segregation operated on the assumption that African Americans accepted unquestioningly their status as second-class citizens. When blacks began to mobilize themselves into a mass-based protest movement, many whites therefore became suspicious. Unwilling to accept that African Americans possessed either the ability or the incentive to attack Jim Crow, they searched for the troublemakers who had secretly stirred racial unrest in the South, and were now manipulating the situation to their own political advantage. This search often led segregationists to the national offices of the Jewish defense agencies. As one newspaper suggested, white supremacists were increasingly of the opinion "that the South's problem—its implacable enemy—is not the Negro but the Northern Jew."[18]

As this quotation would suggest, even hard-line segregationists were often able to distinguish between northern and southern Jews. It would not be long however before the actions of the national organizations tarred all Jews with the same brush. In the ominous words of one southern writer, "The Hebrew who draws criticism upon himself draws it likewise upon Jews everywhere."[19]

In the face of such scarcely veiled threats, it was little surprise that Montgomery Jews should seek to dissociate themselves from the national defense agencies. During a field trip to Alabama in the fall of 1961, Benjamin Muse of the Southern Regional Council met with a number of Jewish leaders, amongst them Montgomery businessman Eugene Heilpern. A man "of liberal convictions," Heilpern had been intimidated into silence by the spread of anti-Semitism. During his conversation with Muse he handed over a leaflet circulated by the White Citizens' Council "which combined rank anti-Semitism with its anti-Negro message." Heilpern was in no doubt as to who was to blame for the deteriorating political situation. As Muse remarked in his report, Heilpern was "in controversy with National Jewish groups" and in particular the ADL, whom he believed were "jeopardizing" the security of Jews in Alabama.[20]

In a determined effort to counter the damage done by the national defense agencies, Montgomery Jews constructed an impenetrable wall of silence around themselves. Their fears were by no means unfounded. Between November 1957 and October 1958, terrorists launched a series of bomb attacks on synagogues across the South. Three temples were destroyed. A further three survived only when the dynamite failed to explode.[21]

Montgomery escaped any such incident. Indeed there was reason to be optimistic that the forces of massive resistance in Alabama would not target Jews. Reports broke in March 1956 that an ideological rift had torn the Alabama Citizens' Council in two. The ultra-segregationist Asa Carter had been expelled from the Alabama White Citizens' Council for inviting anti-Semitic speakers to recruitment drives, and demanding that Jews be removed from the organization's membership roster. His newly formed North Alabama Citizens' Council excluded anyone who did not "believe in the divinity of Jesus Christ," underlining the message by including in its journal "an attack on the 'Hadassah newsletter' for picturing a Negro and white child together." Horrified that this might endow the movement with a reputation for reckless fanaticism rather than responsible leadership, other members had established their own Central Alabama Citizens' Council. According to its initial press release, this latter group was "not interested in religious bias or prejudice," but "concerned only in maintaining segregation." Anti-Semitism indeed proved to be a major fault-line between the Citizens' Councils and more extreme segregationist groups. When the National Citizens' Council held its annual convention in Montgomery in August 1958 it elected Roy Harris as its president. Harris was equally concerned not to allow accusations of anti-Semitism to undermine the respectability of the Citizens' Councils. In his words, "anti-Jews would ruin the meeting." In a similar move, the Montgomery County Citizens' Council deplored anti-Semitism in the pages of its monthly journal, the *States Rights Advocate.*[22]

Expulsion from the ranks of the Citizens' Council was nonetheless not enough to silence the anti-Semitic extremists. Hate groups seized upon the social unrest caused by the bus boycott, hoping to channel white anger toward the Jew. The mails were flooded with anti-Semitic materials, inducing a state of panic amongst Montgomery Jews, and forcing the national defense agencies on to the defensive.[23] As late as 1965 a concerned Jewish citizen wrote to the local office of the Anti-Defamation League to report that the Alabama state legislature had recently been inundated with anti-Semitic literature, including the notorious newsletters *Common Sense* and *The Cross and the Flag.*[24]

City authorities denounced those responsible for distributing hate literature. An editorial in the *Montgomery Advertiser* similarly insisted that "In no other city in this country, could there be a finer group of Jewish citizens."[25] Yet despite the efforts of both politicians and the press to discredit the opinions of anti-Semites, the notion that Jews were the secret masterminds behind the civil rights movement captured the imagination of a worrying number of white Montgomerians. As Harold Fleming, Executive Director of the Southern Regional Council, observed, Montgomery "represents an inflamed situation where racial tension has been accompanied by overt appeals to anti-Semitism; I gather that feelings of insecurity and anxiety in the Jewish community are accordingly greater there than in most other Southern cities."[26]

In 1958, Retired Rear Admiral John C. Crommelin had launched a singularly unsuccessful bid to become the new governor of Alabama, capturing less than half of one percent of the total vote. When the segregationist movement in Alabama split over the issue of anti-Semitism in 1956, Crommelin had been among those who joined Asa Carter in establishing the extremist North Alabama Citizens' Council. Under the influence of Carter, he had, by the time of his gubernatorial campaign, become increasingly outspoken in his belief that the civil rights movement was a "Jewish-Communist conspiracy."[27]

Despite his dismal showing during the election, the old naval officer was still a potent threat to the Jewish community. In 1959 Crommelin sought election as the new mayor of Montgomery. The Rear Admiral had bought air time on one local television channel during his campaign for governor a year earlier. He had used the broadcast to scare voters into believing "that this bombing of the churches in Montgomery—the colored churches—was a planned program by the Communist–Jewish conspiracy to effect the civil rights legislation." His mayoral campaign was marked by equally hysterical accusations. To the dismay of local Jews, Crommelin's rhetoric found a receptive audience. On polling day he captured 1,760 votes, a respectable 10 percent of all ballots cast.[28]

Montgomery Jews had to safeguard not only against extremists such as Crommelin, but also the mainstream segregationist movement. The Citizens' Council was not intrinsically anti-Semitic. Some Jews nonetheless suffered as a consequence of its widespread persecution of suspected liberals. Almost every member of the political establishment in Montgomery was publicly associated with the Citizens' Council, including Mayor William Gayle and Police Commissioner Clyde Sellers. As MIA lawyer Fred Gray asserts, the Council "pretty much expressed the position of the white community." Those who refused to join therefore risked accusations of treachery towards the race. Indeed the Council launched a door-to-door membership drive, threatening to publish the names of those who declined to pay the $5 membership fee. In the words of Fred Gray, "the possibilities of reprisals or ostracism" were all too real.[29]

The intensity of the criticism leveled by Montgomery Jews nonetheless shocked northern officials in the national defense agencies. Albert Vorspan, a social action official of the Union of American Hebrew Congregations, met with Jewish leaders across the South in order to assuage their anxieties. Although he was seldom able to secure complete agreement with southern Jews, he was usually received politely. Such was not the case in Montgomery. Having hoped he might convince his audience that the national Jewish organizations were taking the high moral ground in supporting integration, Vorspan was horrified to hear himself and other New York Jews described as "worse than Hitler," because of the way they "stirred up anti-Semitism." Nor did the overtures of southern officials succeed in striking a more agreeable note. Birmingham lawyer Meyer Newfield, who served on both the ADL's Southeastern Regional Advisory Board and its National Commission, met with Montgomery Jews in 1960 to discuss the local situation. "Upon arrival in Montgomery," he lamented to Arthur J. Levin of the Atlanta ADL, "I was requested to speak about anything but sit-ins and integration."[30]

Despite the most determined efforts of the Jewish community, the desperate struggle to establish its loyalty had yet to be successfully resolved. Having repelled the invading activists from the North, it now had to stamp out the traitors within its own ranks.

During the late 1950s rabbis from across the South overcame not only their own fears, but the objections of their congregations, in asserting their support for desegregation. Inspired by the social activist teachings of their faith, the rabbis often found themselves in the full glare of the public spotlight. In the autumn of 1957 the North Carolina Association of Rabbis had, for example, issued a resolution approving "wholeheartedly and unstintingly" the actions taken in compliance with the Supreme Court decision by the school boards in Charlotte, Greensboro and Winston-Salem. Later that year, six rabbis in Houston announced similar support for the *Brown* ruling.[31]

The political climate in North Carolina and Texas admittedly enabled the rabbis to be more outspoken than their counterparts in Montgomery. Neither state was situated in the Deep South. Such was the strength of liberal sentiment that the rabbis were not at risk of serious recrimination. The rabbis in Houston were, for instance, among a much larger number of 173 clergymen who had added their signatures to the statement in support of school integration. With the worthy exception of the Reverends Robert Graetz and Thomas R. Thrasher, no white minister in Montgomery had offered even tacit support for the bus boycott. Graetz had been rewarded for his bravery with a bomb which tore through his home in August 1956.[32]

With white Montgomerians almost unanimous in their opposition to integration, anyone who dared voice their dissent would be an immediately identifiable target. Should that individual also happen to be Jewish it would provide anti-Semites with concrete evidence of a "Zionist conspiracy" against the citizens of Montgomery. Confronted with such an appalling prospect, it is little wonder that the rabbis should have remained silent.

Elias Levi was rabbi of the small Sephardic congregation Etz Ayahem. His response to the boycott may have been determined by the rabbi of the largest and wealthiest synagogue in the city, Eugene Blachschleger. Blachschleger had served as spiritual leader of the Reform Temple Beth-Or since 1934. Since his arrival in the city he had worked ceaselessly as an "ambassador of good will between the Jews and Christians." His efforts were rewarded when he became the first rabbi ever to be elected to the Montgomery Ministerial Association. Blachschleger had every reason to fear that not only his own reputation but the relationship which he and his congregation had carefully cultivated with the Gentile majority would be ruined if he backed the boycott. "If Martin Luther King passed me on the street," Blachschleger once informed a fellow rabbi, "I would not recognize him. We have never spoken to each other."[33] So assiduously did Blachschleger avoid public attention that his only mention in the *Montgomery Advertiser* throughout the boycott concerned his discussion of the novel *Marjorie Morningstar* at a meeting of a local literary club.[34]

Blachschleger had every reason to retain his anonymity. The rabbi was under no illusion as to the consequences of supporting the civil rights struggle. He had after all only to recall the fate suffered by his Conservative counterpart, Seymour Atlas. Atlas had occupied the pulpit at Agudath Israel for the best part of a decade. Initially he had been seized with the same political paralysis as his congregation. Struggling free of his fears he eventually appeared alongside Martin Luther King on a local television show, and again on a radio discussion of the boycott. Much to the alarm of the congregation, his presence attracted national media attention. *Life* magazine included a photograph of the fastidious rabbi, his hair brylcreemed and thin moustache finely combed, in a feature on events in Montgomery. Atlas was summoned by the board of trustees to an emergency meeting, at which he was told to retract his support for the boycott. In addition he was ordered to submit any public speech to the board "two or three days before printing or delivery of the same."[35]

Atlas was unrepentant. At his next service he offered a defiant prayer in support of the boycott. It was more than the increasingly irate trustees were willing to tolerate. Snubbed by his own congregation, a dispirited Atlas tendered his resignation. Adamant that such an episode should never be repeated the trustees resolved that any future rabbi must consent to avoid the integration issue "in any matter, shape or form whatsoever."[36]

The story of Rabbi Atlas received front page coverage in the national Jewish press. Alarmed at the impression others would have of them, the members of Agudath Israel issued their own interpretation of events. Dr. Irving D. London, a former president of the congregation, insisted that the board of trustees had agreed in November 1955, one month before the boycott even began, not to renew Atlas's contract.[37]

Forty years later it has become all but impossible to separate accusation from counter-accusation. The exact circumstances surrounding the departure of Rabbi Atlas cannot be ascertained. It is nonetheless of note that a similar episode had occurred twenty years earlier. On 25 March 1931, nine black youths were arrested for the alleged rape of two women on a Southern Railway freight train. The Scottsboro case sparked outspoken attacks not only against the defendants but their lawyer, a New York Jew by the name of Samuel Leibowitz. Desperate not to be associated with such a controversial figure, the Alabama Jewish community maintained a distinctly low profile throughout the affair. However, one individual would not be silenced. Rabbi Benjamin Goldstein was at that time the spiritual leader of Temple Beth-Or. At a rally held in support of the Scottsboro boys on 26 March 1933, the rabbi openly decried what he considered to be their wrongful conviction. A dismayed and disgusted congregation ordered Goldstein to retract his statement or resign. Goldstein resigned. As the man who succeeded Goldstein, Eugene Blachschleger must have been all too aware of these events. The resignation of Rabbi Atlas offered him an even more vivid reminder of what might happen were he to risk supporting the boycott.[38]

The ethical dilemma experienced by the rabbis reflects the difficulties faced by the liberal white elite during the desegregation crisis. Southern rabbis were torn between personal sympathy for the integrationist stance of the national Jewish leadership and the need to maintain the support of congregations who virulently opposed change. This precarious position was shared to some extent by southern union officials who struggled to implement the integrationist policy of the AFL-CIO in the face of strident resistance from their local membership. Isolation and a sense of paralysis distinguished liberal white leadership in the South. Rabbi Blachschleger was no exception.[39]

Blachschleger and Atlas were forced to contend with more than fear on the part of their congregations. No matter how legitimate the anxieties of Montgomery Jews, the rise of anti-Semitism does not entirely explain their refusal to support the civil rights cause. As observers such as Murray Friedman and Leonard Dinnerstein have pointed out, southern Jews often enjoyed tremendous financial success and widespread social acceptance, but only because of their willingness to adapt to the strict racial mores of their white neighbors.[40] This was never more true than in Montgomery. As Eugene Heilpern informed Benjamin Muse of the Southern Regional Council, the local Jewish leadership faced an ethical dilemma. Heilpern himself was a successful businessman "closely identified with the power structure" in the city. Such was his personal and professional standing that he openly entertained "some thought of running for Mayor." Although a man "of liberal convictions" Heilpern was alarmed at the intervention of national Jewish organizations in support of integration. The identification of all Jews with the civil rights cause would inevitably undermine any hope that he had of being elected.[41]

While Eugene Heilpern struggled with his conscience over whether to abandon his principles in pursuit of personal gain, other Montgomery Jews had long since decided where they stood on the race issue. Harry Golden included one particularly startling episode in his account of the events leading to the resignation of Rabbi Atlas. According to Golden one of the trustees at Agudath Israel had suggested to the rabbi that were he to become a member of the local Citizens' Council, he could "remain in Montgomery as long as you care." An appalled congregation immediately denied that such a conversation had taken place. Dr. Irving D. London dismissed the accusation that Montgomery Jews were in any way supportive of the Citizens' Council.[42]

Whether or not the deception was deliberate is impossible to tell. What is certain is that Dr. London did not provide reporters with an accurate assessment of the political loyalties of the local Jewish community. "In the entire South," asserted Harry Golden, "there is no one less convincing than a Jewish white supremacist." Such was the prevailing political climate in the South, according to the journalist, that Jews must be seen to support segregation, or risk potentially violent reprisals. Eager to establish their credentials as loyal white Southerners, many Jews had rushed to join the ranks of the Montgomery Citizens' Council. Especially among those Jews more recently settled in the city, there was often an urgent desire not to be seen as outsiders. As one Jewish Council member boasted to journalist Stan Opotowsky: "Look, I hated niggers in Philadelphia and I hate 'em in Alabama."[43]

Arguably most Jews who joined the Citizens' Council did so not out of any ideological conviction, but in order to protect their personal status. Although they had taken out their subscriptions, they provided only the most perfunctory support, parroting the opinions of those around them. It is however not uncommon for an actor who repeats his lines often enough to end up identifying with the part he plays. The individual interviewed by Stan Opotowsky suggests exactly this. Jews were, in fact, active and outspoken supporters of racial segregation. Financier Les Weinstein served on the Board of Directors of the Montgomery Citizens' Council.[44] Fellow businessman Burk Klein was an equally staunch segregationist. Klein corresponded regularly with Charles Bloch, the Jewish lawyer who served as vice-president of the States' Rights Council of Georgia. In one letter, Klein denounced the American Jewish Congress for its active involvement in the civil rights issue. "It is composed of so-called 'liberals.'" he seethed, "residing in the larger Eastern cities and has no membership that we know of in the South." Both Bloch and Klein were determined to drive an ideological wedge between northern and southern Jews. On another occasion the two men discussed plans to attack

"Northern intrusions" at a meeting of the Southeastern Region of the United American Hebrew Congregations.[45]

By the time of the bus boycott there were many Jewish families whose roots in Montgomery stretched back several generations. During its one-hundred-year history the Jewish community had inevitably been shaped by the larger societal forces operating at every level of city life. Interaction with the Gentile majority had led to the fastening of new ties of loyalty besides those which bound together families and members of the same faith. Montgomery Jews had in effect evolved into Jewish Montgomerians.

Acceptance of the caste system was part of this larger process of acculturation. Ever since their arrival in the early nineteenth century, Montgomery Jews had been at best passive supporters of the status quo, at worst, actively involved in the oppression of African Americans. During the antebellum era, they had engaged in the economic exploitation of slaves. When the Civil War erupted they had been willing to fight and die for the preservation of that slave property.[46] Almost a hundred years later Jews opposed the bus boycott not only in order to shield themselves against a segregationist backlash, but because they shared the same attitudes toward African Americans as did other whites. Although some Jews were pressurized through force of white public opinion into supporting segregation, others were active and willing participants in the massive resistance movement. Members of the Montgomery Jewish Federation, for instance, informed the American Jewish Committee that they were morally opposed to integration. As they asserted: "The white community in the South is generally opposed to desegregation. . . . The Jewish community in the South is a part of the white community in the South."[47]

MIA lawyer Fred Gray argues that he was not disappointed by the response of Montgomery Jews to the bus boycott, since he never expected their support. As Gray puts it, he perceived "no basic distinction between Jews and other Caucasians" in terms of their attitude toward the race issue.[48] Martin Luther King had an altogether more idealistic conception of the Jewish community. His opinions were informed by a belief in the essential decency of most human beings, as well as an awareness of the historical experiences of the Jewish people. Nonetheless, he had no substantial evidence to support his faith in the liberalism of local Jews. In the climate of fear and hatred which surrounded Montgomery during the bus boycott, it was arguably unfair to expect Jews to join the civil rights struggle. It is understandable that they should have blurred the "basic distinction" between themselves and other whites.

Similar anxieties determined the decision of Jews in other Alabama cities such as Dothan and Selma to dissociate themselves from the national defense agencies. As Birmingham Jewish community leader Karl Friedman asserts, "they surrendered their B'nai B'rith charters and got out of the Anti-Defamation League because of the pressure." Events in Montgomery therefore provide a microcosmic portrait of the situation which confronted all southern Jews during the desegregation crisis. Friedman also affirms that the Citizens' Council across Alabama attempted to "urge or persuade or cajole" Jews into joining their ranks. Inevitably most paid the subscription fee.[49]

Such actions had by 1960 enabled Jews in Montgomery to avoid confrontation with either African Americans or whites. In the years which followed, however, the city would be confronted with further racial crises. Jews would have to brace for the impact of the Freedom Rides and in particular the struggle to desegregate public facilities, including the downtown stores. Having endeavored to sit out the conflict behind the lines, they would suddenly discover that their businesses occupied the newly shifted battleground.

Notes

1. Henry Hampton and Steve Fayer, eds., *Voices of Freedom: An Oral History of the Civil Rights Movement from the 1950s through the 1980s* (London: Vintage, 1995), 30, 28; Howell Raines, *My Soul Is Rested: Movement Days in the Deep South Remembered* (New York: Penguin, 1983), 56.

2. William S. Malev, "The Jew of the South in the Conflict on Segregation," *Conservative Judaism,* 13:1 (Fall 1958), 45.

3. Martin Luther King Jr. to Rabbi Jacob M. Rothschild, 28 Sept. 1967, Box 8, Folder 1, Jacob M. Rothschild Papers, 1933–85, Special Collections Department, Robert W. Woodruff Library, Emory University, Atlanta; National Jewish Community Relations Advisory Council, Joint Program Plan, 1960–61, 15, National Jewish Community Relations Advisory Council Papers, New York.

4. David L. Chappell, *Inside Agitators: White Southerners in the Civil Rights Movement* (Baltimore and London: Johns Hopkins University Press, 1994), 62, 69–71.

5. As Jack Salzman observes in the introduction to the latest anthology on this subject: "There was a time, not even so long ago, that 'Grand Alliance' would have been a more appropriate title for a volume devoted to the relationship

between African Americans and American Jews." Salzman, "Struggles in the Promised Land," in Jack Salzman and Cornel West, eds., *Struggles in the Promised Land: Toward a History of Black–Jewish Relations in the United States* (New York and Oxford: Oxford University Press, 1997), 1. This theme is also explored in, among others, the following works: Paul Berman, ed., *Blacks and Jews: Alliances and Arguments* (New York: Delacorte, 1994); Murray Friedman, *What Went Wrong? The Creation & Collapse of the Black–Jewish Alliance* (New York: Free Press, 1995); Jonathan Kaufman, *Broken Alliance: The Turbulent Times Between Blacks and Jews in America* (New York: Mentor, 1988); Michael Lerner, *Blacks and Jews: Let the Healing Begin* (New York: Putnam, 1995); Robert G. Weisbord and Arthur Stein, *Bittersweet Encounter: The Afro-American and the American Jew* (Westport, Conn.: Negro Universities Press, 1970).

6. The revisionist interpretation can be found in Leonard Dinnerstein, *Anti-semitism in America* (New York and Oxford: Oxford University Press, 1994), 197–227. See also Salzman, "Struggles," 5, 8–9.

7. Salzman, "Struggles," 13. *Struggles in the Promised Land* is the first volume on the subject of black–Jewish relations to devote substantial attention to the southern states. See the articles by David Brion Davis, Jason H. Silverman, and Deborah Dash Moore. The most comprehensive analysis of the relationship between Jews and African Americans in the South is provided in Mark K. Bauman and Berkley Kalin, eds., *The Quiet Voices: Southern Rabbis and Black Civil Rights, 1880s to 1990s* (Tuscaloosa and London: University of Alabama Press, 1997).

8. Harry Golden, *Only in America* (New York: Permabooks, 1959), 126. A similar line of argument is adopted in Leonard Dinnerstein, "Southern Jewry and the Desegregation Crisis, 1954–1970," *American Jewish Historical Quarterly*, 62:3 (1973), 232–33.

9. *The First 100 Years of Kahl Montgomery* (Montgomery: Paragon Press, 1952); *American Jewish Year Book* (1955), 177.

10. Louis Schmier, ed., *Reflections of Southern Jewry: The Letters of Charles Wessolowsky, 1878–1879* (Macon, Georgia: Mercer University Press, 1982), 72.

11. Jack Salzman et al., eds., *Bridges and Boundaries: African Americans and American Jews* (New York: George Braziller, 1992), 193, 196; John P. Roche, *The Quest for the Dream* (New York: Macmillan, 1963), 134. The American Jewish Committee (AJC) was founded in 1906 by a group of wealthy German Jews. Appalled at the suffering of Russian Jews during the Tsarist pogroms, its members sought to combat anti-Semitism at home and abroad. The Anti-Defamation League (ADL) was established in 1914. Its objective was the elimination of anti-Semitic literature within the United States. A third Jewish defense agency, the American Jewish Congress (AJC) appeared in 1917. In contrast to the other agencies, the Congress was dominated by Eastern European Jews. Unlike the

ADL and AJC, it also lacked any significant southern membership, and therefore avoided the sectional infighting that plagued the other two organizations.

12. *Southern Israelite,* 28 May 1954.

13. Kaufman, *Broken Alliance,* 63.

14. *New York Times,* 24 Mar. 1956, 17; 25 Mar. 1956, 58; *Chicago Daily Tribune,* 24 Mar. 1956, Pt. 2, 12.

15. Will Maslow, "My Brother's Keeper . . . Negro–Jewish Relations in the United States," *World Jewry,* 1:2 (1958), 5; Joshua A. Fishman, "Southern City," *Midstream,* 7:3 (Summer 1961), 42.

16. Herbert R. Moulitz, Report 1957–58 [15 Mar. 1958], Box 1, Folder 2, Anti-Defamation League of B'nai B'rith Records, 1946–82, The Amistad Research Center at Tulane University.

17. Will Maslow, "Negro–Jewish Relations in the United States," Gen-10, 56–61, Box 257: Race Relations: Negroes, American Jewish Committee Papers, Yivo Institute for Jewish Research, New York; Richard Yaffe, "Negro Integration and Jews in the South," *Israel Horizons,* 6:6 (June–July 1958), 30; Leonel Weil to Charles J. Bloch, 16 Jan. 1959, Box 19, Folder 91, Charles J. Bloch Papers, Macon, Georgia Public Library. American Jewish Committee member Cecil Alexander similarly recalls a regional meeting of the organization at which Montgomery Jews spoke openly against any further entanglement in the race issue. Alexander, who was actively involved in the integration of his native Atlanta, was criticized for "exposing" Jews in less cosmopolitan cities including Montgomery. Cecil Alexander, interview with author, 13 Nov. 1993.

18. Harry Golden and Julian Scheer, "Southern Jews and Segregation: Development of attitudes and actions regarding a cardinal issue," *Jewish Life,* 10:7 (May 1956), 26; *Presbyterian Outlook,* 27 Oct. 1958.

19. William D. Workman Jr., *The Case for the South* (New York: The Devin-Adair Company, 1959), 119, 223.

20. Benjamin Muse, confidential memorandum of 18 Oct. 1961, "Alabama: September 15–17 and October 2–5," Series I, Reel 56, Document 1842, 1954, Southern Regional Council Papers, Robert W. Woodruff Library, Atlanta University.

21. Jackson Toby, "Bombing in Nashville: A Jewish Center and the Desegregation Struggle," *Commentary,* 25:5 (May 1958), 385–89; Nathan Perlmutter, "Bombing in Miami: Anti-Semitism and the Segregationists," *Commentary,* 25:6 (June 1958), 498–503; Arnold Shankman, "A Temple Is Bombed—Atlanta, 1958," *American Jewish Archives,* 23:2 (Nov. 1971), 125–53; *National Jewish Post and Opinion,* 29 Nov. 1957; Murray Friedman, "Postscript to an Act of Violence," *ADL Bulletin,* 15:6 (June 1958), 5; *Birmingham Post-Herald,* 29 Apr. 1958.

22. *New York Times,* 6 Mar. 1956; Neil R. McMillen, *The Citizens' Council: Orga-*

nized Resistance to the Second Reconstruction, 1954–64 (Urbana, Chicago, London: University of Illinois Press, 1971), 49–50; Arnold Forster, "The South: New Field for an Old Game," *ADL Bulletin,* 15:8 (Oct. 1958), 1; George Thayer, *The Farther Shores of Politics: The American Political Fringe Today* (London: Allen Lane, 1968), 113–14; Arthur J. Levin, "Since the Supreme Court Decision," *ADL Bulletin,* 15:6 (June 1958), 6.

23. Northern Jewish activists engaged in the civil rights struggle conceded that political tensions within the South had increasingly assumed anti-Semitic overtones. Among those who acknowledged the difficulties faced by southern Jews were Henry E. Schultz of the ADL and Frederick F. Greenman, campaign chairman of the Joint Defense Appeal. *New York Times,* 27 Nov. 1956, 13 Apr. 1956.

24. The local citizen was Raymond E. Cohen, owner of a record store in Montgomery. Monroe Schlactus, ADL Alabama Regional Director, to Raymond E. Cohen, 25 June 1965, Box 1, Folder 30, Anti-Defamation League of B'nai B'rith, Alabama Regional Office, records, 1945–79, Department of Archives and Manuscripts, Linn-Henley Research Library, Birmingham, Alabama, Public Library.

25. Quoted in *National Jewish Post and Opinion,* 25 May 1956. The *Advertiser* also published an article in praise of B'nai B'rith, an organization that "has served American progress in the fields of patriotism, charity, health and brotherly understanding." This was in spite of the conspicuous support for the boycott by the Anti-Defamation League. *Montgomery Advertiser,* 8 Mar. 1956.

26. Harold C. Fleming to Will Maslow, 14 July 1959, Series 1, Reel 3, 0755—0756, Southern Regional Council Papers.

27. "Crommelin," *ADL Facts, 13.* 2 (Apr.–May 1959), 115; James Graham Cook, *The Segregationists* (New York: Appleton, Century, Crofts, 1962); Thayer, 43–44.

28. "Crommelin," 115–16; Cook, Segregationists, 162.

29. James A. Colaiaco, *Martin Luther King Jr.: Apostle of Militant Nonviolence* (New York: St Martin's Press, 1988), 13; David J. Garrow, ed., *The Montgomery Bus Boycott and the Women Who Started It: The Memoir of Jo Ann Gibson Robinson* (Knoxville: University of Tennessee Press, 1987), 111–12; McMillen, citizens council, 44; Fishman, "Southern City," 45; Fred Gray, interview with author, 9 July 1996. The Anti-Defamation League closely monitored the activities of the Montgomery Citizens' Council. In April 1956, ADL assistant director Frederick Routh forwarded a number of clippings and leaflets concerning the Council to the organization's Southeastern Regional Director, Arthur Levin. The cover note remarked that "I think these should interest your people in Montgomery." Frederick B. Routh to Arthur J. Levin, 19 Apr. 1956, Series 1, Reel 4, 0511, Southern Regional Council Papers.

30. Al Vorspan, "Birmingham Revisited," *Reform Judaism* (Fall 1993), 60; Mayer Newfield to Arthur J. Levin, 5 Jan. 1961, Mayer Newfield Papers, 1950–1973, Department of Archives and Manuscripts, Linn-Henley Research Library, Birmingham, Alabama.

31. *Southern Israelite,* 6 Sept. 1957; 1 Nov. 1957.

32. Chappell, *Inside Agitators,* 57; Garrow, *Bearing the Cross,* 8. Both clergymen received local media attention. Graetz was discussed in detail in the *Montgomery Advertiser,* 10 Jan. 1956, 4; 12 Jan. 1956, 4. Thrasher, an Episcopalian minister, made a public appeal for negotiation, and denounced the extremism of the Citizens' Council. *Montgomery Advertiser,* 3 Mar. 1956, 4.

33. *The First 100 Years of Kahl Montgomery,* 22–23; Charles Mantinband to Harry Golden, 19 Dec. 1963, Charles Mantinband Papers, American Jewish Archives, Cincinnati, Ohio.

34. *Montgomery Advertiser,* 5 Jan. 1956. In a further interview Blachschleger admitted that he "made no public pronouncements on this subject [desegregation] either from my pulpit or in the columns of our daily press." P. Allen Krause, "Rabbis and Negro Rights in the South, 1954–1967," *American Jewish Archives,* 21:1 (April 1969), 63.

35. *Life,* 5 Mar. 1956, 41; *National Jewish Post and Opinion,* 17 May 1957.

36. *National Jewish Post and Opinion,* 17 May 1957.

37. Ibid., 14 Jun. 1957.

38. Dan T. Carter, *Scottsboro: A Tragedy of the American South,* rev. ed. (Baton Rouge and London: Louisiana State University Press, 1979), 254–59; Herman Pollack, "A Forgotten Fighter For Justice: Ben Goldstein-Lowell," *Jewish Currents,* 30:6 (June 1976), 14–18.

39. The conflict within southern unions over integration is discussed in Robert J. Norrell, "Labor Trouble: George Wallace and Union Politics in Alabama" in Robert H. Zieger, ed., *Organized Labor in the Twentieth-Century South* (Knoxville: University of Tennessee Press, 1991), 250–72. On tensions between rabbis and their congregations across the South, see Bauman and Kalin, eds., *The Quiet Voices.*

40. Murray Friedman, "One Episode in Southern Jewry's Response to Desegregation: An Historical Memoir," *American Jewish Archives,* 33:2 (November 1981), 171; Dinnerstein, "Southern Jewry," 233.

41. Benjamin Muse, "Alabama," 3.

42. *National Jewish Post and Opinion,* 14 June 1957.

43. Golden, *Only in America,* 127; Stan Opotowsky, "Inside the White Citizens Council: Why Some Jews and Catholics Join Up," *Afro-American,* Afro Magazine Section, 23 Mar. 1957, 3.

44. Stephan Lesher, *George Wallace: American Populist* (Reading, Mass.: Addi-

son-Wesley, 1993), 69. Lesher also observes that a number of Montgomery Jews acted as advisors to Alabama Governor George Wallace. Ibid., 70.

45. Burk H. Klein to Charles J. Bloch, 23 Jan. 1963; Charles J. Bloch to Burk H. Klein, 8 Nov. 1962, Box 27, Folder 119, Charles J. Bloch Papers. For the political career of Charles Bloch, see Clive Webb, "Charles Bloch: Jewish White Supremacist," *Georgia Historical Quarterly* 83 (Summer 1999): 267–92.

46. Leopold Jacob Weil to Josiah Weil, 16 May 1861, photostat copy filed in Box 6, Folder 4, Jacob Rothschild Papers, Robert W. Woodruff Library, Emory University, Atlanta; Eli N. Evans, *The Provincials: A Personal History of Jews in the South* (New York: Atheneum, 1973), 62–63.

47. Yaffe, "Negro Integration and Jews in the South," 30.

48. Fred Gray, interview with author.

49. Karl Friedman, interview with author, 16 Feb. 1994.

V
IDENTITY

INTRODUCTION

According to traditional *halacha,* or Jewish law, a Jew is anyone who was born to a Jewish mother or who officially converted. Nonetheless, a question arises: is Judaism a religion, race, nationality, or ethnicity? In this Part, articles by Langston and Whitfield portray Jews as actors responding to conditions. Wanting both acceptance and continuity, they define themselves as both similar to and different from the majority. In the Rogoff, McGraw, and Langston articles, Jews are defined by others to suit the images and needs of those groups. In every instance, definitions are fluid and ambiguous.

Scott Langston's article illustrates how nineteenth century theologians carefully defined identity as Jews and Americans. Finding common ground with Protestants, rabbinic opinions reflected and facilitated acceptance and acculturation, even as they set Judaism apart as distinctive. Representatives of differing faiths gained understanding of each other's beliefs within an amicable dialog that continued through the twentieth century with shared pulpits, inter-group discussions, and brotherhood weeks.

Yet the pulpit leaders' balance proved fragile. Intermarriage, lackluster attendance at services, and declining observance of the Sabbath and Jewish ritual, and even conversion from Judaism were recurring problems. Some identified as Jews through fraternities like B'nai B'rith; others through charity work or lobbying and aid for Jews at home and overseas, activities reflecting Jewish peoplehood. People identifying as Americans of the Jewish faith were lumped together with the new immigrants by the Christian majority, a sort of forced peoplehood. With widescale acceptance of Classical Reform by descendents of Central European Jews during the 1890s, Jewish practices and education were so diluted that many Jews were more comfortable lighting a Christmas tree than a Hanukah candle. Reform rabbis were asked to fill Unitarian-Universalist pulpits, and some Jews joined churches or supported Jewish Science (an attempt to link faith and healing within Judaism to counteract the perceived appeal of Christian Science to many Jews). Reform partly rose to maintain a religious identity challenged by American secularism. Did it ultimately contribute to the decline of the institution it sought to modernize?

Religious tradition and identity regenerated with each succeeding immigrant wave. East European and Sephardic immigrants melded theirs with Zionism, which was eschewed by most Jews of Central European origin. Although Zionism flourished, identity with labor unions, socialism, and communism (almost the East European equivalent of the Prophetic social justice of Reform's Pittsburgh Platform) only took root in the South as an intellectual exercise and as reverence for Yiddish culture through such organizations as the Arbeiter Ring/Workmen's Circle.

The newcomers acculturated in a process similar to that of those who had arrived earlier. From the late 1930s into the 1950s many East European Orthodox congregations affiliated themselves with the Conservative movement. Second generation East Europeans attended Hebrew Union College and became Reform rabbis. German persecution accelerated under Hitler. Consequently Zionism entered Reform via the Columbus Platform of 1938, although a minority continued opposition. Since the 1950s many Reform congregations have returned to ritual, Hebrew, b'nai mitzvoth, and spirituality. In recent decades Orthodox congregations grew, and Hassidism, havurah groups, and the burgeoning of new congregations and day schools attest to religious renewal.

Western Jews aided overseas brethren from the era of the Balkan Wars through the World Wars and Holocaust. They directed additional assistance to Jews in Palestine and, especially after the Six Day War, to Israel. Aid continued for Soviet refuseniks, Cuban exiles, and Persian Jews who fled after the overthrow of the Shah. Charitable giving, defense of Jews at home and abroad, work in behalf of the Jewish federations, and participation in Jewish community center activities allowed venues for identity even while congregational membership declined and intermarriage increased. Aid flowed regardless of denominational movement or country of origin of the givers, and frequently facilitated the breakdown of such divisions, despite conflicts in leadership, style, and methodology.

The concept of race, a cultural construct, apparently emerged over five hundred years ago as individuals and countries defined themselves as distinctive, especially in relation to others who were conversely condemned as inferior. In the United States, African and Asian Americans, in particular, have borne the brunt of racism. In the transatlantic world Jews, too, were defined by others and themselves as a race. Leonard Rogoff illustrates racialist concepts changing with time and circumstances, and how they were applied positively and negatively to Jews. Neither white nor black but in-between, Jews shared characteristics of each in the ways they were perceived by non-Jews. Whiteness studies analyze when and how Jews "became white," or were gradually accepted as such. Rogoff posits "an underlying confusion about race and ethnicity, heredity and environment," with groups disagreeing among themselves and each

other. Did Jews' actions, including acceptance of majority mores, ease
the way to inclusion? What impact did the black civil rights movement
and the roles of Jews play in the transformation?

Wars offered Jews a means to prove their identity as Americans and to
counteract charges of dual-loyalty. But the Civil War muddled definitions. Before and during the war Jewish opinion tended to reflect that
of their location. Although their positions on slavery and the Civil War
illustrate adaptation to the South, Rogoff finds little distinction concerning the identity of Jews as a race on a regional basis. In fact, regional distinctiveness, or lack thereof, is vigorously debated. Stephen J. Whitfield's article outlines many of the issues and, although he recognizes
nuances, finds in favor of the southern school. Those who support this
position point to Jewish acceptance of slavery, the slave trade, Lost Cause
ideology, and adherence or acquiescence to southern racial mores.
Abraham Peck points to the compatibility of Jewish and southern values
and myths, and Eli Evans notes that southern Jews adapted to regional
idiosyncrasies to succeed. From this perspective, Southern Jews, unlike
Jews elsewhere, avoided controversy. Regardless of whether Jewish behavior transcended region, if they thought of themselves as southern is
not that having a southern identity?

After being the dominant theory for three decades, the identity
of Jews as southern recently came under attack. The development of
Jewish social service agencies followed national patterns as did much individual and group behavior in inter- and intra-group relations. Investigating Jewish life in small towns, the most "southern" of venues, Weissbach, Rogoff, and Deborah Weiner reach identical conclusions. Studying
economics and politics, Ashkenazi and Brown view the southern Jewish
experience as being influenced by Jewish culture and background far
more than regionalism. Jews benefited from the South and responded to
regional peculiarities, but adaptation reflected a broadly-defined Jewishkeit. Even Civil War and Reconstruction experiences illustrate differences as much as similarities with other southerners. Certainly adaptation
to southern life and mores occurred. Nonetheless, from a comparative
perspective, one finds a remarkable degree of similarity for Jews in similar environments, and few Jews fit the profile of the stereotypical southerner. If the majority of characteristics and experiences of Jews in the
South parallel those of Jews elsewhere, by stressing distinctiveness does
not one run the risk of creating a caricature? Are all of the southern traits
associated with Jews southern? If Jews lived with and married African
Americans, as Rothman finds, but Jews fought in duels, as Mark I. Green-

berg observes, does either indicate acceptance or rejection of southern mores, or are the numbers just too small in either case to draw conclusions? Is there one southern Jewry, or do so many sub-regional variations bring into question a generalized southern Jewish identity?

Eliza McGraw's article returns the reader to ambiguous Jewish relations with others. Conservative Christian religious leaders ardently support Israel and see Jewish return to the Promised Land as fulfillment of biblical prophecy and the precondition for the second coming of Christ. Yet they also believe that Jews wrongly fail to acknowledge Christ's divinity or the authenticity of Christianity as Judaism's successor. To Southern Baptists and others, Jews remain a target for proselytizing.

Much has been written on how the South influenced Jews, but McGraw illustrates how Jews influenced other southerners in surprising ways. Like Langston, she finds positive and negative images and interactions as people and groups define themselves in relation to others. Today, perhaps more than any other time in American history, Jews are accepted and express their identities in a variety of fashions. As Jews flock to the South from elsewhere in America and as opportunities and problems transcend regions, even those who believe there was a distinctive southern Jewish identity in the past see a blurring of differences in the present.

13
Interaction and Identity

Jews and Christians in Nineteenth Century New Orleans

Scott M. Langston

On June 11, 1886, James K. Gutheim, rabbi of Reform congregation Temple Sinai of New Orleans, Louisiana, died. His death provoked an outpouring of grief and sadness that enveloped the city as well as the state. Meeting *en banc* [in full court], the Civil District Court heard a eulogy by Judge Frank Adair Monroe and then canceled court and rescheduled cases. The Louisiana Senate adjourned as a symbol of honor and respect after hearing a eulogy and passing a number of resolutions offered by Senator Lawrence O'Donnell regarding Gutheim. Among other traits, the senator noted that the rabbi lived all his life by the Golden Rule. At his funeral, federal, state, and local officials as well as people from all classes and creeds gathered to pay their respects. The Rev. Benjamin Morgan Palmer, longtime pastor of the First Presbyterian Church in New Orleans and a minister influential throughout the South, eulogized Gutheim during the funeral service. In the words of Palmer, Gutheim was "the incarnation of virtue and religion, in whom these are embodied as a living personal agency to renew and bless mankind. This is a kind of gospel which men easily understand, for while they may fail to read the black letter of our different schools of philosophy, or even to interpret aright the dogmas of a religious creed, these are instantly comprehended when translated into the daily actions of a pure and virtuous life. It is the printing in raised type which sets abstract principles in such relief before the eye that he who runs may read."[1] Palmer had used the most Christian of terms—incarnation and gospel—to describe the rabbi and to emphasize how the actions of Gutheim had transcended religious creeds.

Sixteen years later, on May 28, 1902, Palmer died in New Orleans. Rabbi Max Heller, Gutheim's successor at Temple Sinai, extolled Palmer as one who represented the staunchest orthodoxy in his denomination and yet one who "swept away every barrier," and, therefore, "was the minister of all of us."[2] The Reform rabbi made an interesting choice of words by juxtaposing "orthodoxy" with the elimination of all barriers, a characteristic usually not associated with religious orthodoxy unless the barriers are swept away so as to produce uniform beliefs.

Several months after Palmer's death, two old friends of Palmer addressed the audience at his memorial service on November 16. The first was the Rev. Eugene Daniel of the Synod of Virginia and the second was Rabbi Isaac L. Leucht of Touro Synagogue, a Reform congregation in New Orleans. Leucht summarized his relationship with Palmer in the following words: "I have come [to speak] because I loved him and he was my friend for so many years, and because we together were seeking light. Although seeking it upon different paths, we met and never quarreled as to its source." He extolled Palmer's "broadmindedness and large-heartedness," as well as the tenacity with which he clung to his convictions. According to Leucht, Palmer was no bigot or zealot, but "rose to the level of forbearance and broad-mindedness rarely found, pardon me, among theologians."[3]

Were the expressions of Palmer, Leucht, and Heller mere platitudes spoken over the dead, or did they represent a more complex relationship between these Jewish and Christian leaders of New Orleans? Historian Leonard Dinnerstein argued that the understanding of the United States as a Christian-Protestant nation has been a dominant theme in American history but also "an ominous portent for interfaith friction." Therefore Jews always were considered outsiders; the barrier of religion was too difficult to overcome. Leonard Rogoff, in discussing the racial status of the southern Jew, noted that, "In the American South after Reconstruction, a new social line between Jew and white gentile followed the disengagement of white and black." Furthermore, the Gilded Age in New Orleans saw an increase in what one scholar has called "an overt anti-Semitism."[4] Without disputing the validity of these generalizations as applied to the broader southern and national contexts, Jewish-Christian relations in New Orleans seem to offer an exception. As one examines this relationship more closely, it appears that religion helped at least a portion of New Orleanian society to cohere by both integrating and disintegrating religious and ethnic/racial boundaries. While Jews and Christians used religion to strengthen their respective self-identities, they also used it to broaden their conceptions of national identity. They did so by appropriating the religious language and concepts of both traditions, as well as American symbols, and by uniting to combat common threats. Such efforts resulted in redefined religious and national identities for Jews and Christians in New Orleans, and produced communities of faith that cooperated with each other.

Appropriation of Religious Language and Concepts

Benjamin Morgan Palmer was born in Charleston, South Carolina, in 1818. The son and nephew of Presbyterian ministers, he graduated from the University of Georgia in 1838 and the Presbyterian Theological Seminary in Columbia, South Carolina, in 1841. He served as pastor in Georgia and South Carolina and even taught briefly at the Presbyterian Theological Seminary before accepting the pastorate of New Orleans' First Presbyterian Church. In December 1856 he and his family moved to New Orleans and began his new ministry.

A few months prior to his move, Palmer published an article, "The Import of Hebrew History," in the *Southern Presbyterian Review,* in which he reviewed *Post-Biblical History of the Jews* by New York rabbi, Dr. Morris J. Raphall. In essence, Palmer appropriated the Jewish doctrine of monotheism to demonstrate the legitimacy of Christianity, in general, and Protestant Christianity, in particular. Palmer reasoned that "only because there is one God, can there be but one religion; and Judaism, by asserting the first, opened the way for the advent of the second in the Gospel of Christ." By making monotheism crucial to God's plan, Judaism then could be portrayed as preparing the way for Christianity, a monotheistic, but also trinitarian religion.[5] With no conception of coexisting expressions of truth in religion, Palmer saw a divine progression from Judaism to Christianity. Several years earlier, Palmer had argued that the Jewish nation "was only an envelope for the church; the mere shell or rind thrown around it for temporary protection, afterward to be thrown off by its development."[6] Now he applied the same metaphor to describe the relationship between the Jewish religion and nation and concluded, "The Hebrew nation was but the envelope of the Hebrew Church. When the moment should arrive that this Church must be stripped of its exclusiveness and become truly Catholic, the Hebrew nationality must, like the bark or rind of certain fruits, burst open to emancipate the Church it so long enclosed."[7]

In these comments, Palmer acknowledged the necessity of Judaism in

God's plan for the world. He also used Judaism's status to demonstrate the supremacy of Protestantism. His reference to the Jewish religion as the "Hebrew Church," while perhaps not uncommon in nineteenth century discourse, seemed to argue against both the supremacy of Roman Catholicism and of the United States government. Palmer explained the scattering of the Jewish nation as an effort to make it truly catholic. Clearly Palmer intended to emphasize the universal nature of the scattering, but implicitly he seemed to intimate that a truly catholic church existed in opposition to the Roman Catholic Church; that true church— Protestantism—would be the heir to Judaism.[8] Furthermore, he understood the disintegration of the "Hebrew nation" as a prerequisite for the dissemination of the true church. Organized according to self-governing tribes and united under one central government, the Hebrew monarchy, according to Palmer, did not exercise central control. Although unequal in wealth and population, all the tribes were equal in political dignity. Thus, Palmer considered the Hebrew form of government to be a constitutional monarchy, based on popular approval, with two legislative bodies, the Senate and "the body of the people." Furthermore, throughout history, the Jewish religious officials "stood together as conservators of popular rights against regal encroachments, for the stability of the constitution against the innovations of wicked rulers." Why then, asked Palmer, would such a marvelous form of government be destroyed? Divine providence led the people to dissolve the government so that it would not thwart its initial purpose, that is, the dissemination of divine truth. His interpretation gave Palmer a framework from which he could interpret current events and institutional relationships. Foreshadowing the coming Civil War, he surmised that "there are periods in history when secret forces are preparing, to burst out ere long with irrepressible power . . . and such an age is that upon which we are now entering." Concluding that the relationship of Christianity to Judaism argued for Christianity's legitimacy, he asked, "Can that system [Christianity] be false, whose deep foundations are thus laid in the distant past . . . and whose forerunner is this religious race?"[9]

By lashing Protestantism to Judaic notions of monotheism and government, Palmer made religious and political commentary. The truly catholic religion, Protestant Christianity, emerged under God's plan from Judaism. The Hebrew government, while originally intended to house and protect the Jewish religion, had to be destroyed by the people once it departed from its divine purpose. As an analog to the situation in the United States in the mid-1850s, Palmer emphasized the role of the Jewish religious leadership in advocating the rights of the people against the monarchy's efforts to exercise control. He saw southern Protestant ministers performing a similar role in relationship to the government as did the ancient Israelite religious leadership. As the United States government increasingly acted as an autocracy, southern Protestant Christianity stood against it as the legitimate interpreter of God's purposes. Thus, Palmer sought to authenticate southern Protestantism by associating it with Judaism.

Palmer maintained his belief in the vital connection between Judaism and Christianity throughout his life. In a sermon preached on the first day of 1900, he interpreted the progress of the United States in terms of the church of God being held "in the embrace of the ancient Hebrew people." Just as God judged the Canaanites and removed them from the land in order to make room for his chosen people, "when the Indians had, for countless centuries, neglected the soil, had no worship to offer to the true God, with scarcely any serious occupation but murderous inter-tribal wars, the time came at length when, as I view it, in the just judgment of a righteous and holy God, although it may have been worked out through the simple avarice and voracity of the race that subdued them, the Indian has been swept from the earth, and a great Christian nation, over 75,000,000 strong, rises up on this day . . . to give to him the honor which is his due."[10] In his appropriation of Jewish concepts and his associating Judaism and Christianity, Palmer fashioned a boundary, as well as a pathway, between the religions. Just as one peels back the rind to eat the fruit, or opens the envelope to read the letter, so too could one understand the relationship between Judaism and Christianity. Distinctions indeed existed between the two, and, in Palmer's mind, Christianity had superseded Judaism. He, however, conceived of the relationship as progressive or chronological. As a result, the two religions could not be God's chosen instrument at the same time. This understanding highlighted the connection between Judaism and Christianity. Just as the rind and the envelope were essential elements to the fruit and the letter, so too was Judaism essential to Christianity. For Palmer, Jews were not in the same category as Indians. Indians did not worship the true God, and, therefore, were subject to his judgment. Jews, on the other hand, played an essential role not only in the history of Christianity, but also in the history of the United States. This connection created in Palmer a respect for Jews and Judaism that allowed him to embrace Jews in tangible ways without sacrificing the distinctiveness of Christianity. He, therefore, could refer to Gutheim as the incarnation and the gospel.

Appropriation of American Symbols

The embracing of Jews by a leading Protestant figure of New Orleanian and southern society assisted Jews in gaining acceptance and helped legitimate them in the eyes of Christians who misunderstood many Jewish customs and beliefs. This misunderstanding could inhibit Jewish attempts, especially those by Jewish immigrants, to be accepted and could also foster anti-Semitism. Men like Gutheim, Leucht, and Heller welcomed the association with individuals like Palmer. Thus, religion acted as an aid in overcoming ethnic or nationalistic boundaries. Jews could claim to be Americans in spite of their religious differences with the majority and could even find prominent members of that majority who embraced their claim. In so doing, religion fostered Jewish and Christian self-identities while simultaneously broadening American identity.

The use of civil and religious holidays by the three New Orleans rabbis illustrates this process. As a German immigrant, James K. Gutheim exhibited strong American sentiments. Born in 1817 in Westphalia, he immigrated to the United States in the early 1840s. He served Bene Yeshurun in Cincinnati from 1846 until he moved to New Orleans' Gates of Mercy in 1850. He remained there until 1853 when he became the rabbi of Dispersed of Judah, also located in New Orleans. After the Civil War, he returned to Gates of Mercy but soon left for Temple Emanu-El in New York in 1868. He returned to New Orleans in 1872 as the first rabbi of Temple Sinai where he served until his death in 1886.

Among his extant sermons are three that Gutheim preached on Thanksgiving in 1860, 1869, and 1870. In each he appealed to Jewish identity as Americans in order to overcome the religious boundaries between Jew and Christian. In the first he recognized that Thanksgiving originated with the "Pilgrim fathers" and had become a "sacred custom," but he understood the day to be a celebration "for the American people," and that Jews formed "an integral part of this body-politic [*sic*]." Jews, therefore, could claim the founding fathers as their adopted fathers. Gutheim emphasized certain factors that bound together Jews with Americans of different creeds and nationalities, such as the mutual benefits received from liberty and the shared effects of national events. As a result, Jews had the duty to celebrate Thanksgiving with the rest of the nation. Unlike the situation in some other countries, Jews were allowed to participate in national celebrations. Gutheim could thus proclaim, "We are Israelites, but we are at the same time American citizens, in the purest and fullest sense of the word; our fate is bound up with that of our common country." Addressing the coming Civil War obliquely, the rabbi encouraged "every good citizen" to "exhibit a true and pure patriotism" by being ready to make all sacrifices for the right and just cause.[11] The religious boundary that existed between Jews and Christians, therefore, could be overcome by emphasizing their commonality as Americans. This commonality manifested itself apart from religious belief and would be demonstrated not only by the observance of Thanksgiving but also by participation in the imminent Civil War. In this case, shared experience superseded religion in developing American identity.

When New Orleans seceded from the Union, Gutheim continued to appeal to national identity, but, in this case, he meant Confederate identity. His actions on behalf of the Confederacy during the Civil War helped reduce religious barriers created by his Jewishness. Committed ardently to the cause of his nation (now defined as the Confederacy), he chose to leave federally occupied New Orleans in 1863 rather than sign an oath of allegiance to the United States.[12] On May 8, 1863, Gutheim wrote his friend, Isaac Leeser, informing him of his decision to leave the city. Gutheim's reference to President Abraham Lincoln as the "Dictator of Washington" made clear where his sentiments lay. He spent the rest of the war in Montgomery, Alabama, serving two congregations as rabbi.[13] While in Montgomery he delivered a prayer calling on God to bless the Confederacy in the just cause of "the defense of our liberties and rights and independence, under just and equitable laws." He characterized northerners as "those who have forced upon us this unholy and unnatural war—who hurl against us their poisoned arrows steeped in ambition and revenge."[14] These actions won him wide acclaim in the South during and after the war.

As committed as he was to the Confederate cause, Gutheim, however, quickly worked for reconciliation after the war. In 1869, while serving Temple Emanu-El in New York City, Gutheim echoed some of the same sentiments from his Thanksgiving sermon of 1860. Religious law, ceremony, or rite did not command the observance of Thanksgiving nor did it commemorate any Jewish national event. They celebrated this day as Americans, not as Jews. He lauded the peace that had come over the nation, pointing out that material prosperity and civil and religious liberty had brought about such conditions. The prerequisite for peace—independence—was being achieved through the material prosperity of the country. He extolled the American republican system of government since it secured the greatest amount of good for the greatest number of people. Such results sprang from civil and religious liberty. Yet, in spite of these fundamental principles, "some fanatic sectarians" (unidentified by Gutheim) had been attempting to engraft upon the United States Constitution certain religious tenets. These efforts threatened the blessings of civil and religious liberty, which were largely responsible for the prosperity of the nation. "Every good citizen" had the duty to insure freedom.[15] Again, Gutheim had used American identity to combat religious barriers. By defining citizenship in terms of insuring religious liberty, he hoped to negotiate religious differences by appealing to the common American value of liberty. In his eyes, such a value was neither Jewish nor Christian and could be endorsed by all but the fanatical.

The following Thanksgiving Gutheim proclaimed, "All the differences of creed are this day merged into the one controlling sentiment, that the Almighty Creator of the universe is our Father and Protector, who causes the sun to shine and the earth to yield its fruits for the benefit of all His children." Again, he pointed to the material prosperity of the nation as evidence of God's blessing, but the greatest blessings came from the spiritual and moral realm and were ushered in through liberty and peace. Yet many still suffered and were impoverished. Thanksgiving, therefore, called upon the materially blessed to share with those in need.[16] In this sermon, Gutheim merged religious and national identities. Thanksgiving, an American holiday, brought together the varied expressions of religion under two common religious beliefs, divine fatherhood and protection of the nation. Essentially the national identity managed the religious by providing opportunity for religious unity through national unity. This allowed Jews to demonstrate their common interests with Christians by acknowledging God's blessing on members of all creeds and by then seeking to pass on the material blessings not as Jews or Christians, but as Americans.

In his 1870 Thanksgiving sermon, he had observed that "the wounds struck by civil strife are gradually healing. Sectional differences and animosities are fast disappearing under the benign spirit of forbearance and fraternal sympathy."[17] Twelve years later he continued this theme in an address to the Southern Historical Society. He observed that the passions once dividing the nation were receding, and he foresaw the North and the South joining hands and forming a united republic. He then asked why a sectional institution such as the Southern Historical Society was necessary. Gutheim answered by recounting the biblical story of the two-and-a-half Israelite tribes who, after helping the others conquer the Promised Land, decided to settle outside of the land on the east side of the Jordan River (Joshua 22). When the two-and-one-half tribes set up an altar, the remaining tribes took it as an act of unfaithfulness, threatened war, and demanded an explanation. The trans-Jordanian tribes explained that they had built the altar to remind future generations of their connection with the others. Gutheim then explained the mission of the Southern Historical Society as setting up a monument to the strength of the Union. He closed by asserting that the Civil War had obliterated the Mason-Dixon line and called for loyalty to the Constitution, attachment to the Union, and zeal for establishing the fundamental rights of liberty. He was loudly applauded by the audience.[18]

These examples demonstrate Gutheim's use of both American and Confederate identity to navigate obstacles posed by his Jewishness. To him, being an American depended more on one's support of civil and religious liberty than on adherence to a certain dogma. Such an identity was forged and expressed by sharing the fate of the nation and participating in national observances. As Americans, Jews and Christians shared the ravages of war and the blessings of prosperity. Both Jews and gentiles also shared the responsibility to participate in national events and to care for each other. By encouraging Jews to participate in Thanksgiving observances and to sacrifice for the good of the nation, Gutheim, therefore, advocated the active involvement of Jews in creating their American identity. Jews could not expect to live in isolation in the United States without sharing and participating in national events.

Like Gutheim, Rabbi Max Heller also used American identity to overcome barriers constructed by Christian notions of nationalism, but he also applied national identity to overcome barriers erected by Jewish notions. Born in Prague in 1860, Heller came to the United States in 1879. Ordained in 1884 he was a member of the second graduating class of Hebrew Union College. He then became the associate rabbi at Chicago's Zion Congregation. By 1887 he succeeded Gutheim at Temple Sinai. In a sermon given on January 1, 1897, Heller attempted to show how new circumstances often created the need for certain religious expressions, cast in temporary forms, to change. He argued that in the past ghetto life of the Jews, the gentiles had interposed religion as a barrier and a distinguishing factor. In the United States, however, this should not occur in the ordinary relations of life. Heller frankly and bluntly stated, "Jews shall assimilate." This, however, raised an important question concerning the Jewish Sabbath. Was the observance of it unpatriotic? He reasoned that it was not because Sunday had been made the civil day of rest on a humanitarian, rather than a theological, basis. America was not a Christian country. Otherwise, it would indeed be unpatriotic for Jews to observe their Sabbath as opposed to Sunday. Yet, in recognizing the need to assimilate, many Jews had become impatient with or indifferent to the Sabbath ceremony. Heller noted, "We dont [*sic*] know yet how to be loyal to [the] Jewish past without offending."[19] In essence he had emphasized the dilemma facing American Jews. Living in a largely Christian environment, the Jewish Sabbath was not generally recognized by society. Instead, American society was structured around the Christian Sabbath while considering the Jewish Sabbath a day of work. Did being American mean that worship had to be conducted on Sunday while using Saturday as a day of work? By defining American identity in non-theological terms, Heller legitimated what he delineated as non-Christian practices of religion. In short, American identity did not depend on Christian identity. In fact, while he argued that religious barriers were at one time of gentile origin, America had sought to reduce such walls. Therefore, although religion indeed acted as a distinguishing agent, it should not bar Jews access to American society.

A few weeks later, three days before George Washington's birthday, Heller lectured on patriotism and took Washington's life as the focus of his comments. After asking, "Wherein does patriotism consist?" he answered that it consists "not in dying for one's country, but in living for it." He then showed how Washington, through hard work and thriftiness, overcame a childhood bereft of economic and educational advantages. Furthermore, the former president disdained partisanship in religion and politics.[20]

This last idea played an important role in Heller's thinking. By appealing to the example of George Washington, one of the great national icons, Heller attempted to overcome religious barriers to Jews living in a country with a Christian majority. By honoring Washington's birthday and life, Heller showed that being an American did not depend on one's religious affiliation. After all, Washington himself disdained distinctions based on one's religion. Instead, being an American meant rising above those things that divided the nation and working for the betterment of the country. Again, to the gentile, the message was that one's American identity did not depend on one's Christian identity.[21] To his Jewish audience, Heller used Washington to encourage a simplicity of life, consistent idealism, and the fulfillment of responsibilities. Rabbi Leucht expressed similar sentiments in a prayer he wrote for the one-hundredth anniversary of the celebration of Washington's birthday. He too extolled Washington's attributes, praying that these would bind the nation together and lift it to accomplish the highest aim. He entreated

God that prejudices and doubt would not guide humans but that all would look to God for light and truth.²²

The separating of one's religious beliefs from national identity also affected Jewish actions as Americans. Heller believed that Jews in general should not vote as a group when religion had nothing to do with an issue. In fact, to vote for a candidate based primarily on the candidate's like or dislike of the Jews was, in his words, narrow-minded and unpatriotic. Furthermore, to use hyphenated terms (such as German-American) to emphasize one's ethnicity harmed American society since it created divisions.²³ He, therefore, applied the separation of religion from American identity to Jews as well as Christians.

In addition to American history, Heller appropriated current events to oppose religious barriers. The United States had become involved in a war in Cuba and the Philippines toward the end of the nineteenth century. Amid concerns about the safety of American investments in Cuba, the United States went to war with Spain in 1898 in hopes of securing Cuban independence. In a brief war, the Americans defeated Spain and thus helped Cubans gain freedom and drove Spain from the Philippines. President William McKinley sought "to educate the Filipinos, and uplift and civilize and Christianize them." These events provided the backdrop to a sermon delivered by Heller in January 1899.²⁴

In response to a recommendation from the Union of American Hebrew Congregations that Jews devote a Sabbath to remember those in the military, Heller addressed his congregation concerning the Spanish-American War. Linking Judaism with liberty, Heller affirmed the pride of Jews in those who had died fighting for their country. Concerning monuments to commemorate the fallen soldiers, he emphasized the Jewish nature of monuments by turning to Jacob's experience recorded in Genesis 28. After his famous dream of angels ascending and descending upon a ladder extending from heaven, Jacob took the stone he had used for a pillow, set it up as a monument, and declared that "this stone . . . shall be God's house." Heller observed that for a monument to become a house of God, it must commemorate a dream. He then concluded, "the spiritual & imperishable monument will be the liberty of Cuba & of the Philippines." In fact, he called this liberating action "a new flowering out of our traditions." By linking liberty with Judaism, he could conclude, "The U.S. [was] founded upon Jewish aspirations." As examples of this he cited the Puritans, the American Revolution, Abraham Lincoln, and the inspiration found in the biblical concept of the year of jubilee (probably a reference to the Liberty Bell, which was inscribed with a phrase from Leviticus 25:10).[25] Heller was not arguing that the country was a Jewish nation in the same manner that Christians often contended for the Christian nature of the United States. Since the late nineteenth century, Christianity and, more specifically, Protestantism had been linked increasingly with patriotism. Many Americans, especially Christian revivalists, felt the two were synonymous. To be anything other than a Christian, preferably a Protestant, was unpatriotic to many.[26] In a sense, Heller did an "end run" around this argument. Christians may have founded the nation, but the leading attribute of the United States—liberty—actually was a Jewish concept. While Rabbi Gutheim had considered liberty to be neither an exclusively Jewish or Christian value, Heller explicitly identified it as having Jewish roots.

What were the implications of such a view? Jews no longer would have to speak, as Gutheim had, of the founding fathers as their adopted fathers. The majority of the founding fathers may not have been Jewish literally, but they operated from a Jewish principle. Thus Judaism played a leading role in the founding of the nation in a spiritual sense. Furthermore, to support the spread of liberty to Cuba and the Philippines not only was an American ideal, it also was a Jewish ideal. Jews could cross any barrier imposed by religion and wholeheartedly support this national goal as Americans, although President McKinley had identified the Christianizing of Filipinos as one objective of the war. Heller used religion to redefine or broaden American notions of identity to give Jews a significant part in the founding of the country. Like Gutheim, Heller called for active participation by Jews in national events and in the creation of their American identity. He, however, went a step further in his appropriation of the concept of liberty. Liberty was indeed the quintessential expression of American identity. As a Jewish ideal, however, Americans had "borrowed" it. Jews were not merely "foreigners" living in the land. They were virtual founders of the nation.

Heller's redefinition of liberty and support of the Spanish-American War also reflected what Sidney E. Mead has called an amalgamation or syncretization of theology with American society. Accordingly, during the last half of the nineteenth century, the ideas and ideals of a democratic society with a "free enterprise" system were generally accepted by Protestants. He explained that as "activistic American Protestants lost their sense of estrangement from the society, [they] began to argue that it (i.e., American society) was profoundly Christian, and to explain and vindicate it in a jargon strangely compounded out of the language of traditional Christian theology, the prevalent common-sense philosophy, and laissez-faire economics." Heller and other Jews confronted a society that was increasingly intertwined and identified with Protestant Christianity. Yet, through their efforts to redefine terms often understood in the context of Protestantism, Jews sought to fortify their status as Americans and to challenge Protestant notions.[27] This broadening of American identity nurtured cooperation between Jews and Christians of New Orleans in a variety of settings.

Jewish-Christian Unity

Palmer, Gutheim, Leucht, and Heller used religion to overcome barriers that might otherwise have inhibited intergroup dialogue. By doing so, they engaged in the redefinition of religious and national identities. Did, however, their words indicate what some scholars have called a "surface cordiality"? Did the actions of Gutheim, Leucht, and Heller represent protective measures designed to interpret Jewishness in manners acceptable to a gentile majority? Did Palmer join with Jews merely to advance Christian goals? While the role of southern rabbis has been understood to be that of an interpreter or broker of Jewish values and culture to the gentiles,[28] Palmer also seemed to perform the same function on behalf of Christians. Furthermore, Gutheim, Leucht, and Heller transmitted images of Christians to their Jewish audiences. Palmer likewise transmitted Jewish images to Christians. All four sought to explain the other's faith within the framework of their respective religions.

Concerning the early religious environment of the United States, Sidney E. Mead has observed, "Because religious commitment is an all-or-nothing matter, each religious group tended to absolutize the particular tenets of its generally Christian theology and polity that distinguished it from all others. For in these its sense of peculiar and significant identity and its justification for separate existence were rooted." If this statement is true regarding the relationship between Christian denominations, it seems to be even more applicable regarding the relationship between Judaism and Christianity. Mead argued further, "It is for this reason that every religious group tends to resist emphasis on the tenets it shares with all others." Accordingly, religious freedom caused each group to compete with the others for the uncommitted.[29] Mead's idea helps explain partially why Christian denominations maintained their distinctive doctrines; it was a matter of survival. Maintaining doctrinal distinctiveness paradoxically became all the more important as Jews and Christians in New Orleans began to find issues on which to unite. As the two groups began to explore ways of negotiating the traditional barriers between them, the respective assertions concerning the true or superior nature of their religions kept them from losing their distinctive identities.

All four ministers saw the value of maintaining religious particularism, and each, in fact, stressed the superiority of his denomination while recognizing the contributions of others. As previously noted, Palmer, like most Christians, believed that Christianity had superseded Judaism in God's plan as his instrument in the world. Thus in explaining why the central tenet of Christianity (the death and resurrection of Jesus) provoked Jewish opposition, he asserted that Jews did not disagree with Christians concerning the commonly shared doctrines of supernatural revelation, mediation, redemption, sacrifice, atonement, and priesthood. Instead, "the trouble with the Jew is that all these are assumed by Christianity into itself, and thus Judaism is vacated; by which all his religious associations are offended, and he is led to reject the Cross." In simple terms, Christianity had assumed Judaism's earlier role.[30]

The belief in the superiority of one's religion, however, was not unique to Christians like Palmer. Gutheim manifested the same ideas, albeit applied to Judaism, and did not hesitate to chastise and confront Christianity. In 1849, for example, at the consecration of congregation Adath Israel of Louisville, Kentucky, he proclaimed the mission of Judaism "to be the bearer and guardian of the Revelation of God and of the Doctrine of the Unity of His Being for all times and to all nations."[31] In his inaugural sermon at Temple Emanu-El in New York, given on November 14, 1868, he referred to Christian stereotypes by asking, "Has not, for the last 1,800 years, our truthful religion been decried as an exploded system, and our faithful adherence to it been styled blinded stubbornness?" He then argued for the necessity of recognizing truth, comparing the spiritually blind with the physically blind. One who has been born blind can never see the light of day. So, too, one who is spiritually blind cannot "appreciate properly and truly the mysterious workings of Providence" because his "mental eye is overclouded and darkened by superstition and irreligion." Thus the "preacher in Israel" must impart truth and dispel "the clouds of error and prejudice." The following week he contended that gentile interest in Judaism came more from curiosity rather than from true appreciation. He challenged his congregation to spread "enlightened religious views . . . for the triumph of truth, light and love, in this great Western World."[32] Gutheim, therefore, sought to overcome prejudice and misunderstanding by dispelling erroneous notions of Judaism. He also hinted at the inferiority of Christianity by emphasizing the spiritual blindness that it had produced.

Yet, Gutheim could be even more direct. The idea of Israel's mission arose often in his preaching. He used this concept to orient Jews to their role as a people scattered among the nations and without a homeland. In an undated sermon on Numbers 4:14–20, he illustrated the relationship of the Jews to the world by comparing it to the relationship of the biblical tribe of Levi, and especially the priests, to the rest of the biblical Israelites. The tribe of Levi acted as the divinely chosen tribe to perform religious duties. In the same way, "the people of Israel, were selected by the Most High, to be the guardians and conservators of his word, the ministers of the human race, the priests in the sanctuary." This mission explained why Israel had been dispersed throughout the world. Jews were to be a blessing to all humanity so that all people, including "those who imagine to preach the highest truths enveloped in irreconcilable mysteries and forced human dogmas," clearly a reference to Christians, would one day "learn the true Knowledge of God from Israel."[33] Gutheim utterly rejected the notion of Christianity as the divine bearer of truth to the world. To him Judaism had not become bankrupt by the advent of Christianity. If anything, Christianity was based on empty claims and biblical misunderstanding.

Gutheim explicated the complete lack of basis for Christian claims in a sermon he delivered on March 18, 1854. Using Exodus 32:30–33 as his text, he argued for the individual's responsibility for sin. He warned against efforts to obtain divine pardon and grace by "false means." Each person individually possessed the power to restore his or her relation with God. Twice in his sermon manuscript, Gutheim underlined the sentence, "The Bible sanctions no vicarious atonement, no expiation of sin by proxy." He concluded his message by asserting that, "The idea of a vicarious atonement as being necessary to the salvation of mankind, of a nation or of a single individual is, therefore, in direct opposition to the letter and spirit of the Bible."[34] By attacking the idea of vicarious atonement, Gutheim struck at the heart of Christianity. Without the doctrine of the vicarious atoning death of Jesus, Christianity would not exist. Therefore, like Palmer, Gutheim held strong beliefs regarding the superiority of his religion.

Max Heller, on the other hand, presented a more ambiguous position toward Christianity. This may be explained, in part, by his view of religious truth. To him, rather than being singular, the latter exhibited a variety of manifestations (unlike Palmer's idea of truth progressing from

Judaism to Christianity). As a result, Judaism could never claim infalli-
bility or a monopoly of truth.[35] True tolerance, therefore, was to "thank
[our] brother for differing, instead of forgiving him."[36] He counseled
his congregation to be tolerant toward other religions. Anticipating the
question whether or not tolerance meant unfaithfulness to "our truth,"
he answered negatively because "there is no absolute truth; true is to
each what makes him noble."[37]

With sentiments such as these, it would seem that Heller would hardly have a harsh word to say about other religions, especially Christianity.
Yet, he did. Although he preached toleration, he also asserted that every
religion answered a human need. What need did Judaism answer? To use
Heller's words, it "suits most, fits highest intelligences, lifts them up &
progresses with us."[38] He apparently conceived of Judaism to be among
the highest of religions. While all religions had positive values and contained truth, most, if not all, fell short of Judaism. Heller cautioned
against assuming that Judaism contained all truth, but he apparently believed it contained the most truth. Naturally rejecting Christianity's ultimate claims, he affirmed, "We can venerate the Christ-character, even
though we cannot accept the Christ-faith; but even the latter we can hon-
or and admire in others where it gives rise to childlike trust and elevated sentiment."[39] Admiration of Christian ideals, thus, did not prevent
Heller from viewing it as inferior to Judaism.

Given Judaism's mission of living its faith in a world "brutally materi-
alistic in its greed," Judaism was the antidote needed by everyone.
Nonetheless the ideals and truths of Judaism had been preached by men
"not of Israel's blood" and spread throughout the world with the use of
the Hebrew Bible (the Christian Old Testament). To Heller, although
these truths had been preached, they had not been lived. From this necessity he found a mission for Jews because out of all "history's great
teacher-nations," Israel alone had survived so that it could embody these
truths. Christianity had failed in this effort. Heller juxtaposed the influence of Jesus with the mission of the Jews

> That sweet personality of the Christian savior, with all its purity and
> all its impossibility, has affected but imperceptibly the military and
> imperialistic barbarism of our age; the world's Messiah must be a
> whole people which will bring peace to the individual, as it will
> teach righteousness to the nations.
>
> Israel is the world's divinely appointed Messiah.

Christianity had good points, but it had essentially failed. The world needed Judaism, the true messianic vehicle, to live the Jewish truths that Christians had appropriated but not lived. This would best be accomplished through Zionism. Ironically, Heller saw the need for a physical nation to aid Jews in accomplishing their divine mission. This idea was not far removed from Christians' efforts to use the United States to further their ideals.[40]

Each of the four ministers, therefore, transmitted to their audiences similar pictures of the other's religion. The two religions were connected, but their counterpart had departed from the divine mission either through spiritual blindness or error. In spite of strongly-held beliefs that their respective religion was the superior and divinely chosen creed of the modern era, Jews and Christians in New Orleans found common ground on which to unite. Furthermore, these religious ideas were not impenetrable barriers prohibiting the two groups from joining hands on religious issues. To the contrary, religion often provided the forum for cooperation.

Palmer and other Christians could unite with the Jews of New Orleans to denounce the persecutions of Jews in Russia. At a rally held on March 16, 1882, Palmer, along with Percy Roberts, a local lawyer, the Rev. Father O'Connor (probably John F. O'Connor, assistant pastor of Jesuits' College and Church of the Immaculate Conception), and T. J. Semmes, also a local lawyer and former Confederate senator, spoke to a large crowd. According to the *New Orleans Times-Democrat,* this event attracted an unprecedented number of people. The mayor of New Orleans, Joseph A. Shakespeare, called the meeting to order and then called for the reading of a number of resolutions previously composed by a committee chaired by the Rev. Henry M. Smith, pastor of the Third Presbyterian Church. Other notable local and state businessmen and politicians participated in various capacities. Members of the Jewish community served alongside Christians as vice presidents. Invoking humanity, justice, and Christianity, the resolutions denounced the treatment of Russian Jews, calling it unparalleled in modern history. They endorsed the policy of settling the refugees in agricultural colonies and the offer of Gov. Samuel D. McEnery to give homesteads to Russian Jews. The committee pointed to the Sicily Island agricultural colony for Russian Jews, located in Catahoula Parish, as a foreshadowing of future success. They encouraged the mayor to appoint a committee to receive and disburse contributions for the relief of Russian Jews. Finally, they requested Louisiana's congressional delegation in Washington to bring the city's sentiments before the president. All resolutions carried unanimously.[41]

Following the approval of the resolutions, the four speakers addressed the crowd. Roberts spoke first, describing the Jewish race as "the most remarkable people" and "God elected," "God ordained," and "God producing." He emphasized the Jewish support of Christian victims of persecution, specifically referring to a speech given by Rabbi Gutheim in New Orleans in 1851. According to Roberts, twenty thousand Christians had been "inhumanly slaughtered in Syria by their Mohammodan enemies." In reply to his question, concerning who led in crying out against such atrocities and in gathering relief for the victims, Roberts had C. F. Buck, the city attorney, read an excerpt from Gutheim's address. The excerpt included letters written by Moses Montefiore and the Chief Rabbi of Great Britain encouraging Jewish support of the suffering Christians, and in Montefiore's case, including a one thousand dollar contribution for relief. Roberts then resumed his argument for aid by developing the idea of the Christians' debt to the Jews. He observed, "We owe them all that we hold highest and dearest of our possessions." Among these things, he included "our" law, code of morals, religion, and "on his human side, our very God himself."

Father O'Connor next highlighted factors that united Jew, Protestant, and Catholic on this occasion. Among them, he pointed to the common sentiment of human sympathy in the face of persecution, the assault on everyone's inalienable right to peace, prosperity, and life, and the outrages against Christian principles in a Christian country. The priest labeled the persecution of Russian Jews as attacks on human rights, the spirit of Christianity, and civilization. Semmes then noted how the previous speakers had fully explored the Christian point of view regarding the issue at hand. He would address the crowd not as a Christian, but as an American citizen. As such, he protested the Russian persecutions because they violated the great American principle espousing the right of all to express their opinions. When he encouraged the audience to register their protests as Americans against the attack on the Jews, he was met with loud and long cheering.

Palmer rose as the final speaker of the evening. He advocated the cessation of Russian persecutions and the reception of Russian Jewish immigrants by the United States. He borrowed Semmes' idea of speaking as an American when he asserted that the voice of protest must come from American soil. In order to be true to "the great sentiment engraved upon the cornerstone of our civil government," namely the right to life, liberty, and the pursuit of happiness, Americans must protest and offer refuge to the oppressed. He then addressed the religious aspect of the matter. Reflecting on the biblical history and associations with the Jews, he referred to the fact that Christianity had derived from Judaism. The sacred books of the Jews were the sacred books of Christians. Due to this connection, which he had long espoused, he would support Jews whenever necessary. In Palmer's words, "Whenever persecution burst upon the Jew there would I be at his side—an Hebrew of the Hebrews—to suffer and to do. If we cannot stay the hand of persecution abroad, let us welcome them to our homes and our bosoms here, and roll up such a sentiment in favor of civil and religious freedom on this new continent that it shall never be darkened with the stain which rests upon the old."[42] After a long and loud applause, the meeting ended. Palmer's last words apparently struck a chord with some in the Jewish community, for at his death twenty years later, Rabbi Leucht paraphrased Palmer at his memorial service, "When a Hebrew suffers, I suffer with him . . . these words since then have been the bonds that linked us to him—even unto death."[43] Jews like Leucht regarded Palmer's statements as concrete evidence of his support of Jews and not as mere rhetoric.

All four speakers emphasized different connections with Jews. Percy Roberts highlighted the idea of Christian indebtedness to the Jews. Father O'Connor pointed to the Christian responsibility to respond to suffering. T. J. Semmes moved away from the religious aspects of the meeting and addressed an American reaction, and Palmer combined the religious and American responses. His speech accentuated how these two great influences, national and religious (in this case, Christian) ideals, worked simultaneously to overcome barriers that both, taken in isolation, often constructed. In terms of religion, Jews and Christians disagreed deeply over the nature of God and his work in the world, and their theological claims often contradicted one another. If one's American identity depended on one's Christian identity, then Jews and Christians could never be united as fellow citizens. In this case, American ideals of liberty helped overcome religious barriers by associating religious liberty with American identity. Being an American meant, at least theoretically, looking past distinctions raised by religion. In other words, Palmer's status as an American helped keep his claims of Christian superiority in check. This idea differed dramatically from other forms of American identity present since at least the 1870s. Evangelicalism, such as that represented by Dwight L. Moody and the home missionary movement, often equated Americanization with evangelization.[44] On the other hand, religious identity also enabled Jews and Christians to find common ground. Christians in New Orleans protested the Jewish persecution precisely because they were linked to Jews based on religion.

The Jewish response to the mass meeting revealed several points of contact with the Christian expressions of support. Rabbi Gutheim addressed his congregation at Temple Sinai on Saturday, the day after the mass meeting. Many gentiles attended the service, as well as a large number of Jews. Gutheim predicted that the outpouring of Christian support on behalf of the Jews would not be forgotten; "it was an era in the life of the Jewish people, and an event that time should not be able to efface." Furthermore, he hoped that "by our acts and liberality [we can] show that we are all of one blood." (This portrayal differed from Heller's later assertion that Christians were "not of Israel's blood.") The ideas of indebtedness and shared values had again arisen.[45]

Gutheim also addressed the source of the persecutions. He attributed it to "bigoted religionists" who sought "to force upon the world their peculiar tenets, and would gladly compel all men to follow their leaders." While in antiquity, nations worshipped their own gods and asserted their superiority, "now all nations recognize that there is only one true God." The Russian persecutions reflected a retrogression to the ancient days of polytheism. According to Gutheim, however, "our scriptures" encouraged a different response to religious pluralism, namely, "that we should love our neighbors as ourselves." He defined this idea as respect for the views and opinions of other citizens. The rabbi remarked, "Obedience to this divine principle does not necessitate an abandoning of our faith, not at all, but that we shall recognize the rights of the stranger."[46]

Gutheim's appropriation of the "love thy neighbor as thyself" principle must have struck a chord with Christians. This principle occurred in Leviticus 19:18, but according to Matthew 22:34–40, Jesus used it to help define the essence of the Law and the Prophets of the Hebrew Bible. According to the Matthew account, a Pharisee asked Jesus which commandment was the greatest. Jesus responded by quoting Deuteronomy 6:5, which enjoined complete devotion to God. He also said that the second commandment was similar to the first; "you shall love your neighbor as yourself." Christians undoubtedly knew this episode well because it represented a bare-bones expression of the foundational principles of their religion. When Gutheim identified this ideal as Jewish, Christians certainly noticed the connections between the two religions. Gutheim had subtly shown that the agreement of Judaism and Christianity on two major core values could lead to cooperative action in the national arena. By defining love of one's neighbor in terms of respect for his or her views and opinions, Gutheim wedded religious ideas with civil liberty. Thus, the religious found expression in the civil by granting religious liberty. In essence when Jews and Christians practiced religious liberty, they were practicing a fundamental principle of their respective faiths and were not being unfaithful to their respective religions.

Rabbi Leucht also addressed his congregation at Touro Synagogue regarding the mass meeting. Leucht had been born in Darmstadt and immigrated to the United States in 1864. He served as the assistant rabbi to Rabbi Henry Hocheimer at the Fell's Point congregation in Baltimore before becoming Gutheim's assistant in 1868, first at Gates of Mercy and later at Temple Sinai. In 1879 he became the rabbi of Gates of Mercy, which merged with Dispersed of Judah in 1882 to form Touro Synagogue. In response to the mass meeting, Leucht chose to address his newly reconstituted congregation on the issue of Jews and agriculture. Pointing out that in antiquity Israel had been composed of agriculturists, Leucht contended that hundreds of years of persecution had forced Jews to switch to mercantile pursuits. He agreed that far too many Jews were working as merchants, and he encouraged Jewish parents to teach their children other trades, "and prove to the world we are willing to definitely solve the Jewish question." To Leucht, Jews bore the primary responsibility for ridding their gentile neighbors of prejudice against them. In this context he viewed the mass meeting as a symbol of the willingness of gentiles to assist Jews in this endeavor. He also understood it to be a sign that God would never forsake Israel. In reference to Palmer's address, Leucht said, "When that great and eloquent divine, with tears in his voice proclaimed, 'Whenever a Hebrew suffers I suffer with him,' it was to me as if that God who proclaimed himself to be the Father of all mankind had spoken with his eloquent tongue."[47]

Leucht's response reveals two aspects of the issue. First, Jews were not passive spectators watching Christians fight their battles for them. Leucht interpreted Christian efforts at the mass meeting as welcome assistance, but he placed the primary responsibility for resolving their plight at the feet of the Jewish people. Indeed the Jews of New Orleans had worked previously for the relief of Jews in Russia. Jews had settled Sicily Island in 1881, the first Russian Jewish agricultural colony in the United States. The New Orleans Agricultural Society lent assistance to this endeavor. The New Orleans Immigrant Aid Association also raised funds to assist the Russian Jews. Jews in Elizabethgrad wrote a letter to the society on March 10, thanking the association for its assistance. Unfortunately, the assistance proved inadequate. Located in a swamp some distance from New Orleans, the Sicily Island affair failed in less than a year.[48] In fact, while the mass meeting was going on, the Jews at Sicily Island were struggling with a devastating flood that eventually doomed their colony. Yet, the whole movement represented active participation on the part of Jews to address the suffering of Russian Jews. Second, Christian assistance arose from their common association with Jews in the realm of religion. Palmer had identified religious connections as the tie binding Jews and Christians together. Leucht affirmed it by acknowledging the act of the "Father of all mankind" in the words and actions of Palmer and others. Once again, religious identity allowed Jews and Christians to unite.

This identity expressed itself again a few weeks after the mass meeting. On March 27 many ministers of the city came together to explore the possibility of creating a league dedicated to the better observance of the Sabbath. Palmer played a leading role in convening the meeting. Sabbath movements were not uncommon in the United States and also internationally. In the 1820s and 1830s, the Christian Sabbatarian movement began in the United States as part of a social and religious reform effort. These efforts contributed to the creation of a six-day work week.[49] The New Orleans movement also identified religious, as well as social, reasons for agitating for the better observance of the Sabbath.

Palmer called the meeting to order and nominated Methodist Bishop J. C. Keener as president of the fledgling organization. After his election, the bishop remarked that Louisiana was the only state without a Sunday law, noting the failure of previous efforts to pass such an act. He indicated that an indirect impetus for the present meeting may have arisen after the United States Supreme Court declared unconstitutional a local option Sabbath law that had been adopted by several parishes. He expressed confidence that the next legislature would deal with the constitutional objections if pressed by public opinion.[50]

After electing the Rev. J. W. Flinn, pastor of Memorial Presbyterian Church, as secretary, the conference next heard an address by Palmer. In an effort to show the broad appeal of the movement, he read a note from the Roman Catholic Archbishop, J. N. Perche, expressing regret over his being unable to attend. Palmer noted that he had conferred with Gutheim about the meeting and that the rabbi was present. Palmer, therefore, demonstrated that the major religious groups of New Orleans—Catholic, Protestant, and Jewish—had declared their interest in the Sabbath observance movement.[51] Palmer's inclusion of Judaism marked an important step in the recognition of Judaism by Christians as a legitimate religious expression.

Palmer hoped that consensus would arise from agreement on three broad principles. The first justified the movement's existence based on the desecration of the Sabbath. Not only did ministers want to see the desecration halted, but so did "men of the world." The second asserted that the Sabbath belonged to God. Due to the divine ownership of this day, it ought to be spent in worship, rest from work, and absence of worry. Palmer, however, acknowledged that in order to impress upon all people the need for Sabbath observance, not only would all the ministers need to address the issue from their pulpits, but the publicity from newspapers and journals would be necessary. The latter would help reach the non-religious segment of New Orleanian society. Lastly, he indicated that God had given the Sabbath to man. By affirming these three principles, Palmer believed that a platform broad enough for all shades of belief could be fashioned. He did express concern over the issue of the relationship between the church and state. While believing that individuals could address the legislature concerning these issues, he expressed reticence over organized religious bodies doing so. He believed it best to leave out of the movement's platform any reference to organized legislative action. Although Palmer did not want to establish a Sabbath observance league that would lobby the Louisiana legislature, he hoped that the league would influence public opinion.[52]

After several other speakers expressed their opinions, Gutheim addressed the meeting. He began by saying that his presence might be "out of place" but Keener responded, "Not at all. We are glad to have you with us." According to the newspaper account, many others in the audience added, "We are glad to see you here." The rabbi affirmed the necessity and value of keeping the Sabbath to any religion. He cautioned, however, against relying on legislative action to further the cause of Sabbath observance. Instead, he encouraged the use of moral persuasion, noting that in his thirty-two years of residence in New Orleans, he had seen a gradual improvement in Sabbath observance. He concluded by stating that his "peculiar situation" prohibited him from voting on the resolutions. Others concurred with Gutheim's warning. In the end, Palmer's three resolutions were adopted unanimously, and the meeting adjourned until the next week.[53]

On March 31 Rabbi Leucht delivered a sermon to his congregation in support of the aims of the Sabbath Observance League. From his point of view, anything that raised the moral sentiment of the community as well as alleviated the burden on the poorer classes and freed them from "the bondage of their taskmasters" warranted discussion. Freedom and liberty played integral roles in Leucht's interpretation of the Sabbath. Extrapolating from the fourth commandment's historical context (Exodus 20:8–11), he argued that it served to show the recently freed Israelites that they indeed were free and now could choose to work, rather than be forced to do so.[54]

From the historical, Leucht proceeded to cultivate the Sabbath's value to modern society. The underlying principle of Sabbath celebration was the "moral elevation of man through physical rest." Thus the Sabbath brought a great moral influence upon the Jews and was even responsible for the survival of the Jewish race. He reminded his congregation that the Sabbath they observed on foreign shores had not accompanied them to the United States. He attributed this primarily to the fact that "in the chase after gain we have had no time for its blessed comforts." Leucht, therefore, recognized the deleterious effects of materialism upon his congregation.[55]

Both Jew and Christian shared in the threat of materialism on moral and spiritual sensitivities of people. As a result, Leucht could proclaim, "I believe a better observance of Sunday by the Christian community will have the effect of inducing you to hallow and reverence your own Sabbath." In fact, he considered it the "sacred duty" of Jews to assist in the "noble undertaking" of the league. How could this be done? Governmental enforcement clearly was not a viable option. He reasoned that the religious denomination in the majority in the legislature would dictate how the Sabbath would be observed. Invariably, religious hatred and jealousy would take over and even threaten the survival of the republic. Furthermore, he found unacceptable the proposal that Jews should be allowed to close their businesses on Saturday and reopen them on Sunday. Jews did not want laws enacted, either positively or negatively, on their behalf based on their status as Jews. According to Leucht, "We are—and must be in the eyes of the law—nothing but citizens of the United States, with equal burdens and equal rights." For Leucht, a Sunday law dictating how the Sabbath should be observed was unacceptable and a violation of individual freedom. On the other hand, he would support a law declaring that no one could be forced to work on the Sabbath.[56]

Both Leucht and Gutheim agreed that people would best be incited to a better observance of the Sabbath only by appealing to morality and humanity. Leucht strongly urged members of his congregation to join the league, and he closed his sermon with one final appeal. By joining the league, "we will be able to repay that noble band of men who so eloquently and heartfully stood by the Jew when he was in want of sympathy, when persecuted by his adversaries." In doing so they would exemplify the words found in Malachi 2:10: "Have we not all one Father? Has not one God created us? Why, then, should we deal treacherously, one against the other, to profane the covenant of our Father?" These closing words of Leucht are most interesting because they reveal a sense of debt on the part of some Jews toward Christians. Undoubtedly Leucht was referring to the efforts of the people of New Orleans, led by Christian ministers, to support the Russian Jews at the mass meeting held earlier in the month. Jews and Christians felt a strong sense of debt springing from actions motivated by religion. This joint indebtedness helped them overcome the exclusive claims of their respective religions. His use of Malachi 2:10 also is interesting. In its biblical context, these words addressed the faithlessness of Jews living in the post-exilic (post 539 B.C.E.) community of Judah to the covenant as demonstrated by their intermarriage with gentiles. Leucht now used this verse to illustrate the brotherhood of Jew and gentile.[57]

The Sabbath Observance League exemplified several aspects of Jewish-Christian relations. First, it showed the ability of Jews and Christians to unite voluntarily on religious issues. Sabbath observance was an integral part of both faiths, and both suffered from a general neglect of it by the populace. By joining forces they hoped to achieve mutual benefit. The league also demonstrated the ability of Jews to exert influence on Christians. Gutheim and Leucht helped persuade the league not to seek legislative action in order to achieve its goal. The effort by Christians to include Jews in the league further showed the growing importance of Jews to the religious community. Finally, the league represented the continuing dialogue about the meaning of religious liberty. Jewish opposition to Sabbath laws potentially put them in a dangerous situation. Besides the financial burden they would have to bear by not conducting business on Saturdays and Sundays, their patriotism might also be questioned. In 1885 the Rev. Wilbur F. Crafts wrote *The Sabbath for Man,* a book wherein he detailed the history of Sabbath observance. He supported Sabbath (Sunday) laws in the United States in light of the many benefits of such observance. He also linked it to the preservation of American society. Those who opposed Sunday laws, therefore, threatened the very existence of the United States. Linking Sabbath obser-

vance to the founding of the country and noting that "Christianity is in-
terwoven with the entire structure and history of the American government," Crafts questioned the patriotism of any who would oppose laws
enforcing a quiet observance of the Christian Sabbath. He further argued that this opposition was based on false ideas of liberty, and he concluded that, "The first thing that emigrants of the baser sort need to
learn on arrival in America is that American liberty includes obedience
to the laws which protect the rights and liberties of all." Distinguishing
between the "better class of Jews" and the "baser sort," Crafts believed
that the latter needed to "take the scales of personal selfishness from
their eyes" and rejoice in the benefits obtained by Sunday laws. The opposition voiced by Gutheim and Leucht to Sunday laws combined with
their support of a Sabbath observance league challenged notions of
Christian patriotism and liberty such as that expressed by Crafts. Remarkably, although the Sabbath Observance League was dominated by
Christians, it refrained from pursuing the passage of Sunday laws. This
was due, at least partially, to the efforts of Gutheim and Leucht. More
importantly, the league's restraint in seeking legislation reflected more
Jewish than typical Christian notions of liberty. Jewish presence and activity, therefore, helped broaden Christian concepts of religious liberty
and American identity.[58]

William G. McLoughlin Jr. has noted that from 1875 to 1915 several
forces caused a reconstruction of American life. One of those factors was
the massive influx of immigrants with different cultural and religious values. This migration caused a redefinition of many of the traditions of
American life.[59] Similarly, the prominent presence of Jews among Christians in New Orleans forced the latter to reconceptualize their ideas of
religious liberty. Some Christians began to grasp that religious liberty did
not simply mean the freedom of Christian expressions of religion. It also
included non-Christian expressions. Christians' understanding of American identity, so steeped in the idea of freedom, slowly began to expand
beyond the criterion of adherence to Christian dogma. Nineteenth century Christians, and especially Protestants, often tried to "Christianize"
American culture to ensure that their values would prevail.[60] The inclusion of Jews in the Sabbath League represented at least a small change
in Christians' views of religious liberty. While they still attempted to
"Christianize" society, they now included Jews in the efforts to change society through Sabbath observance.

One final area in which the Jews and Christians of New Orleans united arose from the confrontation with common enemies. Historian Bob-

bie Malone has aptly described Palmer as Heller's mentor.[61] Both believed strongly in the supremacy of their respective faiths, yet they could work together on such issues as the Louisiana anti-lottery campaign as well as threats to religious awareness like materialism and pragmatism.

In 1892 electors had to decide whether to renew the charter of the Louisiana State Lottery. The daily, monthly, and semi-annual lottery drawings brought in large amounts of revenue for the state. While the lottery wielded great political and monetary power, citizens of Louisiana divided bitterly over the issue. The anti-lottery campaigners had been working in earnest for the past two years to defeat the charter renewal. The lottery, however, presented a formidable opponent, especially since the 1880s had been its most prosperous decade. Heller and Palmer played prominent roles in the opposition movement, as did Episcopal Bishop David Sessums, Catholic Archbishop Francis Janssens, and the Rev. Beverly Carradine, pastor of the Carondelet Street Methodist Church. According to one historian, Palmer delivered "the most stirring oratory in the antilottery campaign" at a rally held in New Orleans' Grand Opera House on June 25, 1891.[62] Heller also delivered an influential speech on August 13, 1891, in Shreveport that helped in the eventual overwhelming rejection of the lottery amendment by the voters, although many in his congregation, including the congregation's president, opposed Heller on this issue.[63]

The lottery represented to Palmer and Heller the encroachment of materialism and greed on society. This loomed as a serious threat to both religions. Rather than view each other as enemies, Jews and Christians found allies in one another as they confronted mutual threats. Heller noted as much in "The Cowardice of Prosperity," a sermon given either in 1897 or 1898. He described the current generation as being one of "boundless wealth, inexhaustible opportunity and well-nigh riotous freedom; an age whose children are born to an intoxicating heritage of enjoyment and privilege." Consequently, "the sterner notes of religious duty are laughed into the wind" and "drowned out in spiritual chaos." This situation, however, was not confined to Judaism, for even "the most orthodox and rigid of Christian denominations" complained "that prayer and worship are losing their hold upon the people, that the sermon becomes emasculated, a mere feature of attraction and entertainment."[64] Thus, some Jews and Christians formed alliances in their efforts to maintain their religions in the face of an encroaching materialism. Religion acted as a catalyst, rather than an obstacle, in bringing Jews and Christians together.

These actions by the four ministers seem to indicate genuine attempts to cross boundaries. The relationship of Jews and Christians in New Orleans as represented by Benjamin Morgan Palmer, James K. Gutheim, Isaac L. Leucht, and Max Heller reveals different notions of American and religious identity. While barriers erected on the basis of ethnic or religious associations existed, gateways were cut into the barriers, thereby allowing access between the two groups. At times, religion worked as a conduit through ethnic barriers, while at other times national and regional associations allowed religious boundaries to be negotiated. Ultimately these gateways allowed each group to maintain distinctive identities while forging a relationship that proved beneficial to both. Perhaps Rabbi Leucht summarized best the relationship between Jews and Christians in New Orleans as he closed his eulogy at Palmer's memorial service in 1902.

> At the sacred shrine of his memory let me say that I believe that it is eminently due to the life and influence of Dr. Palmer that a deep, religious peace reigns supreme in our midst. Thank God, we live in a community wherein all public endeavors, in all that tends toward the good of our people, we know of no separating walls. We never ask our neighbor: "What dost thou believe? But, what art thou willing to do for the best interests of our Commonwealth?" We take each other by the hand, exclaiming: "Let there be no strife between me and thee," and together we help to build on that great structure where in time to come will be sung a hallelujah by a united mankind.[65]

Two years later Leucht stated in a newspaper article detailing the celebration of his sixtieth birthday and his twenty-fifth year as rabbi at Touro, "I am a Jew, and yet am a Protestant and also a Catholic, for I always protest against anything that opposes light and progress, and I am universal in my belief in the fatherhood of God and the brotherhood of man."[66] Leucht was not unaware of the theological and social issues dividing Jews and Christians, but he had identified how the two groups had forged a working relationship. They had emphasized mutual interests, springing from both religious and nationalistic sources, that bound them together. They had indeed become cooperating communities of faith even in the midst of anti-Semitism. In their working together, the leaders of these two communities redefined their identities as Jews, Christians, and Americans.

Jewish ideas of American identity included religious freedom as well as the duty of all Jews to participate in national observances and events. American identity had no room for distinctions based on religion. For Christians like Palmer, American identity was bound up with Christianity, but his understanding of Christianity allowed Jews to play an important role in God's efforts to establish Christianity and later, the United States. He even left the possibility open for Jews being used again in God's plan.[67] For Palmer and others like him, however, American identity moved away from Christian identity. For both groups, American liberty did not mean the absence of claims of religious superiority. Jews and Christians maintained belief in the supremacy of their respective religions, but they could cooperate on many national and religious issues either as Americans or as people of God.

Notes

A version of this chapter was read at the annual meeting of the Southern Jewish Historical Society held in Richmond, Virginia, on November 5–7, 1999.

1. *New Orleans Times-Democrat,* June 15, 1886.

2. Ibid., May 31, 1902.

3. *In Memory of Rev. Benjamin Morgan Palmer, D. D.,* n.d., 17; also see Thomas Cary Johnson, *The Life and Letters of Benjamin M. Palmer* (Richmond, 1906; reprint, Great Britain, 1987), 645–50 (page citations are to the reprint edition).

4. Leonard Dinnerstein, *Antisemitism in America* (New York, 1994), 13–14, 246; Leonard Rogoff, "Is the Jew White? The Racial Place of the Southern Jew," *American Jewish History* 85 (September 1997): 195; Bobbie Malone, *Rabbi Max Heller: Reformer, Zionist, Southerner, 1860–1929* (Tuscaloosa, 1997), 37.

5. Benjamin Morgan Palmer, "Import of Hebrew History," *Southern Presbyterian Review* 9 (April 1856): 591, 608.

6. Palmer, "Narrative of a Mission of Inquiry to the Jews," *Southern Presbyterian Review* 1 (December 1847): 40.

7. Palmer, "Import of Hebrew History," 590.

8. As an example of Palmer's attitude toward the Roman Catholic Church, his statement in "Narrative of a Mission of Inquiry to the Jews," (p. 53) is helpful. In commenting on the negative effect that rabbinical studies had on the Hebrew mind, Palmer said, "The dialectics of the Talmudists produced a race of sophists precisely similar to those whom the dialectics of the schoolmen produced in the Romish Church."

9. Palmer, "Import of Hebrew History," 598–601, 610.

10. Benjamin Morgan Palmer, *The Address of Rev. B. M. Palmer Delivered on the First Day of the New Year and Century,* January 1, 1900, 6, 10–11.

11. James K. Gutheim sermon, November 29, 1860, James K. Gutheim Papers, Jacob Rader Marcus Center of the American Jewish Archives, Cincinnati, Ohio (hereafter cited as Gutheim Papers).

12. William Warren Rogers Jr., "'In Defense of Our Sacred Cause': Rabbi James K. Gutheim in Confederate Montgomery," *Journal of Confederate History* 7 (1991): 115.

13. Bertram W. Korn, *American Jewry and the Civil War* (Philadelphia, 1951), 47–51.

14. Small collections, SC-4414, Miscellaneous, Jacob Rader Marcus Center of the American Jewish Archives, Cincinnati, Ohio.

15. Gutheim sermon, November 18, 1869, Gutheim Papers.

16. Gutheim sermon, November 24, 1870, Gutheim Papers.

17. Gutheim sermon, November 24, 1870, Gutheim Papers.

18. James K. Gutheim, "Addresses of Rev. J. K. Gutheim and Rev. Dr. Palmer, at the Great Meeting in New Orleans," *Southern Historical Society Papers* 10 (June 1882): 250. Palmer spoke at the same meeting and used much of his time to rebut the idea of the Lost Cause.

19. Max Heller sermon, January 1, 1897, Friday Lectures 1896–1897, Box 9, folder 1, Max Heller Papers, Jacob Rader Marcus Center of the American Jewish Archives, Cincinnati, Ohio (hereafter cited as Heller Papers). The vast majority of the extant Heller sermons are sermon notes rather than manuscripts. Often only words or phrases are written, making it difficult on occasion to determine what Heller meant.

20. Heller sermon, February 19, 1897, Friday Lectures 1896–1897, Box 9, folder 1, Heller Papers. In earlier sermon notes, Heller stated that Washington "deprecated partisanship." Later Heller gave the following note from which I extrapolate his argument for Washington's avoidance of partisanship: "Above part in religion & politics."

21. See also Heller sermon, March 30, 1894, Friday Lectures 1893–1894, Box 9, folder 1, Heller Papers. In this sermon, Heller argued that it was un-American to put religious beliefs into the Constitution.

22. Box 2, folder 1, Rabbi Isaac L. Leucht Papers, Manuscript Collection 853, Manuscript Department, Howard-Tilton Memorial Library, Tulane University, New Orleans, LA.

23. Max Heller, *Jewish Ledger,* May 8, 1896; Heller sermon, May 17, 1895, Friday Lectures 1894–1895, Box 9, folder 1, Heller Papers.

24. John Mack Faragher, Mari Jo Buhle, Daniel Czitrom, and Susan H. Armitage, *Out of Many: A History of the American People,* 2d ed. (New Jersey, 1997), 640–41; President McKinley quoted in Samuel Flagg Bemis, *A Diplomatic History of the United States* (New York, 1955), 472.

25. Heller sermon, January 27, 1899, Friday Lectures 1898–1899, Box 9, folder 2, Heller Papers; David Hackett Fischer, *Albion's Seed: Four British Folkways in America* (New York, 1989), 595–97. Leviticus 25:10 addresses the year of Jubilee wherein those who had been enslaved due to debt were freed and land sold for pressing economic reasons was restored. Inscribed on the Liberty Bell was the phrase, "Proclaim Liberty throughout all the Land unto all the inhabitants thereof."

26. William G. McLoughlin Jr., *Modern Revivalism: Charles Grandison Finney to Billy Graham* (New York, 1959), 444–45.

27. Sidney E. Mead, *The Lively Experiment: The Shaping of Christianity in America* (New York, 1963), 138–39. Jon Butler has noted that between 1790 and 1860, Christianity in America changed from its colonial state-church pattern. As traditional church-state relations declined, the concern shifted from the relationship of government to the church to the relationship of the government to religion. While the post-revolutionary governments tended to support Christianity in general, the state's authority in religious matters declined and denominational authority increased. As denominations proliferated, some Christians wanted governmental recognition of America's Christian and Protestant identity. In response to indifference by some and to religious pluralism introduced by immigration, some Christians in the 1850s "evolved a myth of the American Christian past." This myth "pressed new historical 'facts' on antebellum America as moral obligations." See Butler, *Awash in a Sea of Faith: Christianizing the American People* (Cambridge, MA, 1990), 257–64, 284–86 (quote).

28. Dinnerstein, *Antisemitism in America*, 177, 180; Malcolm H. Stern observed that "A prime function of the Southern rabbi became interpreting the Jew to the non-Jewish community." See Stern, "The Role of the Rabbi in the South," in *"Turn to the South": Essays on Southern Jewry*, ed. Nathan M. Kaganoff and Melvin I. Urofsky (Charlottesville, 1979), 27; Mark K. Bauman and Arnold Shankman, "The Rabbi as Ethnic Broker: The Case of David Marx," *Journal of American Ethnic History* 2 (Spring 1983): 51–54.

29. Sidney E. Mead, *The Nation with the Soul of a Church* (New York, 1975), 37–38.

30. Benjamin Morgan Palmer, "Offence of the Cross, Unreasonable," in *A Weekly Publication Containing Sermons* by Rev. B. M. Palmer (New Orleans: November 19, 1876), 83. The text of this sermon came from 1 Corinthians 1:23: "But we preach Christ crucified, unto the Jews a stumbling block, and unto the Greeks foolishness."

31. James K. Gutheim, *Sermon Delivered at the Consecration of the Synagogue Adas Israel, at Louisville, KY,* March 30, 1849, 4. See also his sermon of December 1, 1853, where he defined Israel's peculiar destiny as "Israel should be the people of religion among the nations of the earth." Gutheim Papers.

32. Gutheim, *The Temple Pulpit* (New York: 1879), 19–20, 35.

33. Gutheim undated sermon on Numbers 4:14–20, Gutheim Papers.

34. Gutheim sermon, March 18, 1854, Gutheim Papers.

35. Heller sermon, April 24, 1891, Friday Lectures 1890–1891, Box 9, folder 1, Heller Papers.

36. Heller sermon, November 23, 1888, Friday Lectures 1887–1888, Box 9, folder 1, Heller Papers.

37. Heller sermon, May 26, 1893, Friday Lectures 1893, Box 9, folder 1, Heller Papers.

38. Heller sermon, March 25, 1887, Friday Lectures 1887–1888, Box 9, folder 1, Heller Papers.

39. Heller, *Jewish Ledger,* January 3, 1896.

40. Heller, *The American Hebrew,* May 8, 1903, 827–828. Gutheim would have agreed with this assessment. In a sermon preached in 1870, he proclaimed, "Israel, by its steady adhesion to this truth [humanity's creation in the image of God], has thus become the Messiah, the redeemer of mankind." He went on to show the superiority of Judaism to Islam and Christianity. The latter two religions sought conversions through force and brutality, but Judaism, the bearer of genuine religious truth, appealed to reason and waited patiently for the ultimate triumph of its cause. Gutheim, sermon dated 1870, "The episode recorded here . . ." Gutheim Papers.

41. Unless otherwise noted, the account of the mass meeting comes from the *New Orleans Times-Democrat,* March 17, 1882.

42. A portion of Palmer's speech can also be found in Johnson, *The Life and Letters of Benjamin M. Palmer,* 487–90.

43. *In Memory of Rev. Benjamin Morgan Palmer, D. D.,* 20.

44. McLoughlin, *Modern Revivalism,* 267.

45. *New Orleans Times-Democrat,* March 18, 1882.

46. Ibid.

17. *Southwestern Presbyterian,* March 23, 1882.

48. Pearl W. Bartelt, "American Jewish Agricultural Colonies," in *America's Communal Utopias,* ed. Donald E. Pitzer (Chapel Hill: 1997), 358; *New Orleans Times-Democrat,* April 23 and May 21, 1882.

49. Benjamin Kline Hunnicutt, "The Jewish Sabbath Movement in the Early Twentieth Century," *American Jewish History* 69 (December 1979): 196–97.

50. *New Orleans Times-Democrat,* March 28, 1882; *Southwestern Presbyterian,* March 30, 1882.

51. Ibid.

52. Ibid.

53. Ibid.

54. *New Orleans Times-Democrat,* April 3, 1882; *Southwestern Presbyterian,* April 6, 1882.

55. Ibid.

56. Ibid.

57. Ibid.

58. Wilbur F. Crafts, *The Sabbath for Man* (New York, 1885), 193, 251, 255–61.

59. McLoughlin, *Modern Revivalism,* 168.

60. Milton J. Coalter, John M. Mulder, and Louis B. Weeks, *The Re-Forming Tradition: Presbyterians and Mainstream Protestantism* (Louisville, 1992), 37–38.

61. Malone, *Max Heller,* 50, 69.

62. Joy J. Jackson, *New Orleans in the Gilded Age: Politics and Urban Progress, 1880–1896* (Baton Rouge, 1969), 115, 121, 129.

63. Malone, *Max Heller,* 54.

64. Max Heller, "The Cowardice of Prosperity," Friday Lectures 1897–1898, Box 9, folder 1, Heller Papers.

65. *In Memory of Rev. Benjamin Morgan Palmer, D. D.,* 21.

66. *New Orleans Daily Picayune,* January 24, 1904.

67. Palmer, "Narrative of a Mission," 54.

14
Is the Jew White?

The Racial Place of the Southern Jew

Leonard Rogoff

In 1910 the Dixie Publishing Company of Moravian Falls, North Carolina, published *The Jew a Negro, Being A Study of the Jewish Ancestry from an Impartial Standpoint,* by the Rev. Arthur T. Abernethy, A.M., Ph.D. Abernethy—a preacher, professor, and rustic journalist—sought to demonstrate through "ethnology" and "Scriptural proofs" how "the Jew of today, as well as his ancestors in other times, is the kinsman and descendant of the Negro."[1]

Behind *The Jew a Negro* lay a century of transatlantic speculation on the racial status of the Jew. In the American South the problem of the Jew's racial identity was a footnote to the larger debate on white-black relations, a question pushed forward in the racially unsettled period between 1850 to 1915. Jews were accepted as white, but their precise racial place was not fixed. A long tradition of European folklore, reinforced by an emerging racial science, cast the Jew on the black side of the color line. Southern racial ideology was not distinctly regional but borrowed from the international debate. Ideologies born in the salons of European intellectuals and the academies of New England professors found their way into the sermons of backwoods Southern preachers like Abernethy. Such a work as *The Jew a Negro* is representative of texts that transmitted cosmopolitan racial ideologies into Southern popular culture.

Jews were a racial tabula rasa upon which anything could be written. Over the course of the nineteenth century, nationalists split races into increasingly discriminating categories. Whether racial theorists defined Jews as Semites or—as became more common later in the century—Orientals, the Jews' status as Europeans was questioned. The Jews' color was described variously as white, black, or mixed. The anthropological status of the Jews reflected their social standing. In the American South after Reconstruction, a new social line between Jew and white gentile followed the disengagement of white and black. This separation occurred at a time when the Jews' color was being questioned. The immigration of millions of "swarthy" East European Jews exacerbated these racial anxieties, although very few settled in the South.

The Jews who came South entered a bipolar racial society. Did Southern race thinking on the black affect the Jew's social status? What was the place of the Jew in the Southern racial hierarchy? Southerners as Christians inherited a folkloric prejudice, a color symbolism, that attributed virtue to white skin and evil to black. This bias drew on more ancient theologies and folk beliefs that physiology reflects character. A folklore evolved of the Jew as "dark and ugly" in contrast to the fair and handsome gentile. This folk belief, Sander Gilman observes, originated in the Middle Ages. The Jews' inner depravity as children of Cain or Satan had a physical sign, traditionally rendered as horns, hooked noses, or discolored skin. Jews were thought to exude a peculiar body odor, and their men were said to menstruate. The Jew's sallow complexion reflected a diseased soul. The liberal Bavarian writer Johan Pezzl in the 1780s compared the Polish Jew to an "Orang-Utan . . . their necks exposed, the color of a Black." Adam Gurowski, a Polish nobleman visiting America in the 1850s, "took every light-colored mulatto for a Jew." John Quincy Adams disdained Florida Senator David Levy Yulee for "the dash of African blood in him," and Confederate statesman Judah Benjamin, olive skinned and black haired, was immortalized as the "dark prince."[2]

The folkloric biases against Jews found reinforcement in the racial science that emerged from the Enlightenment. Proponents of racial science believed race to be more than a criterion of head size and shape, skin color, or hair texture. They argued that race also implied moral, intellectual, and psychological character, the capability to be assimilated into civil society and granted political rights. Natural scientists and racial philosophers like Carolus Linnaeus and Georges Louis Leclerc, comte de Buffon, promulgated taxonomies that placed the Caucasian on top and the African at the bottom. Race thinkers usually classified race by three colors—white (Caucasian), yellow (Oriental), and black (African) —or by five, adding brown (Malay) and red (Indian).

Given human diversity, natural scientists debated whether human races emerged from a common origin or derived from separate creations, whether racial characteristics were innate or environmental, and whether acquired traits could be inherited. As these scientists examined zoological evidence they questioned whether race mixing debilitated or improved the human stock. Across continents scientists, ministers, and self-anointed racial experts debated black origins, assuming the African's inferiority. Environmentalists, attributing black skin to the effects of the tropical sun, assumed each race was peculiarly adapted to its geography and climate.

Into these arguments race thinkers dragged the Jews. They regarded Jews as a "litmus test" of racial purity because of the Jews' antiquity, resistance to intermarriage, and geographical dispersion. In 1775 the German anthropologist Johann Friedrich Blumenbach wrote that the Jewish type was instantly recognizable, but he did not define the distinguishing Jewish characteristics. This assertion of a recognizable but undefinable Jewish type provoked debate for centuries. In 1787 the Reverend Dr. Samuel Stanhope Smith, professor of moral philosophy at Princeton, argued that "no example can carry with it greater authority . . . than that of the Jews" to prove that race was merely the product of "the peculiar characteristics of every climate." Although Jews "descended from one stock," Smith observed, they are fair in Britain and Germany, brown in France and Turkey, swarthy in Portugal and Spain, olive in Syria and Chaldea, and tawny or copper in Arabia and Egypt. James Cowles Prichard, the English physician and ethnologist whose *Researches into the Physical History of Man* (1808) became the authoritative text of early British racial science, denied Smith's claim that climate alters skin color. He argued that Jews were originally a white people, not racially different from Europeans. The Jewish type remains fixed, Prichard claimed, although intermarriage had varied skin colors.[3]

Missionaries and explorers brought to public attention the black Cochin Jews of Malabar, African Jews of Abyssinia, and Chinese Jews of Kaifeng. A new scientific historicism opened Hebrew origins to debate. Jews were described variously as purely Caucasian Semites, dark Egyptians, ruddy Edomites, black Cushites, mixed-blood Chaldaeans, and so on. Such disparate authorities as Dutch-Jewish leader Menasseh ben Israel, British historian James Adair, Puritan clergyman Cotton Mather, and Quaker colonist William Penn speculated that Native Americans were the Lost Tribes of Israel.[4]

America with its white, red, and black races was a testing ground for racial speculation. De Crevoceur hailed the new man, the American, whose nationhood, infusing the best of all peoples, was defined by creed, not race. Yet Thomas Jefferson, who declared in the Declaration of Independence that "all men are created equal," wrote in *Notes of the State of Virginia* that only "natural history" could resolve his "suspicion" about the "different qualifications" of the red and black races.[5]

Although the agrarian South was a scientific backwater distant from Northern and European academic capitals, Southern planters, ministers, physicians, and professors read the racial science literature and corresponded with the leading intellectual lights to answer their questions on the humanity of blacks or the legitimacy of slavery. Port cities like Charleston or New Orleans imported fashionable ideologies as well as merchandise. These cosmopolitan centers hosted scientific societies that debated the latest intellectual developments. In their journals and learned societies Southerners argued science and revelation, citing a Buffon or a Blumenbach in defense of their positions. When the Reverend Buckner H. Payne of Nashville found himself engaged in a pamphlet war on the biblical roots of race, he wrote to a Dr. Blackie in Scotland, asking, "What do the Universities of Edinburgh and Bonn teach concerning the origin of the Negro?"[6] Natural scientists like Swiss-born Louis Agassiz, the famous Harvard zoologist, worked the Southern lecture circuit. One influential Southern natural scientist, the Reverend John Bachman of Charleston, held a Ph.D. from the University of Berlin.

Science in the South deferred to scripture. As orthodox Christians, most Southerners were monogenists, holding for the common origin of the various races as children of one God. They drew elaborate genealogies of racial origins that reconciled Genesis and anthropology. Jews were descendants of Adam and Eve whose tribal roots traced to Noah's son Shem while blacks were commonly regarded as descendants of Noah's son Ham. Some ministers noted that Noah's curse of servitude actually fell on Canaan, and the scriptural authority of the black's Hamitic descent was heatedly debated. Although some thought that the races diverged after the fall of Babel, most ascribed racial divisions to the Flood. A diverse group of anticlerical racial scientists and radical fundamentalists traced the black to a separate creation of pre-Adamite origin. For some of these polygenists the black was not human but a beast. An anonymous minister in Augusta, Georgia, answered the question "Who and what is the Negro?" by arguing that the black was Nachast, the snake in the Garden of Eden.[7] The mythology of the black's beastly origins endured into the twentieth century.

As the nineteenth century progressed, racial science grew in its determinism. By midcentury Americans were increasingly speaking of their manifest destiny as Anglo-Saxon racial destiny. In achieving their national ambitions white Americans enslaved the African and vanquished the Indian. Nativist fevers gave rise to the anti-immigrant, anti-Catholic Know Nothings, whose popularity peaked at midcentury. White Southerners, committed to the defense of slavery, began asserting their region's distinct values and their superiority to those of the North. Racial extremists saw mixed blood as degeneration into negroid bestiality and incivility. In 1850, Robert Knox's *Races of Men* appeared in England and was well-received in America. "Race is everything," Knox declared. He did not think that Jews could be assimilated into the Anglo-Saxon race, referring to the "African character of the Jew, his muzzle-shaped mouth and face removing him from certain other races."[8]

The most influential racial thinker of the nineteenth century was Count Arthur de Gobineau, whose *Essai sur l'inégalité des races humaines* (1853–1855) became the bible of scientific racism. Abstracting from linguistics, Gobineau posited the concept of an Aryan race, particularly its Nordic strain, that sat atop the racial hierarchy. Whether Arabian, French, or Polish, the Jewish type, he argued, remained "relatively pure." Consequently, he found that "they all look alike. . . . The Semitic face looks exactly the same . . . as it appears on the Egyptian paintings of three or four thousand years ago, and more." While Gobineau wrote admiringly of the Jews as an intelligent white people who had created a civilization in barren Palestine, he later warned that historically Jews had undergone a "Semitic fusion," a "blending with black blood," that made them a threat.[9]

A goateed Southern gentleman, Josiah Nott of Mobile, Alabama, proved to be America's most indefatigable propagandist for racial science. Educated in New York and Philadelphia medical schools, Nott was well versed in continental racial theory. He traveled in European intellectual circles, where he was well received as the spokesperson for what became known as the American School of Anthropology. Nott was a polygenist who wanted to "cut loose the natural history of mankind from the Bible" and place anthropology on a scientific footing. In 1856 he selectively edited and published Gobineau in English as *The Moral and Intellectual Diversity of the Races*. He embarked on the lecture circuit as the frontman for the father of American racial science, Quaker physician Samuel Morton of Philadelphia. Morton had assembled nearly a thousand skulls to support his thesis that the races were separate creations traceable to specific geographic regions. Pouring mustard seed and lead shot into hundreds of skulls, Morton divided humanity into five races. Morton's measurements of brains in cubic inches yielded 92 for the Teuton, 89 for the Semite, and 83 for the African. In *Crania Aegyptica* Morton reported that the sculpture of the temples of Luxor and Karnak demonstrated the persistence of African and Jewish racial types to the present day.[10]

In 1850, at a conference of the newly founded American Association for the Advancement of Science in Charleston, Nott lectured on "An Examination of the Physical History of the Jews in Its Bearings on the Question of the Unity of the Races." His magnum opus *Types of Mankind* (1854), which he published with the English-born Egyptologist George R. Gliddon, contains a chapter entitled "Physical History of the Jews." It opens as follows: "This historical people furnishes so striking an example of the permanence of a *Caucasian* type." Morton had measured the mummified skull of an Israelite from the catacombs of Memphis, Nott reported. Its measurements compared exactly with modern Jewish crania and differed markedly from antique crania of Africans and Egyptians. Comparing a Chaldaean effigy to a prominent Alabama Jew, Nott observed that Jews have remained unchanged "from Mesopotamia to Mobile for at least 5,500 years." Though Jewish skin may be bleached in the North, tanned in the South or "occasionally mingled," these were merely "temporary" changes.[11]

In "Physical History of the Jews" Nott included letters from Jewish authorities endorsing his views. Isaac Leeser, mentor of traditional Judaism in America, concurred that "in all essentials, the Jews are the same [as] they are represented on the Egyptian monuments . . . fair . . . identical with the Europeans like all other white inhabitants of this continent. All Jews that ever I have beheld are identical in features." A letter from Rabbi Morris Raphall of New York, who believed that slavery was justified biblically, explained that black Malabar Jews and Jewish Negroes in Africa were descended from slaves manumitted by Jewish masters. Chinese and North African Jews were "of really Jewish descent" and were therefore "white."[12]

In his Charleston lecture Nott used the example of Jewish racial fixity and purity not to comment on the social or political status of modern American Jews but to advance his anthropology. His larger intent was to attack the biblicism and monogenism of the English ethnologist James Prichard. Among those attending Nott's lecture on the Jews were the zoologist Louis Agassiz of Boston and the Reverend John Bachman of Charleston. Like many Southern clergymen, Bachman was affronted by the polygenist challenge to Genesis and was shocked to hear Agassiz support Nott. In print and pulpit the two locked into a public debate that echoed across the South. Their issues were the fertility of hybrid species in zoology, the accuracy of Genesis, and the sources of African inferiority, which both monogenists and polygenists assumed. Their arguments made more reference to the mule than to the Jews, the ostensible subject of Nott's lecture that provoked the debate.[13]

The Jewish racial question was not a social or political issue in the antebellum South: whatever anti-Semitism Southern Jews encountered was primarily economic or religious. Jews suffered office-holding disabilities under constitutional religious tests in Maryland until 1826 and in North Carolina until 1868. Jews were widely suspected as financial speculators. In 1846 John C. Calhoun complained that Jews were "notoriously a race of brokers, bankers, and merchants." "Race" in the vernacular lacked its scientific connotations other than to suggest that Southerners looked upon Jews as a class. Such categorical denunciations of Jews became more commonplace during the Civil War and Reconstruction. In 1862 a public meeting in Thomasville, Georgia, called for the "banishing" of the town's Jews. Yet across the South Jews gained racial acceptance. Along with its code of race the South held a code of hospitality. The demonizing of the Jew was directed against the mythic Shylock and Christ-killer rather than the local Jewish merchant, who was more often welcomed as a neighbor and honored as a citizen. In Raleigh, Charleston, Richmond, and New Orleans Jews intermarried with leading gentile families.[14]

As historian John Efron notes, the "relative insignificance" of Jews in a country's anthropological literature reflected social tolerance and acceptance. In neither British nor American ethnology were Jews an obsessive theme. Monogenists and polygenists cited the example of the Jews in proof or refutation of ideological positions on the innate or environmental origins of race. When in 1867 the Reverend Young of Nashville wrote Dr. Blackie of Scotland to inquire about European thinking on black ethnology, Blackie cited the Jew as but one case study among many that illustrated how all races were a "cosmopolite" mixture descended from a common ancestor. "The Negro and European were two extremes of a very long gradation," Blackie argued, and he discussed the "Jew" in the context of the "Arab" and the "Hindoo." Although Blackie noted a distinctively Jewish nose and lips, he observed that the Jews "have assimilated in physical character to the nations with whom they reside." Young turned to Blackie for confirmation that "ethnology" was subordinate to "divine truth;" the Nashville minister's real concern was the challenge that Nott's polygenism presented to the orthodox interpretation of scripture.[15]

The science that placed the Jew as racially similar to Europeans denigrated the African as an inferior race or species that could not be improved by emancipation, suffrage, or education. As a justification for white supremacy, the American School of Anthropology found fertile ground in the South. By 1871 *Types of Mankind* had gone through 10 editions, and by 1900 it was still in print. Although leading racial thinkers like Morton claimed to be in service of science and eschewed politics, Nott was an ardent Southern apologist and propagandist for "niggerology." One of the American School's intellectual citadels was Charleston, where a medical college and natural history museum sponsored publications and conferences. John Hammond, governor of South Carolina, stated that the "doctrine of Races" proved the "philosophy of subjugation." William Gilmore Simms's *Southern Quarterly Review* praised Nott's *Types of Mankind* as "highly creditable to the learning and talent of the south."[16]

The racial literature added fuel to feelings of "white racial exclusiveness" in the South. In antebellum Southern society blacks and whites had lived together in separate spheres but in close proximity. After the upheaval of war and Reconstruction, the South renegotiated its race relations. For over sixty-five years following Emancipation, customs and then codes of segregation became established. In response to black aspirations in politics, economics, and education, whites sought to separate themselves from blacks by law. In the lower South, mulattos, who before 1850 had enjoyed special social status by virtue of their white blood, were now seen as part of an undifferentiated black mass, and Southern society became biracial, intolerant of ambiguity.[17]

As the postbellum South reinvented its social order, the question of the Jews' race became significant not merely as a case study of biblical interpretation or anthropological speculation on the origins of the African but also in terms of the Jews' position in the Southern hierarchy of social place. In 1867 "Ariel," Nashville clergyman and journalist Buckner H. Payne, published *The Negro: What Is His Ethnological Status?* It reiterated polygenist arguments that dehumanized the African as a species apart. "The Jews, the descendants of Shem, in every country . . . belong to the white race," Ariel wrote. "We know then, on Biblical authority, with mathematical certainty, that they are not Negroes, either before, at nor since the flood, but white." In 1875 a pseudonymous racial pamphleteer, Sister Sallie, endorsed Ariel's views in *The Color Line,* a book dedicated to "Organizing the White People of the South." Sister Sallie contrasted the beastly Negro with the children of Abraham: "Jews, as far as we know anything of them, are all white persons, and all history concurs in the same."[18] At this time, too, Zebulon Vance, North Carolina's most venerated politician, began delivering a philo-Semitic speech, "The Scattered Nation," on the Chatauqua circuit with the expressed intention of rebutting "objections to the Jew as a citizen." He claimed that "whilst no people can claim such an unmixed purity of blood, certainly none can establish such antiquity of origin, such unbroken generations of descent" as can Jews. Identifying the Jews as a Semitic race, he found them closer statistically in height, reach, and width to Europeans than to Africans. Vance expressed outrage that civilized Jews, flesh of the Savior, should suffer discrimination as if they were barbaric, uncivilized Africans. Vance called the Hebrews "our wondrous kinsmen."[19]

The encomium on the Jews became a setpiece in popular lectures and journalism into the early twentieth century. For fifteen years after its first delivery in 1874, "The Scattered Nation" was preached repeatedly from lecterns and reprinted in virtually every journal and newspaper across the South. In 1888 the North Carolina *Tobacco Plant* newspaper rhapsodized, "What a wonderful race of people is this Jewish race . . . well may they be proud of their race." Widely published was the famous retort to an anti-Semitic insult, attributed variously to Benjamin Disraeli or Judah Benjamin, that the Jews were priests in the temple of Solomon when the Anglo-Saxons were barbarians in the caves of Gaul. So commonplace were these paeans that in 1894 H. T. Ezekiel of Richmond thought that the philo-Semite "must have his doubts or there would be no need for such asseverations." In 1901 Dr. A. B. Arnold of Baltimore complained testily about "the incessant laudations lavished on the Jewish people."[20]

More often, Southern Jews shared the Southerners' "romantic racialism" and assented to the view of themselves as members of a pure, fixed, uniform white race which had preserved its lineage since antiquity. Taking the environmentalist position, in 1879 an editorial writer in *The Jewish South* of Atlanta asserted that "the clime of the South is about the same as in the Holy Land, and the peculiar features of our race are therefore better preserved here." Thirty years later a Jewish newspaper, *The Temple* in Louisville, quoted Jewish communal leader Charles Morris: "From the sunny cotton fields of our southland to the icy gold fields of the north, you will find the Jew—the same." On scientific authority, Morris claimed "by virtue of their aristocracy of blood . . . the Jews are the purest blood people." When Chicago's Rabbi Emil Hirsch in the *Reform Advocate* scorned claims of Jewish racial purity with the comment "race pride is ridiculous," the *Jewish South* conceded that Jewish blood had become mixed, but "dissented when [Hirsch] characterizes race pride as ridiculous." The editorial admonished Hirsch, who had held rabbinical posts in Baltimore and Louisville, that "religion or race . . . shows in a man's face . . . the 'race' lives."[21]

Though classifying Jews as white, the racial literature also contained seeds that ultimately undermined the Jewish position. Race theorizers invariably claimed the authority of logic and evidence, but their arguments were confused, contradictory, and incoherent. Even when establishing the Jew as purely white, racial thinkers assumed the persistence of a Jewish Ur-type in dark Persian or blond French Jews, but the uniquely Jewish element eluded definition. Hereditarian claims of Jewish racial purity conflicted with obvious Jewish diversity across environments. Citing a Dr. Pressell, Vance ranked Jews from the "lowest" unintelligent Arab-Asians, to the "Talmudical" North African East Europeans, to the "most intelligent and civilized" Central and West Europeans, who "have become simply Unitarians or Deists." Vance's racialism was Eurocentric rather than philo-Semitic. Over the course of the century, racial splitting became increasingly discriminatory as whites sought new labels—Teuton, Nordic, or Anglo-Saxon—to dissociate themselves from other races. Morton's own craniometry had shown the Semite skull to be inferior to the Teuton. In *Types of Mankind* Nott listed the Hebrew as Caucasian, but then observed in *The Negro Race: Its Ethnology and History* (1866) that Jews are a "very mixed race."[22] For racial radicals it was an easy segue from the scientific "mixed" to the inflammatory "mongrel."

Darwinism overthrew the American School of Anthropology. Evolution documented the common origin of the races and made mockery of the thousands of years of evidence that Morton and Nott cited on the walls of Egyptian temples. Natural selection and variation accounted for human variety. But the prejudicial belief in the existence of a racial hierarchy merely shifted its scientific ground.

Social Darwinism revived racial consciousness as the naturalistic survival of the fittest. Its proponents ranked races on an evolutionary scale and justified imperialism abroad and white supremacy at home as race war—the subjugation everywhere of supposedly inferior peoples of color. The new science of genetics, which was consonant with Darwinism, gave racialism authority. The writings of Francis Galton, the Englishman who coined the term "eugenics" in 1883, were well received in America. Although Galton felt "honoured" to chair a London conference of "eminent Jews" on the race question, he also decided "that the Jews are specialized for a parasitical existence upon other nations."[23]

As the century progressed, European race literature grew increasingly vitriolic in its determinism. The formation of a unified German nation state had unleashed an anti-Semitic reaction against newly emancipated Jews as they aspired to attain political rights and join the majority culture. German anthropologists justified a racial nationalism that effectively removed Jews from the body politic. England was more liberal and by midcentury had removed most Jewish political disabilities. English racial literature (with the notable exception of Knox) had not been overtly antagonistic toward Jews. The link between race and religion was fully expressed by Anglo-Israelites, who believed that the English (and northern Europeans) were blood descendants of the northern kingdom of ancient Israel—the B'rit Ish. Anglo-Israelitism spread in middle-class Protestant circles after 1840 and peaked at the turn of the century. Queen Victoria herself claimed Davidic descent for the English royal family. John Wilson, whose *Lectures on Our Israelitish Origin* (1840) popularized the idea, affirmed the biblical origins of modern Jews as descendants of the southern kingdom of Judah but then argued that these Jews had contaminated their blood by intermarrying with heathen tribes. Jesus, some Anglo-Israelites argued, was not a Jew but an Aryan; a Gaulilean, not a Galilean.[24]

The idea that Jews were "'black' or, at least, 'swarthy'" prevailed in late nineteenth-century literature and persisted well into the twentieth century, particularly in Germany. Karl Marx labeled Ferdinand Lassalle "the Jewish nigger," questioning his head shape and parentage. Houston Stewart Chamberlain thought Jews had interbred with Africans during their Alexandrian exile. Freud was labeled a "'black' Jew" and wrote of himself as a Mischling, a half breed with "Jewish-Negroid features."[25]

Eugenics and physical anthropology only exacerbated the taxonomic confusion. Commonly, Jews were categorized as Asiatic or Oriental, and thus not European. Anthropologists, including some Jews, used such terms as West Asian-Oriental, Western Asiatic, Semitic Oriental, Nomadic Oriental, Eurasian, or Alpine-Himalayan. Speculations were rife about the Jews' descent from Mongoloid or Turkic Khazars. Even the great debunker of racial science, Franz Boas, wrote, "What we ordinarily designate as a Jewish type is, as a matter of fact, simply an Oriental type." When American immigration laws excluded Asians—the Chinese in 1882 and the Japanese in 1907—voices were raised that "the Hebrew race is essentially Oriental . . . there is at least ground for objection to unrestricted Jewish immigration."[26]

Jews, in the prevalent spirit of race pride, often referred to themselves as Oriental, but the label also carried connotations that pushed Jews on the wrong side of the color line. Orientalism was a transitional step in discoloring Jews as whites. The *Jewish Chronicle* of Mobile in 1909 quoted Rabbi Emil Hirsch: "The American looks upon the Jew as an Oriental and upon Orientals as a people fond of extravagant display and personal show and careless of personal cleanliness." Oriental racial attributes—sensuality and dirtiness—stereotypically belonged to the darker races.[27]

The eugenics movement intensified racial anxieties, and antiimmigrant proponents played on fears of racial contamination. Charles Davenport, founder of American eugenics, called the offspring of intermarried Jews "halfbreeds" who were more likely to be infertile. Race scientists reported the Jew's short stature and diminished lung capacity, warning of signs of "physical degeneracy" that would pollute American blood. Dr. J. G. Wilson of New York in a *Popular Science* article, "The Crossing of the Races," warned: "We are becoming a smaller and a darker race . . . instead of the race of tall blondes we once were." Among all immigrant groups, Wilson pointedly feared that a Jewish "racial substitution" threatened to diminish "Anglo-Saxon ideals."[28]

In the late nineteenth century a Jewish racial science emerged in defense. Russian-born German anthropologist Samuel Weissenberg systematically studied the physical anthropology of diverse Jewish populations across Europe. He argued that Jews comprised several racial types not distinguishable from other Europeans. The Southern Jewish press reported Weissenberg's scientific explorations of Jewish types. Even more widely distributed were the writings of English folklorist Joseph Jacobs, who claimed Jews were racially pure. Jewish blood had a "prepotency" that allowed it to dominate any racial mix. He claimed "cerebral development" had enlarged Jewish skulls. Jacobs, who relocated to New York in 1900 to edit the *Jewish Encyclopedia,* became the recognized authority on the Jewish race question in both the popular and Jewish media.[29]

Southern Jews had no regional perspective on the question of their racial identity but expressed views as varied as the international debate. Southern Jews, too, took up the race-war battle cry—with all its categorical confusions. Texan Leo Levi, in an 1895 address to the New Orleans YMHA, admitted that Jews possess some undesirable Oriental traits, but he asserted that Jews have endured for two thousand years by "survival of the fittest" and "natural selection." Jews "abstained very generally from intermixture of blood." In 1900 Omaha's Rabbi Abram Simon, a native Tennessean, endorsed the view that selective breeding could only improve the stock. He claimed that "only savages are racially pure." The Jew was a "composite racial type" like all "the highest civilizations." Ten years later Rabbi Barnett Elzas of Beth Elohim in Charleston argued against intermarriage on the basis of the "stern law of preservation." He denied that mixing would improve the race and condemned the "suicidal policy of self-extinction by means of assimilation." Jews sought to dignify their heritage as a people apart while minimizing their difference with their neighbors. Echoing Blumenbach from the eighteenth century, *The Temple* editorialized, "Nearly everybody can tell a Jew on sight, and yet it is very difficult to define the typical Jewish characteristics."[30]

In the South as whites closed ranks after Reconstruction those without racial definition were suspect. Racial intermingling became less commonplace, and in the 1870s Southern states began enforcing laws forbidding interracial marriage. From 1889 to 1915 racial extremism ascended in the South. Race radicals depicted a "new Negro" who, freed from civilizing slavery, was retrogressing toward a natural state of savagery. By the 1890s mulattos and miscegenation became obsessive themes in Southern writing, and after 1905 "race suicide" became a popular subject. Southern rustic journals, like Wilber Franklin Phelps' *Menace,* spread the racial gospel to hundreds of thousands. In contrast to liberals who saw assimilation as improving the national stock, eugenicists cited statistics demonstrating that hybrid, mongrel, mixed, or amalgamated species were infertile, inferior, and debilitated. From 1880 to 1910 customs of racial separation were encoded in laws of segregation, beginning with railroad cars and then moving toward political disfranchisement. With the defeat of black-Republican government, Southern Redeemers reestablished white supremacy as a ruling principle.[31]

In the South fears of racial amalgamation evolved into a paranoid concern with "invisible blackness," observes historian Joel Williamson. That Jews were sensitive to black stereotyping is suggested by an 1898 advertisement in the *Jewish South* of Richmond for "anti-kink for straightening kinky and curly hair." Forced to choose by the color line, some light-skinned African Americans "passed" as whites while others, like author Charles Chesnutt or NAACP leader Walter White, chose to identify as black. A Charlottesville African American editor found himself unable to answer the question, "What is a Negro?" Negro was "an idea," a social and political construct.[32]

Certainly the social discrimination that American Jews began experiencing in the late nineteenth century owed to class resentments against

Jews as parvenus, but the distaste was expressed as racial. Hoteliers Henry Hilton and Austin Corbin set off a national storm when they excluded Jews beginning in 1877 with the celebrated rebuff of Joseph Seligman in Saratoga. Dismissing the testimony of a converted Jew at an 1879 meeting of the Society for Suppressing the Jewish Race, Corbin retorted that the "society opposed the Jews only as a nasty and vulgar race and not on account of their religion." Mr. Hilton "quite agreed."[33]

Jews were too small a minority in the South to present the social, political, or cultural challenge to Southern whites that their coreligionists had posed for Northern whites, but discrimination followed the South's urbanization and integration into the national economy. In 1879 a Jewish Atlantan observed, "The Hiltonian process, is thus far, not introduced in the South, for in this section of the country there does not exist these race prejudices." That same year an Atlanta Jewish clothier dismissed the Seligman episode as "literally impossible in this city or state . . . there is no distinction of race or religion. Jews who are respectable go everywhere." Twenty years later Atlanta's *Jewish Sentiment* lamented, "there is prejudice against the Jews everywhere."[34]

Jews in New South cities experienced this discrimination most forcefully. In 1897 a Jewish newspaper in Richmond reported "Jews and the Gentiles do not mix." In 1901 an article in a Jewish journal in Mobile observed, "The Jew is seldom assailed because of his profession of Jewish faith . . . yet the association between Jew and Gentile" was greater in the nineteenth century than in the twentieth. In 1887 a Jew was a founding member of Altanta's exclusive Gentlemen's Driving Club, but by 1915 neither its successor, the Piedmont Driving Club, nor the Capital City Club counted another Jew among its 600 members—despite the Jews' acceptance into high circles of commerce. Southern elite anti-Semitism, in the absence of many Jews, reflected the region's adoption of national mores.[35]

Race became the criterion of social standing. Philo-Semitic Mark Twain wrote in 1899 that the "persecution of the Jews . . . on the score of religion, I think it has already come to an end. On the score of race prejudice and trade, I have an idea it will continue . . . race prejudice cannot be removed." Who can fail "to realize that social recognition has a biological basis?" asked Thomas Pearce Bailey, a leading race apologist (though not an anti-Semite), in *Race Orthodoxy in the South* (1914). "Blood will tell."[36]

The origins of this stereotyping of Jews as a racially dark people predated the massive East European immigration, but the arrival of two million Jews from Eastern and Central Europe between 1880 and 1924 intensified anxieties. In the early 1900s, with the black subordinated by legalized segregation, race baiters stirred up hatred against Southern and Eastern Europeans, primarily Italian and Slavic Catholics and Russian Jews, who were seen as a threat to Anglo-Saxon cultural and political hegemony. Though many racial thinkers split Jews—generally along Sephardic and Ashkenazi lines—belief in the uniformity of race persisted. Native-born Southern Jews of German origin unhappily found themselves categorized with their newly arrived East European coreligionists.

While some German Jews in the South affirmed their racial solidarity with the East Europeans—glorifying the spiritual unity of Israel, expressing race pride in the immigrants' industriousness and rapid rise—others adopted attitudes of racial disparagement toward the greenhorns. The Russians were "cattle." The *Jewish South* quoted English novelist Hall Caine, who used a typically racist stereotype in describing the Russian Jew as "a child of nature." In 1909 Mrs. Adelaide Hirshfield of Mobile devised a grand plan to place immigrant Romanian Jews in the Alabama cotton fields "to supplant the lazy negro."[37]

The South, even more than other regions, had at first welcomed immigration as a means to alleviate agrarian and industrial labor shortages and to ensure continued white dominance. In the 1880s Southern states formed boards of immigration to attract farm and industrial workers. From 1903 to 1907 several Southern states sent agents to Europe, but few immigrants settled in the South. Even though the numbers remained low, Southern congressmen, who had once endorsed free immigration, later turned solidly antiimmigrant as the Eastern and Southern Europeans began surpassing northwestern Europeans. Antiblack Southerners joined a coalition of restrictionists that included labor unionists, patrician New Englanders, anti-Catholic midwesterners, and anti-Mexican and anti-Asian Westerners.

Swarthy Jews and Italians might be invisible blacks. Southern antiimmigrant rhetoric reflected antiblack anxieties. Senator Furnifold McLendel Simmons, boss of the North Carolina Democratic machine, cautioned "men of Anglo-Saxon blood" against "negro domination" and "the degenerate progeny of the Asiatic hoards" [*sic*]. Congressman John Abercrombie of Alabama warned, "The color of thousands of them differs materially from that of the Anglo-Saxon." His fellow Alabaman, Oscar Underwood, contrasted the "pure whiteness" of the older immigration to the tainted "Asian and African blood" of the new. In 1904 South Carolina limited its immigration bureau to "white citizens . . . of Saxon origin," while in 1910 North Carolina specified "Teutonic, Celtic, or Saxon."[38]

In polite society the Jew, like the black, became a Problem or a Question. Nathaniel S. Shaler of Kentucky, who served as Dean of the Lawrence School of Science at Harvard, in *The Neighbor: The Natural History of Human Contacts* (1904) wrote consecutive chapters on "The Hebrew Problem" and "The Problem of the African." Shaler, a Southern apologist, noted that racially "the Israelite has not the tenth part of the value of that which parts us from our African neighbors." Shaler wrote sympathetically of Jews, yet he wondered why personal acquaintance with blacks decreased prejudice while the opposite seemed true with Jews. An immigration restrictionist, he advocated forbidding entry to "those who are not of our race except the Jews," although he did not want the "degraded among these."[39]

Eugenics and race science provided a vocabulary that reinforced Southern antiimmigrant prejudices. Particularly Southern was the sexual obsession with racial intermingling. Southern anti-Semites employed racial imagery that evoked the Jew as a perverted dark Other. In 1898 a Virginian, a Jewish convert to Christianity charged with wife beating, was described as "swarthy of complexion and of Jewish extraction." Tom Watson, the agrarian Georgia demagogue, appealed to class and economic resentments, but he used racial language to inflame the masses against Leo Frank. In 1915 Watson wrote, "Every student of sociology knows that the black man's lust after the white woman *is not much fiercer than the lust of the licentious Jew for the Gentile.*" Though Watson denied any "racial dislike" of Frank, he captioned a picture of him in *Watson's Magazine* with imagery that evoked African stereotypes: "Note the Horrible Lips, the Nose, and the averted eyes of Leo Frank—a typical pervert." Rape, in eugenic terms, constituted racial defilement. Southerners, with their romantic exaltation of race, glorified Southern white womanhood and reacted violently to its violation. The two most brutal outbursts of Southern anti-Semitism—the lynching of Leo Frank and the castrating of Joseph Needleman in North Carolina in 1925—both involved alleged attacks on women.[40]

"The more closely linked to sexuality," E. J. Ayers notes of Southern black-white relations, "the more likely was a place to be segregated." Harry Golden observed that a Southern Jewish merchant may have civic and business dealings with white gentile men for twenty years without the "social union" of "meeting the wife." Jews and gentiles separated at clubs and resorts. Golden called this custom "segregation at sundown."

In 1910, when Senators Joseph Bailey of Texas and Hernando Money of Mississippi praised Jews for "their race pride and persistent efforts to preserve their racial identity," they were also, by implication, lauding Jews for racially segregating themselves. On Klan Day at the Texas State Fair in 1923, Imperial Wizard Hiram Evans asked the crowd, "Would you have your daughter marry a Jew?"[41]

Fears of Jewish racial contamination had roots in religious difference. The folklore of Jews as racially pure and venerable coexisted with the countermyth of Jews as racially mixed and sinful. In *The Negro a Beast* (1900) the fundamentalist Charles Carroll of Missouri laid the groundwork for *The Jew a Negro*. Caroll's book sold into the thousands, its message appealing to poor rural whites likely unacquainted with Jews. Carroll argued that blacks were high-grade apes who imitate humans but lack souls, "monstrosities" without "rights social financial political or religious . . . not even the right to live." He described race mixing as original sin and traced it to biblical Hebrews who will someday perish in a well-deserved apocalypse. Implying the Jews' invisible blackness, Carroll wrote that the ancient "Israelites had persisted in amalgamation for so long a period that their mixed-blooded progeny were not distinguishable from pure whites." Although Carroll did not concern himself with modern Jews, his demonizing of ancient Hebrews paved the way for modern racial anti-Semites like Abernethy. Southern Christians saw the Jews among them as living relics of the biblical people. If a tenet of Jim Crow stated that "a person having any Negro blood whatsoever is, with all his descendants, forever and eternally of the Negro race," then the modern Jew bore the taint of his or her ancestors.[42]

Abernethy did not specifically cite Carroll, nor did he share Carroll's antiscientific bias. But the parallelism of the books' titles suggests a desire to emulate Carroll's success by pandering to popular race prejudice. As a self-promoting hack, Abernethy purveyed viewpoints that were unoriginal. He advertised dubious degrees and claims of ordination, but he was not a marginal figure. Abernethy held editorial and ministerial posts in New York as well as North Carolina. He was later Poet Laureate of North Carolina, and President Franklin Roosevelt honored him as "Ambassador of Sunshine." Author of 50 books, he claimed that his syndicated columns reached 7,125,000 readers.[43]

Although Professor Abernethy tried to maintain the disinterested tone of the natural scientist in *The Jew a Negro*, the minister proved incapable of sustaining it, and the "impartial standpoint" yielded to a racist, pulpit-pounding, anti-Semitic screed. Southerners wrestled more with making biblical sense of race than with coming to terms with its anthropology, and their ears were more attuned to evangelists than to scientists. Severing Christianity from its Jewish roots, some religious white supremacists annointed the Anglo-Saxons as the chosen people. In *The Jew a Negro* Abernethy wrote that Christ "was exalted into the Godhead" as a "tall blond with amber hair and beard, blue eyes, clear complexion." One popular Protestant hymn underscored the color symbolism that linked race and religion: "precious is the flow that makes me white as snow . . . nothing but the blood of Jesus."[44]

The "one-drop" rule meant that even the slightest suggestion of African blood typed a person as irredeemably black. Whites began looking beyond skin color to hair, feet, and fingernails in search of telltale clues of African origin. In *The Jew a Negro* Abernethy rested his case on a study in 14 Southern states of "the tell-tale finger nail formation," a trait that he felt indicated the Jews' African origin even when skin turned white and hair grew blonde. Abernethy concluded, "Thousands of years of effort to throw off their nigresecence have failed to eradicate those race characteristics, and the Jew of to-day is essentially Negro in habits, physical peculiarities and tendencies."[45]

Abernethy's two primary cited sources, W. Z. Ripley and Charles Woodruff, wrote popular, foundational texts of the eugenics movement. In *The Effects of Tropical Light on White Men* (1905) Woodruff, a U.S. military physician in the Philippine service, warned of the threat to American hegemony here and abroad by unrestricted immigration. Abernethy's preface included his lengthy correspondence with Woodruff, whom he quoted: "The original Jews were . . . short, dark people of the long headed type . . . It would be better to say that the Negro descended from the ancient Jewish type or Mediterranean race. It is hardly correct, ethnically, to reverse the sentence." Woodruff claimed that the Ashkenazim, who comprise ninety percent of Jews, are "Asiatic converts," while the Sephardim, who comprise but ten percent, are of Semitic blood, African in origin. Although he claimed that "some of our best and most valuable citizens are of the Jewish faith," Woodruff also warned against the "dense masses" in city slums, those of "lower races in civilization" who comprised "actually a species of animal under domestication" kept alive by Aryan sanitation. Abernethy took Ripley's *Races of Europe* (1899) as his second major source. Based on his claims of 2,500 physical measurements of Jews, Ripley concluded that "the boasted purity of descent of the Jews is . . . a myth. . . . The evidence of the sacred books bears out the . . . theory of an original dark type." He left it to the reader to decide whether "modern Jews" descended from the biblical people.[46]

Curiously, the word "immigration" never appeared in *The Jew a Negro*, although that was the focus of national eugenicist literature. Racial nativism was stronger where immigrants were fewer. Abernethy wrote from a mountain town with few blacks and no Jews in a state with the smallest percentage of Jews in the country. Little in rural Southerners' experience acquainted them with modern Jews. Southerners like Abernethy received a traditional education built on the twin pillars of the Bible and classical literature. Southerners took less comfort from the modernist language of eugenics and anthropology than from the regional vocabulary of race, family, ancestry, and religion. As a program, eugenics made less headway in the South than it did in the North or West. But blood, exalted by romantic cults of the Teuton and Anglo-Saxon, remained important to Southerners. While Southerners like Abernethy claimed aristocracy of blood for themselves (as indeed did the Jews), other Americans looked upon the South as the most illiterate, diseased, and impoverished of all the nation's regions. The craniometrists and eugenicists not only disparaged the African American and immigrant Jew but also ranked the poor Southern white, the hick and hillbilly, among the "feeble-minded," retrograde classes.[47] In diminishing the Jew as a "Negro," Abernethy, as a race-proud Appalachian, advanced his own position.

The appeals to American blood resonated among poor Southern whites, particularly among agrarians dislocated by the New South industrial economy. Abernethy reclaimed the blood privilege of the Anglo-Saxon American and blamed Jews for every alien, modern import, from Wall Street finance to the Higher Criticism. He wrote in defense of poor rural whites and spoke the country prejudices of the dispossessed. Mary Phagan, the murdered girl in the Frank case, came from such a newly urbanized, millworking family. Frank's opponents passed out cards asking Georgians of "true American blood" to boycott the stores of those whose blood was "streaked." In Faulkner's *Sanctuary* Clarence Snopes, a lowlife Southern white personified, speaks as an "American" against a Memphis lawyer: "The lowest, cheapest thing on earth aint a nigger: it's a jew. We need laws against them. Drastic laws."[48]

Politically, nativist forces in both North and South called for limits on the immigrant franchise. In the urban North the rising number of immigrants presented an electoral threat to Anglo-Saxon political hegemony. Without necessarily singling out Jews among the immigrants, Ripley, Shaler, and Woodruff as well as some New England patricians had spoken of limiting the franchise to save "our government in the future, when our higher types begin to die out," as Woodruff put it.[49] Significant numbers of immigrant voters did not reside in the South, but the South had the political precedent of Jim Crow. Writing in the era of poll taxes, literacy tests, and white primaries, Abernethy argued that after "the Negro is eliminated from the citizenship of the United States . . . the American government will turn its attention to the alien Hebrew." Evangelist Sam Jones, too, wanted "foreign hoards" [*sic*] removed from the ballot. In 1890 former governor of South Carolina Wade Hampton linked Negro franchise with suffrage for "the Anarchist, the Communist, the Nihilist, and all the other scum of the European nations." In 1913 Bryan County, Georgia, eliminated Jews from grand and petit juries.[50]

Eugenics drew a line of hygiene, of "cleanliness," that quarantined Jews socially. Anti-Semitic rhetoric had long characterized Jews as "dirty" —in the 1860s Richmond newspapers complained of a "dirty greasy Jew" and "unkempt Israelites"—but eugenics injected new connotations into these epithets. Immigrant Jews with their supposedly weak constitutions, ghetto filth, and gross sensuality were thought to be a public health menace. A Lithuanian immigrant child in a Southern town recalled how a non-Jewish playmate's mother, fearing contamination, would not let him share a glass with her son. Eugenicists traced social ills to disease, and the Progressive Era was obsessed with campaigns for public health. Not only were Jews allegedly dirty, they were also parasites who finance but do not produce. Eugenicists considered economic parasitism the Jewish racial disease just as they thought the Irishman was susceptible to alcoholism, the Italian to crime, and the African to lust or laziness. Southern agrarians like Tom Watson appropriated this rhetoric against "parasitic" Jews in their defense of the "worthy working poor." Jews were socially segregated.[51]

From at least the early 1800s and continuing into the 1960s, Jews were often distinguished from whites in common speech. This stereotyping prevailed among both blacks and whites regardless of region. In the American vernacular a "white" Jew might denote an honest businessman or a Jewish friend in contrast to a "black" Jew, who was not to be trusted. An R. G. Dun agent's credit report noted of one Indianapolis Jewish merchant: "We should deem him safe but he is not a white man. He is a Jew." When Felix Frankfurter was nominated for the Supreme Court, Senator William Borah of Idaho received a protest letter that whites, not Jews, belonged on the Court.[52] This language also prevailed in the Southern lex-

icon. In 1893 *The Times* of Richmond cited a police report on an alter-
cation between a "white man" and a "Polish Jew." The owner of a Georgia resort explained to his Jewish friend that as a "white Jew" he could
swim in the lake, but other Jews were unwanted. Some white Protestants
in Atlanta spoke of the Russians as "black Jews." "Everyone was black or
white and then there were the Jews," Atlantan Nancy Thal recalled of the
1950s. As late as 1961 Dean John Buhler of the Emory University Dental
College was still asking applicants to indicate whether their "race" was
"Caucasian, Jew, Other." Blacks, too, both North and South, spoke of
Jews and whites. As defense lawyers in the Leo Frank trial pointed to a
black suspect, a black newspaper in Chicago questioned, "Is the Jew a
white man?" Black folklore included a genre of jokes about a "Colored
Man, a Jew, and a White Man."[53]

There were instances in the South where a Jew was taken for a black.
An anthropologist observed that Southerners commonly regarded a Jew
as a mulatto and recalled a New York Jew who complained about his
problems traveling in Southern states. In 1912 in Pine Bluff, Arkansas, a
darkly complexioned Russian Jewish man entered a stylish cafe with a
fair-skinned white woman and was chased from the premises by enraged
whites who took him for a black.[54]

When white Southerners looked at Jews, they saw blacks in close proximity. In a society where consorting with blacks rendered one a social
outcast, Jewish merchants, starting with the Germans, catered to black
trade. When impoverished East Europeans arrived in Southern cities,
they often found homes bordering black neighborhoods. White Southerners saw prominent Northern Jews identify with blacks as a black-Jewish alliance formed in the early twentieth century. Brothers Joel and
Arthur Spingarn served as leaders of the National Association of Colored People, founded in 1910, and Julius Rosenwald built black schools
across the rural South. Communist labor organizers, many of them Jews,
were suspected of radicalizing black workers. And in 1931 New Yorker
Sam Leibowitz provoked an anti-Semitic storm in coming to Alabama to
defend the Scottsboro Boys.[55]

With the African American migration to the North after 1915, Southern black folklife flowed into the national mainstream, often through
Jewish interpreters. Jews, racially less threatening than blacks, became
purveyors of African American culture to whites. When an Al Jolson,
George Jessel, George Burns, Fanny Brice, or Eddie Cantor blackened
up, their racist caricatures marked them as having assimilated into Americans, but they were also confirming one way Americans looked at Jews.

Jolson introduced jazz style into the minstrelsy: "I like to sing the low down blues." In the 1920s Sophie Tucker, the first Red Hot Mama, brought African American blues to white audiences. Black music and literature redefined American culture. Music critics attributed the popularity of jazz not to the African Americans who originated it but to the Jews who became agents of its dissemination. *The Dearborn Independent* headlined, "Jewish Jazz Becomes Our National Music" and dismissed the African American art form as "Yiddish moron music."[56] George Gershwin, Aaron Copland, and Ernst Bloch brought Afro-American themes into the concert-hall, the temple of high culture. Music critic John Tasker Howard characterized jazz as the "Jewish interpretation of the Negro," and high-brow cultural guardians accused Jews of infecting American culture with African primitivism, sensuality, and sexual depravity. Jews numbered among the most prolific writers and performers of coon show songs. Jewish vaudeville companies toured the South, and by 1920 radio brought Tin Pan Alley into living rooms. Abernethy, citing the New York press, castigated popular music and blamed it on the Jew's lack of artistic taste.[57]

In a reversal of roles, an ethnic caricature of black Jewface emerged. Tom Heflin of Alabama spoke sardonically on the House floor of a Yiddish-speaking "Negro" who was arrested in New York by a Yiddish-speaking Irishman and was taken before a Yiddish-speaking judge. In 1909 *The Temple* of Louisville reprinted the satire, "That Jewish Nigger," about a black youth, Chaim Rosenwasser, who explained to his greenhorn Russian relatives "in good Yiddish" that "Russian people get burned coal-black within a few years after landing on account of that fierce American sun." Such parodies, which drew on vaudeville stage types, were intended as spoofs, but they revealed the underlying confusion about race and ethnicity, heredity and environment. In what became a literary museum of Jewish curiosities, the Southern Jewish press printed reports of black Jews in the Sahara and Timbuctoo, of the black Jews of Cochin, of a black African in Hartford fluent in Hebrew, and of Sam Wolskowi, a black Jew in New York from northeastern Egypt. "What the public mainly wants to know," a newspaper asked, "is there really a Jewish negro tribe anywhere on the globe?"[58]

Jews and gentiles, both black and white, commonly drew parallels between the oppression of Russian Jews and Southern blacks. Northern Jews were far more likely than Southern Jews to assert such commonalities. When the *Jewish Exponent* of Philadelphia described the 1898 Wilmington race riot as a pogrom, Herbert Ezekiel of Richmond responded indignantly, "The comparison of Jews and negroes is, we had always thought, a pastime of our Christian neighbors and one which we, of all people, should not countenance." Ezekiel admonished, "There is nothing in common between the two races in this section." When the Northern *Jewish Review* stated that "the negro is what he has been made to be by those who should have raised and educated him, the same has been the case with the Jew," the *Jewish South* rebutted: "The fact of the whole business is that physiology and contemporaneous events are to the effect that negroes are intellectually, morally and physically an inferior race—a fact that none can deny."[59]

Jews were not exclusively regional in their racial thinking anymore than other Americans. Rabbi Max Heller of New Orleans was one Southerner who acknowledged parallels in the Jewish and African American experiences of oppression. He also spoke admiringly of Booker T. Washington. Heller was unable to comprehend why "scholarship or gentlemanliness in the negro . . . does not or can not make him the superior of any white man." Heller's "respect" and "esteem" for an African American like Washington contrast sharply with the illiberal views of Isaac Mayer Wise of Cincinnati. In 1894, when Washington wrote that "the black man, like the Jew or white man" should choose carefully his branch of business, Wise retorted that Washington had committed a "scientific blunder" and needed "a lesson in primary ethnology." "All Jewish Americans are Caucasians," Wise responded and chastised Washington for expressing a "secret malice that invariably marks a servile nature seeking to assume a feeling of equality with something higher, which it does not possess."[60] Wise, who had scolded abolitionists, was sensitive to Southern Jewish feelings.

Jews themselves never achieved any consensus on their racial identity nor even what to call themselves. Judaism's leading lights had pontificated on the meanings of "Jew," "Hebrew," and "Israelite," some echoing assimilationist German Jews by describing themselves as Americans of the Mosaic faith. J. L Ezekiel of Richmond argued that the terms were "synonymous," though he admitted the label "Jew" had "in popular estimation . . . an unsavory odor" in that it designated race. In 1911 the congressional Dillingham Commission on immigration published 41 volumes of documents and testimony on whether the Jew ought to be classified as a separate race. Communal leaders Mayer Sulzberger, Cyrus Adler, Simon Wolf, Simon Guggenheim, and Louis Marshall asserted unequivocally that Jews did not constitute a race. Solomon Schechter and

Lewis Dembitz of Kentucky countered that indeed "the Jews are a race." Professor Morris Jastrow of Philadelphia argued that the Jews could be considered a race for "anthropological and sociological purposes" but not in a "political sense." Leo Levi, B'nai B'rith president, wisely warned that it was hopeless for the State Department to resolve the issue when it posed one of the most "vexing questions of controversy among Jews."[61]

In 1912 Nahum Wolf reflected in the *North American Review*, "Recent anti-Jewish publications abroad are zealously disseminating the idea that the Jews are an inferior race." The turn of the century witnessed a rash of racialist literature in the popular media by anti-Semites like Burton Hendrick, a New England historian, and E. A. Ross, a Wisconsin sociologist. Werner Sombart's *The Jews and Modern Capitalism* and Houston Stewart Chamberlain's *Foundations of the Nineteenth Century,* fundamental works of German anti-Semitism, were published in English translation. Madison Grant's *Passing of the Great Race* (1916) drew the one-drop analogy that "the cross between a white man and a Negro is a Negro . . . The cross between any of the three European races and a Jew is a Jew." The national advocates of psychological testing—Carl Brigham, Robert Yerkes, Lewis Ternan, and H. H. Godard—warned that America had imported 2,000,000 immigrants whose "average intelligence" was nearer that of the African than of the white. They disputed assumptions of Jewish intellectual superiority. The Jews were a "racial medley," claimed eugenicist Lothrop Stoddard in a widely quoted popular magazine article, "The Pedigree of Judah" (1926). Stoddard described a Jewish "Negroid strain" that showed itself in "frizzy or woolly hair, thick lips, and prognathous jaws."[62] This international racialist literature persisted little changed from 1900 into the 1930s.

Southern literature on race drew from that of the North. A national mass-circulation media disseminated racial ideology. In 1900 the *Jewish Chronicle* of Mobile asked, "Is there a Jewish question?" The *Chronicle*'s answer was, "Pick up the newspapers and the magazines . . . Why, one would think from the number of articles appearing in the prints on the Jew that all other subjects have been worn threadbare." Newspapers and popular magazines like *McClure's, Popular Science,* or *Saturday Evening Post* brought eugenic debates down South. In espousing anti-Semitism, provincial Southerners like Abernethy were aspiring to join the cosmopolitan world. Southerners found justification for their antiblack views in Northern antiimmigrant racial rhetoric. Products of Eastern campuses, the South's leading academicians brought cosmopolitan ideologies to provincial campuses. Many of these professors, including Abernethy, had studied at Johns Hopkins, which served as an intellectual bridge between North and South.[63]

"The whole world is interested in the subject of the Jews as a race," the physician and anthropologist Maurice Fishberg observed in 1911. Contemporary writers on racial subjects cited Fishberg, a Russian-born Jewish immigrant, as the foremost scientific authority in America on the Jewish racial question. He collaborated with Franz Boas and Joseph Jacobs and corresponded with Samuel Weissenberg. Studying surveys comparing 150,000 Jewish and non-Jewish European children, Fishberg stated bluntly, "we do not know of any *absolutely pure races.*" After personally measuring 4,200 Jewish noses in New York, he reported the "head form of the Jews agrees closely with that of the non-Jewish races and peoples." In *The Jews: A Study in Race and Environment* (1911), Fishberg identified a Jewish "negroid type." Although East European Jews have "not come in contact with Negroes for centuries," Fishberg observed a Jewish physiognomy characterized by "very dark skin, black and woolly hair, elongated head, prognathous face, muzzled jaws, large thick lips, and broad flat nose."[64]

Sponsored by the United Hebrew Charities of New York, Fishberg worked to divorce anthropology from racial science, undermining the foundations of anti-Semitism. An assimilationist, he stated that the question "of incorporating the Jews into the body politic of Anglo-Saxon communities" motivated his anthropological research. Speaking at a eugenics conference, Fishberg assured "those interested in improving the human breed . . . [that] the flow of Jewish blood into the veins of European and American peoples does not infuse any new racial elements."[65] Yet Abernethy, Woodruff, and Stoddard all cited Fishberg when they argued for the black origins of Jews. The popular media distorted Fishberg by suggesting that his evidence of a Jewish African type characterized the whole Jewish people. The route of dissemination can be traced in an article that appeared in a Jewish newspaper, *The Temple* of Louisville in 1910: "In the popular mind there is a clearly defined Jewish type—black haired, black-eyed, thick-lipped, swarthy-complexioned." Interestingly, *The Temple* article was a reprint from the Newark [N.J.] *Star* which, in turn, summarized a piece in *McClure's. McClure's* cited Maurice Fishberg.[66]

In 1913, Rabbi Max Heller of New Orleans responded at length to "the pseudo-scientific spectre of Antisemitism" in the *Year Book* of the Central Conference of American Rabbis. Heller's "The Place of the Jew in a Racial Interpretation of the History of Civilization" (1913) was the most extensive Southern Jewish statement on race, but it made no specific reference to the South. The article was a detailed rebuttal of the Anglo-German Houston Stewart Chamberlain's *Foundations of the Nineteenth Century*. Heller feared that the importation of European racial ideology was undermining the social acceptance of American Jews. He acknowledged that this "poison science" had wrought "havoc" in the "political, social, economic . . . life of the modern Jew." He attacked the Frenchmen Ernest Renan and Edouard Drumont, but he reserved his artillery for Chamberlain, who had labeled Jews a "bastardized race" with a negroid strain. Heller was distressed that educated Americans were greeting newly published English translations of Chamberlain's work with "much enthusiastic commendation." To refute Chamberlain, Heller drew on Boas and Weissenberg and cited as correctives the Zionists Ignaz Zollschan and Arthur Ruppin. Heller did not think that the Jews could be "scientifically delimited" as a race but instead constituted a "group . . . unified by spiritual heritages, home disciplines, life experiences, and exalted hopes."[67]

Born in Prague and educated at the University of Cincinnati and Hebrew Union College, Heller had a cosmopolitan perspective on race. He saw the race problem in universal terms, as historian Bobbie Malone notes, for reasons of both principle and self-interest. In speaking of social justice for African Americans, Heller championed "the cause of the oppressed and downtrodden of all races and climes" from "unreasoning racial antipathies." Heller linked Negrophobia and anti-Semitism. In 1898, as a Louisiana constitutional convention debated black disfranchisement, Heller delivered a sermon on "Modern Intolerance" which discussed black civil liberties in the context of the Dreyfus Affair. As late as 1909 Heller still found it necessary to refute "stupid" and "inhuman" polygenist arguments that the African lacked a soul or Adamic descent. He argued for the common parentage of white and black races. Living in a segregated society no doubt sharpened Heller's racial consciousness. After the New Orleans race riots of 1900 he abandoned his faith in assimilation and turned Zionist.[68]

Such Jewish defense efforts as Fishberg's and Heller's were part of a larger campaign by social progressives to delegitimize racial science's premises of fixed, pure races. In 1911 the Dillingham Commission published Franz Boas' *Changes in Bodily Form of Descendants of Immigrants*. Boas demonstrated that over several generations the American environment transformed the head shapes of Italians and Jews toward a "uni-

form type." The literature that racially elevated the Jew often continued
to devalue the black. The Commission's *Dictionary of Races or Peoples*—
with some 600 entries—defined the "Hebrew, Jewish, or Israelite" as a
race "of Semitic origin" but today a "mixed race . . . although to a less
degree than most . . . more truly European than Asiatic or Semitic." According to the *Dictionary*, the Bureau of Immigration classified the Hebrews as members of "the Slavic grand division of the Aryan family." The
"Negro," the *Dictionary* reported, was also "mixed" although "belonging
to the lowest division of mankind from an evolutionary standpoint."[69]

Nativism and racial radicalism declined after 1915 but revived in the
early 1920s when a Red scare and a renascent Ku Klux Klan focused their
sights on the alien, radical Jew. Congress passed immigration quota laws
in 1921 and 1924. Henry Ford's *Dearborn Independent* spouted calumny
against the "International Jew." Anglo-Israelites, centered in the Dayton
Theological Seminary, enjoyed popularity in the 1920s and published a
stream of anti-Semitic tracts with titles like "The Modern Canaanites" or
"Jesus Christ Was Not a Jew." Yet by the late 1920s, as prosperity and the
immigrants' rapid assimilation eased social tensions, racial bigotry was
losing its force. Lynching declined. Social progressives and Christian liberals extolled brotherhood, cited the upwardly mobile Jewish immigrants as exemplars of Americanism, and lauded their cultural gifts to
the nation.[70]

In explaining Jewish acceptance in the segregated South, Eli Evans
observes that "Jews were, first of all, white, or at least . . . could pass for
white." Philo-Semitism was never incompatible with Negrophobia. In rebutting anti-Semites, archsegregationist James Denson Sayers wrote in
Can the White Race Survive? (1929): "There are some people who make
themselves ridiculous by comparing" the "highly moral" Jew to the "Negro," whose character was cursed by "savagery."[71]

For anti-Semitic Southerners, their positive experiences with local
Jews created cognitive confusion, and they sought to make racial sense
of their discomfiture. Some non-Jewish Southerners testified to the ex-
ceptionality of the Southern Jew even as they expressed a generalized
anti-Semitism. In small towns especially, non-Jews welcomed Jewish
neighbors but considered outsiders suspect. A Theodore Bilbo could
nastily Jew-bait New Yorkers in Congress while professing brotherly love
for his fellow Southern Jew. In 1936 Kemp Battle, former president of
the North Carolina bar, protested the admission of out-of-state Jewish
students to the University of North Carolina. Battle, grandson of a UNC
president, wrote a letter to then President Frank Graham, who was an

outspoken friend of the Jewish people. The Southern Jew was an "entirely different personality" from the Northern Jew, Battle argued, "and the difference is doubtless racial as well as environmental." He included an unsigned statement from a "liberal" Southern academic explaining that "southern Jews are mostly the Sephardim [*sic*] Jews" from Spain, England, and Germany while Northern Jews come from Russia and Poland. These "racially quite different" Northerners, vulgarly known as "kikes," are "Jews only by religion," Battle explained. Such Jews should be regulated by quotas.[72] Battle revealed a Southerner's predilection to view Jews in the context of segregation and racial hierarchy.

Battle's nonsensical anthropology demonstrated the persistence of anachronistic theories of race science. UNC medical professor W. C. George, a renowned expert on blood, wrote Graham that without "restrictive measures agains[t] the Jews" there would be race war. George, who served as a scientific apologist for white supremacy during the civil rights era, wrote in 1936 that one race is "going to dominate and determine the nature of civilization, and the other will be submissive or it will be exterminated."[73]

In the 1930s Nazi propaganda raised the racial banner here and abroad, and American eugenicists like Stoddard were lauded in Germany. The inflammatory racial rhetoric discomfited Jews in the South no less than in other regions, but Nazi sympathizing was an American rather than a Southern phenomenon. Although William Dudley Pelley, the self-proclaimed American Hitler, established headquarters for his fascist Silver Shirt Legion in Asheville, North Carolina, from 1932 to 1941, he was a New Englander. Hounded by local authorities, he relocated to Indiana. U.S. Senator Robert "Our Bob" Reynolds of North Carolina was an isolationist who revived populist canards about Jewish international conspiracies, but, facing certain defeat for his unpopular views, he declined to seek reelection in 1944. The South, with its army camps and traditions of militarism and patriotism, rallied behind the war effort.[74]

The Nazi link stigmatized the eugenics movement in America. With the horrors of racial classification revealed after the Holocaust, eugenics was greeted with revulsion. The newer sciences of genetics and blood typing demonstrated the absurdity of pure races and discredited race as a scientific term. With the example of Franz Boas before them, cultural anthropologists like Margaret Mead, Robert MacIver, Melville Herskovits, and Ruth Benedict campaigned to educate the public on the fallacies of scientific racism. Natural scientists—Jews like Ashley Montague and Stephen Jay Gould prominent among them—have abandoned the term "race" altogether. Race has become a social and political construct largely promulgated for reasons of self-definition or governmental entitlement.

The idea of Jew as black persisted only among the fringe of fervid segregationists and anti-Communists. Their beliefs, again, did not derive from specifically Southern ideologies but resonated as a civil-rights movement challenged the white-supremacist political order. One tract from Chicago warned that "Semitism and Communism are interchangeable terms and Jews should never be regarded as a white. Their origin is . . . black." In *The Negro's Place in Call of the Race* (1948) William Murray, former governor of Oklahoma, expressed alarm about the visit to Tulsa of an eastern communist journalist whose picture revealed "a Negro face (if you look at his eyes, wide flat nose and thick lips) with a Jew name—Max Lerner." Southerners, Harry Golden observed, "mostly think of a Jew as a substitute Negro."[75]

Archsegregationists characterized Jews as "white niggers" or as pure-bloods who were debilitating the white race by encouraging race mixing. J. B. Stoner and his National States Rights Party (NSRP) of Georgia picked up the Anglo-Israelite theme. In his newspaper *The Thunderbolt* Stoner railed against "Jews and other mongrelizers" and cited the science of Gobineau, Grant, and Stoddard. In Durham the populist weekly *Public Appeal* carried Anglo-Israelite columns from Dayton: "Jesus is against integration. . . . Only a small number of the dark, hooked-nose, kinky haired racially mixed Jews returned to Israel from Babylonian captivity. The most pure Semitic White Race is to be found today in the Anglo-Saxon."[76] John Crommelin of Alabama, NSRP vice-presidential candidate in 1960, quoting Stoddard, thought that "Jews picked up their first traces of Negro blood" in Egypt. Crommelin described such a mixblooded person as a "Jewlatto." These themes survive among some members of the Christian Identity Movement that derives from Anglo-Israelitism. The Aryan Nation's creed states that "the Canaanite Jew is the natural enemy of our Aryan (White) Race." Jews are "children of darkness" while Aryans are "children of light." In *Proof: God's Chosen are White Adamic Christians* (1974), Thomas O'Brien of the New Christian Crusade Church of Metairie, Louisiana, writes that Jews "are the mongrelized descendants of Satan through Cain."[77]

At the other extreme, small numbers of African American Judaizers insist that blacks are true Israel. This movement has roots in Southern black fundamentalism. African American folklore was abundant with images of blacks as children of Israel crossing from slavery to freedom. Starting in the 1890s, black Jewish sectarians emerged in the urban North, and in the 1920s congregations could be found in five cities. Such works as W. L. Hunter's *Jesus Christ Had Negro Blood in His Veins* (1901) and Alonzo P. B. Holly's *God and the Negro* (1937) popularized the black origins of ancient Israelites. More recently, Minister M. Nasi, a member of a sect of 400 black Jews in Israel and America, asserted that slaves brought to America "were truly the Hebrew Israelites." Abernethy's claim that Jews were originally black Egyptians is now repeated by some Afrocentricists like George Stallings of the Imani Temple in Washington or Emmanuel Twesigyue, author of *The African Origin of Humanity, Monotheism, and Civilization* (1991).[78]

Jewish racial identity has never been fixed—in the South or elsewhere—and it has been alloyed invariably with social, economic, and religious elements. Significantly, racial ideology did not necessarily intrude on the Southern Jews' social reality, and Jews generally gained entry where blacks were refused. Whatever racism Southern Jews experienced was rarely more than impolite. Jews suffered from discriminatory social customs, not legal codes. With very few exceptions, Jews did not face the lynch mobs, the political disfranchisement, nor the daily humiliations of legalized segregation of blacks, but they did confront residential restriction, social isolation, and university quotas even though, unlike in the North, their numbers were too small to be consequential. Jews did not pose the same cultural or political challenge in Atlanta or Richmond as they did in Berlin, Vienna, Boston, or New York. Why indeed should Southern Jews have faced any prejudice when the conditions that fomented European racial nationalism or Northern American social discrimination were lacking in the South? At least part of the answer can be found in Southern race consciousness.

The race factor has generally been disparaged in explaining Southern attitudes toward Jews. Leonard Dinnerstein points to "Protestant fundamentalist culture" as the source of Southern anti-Semitism. Steven Hertzberg writes, "There is no indication that the Caucasian standing of southern Jews was ever seriously challenged." John Higham argues that the "traditional American racism" that excluded "dark-skinned people" from "equal social status in white society" did not apply to Jews; the color issue was raised only to identify Jews with whites. Higham stresses American anti-Semitism's "weak ideological sources and its more substantial basis in the new social relationships in the Gilded Age."[79]

Yet race did color Southern attitudes to the Jew. Even if the Jews were not black, their racial difference was still assumed. The disengagement of Jews and white Southerners occurred at the time when Jim Crow was being established and the Jews' racial status as white was questioned. Racial ideology was both cause and effect. Whether white Southerners saw Jews as pure, mixed, or mongrel reflected social, economic, and religious attitudes. Race-science ideologies, repeated in countless articles and propagated by rustic journalism, also influenced popular feelings, adding authority to prejudice. The premises of race science lacked the coherence to coalesce into programmatic anti-Semitism. Nor, by and large, were white Southerners predisposed to institute an anti-Semitic campaign. Southerners were also strongly inclined to see Jews as flesh and blood of Jesus.

Southern anti-Semitism borrowed from the national culture. Southern Jewish fears of anti-Semitism often had less to do with the local situation than with the immigrants' anxious memories of their European Jewish experience. Jews kept their eyes on events abroad and expressed concern that European anti-Semitic fevers would infect America. The Southern Jews' cosmopolitan perspective on their racial identity lends evidence to Mark Bauman's assertion that "Jews in the South were influenced by the regional subculture in a relatively marginal fashion."[80] The Southern factor was the Jim Crow context. Violence threatened those who crossed black/white lines. The Southerners' romantic religiosity and racialism heightened Jewish racial consciousness. In contrast to their Northern coreligionists, Southern Jews were more likely to voice race pride, to assert the purity of Jewish blood, and to reject parallels between blacks and themselves. These defense efforts were not exclusively regional, however, and Southern Jews identified themselves in racial terms common among Jews elsewhere.

The idea of the Jew as other-than-white flowed underground through much of the nineteenth century, surfaced in the late nineteenth and early twentieth centuries, and then submerged again. In the Southern marketplace of ideas it was a product that ultimately failed to sell. *The Negro a Beast* was a best seller, *The Jew a Negro* sold poorly, but the conclusion of the syllogism, *The Jew a Beast*, never made it to market. No mainstream voice asks anymore, "Is the Jew white?"

As Jews assimilated they ceased to be a marginal people. Jews were recognized as racially indistinguishable from non-Jewish whites and gained acceptance on campuses, in corporations, and—excepting some vestiges of elite social anti-Semitism—at resorts and country clubs. If race matters, then the extinction of the idea of the Jew as racially different may be a factor in explaining the breakdown of Jewish-African American relations. Jews drew closer to blacks at a time when their own color was called into question and have parted as they have assimilated into the larger white society. Despite their own sense of difference, Jews are by now firmly and indelibly on the white side of the color line.

Notes

1. Arthur T. Abernethy, *The Jew a Negro, Being a Study of the Jewish Ancestry from an Impartial Standpoint* (Moravian Falls, N.C., 1910), 11. I wish to thank Cyma M. Horowitz, library director of the American Jewish Committee, and Kevin Proffitt of the American Jewish Archives for their assistance.

2. Sander Gilman, *Freud, Race, and Gender* (Princeton, N.J., 1993), 20; Sander Gilman, *The Jew's Body* (New York, 1991), 172, 174; Geoffrey Wigoder, *Dictionary of Jewish Biography* (New York, 1991), 560; Stephen Vincent Benét, *John Brown's Body* (New York, 1968), 66.

3. John Efron, *Defenders of the Faith: Jewish Doctors and Race Science in Fin-de-Siècle Europe* (New Haven, Conn., 1994), 41–45.

4. Efron, *Defenders of the Race*, 37.

5. Thomas Jefferson, *Notes on the State of Virginia*, in *The Portable Thomas Jefferson*, ed. Merrill D. Peterson (New York, 1984), 192–93.

6. Robert Young, *The Negro: A Reply to Ariel* (Nashville, 1867), 38; reprinted in John David Smith, *Anti-Black Thought: 1863–1925, The "Ariel" Controversy*, Volume V (New York, 1993).

7. A Minister (anon.), *Nachash: What Is It? or An Answer to the Question, "Who and What Is the Negro?"* (Augusta, Ga., 1868); reprinted in John David Smith, *Anti-Black Thought: 1863–1925, The Biblical and "Scientific" Defense of Slavery*, Volume VI (New York, 1993). See also Charles Carroll, *The Negro a Beast* (New York, 1980).

8. Reginald Horsman, *Race and Manifest Destiny: The Origins of American Racial Anglo-Saxonism* (Cambridge, Mass., 1981), 1; John Efron, *Defenders of the Race*, 50–51. Racially deterministic views contrast with the American liberal tradition of Emerson, Whitman, and Holmes, who celebrated Americans as the "great assimilating people."

9. William Stanton, *The Leopard's Spots: Scientific Attitudes toward Race in America, 1815–1859* (Chicago, 1960), 174; Arthur de Gobineau, *The Inequality of Human Races,* trans. Adrian Collins (New York, 1915), 122; Michael Biddiss, *Father of Racist Ideology: The Social and Political Thought of Count Gobineau* (New York, 1970), 124–25.

10. Josiah C. Nott, *Two Lectures on the Black Race,* 7; John S. Haller Jr., *Outcasts from Evolution: Scientific Attitudes of Racial Inferiority, 1859–1900* (Urbana, Ill., 1971), 81; Josiah C. Nott and George R. Gliddon, *Types of Mankind* (Philadelphia, 1857), 454.

11. Nott and Gliddon, *Types of Mankind,* 111, 115, 116, 121–22; Efron, *Defenders of the Race,* 55.

12. Nott and Gliddon, *Types of Mankind,* 120–22.

13. See Reginald Horsman, *Josiah Nott of Mobile: Southerner, Physician, and Racial Theorist* (Baton Rouge, 1987), 113–88, 199–200.

14. John C. Calhoun, *The Papers of John C. Calhoun* (Columbia, S.C., 1983), 22: 9; Bertram Korn, *American Jewry and the Civil War* (Philadelphia, 1951), 179; See Jonathan Sarna, "The 'Mythical Jew' and the 'Jew Next Door,'" in *Anti-Semitism in American History,* ed. David Gerber (Urbana, Ill., 1986), 57–78. The case of Jacob Henry demonstrated the complexity of Southern attitudes. Although as a Jew he was constitutionally disqualified from public office, he was allowed to take a seat in the North Carolina state legislature in 1809.

15. Efron, *Defenders of the Race,* 11; Young, *The Negro: A Reply to Ariel,* 41, 43, 47.

16. Horsman, *Josiah Nott,* 179; Stanton, *The Leopard's Spots,* 52, 62, 85, 122.

17. Joel Williamson, *New People: Miscegenation and Mulattoes in the United States* (New York, 1980), 2, 87, 92.

18. Ariel [Buckner H. Payne], *The Negro: What Is His Ethnological Status?* (Cincinnati, 1867), 9; reprinted in John David Smith, *Anti-Black Thought: 1863–1925,* Volume V; Sister Sallie, *The Color Line* (n.p., 1875), 9; reprinted in John David Smith, *Anti-Black Thought: 1863–1925, Volume VI.* See also John David Smith, introduction to *Anti-Black Thought* for a discussion of the Ariel controversy.

19. Zebulon Vance, *The Scattered Nation* (New York, 1904), 12, 28, 34, 36, 41.

20. Leonard Dinnerstein, *Antisemitism in America* (New York, 1994), 177–78; *Tobacco Plant,* 11 December 1888; *Jewish South,* 19 January 1894; *Jewish Chronicle,* 8 February 1901.

21. *Jewish South,* 15 November 1879; see George Fredrickson, *The Black Image in the White Mind: The Debate on Afro-American Character and Destiny, 1817–1914* (New York, 1978); *The Temple,* 26 August 1910; *Jewish South,* 13 April 1894.

22. Horsman, *Race and Manifest Destiny,* 70; Vance, *The Scattered Nation,* 27–28; Josiah C. Nott, *The Negro Race: Its Ethnology and History* (Mobile, 1866), 16.

23. Efron, *Defenders of the Race,* 81; Raphael Patai and Jennifer Patai Wing, *The Myth of the Jewish Race* (Detroit, 1975), 146.

24. See Efron, *Defenders of the Race,* 13–57; Michael Barkun, *Religion and the Racist Right* (Chapel Hill, 1994), 7, 126.

25. Gilman, *The Jew's Body*, 171, 175; Efron, *Defenders of the Race*, 50–52; Gilman, *Freud, Race, and Gender*, 19.

26. Patai and Wing, *Myth*, 36–37; Robert Singerman, "The Jew as Racial Alien: The Genetic Component of American Anti-Semitism," in Gerber, *Anti-Semitism in American History*, 110.

27. *Jewish Chronicle*, 22 October 1909.

28. J. G. Wilson, "The Crossing of the Races," *The Popular Science Monthly* 79, 29 (November, 1911), 486, 495; Singerman, "The Jew as Racial Alien," 106, 111.

29. *Jewish South*, 31 July 1896; Joseph Jacobs, "Anthropology," *Jewish Encyclopedia* (New York, 1901), 619.

30. *The Temple* 29 April 1910; 17 June 1910; 16 September 1910; *Jewish Chronicle*, 9 February 1900, 23 August 1901; *Jewish South*, 3 May 1895.

31. Williamson, *New People*, 6.

32. Williamson, *New People*, 98, 108.

33. *Bridges and Boundaries: African Americans and American Jews*, ed. Jack Salzman (New York, 1992), 172.

34. *The Jewish South*, 1 August 1879, 9 April 1897; Steven Hertzberg, *Strangers within the Gate City: The Jews of Atlanta, 1845–1915* (Philadelphia, 1978), 170, 180.

35. *The Jewish South*, 1 August 1879, 9 April 1897; Hertzberg, *Strangers within the Gate City*, 170–71, 180; *Jewish Chronicle*, 30 August 1901.

36. Mark Twain, "Concerning the Jews," in *Collected Tales, Sketches, Speeches & Essays, 1891–1910* (New York, 1995), 368; Thomas Pearce Bailey, *Race Orthodoxy in the South and Other Aspects of the Negro Question* (New York, 1914), 324.

37. *Jewish South*, 3 November 1893, 9 March 1894; *The Temple*, 31 December 1909.

38. John Higham, *Strangers in the Land: Patterns of American Nativism, 1860–1925* (New Brunswick, N.J., 1988), 164–66, 168; Randall Miller, "Ethnic Life," in *Encyclopedia of Southern Culture*, eds. Charles Wilson and William Ferris (Chapel Hill, 1989), 417. The anti-Italian and anti-Catholic drum was beaten even louder than the anti-Semitic one. The lone lynching of a single Jew contrasts with some 20 Italians murdered by mob violence. Italians were widely suspected of having black blood.

39. Nathaniel S. Shaler, *The Neighbor: The Natural History of Human Contacts* (Boston, 1904), 166, 327.

40. *Watson's Magazine*, 20, 3 (January 1915), 143; 20, 5 (March 1915), 257; 20, 3 (January 1915), 140; Arnold Shankman, *Ambivalent Friends: Afro-Americans View the Immigrant* (Westport, Conn., 1982), 129.

41. E. J. Ayers, *The Promise of the New South* (New York, 1992), 140; Mark Haller, *Eugenics: Hereditarian Attitudes in American Thought* (New Brunswick, N.J.,

1963), 156; *The Temple*, 4 March 1910; Harry Golden, "Jew and Gentile in the New South: Segregation at Sundown," *Commentary* 20 (November 1955), 403.

42. Charles Carroll, *The Negro a Beast*, 106; Charles Carroll, *The Tempter of Eve* (St. Louis, 1902), 493; Robert Weisbord and Arthur Stein, *Bittersweet Encounter: The Afro-American and the American Jew* (Westport, Conn., 1970), xi.

43. "An Evangelist Who Comes Free" (n.p., n.d.), pamphlet in North Carolina Collection.

44. Joel Williamson, *A Rage for Order: Black/White Relations in the American South since Emancipation* (New York, 1986), 197; Michael Barkun, *Religion and the Right*, 7; Edward Larson, *Sex, Race, and Science: Eugenics in the Deep South* (Baltimore, 1995), 5, 13; Abernethy, *The Jew a Negro*, 94.

45. Williamson, *New People*, 1; *Jewish South*, 10 June 1898; Abernethy, *The Jew a Negro*, 105.

46. Abernethy, *The Jew a Negro*, 13–14; Charles Woodruff, *Expansion of Races* (New York, 1909), 325, 333, 379–81; W. Z. Ripley, *The Races of Europe* (New York, 1899), 390.

47. Charles Davenport, "The Eugenics Programme and Progress in America," in *Eugenics: Twelve University Lectures*, ed. Lewellys Barker (New York, 1914), 5.

48. Hertzberg, *Strangers within the Gate City*, 203, 213; William Faulkner, *Sanctuary* (New York, 1931), 211.

49. Charles Woodruff, *The Effects of Tropical Light on White Men* (New York, 1905), 312.

50. Arthur Abernethy, *The Jew a Negro*, 107; Kathleen Minnix, *Laughter in the Amen Corner: The Life of Evangelist Sam Jones* (Athens, Ga., 1993), 193; Thomas Curran, *Xenophobia and Immigration* (Boston, 1975), 117; Arnold Shankman, *Ambivalent Friends*, 129–30.

51. Howard Sachar, *A History of the Jews in America* (New York, 1992), 75; Henry Bane interview with Leonard Rogoff, 18 November 1986. Quoted in Leonard Rogoff, *Homelands: Southern Jewish Identity in Durham and Chapel Hill, North Carolina* (Tuscaloosa, 2001).

52. Leonard Dinnerstein, *Antisemitism in America*, 20.

53. Melissa Greene, *The Temple Bombing* (Reading, Ma., 1996), 127, 114; *Jewish South*, 9 September 1893, 1 July 1898; *Chicago Defender*, 2 January 1915; Dinnerstein, *Antisemitism in America*, 202.

54. Maurice Fishberg, *The Jews: A Study in Race and Environment* (New York, 1911), 120; Shankman, *Ambivalent Friends*, 145–46.

55. See Dan Carter, *Scottsboro: A Tragedy of the American South* (Baton Rouge, 1979).

56. Albert Lee, *Henry Ford and the Jews* (New York, 1980), 29; John Joyce, Bill

Malone, and Bruce Raeburn, "Sons of David and Stars of Jazz," Panel discussion at the Southern Jewish Historical Society's annual conference, New Orleans, La., 28 October 1995.

57. Melissa Greene, *The Temple Bombing*, 38; Macdonald Smith Moore, *Yankee Blues: Musical Culture and American Identity* (Bloomington, Ind., 1985), 143, 160; Abernethy, *The Jew a Negro*, 80.

58. Edward Larson, *Sex, Race, and Science*, 103; *The Temple*, 1 October 1909; *Jewish South*, 5 November 1897, 6 September 1895, 15 October 1897, and 14 October 1898.

59. *Jewish South*, 24 November 1898.

60. Bobbie Malone, "Rabbi Max Heller and the 'Negro Question,' New Orleans, 1891–1911," in *The Quiet Voices: Southern Rabbis and Black Civil Rights*, eds. Mark Bauman and Berkley Kalin (Tuscaloosa, Ala., forthcoming); *The Booker T. Washington Papers*, 1889–95, ed. Louis Harlan (Urbana, Ill., 1974), 409; *American Israelite*, 26 July 1894.

61. *Jewish South*, 8 November 1895; The Immigration Commission, *Statements and Recommendations by Societies*, 288, 292.

62. Nahum Wolf, "Are the Jews an Inferior Race?" *North American Review* 195 (April 1912), 492; Madison Grant, *The Passing of the Great Race* (New York, 1921), 16, 18; Leo Kamin, *The Science and Politics of IQ* (Potomac, Md., 1974), 25; Lothrop Stoddard, "The Pedigree of Judah," *The Forum*, 75, 3 (March 1926), 326.

63. *Jewish Chronicle*, 16 February 1900; Ayers, *The Promise of the New South*, 422–23.

64. Maurice Fishberg, "Materials for the Physical Anthropology of the East European Jews," *Memoirs of the American Anthropological Association* (Lancaster, Pa., 1905–1907), 6, 84; Maurice Fishberg, The Jews, 120.

65. Singerman, "The Jew as Racial Alien," 111.

66. *Jewish Chronicle*, 16 February 1900; *The Temple*, 16 September 1910; Fishberg, *Memoirs*, v, 5.

67. Max Heller, "The Place of the Jew in a Racial Interpretation of the History of Civilization," *Year Book of the Central Conferences of American Rabbis*, 23, (1913), 305, 311, 315, 338.

68. Quoted in Bobbie Malone, *Rabbi Max Heller: Reformer, Zionist, Southerner, 1860–1926* (Tuscaloosa, 1997).

69. Franz Boas, "Changes in Bodily Form of Descendants of Immigrants," *Reports of the Immigration Commission*, 61st Cong., 2nd sess., 1911, Sen. Doc. 208, 5; *Dictionary of the Races or Peoples: Reports of the Immigration Commission* (Washington, D.C., 1911), 73, 100.

70. Tom McIver, "The Protocols of Creationism: Racism, Anti-Semitism, and

White Supremacy in Christian Fundamentalism," *Skeptic* 2, 4 (1994), 81; I. A. Newby, *Jim Crow's Defense: Anti-Negro Thought in America, 1900–1930* (Baton Rouge, 1965), 2.

71. Eli Evans, *The Provincials: A Personal History of Jews in the South* (New York, 1976), 40; James Denson Sayers, *Can the White Race Survive?* (Washington, D.C., 1929). Sayers was responding to Ernest Sevier Cox who in *White America* (Richmond, Va., 1923) warned against Northern Europeans breeding with Southern and Eastern Europeans.

72. Letter from Kemp Battle to Frank P. Graham, 17 November 1936, Southern Historical Collection. In 1936 15 percent of the freshman class at Chapel Hill was Jewish.

73. Letter from W. C. George to Frank Graham, 30 September 1936, Southern Historical Collection.

74. H. G. Jones, "Pelley, William," *Dictionary of North Carolina Biography*, ed. William S. Powell (Chapel Hill, 1991), 5:60–61; Julian Pleasants, "The Senatorial Career of Robert Rice Reynolds, 1933–1945" (Ph.D. diss., University of North Carolina, 1971), 465–66, 496–97.

75. William Murray, *The Negro's Place in Call of Race* (Tishomingo, Okla., 1948), 35; William Hamilton, *Salute the Jew* (Chicago, 1935), 7; Eli Evans, "Harry Golden," *Encyclopedia of Southern Culture*, 957.

76. *The Public Appeal*, 27 May 1955; James Graham Cook, *The Segregationists* (New York, 1962), 162–63.

77. James Graham Cook, *The Segregationists* (New York, 1962), 162–63; McIver, 84.

78. Morris Lounds, *Israel's Black Hebrews: Black Americans in Search of Identity* (Washington, D.C., 1981), 19, 38; W. L. Hunter, *Jesus Christ Had Negro Blood in His Veins* (Brooklyn, 1901); Alonzo Potter Burgess Holly, *God and the Negro* (Nashville, 1937); Emmanuel Twesigye, *The African Origin of Humanity, Monotheism and Civilization* (New York, 1991).

79. Dinnerstein, *Antisemitism in America*, 197; Hertzberg, *Strangers within the Gate City*, 196; John Higham, *Send These to Me: Immigrants in Urban America* (Baltimore, 1984), x, 149.

80. Mark Bauman, *The Southerner as American: Jewish Style* (Cincinnati, 1996), 5.

15
The Braided Identity of Southern Jewry

Stephen J. Whitfield

Connoisseurs of the complications of ethnicity can find much to meditate upon in the experience of Southern Jewry. From the early national period, throughout the nineteenth century and to some extent thereafter, the small town exerted a decisive influence in Southern Jewish life; urban life and the cosmopolitanism that can be fostered there, if anywhere, have been rare—and recent—in Southern history. The predominance of the village has imposed huge if not insuperable difficulties in sustaining the dynamics of Yiddishkeit, not only because of the religious requirements of the *minyan* but also because such towns, especially in the South, have not exactly defined themselves as havens for nonconformists. Children of religious dissidents growing up there have amply felt the pressures placed upon them to comply with the mores of a rather homogeneous white majority.

Though over 1,200,000 Jews now live in the eleven states of the former Confederacy, the region has been—at least historically—generally impervious to Jewish life; and the consequences of this demographic limitation are what this paper is designed to explore. Despite the hemorrhaging of population from the Northeast to the Sunbelt, which has given Florida a larger Jewish population than France, the proportion of Jews in most of the former Confederacy remains a fraction of one per cent. More are still packed into one borough—Brooklyn—than live in ten Southern states combined. For what has eluded Southern Jewry is the urban density that has enabled Jewish life to flourish in New York, in Chicago, in Philadelphia, in Boston, perhaps even in Los Angeles and San Francisco. Unlike the fertile crescent that begins in Boston and stretches down to Washington, D.C., where the creativity and influence of Jews have been so conspicuous, the matrix of Jewish culture even in New Orleans and Richmond and Atlanta has generally been too thin to replenish itself, and the pressures from the general environment have been too corrosive.

Southern Jews have been more vulnerable than co-religionists in, say, the Northeast to the impact of their neighbors; and it is virtually tautological to infer that assimilation will be accelerated where weak counter-influences radiate from Judaism and Jewishness itself. Such conditions encouraged frequent gestures to conciliation and special sensitivity to the opinions of the Gentiles, who were numerically and politically so powerful. That had its effect upon the values and attitudes of Southern Jews. Demographic vulnerability also stimulated a high number of Southern Jews to consecrate their lives to full acceptance within the region; they were not numerous enough to dare to consider transforming that overwhelmingly Protestant but biracial community. The very distinctiveness of Dixie, its singularity in comparison to the rest of America, also meant the accentuation of certain differences with Yiddishkeit elsewhere.[1] The repercussions can be traced in relations with Gentiles, in politics, in religion and in culture. For maturation within the region tended to produce a braided identity, in which the primordial heritage of both the Jews and other Southerners was inextricably intertwined.

The historical rarity of Southern Jews has meant that anti-semitism, for instance, has sometimes been a product of ignorance, a function of the abstractness that could be projected against the unseen, without necessarily directing any antagonism against "the Jew next door."[2] When the Jew has in fact turned up in the vicinity, neighbors may be nonplussed. Several years ago the author met a woman in Youngstown, Ohio, whose husband's company had transferred them to a hamlet in Arkansas, where they had been invited to a neighbor's home for dinner. But when they arrived at the door, the hostess, not knowing how to properly address a non-Christian, asked: "Do you prefer to be called Hebrew or Jewess?" The husband immediately solved the delicate dilemma by saying, "Just call her Barbara." And social relations went smoothly thereafter.

Personal testimony is the best evidence of the tenuousness of Jewish life in the South. The early chapters of the autobiography of Morris B. Abram (b. 1918) are invaluable for conveying the ambience of small-town Jewry. Growing up in Fitzgerald, Georgia, Abram "resented my Roumanian father's humble circumstances, lack of education, and unmistakably foreign ways. I hated, then, his heavily accented . . . speech.

. . . I felt more comfortable with my mother—particularly with Gentiles present—and even emulated her prideful disdain of East European Jews, a form of snobbery I would later deplore. . . . She regarded Judaism as a religion [which] . . . blurred the outward distinctions between Jews and Gentiles." Though he never became bar mitzvah and did not travel the ninety miles to Albany to a synagogue, the studious and puny Abram "was wholly at odds with the life around me." The public school "began with prayer, featured New Testament scriptures, including . . . the most offensive tirades against the Jews in the Book of John." No wonder then that "the Baptist sensibility that surrounded me" affected the future president of both the American Jewish Committee and of Brandeis University "as tellingly as Jewish characteristics from my family."[3]

Diane Ravitch (*née* Silvers), was born in Houston in 1938. Her father had been born in Savannah, himself the son of a former Confederate Army drummer boy. Her mother, born in Bessarabia, got to Houston at the age of 10, where both Diane Ravitch's parents operated a liquor store for their entire lives. She remembers Jewish country clubs, Jewish secret fraternities and sororities, and friendship circles dependent on the synagogue to which one's family belonged. A reader and something of a loner, she fell under the influence of the only learned person she knew in Houston, the Reform rabbi Hyman Judah Schachtel, a noted anti-Zionist. Diane Ravitch remembered that "the Houston Jews I knew tried extra hard to show that they were as patriotic as non-Jews. I recall a strong sense that it was gauche to seem *too* Jewish. . . . My parents did not want us to learn Yiddish; it was the language of the Old World and of a rejected past."[4]

Now one of the nation's leading scholars of education, she had her own "Jewish education . . . limited to Sunday school in our Reform temple. We learned a smattering of Jewish history. I was so poorly educated as a Jew that I didn't know how poorly educated I was. At [Wellesley] college, I came across an article by Milton Himmelfarb in *Commentary* . . . [that] had to do with certain Jewish traditions like love of learning and social activism. I thought to myself, 'So *these* are Jewish traditions.' *I didn't know that.* The Jews I knew and grew up with didn't seem to be distinguished from non-Jews in either. There was no evidence of intellectual drive among the people I went to school with." She added that most were engaged in "succeeding, assimilating, being very low-key on Jewish issues in order not to antagonize non-Jews, and becoming just as Texan as other Texans. Our parents dinned into us the importance of being Jewish but never communicated why. The reasons seemed to be largely negative."[5] It is not necessary to exaggerate or to romanticize the depth of Judaic learning in homes elsewhere in the United States to detect here a distinctive Southern accent, a representative childhood.

Janice Rothschild Blumberg (b. 1924) remembers her own Reform background in Georgia as rather typical: "We . . . had been brought up to believe that assimilation was highly desirable, that ritual was an anachronism to be avoided as far as possible, that Zionism implied dual loyalty, and that even a passing acquaintance with Hebrew branded one as slightly déclassé." After marriage to the rabbi of The Temple (Hebrew Benevolent Congregation) in Atlanta, she dreaded parties in December, when Jews would confront her husband's opposition to the Jewish celebration of Christmas: "All of us had enjoyed Christmas trees in our homes when we were children and never seen the slightest bit of guilt on the part of our parents or grandparents who provided them."[6] Two final examples of the convergence of the Judeo-Christian tradition can be cited. An employee of the Jewish Federation of Greater New Orleans, Florence Ann Midlo, grew up in Lufkin, Texas, where her Polish-born grandfather had become a bank director. "We celebrated all the holidays, both Jewish and Christian," she has recalled. "For Passover we'd clear the flour from the house. The next week we'd dye Easter eggs." Jeanne Weill, a journalist who grew up in Lafayette, Louisiana, enjoyed one seder that culminated with jambalaya, the spicy dish that contains forbidden delicacies like shrimp, sausage and ham.[7]

Mixed signals and tiny numbers were bound to have consequences for the perpetuation of a sense of peoplehood. Consider the implications for endogamy. "A Hebrew never marries outside his own race," proclaims the drunken and embittered film director in Mordecai Richler's novel, set in Canada, *The Apprenticeship of Duddy Kravitz* (1959).[8] This generalization was certainly never true, but was perhaps especially false in the South.[9] Though accurate statistics on Southern rates of intermarriage are not available, the case of the Sheftall family may be taken as symptomatic. Benjamin Sheftall and his wife Perla arrived in Savannah in 1733 and were pivotal in establishing a Jewish community there, including the third oldest synagogue in America, Mickve Israel. "The first three generations of Savannah Sheftalls were united by their dedication to Judaism and their physical proximity. However, in the fourth and fifth generations this important unity began to crumble," according to a Gentile descendant who has summarized the fate of his family. "Today Benjamin Sheftall's family numbers about one thousand and covers the United States. Only a few family members are practicing Jews."[10]

Such evaporation of religious loyalty was true of many other colonial
families, not only in the South, and elsewhere in the region the tempo
of assimilation was about as rapid. In New Orleans the first president of
congregation Shaarei Chesed (Gates of Mercy), founded in 1828, was
married to a Catholic, and in a sermon to the congregation reportedly
condemned fasting on Yom Kippur as "damned nonsense." Shaarei
Chesed also broke with Jewish law by permitting the non-Jewish spouses
of its members to be buried in its cemetery.[11] In some Southern communities today, the accelerated pace of exogamy is so great that more
Jews appear to be marrying Gentiles than other Jews.

Probably none of the features of Jewish life in the South has been
unique, unknown elsewhere in the United States or, for that matter, in
the Diaspora; and assimilation is at least as ancient as the worship of the
Golden Calf. But the expression of Jewish identity was distinctive below
the Mason-Dixon line. Acculturation may or may not have proceeded
more quickly there than other sparsely settled regions like, say, the West;
but it did assume a discernably different form.

In illuminating the character of Southern Judaism, the unpreten-
tiousness of a recent memoir by the widow of Rabbi Jacob Rothschild
should not conceal its importance. The rabbi, who was from Pittsburgh,
did much to conform outwardly to the mores and values of the community in which he had settled, even to the point of looking forward to the
opening prayer he delivered at a Georgia Tech football game. He even
took up horseback riding, as did his Orthodox colleague Emanuel Feldman, who came to Atlanta in 1952. Such equestrian enthusiasm aston-
ished one lay leader, whom Feldman then asked: "You think only Reform
rabbis can ride horseback?" To which the lay leader slowly replied: "No.
But when a Reform rabbi falls off a horse, the people ask: 'Did he get
hurt?' When an Orthodox rabbi falls off a horse, the people ask: 'What
was he doing on a horse?'"[12] In a region that has placed such a high premium on piety as well as on athletic prowess, no conflicts between such
values were supposed to erupt. Hence the uniqueness of the choice that
faced Al Rosen of Spartanburg, South Carolina, and of Miami in 1953.
The third baseman refused to play for the Cleveland Indians during the
High Holy Days, even though such self-denial may have cost Rosen the
American League batting championship.[13]

This braided identity has taken some peculiar twists. Hard as it may be
for occupants of Southern pulpits to believe, Southern Jews (except in
Florida) are somewhat more likely to attend synagogue than Jews outside the region, by a margin comparable to the difference in regular

church attendance between white Protestants in the South and those elsewhere. Here then is a paradox that Professor John Shelton Reed has noticed: "By being more Southern—that is, by participating in organized religious activities—Southern Jews are at the same time more Jewish."[14]

But however subtly Southern culture may have reinforced religious worship, its contours did not necessarily have positive effects upon the Jews who lived in the region that H. L. Mencken dismissed as "the Sahara of the Bozart." The Southern legacy includes considerable illiteracy and ill will toward intellectuality. While studying at Oxford, Willie Morris of Yazoo City, Mississippi met Robert Frost, who asked the young Rhodes Scholar where he was from. Morris's answer prompted the junketeering poet to mutter: "Hell, that's the worst state in the Union." Morris rebutted that Mississippi had produced some superb writers, to which Frost responded: "Can't anybody down there read them."[15] Even if such disdain can be discounted as a *jeu d'esprit,* the South has nevertheless struggled with a heritage that has not exalted what can be termed high culture. Among the greatest of American writers to emerge from Mississippi, and certainly the most important black writer to come from the Deep South, was Richard Wright. While living in Memphis, he contrived to get library books by pleading with a white co-worker to let him borrow his library card, and then forged the white man's name beneath a note that beseeched the white librarian: "Dear Madam, Will you please let this nigger boy have some books by H. L. Mencken?" Wright, who was then eighteen years old, later recalled standing "a respectful distance from the desk, looked as unbookish as possible, and waited for the white patrons to be taken care of." Before his request was fulfilled, the librarian asked him: "You're not using these books, are you?" To which Wright replied reassuringly, "Oh, no, ma'am, I can't read."[16]

The opportunities available to Jews growing up in New York constitute an extraordinary contrast. Alfred Kazin and his sister Pearl K. Bell, both of whom grew up to become prominent literary critics, forged *several* library cards—to "be sure of enough reading."[17] They personified a people whose God intended them to live by the Book. It is also widely acknowledged that theatrical audiences are very disproportionately Jewish, so much so that Broadway performances have been cancelled on Kol Nidre. Clive Barnes, the drama critic for the New York *Post,* has remarked that, if no Jews lived in New York, Broadway would have to shut down; *every* night would be Yom Kippur.[18]

But compare that avidity to the fate of what is probably the most important play written since the Second World War, Samuel Beckett's *En attendant Godot*. By a set of bizarre circumstances whose recounting need not hold us up, its American premiere was scheduled for Coral Gables. It was directed by the Russian-born Alan Schneider and starred the undoubtedly bemused comedy team of Tom Ewell and Bert Lahr. The marquee of the Coconut Grove Playhouse billed the future Nobel laureate's unbearably bleak vision of the emptiness and estrangement of human existence as "the laugh sensation of two continents." Although south Florida has been home to writers as distinguished as Tennessee Williams, who applauded loudly at the curtain, and Ernest Hemingway, most of the audience scarcely appreciated *Waiting for Godot.* "By the intermission," the director recalled, "at least a third of the house had left. Another third didn't come back afterward; they were too busy drowning their resentment in the theater bar, where the dialogue was more familiar." Schneider mordantly concluded: "We should never have gone to Miami."[19] In defense of the Coconut Grove audience, however, it should be added that Beckett's play did not do significantly better on Broadway; and Parisian audiences were considerably less gracious to Stravinsky's avant-garde *Rite of Spring* when it opened in 1913. But Miami's citizenry nevertheless botched a unique opportunity to welcome one of the masterpieces of modern drama.

Even though too few Jews have lived in the South to contribute much formally and directly to its culture, and others—like Lillian Hellman—moved north, Jews from outside the region were not unimportant in affecting it. Let two examples suffice to be suggestive, even though it is a slice of Jewish folk wisdom—as well as good social science—that "'for instance' is not proof."

While browsing in the Chicago Public Library, Richard Wright stumbled across Gertrude Stein's *Three Lives* (1909). In the section devoted to "Melanctha," Stein attempted to capture the experience of a simple black woman, even though the author, the granddaughter of German Jewish immigrants, was herself born in Allegheny, Pennsylvania, raised in Oakland, California and educated at Radcliffe and at the Johns Hopkins Medical School. Wright later recalled the effect of Stein's literary feat: "As I read it my ears were opened for the first time to the magic of the spoken word. I began to hear the speech of my [Mississippi] grandmother, who spoke a deep, pure Negro dialect and with whom I had lived for many years. All of my life I had been only half hearing, but Miss Stein's struggling words made the speech of the people around me vivid. From that moment on, in my attempts at writing, I was able to tap at will the vast pool of living words that swirled around me."[20]

Consider also the Jewish influences present at the creation of possibly the single most famous entertainer in history, though by itself the music of Elvis Presley was not strong enough to do without a singular look as well. For his clothes the high school kid from Tupelo, Mississippi, went to the black section of Memphis, to Lansky Brothers' store on Beale Street, an establishment that black pimps patronized. Bernie Lansky's standard greeting ("Hey, man, what you need today?") led to the selection of the once and future king's outlandish pants, belt and shirt, just as in Augustus Baldwin Longstreet's nineteenth-century yarns of the early "Southwest," Sut Lovingood is described as "a queer looking . . . funny sort of genius, fresh from some bench-legged Jew's clothing store."[21] In 1951 Presley selected a hair-style that he himself called "the Tony Curtis Cut," named for the former Bernard Schwartz of the Bronx, whose second screen appearance was in *City Across the River* (1949), a movie based on a novel about a Brooklyn Jewish youth gang, *The Amboy Dukes*. Presley's "act of self-creation," one of his biographers argues, "marks the true beginning of . . . [his] career as a pop culture hero. Though he [was] still years away from rock music and the Sun Studio, he [was] already very close to the classic Presley image. The image precedes the talent, as it was destined to outlive the talent, becoming an imperishable pop eidolon."[22]

Jews might tincture the values and lives of other Southerners; but they lacked the numbers or the will to form a vigorous, cohesive and self-sustaining subculture of their own. They were therefore especially susceptible to the regional pride and mores that, beginning in the nineteenth century, were so pervasive and intense. For example, the sculptor Moses Jacob Ezekiel was born in Richmond in 1844; and though he did not attempt to conceal his origins, he was raised in a home devoid of religious observance. Though Ezekiel was anti-slavery (like General Robert E. Lee himself), he volunteered to fight for the Confederacy, and in 1914 completed the monument to it located at Arlington National Cemetery.[23] There is a logic, not just within American history but within Jewish history as well, to Emma Lazarus's apostrophe to the immigrants at the base of the Statue of Liberty, welcoming them to a nation that so closely approximated the end of exile. Whatever the satisfaction that Southern Jewry gained from social and political acceptance, no such logic informs Ezekiel's memorial.

Perhaps the most famous Southern Jew of his day, Bernard Baruch, was emblematic of a mentality that had originated in third-century Babylonia and flourished in the Middle Ages but which was intensified in the

South: *dina de-malkhuta dina* ("the law of the kingdom is the law"). A son of a Ku Klux Klansman of the Reconstruction era, Baruch was immunized against the appeal of Jewish peoplehood. He did not attend religious services except on Yom Kippur, and even then—according to cynics well aware of Baruch's egotism—it was only to hear the other worshippers repeat his surname ("blessed" in English). The Episcopalian whom he married raised their children in that faith. He denied one request to buy Israel Bonds by claiming that he only bought U.S. Bonds. He also enjoyed a reputation for buying Congressmen (FDR once said that the financier "owned" sixty of them), which made him a special target of antisemites like the crackpot Ezra Pound, who called the United States "Baruchistan." In referring to "the land of my forebears," Baruch meant the South, where he complied with his mother's request to keep a home. Yet after the Second World War and the Holocaust had made the quest for a national haven for the Jews so desperate, the South Carolinian's "Jewish heart" began to tick. Despite his own view that the Jews belonged only to a religious category, he came to support—publicly and financially—their political claims to Palestine.[24]

Southern Jews rarely thought of themselves as belonging to a distinct people pursuing claims of national existence. Nor did they consider themselves (as Chief Justice Rehnquist's Vermont real estate deed quaintly put it) members "of the Hebrew race." In the first half of the twentieth century, anti-Zionism was probably stronger in the South than in other Jewish communities. Of the twenty rabbis on the initial board of the American Council for Judaism, which was the marrow of organized opposition to Jewish nationalism, a third were from the South, and with laypeople from the Southwest as well constituted half of its entire board.[25]

The most extreme instance of anti-Zionism erupted in Houston in the 1940s, when a Reform congregation sought to make acceptance of a particular creed a condition of full membership. In defiance of the Union of American Hebrew Congregations and the Central Conference of American Rabbis (and especially their Columbus Platform of 1937), the board of Beth Israel stipulated in 1943 that Jews "consider ourselves no longer a nation. We are a religious community, and neither pray for nor anticipate a return to Palestine. . . . Our nation is the United States of America. Our nationality is American. Our race is Caucasian. With regard to the Jewish settlement in Palestine[,] we consider it our sacred privilege to promote the spiritual, cultural and social welfare of our co-religionists there."

Though the Beth Israel board gained the support of another Reform synagogue in Baton Rouge, a fire-storm of criticism ensued. The "Basic Principles" were not formally rescinded, however, until 1968, well after Beth Israel had already lost its struggle to throttle Zionism in the name of "Americanism."[26] When the bulk of Southern Jews finally came to terms with Zionism, especially after the establishment of the state of Israel, it became an acquired taste, based upon insufficiently right reasons—not so much because of the pluralist tolerance and social democratic institutions that are unique to the Middle East, but more because of its swaggering reputation for military prowess and eye-for-an-eye toughness. For the male character ideal that was forged in the Promised Land resembled more the protagonist of *Walking Tall*, Buford Pusser, than Marcel Proust. Pride in Israel thus harmonized with what their fellow Southerners admired as well.[27]

Success in politics also meant conformity to the region's *sancta*. During the Great Depression, the governor of Florida was David Sholtz, who had been born in Brooklyn of immigrant parents and had graduated from Yale. He had lived in the state only fifteen years before he was elected governor. This is not the sort of résumé that, in the era of Jim Crow, Deep South politicians would be expected to brandish. His parents, having fled Russian persecution, made a fortune in real estate investments; and during a visit to Daytona Beach, Sholtz's father was impressed with its climate and waterways. David liked it so much that he settled in Volusia County after obtaining his law degree.

He enjoyed a number of advantages: service in the Navy in the Great War, grand exalted ruler of the Florida Elks, president of the state's Chamber of Commerce. Perhaps most importantly, Sholtz was a practicing Episcopalian, though he did not disclaim his Jewish origins. He thus enjoyed the social acceptance that eluded even Al Capone who, upon moving from Cicero, Illinois, to Miami, tried without success to become a member of the Rotary Club.[28] And Sholtz's father had brought the Dodgers from David's native Brooklyn for spring training in Daytona Beach. Sholtz was an effective campaigner for the governorship in 1932, when too few Jews lived in the state to arouse fears of "bloc" voting. An opponent in the second primary nevertheless yielded to the temptation of pressing antisemitic charges, which proved ineffective. Sholtz opposed the Eighteenth Amendment, which was unpopular among voters, for whom Prohibition offered the solace of being better than no liquor at all. He worked especially hard for public education but left office under a cloud, accused of association with gambling interests, and was unsuccessful in his legal practice in Jacksonville. Most of his life after serving as governor was spent in New York.[29]

The South has produced more than its share of sulphuric demagogues, but only two of them could be described as virulently antisemitic: Senator Theodore Bilbo and Congressman John Rankin. Against some stiff competition, these two Mississippians were probably the most racist Southerners ever to contaminate Capitol Hill. Yet oddly enough Bilbo had a Jewish campaign manager in 1940, and he was sympathetic to Zionism (hoping that American blacks would emulate the movement by emigrating to Africa). By distinguishing between "good" Jews and "Kikes," Bilbo could gain political mileage from rhetorical assaults on New York without necessarily forfeiting the tiny Jewish vote in his own state. Rankin was more convinced that the world was locked in an apocalyptic struggle between "Yiddish Communism" and "Christian civilization," warning that "international Jews" who did not give American patriotism priority were "making the greatest blunder since the Crucifixion." But when Rankin tried to succeed Bilbo in the United States Senate, he finished last in the Democratic primary, losing even his own district (where fewer than a third of his constituents had managed to complete high school).[30] Fortunately for the Anti-Defamation League, neither demagogue lived long enough to track the career of the New York-born Morris Cohen, who may well have been the only Jew ever to win a football scholarship to Ole Miss. But matriculation was apparently too brief for the patriotism of the region to affect Cohen, who became the only such athlete ever to be accused of espionage for the Soviet Union. He and his wife were convicted in London in 1961 for having conspired to transmit military secrets; they were later traded for British spies and re-settled in Poland.[31]

Southern Jewish marginality, one scholar has argued, "has placed a high premium on conformity to the regional mores," so that even when the actual level of bigotry is overestimated, "there has been enough *latent* anti-Semitism . . . to make good southerners out of many Jews."[32] A few—very few—Southern Jews became rabid segregationists, such as Rabbi Benjamin Schultz of Mississippi, himself a recent arrival from New York who openly backed the Citizens' Councils, or Charles J. Bloch, a Macon attorney who helped spark the Dixiecrat revolt from the Democratic party in 1948. Bloch was also the main author of a bill in the Georgia legislature that proposed closing public schools if even token desegregation were attempted.[33] In their zeal to ingratiate themselves with the worst anti-democratic and racist instincts of their neighbors, in the completeness of their desire to save themselves whatever the moral cost, they were the mild counterparts of the Nationale Deutschenjuden, German Jews who supported the Nazis and whose slogan—their enemies quipped—ought to have been, *"Raus mit Uns!"* ("Kick Us Out"). But the Nationale Deutschenjuden were as statistically freakish as virulently segregationist Southern Jews.

For even though the community could not be mobilized against social injustice with the passion of their Prophetic ancestors, no instinctive, primitive hostility to desegregation surfaced either. Sociologist John Shelton Reed has shown how the 1968 elections highlight the political differences between Jews and other white Southerners, even while he has stressed the difficulties of investigating so marginal a minority as Southern Jews. In that election, out of every five white Southern votes, Humphrey got one, Nixon two and Wallace the other two. Even among college-educated white Southerners, the American Independent Party candidate and his running mate, General Curtis LeMay, got one of five votes. At the same time, Jewish voters throughout the United States were ignoring Wallace altogether, while giving Nixon one in five votes and bestowing the other four on Humphrey. (No subsequent Presidential candidate has exceeded the liberal Democrat's margins among Jews in 1968; for recent comparisons in the Western Hemisphere, one almost has to turn to the landslides that Haitian voters gave the unopposed President for Life, "Baby Doc" Duvalier.)

Though it is difficult to beguile information from so small a sample, Professor Reed has concluded that Southern Jewish voters were more likely to be for Nixon than Jews exercising the franchise elsewhere, and more likely than other Southerners to be for Humphrey. But the biggest difference was that virtually no Southern Jews voted for Wallace, even though 37% of white Southerners cast ballots for the former Alabama governor. "To judge by this single indicator," Reed summarized, "Southern Jews do show the effects of their regional environment. . . . But their acculturation has not been so great as to blot out their differences from Southern gentiles, or to lure them into the Wallace camp in any significant number."[34] Though few risked becoming either heroes or martyrs, scholars like Milton Konvitz were therefore wrong to conclude that Southern Jews "were hardly differentiated from their neighbors in the cities and towns . . . in attitude toward the civil rights movement."[35]

Even though Southern Jewry as a whole merits no epilogue in *Profiles in Courage,* a few did speak out against the evils of white supremacy. One early voice belonged to Louis Isaac Jaffe, an editorial writer for the Norfolk *Virginia-Pilot,* who won a Pulitzer Prize in 1929 for his denunciation of lynching and of the Byrd machine.[36] Probably the most important Southern Jewish critic of segregation, however, was Atlanta's Rabbi Rothschild, who tried to live in opposition to the color line that, more than anything else, separated Southerners from other white Americans. His widow's memoir often poignantly records the human price that white Southerners paid for their refusal to accept blacks as their equals. *One Voice* distills how her fellow Southern Jews sought to negotiate their way through the turmoil that segregation wrought.

Those whose roots had been sunk deepest in Southern soil often felt the most insecure, the most eager to escape the claims of Judaism and of conscience. In the immediate aftermath of the *Brown* v. *Board of Education* decision, Rabbi Rothschild realized that "scions of old, established families well settled in the South for generations . . . ran for cover first. It was they who claimed to be completely accepted by the Gentiles in their communities and they who insisted that for them Judaism was a religion only."[37] (How ironic that one Prophet of that religion had dreamed of a day when "none shall make them afraid.") When in 1958 another Southern rabbi urged prudence, Rothschild replied: "How can we condemn the millions who stood by under Hitler or honor those few who chose to live by their ideals . . . when we refuse to make a similar choice now that the dilemma is our own?. . . . When you—and many others in the South—seek to silence those who would speak out, then you really do more than just remove yourselves from the battle. You also seek to deny the right of those who want to act with courage to do so."[38]

How many rabbis and rebbetzins elsewhere in the United States had to challenge the racial segregation and racial etiquette that impeded the formation of ordinary human contact? Consider the question of guessing who's coming for dinner, and the answer—unprecedented in the early 1960s—turned out to be Dr. and Mrs. Martin Luther King. This was not a topic discussed by the "worthy editor" of the "bintel brief," the advice column of the *Jewish Daily Forward.* The Kings found themselves in an unfamiliar Atlanta neighborhood, where the signs and numbers were poorly lit, and got lost. They had to ask someone for directions, but Dr. King later explained when they finally arrived: "We were careful not to embarrass you with your neighbors. I let Coretta go to the door so they'd think we were just coming to serve a party." The author comments: "I still get a lump in my throat when I think of it." The entree she had intended to serve was coquilles St. Jacques—not the sort of dish that households on the Old East Side favored. But Mrs. Rothschild was overruled by her own maid, who insisted: "I knows what colored preachers likes to eat. We are having barbecued chicken!"[39] Less than three years later, King would be in Oslo to accept his Nobel Prize, an astonishing measure of the velocity of change.

In considering the transformation from the Old South to the New, in reflecting upon how that modernization finally occurred, the historian cannot ignore the role of law. Jewish members of this profession have been noteworthy for their own involvement in eroding the ugly legacy of racial supremacy and political primitivism. The struggle against segregation was by far the most decisive, but it was not the only battle that Jewish attorneys have waged. Sometimes such lawyers have arisen within the region itself, most notably Morris Abram, whose victory in the case of *Sanders v. Gray* (1963) finally cracked the county-unit system that ensured the rural domination of states like Georgia itself.[40] Morris Ernst was born in Uniontown, Alabama in 1888; but he was raised and practiced law in New York. Part of the importance of being Ernst was his service on President Truman's Civil Rights Commission. It might be added that David Addlestone of South Carolina served as an ACLU attorney, and was perhaps most important for defending the equal rights of homosexuals serving in the military, who have also enlarged the public space of the region.

The Tennessee Valley Authority is the nation's largest and only Federally-owned utility, annually generating about $2 billion in sales. To be its chairman, President Jimmy Carter appointed Simon David Freeman, the son of an Orthodox Jewish umbrella maker in Chattanooga. Born in 1926, Freeman was old enough to remember how floods had ravaged the area before the dams of TVA could control the Tennessee River: "TVA and religion were the two biggest things in my life." He graduated from Georgia Tech, then financed his way through the University of Tennessee Law School, finishing first in his class while working part-time at TVA. It is one index of Freeman's zeal for conservation and for public power that one energy industry representative called him "bad news."[41]

The landmark case of *Gideon v. Wainwright* (1963), which established the right of indigents charged with a felony to be represented by counsel in state courts, was successfully argued before the Supreme Court by Abe Fortas, born and raised in Memphis. (Miami's Tobias Simon of the Florida chapter of the ACLU was designated to represent Clarence Gideon in the criminal proceeding thereafter.) Of course Fortas himself later served on the Supreme Court, and was nominated by President Johnson to serve as Chief Justice. But he was forced to resign in the wake of a scandal, in which he had accepted a consulting fee from a foundation that a Jewish entrepreneur created, Georgia-born Louis Wolfson. The appearance of impropriety was enough to expel him from the bench. A panel of legal experts later rated Fortas among the "near great" Justices to have served on the U.S. Supreme Court.[42]

But the pursuit of equal justice, especially in opposition to Jim Crow, has mostly been the achievement of attorneys who were of necessity "outside agitators." Samuel Leibowitz achieved fame (or notoriety) as the champion of the Scottsboro "boys," nine blacks who were framed and (with one exception) sentenced to die, falsely accused in 1930 of raping two white women. He lost one of the trials, in part because the Morgan County solicitor screamed at the xenophobic jurors to ensure that "Alabama justice cannot be bought and sold with Jew money from New York." Leibowitz eventually won on appeal, even while the Scottsboro boys themselves languished in prison. As the NAACP's attorney, he battled for control of the case against Joseph Brodsky of the Communist-sponsored International Labor Defense, whose eloquence, in arguing one appeal before the Alabama Supreme Court, was acknowledged even by the Montgomery *Advertiser*. (One of that newspaper's headlines was "Negro Partisans 'Dictate' Course to High Court.") Two important Supreme Court decisions resulted from ILD and NAACP efforts: *Powell* v. *Alabama* (1932), which condemned the state's initial local counsel as inadequate to represent the Scottsboro boys; and *Norris* v. *Alabama* (1934), which struck down the county's systematic exclusion of blacks from jury rolls.[43] These decisions eventually strengthened the protections promised in the Sixth Amendment.

Other "outside agitators" should also be recognized. In one of the most celebrated autobiographies to emerge from the region in recent years, Theodore Rosengarten's reconstruction of the life of an illiterate black farmer from Alabama named Ned Cobb ("Nate Shaw"), the white lawyer from the North who tries to help establish the Sharecroppers Union is given the pseudonym of Stein.[44] Arthur Garfield Hays of the ACLU assisted in the defense of biology teacher John T. Scopes in the "monkey trial" in Dayton, Tennessee—a momentarily lost battle for freedom of thought. In the 1940s the future New York Congressman Allard Lowenstein was an undergraduate at the University of North Carolina, where he fought for racial integration, and was later a civil rights attorney and activist in Mississippi in the 1960s.

William Moses Kunstler showed true grit as counsel for Dr. King, Stokely Carmichael and H. Rap Brown, as well as the civil rights organizations which they led. His memoir of his civil rights work in the South, *Deep in My Heart* (1966), is a stirring account of the injustices that he and his clients faced, though Kunstler does not credit his own Jewish background with helping to arouse his own sense of social justice. Mel Leventhal moved from Brooklyn to serve as an NAACP attorney in Jackson, Mississippi, fighting especially for school desegregation. He also married Alice Walker, the Georgia sharecroppers' daughter who later won a Pulitzer Prize for her novel *The Color Purple*.[45] Though they were divorced and Leventhal moved back to New York, he remained with the NAACP Legal Defense and Education Fund, which Jack Greenberg has long directed from New York. Another crucial organization in the defense of civil rights in the South was the Lawyers' Constitutional Defense Committee, whose executive director was Henry Schwarzchild; and a key figure in it was Richard Sobel. On behalf of the NAACP's Legal Defense and Education Fund, Michael Meltsner helped win the case of *Furman v. Georgia* (1972), which, since blacks in the South were so disproportionately executed, made it more difficult for states and juries to inflict capital punishment. Anthony Amsterdam of Philadelphia was active in both civil rights and the struggle against capital punishment. Alvin Bronstein served as executive director of the ACLU's National Prison Project, and in the case of *James v. Wallace* (1976) was pivotal to a class action suit requiring minimal, humane standards of incarceration in the state of Alabama—if need be, under Federal judicial auspices.[46] Such champions of justice may well have appeared more often in the history books than in history, which tends to be less romantic. But they did exist.

One of the dramatic signs of the change which they helped achieve has been in the calibre and personnel of law enforcement. The latitude of Southern cops in giving vent to their prejudices and in abusing their authority has long been the stuff of legend that is composed of about equal parts of Bull Connor of Birmingham, Jim Clark of Selma and Rod Steiger in *In the Heat of the Night*. But consider two counter-examples.

Until 1820 the largest Jewish minority in the United States was in Charleston, which did not select a Jewish police chief until recently; and for sheer exoticism Reuben Morris Greenberg trumps everyone. He is an active member of Congregation Emanu El, a Conservative *shul* in which he served on the board of trustees and co-chairs the adult education committee. But he is also the first black ever to be Charleston's top cop. Born in Texas in 1946, Greenberg had a paternal grandfather who was Jewish. Yet he himself did not tap that aspect of his heritage until moving to the San Francisco area, where he discovered that most of the white allies of the blacks who were fighting racial discrimination were Jews. He converted first in a Reform ceremony and more recently in a Conservative ceremony. Greenberg has apparently been a very effective police officer, credited with sharp reductions in the city's crime rate; and he has consulted with the Jerusalem police force. But he has admitted that the oddest adjustment since moving to Charleston has been listening to the other members of Congregation Emanu El *daven* with Southern accents.[47]

Given the ethnic composition of Miami Beach, it may not be astonishing that its police chief would be born in the Bronx; his name is Rocky Pomerance. But though weighing the 260 pounds that has been the obligatory minimum for Southern policemen, no one could be further from the traditions of their guild. Wearing his "Se Habla Español" armband, Pomerance was the first member of the Miami Beach police department to learn Spanish. He now wears no uniform and carries no gun, though he does smoke a pipe and professes great fondness for the ballet and other arts; his daughter Gayle, incidentally, is a rabbinical student. Savvy and sophisticated, Pomerance is given credit for eliminating graft on the police force itself, and for ensuring that Miami Beach enjoys one of the lowest crime rates of any city of its size in the country. His term as president of the International Association of Police Chiefs completes this picture of exoticism.[48]

The Jews then represented forces of change, agents of modernization, and especially throughout south Florida they eventually hit with the force of Hurricane Esther. But first was the daunting task of defying the limits of demography, the challenge of convincing Jews (and other Northerners) to take their stand to live and die in Dixie.

The first to promote such a migration was Moses Elias Levy (1782–1854), a Moroccan who sank an incredible $54,000 into lands and plantations while Florida was still under Spanish rule. Levy intended to attract his fellow Jews initially according to common religious principles and customs. At the outset of the Second Seminole War, however, part of the work in what became Alachua County was destroyed; and he reached the melancholy conclusion that "it is not easy to transform old clothes men or stock brokers into practical farmers." Having promoted the introduction of sugar cane into the United States, Levy eventually got his money back, however; and his son David, who changed his name to Yulee, became Florida's first U.S. Senator.[49]

A more successful real estate promoter arrived well over a century later. Leonard Rosen, along with his brother Jack, had made a fortune marketing lanolin out of Baltimore. In 1957, while on vacation in Miami, Rosen missed his return flight and drove a rented car instead to a health spa near Fort Myers to soothe his arthritic feet. Instead he saw the possibilities of marketing Florida real estate. In association with Milt Mendelson, Rosen figured out how to sell a place they called Cape Coral without buying the land out-of-pocket. As one author has explained it, "Rosen could buy a small parcel and take out options on the rest as the orders came in, acquiring this product . . . with the customers' money. Customers would pay more than twenty times retail what Rosen would have to pay wholesale." The Rosens' Gulf American Land Corporation used the following techniques: "If you lived in a northern city, you were likely to be invited to a free dinner at which a speaker would give a talk on Florida or where a movie would be shown, and you would end up in a banquet hall, unaware that some of your table-mates were Gulf American employees . . . After the movie, a large display board would be uncovered, various lots would be put up as available for sale, and a Gulf American employee, still incognito, would jump up and say, 'Put a hold on Lot Number 239.' Another Gulf American employee, also incognito, would be visibly distressed that he had lost out on that one, and in this stock-exchange-like frenzy you could begin to believe that unless you put the hold on Lot 240 you would miss a wonderful opportunity, never suspecting that there was an infinite supply of lots, and so you would jump up and yell 'sold.'"

For the obtuse shnooks who were still unable to perceive the splendid advantages of such residences, a free weekend at Cape Coral was offered; "and in the confusion of whether they were vacationers, guests, investors or ingrates[,] the populace bought the lots." John Rothchild's *Up For Grabs* adds that "Gulf American installed its most persuasive employees at the site," where they "were aided by secret intercom systems in the rooms, through which they could eavesdrop on the units and learn whether a husband or a wife was resisting the purchase and how best the resistance could be overcome." But Gulf American discovered valuable minerals under 1,300 lots that it had sold, and it ran into a little trouble when it was caught switching them to several miles away and changing the legal description. Coral City was the first of several spectacular successes in the creation of such communities in south Florida. In 1969 Rosen and his partners sold Gulf American at its peak, and he himself left Florida for good. Mendelson stayed long enough to create a new subdivision, but was charged with fraud in the sale of securities in his company and was jailed for several months.[50]

These promotional efforts helped propel Miami Beach and environs into a unique niche in the milieu of Southern Jews, despite the odds against them. For Carl Fisher, who created Miami Beach virtually *ex nihilo,* intended the city to be restricted, off-limits to Jews (except the extremely wealthy), just as he wanted visitors and vacationers and settlers to ignore mortality itself—so he prohibited cemeteries within the city limits of Miami Beach.[51] But the actuarial tables pressed their inexorable claims; and the Jews, a people which had experienced an earlier exodus to the promised land, were almost as unstoppable. For in defying Carl Fisher's snobbish residential ban, the Jews recognized the fulfillment of the divine promise made to Abraham for having offered to sacrifice his son. It is re-read every Rosh Hashanah: "Thy seed shall possess the gate of his enemies" (Genesis 22:17).

So many of Isaac's descendants came that Miami has surpassed Chicago and Philadelphia to become the third largest Jewish community in the United States. Three counties, Miami-Dade, Broward, and Palm Beach, now account for ten percent of American Jewry. One Floridian in twenty is now Jewish, putting it third in proportion (behind New York and New Jersey) and—with over half a million Jews—third in actual numbers (behind New York and California). If the former Confederacy now ranks as the fourth largest concentration of Jews in the world (with only the rest of the United States, Israel itself and the Soviet Union currently harboring more Jews), it is because of the attraction of the Sunshine State. While some states like Alabama, Louisiana, North Carolina and South Carolina have recorded slight losses of their Jewish population, Florida has become home for the third biggest population of Jews in the United States, giving a jolting jump-start to the communal life of Southern Jewry.

But consider as well the novelty of this concentration of Jewish life in the South: Miami Beach is not much older than the *average* age of its residents, which is 68. Its population is so geriatric that, to borrow George Burns' quip, a typical citizen who wakes up in the morning with a song in his heart has probably had an FM amplifier installed in his pace-maker. But the community itself—the unit that Jewish social historians prefer to study—is fresh. Miami Beach is younger, for example, than certain Jewish residents of Florida such as the author's own grandmother (born in 1892) who, incidentally, by the year Miami Beach was invented, had already married her husband. Miami proper, which Cuban immigrants have utterly transformed, was only 90 years old in 1985. It took Greater Boston three centuries to attract the same size general population that Greater Miami achieved in three decades.

The change has been of such magnitude that south Florida is commonly described as if it were "not really the South" at all, as if Scarlett O'Hara's beloved Tara had suddenly undergone a condo conversion. One historian has argued that, in the twentieth century, the geographically most southern state "is not a Southern state . . . It should be excluded from regional generalizations."[52] Historically a rural society and an agrarian economy, the region is now tipped at the bottom with what the Census Bureau terms the Miami–Fort Lauderdale Standard Consolidated Statistical Area, which is the nation's sixth largest metropolitan area. Historically the poorest section of the United States, the South that Franklin Roosevelt defined as the country's #1 economic problem now boasts of a city which, if Miami were independent, would have a gross national product greater than any Latin American nation other than Brazil and Argentina.[53]

One wonders what the Bible Belt slightly to the north makes of Eugene Weisman, who has gone into partnership with a tribe of Seminoles who live on a reservation near Hollywood. They are exempted from many state civil laws, among them the limitation that the top prize in bingo is $100. So, with the 397 Seminoles, Weisman has run a bingo emporium where the super-jackpot each night can run as high as $19,000. As manager of the operation, he gets 45% of the earnings, which annually total about $3 million.[54] This circumvention of the law, in which Indians are brought in to steam up the get-rich-quick atmosphere, may not resemble an idealized picture of the placid Old South or the "real" South. But Weisman's ploy would have shocked very few members of Faulkner's Snopes clan either.

If urban vitality and optimism and go-for-broke entrepreneurship are not "Southern," then the definition of regional identity would be forever frozen in a time warp. It would mean that its destiny would be fixed only by rustics—by plantation overseers and owners, by black field hands and sharecroppers, by benighted but charming good ol' boys and girls and their kin endlessly confined to chomping on hominy grits and hush puppies. It would mean that the Old South would never be allowed to take its first baby steps into the New. Such a definition is simply too rigid and ahistorical to make allowances for the forms of modernization familiar to the rest of the country.

The legacy of Southern Jewry therefore consists of venturousness as well as tradition, iconoclasm as well as filiopietism, resistance as well as compliance. Many of its representatives have come to believe in the compatibility of Southern and Jewish traditions, have wanted in effect to feast on matzoh brei as well as moon pie and to keep Judaism alive even in unpromising circumstances. In the poem "Eulogy," Shael Herman (b. 1943) has memorialized his Hebrew instructor, Ephraim Lizitsky, "teaching for 50 dollars a month/in good times/for nothing in bad ones," a scholar who "spoke with a heavy Polish accent/his voice always sounding like it/came through a cheap tape recorder/he begged softly/always for the sake of your people/your heritage/not to play baseball/when you had lessons." Joseph Cohen grew up in Clarksdale, Tennessee, in the 1930s; he has recalled family trips to the kosher butcher in Nashville, 45 miles away, long before superhighways.[55] At Tulane, where Cohen taught English literature, no course in Jewish history or religion or languages was included in the curriculum as late as the 1960s. In the mid–1980s Professor Cohen directed the program in Jewish Studies at Tulane that offers a dozen courses, and many of the students taking them may be experiencing a sensation akin to finding buried treasure.

There is something valiant and impressive about the Jewish capacity to survive, to defy odds so long that it is not awkward to label such resilience a miracle. That is a common description of the rebirth of a Jewish commonwealth and homeland in the Middle East; and something that Chaim Weizman once said is applicable to Jewish life elsewhere: "Miracles do happen, but one has to work very hard for them."[56] That is the way one might think about how the springs of Jewish life can sometimes get renewed in the South as well, where certain observances and traditions were imperiled but could still be fought for, where a sense of solidarity and identity could be achieved against conformist pressures in the other direction, where the transmission of at least a smattering of learning to one's children and grandchildren was sometimes more than a forlorn hope.

These have been efforts worthy of respect, ensuring that communities are preserved from one generation to the next (so far), in an ambience often so indifferent to such purposes. Sometimes manning the bilge pumps, some Southerners have therefore worked very hard for the miracles of maintaining their own connections to Jewishness; and that is why, having lasted six millennia, Jewish history might be expected to continue, to extend itself even in places that their Biblical ancestors could not have foreseen, like Baton Rouge and Beaumont and Boca Raton.

Notes

1. Eli N. Evans, *The Provincials: A Personal History of Jews in the South* (New York: 1973), pp. 39–49, *passim;* Melvin I. Urofsky, "Preface: The Tip of the Iceberg," in Nathan M. Kaganoff and Melvin I. Urofsky (eds.), *"Turn to the South": Essays on Southern Jewry* (Charlottesville: 1979), p. xii; Abraham D. Lavender, "Jewish Values in the Southern Milieu," in ibid., pp. 124–34.

2. Stephen J. Whitfield, "Jews and Other Southerners: Counterpoint and Paradox," in ibid., pp. 81–88; Jonathan D. Sarna, "The 'Mythical Jew' and the 'Jew Next Door' in Nineteenth-Century America," in David A. Gerber (ed.), *Anti-Semitism in American History* (Urbana: 1986), pp. 57–78.

3. Morris B. Abram, *The Day is Short: An Autobiography* (New York: 1982), pp. 9–13, 17–18, 25, 35–36.

4. Diane Ravitch, "The Educational Critic in New York," in Bernard Rosenberg and Ernest Goldstein (eds.), *Creators and Disturbers: Reminiscences by Jewish Intellectuals of New York* (New York: 1982), pp. 388–90.

5. Ibid., p. 391.

6. Janice Rothschild Blumberg, *One Voice: Rabbi Jacob M. Rothschild and the Troubled South* (Macon, Ga.: 1985), pp. 27, 29.

7. Roy Hoffman, "Passover Tradition in American South," *New York Times,* March 23, 1983, III, p. 3.

8. Mordecai Richler, *The Apprenticeship of Duddy Kravitz* (New York: 1974), p. 145.

9. Evans, *Provincials,* pp. 183–91; Sidney I. Goldstein, "Mixed Marriages in the Deep South," in Leonard Dinnerstein and Mary Dale Palsson (eds.), *Jews in the South* (Baton Rouge: 1973), pp. 283–87.

10. John McKay Sheftall, "The Sheftalls of Savannah: Colonial Leaders and Founding Fathers of Georgia Judaism," in Samuel Proctor and Louis Schmier, with Malcolm Stern (eds.), *Jews in the South: Selected Essays from the Southern Jewish Historical Society* (Macon, Ga.: 1984), pp. 65–69, 78.

11. Leon Jick, *The Americanization of the Synagogue, 1820–1870* (Hanover, N.H.: 1976), pp. 54–55.

12. Blumberg, *One Voice,* pp. 49, 199.

13. Robert Slater, *Great Jews in Sport* (Middle Village, N.Y.: 1983), pp. 172–74.

14. John Shelton Reed, *One South: An Ethnic Approach to Regional Culture* (Baton Rouge: 1982), p. 111; Alfred O. Hero, Jr., "Southern Jews," in Dinnerstein and Palsson (eds.), *Jews in the South,* p. 246.

15. Willie Morris, *North Toward Home* (New York: 1967), p. 196.

16. Richard Wright, *Black Boy: A Record of Childhood and Youth* (New York: 1966), pp. 267–74.

17. Alfred Kazin, "New York Jew," in Rosenberg and Goldstein (eds.), *Creators and Disturbers*, p. 195.

18. Harold Clurman, "The Yiddish Influence on American Theater," in ibid., p. 177.

19. Alan Schneider, *Entrances: An American Director's Journey* (New York: 1986), pp. 228–36.

20. Quoted in Carl Van Vechten (ed.), *Selected Writings of Gertrude Stein* (New York: 1972), p. 338.

21. Quoted in Walter Blair and Hamlin Hill, *America's Humor: From Poor Richard to Doonesbury* (New York: 1978), p. 193.

22. Albert Goldman, *Elvis* (New York: 1981), pp. 80–82.

23. Stanley F. Chyet, "Moses Jacob Ezekiel: A Childhood in Richmond," *American Jewish Historical Quarterly*, 62 (March 1973), 286–94.

24. Bernard Baruch, *My Own Story* (New York: 1957), p. 289; Ben D. Kimpel and T. C. Duncan Eaves, "Ezra Pound's Anti-Semitism," *South Atlantic Quarterly*, 81 (Winter 1982), 58; Jordan A. Schwarz, *The Speculator: Bernard M. Baruch in Washington, 1917–1965* (Chapel Hill, N.C.: 1981), pp. 9–10, 274, 559–66.

25. Myron Berman, "Rabbi Edward Nathan Calisch and the Debate over Zionism in Richmond, Virginia," *American Jewish Historical Quarterly*, 62 (March 1973), 301.

26. Howard R. Greenstein, *Turning Point: Zionism and Reform Judaism*, Brown Judaic Studies 12 (Chico, Cal.: 1981), pp. 51–71.

27. Evans, *Provincials*, pp. 107–09.

28. John Kobler, *Capone: The Life and World of Al Capone* (New York: 1971), p. 215.

29. Merlin G. Cox, "David Sholtz: New Deal Governor of Florida," *Florida Historical Quarterly*, 43 (October 1964), 142–52; Hank Drane, "Depression-weary voters opted for Sholtz," Jacksonville *Florida Times-Union*, March 23, 1981, section B, pp. 1–2.

30. Edward S. Shapiro, "Anti-Semitism Mississippi Style," in Gerber (ed.), *Anti-Semitism*, pp. 129–51; Chester M. Morgan, *Redneck Liberal: Theodore G. Bilbo and the New Deal* (Baton Rouge: 1985), p. 238.

31. New York *Times*, March 19, 1961, IV, p. 6, and March 23, 1961, p. 2; Rebecca West, *The New Meaning of Treason* (New York: 1964), pp. 275–88.

32. Lewis M. Killian, *White Southerners*, rev. ed. (Amherst, Ma.: 1985), pp. 80–81.

33. Blumberg, *One Voice*, pp. 118–20; Killian, *White Southerners*, p. 80.

34. Reed, *One South*, pp. 105, 108–10; Leonard Dinnerstein, "Southern Jewry and the Desegregation Crisis, 1954–1970," *American Jewish Historical Quarterly*, 62 (March 1973), 231–41; Murray Friedman, "Virginia Jewry in the School

Crisis: Anti-Semitism and Desegregation," in Dinnerstein and Palsson (eds.), *Jews in the South,* pp. 341–50; Allen Krause, "Rabbis and Negro Rights in the South, 1954–1967," in ibid., pp. 360–85.

35. Milton R. Konvitz, "Jews and Civil Rights," in Peter I. Rose (ed.), *The Ghetto and Beyond: Essays on Jewish Life in America* (New York: 1969), p. 286; Killian, *White Southerners,* p. 70.

36. John Hohenberg, *The Pulitzer Prizes* (New York: 1974), p. 77.

37. Blumberg, *One Voice,* pp. 68–69.

38. Quoted in ibid., pp. 76–77; Steven Hertzberg, *Strangers Within the Gate City: The Jews of Atlanta. 1845–1915* (Philadelphia: 1978), p. 221.

39. Rothschild, *One Voice,* pp. 144–45.

40. Abram, *Day is Short,* pp. 48–51, 78–86, 101–09.

41. "A Conservationist Shakes the TVA," *Time,* 111 (May 29, 1978), 81.

42. Anthony Lewis, *Gideon's Trumpet* (New York: 1964), pp. 48, 50–53, 118–21, 169–74, 223–27; *New York Times,* November 19, 1972, p. 74.

43. Dan T. Carter, *Scottsboro: A Tragedy of the American South* (New York: 1971), pp. 156–58, 161–63, 235–41, 322–24.

44. Theodore Rosengarten, *All God's Dangers: The Life of Nate Shaw* (New York: 1975), pp. 342–44, 353–56, 554.

45. Willie Morris, *Yazoo: Integration in a Deep-Southern Town* (New York: 1972), pp. 111–14.

46. Robert Francis Kennedy, Jr., *Judge Frank M. Johnson, Jr.: A Biography* (New York: 1978), pp. 235–48.

47. Dean Calbreath, "Charleston's Jewish Top Cop Visits Old Friends in East Bay," *Northern California Jewish Bulletin,* April 11, 1986, p. 23; *Time,* 125 (February 18, 1985), 85; *New York Times,* June 14, 187, p. 33.

48. Richard Reeves, "A Police Chief in the Spotlight—and on the Spot," *New York Times,* July 9, 1972, X, p. 1; Jon Nordheimer, "Miami Beach Peace Keeper," *New York Times,* August 25, 1972, p. 38.

49. Joseph Gary Adler, "Moses Elias Levy and Attempts to Colonize Florida," in Proctor and Schmier (eds.), *Jews of the South,* pp. 17–29; Leon Hühner, "Moses Elias Levy: An Early Pioneer and the Father of Florida's First Senator," *Florida Historical Quarterly,* 19 (April 1941), 319–45, and *idem.,* "David L. Yulee, Florida's First Senator," in Dinnerstein and Palsson (eds.), *Jews in the South,* pp. 52–65.

50. John Rothchild, *Up for Grabs: A Trip through Time and Space in the Sunshine State* (New York: 1985), pp. 82–105.

51. Ibid., pp. 35, 38–43, 76–77, 209.

52. Jack Temple Kirby, "The Southern Exodus, 1910–1960: A Primer for Historians," *Journal of Southern History,* 49 (November 1983), 587–88.

53. For these and previous statistics, see Ira Sheskin, "Ten Percent of American Jews," in *Jews of South Florida,* Andrea Greenbaum, ed., (Hanover NH, 2005), 4; "Jewish Population in the United States," David Singer and Lawrence Grossman, eds., *American Jewish Yearbook* (New York, 2004) 125; T. D. Allman, "The City of the Future," *Esquire,* 99 (February 1983), 42, 44.

54. "Bingo is the Best Revenge," *Time,* 116 (July 7, 1980), 18.

55. Shael Herman, *Offshoots* (New Orleans: 1967), pp. 42–43; Hoffman, "Passover Tradition in American South," p. 3.

56. Quoted in Isaiah Berlin, *Personal Impressions* (New York: 1980), p. 61; Roy Hoffman, "Southern Jews Act to Rescue a Past," *New York Times,* November 12, 1986, C, pp. 1, 3; Janice R. Blumberg, "Southern Jews Act to Preserve History," *Reform Judaism,* 15 (Spring 1987), 16–17.

16
"How To Win the Jews for Christ"

Southern Jewishness and the Southern Baptist Convention

Eliza R. L. McGraw

When Flannery O'Connor famously referred to the South as "Christ-haunted," she created a label for the influence that Christianity wields for many Southerners.[1] As Walker Percy asks, "How do you blaspheme in California?"[2] Within Southern Baptist representations of Jewishness, Jews typically function paradigmatically, either negatively as the executioners of Jesus, or positively as the model witnesses, waiting to be converted, and thereby signal the advent of the Messiah's Second Coming. While some critics argue that this concept of the Jewish people prevents Jewish "normalization" in the South, where symbol tends to thrive, the resistance of Jewishness to such absorption gives it power. Eric Voegelin writes that "Israel did not sink into a dead past, but survived in symbolic forms,"[3] calling up the biblical potency of Jewishness. Religious meaning prospers in the South, and Southern Jewishness harnesses its power through its refusal to "sink into a dead past," preserving its concurrent symbolic agency.

Voegelin writes of the nature of Israel as both a concept and a people:

> The constitution of Israel as a carrier of the truth, as an identifiable and enduring social body in history, could be achieved only through the creation of a paradigmatic record which narrated (1) the events surrounding the discovery of the truth and (2) the course of Israelite history, with repeated revisions, as a confirmation of the truth. . . . Precisely when its dubiousness as a pragmatic record is recognized, the narrative reveals its function in creating a people in politics and history.

Hence, there is an intimate connection between the paradigmatic narrative of the Old Testament and the very existence of Israel (p. 123).

Because the South houses the intimacy Voegelin describes, it has need for Jewishness in some of its Christian contexts. Jewishness provides a template for the integration of myth and history, which Southern Jewishness foregrounds. Overall, Voegelin's concept of Jewishness in text and history forms a close parallel with Southernness and thus provides a space for an inevitable mutual recognition.

Commingling concepts of Israel and the South go back to the Confederacy's vision of itself as a chosen people and endure in the present day, as the Southern Baptists who support the state of Israel attest. Israel frames a natural typology for the South. In a land where, as William Faulkner writes in *Intruder in the Dust* (1948), "for every Southern boy, not once but whenever he wants it . . . there is the instant when it's still not yet two oclock on that July afternoon in 1863,"[4] myth is a quotidian presence. The "dubious" nature, as Voegelin notes, of such symbol systems creates a narrative and, thus, a political and historical people.

In turn, the symbolic nature of Jewishness and its narrative underpin various strains of Southern Christianity. Some Southern Baptist representations in particular position Jewishness as synonymous with Jesus, and seek Jewish conversion. The Southern Baptist Convention (SBC) strives to contain and thus comprehend Jewishness, which it otherwise confoundingly reinforces and repudiates. As one recent tract calling Southern Baptists to convert Jews urges, "Use terminology that emphasizes the Jewishness of our faith."[5] Jewishness, the rhetoric implies, already lies within Southern Baptist belief. If Jewish people would accept Jesus as the Messiah, they could be subsumed beneath the canopy of Southern Baptist doctrine, and the SBC would have proof of its contention that its brand of Christianity supersedes Judaism. Missionaries for the SBC attempt to claim Jewishness specifically to prove that the Second Coming is at hand, but their overweening mission points toward a desire to contain Jewishness and make it safe for Southern Baptists. Southern Baptists strive to own and therefore demonstrate that they have advanced beyond Southern Jewishness. As one tract advises, "The main argument to be used in the Christian approach to the Jew is that Christ came not to destroy the Jewish faith but to fulfill it."[6]

In his study of blackface minstrelsy, *Love and Theft* (1993), Eric Lott writes that "underwritten by envy as well as repulsion, sympathetic identification as well as fear, the minstrel show continually transgressed the color line even as it made possible the formation of a self-consciously white working class."[7] The SBC's relationship with Jewishness reflects some of the tensions Lott describes as inherent in minstrelsy. Jewishness, like the minstrel show, enables a dominant culture to define itself more concretely. If the SBC forms a less transgressive force than the minstrel show, its connection to Jewish people and their position as would-be converts fulfills Lott's description of a gnarled association that encompasses sympathy as well as fear.

These anxieties of affiliation reach far back into the history of the SBC, which foregrounds region along with dogma. Baptists in America split with the rest of the country in 1861. While the Northern—or American, as they came to be known—Baptists decreased in number and became more liberal, Southern Baptists prospered.[8] Baptists and Southernness dovetailed at the Jewish-informed issues of chastisement and chosenness. For Southern Baptists, the Confederacy lost the Civil War because, as Edward Queen writes, "God had other plans for the Southern people and had to chastise them for their sins—like the Israelites of old" (p. 16). The Southern Baptists' zenith of unity with other churches came during the Civil War, since all supported the Lost Cause. After the war, Southern Baptists resisted joining the National Council and World Council of Churches because the idea of a union "conjured up memories of the Union from which the Confederate States had seceded."[9] Even one hundred and thirty years after the Civil War, Southernness remains central to the Convention. During Jimmy Carter's campaign for president the press called Carter a "Southern Baptist evangelical" and the head of one SBC agency said, "We are not evangelicals. That's a Yankee word."[10] As Victor I. Masters wrote in 1920: "in the South is the Baptist center of gravity" (Queen, p. 16).

Tracts on evangelizing Jews reinforce the Southern Baptist preoccupation with Southernness. *An Open Letter To the Jewish People of the South* proclaims that "since [the Southern Jew] set foot on Southern soil there has been a kindly feeling between him and his neighbor. . . . This is because the average Southern Gentile is a gentleman."[11] The tract deploys the banner of Southern honor to entice putative converts, placing Southernness above differences in religion. In the companion tract *The Jew's Contribution to the South,*[12] Southerners read of Judah P. Benjamin and David Yulee, who both contributed to the Lost Cause, Benjamin as the treasurer of the Confederacy and Yulee as a Confederate senator. Southern Jewish people are desirable coreligionists because "The Southern Jew . . . does not harbor the prejudice that poisons the mind of his foreign-born brother, and is able to form a better conception of Christianity. He has associated, more or less, with the better brand of Christians, and is not confined to a ghetto life as is the case in other sections" (p. 13). According to Gartenhaus's rhetoric, Southern Jews stand as exemplars of their type. Southerners need not fear the alien or the filthy immigrant, since a better class of Jewish people live in the South. Regional and class status make the Southern Jews non-threatening and perfect candidates for conversion, since Southern Baptists can teach them that "Christianity is not a foreign religion but the full flower of Judaism" (p. 15).

Like Southernness, evangelism has long been a part of Southern Baptist doctrine. As Christine Leigh Heyrman writes, "evangelicalism in contemporary America hews to the shape it had assumed in the South in the mid-nineteenth century. But even more striking are the ways in which social changes unfolding over the latter half of the twentieth century have encouraged evangelicals to reclaim territory they were long ago obliged to cede."[13] Evangelism and conversion underpin the Southern Baptist tradition, and in Heyrman's words "reclaim" some territory through one more extension of Southern Baptistness to everyday life. In 1954, for example, the slogan for the Convention read "A Million More in '54."[14] One Southern Baptist tract's preface says, "Southern Baptists are especially fitted to render this service [of conversion] because there are seven members of our churches to each Jew in the South."[15] On a doctrinal level, the conversion of the Jews will signal to Southern Baptists that Jesus's Second Coming is near, and the close yet vexed relationship of Judaism to Christianity makes Jewish people desirable converts. As Mrs. F. W. Haberer writes in a 1938 issue of the Virginia Woman's Missionary Union *Religious Herald*, "in a peculiar, special way, the Jews are God's own chosen people. They have been set apart for a special Mission, through them God made Himself known to the rest of humanity."[16] As Keith Harper writes, "[R]ather than turning to politics to effect social change, Baptists relied on personal evangelism. . . . Their reasoning was simple. They believed that creating a better society depended upon supplying the society with better people. . . . Between 1890 and 1920, Southern Baptist social criticism hinged not only on the assumption that better societies were built on better people but also upon a set of cultural assumptions inherited from the Populists."[17] These inherited assumptions saw Jewish people as alien and America as white. Combined with a drive toward personal evangelism, Southern Baptists came from a tradition prepared to convert Jews to make them the "better people" Southern society depends upon.

Around 1921, the Woman's Missionary Union published a tract called *Pioneer Work Among Southern Jews*.[18] When missionaries would try to convert Jewish people, the tract says, they would be pelted with stones: "Sometimes the stones would find their mark and missionaries would stand, testifying for their Lord, with the blood streaming down their faces." Once Jewish attention is gained, however, missionaries witness "an amazing change" from violence: "While we cannot report a large number of conversions, yet we say that God's Spirit has been working in Jewish hearts" (Women's Missionary Union). The Southern Baptist martyrs approximate Jesus, bleeding as he bled, testifying as he and his followers did. Preaching to Jewish people constitutes a central enough tenet to bleed for and an opportunity for sanctification. A 1928 *Baptist Messenger* article takes a more tactical stand and reminds Southern Baptists of Evans's "ace in the hole," if for a different purpose: "if we will realize that our Savior was a Jew and died for Jews as well as Gentiles, we may win them to Jesus Christ."[19] Remembrance of Jesus's Jewishness can enlarge Christian understanding. Jewishness is crucial to the Southern Baptist understanding of responsibility and "witness," whether the Jews represent stone-throwing apostates or Jesus's brethren.

Jacob Gartenhaus contributed steadily to the advances of missions embracing both these ideologies through the early to mid twentieth century. After attending European rabbinical schools, the Austrian Gartenhaus studied at the Southern Baptist Theological Seminary in Louisville, Kentucky, to become a Southern Baptist evangelist. He was the superintendent of the SBC's Department of Jewish Evangelism, under the auspices of what was originally called the Home Mission Board and is now the North American Mission Board. This board was devoted to domestic evangelism from 1921 to 1958. As he saw it, Gartenhaus never left his Jewish past entirely behind, committing himself to mission work among his former coreligionists. His zeal showed. At the 1922 SBC annual meeting he reported: "I have made 955 personal visits, had 1,220 conversations, distributed 196,000 pages of tracts; Gospels distributed, 216; New Testaments sold, 44; addresses, 1091; conversions, two; collections for Jewish work, $171.57."[20] Gartenhaus utilized Jewishness to convince Jewish people to convert. In 1935, he addressed a Shreveport audience to spread the message that "every Jew today is a living proof that the Bible is God's word, that the existence of the Jew today, in spite of the persecution and dispersion, is an enigma which none of the philosophers and historians can explain."[21]

Many other Southern Baptists joined Gartenhaus in conversion efforts. Tracts moved from reifying the myth of Jew as Christ-killer to debunking it in order to demonstrate sympathy for putative Jewish converts. In *If I Were A Jew* Henry Alford Porter writes that "The Jews as a race are no more to be blamed for the crucifixion of Jesus than are the people of Missouri to be blamed for the recent lynching that took place" (n.p.).[22] Porter's formulation offers Southerners a way not to feel culpable for lynchings and to forgive Jews all at once. Only a few years after Leo Frank, a Northern Jewish factory manager, was hanged from a tree in Georgia, Southern Baptists encouraged their audiences to excoriate lynchings in place of mission work. The displacement of the lynching to Missouri also portrays it as a problem not necessarily Southern. Porter further asserts that race tension plagues the whole country and Southern Baptists, by refusing to imagine Jews as Christ-killers, are by proxy countering lynching. Couching conversion as philo- rather than antisemitic allows Southern Baptists to depict conversion as loving, combating lynching as well as apostasy. Porter also indicts Henry Ford's antisemitism. Ford embraced as genuine *The Protocols of the Elders of Zion,* a fraudulent document that ostensibly outlined the sinister aims of a global Jewish cabal that controlled the world's finances. Porter derides the *Protocols* as "rank forgery," to emphasize his stance against antisemitism. As the South struggled to shed the backward reputation H. L. Mencken foregrounded when he dubbed the region "The Sahara of the Bozart" in 1917, Porter calls for Southern Baptists to add to their own Americanization and sophistication by Christianizing Jewish Southerners.

Commercial influence also molded Southern Baptist rhetoric. Business templates made the conversion mission seem relevant to Southern Baptists during the 1930s. Dale Carnegie's boosterish imprint shows in Gartenhaus's *How To Win the Jews for Christ*[23] both in its title, which mimics Carnegie's *How To Win Friends and Influence People*[24] (1936), and style. After categorizing Jewish people as either "Orthodox," "Reformed," "Zionist" or "Socialistic," Gartenhaus recommends "the simple rules of salesmanship . . . 1. Getting one's attention. 2. Make him interested. 3. Create in him a desire for what you have to offer him. 4. Then come to the final appeal foreclosing the deal" (p. 6). Using a more detailed version of Carnegie's injunction to "Begin with praise and honest appreciation" (p. 180), he also reminds his readers that "The Jew likes to be flattered. You may use your judgment how far you may go in this, but don't exaggerate it. Remember that the keen Jew will at once recognize whether your words are sincere or not" (p. 11). Gartenhaus's contemporary pamphlet *A New Emphasis on Jewish Evangelization Through The Local Church* warns on its first page "This Tract is for Christians Only."[25] This caveat points toward the idea that, throughout the tract, "the Jew" is treated as an exotic animal, just as potential customers are in Carnegie's work. "The literature must be adapted to the particular type of Jew we have in the South," Gartenhaus warns (p. 7). The *How to Win Jews* approach tried to show Southern Baptists that effort and vim will prevail after President Roosevelt, determined to spread the New Deal in the South even as Southern conservatives opposed it, described the South as "the nation's No. 1 economic problem" in 1938. As the Depression wore on, many Southerners needed to hear that effort could produce results. Gartenhaus's approach appropriates hopeful thinking, placing conversion under the rubric of New South business endeavors.

World War II and the creation of the State of Israel offered new insights into the Jewish mind for Southern Baptist missionaries. In *How To Approach the Jew With the Gospel* (1966), Gartenhaus writes that "The Nazi onslaught nearly crushed the Jew. But the emergence of the State of Israel raised him up from the dust, straightened his back, lifted his head so that he could look any man straight in the eye and say, 'I am as good as any other man'" (p. 1). Pairing these two events lends Jewishness an import that makes their conversion all the more important for Southern Baptists. If the State of Israel is a sign of God's chosen people, it also demonstrates that the Jewish role of witness is all the more germane to Southern Baptist theology. As the South underwent changes ranging from President Truman's 1946 appointment of the President's Committee on Civil Rights to the victories of the Dixiecrats in 1948, the Southern Baptists continued to campaign for Jewish mission work. In 1952, Frank Halbeck, the Field Worker in the Home Mission Board's Jewish Department after Gartenhaus vacated the position, claimed eighty-two responses for baptism at the annual SBC meeting.[26] Three years later he could report that "The year 1955 has been our greatest year thus far," with 108 conversions and 100,000 tracts distributed.[27]

After that high point, the post–Civil Rights era Southern Baptists posited understanding Judaism as the key to conversion. As songs such as "Free To Be You and Me" rang from American classrooms, the Southern Baptists responded with a more evenhanded—if no less radical—approach to Jewish conversion. In A. Jase Jones's pamphlet *The Jewish*

People and the Baptist Witness, information on Jewish holidays appears alongside entreaties for mission work.[28] Jones notes that "Rarely, if ever, should one mail unsolicited tracts, even to Jewish friends. They receive too much hate literature by mail, and even good Christian tracts may be put in the same category with the hate literature" (p. 22). Even with a more measured tone, however, the bottom line prevails: "to ask the Christian to forego all missionary activity is to ask him to cease to be authentically Christian" (p. 14). At the pamphlet's end, Jones recommends older traditional tracts such as *If I Were A Jew,* reestablishing the older currents of stricter doctrine beneath the moderate pages of his work. In another change of tone, the Home Mission Board changed the name of the committee from Department of Jewish Evangelism to Department of Interfaith Witness, and at the 1968 annual meeting of the SBC, the Board reported that "Jewish work is being promoted more widely than ever," and that in addition to the tracts earlier missionaries handed out, "Slide sets were made available."[29]

By the late seventies, internal conflict plagued the SBC. From 1979 to 1991, moderates were pushed away from the convention, and "In the process its leaders changed the course of the nation's largest Protestant denomination and put fundamentalism, a movement nearly invisible for more than five decades, on the national agenda."[30] Moderates called the 1979 annual meeting a "takeover" while fundamentalists dubbed it a "take-back."[31] The titles of books about the conflict illustrate its timbre: *The Southern Baptist Holy War, Baptist Battles; The New Crusades, The New Holy Land; The Struggle for the Soul of the SBC.* A major polarizing question was over "inerrancy"—whether the Bible contains slippage between certain translations and versions. Fundamentalists believed that not accepting the Bible as infallible constitutes heresy, while moderates saw the struggle as about power, not inerrancy, which they could not support.[32] As America leaned rightward with Ronald Reagan's election in 1980, the fundamentalists who preached inerrancy ascended within the Convention ranks, and their agenda became the foremost of the Convention, and remains so today. Pressure to evangelize increased along with fundamentalist domination.

Probably the most publicized event concerning Jews and Southern Baptists in the 1980s, however, did not concern conversion. In August 1980, at a national affairs briefing for evangelical leaders in Dallas, Bailey Smith, then president of the SBC, said: "It is interesting at great political rallies how you have a Protestant to pray and a Catholic to pray, and then you have a Jew to pray. With all due respect to those dear people, my friends, God Almighty does not hear the prayer of a Jew."[33] Smith's comment resonated through the country, providing fodder for editorial pages and causing President Reagan to decry Smith's statement.[34] Other Christian groups, including Catholics and Episcopalians, followed suit. Richard Fisher, a political cartoonist, addressed Smith's remark by reminding readers that Jesus was Jewish.

Fisher depicts Jesus, halo intact, entreating heaven, his hands entwined in worship above a reprint of Smith's comment. His cartoon appeared in the *Arkansas Gazette*, reminding Southerners of the ultimate importance of Jewishness as Jesus's origin. That the cartoon was reprinted in the Best Cartoons of 1980 demonstrates its nationwide impact.

Part of the more fundamentalist agenda of the late twentieth century included an increase in evangelism, which led in turn to a resolution to renew vigor in converting Jews. On June 11–13, 1996, the SBC adopted a resolution titled "On Jewish Evangelism" at its annual meeting.[35] The resolution reads in part: "Be it further RESOLVED that we recommit ourselves to prayer, especially for the salvation of the Jewish people as well as for the salvation of 'every kindred tongue and people and nation' (Revelations 5:9); and Be it finally RESOLVED, That we direct our energies and resources toward the proclamation of the gospel to the Jewish people."[36] Resolutions passed at SBC meetings are nonbinding, but do set goals for congregations during the year to come and provide a template for Southern Baptist behavior and issues. Recently, the SBC has passed injunctions such as renewing the prohibition of gambling and boycotting the Walt Disney company because of its tolerance of gay people.[37]

When Resolution 10 became public, Jewish groups responded immediately. B'nai B'rith issued a press release casting the resolution as hostile: "Pluralism is a basic tenet of our American way of life. It means respecting each other's traditions and religious paths. We cannot believe that creating such tensions between Jews and Christians can possibly advance humankind toward the ultimate Messianic Age that both Christians and Jews look forward to with hope and faith. We urge the Southern Baptists to reconsider these steps."[38] The National Conference (formerly the National Conference of Christians and Jews) reacted with similar chagrin: "We recognize that a dedication to converting others may be a doctrinal belief of a faith group . . . however. . . . Targeted faith communities understandably feel diminished, angry, and threatened. . . . We call on members of the Southern Baptist Convention to reconsider."[39] Some laughed bitterly at the idea, such as columnist

Howard Kleinberg, who asked, "Or is the Southern Baptist goal simply to vanquish Judaism? That's been tried before. Many times. Hasn't worked. History has shown that the Jews are much like the U.S. Marines: they only need a few good men and women."[40]

The message was conveyed to local levels as well. Ray Waddle reported in the *Nashville Tennessean* that pastor Don Finto preached evangelizing Jews to his congregation, saying that he wanted to convert Jewish people because he "loves Jews." Steve Fuchs, a local Reform rabbi, said, "With all their talk of love, love, love, what they want to accomplish is what Hitler tried to accomplish—no more Jews."[41] Most telling of the preeminence that the evangelical viewpoint retains in the South is the sidebar that ran adjacent to the story, which Waddle also wrote. Its headline reads "Christians' missionary efforts based on Scripture," suggesting that the conversion effort is virtuous and supported by a confirmed text. The article goes on to explain that "Jesus said, 'Go therefore and make disciples of all nations'."[42] While Waddle's article appears to exist to illuminate disinterested readers, it instead demonstrates a Christian fundamentalist understanding of the conflict by casting Jewish people as stiff-necked Jesus-rejecters. He reminds readers, "Judaism was the faith from which Christianity sprung; it was the Jewish community that first rejected Jesus." Waddle associates Christianity with words such as "concentrate," "vital," "strength," and "produce" while Jewish people "insist," "argue," and "recoil." Most significantly, Jewish people "reject" Jesus three times in this ten paragraph, two-column article. Few symbols represent the Americanization of the South as glaringly as *The Tennessean* with its colorful Gannett graphs and editorials from all over the country. The Waddle article, in contrast, reinforces the local tradition of Southern Baptist predominance, as the rhetoric of the would-be converters informs the items in the hometown newspaper of the SBC.

In the wake of 1996's Resolution 10, Jewishness remains at issue for the Convention. In 1999, the High Holy Days spurred a refreshed conversion campaign from the SBC, who took the Jewish New Year as an opportunity to release a booklet directed at Jews. My request for materials on Jewish evangelism from the North American Mission Board in 1999 yielded one of Gartenhaus's tracts from the thirties, information on Judaism, such as an "Interfaith Witness Belief Bulletin" that includes Jewish demographics and pamphlets explaining Jewish holidays, a list of messianic prophets and fulfillments to bolster the evangelistic point, and an article on "messianic Judaism."

The Convention yet strives to contain Jewishness as the century closes,

envisioning mission work and conversion as Southern Baptist responsibilities. The mellower terminology and Jewish calendar point toward a
less didactic trend, but the inclusion of Gartenhaus's work forty years after he left the Home Mission Board indicates a patent claim to traditional patterns of evangelism. For the Southern Baptist Convention, the
mission to make Jews into Southern Baptists remains unfinished, and
will until Jewishness represents no more than a crucial but superannu-
ated phase. If in the South, the Baptists are indeed the center of gravity,
then, as Voegelin writes, Israel is "the center from which radiates the order of history" (p. 472). As the aims of the SBC demonstrate, Jewishness
provides a design within its religious economy. The Southern Baptists
still want to win the Jews.

Notes

I would like to thank Bill Sumners, the archivist at the Southern Baptist Historical Library and Archives, who let me sort through uncatalogued material and
answered many questions. I would also like to thank Michael Kreyling, who read
many versions of this essay.

1. O'Connor's "Christ-haunted" comment appears in her essay "Some Aspects of the Grotesque in Southern Fiction," in the collection *Mystery and Manners: Occasional Prose* (ed. Sally and Robert Fitzgerald [New York: Farrar, Straus,
Giroux, 1969]). The essay was originally delivered as a paper in 1960 at Wesleyan
College for Women in Macon, Georgia, and then published in 1965 (after O'-
Connor's death) in the *Cluster Review* (March 1965, pp. 5–6, 22). The phrase has
gained popularity, and has been used in such instances as the titles of a 1994 essay collection dealing with Southern faith and of a 1998 conference on Southern religion at Baylor University.

2. Walker Percy, "How to Be an American Novelist in Spite of Being Southern and Catholic," *Signposts in a Strange Land* (New York: Farrar, Straus, Giroux,
1991), p. 177.

3. Eric Voegelin, *Order and History* (Baton Rouge: Louisiana State University
Press, 1956), p. 314.

4. William Faulkner, *Intruder in the Dust* (New York: Vintage, 1987), p. 190.

5. Jim R. Sibley, *Judaism* (Alpharetta, Georgia: North American Mission
Board of the Southern Baptist Convention, 1998), p. 4.

6. Jacob Gartenhaus, *How to Approach the Jew With the Gospel* (Alpharetta, Georgia: North American Mission Board of the Southern Baptist Convention, 1966),
p. 3. Located in the Southern Baptist History Library and Archives, Nashville,
Tennessee.

7. Eric Lott, *Love and Theft: Blackface Minstrelsy and the American Working Class* (New York: Oxford University Press, 1993), p. 8.

8. Edward L. Queen, II, *In the South the Baptists are the Center of Gravity* (Brooklyn: Carlson Publishing, 1991), p. 15.

9. E. Luther Copeland, *The Southern Baptist Convention and the Judgment of History* (Lanham, Maryland: University Press of America, 1995), pp. 70, 79.

10. Timothy George, "Toward an Evangelical Future," in *Southern Baptists Observed,* ed. Nancy T. Ammerman (Knoxville: University of Tennessee Press, 1993), p. 283.

11. Jacob Gartenhaus, *An Open Letter to the Jewish People of the South.* Most of the SBC tracts are not dated, so I have attempted to place them historically through examining their typefaces and historical references. For example, Henry Alford Porter's *If I Were A Jew* ([Atlanta: Home Mission Board, Southern Baptist Convention, n.d.], Southern Baptist Archives) refers to the fraudulent antisemitic document *The Protocols of the Elders of Zion* as recent. Since *The Protocols* became widely available in the United States around 1920, I have placed the tract near that date. Some tracts also recommend other, obviously earlier, pamphlets, so I have construed a rough chronology.

12. Jacob Gartenhaus, *The Jew's Contribution to the South* (Atlanta: Home Mission Board, SBC, n.d.), Southern Baptist Archives.

13. Christine Leigh Heyrman, *Southern Cross* (New York: Knopf, 1997), p. 258.

14. Samuel Hill, "The Story Before the Story: Southern Baptists Since World War II" (in Ammerman, *Southern Baptists Observed,* p. 32).

15. M. E. Dodd, Preface to *Jewish Trophies of Grace,* by Jacob Gartenhaus (Atlanta: Home Mission Board of the Southern Baptist Convention, n.d.), Southern Baptist Archives.

16. Mr. F. W. Haberer, *Religious Herald,* 1938, Southern Baptist Archives.

17. Keith Harper, *The Quality of Mercy* (Tuscaloosa: University of Alabama Press, 1996), p. 16.

18. Women's Missionary Union, *Pioneer Work Among Southern Jews* (Birmingham: Southern Baptist Convention, 1921), n.p. Southern Baptist Archives.

19. E. C. Routh, "The Gospel and the Jew," *Baptist Messenger,* December 20, 1928, n.p. Southern Baptist Archives.

20. Southern Baptist Convention, *Record of the 1922 Annual Meeting* (Nashville: Marshall Bruce, 1922), p. 191.

21. Jacob Gartenhaus, *Traitor? A Jew, A Book, A Miracle* (Nashville: Thomas Nelson, 1980), p. 183.

22. Porter's calling Jewishness a "race" is typical for the parlance of his day. The confusion between ideas of Jewishness as an ethnicity and as a faith pervades the Southern Baptist understanding. Indeed, this slippage pervades many

discussions of Jewishness. It would be naive to ignore the possibility of any racial or ethnic nuances inherent in the SBC's or any other group's understanding of Jewishness; however, as the focus of the tracts indicates, Jewishness typically represents a religious force to the Convention.

23. Jacob Gartenhaus, *How To Win the Jews for Christ* (Atlanta: Home Mission Board of the Southern Baptist Convention, n.d.), Southern Baptist Archives.

24. Dale Carnegie, *How To Win Friends and Influence People* (1936 rpt; New York: Pocket, 1962).

25. Jacob Gartenhaus, *A New Emphasis on Jewish Evangelization Through the Local Church* (Atlanta: Home Mission Board of the Southern Baptist Convention, n.d.), Southern Baptist Archives.

26. Southern Baptist Convention, *Record of 1952 Annual Meeting* (Nashville: Southern Baptist Convention, 1952), p. 217.

27. Southern Baptist Convention, *Record of 1955 Annual Meeting* (Nashville: Southern Baptist Convention, 1955), Southern Baptist Archives.

28. A. Jase Jones, *The Jewish People and the Baptist Witness* (Atlanta: Home Mission Board of the Southern Baptist Convention, n.d.), Southern Baptist Archives.

29. Southern Baptist Convention, *Record of 1968 Annual Meeting* (Nashville: Southern Baptist Convention, 1968), p. 162.

30. Diane Winston, "The Southern Baptist Story" (Ammerman, p. 29).

31. David T. Morgan, *The New Crusades, The New Holy Land* (Tuscaloosa: University of Alabama Press, 1996), p. 37.

32. For a detailed account of the inerrancy debates see Morgan, chapter 3.

33. Kenneth L. Woodward, "The Evangels and the Jews," *Newsweek*, November 10, 1980, p. 76.

34. See for example Leonard Garment, "Holier Than Us?," *New York Times,* June 27, 1996, p. A23; Benjamin J. Hubbard, "Southern Baptists Read Selectively," *Los Angeles Times,* June 30, 1996, p. 9; Jacob Neusner, "Firmly Held Beliefs Often Require Judgments; Religion: The Southern Baptist Movement to Convert Jews Deepens the Faith of All," *Los Angeles Times,* July 26, 1996, p. 9.

35. Even though this is a misnomer, apparently suggesting that Jews themselves proselytize, the Southern Baptist term means evangelizing to Jews.

36. Southern Baptist Convention, *Record of 1996 Annual Meeting* (Nashville: Southern Baptist Convention, 1996), p. 97. Southern Baptist Archives.

37. When the *Today* show interviewed Michael Eisner, the president of Disney, about the SBC resolution to boycott his company, he took the opportunity to comment also upon the resolution supporting evangelizing Jewish people, equating it with Nazi aims. "That was something that hasn't been recommend-

ed since the forties in Europe," Eisner said of Resolution 10 (*Today*, NBC, April 21, 1997).

38. Tommy B. Baer, *B'nai B'rith Urges Southern Baptist Convention To Reconsider Formal Resolution Actively Seeking To Convert Jews To Christianity*, June 4, 1996; October 1998, <http://bnaibrith.org/pr/sbaptist.html>.

39. Sanford Cloud, *Statement on The Southern Baptist Convention Resolution On Evangelizing Jews*, July 1, 1996, National Conference, October 9, 1998, <http://members.aol.com/natlconf/baptists.html>.

40. Howard Kleinberg, "Baptists Aim to Convert Disney, Jews," *New Standard*, June 18, 1996, pp. 1–2; October 1998, <http://www.s-t.com/daily/06-96/06-18961/b040p070.htm>.

41. Ray Waddle, "Temple's Rabbi Offended By Call to Convert Jews," *The Tennessean*, April 18, 1997, pp. 1A–2A.

42. Ray Waddle, "Christians' Missionary Efforts based on Scripture," *The Tennessean*, April 18, 1997, p. 2A.

Bibliographical Essay

AJH = *American Jewish History* and its antecedents
AJA = *American Jewish Archives Journal* (previously *American Jewish Archives*)
SJH = *Southern Jewish History*
* = works with extensive citations for further reading; see also citations in articles

The definitive academic history of southern Jewry remains to be written. Two insightful, journalistic accounts are Eli N. Evans, *The Provincials: A Personal History of the Jews in the South* (New York, 1973; reprinted 1998) and Harry Golden, *Our Southern Landsman* (New York, 1974). Leonard Dinnerstein and Mary Dale Palsson, eds., *Jews in the South* (Baton Rouge, 1973), Nathan M. Kaganoff and Melvin I. Urofsky, eds., *"Turn to the South": Essays on Southern Jewry* (Charlottesville, 1979), Abraham D. Lavender, ed., *A Coat of Many Colors: Jewish Subcommunities in the United States* (Westport CT, 1977), and Samuel Proctor and Louis Schmier with Malcolm Stern, eds., *Jews of the South: Selected Essays From the Southern Jewish Historical Society* (Macon, 1984), offer good essays. Interpretations are also found in Mark K. Bauman, *The Southerner as American: Jewish Style* (Cincinnati: American Jewish Archives, 1996),* Mark K. Bauman, "The Flowering of Interest in Southern Jewish History and its Integration into the Mainstream," *Religion in the Contemporary South,* Corrie E. Norman and Don S. Armentrout, ed.s (Knoxville, 2005),* Mark I. Greenberg, "Becoming Southern: The Jews of Savannah, Georgia, 1830–1870," *AJH* 86 (March 1998): 55–75, Abraham J. Peck, "That Other 'Peculiar Institution': Jews and Judaism in the Nineteenth Century South," *Modern Judaism* 7 (February 1987): 99–114, Stephen J. Whitfield, *Voices of Jacob, Hands of Esau: Jews in American Life and Thought* (Hamden CT, 1984), and Gary P. Zola "Why Study Southern Jewish History?" *SJH* 1 (1998): 1–22. *SJH 16* (2003) has a complete list of articles in *AJH, AJA,* and *SJH.* For a thorough bibliographic essay, see Mark K. Bauman, "A Century of Southern Jewish Historiography," *American Jewish Archives Journal* (forthcoming).

The best city histories are James William Hagy, *This Happy Land: The Jews of Colonial and Antebellum Charleston* (Tuscaloosa, 1993), Steven Hertzberg, *Strangers Within the Gate City: The Jews of Atlanta, 1845–1915* (Philadelphia, 1978), and Leonard Rogoff, *Homelands: Southern Jewish Identity in Durham and Chapel Hill, North Carolina* (Tuscaloosa, 2001). Wendy Lowe Besmann, *A Separate Circle: Jewish Life in Knoxville, Tennessee* (Knoxville, 2001), Myron Berman, *Richmond's Jewry, 1769–1976: Shabbat in Shockoe* (Charlottesville, 1979), and Mark H. Elovitz, *A Century of Jewish Life in Dixie: The Birmingham Experience* (Tuscaloosa, 1974) are also good. For a specialized work in urban studies, see Ronald H. Bayor, "Ethnic Residential Patterns in Atlanta, 1880–1940," *Georgia Historical Quarterly* 63 (Winter, 1979): 435–46. Other state and local histories include Fedora Small Frank, *Five Families and Eight Young Men (Nashville and Her Jewry, 1850–1861)* (Nashville, 1962), Frank, *Beginnings on Market Street: Nashville and Her Jewry, 1861–1901* (Nashville, 1976), Henry Alan Green and Maricia Kerstein Zerivitz, *Mosaic: Jewish Life in Florida; A Documentary Exhibit from 1763 to the Present* (Coral Gables, 1991), Bertram Wallace Korn, *The Early Jews of New Orleans* (Waltham MA, 1969), Korn, *The Jews of Mobile, Alabama, 1763–1841* (Cincinnati, 1970), Carolyn Gray LeMaster, *A Corner of the Tapestry: A History of the Jewish Experience in Arkansas, 1820s–1990s* (Fayetteville AR, 1994), Selma S. Lewis, *A Biblical People in the Bible Belt: The Jewish Community of Memphis, Tennessee, 1840s–1960s* (Macon GA, 1998), Deborah Dash Moore, *To the Golden Cities: Pursuing the American Jewish Dream in Miami and LA* (New York, 1994), Natalie Ornish, *Pioneer Jewish Texans: Their Impact on Texas and American History for Four Hundred Years, 1590-1990* (Dallas, 1989), Theodore and Dale Rosengarten, eds., *A Portion of the People: Three Hundred Years of Southern Jewish Life* (Columbia SC, 2002), Saul Jacob Rubin, *Third to None: The Saga of Savannah Jewry, 1733–1983* (Savannah, 1983), Leo E. and Evelyn Turitz, *Jews in Early Mississippi* (Jackson MS, 1983), and Melvin I. Urofsky, *Commonwealth and Community: The Jewish Experience in Virginia* (Richmond, 1997). Belinda and Richard Gergel, *In Pursuit of the Tree of Life: A History of the Early Jews of Columbia, South Carolina, and the Tree of Life Congregation* (Columbia SC, 1996), Hollace Ava Weiner, *Beth-El Congregation, Fort Worth, Texas, Centennial, 1902–2002* (Fort Worth, 2002), and Jerry Cristol, *A Light in the Prairie: Temple Emanu-El of Dallas, 1872–1997* (Fort Worth, 1998) are analytic congregation histories. For small towns see Lee Shai Weisbach, *Jewish Life in Small Town America* (New Haven, 2005), Weissbach, "Stability and Mobility in the Small Jewish Community: Examples from Kentucky History," *AJH* 79 (Spring 1990): 355–75, Weissbach, "Kentucky's Jewish History in National Perspective: The Era of Mass Migration," *Filson Historical Quarterly* 69 (1995): 255–74, Terry Barr, "A Shtetl Grew in Bessemer: Temple Beth-El and Jewish Life in Small Town Alabama," *SJH* 3 (2000): 1–44, *We Call This Place Home: Jewish Life in Maryland's Small Towns* ed. by Karen Falk and Avi Y. Dector (Baltimore, 2002), Gerald L. Gold, "A Tale of Two Communities: The Growth and Decline of Small Town Jewish Communities in Northern Ontario and Southwestern Louisiana," *The Jews of North America* ed. by Moses Rischin (Detroit, 1987), 224–34, Charles Joyner, "A Community of Memory: Assimiliation and Identity Among the Jews of Georgetown," in *Shared Traditions: Southern History and Folk Culture* (Urbana IL, 1999), 177–92, James Lebeau, "Profile of a Southern Jewish Community: Waycross, Georgia," *AJH* 58 (June 1969): 429–46, Leonard Rogoff, "Synagogue and Jewish Church: A Congregational History of North Carolina," *SJH* 1 (1998): 43–81, Louis Schmier, "The First Jews of Valdosta," *Georgia Historical Quarterly* 62 (Spring, 1978): 32–49, Deborah R. Weiner, "The Jews of Clarksburg: Community Adaptation and Survival, 1900–60," *West Virginia History* 54 (1995): 59–77, Weiner, "The Jews of Keystone: Life in a Multicultural Boom Town," *SJH* 2 (1999): 1–23, Weiner, "Middlemen of the Coalfields: The Role of Jews in the Economy of the Southern West Virginia Coal Towns, 1890–1950," *Journal of Appalachian Studies* 4 (Spring 1998): 29–56, and Canter Brown Jr., *Jewish Pioneers of the Tampa Bay Frontier* (Tampa FL, 1999). On Gaunse, see Lewis S. Feuer, *Jews in the Origins of Modern Science and Bacon's Scientific Utopia: The Life and Work of Joachim Gaunse, Mining Technologist and First Recorded Jew in English-Speaking America* (Cincinnati, 1987), and Gary Grassl, "Joachim Gans of Prague: The First Jew in English America," *AJH* 86 (June 1998).

On the origins of Reform Judaism see Gary P. Zola, *Isaac Harby of Charleston, 1788–1828: Jewish Reformer and Intellectual* (Tuscaloosa, 1994),* and Zola, "The First Reform Prayer Book in America: The Liturgy of the Reform Society of Israelites," *Platforms and Prayer Books: Theological and Liturgical Perspectives on Reform Judaism* ed. by Dana Evan Kaplan (Lanham MD, 2002): 99–118.

Family works illustrating linkages as well as problems with intermarriage and maintaining identity are Myron Berman, *The Last of the Jews?* (Lanham MD, 1998), Emily Bingham, *Mordecai: An Early American Family* (New York, 2003), and Kaye Kole, *The Minis Family of Georgia, 1733–1992* (Savannah, 1992).

For the rabbinate and religion see Mark K. Bauman and Arnold Shankman, "The Rabbi as Ethnic Broker: The Case of David Marx," *Journal of American Ethnic History* 3 (Spring 1983): 51–68, Bauman, *Harry H. Epstein and the Rabbinate as Conduit for Change* (Rutherford, NJ, 1994), Myron Berman, "Rabbi Edward N. Calisch and the Debate over Zionism in Richmond, VA," *AJH* 62 (March 1973): 295–305, Janice Rothschild Blumberg, "Rabbi Alphabet Browne: The Atlanta Years," *SJH* 5 (2003): 1–42, Mark Cowett, *Birmingham's Rabbi: Morris Newfield and Alabama, 1895–1940* (Tuscaloosa, 1986), A. Stanley Dreyfus (compiler), *Henry Cohen, Messenger of the Lord: A Tribute to the Memory of its Beloved Rabbi on the One Hundredth Anniversary of his Birth by Congregation B'nai Israel of Galveston* (New York, 1963), Israel Goldman, "Henry W. Schneeberger: His Role in American Judaism," *AJH* 57 (December 1967): 153–90, Henry M. Green, *Gesher VaKesher/Bridges and Bonds: The Life of Leon Kronish* (Atlanta, 1996), Yitzchak Kerem, "The Settlement of Rhodesian and Other Sephardic Jews in Montgomery and Atlanta in the Twentieth Century," *AJH* 85 (December 1997): 373–91,* Abraham J. Karp, "Simon Tuska Becomes a Rabbi," *AJH* 50 (December 1960): 79–97, Scott M. Langston, "James K. Gutheim as Southern Reform Rabbi, Community Leader, and Symbol," *SJH* 5 (2003): 69–102, Irwin Lachoff, "Rabbi Bernard Illowy: Counter Reformer," *SJH* 5 (2003): 43–68, Bobbie Malone, *Rabbi Max Heller: Reformer, Zionist, Southerner* (Tuscaloosa, 1997), Karl Preuss, "Personality, Politics, and the Price of Justice: Ephraim Frisch, San Antonio's 'Radical' Rabbi," *AJH* 85 (September 1997): 263–88, Israel Tabak, "Rabbi Abraham Rice of Baltimore: Pioneer of Orthodox Judaism in America," *Tradition* 7 (Summer 1965): 100–120, Ellen M. Umansky, "Christian Science, Jewish Science, and Abraham Geiger Moses," *SJH* 6 (2003): 1–36, Umansky, *From Christian Science to Jewish Science* (NY, 2005), Peggy K. Pearlstein, "Macey Kronsberg: Institution Builder of Conservative Jidaism in Charleston, SC, and the Southeast," *SJH* 8 (Fall 2005), Joel Ziff, ed, *Lev Tuviah: On the Life and Work of Rabbi Tobias Geffen* (Newton MA, 1988).

For re-routing plans for immigration into the South see Bernard Marinbach, *Galveston: Ellis Island of the West* (Albany, 1983) and Hollace Ava Weiner, "Removal Approval: The Industrial Removal Office Experience in Fort Worth, Texas," *SJH* 4 (2001): 1–44.

For Jewish women see Mark K. Bauman, "Southern Jewish Women and Their Social Service Organizations," *Journal of American Ethnic History* 22 (Spring 2003): 34–78* and Mark I. Greenberg, "Savannah's Jewish Women and the Shaping of Ethnic and Gender Identity, 1830–1900," *Georgia Historical Quarterly* 82 (Winter 1998) 751–74.

For social services see Bauman, "The Transformation of Jewish Social Services in Atlanta, 1928–1948," *AJA* 53 (2001): 83–111,* and Peter K. Opper, *"Like a Giant Oak": A History of the Ladies Hebrew Benevolent Association and Jewish Family Services of Richmond, Virginia, 1849–1999* (Richmond, 1999), and Wendy Besmann, "The Typical Homekid Overachievers: Instilling a Success Ethic in the Children's Home of New Orleans," *SJH* 8 (2005).

For business see Elliott Ashkenazi, *The Business of Jews in Louisiana, 1840–1875* (Tuscaloosa, 1988), Don M. Coever and Linda D. Hall, "Neiman-Marcus: Innovators in Fashion and Advertising," *AJH* 66 (September 1976): 123–36, Hasia Diner, "Entering the Mainstream of Modern Jewish History: Peddlers and the American South," *SJH* 8 (2005), Gary R. Freeze, "Roots, Barks, Berries and Jews: The Herb Trade in Gilded-Age North Carolina," *Essays in Economic and Business History* 13 (1995): 107–27, Richard Hawkins, "Lynchburg's Swabian Jewish Entrepreneurs in War and Peace," *SJH* 3 (2000): 45–82, Clifford M. Kuhn, *Contesting the New South Order: The 1914–1915 Strike at Atlanta's Fulton Mills* (Chapel Hill, 2001), Chris Monaco, *Moses Levy of Florida: Jewish Utopian and Antebellum Reformer* (Baton Rouge, 2005), Leon J. Rosenberg, *Sangers': Pioneer Texas Merchants* (Austin, 1978), Morton Rothstein, "Sugar and Secession: A New York Firm in Antebellum Louisiana," *Explorations in Entrepreneurial History* 5 (1968): 115–31, Richard E. Sapon-White, "A Polish Jew on the Florida Frontier and in Occupied Tennessee," *SJH* 4 (2001): 93–122, Louis Schmier, "Helloo! Peddler Man! Helloo!" in *Ethnic Minorities in Gulf Coast Society* ed. by Jerrell Schopner (Pensacola, 1979), 75–88, Schmier, "For Him the 'Schwartzers' Couldn't Do Enough: A Jewish Peddler and his Black Customers Look at Each Other," *AJH* 73 (September 1983): 39–55, Susan E. Tifft and Alex S. Jones, *The Trust: The Private and Powerful Family Behind the New York Times* (Boston, 1999), Bennett H. Wall, "Leon Godchaux and the Godchaux Business Enterprise," *AJH* 66 (September 1976): 50–66, and Patricia Spain Ward, *Simon Baruch: Rebel in the Ranks of Medicine, 1840–1921* (Tuscaloosa, 1994). Harold Melvin Hyman, *Oleander Odyssey: The Kempners of Galveston, Texas, 1854–1980s* (College Station TX, 1990) mixes economics and politics. For politics see Mark K. Bauman, "Factionalism and Ethnic Politics in Atlanta: German Jews from the Civil War through the Progressive Era," *Georgia Historical Quarterly* 82 (Fall 1998): 533–58, Merlin G. Cox, "David Sholtz: New Deal Governor of Florida," *Florida Historical Quarterly* 43 (October 1964): 142–52, Mark I. Greenberg, "Tampa Mayor Herman Glogowski: Jewish Leadership in Gilded Age Florida," *Florida's Heritage of Diversity* ed. by Greenberg and Canter Brown Jr., (Tallahassee, 1997), and Robert N. Rosen, *The Jewish Confederates* (Columbia SC, 2000).*

For agricultural utopias see Eli Ginsberg, "The Jewish Colony in Waterview," *Virginia Magazine of History and Biography* 66 (October, 1958): 460–62, Arnold Shankman, "Happyville: The Forgotten Colony," *AJA* 30 (1978): 3–19, and Margalit Shilo, "Sicily Island and Rishon-LeZion: A Comparative Analysis," *AJA* 47 (1995): 182–212.

For antisemitism see Morton Borden, *Jews, Turks, and Infidels* (Chapel Hill, 1984), Leonard Dinnerstein, *Uneasy at Home: Antisemitism and the American Jewish Experience* (New York, 1987), *Anti-Semitism in American History* ed. by David A. Gerber (Urbana IL, 1986), Jeffrey Melnick, *Black-Jewish Relations on Trial: Leo Frank and Jim Conley in the New South* (Jackson MS, 2000),* Steve Oney, *And the Dead Shall Rise: The Murder of Mary Phagan and the Lynching of Leo Frank* (New York, 2003). On other incidents of overt violence, see Patrick Q. Mason, "Anti-Jewish Violence in the New South," *JSH* 8 (2005); Daniel R. Weinfield, "Samuel Fleishman: Tragedy in Reconstruction Era Florida," *SJH* 8 (2005). See also Rosalind Benjet, "The Ku Klux Klan and the Jewish Community of Dallas, 1921–23," *SJH* 6 (2003), Mark I. Greenberg, "Ambivalent Relations: Acceptance and Anti-Semitism in Confederate Thomasville," *AJA* 65 (Spring/Summer 1993): 13–30, Melissa Fay Greene, *The Temple Bombing* (Reading MA, 1996), Edward C. Halperin, "Frank Porter Graham, Isaac Hall Manning, and the Jewish Quota at the University of North Carolina Medical School," *North Carolina Historical Review* 67 (1990): 385–410, William F. Holmes, "Whitecapping in Late Nineteenth Century Georgia," in *From the Old South to the New* ed. by Walter J. Fraser, Jr. and Winfred B. Moore (Westport, 1981), 121–32, Tom Keating, *Saturday School: How One Town Kept out the "Jewish", 1902–1932* (Bloomington, 1999), Lawrence N. Powell, *Troubled Memory: Anne Levy, The Holocaust, and David Duke's Louisiana* (Chapel Hill, 2000), Louis Schmier, "An Unbecoming Act: Anti-Semitic Uprising in Thomas County, Georgia," *Civil War Times Illustrated* 23 (October 1984), and Beverly Williams, "Anti-Semitism and Shreveport,

Louisiana: The Situation in the 1920s," *Louisiana History* 21 (Fall 1980): 387–98. Studies in Jewish-Christian relations include Harry E. Moore Jr., "The National Council of Christians and Jews in Memphis, 1932–1989," *West Tennessee Historical Society Papers* 45 (1991): 48–67, George H. Shriver, "Christian Ecumenicism and Judeo-Baptist Relations in Savannah, Georgia," *Baptist History and Heritage* 38 (Spring 2003): 6–19, and Holly Snyder, "A Tree with Two Different Fruits: The Jewish Encounter with German Pietists in the Eighteenth Century Atlantic World," *William and Mary Quarterly* 58 (2001): 855–82.

On Black-Jewish relations see Clive J. Webb, *Fight Against Fear: Southern Jews and Black Civil Rights* (Athens GA, 2001),* *Quiet Voices: Southern Rabbis and Black Civil Rights* ed. by Mark K. Bauman and Berkley Kalin (Tuscaloosa, 1997),* Debra L. Schultz, *Going South: Jewish Women in the Civil Rights Movement* (New York, 2001), Eric L. Goldstein, *The Price of Whiteness: Jews, Race, and American Identity* (Princeton, 2006), Cheryl Greenberg, "The Southern Jewish Community and the Struggle for Civil Rights," in *African Americans and Jews in the Twentieth Century* ed. by V.P. Franklin, et.al., (Columbia MO, 1998), Greenberg, *Troubling the Waters: Black-Jewish Relations in the American Century* (Princeton, 2006), S. Jonathan Bass, *Blessed are the Peacemakers: Martin Luther King Jr., Eight White Religious Leaders, and the "Letter from Birmingham Jail,"* (Baton Rouge, 2001), Raymond A. Mohl, *South of the South: Jewish Activists and the Civil Rights Movement in Miami, 1945–1960* (Gainesville FL., 2004), and Adam Mendelsohn, "Two Far South: Rabbinical Responses to Apartheid and Segregation in South Africa and the American South," *SJH* 6 (2003): 63–132.

Helpful works on identity include Karen I. Blau, "Varieties of Ethnic Identity: Anglo-Saxons, Blacks, Indians, and Jews in a Southern County," *Ethnicity* 4 (1977): 263–86, Anny Bloch, "Mercy on Rude Streams: Jewish Emigrants from Alsace-Lorraine to the Lower Mississippi Region and the Concept of Fidelity," *SJH* 2 (1999): 81–110, Caroline Bettinger-Lopez, *Cuban-Jewish Journeys: Searching for Identity, Home, and History in Miami* (Knoxville TN, 2000), Marcie Ferris, *Matzoh Ball Gumbo* (Chapel Hill, 2005), David Goldfield, "Sense of Place: Blacks, Jews, and White Gentiles in the American South," *Southern Cultures* 3 (1997): 58–79, Eliza R. L. McGraw, *Two Covenants: Representations of Southern Jewishness* (Baton Rouge, 2005), Bryan Stone, "'Ride 'em Jewboy': Kinky Freedman and the Texas Jewish Mystique," *SJH* 1 (1998): 23–42; and Stone, "Edgar Goldberg and the *Texas Jewish Herald:* Changing Coverage and Blended Identity," SJH 7 (2004) 71–108.

Contributors

Elliott Ashkenazi is an independent historian with training at the London School of Economics, a BA in history from the University of Pennsylvania, a JD from Harvard, and a Ph.D. in business history from George Washington University. His book *The Business of Jews in Louisiana, 1840–1870* first appeared in 1988 and was republished in 2003. He edited and wrote an introduction to *The Civil War Diary of Clara Solomon, Growing Up in New Orleans, 1861–1862* (1995). Ashkenazi is interested in American and European Jewish business history during the nineteenth and early twentieth centuries and is presently investigating the contributions of European private Jewish banks to international development between 1870 and 1914 and the transatlantic ties between the Southern Jewish business community and its counterparts in England during the nineteenth century.

Mark K. Bauman is the editor of *Southern Jewish History,* co-editor (with Berkley Kalin) of *Quiet Voices: Southern Rabbis and Black Civil Rights* (1997), and editor of three special issues of *American Jewish History* (1989, 1997 [co-edited with Bobbie S. Malone]). The author of biographies of Southern Methodist Bishop Warren A. Candler (1981) and Rabbi Harry H. Epstein (1994), he has published over forty articles in scholarly journals and anthologies, and a pamphlet, *The Southerner as American: Jewish Style* (1996). Bauman earned a BA from Wilkes College (now University), MAs from Lehigh and the University of Chicago, and a Ph.D. from Emory. He retired as Professor of History from Atlanta Metropolitan College. He served as the Mason Fellow in the Department of Religion

at the College of William and Mary in the fall of 2005. Former president
of the Georgia Association of Historians, he received that organization's
Outstanding Service Award (2002). The recipient of the Jesse Lee Prize
from the Methodist Episcopal Church and fellowships from the American Jewish Archives, Bauman investigates southern Jewish history to gain
a better understanding of individual and group behavior patterns.

Canter Brown Jr., Professor of History at Florida A&M University, received a JD and Ph.D. from Florida State University. His numerous works
in Florida and southern history include *Ossian Bingley Hart, Florida's Loyalist Reconstruction Governor, Florida's Black Public Officials, 1867–1924,
Florida's Peace River Frontier, The Supreme Court of Florida and Its Predecessor
Courts, 1821–1917* (with Walter W. Manley and Eric W. Rise), and *Laborers in the Vineyard of the Lord: The Beginnings of the AME Church in Florida, 1865–1895* (with Larry Eugene Rivers). Brown is the recipient of the
Southern Jewish Historical Society's B.H. Levy Prize, the Florida Histor-
ical Society's Governor LeRoy Collins Prize, Rembert W. Patrick Book
Award, and Harry T. and Harriette V. Moore Award, and the American
Association of State and Local History's Certificate of Commendation.
He is a native of Fort Meade, Florida.

Mark I. Greenberg received a BA from the University of Toronto, an MA
from the University of Western Ontario, and a Ph.D. in American history from the University of Florida under the supervision of Samuel Proctor. While at UF, he served as assistant editor of the *Florida Historical
Quarterly* and in the Samuel Proctor Oral History Program. He and Canter Brown Jr. co-edited *Florida's Heritage of Diversity: Essays in Honor of
Samuel Proctor* (1997), which contains his award-winning essay. "Tampa
Mayor Herman Glogowski: Jewish Leadership in Gilded Age Florida." In
addition to his work on Florida, Greenberg has published and lectured
extensively on Jewish history in the southern United States. His articles
appear in *American Jewish History, American Jewish Archives Journal,* and *The
Georgia Historical Quarterly.* Before joining the Florida Studies Center
as its director in November 2001, the Mississippi Humanities Council
named Greenberg its 2000 Humanities Scholar of the Year.

Scott M. Langston teaches religion and biblical studies at Texas Christian University in Ft. Worth, Texas, and American history at Weatherford College, Weatherford, Texas. He received a Ph.D. and a Master
of Divinity from Southwestern Baptist Theological Seminary in Ft.

Worth, Texas, an MA from the University of Texas at Arlington and a BA from Houston Baptist University. He is the author of *Exodus Through the Centuries* (Blackwell Bible Commentary series, 2005), as well as numerous articles, including "James K. Gutheim as Southern Reform Rabbi, Community Leader, and Symbol" *Southern Jewish History* (2002), and "Reading a Text Backwards: The Book of Esther and Nineteenth Century Jewish American Interpretations" in *The Book of Esther in Modern Research* ed. by Leonard Greenspoon and Sidnie White Crawford (2004).

Eliza R. L. McGraw received a Ph.D. in English from Vanderbilt University in 1999. Her work on southern Jewishness has appeared in journals including *Southern Cultures, South Atlantic Review, Religion and Literature,* and *Mississippi Quarterly.* Her book *Two Covenants: Representations of Twentieth-Century Southern Jewishness* was published by LSU Press in 2005. She lives in Washington, D.C.

Howard N. Rabinowitz received a BA from Swarthmore College and a Ph.D. from the University of Chicago. An expert on the history of race relations, ethnicity, cities, and the South, Rabinowitz spent most of his academic career at the University of New Mexico. His major publications include *Race Relations in the Urban South, 1865–1890* (1982), *The First New South, 1865–1920* (1992), *Race, Ethnicity, and Urbanization: Selected Essays* (1994), and the edited collection *Southern Black Leaders of the Reconstruction Era* (1982). At the time of his death in 1998 at age 56, he was nearing completion of a comprehensive study of the development of Albuquerque since World War II.

Leonard Rogoff is Research Historian for the Jewish Heritage Foundation of North Carolina and visiting assistant professor at Duke University. He earned a Ph.D. from the University of North Carolina at Chapel Hill and taught at North Carolina Central University. He is the author of *Homelands: Southern-Jewish Identity in Durham and Chapel Hill, North Carolina* (2001). His articles have appeared in *Southern Jewish History, American Jewish History,* and *Quiet Voices: Southern Rabbis and Black Civil Rights.* He is the editor of *The Rambler,* the newsletter of the Southern Jewish Historical Society. He conceived and wrote text for the exhibition "Migrations: Jewish Settlers of Eastern North Carolina" and is currently working on a multi-media project, "Down Home: Jewish Life in North Carolina."

Joshua D. Rothman received a Ph.D. in history from the University of Virginia. He is Assistant Professor of History at The University of Alabama and the author of *Notorious in the Neighborhood: Sex and Families across the Color Line in Virginia, 1878–1861* (2003), which won the 2004 Outstanding Book Award from the Organization for the Study of Communication, Language, and Gender. His current project is a study of America's southwest cotton frontier during the economic boom of the 1820s and '30s known as the "flush times."

Ira M. Sheskin is Associate Professor in the Department of Geography at the University of Miami and Director of the Jewish Demography Project at the Sue and Leonard Miller Center for Contemporary Judaic Studies. He earned an MA from SUNY-Buffalo and a Ph.D. from the Ohio State University. Recent publications include "American Jewish Ethnicity" and "The Changing Spatial Distribution of American Jews." His books include *Survey Research for Geographers* and *How Jewish Communities Differ.* He is also the author of more than 35 demographic/geographic studies of Jewish communities throughout the United States.

Clive Webb is Lecturer in North American History at the University of Sussex in Brighton, England. He received a BA from the University of Warwick, an MA from the University of Sheffield, and a Ph.D. from Cambridge University. Webb is the author of *Fight Against Fear: Southern Jews and Black Civil Rights* (2001), which received the Southern Jewish Historical Society's award for the "most significant contribution to the field of Jewish history of the American South," and of several articles and book chapters. He edited *Massive Resistance: Southern Opposition to the Second Reconstruction* (Oxford University Press, 2005). He is currently working on a study of the lynching of Mexicans in the United States with William Carrigan of Rowan University.

Deborah R. Weiner serves as Research Historian and Family History Coordinator at the Jewish Museum of Maryland in Baltimore. She received a Ph.D. in history from West Virginia University. Her book *Coalfield Jews: An Appalachian History* (University of Illinois Press, 2006) explores nine small Jewish communities in the coal mining regions of Kentucky, Virginia, and West Virginia. Her work has been published in several scholarly journals and general audience publications, including *American Jewish Archives Journal, Southern Jewish History, Journal of Appalachian Studies, Encyclopedia of Appalachia, West Virginia Encyclopedia,* and the essay collection *Transnational West Virginia: Ethnic Communities and Economic Change, 1840–1940.*

Hollace Ava Weiner's research into Texas Jewry has appeared in *American Jewish History, Southern Jewish History, Western States Jewish History,* the *Southwestern Historical Quarterly,* and *Quiet Voices: Southern Rabbis and Black Civil Rights* (1997). A former journalist with the *Fort Worth Star-Telegram,* Weiner is the author of *Jewish Stars in Texas: Rabbis and Their Work* (1999). An excerpt from her rabbinical research appears in *Literary Fort Worth* (2002). Weiner, past president of the Southern Jewish Historical Society, is archivist at her synagogue, Beth-El Congregation in Fort Worth, and in 2002 wrote the congregation's centennial history. Weiner was awarded a Jewish Women's Archive fellowship to research the role the local National Council of Jewish Women played in building community in Fort Worth. She is co-editing an anthology tentatively titled *Lone Stars of David: the Jews of Texas* that will be part of the Brandeis Series on American Jewish History, Culture, and Life.

Lee Shai Weissbach is Professor of History at the University of Louisville, where he has also served as department chair and as Associate Dean of the College of Arts and Sciences. He received his undergraduate training at the University of Cincinnati and earned his Ph.D. at Harvard University. Weissbach has written extensively on nineteenth- and early twentieth-century French and American history, with special emphases on synagogue architecture and the experience of Jews in small towns. He has held a fellowship from the National Endowment for the Humanities and has been Vice President of the Society for French Historical Studies, a member of the Executive Committee of the Academic Council of the American Jewish Historical Society, a trustee of the Southern Jewish Historical Society, and a Fellow at the American Jewish Archives. Weissbach's publications include *The Synagogues of Kentucky: Architecture and History* (1995) and articles in journals such as the *Journal of Social History,* the *AJS Review, Jewish History, Shofar, American Jewish History,* and *American Jewish Archives Journal.* His book, *Jewish Life in Small-Town America: A History,* was published by Yale University Press in 2005.

Stephen J. Whitfield holds the Max Richter Chair in American Civilization at Brandeis University, from which he received his Ph.D. Born in Houston, Texas, and raised in Jacksonville, Florida, he is a Tulane graduate with eight books to his credit, including *A Death in the Delta: The Sto-*

ry of Emmett Till (1988) and In Search of American Jewish Culture (1999). Most recently, he edited an anthology of original essays in US historiography, A Companion to 20th-Century America (2004).

Gary P. Zola is the Executive Director of The Jacob Rader Marcus Center of the American Jewish Archives and Associate Professor of the American Jewish Experience at Hebrew Union College-Jewish Institute of Religion in Cincinnati. He also serves as the editor of the American Jewish Archives Journal. Zola specializes in the history of American Reform Judaism and Southern Jewish history. His edited volumes include The Dynamics of American Jewish History: Jacob Rader Marcus's Essays on American Jewry (Waltham, MA, 2003) and Women Rabbis: Exploration and Celebration (Cincinnati, 1996). His book Isaac Harby of Charleston, 1788–1828 (Tuscaloosa, 1994) is an authoritative analysis of the first organized attempt to reform Judaism in North America. Zola earned a Ph.D. in American Jewish history at Hebrew Union College-Jewish Institute of Religion.